Baking and Pastry

Baking and Pastry

MASTERING THE ART AND CRAFT

The Culinary Institute of America

JOHN WILEY & SONS, INC.

THE CULINARY INSTITUTE OF AMERICA
Tim Ryan, CMC, PhD, *President*
Victor Gielisse, CMC, PhD, *Vice President and Dean of Culinary and Baking and Pastry Arts*
Mark Erickson, CMC, *Vice President, Continuing Education*
Thomas Gumpel, CMB, *Associate Dean of Baking and Pastry Arts*
Susan Cussen, *Director of Marketing and Product Development*
Lisa Lahey, *Editorial Project Manager*
Mary Donovan, *Editorial Project Manager*
Margaret Otterstrom, *Editorial Assistant*
Rachel Toomey, *Editorial Assistant*

JOHN WILEY & SONS, INC.
Robert Garber, *Vice President and Executive Group Publisher*
Natalie Chapman, *Vice President and Publisher*
Pamela Chirls, *Senior Editor*
Diana Cisek, *Production Director*
Monique Calello, *Senior Production Editor*
Pamela Adler, *Assistant Editor*
Edwin Kuo, *Art Director*
Valerie Peterson, *Associate Marketing Director*
Adrianne Maher, *Marketing Manager*

Published by John Wiley & Sons, Inc., Hoboken, New Jersey
Published simultaneously in Canada

For general information on our other products and services or for technical support, please contact our Customer Care Department within the United States at (800) 762-2974, outside the United States at (317) 572-3993 or fax (317) 572-4002.

Wiley also publishes its books in a variety of electronic formats. Some content that appears in print may not be available in electronic books. For more information about Wiley products, visit our web site at www.wiley.com.

Library of Congress Cataloging-in-Publication Data:

Baking and pastry : mastering the art and craft / Culinary Institute of America.
    p. cm
  Includes bibliographical references and index.
  ISBN 0-471-44382-4 (cloth)
   1. Baking. 2. Pastry. 3. Desserts. I. Culinary Institute of America.

  TX763 .B3234 2004
  641.8'15—dc21

                                                    2002070202

Printed in the United States of America

All Photographs by BEN FINK

Cover and Interior Design by VERTIGO DESIGN, NYC

Color Separations by ULTRAGRAPHICS, LTD.

10 9 8 7 6 5 4 3 2 1

Acknowledgments

The Culinary Institute of America wishes to acknowledge the following individuals for their dedication to excellence in every aspect of this book—reading and critiquing the text; testing and reviewing recipes; and being the baking and pastry professionals in the photographs throughout the book: Daniel M. Budd; Kate Cavotti; Richard J. Coppedge, Jr., CMB; Stephen Eglinski; Christophe Gaumet, CMB; Nick Greco; Peter Greweling, CMB; George Higgins, CMB; Eric Kastel; Todd Knaster; Alain Levy; Joseph McKenna, CMPC; Andrew Meltzer; Patricia Mitchell; Paul Prosperi; Dieter Schorner, CMB; Rudolph Spiess; Betty L. Van Norstrand; Frank Vollkommer; and Stephane Weber.

The images in this book were created in The Culinary Institute of America's studio, bakeshops, and kitchens and in the Apple Pie Bakery Cafe. Many thanks to Ben Fink, the photographer whose work enhances the words throughout the book. We also thank our partners at John Wiley & Sons, Inc. for their tireless attention to detail, Alison Lew and Renata De Oliveira at Vertigo Design, NYC for their creativity and dedication, and Sarah Bales and Jessica Bard for their assistance.

To all those students and recent graduates who helped with research, recipe testing, and photography, we wish to express our appreciation. So many students participated that we are unable to list all of them here, but we acknowledge the special contributions of Michael Brady, Hollis Carr, Jana Dedek, Kathleen Delehanty, Debbie Hartman, Cheryl Hecht, Tim Kitzman, Peter and Eleanor Lenich, Jill McClennen, Sheryl Norton, Cindy Ranalli, Matt Ratliff, Amy Smith, Sherri Tan, and Lynn Tonelli.

Finally, we wish to acknowledge the heritage of all bakers, extending back through the ages. We look forward with anticipation to see how advances emerging in the field contribute to the ever-evolving future of the baking and pastry arts.

Contents

Preface

The audience for which *Baking and Pastry: Mastering the Art and Craft* is written includes baking and pastry professionals and serious home bakers who want to continue their education or refer to a complete guide of baking and pastry techniques, formulas, and presentations. In addition, our students at The Culinary Institute of America in Hyde Park, New York, and at our Greystone campus in St. Helena, California, as well as students in other culinary programs, will use this book as an important part of their education. Within these twenty chapters the reader will find a tremendous amount of information presented in text, formulas, photos, and detailed drawings.

At The Culinary Institute of America, our curriculum is presented to students in a building-block manner, with each course building upon the foundation laid by the previous one. As students move through the curriculum, they gain the experience and knowledge necessary to become baking and pastry professionals.

We used this same philosophy in developing the chapters and organization for this book. The first five chapters set the stage for understanding the baking and pastry profession and using the specialized equipment and products that are common to the bakeshop. In these chapters we explain the role that science plays in baking and the importance of serving safe food. We introduce some fundamental baking mathematics such as bakers' percentages and metric conversions that are crucial for a full understanding of the craft.

In Chapter 6 we explore various fermentation principles and ingredient variations for yeast doughs before delving into shaping and finishing techniques for hearth breads and rolls in Chapter 7.

In Chapters 8 through 12, the reader is exposed to a wide range of formulas and production techniques that make up the foundation for a quality bakeshop. Pastry doughs and batters, quick breads and cakes, cookies, creams and custards, and glazes and sauces are the basis for many baking and pastry presentations.

Frozen desserts continue to be a favorite dessert choice. In Chapter 13 we introduce a wide range of techniques and formulas for making high-quality sorbets, ice creams, granitas, and parfaits. In addition, we demonstrate the versatility of frozen desserts and encourage exploration of different flavoring methods and ingredients.

Pies and tarts have risen to an all-time popularity due to their simplicity in production and America's new-found love of rustic, homespun desserts. In Chapter 14 we show different ways of shaping, filling, and baking pies, tarts, and fruit desserts.

Filled and assembled cakes and tortes are the focus of Chapter 15. Here we present the proper assembly techniques while stressing the importance of combining flavors and textures. We separate the chapter into two parts, making a distinction between classic and contemporary cakes and tortes. We celebrate the origin of classic cakes and tortes, which have come to us from France, Austria, and Germany. Contemporary cakes and tortes, on the other hand, are creations that stretch the imagination of the pastry chef. Here modern equipment and global ingredients are combined to create sensible flavor and textural combinations.

In the later chapters, readers draw upon lessons learned earlier in the book. We present formulas for making individual pastries in Chapter 16, and in Chapter 17 we introduce hot, cold, and frozen plated desserts that have multiple components. Many of these components, such as cookies, glazes, and ice creams and sorbets, are cross-referenced to other chapters.

One of the fastest-growing trends in the baking and pastry industry centers on chocolates and confections. The principles, techniques, and applications involved in working with chocolate and sugar can be complex and challenging; therefore, in Chapter 18 we guide the reader through the fundamentals. These principles are then applied to create intricate and dramatic confections.

Décor principles, techniques, and materials are addressed in Chapter 19. Piping, lettering, marzipan, gum paste, sugar, and chocolate are just some of the décor techniques and materials presented. We also focus on the hand tools, equipment, and proper storage and handling of the materials.

In Chapter 20, the final chapter, we concentrate on wedding and specialty cakes. This chapter is a synthesis of many of the techniques and applications presented in earlier chapters. However, we also introduce some new decorating techniques and specialized equipment and materials.

Being involved with this book has altered the way we feel about the industry. We have gained a much richer appreciation not only for the process but for the art and craft. We are confident that the reader will not only enjoy this book but also gain a renewed respect for the field. I consider myself fortunate to be involved at this level of the industry and to have the opportunity to play a part in the development of future industry leaders. I believe this book will prove to be the perfect bakeshop companion.

Thomas Gumpel

CHAPTER 1

The Professional Baker and Pastry Chef

ANY PROFESSION HAS A GREAT MANY SIDES, AND THE BAKING AND PASTRY

PROFESSION IS NO EXCEPTION. A BAKING AND PASTRY PROFESSIONAL IS AN

ARTIST, A BUSINESSPERSON, AND A SCIENTIST, AMONG OTHER THINGS.

ACQUIRING THE SKILLS AND KNOWLEDGE NECESSARY TO SUCCEED IN THIS

PROFESSION IS A LIFELONG ENDEAVOR.

The craft of baking finds its origins thousands of years ago in ancient civilizations. Baking is an integral part of humankind's history, as bakers have been and continue to be the source of some of the most common and basic of foodstuffs. Because of this closely tied relationship, baking, as a profession, evolved in relationship to the progression of civilization. For example, perhaps because bread is one of the most important baked products, throughout recorded history governments have regulated the production of bread: its production methods, its quality, its weight, and its price. Bakers were among the first tradesmen organized into guilds; one of the first bread bakers' guilds was established in Rome in 150 B.C.

The pastry chef, as the position exists today in restaurants and hotels, evolved through the brigade system. This system of organization, instituted by Escoffier, served to streamline and simplify work in hotel kitchens. Under the brigade system, each position has a specific workstation and defined responsibilities. In this system the production of pastries was the responsibility of the pâtissier (pastry chef). Later, this position was often separated from the brigade and developed an organizational structure of its own. This branch of the culinary arts also owes a debt to the work of Marie-Antoine Carême (1784–1833), a Parisian chef and pastry chef who sought to make the work of all culinary professionals more logical and organized. Two of the most influential books written on the pastry arts, *Pâtisserie Royal* and *Pâtisserie Pittoresque,* are part of his enormous legacy, and his work continues to have an effect to this day.

Today, as then, individuals in the baking and pastry profession may want to, and often do, specialize in one area of the craft. However, an individual embarking on a career in the baking and pastry arts will most likely initially work with a variety of other baked goods including breads, breakfast pastries, cookies, and cakes.

When you first start out, you will work under direct supervision, preparing basic items and using standard formulas. As you gain skill and take on more responsibility, you may develop menus, specials, or signature items; manage, or develop products for, large-scale production; hire and train staff; promote yourself or your business; and/or take on a host of other activities and functions.

Career Opportunities for Baking and Pastry Professionals

Both bakers and pastry chefs can pursue a wide array of options over the course of their careers. You might own your own shop or company or work for someone else. You could work in a commissary setting, in a restaurant, or in a small custom shop such as one specializing in chocolate work, confections, wedding cakes, or hand-crafted breads. To get a well-rounded foundation as a professional you may want to work in a cross section of bakeries, pastry shops, and kitchens. After you have a solid foundation, you may choose to specialize in a specific discipline. These decisions will affect the path of your career.

The executive pastry chef is responsible for all bakeshop and pastry kitchen operations, including ordering, staff supervision, and menu development and pricing. The pastry chef (*pâtissier*) is responsible for baked items, pastries, and desserts. In larger operations, the pastry chef frequently supervises a separate kitchen area or a separate shop. The position of pastry chef may be further broken down into the areas of specialization such as the *confiseur* (prepares chocolates and confections) and *boulanger* (prepares yeast-raised baked goods), among other positions.

Bakers will most often follow one of two paths, working either in large commercial bakeries that specialize in high-volume production or in smaller bakeries that produce lower volume.

Wholesale bakeshops focus on large-scale production. They sell finished or par-baked items, as well as unbaked and unformed doughs and batters, to a variety of outlets, such as supermarkets, cafés, smaller bakeshops, gourmet shops, individual or chain restaurants, catering halls, and cafeterias.

Individually owned shops may provide a wide range of services, from a full-service bakeshop offering a variety of baked goods to one that specializes in chocolates and confections or wedding cakes. For some bakers and pastry chefs such private enterprises are a sideline to their career, while for others, they are a full-time occupation.

Large hotels rely upon the skills of the pastry chef and baker. Depending upon the size of the hotel and the number of food outlets it has—fine-dining restaurants, room service, coffee shops, and banquet rooms—it may operate the bakeshop and pastry kitchen as a commissary, responsible for a wide range of items from breakfast pastries to elaborate pastry displays, wedding cakes, and plated desserts. The pastry chef may report directly to the executive chef or to the executive pastry chef.

A special pulled
sugar piece
prepared by the
décorateur

Full-service restaurants, such as white-tablecloth establishments, bistros, and family-style restaurants, feature full menus with a choice of selections for each course, including dessert. The pastry chef in a restaurant, as in a hotel, needs a wide range of baking and pastry skills to meet the challenges of making a variety of items, from ice cream and cakes to chocolates served as mignardises and petits fours to pizza dough and more. Private clubs and executive dining rooms provide food service to their members or clients. While some operations may employ a baker or a pastry chef, or even have a modest-size staff, it is often the chef's job to locate and purchase high-quality baked goods and pastries.

Institutional catering and volume food operations, such as those you find in schools, hospitals, colleges, and airlines, rely upon executive pastry chefs and master bakers to develop items that can be prepared by a staff with relatively few professional culinary skills. Manufacturers and producers operate research and development kitchens to test products and formulas and fine-tune them. These large business operations can offer employees benefits and the opportunity for career advancement within the corporation.

Caterers provide a particular service, often tailored to meet the desires of a special client for a particular event, whether a trade convention, wedding, birthday party, cocktail reception, or gallery opening. Caterers may provide on-site services (the client comes to the caterer's premises), off-site services (the caterer goes to the client's premises), or both. Pastry chefs and bakers may be part of the permanent staff at larger halls or centers, or they may work in partnership with caterers or directly with clients as needed.

The dessert station on a busy night in a full-service restaurant

Grocery stores and department stores hire a significant number of baking and pastry professionals. Their responsibilities may include developing the dessert components of home meal replacement (carryout) offerings, signature breads for the bakeshop, and/or specialty items such as pastries and chocolates, as well as assisting with research, focus groups, packaging, pricing, and promotion strategies.

Research-and-development kitchens employ baking and pastry professionals to develop formulas for manufacture, create signature items for restaurant chains, develop training materials and programs for new equipment, generate formulas that highlight specific products, and much more.

Many professional and consumer publications maintain test kitchens to develop and test formulas and recipes for publication.

Working in an industry with so many niche markets and areas of specialization means the desire to turn your own particular experience and expertise into a marketable skill can lead you into a dynamic aspect of the industry: consulting. Consultants may work with clients to develop formulas or menus, staffing strategies, marketing plans, packaging, and the like. Or they may help design work areas, retail areas, and storage areas to maximize production and minimize costs.

Working in the "front of the house" as a salesperson is also an important function. People who really understand the needs of today's bakeshops, restaurants, hotels, and pastry shops can help bakers, chefs, managers, and executives to learn about new products, or about new ways to use familiar products or equipment. They

The bakeshop as a classroom

act as a liaison between the people on the job and the company or companies whose products they represent, keeping the lines of communication open.

Teachers in the baking and pastry arts are vital to the success of the degree- and certificate-granting programs offered nationwide and around the globe. Teaching jobs may require additional training, education, or certification. Professionals who turn to teaching bring a special awareness of industry needs, as well as knowledge of how things work in a business environment.

Food writers and critics report on industry or societal trends, products, shops, restaurants, and chefs, among other topics. They write books, articles, columns, screenplays for video, and content for multimedia and on-line media. It always means more when the writer is well versed in the baking and pastry and culinary arts.

Formal Education

The fact that the baking and pastry arts are professional careers today is clear from the expectations both employees and employers bring to their work. All employers look for both experience and education when they hire at virtually any position above entry level, and at the most prestigious shops, even entry-level positions may require a degree or some formal training. Employees look for positions that let them learn the skills they need to advance, and they know that a formal education can tip the scales in their favor.

The increasing emphasis on a formal education in the baking and pastry arts grows hand in hand with the number of programs dedicated exclusively to baking and pastry. Employers rely upon the general and specific skills of the craft as taught by these schools to establish a common ground of ability, saving them hours of on-the-job training. The best education couples theoretical training (bookwork) with plenty of hands-on experience to develop confidence and ability in all areas of baking and pastry arts.

Both employers and schools, however, recognize that formal education on its own is not enough to ensure excellence. Baking and pastry are practical arts. To master them, you need to work. Whether you are working on your own or for someone else, you must make job choices carefully. It is tempting to make a decision based solely on salary, location, or a similar immediately tangible reward. However, if you consider each job as an investment in your future, it is far easier to evaluate the long-lasting rewards.

Continuing Education

Just as a formal education has become an important first step in launching a career, certification and continuing education programs are means to advancing a professional career in the baking and pastry arts. Because the industry is constantly evolving, continuing education can be as important as initial training. Attending classes, trade shows, workshops, and seminars helps practicing professionals hone skills in specialized areas while keeping up with new methods, ingredients, techniques, products, and business skills.

Contests and competitions offer you a chance to really stretch yourself. Professional magazines, journals, newsletters, and Web sites have information about contests at the local, national, and international level. Whenever you submit your work to the scrutiny of a panel of judges, you will learn more about the profession. Critical review provides you with a means to keep improving in ways that daily production work never can. Practice, research, and the stress of competition exercise your professional muscles in the same way competing in a sporting event strengthens an athlete.

Throughout your career, continue to evaluate your achievements and goals, and take the appropriate steps to keep on top of the latest information in the areas you are most concerned about. Read newspapers to find out about events, trends, or specific issues that affect your community. Read national and international publications such as magazines and newsletters geared to both professionals and the public. Web sites, government publications, and books are all excellent sources of information for topics such as nutrition, the environment, health, business, and the economy.

Educate yourself and learn to use the important tools of your business; budgets, accounting systems, and inventory control systems all play a role. Many organizations, from the largest chains to the smallest one-person catering company, rely upon software programs that allow them to manage a number of areas efficiently: inventory, purchases, profits and losses, sales, food costs, reservations, payroll, schedules, and budgets. If you are not using a system capable of tracking all this information and more, you cannot be as effective as you must be to survive and succeed.

Culinary schools, professional organizations, trade shows, and seminars all offer professional-level courses and workshops, as do some high schools and community colleges. A growing number of on-line and long-distance learning options also exist, offered by schools and businesses. Travel programs provide an excellent opportunity to learn more about various cuisines and cultures, to do original research, or to expand your professional horizons.

There are also classes and workshops that offer continuing education units (CEUs), essential to achieving certain certifications or diplomas.

Certification

The Retailer's Bakery Association (RBA) and the American Culinary Federation (ACF) have established standards for certifying bakers and pastry chefs. The RBA's certification levels begin with Certified Journey Baker (CJB); the ACF certifies Pastry Culinarians.

With each level of certification, your work history must meet certain criteria for you to be eligible to take the exams. The exams given by the RBA have both a written and practical component.

The RBA's next level includes three designations: Certified Baker (CB), Certified Decorator (CD), and Certified Bread Baker (CBB).

The ACF gives the certification of Working Pastry Chef (WPC) as an entry-level certification and requires the participants to pass only a written test for this certification. Individuals working at this level are typically responsible for a shift or a section within a food-service operation. The next certification given by the ACF is that of

Certified Executive Pastry Chef (CEPC). Individuals at this level are often department heads, typically reporting to the executive chef or the management team of a corporation, or working in research or other areas of specialization.

Certified Master Baker (CMB) is the highest certification given by the RBA, while the ACF grants Certified Master Pastry Chef (CMPC) certification, a ten-day exam that combines a written and practical examination that covers classical and contemporary applications.

Both the RBA and the ACF have specific minimum criteria that must be met before you can apply for certification. Typically, you must show an accumulation of several hours, or "points," in education and work experience. Once certification is granted, you may also be required to maintain your certification through continuing education, competitions, and similar professional activities.

Networking

Developing a professional network is a task to take seriously. Networks can be formal or informal. The way to begin is simply to introduce yourself to others in your field. Always have your business cards with you when you go to other restaurants or to trade shows. Join professional organizations and read their material. Most organizations maintain Web sites that enable you to contact other professionals, get in on chats or message boards, and make new professional contacts.

Make sure that you record names, titles, work numbers for voice and fax, and e-mail and regular mail addresses in a safe place. You can use a variety of systems, from a simple address book to a computerized database. If using a computer, protect your information; if it is somehow destroyed or lost, you will rarely be able to recapture it all. Make copies or backups regularly. Some of the information you collect may be confidential. If you want to keep your network healthy, respect that confidentiality at all times.

When you first make a good contact, follow up with an e-mail, phone call, or a note. The communication that you develop with your peers will keep your own work fresh and contemporary, and an established network will also make it much easier for you to find your next job or your next employee.

The Business of Baking and Pastry

As your career evolves, you will move up from positions where your technical prowess is your greatest contribution into those where your skills as an executive, an administrator, and a manager are more in demand. At this level, fiscal responsibility for food and labor costs becomes especially important. This does not mean that your ability to make breads or produce pastries is any less important, simply that you must learn and assume more managerial or administrative tasks and responsibilities. You may be developing new menu items or signature dishes. Keeping costs under control to improve profit will be a constant concern. You must develop effective and appropriate production schedules and train yourself and those working with you to improve. Plating, presentation, and pricing are part of the daily concerns of any executive pastry chef or baker. Performing these important business tasks all stretch your skills as a manager.

Managing a bakery or pastry shop requires the ability to handle four areas effectively: physical assets, information, people (human resources), and time. The greater your management skills in any of these areas, the greater your potential for success. Many management systems today emphasize the use of quality as a yardstick. Every area of your operation can be used to improve the quality of service you provide your customers.

MANAGING PHYSICAL ASSETS

Physical assets are the equipment and supplies needed to do business: large and small equipment, food and beverage inventory, tables, chairs, linens, china, flatware, glassware, computers and point-of-sale systems, cash registers, kitchen equipment, cleaning supplies, and ware-washing machines. In short, physical assets include anything, other than services you must purchase or pay for, that affects your ability to do business well.

The first step in bringing the expenses associated with your physical assets under control is to determine what your actual expenses are. Then you can begin the process of making any necessary adjustments and instituting control systems that will keep your organization operating at maximum efficiency.

One of the biggest expenses for any baking and pastry operation is food and beverage costs. You or your purchasing agent will have to work hard to develop and maintain a good purchasing system. Because each operation has different needs, there are no hard-and-fast rules, just general principles that you can apply to your own situation.

MANAGING INFORMATION

You may sometimes feel that it's impossible to keep current in all the important areas of your job. Given the sheer volume of information being generated each day, you may be right. However, the ability to tap into the information resources you need, using all types of media and technology, has never been more important. You must not only keep yourself informed of the latest trends, but also develop the ability to look beyond what is current to predict future trends. This will help to keep your business thriving.

Restaurants, menus, and dining room design have all been dramatically affected by such societal trends as busy, on-the-go lifestyles and the increasing interest in world cuisines. Current tastes in politics, art, fashion, movies, and music have an effect on what people eat and where and how they want to eat it. The Internet is a powerful influence as well.

Information gathering can become a full-time task on its own. To make effective use of the information available, you must be able to analyze and evaluate the material at your disposal and sift out what is important.

MANAGING HUMAN RESOURCES

Every shop relies directly on the work and dedication of a number of people, from the executive pastry chef to the bakers and pastry cooks to the wait staff and maintenance and cleaning staff. No matter how large or small your staff may be, the ability to engage all your workers in a team effort is one of the major factors in determining whether or not you will succeed.

One of the hallmarks of the true professional is skill at being a team member. (Even if you are the only person on the staff, your business is still a team effort involving you, your customers, and your suppliers.) The larger the staff, the more important it is that each member learns to work as part of a team. Teamwork can be one of the most difficult skills to master, and it requires as much practice and concentration as any baking or pastry technique. The best teams are made up of talented individuals. These professionals bring not just technical skills but also a passion for excellence and a commitment to the success of both the team and the profession.

You can recognize a strong team approach in a successful bakeshop or pastry kitchen. Everyone feels he or she has a distinct and measurable contribution to make within the organization. Everyone knows the clear criteria for the work to be done (otherwise known as a job description). To do a job well, it's important to know exactly what the quality standards are. Providing feedback, constructive criticism, and suggesting or providing additional training or disciplinary measures continually reinforce those standards, as does clear, objective evaluation of an employee's work.

The management of human resources entails several legal responsibilities. Everyone has the right to work in an environment that is free from physical hazards. This means that, as an employer and an employee, you deserve a workspace that is well lit, properly ventilated, and free from obvious dangers, such as improperly maintained equipment. Employees must have access to drinking water and to bathroom facilities. Beyond this bare minimum, some shops or companies may offer a locker room, a laundry facility that provides clean uniforms and aprons, or other such amenities. The employer is also responsible for making the appropriate legal deductions from each employee's paycheck and for reporting all earnings properly to state and federal agencies.

Liability insurance (to cover any potential harm to your facility, employees, or guests) must be kept up to date and at adequate levels. Individual employers or companies may also offer additional benefits as part of an employment package, including life insurance, medical and dental insurance, assistance with such things as dependent care, adult literacy training, and access to (and support for those enrolled in) substance abuse programs. In an increasingly tight labor market, a generous benefits package can make a difference in the caliber of employees any company or shop is able to attract and retain.

MANAGING TIME

It may seem that no matter how hard you work or how much planning you do, the days are not long enough. Learning new skills so that you can make the best possible use of the time you have should be an ongoing part of your career development. If you look over your operation carefully, you will discover how time is wasted. In most operations, the top five time wasters are lack of clear priorities for tasks; poor staff training; poor communication; poor organization; and inadequate or nonexistent tools for accomplishing tasks. To combat these time wasters, use the following strategies:

Invest time in reviewing daily operations. Until you are clear about what needs to be done and in what order, you cannot begin the process of saving time. Consider the way you, your coworkers, and your staff spend the day. Does everyone have a basic understanding of which tasks are most important? Do they know when to begin a particular task in order to finish it on time? It can be an eye-opening experience to take a hard look at where everyone's workday goes. Once you determine, for example, that your staff requires less manpower to prepare a particular basic item, but more staff is needed for plating during the dinner rush, or that the dishwasher is sitting idle for the first two hours of his or her shift, you can take steps to rectify the problem. You could reorganize the hours you have scheduled people, taking one staff member off the prep schedule and adding one for the dinner service. You might decide to train the dishwasher to stock shelves or measure ingredients during down time, or you could revise the schedule so that the dishwasher's shift begins two hours later.

Invest time in training others. If you expect someone to do a job properly, you need to take enough time to explain the task carefully. Walk yourself and your staff through the jobs that must be done, and be sure that everyone understands how to do the work, where to find necessary items, how far individual responsibility extends, and what to do in case a question or emergency comes up. Give your staff the yardsticks they need to evaluate their jobs and to determine if they have done what was requested in the appropriate fashion, and on time. If you do not invest this time up front, you may find yourself squandering precious hours following your workers around, picking up the slack, and doing work that should not be part of your day.

Learn to communicate clearly. Whether you are training a new employee, introducing a new menu item, or ordering a piece of equipment, clear communication is essential. Be specific, use the most concise language you can, and be as brief as possible without leaving out necessary information. If certain tasks are handled by a number of people, be sure to write that task out, from the first step to the last, so that everyone will execute the task in the same way. Encourage people to ask questions if they do not understand you. If you realize you need help learning communication skills, consider taking a workshop or seminar to strengthen weak areas.

Take steps to create an orderly work environment. If you have to dig through five shelves to find the lid to a storage container for buttercream, you are not using your time wisely. Organize work areas carefully, so that the tools, ingredients, and equipment needed are readily available. Schedule like activities so they are performed at the same time. Set up ample, easy-to-access storage space for common items such as whips, spoons, ladles, and tongs. Electrical outlets for small equipment ought to be within reach of everyone. While you may be forced to work within the limits of your existing floor plan, be on the lookout for strategies, equipment, or products to turn a bad arrangement into one that works smoothly.

Purchase, replace, and maintain all tools as necessary. A well-equipped kitchen has all the tools necessary to prepare every item on the menu. If you are missing something as basic as a sieve, your crème anglaise will not be perfectly smooth. Learn to operate equipment safely and teach others to do the same.

The Profession

A professional makes a living from the practice of a craft. Rather than viewing work as simply a means to an end, true professionals have a passion for their craft and a drive for excellence. Some professionals may tell you that they baked for their families or worked in a bakeshop when they were young. They may have entered baking contests, clipped recipes, and collected books about baking. Others come to the baking and pastry field after establishing themselves in other areas in the food-service industry. Still others make a switch to the baking and pastry profession as a second or third career.

All professionals must learn the foundations of the profession — handling ingredients and equipment and standard or basic formulas. At the next level, they apply those foundations, adapting and modifying formulas or finding ways to improve quality and efficiency in their own work. At the highest level, they draw on all they know and use their knowledge, skills, and creativity to produce something — as specific as a new pastry or as intangible as a successful career — that was not there before.

Every member of any profession, whether he or she is a teacher, lawyer, doctor, a baker, or a pastry chef, is responsible for its image. Those who have made the greatest impression know that the cardinal virtues of the baking and pastry profession are an open and inquiring mind, an appreciation of and dedication to quality, and a sense of responsibility. Success also depends on certain specific character traits, some of which may be inherent, some of which are diligently cultivated throughout a career.

A commitment to service. The food-service industry is predicated on service, and professionals must never lose sight of what that word implies. Good service includes (but is not limited to) providing quality items that are properly and safely prepared, appropriately flavored, and attractively presented — in short, that make the customer happy. The degree to which an operation can offer satisfaction in these areas is the degree to which it will succeed in providing good (or, ideally, excellent) service. The customer must always come first.

A sense of responsibility. A professional's responsibility is fourfold: to him- or herself, to coworkers, to the business, whether it be a bakery or restaurant, and to the customer. Waste, recklessness, disregard for others, and/or misuse or abuse of any commodity are unacceptable. Abusive language, harassment, ethnic slurs, and profanity do not have a place in the professional bakeshop or pastry kitchen. When employees feel that their needs are given due consideration, their self-esteem will increase and their attitude toward the establishment will become more positive; both results will increase productivity and reduce absenteeism.

Good judgment. Although it is not easy to learn, good judgment is a prerequisite for becoming a professional. Professionals learn what is right and appropriate over a lifetime of experience. Good judgment is never completely mastered; rather, it is a goal toward which one can continually strive.

CHAPTER 2

Ingredient Identification

CHOOSING INGREDIENTS WITH CARE, BASED UPON QUALITY, SEASONALITY, AND OTHER CONSIDERATIONS, INCLUDING COST, IS A PREREQUISITE FOR HIGH-QUALITY BAKED GOODS. EACH INGREDIENT HAS ITS OWN SET OF CHARACTERISTICS, AND IT IS THE PASTRY CHEF OR BAKER'S JOB TO LEARN TO HANDLE ALL INGREDIENTS PROPERLY, FROM THE TIME THEY ARE RECEIVED THROUGHOUT EACH PHASE OF STORAGE, HANDLING, AND PREPARATION.

Flours, Grains, and Meals

This broad category encompasses both whole grains, such as rice and barley, and milled or otherwise refined products, such as cornmeal and pastry flour. The fruits and seeds of cereal grasses and grains are versatile, universal foods, part of every cuisine and culture. For the most part, they are inexpensive and widely available, providing a valuable and concentrated source of nutrients and fiber.

Whole grains are grains that have not been milled. They usually have a shorter shelf life than milled grains.

Milled grains are polished to remove the germ, bran, and/or hull. They may have a longer shelf life than whole grains, but some of their nutritive value is lost during processing.

Milled grains that are broken into coarse particles may be referred to as *cracked*. If the milling process continues, *meals* and *cereals* (cornmeal, farina, rye meal) are the result. With further processing, the grain may be ground into a fine powder, known as *flour*, whether wheat, rice, or another type.

Various methods are used for milling: crushing the grains between metal rollers, grinding them between stones, or cutting them with steel blades. Stone-ground grains are preferable in some cases, because they are subjected to less heat during milling than with other methods and so retain more of their nutritive value.

WHEAT FLOUR

Flour is a staple ingredient in the bakeshop, used in baked goods of all types. Flours can also be used to coat work surfaces and to dust molds and pans so that dough and batters do not stick or tear. They thicken liquids by forming a gel. (For more about gelatinizing starches, see pages 85–88.)

Each flour has its own characteristics, but wheat flour is the most common type used in the bakeshop. It is the only flour that contains enough gluten-forming proteins to provide the structure essential to baked goods. (For more about gluten in flour, see page 76.) And wheat flour can be used to achieve a range of effects, from the resiliency of a hearty bread to the delicate flake of a pastry. (For more about gluten development, see pages 76–77.) Flours made from other grains, such as rye, rice, corn, millet, barley, oats, amaranth, kamut, quinoa, and spelt, add distinctive flavors and textures to baked goods.

The Wheat Kernel

Before the baker can understand the different varieties of wheat flour, he or she must understand what makes up wheat. The wheat kernel is made up of the following components:

Bran constitutes 14.5 percent of total kernel weight. The bran is the dark outer coating of the wheat kernel and contains large amounts of insoluble dietary fiber.

Endosperm comprises 83 percent of total kernel weight. The endosperm is the internal portion of the wheat kernel and contains the largest amount of protein and starch. White flour is produced from the endosperm.

Germ is 2.5 percent of total kernel weight. The germ is the embryo of the wheat kernel and contains fats, vitamins, minerals, and some protein.

FROM UPPER LEFT: 9-grain cereal, whole spelt berries, spelt flour (in metal pint measure), whole wheat flour (on scale), cracked wheat, whole wheat berries, rye meal, cornmeal, rolled oats, steel-cut oats, millet, roasted buckwheat, raw buckwheat, buckwheat flour (in bag with measuring cup)

Wheat is classified by season and color, as follows: *hard red winter wheat, hard white winter wheat, hard red spring wheat, soft red winter wheat,* and *soft white winter wheat; durum wheat* is a particular type of hard wheat. Winter wheat is planted in the winter and harvested the following summer; spring wheat is planted in the spring and harvested that summer. Generally, spring wheat produces the hardest flours and winter wheat the softest.

Milling

Milling is the process that separates the wheat kernel into its three parts: bran, germ, and endosperm. Once the bran and germ have been removed, the endosperm is sifted to reduce the particle size to the correct quantity for flour.

Extraction Rate

The extraction rate is the percentage of flour obtained after a grain has been milled. The extraction rate will vary with flour refinement. For example, flour with an 80 percent extraction rate indicates that 80 lb/36.29 kg of flour was obtained from 100 lb/45.36 kg of grain. Whole wheat flour, which has nothing removed, has a 100 percent extraction rate.

Ash

The ash content is a milling standard that determines the mineral (inorganic) material remaining in the flour after milling. Ash content is determined by burning a measured amount of milled flour and weighing the mineral (inorganic) material that remains after incineration. Ash content is related to flour color and type. This information can be found for any flour by checking individual specifications.

Flour Treatments

Aging and **bleaching:** Newly milled flour is not ready for the bakeshop. Bakers refer to freshly milled flour as "green flour." Dough made using "green flour" tends to absorb more water and is not elastic, due to the immature proteins found in the flour. In addition to having weak proteins, freshly milled flour is yellow in color. When flour is allowed to age naturally, for approximately 2 to 3 months, the oxygen in the air will whiten the flour and develop the proteins. Chemicals are sometimes used to synthetically replicate the aging and whitening process. Benzoyl peroxide and chlorine dioxide are two of the products used to chemically age and bleach flour. Flour that has been chemically aged and bleached will bear a "bleached flour" label.

Oxidizing: Potassium bromate, an inorganic compound, is an oxidizing agent added to flour to improve bread volume. When potassium bromate is present in flour, product volume increases by approximately 10 to 15 percent.

Enrichment: Enriched flour has nutrients replaced that were lost during milling. Nutrients added include thiamine, niacin, riboflavin, iron, and calcium. Flour that has been enriched will bear an "enriched flour" label. Enriched flour has no effect on baking performance.

Types of Flour

All-purpose flour is a blend of hard and soft wheat flours milled from the endosperm of the wheat grain; the specific blend varies from region to region. Southern all-purpose flour generally has more soft wheat than all-purpose flours in other parts of the county. The protein content in all-purpose flour can range from 8 to 12 percent.

Bread flour, also known as patent flour, is a hard wheat flour made from the endosperm and is used for breads and soft rolls. Its protein content ranges from 11 to 13 percent.

High-gluten flour is milled from the entire endosperm; it is used for bagels and hard rolls. Its protein content is typically 13 to 14 percent.

Clear flour is a hard wheat flour made from the endosperm that has a darker color than bread or high-gluten flour and is typically used in rye breads. The protein content of clear flour ranges from 13 to 15 percent.

Whole wheat flour is a hard wheat flour milled from the entire wheat kernel, including the bran and germ; because the germ is high in lipids, whole wheat flour can quickly become rancid. Its protein content ranges from 14 to 16 percent.

Durum flour, milled from the endosperm of the durum wheat kernel, is a hard wheat flour used in bread making. Its protein content ranges from 12 to 14 percent.

Semolina is a more coarsely ground durum wheat flour, used most typically in pasta making.

Cake flour is a soft wheat flour with a protein content ranging from 6 to 9 percent. It is used for cakes and cookies.

Pastry flour has a protein content ranging from 8 to 10 percent. It is used for pie dough, muffins, and some biscuits, as well as pastries.

Other Wheat Products

Cracked wheat is coarsely cracked or cut wheat kernels, including the bran and germ. It lends texture and flavor to breads.

Vital wheat gluten is produced from the insoluble gluten protein extracted from flour during the milling process. The protein is dried and ground into a powder. It is used to fortify dough.

RYE

Although **rye flour** behaves quite differently from wheat flour in baking (see page 16), rye kernels are milled in a manner similar to that used for wheat kernels. *White rye flour* is the mildest-flavored and lightest-colored rye flour, with a protein content of 8 to 10 percent. *Medium rye flour* has a slightly higher protein content, 9 to 11 percent, and is somewhat darker. *Dark rye flour,* which is milled from the outer portion of the endosperm, has a protein content of 14 to 17 percent. *Pumpernickel flour* (or *rye meal*) is a coarse grind made from the entire rye kernel with an intense flavor and a dark color.

OTHER GRAINS AND CEREALS

Oats are cleaned, toasted, and hulled before use. Cleaned whole oats are referred to as **oat groats.**

Oat flour is made from oat groats ground into a fine powder; it contains no gluten.

Steel-cut (or Scotch or Irish) **oats** are milled by cracking oat groats into smaller pieces.

Rolled oats, sometimes called old-fashioned oats, are made by steaming and flattening oat groats.

Instant oats are cracked oat groats that are precooked, dried, and rolled.

Buckwheat has a distinctive strong, nutty whole-grain flavor and a relatively high fat content. Buckwheat may be roasted or unroasted. *Roasted buckwheat groats,* sold as kasha, have an intense flavor. *Unroasted groats* have a slightly milder flavor. Both are also milled into meal or flour.

Spelt is a cereal grain that contains less gluten and more protein than wheat. It is used in a variety of baked goods. It is available for use as a whole grain or a white or whole-grain flour.

Millet is a gluten-free seed with a mild flavor. It is available whole, cracked, or ground into flour.

Cornmeal is made by grinding dried corn kernels. Its color is determined by the color of the corn kernels used. Cornmeal is available in varying consistencies, from fine to coarsely ground.

RICE

During processing, rice is polished to remove some or all of the bran. **White rice** has had all the bran removed, while **brown rice** is only partially polished, leaving behind some of the bran. Rice is categorized generally by the length of the grain: short, medium, or long. Rice flour is made by grinding white, brown, or sweet rice.

Rice flour has a mild flavor and is commonly used to make gluten-free baked goods.

Sugars, Syrups, and Other Sweeteners

Granulated sugar is pure refined sucrose derived from either sugarcane or from sugar beets. Granulated sugar has small, evenly sized crystals, and it is the most commonly used sugar in the bakeshop.

Superfine sugar has very small crystals and dissolves quickly. It is sometimes used in cake batters and meringues.

Sanding sugar has large crystals and is used primarily to decorate baked goods.

Pearl or **decorating sugar** has large pearl-shaped crystals and is used as a decoration for baked goods.

Brown sugar is granulated sugar with added molasses. *Light brown sugar* has a milder molasses flavor; *dark brown sugar,* which contains more molasses, has a more pronounced flavor. Store brown sugar in an airtight container to prevent loss of moisture.

Turbinado sugar is a coarse granular partially refined sugar with a light brown color and a very mild molasses taste.

Confectioners' sugar, also called powdered sugar or icing sugar, is granulated sugar ground to a powder with added cornstarch (up to 3 percent by weight) to keep it from caking. Confectioners' sugar is available in different grades of fineness (the number in the name reflects the mesh size of the screen used to sift the powdered sugar); 10X sugar is finer than 6X sugar.

Isomalt is a white crystalline "sugar-free" sweetener made from sucrose used in diabetic baking. Because it does not break down when heated and absorbs very little water, some pastry chefs like to use isomalt for pulled sugar work.

Corn syrup is produced from cornstarch. It contains 15 to 20 percent dextrose (glucose), other sugars, water, and often flavorings. *Light corn syrup* has been clarified to give it its light color; *dark corn syrup* includes refiner's syrup and caramel color and flavor, giving it a darker color and a molasses flavor. Corn syrup resists crystallization, making it suitable for some confectionery work.

Glucose syrup is 42 DE corn syrup (see sidebar on page 22) used in icings, confections, and pulled sugar work.

BACK ROW, FROM LEFT TO RIGHT:
Confectioners' (or powdered) sugar, granulated sugar, superfine sugar

MIDDLE, FROM LEFT TO RIGHT:
Isomalt, light brown sugar, dark brown sugar, turbinado sugar

FRONT:
Sanding sugar

Molasses is a thick dark brown liquid by-product of sugar refining; it contains sucrose and invert sugars. Molasses has a rich flavor but it is less sweet than sugar. Molasses is available as light, dark, or blackstrap. Light, dark, and blackstrap are rendered, respectively, from the first, second, and third boiling of the sugar syrup in the refining process and range from light in color and flavor (light molasses) to very dark and intensely flavored (blackstrap molasses). Molasses may also be labeled "sulfured" or "unsulfured," depending on whether or not sulfur was used during processing. Sulfured molasses has a stronger flavor than lighter, more delicate unsulfured molasses.

Corn Syrup and Glucose Syrup

Corn syrup and glucose syrup are very similar syrups commonly used as an ingredient in pastries, cakes, and confections. Both are made through the conversion of starches into sugars. Cornstarch is typically used for syrup manufacture in America because it is widely available and inexpensive. Most European manufacturers, however, use potato starch to make syrups. The end result can be the same regardless of the starch used if the same process in manufacture is used and neither starch is inherently superior for syrup production.

There are two methods used to manufacture syrups from starches. The first method is to treat the starch with an acid and heat to convert it to sugar. After the conversion is complete, the acid is neutralized with an alkali. However, today, more and more syrups are manufactured with the use of enzymes. The enzymes used in syrup manufacture act to break down the polysaccharides in the starch. Using enzymes allows for more precise control of the process and it is therefore specialty corn syrups such as high fructose syrup and high maltose syrup that are manufactured using this method.

Corn syrup is purchased by a specification called DE, which stands for dextrose equivalence. Simply stated, DE is the amount that the chains of starch are broken down. The more the chains are broken down, the higher the DE rating. The DE of corn syrup provides you with some important information about that syrup. Syrups with higher DE ratings will be sweeter, thinner in consistency, and able to caramelize more readily. Flavor, viscosity, and caramelization are all of vital importance to the pastry chef. Most of the corn syrup used in the pastry kitchen is 42 DE syrup, which is a fairly thick syrup of only moderate sweetness, and will not discolor easily when cooked. Other available syrups are 63 DE, which is a very sweet, thin syrup, and 27 DE, which is a thick syrup that is only slightly sweet. Knowing the DE of the syrup in question doesn't tell everything about that syrup. Due to differences in manufacturing processes, even syrups with the same DE may behave slightly differently when used in a formula, particularly one that is cooked to a high temperature such as pulled sugar or hard candy.

Although these syrups may not be completely identical, they may be used interchangeably for 95 percent of their uses in pastry and confectionery. It is only when a syrup constitutes a very large part of the formula, as for example in pulled sugar, that the differences can be detected. However, even for formulas such as these, there is no guarantee of which syrup will perform better.

Malt syrup, made from sprouted barley and corn, is used in some yeast breads. *Diastatic malt syrup* contains enzymes that break down the flour's starch into sugars. *Nondiastatic malt syrup,* which contains no diastase enzymes, is used to flavor and enhance the color of doughs.

Golden syrup (or light treacle syrup) is processed from sugarcane juice. It can be used in place of corn syrup in confections and baked goods.

Honey, a naturally inverted sugar (see page 83), is a sweet syrup produced by bees from flower nectar. The flowers, not the bees, determine honey's flavor and color. Honey can range in color and flavor from pale yellow and mild to dark amber and robust, depending on the source of the nectar.

Maple syrup is a liquefied sugar made from the concentrated sap of the sugar maple tree. Maple syrup is available in several different grades, ranging from Grade AA, which is thin and mild in flavor to Grade C, which is thick and strongly flavored.

Inverted syrup is derived from sucrose that has been broken down into equal parts of glucose and fructose. Inverted sugar is manufactured by adding an acid, or invertase, to sucrose.

Thickeners

A thickener is any ingredient that is capable of gelling, stabilizing, or thickening. The list of thickeners used in the bakeshop includes gelatin, pectin, plant gums such as agar-agar, and starches. (For an explanation of how starches, gelatin, pectin, and gums thicken liquids, see pages 85–88.)

GELLING AGENTS

Gelatin is a protein processed from the bones, skin, and connective tissue of animals. It may be used as a gelling agent, thickener, stabilizer, emulsifier, and/or foaming agent. It is available in granulated or sheet form. Sheet gelatin is sold in different bloom strengths, or gauges, but as there is no universal standard of identification, the strengths of different gauge numbers may vary depending on manufacturer.

Pectin is a gelatinizing agent that occurs naturally in many fruits. It is produced commercially by extraction from citrus or apple skins. Pectin is the gelling agent commonly used in jams, jellies, and preserves. Pectin is also used to make the centers of high-quality jelly beans.

Agar-agar is a gum derived from sea vegetables. It is available powdered, in flakes or blocks, or as brittle strands. It has very strong gelling properties (stronger than those of gelatin), but its higher melting and gelling points make it unsuitable for some uses. Agar-agar is used in some vegetarian products and confections.

STARCHES

Processed and refined starches are used to thicken and stabilize liquid mixtures. They result in a range of textures and consistencies once they set into a gel.

Arrowroot, which is sometimes known as arrowroot flour, is derived from the arrowroot plant, a tropical tuber. It is often used for thickening sauces because of the transparent and high-gloss finish it yields.

Potato starch comes from potatoes that are cooked, dried, and then ground into a fine powder; it may also be called potato flour.

Cornstarch, ground from corn kernels, is used primarily as a thickener, but it is also sometimes used in conjunction with wheat flour to yield softer results in baked goods.

Tapioca is derived from the root of the tropical plant cassava, also called manioc. It is available as flakes, granules, and, most commonly, small balls or pellets (called pearl tapioca), and flour; the flour, or starch, is sometimes called cassava or manioc flour or starch.

Modified (or converted) starches are modified through a process involving an acid and hydrolysis. The starches produced in this manner function more efficiently as thickeners for frozen items that will be thawed, as they resist separation.

Sheets of leaf gelatin and granulated gelatin

Dairy Products

Milk, cream, and butter are among the dairy products used daily in most bakeshops and pastry kitchens. Customarily, containers and packages are dated to indicate how long the contents will remain fresh; because the freshness periods vary from container to container, the contents of different containers should not be combined.

When storing dairy products, flavor transfer is a particular concern. Store milk, cream, and butter away from foods with strong odors. Wrap cheeses carefully, both to maintain their texture and to prevent their aromas from permeating other foods.

MILK AND CREAM

Unless milk is homogenized, it will separate, allowing the cream to rise to the top as the milk sits. The milk sold today is typically forced through an ultrafine mesh at high pressure to break up the fat globules, dispersing them evenly throughout the milk in the process known as homogenization. Milk is also pasteurized to kill bacteria and other harmful organisms by heating it to a specific temperature for a specific period of time (140°F/60°C for 30 minutes, or 161°F/72°C for 15 seconds).

Milk is labeled according to its milk fat content. *Whole milk* contains at least 3 percent milk fat. *Reduced-fat milk* contains 2 percent milk fat, *low-fat milk* contains 1 percent, and *fat-free milk* contains less than 0.1 percent.

Cream, like milk, is homogenized and pasteurized, and it may be stabilized to help extend shelf life. Some chefs prefer cream that has not been stabilized or ultrapasteurized because they believe it will whip to a greater volume. *Heavy* or *whipping cream* must contain at least 35 percent milk fat and is used for whipping. *Light cream* has between 16 and 32 percent milk fat, and it does not whip easily. It is sometimes used instead of milk to add a richer flavor and creamier texture.

Evaporated milk is whole or fat-free milk that is heated in a vacuum to remove 60 percent of its water content. **Sweetened condensed milk** is evaporated milk that has been sweetened. These are sold in cans of varying sizes.

Nonfat dry milk (powdered milk) is made by removing the water from de-fatted milk. Sold in boxes, it does not contain any milk fat and can be stored at room temperature.

FERMENTED AND CULTURED MILK PRODUCTS

Buttermilk, crème fraîche, sour cream, and yogurt are all produced by inoculating milk or cream with a bacterial strain under precisely controlled conditions. The reaction of the culture with the milk product thickens the milk or cream and gives it a pleasant tangy flavor.

Traditionally **buttermilk** was the by-product of churning milk into butter. Most buttermilk sold today is nonfat milk to which a bacterial strain has been added and, despite its name, contains only a very small amount of butterfat. Buttermilk has a thick texture and a slightly sour flavor.

Sour cream is cultured cream with 16 to 22 percent fat. Low-fat and nonfat versions of sour cream are also available.

Yogurt is a cultured milk product made from whole, low-fat, or nonfat milk; it may be plain or flavored.

Crème fraîche is made by adding an acid to cream that has 30 percent milk fat. The acid thickens the cream but does not cause it to ferment, so crème fraîche has a sweet flavor. Its high fat content gives it a velvety texture.

CHEESES

Soft and/or Fresh Cheese

Soft or fresh cheeses are soft enough to spread or spoon easily. They typically have a mild, slightly tangy flavor and are low in fat. They are able to absorb liquids, making them a good ingredient for baking. Soft cheeses usually have a high moisture content and are relatively perishable.

Farmers and baker's cheeses are cow's milk cheeses with a mild, tart flavor and soft grainy texture. **Ricotta cheese** is a cow's milk cheese with a very mild, delicate flavor; it can be drained to produce a drier, grainy cheese. *Ricotta impastata* is a smooth, spoonable, dry cheese used when regular ricotta would add too much moisture to a formula, such as cannoli filling.

Cream cheese has a mild, slightly tangy taste and a soft, spreadable texture. The *reduced-fat cream cheese* sometimes called Neufchâtel (not to be confused with French Neufchâtel, a soft unripened cheese) has less fat than regular cream cheese, but it also has more moisture. This Neufechâtel may often be used interchangeably with regular cream cheese without requiring changes to the formula to compensate for the lower fat and higher moisture. Other types of cream cheese include low-fat, nonfat, whipped, and flavored; cream cheese is sold in blocks, tubs, or packages.

Mozzarella cheese, made from either cow's or water buffalo's milk, has a mild, slightly tangy flavor and a soft, creamy, slightly elastic texture. Mozzarella is sold fresh or aged, in balls or blocks; it is also available grated.

Hard and Grating Cheeses

Hard cheeses have a dry texture and firm consistency. They slice and grate easily. Grating cheeses are typically grated or shaved rather than cut because they have a hard crumbly texture and will not create a uniform slice with out breaking apart.

Cheddar cheese is a dry semi-firm cheese made from cow's milk. During manufacture it undergoes a cheddaring process where the curds are piled and pressed which causes the expulsion of whey allowing for the development of characteristic cheddar texture. Cheddar cheese originated in England, but is now commonly made in America and elsewhere.

Parmesan cheese (Parmigiano-Reggiano) is a very hard, crumbly grating cheese. It gets its special flavor and texture from an extended aging period, during which it dries and develops an intense, pungent flavor.

BUTTER

The best-quality butter has a sweet flavor, similar to fresh heavy cream; if salt has been added, it should be barely detectable. The color of butter will vary depending upon the breed of cow, the diet of the cow, and the time of year, but is typically a pale yellow. Both **salted and unsalted butter** are available. The designation "sweet butter" indicates only that the butter is made from sweet cream (as opposed to sour). If unsalted butter is desired, be sure that the word "unsalted" appears on the package.

According to USDA regulations, salted butter may contain no more than a maximum of 2 percent salt. The salt can extend the butter's shelf life, but it can also mask slightly off flavors or aromas. Old butter takes on a very faintly cheesy flavor and aroma, especially when heated. As it continues to deteriorate, the flavor and aroma can become quite pronounced and unpleasant, much like sour or curdled milk.

Grade AA butter has the best flavor, color, aroma, and texture. Grade A butter also is of excellent quality. All grades of butter must contain a minimum of 80 percent milk fat. Grade B may have a slightly acidic taste, as it can be made from soured cream.

EGGS

Eggs are graded by the U.S. Department of Agriculture based on appearance and freshness. The top grade, AA, indicates a very fresh egg (if they have been properly stored and recently purchased) with a white that will not spread unduly once the egg is broken and a yolk that rides high on the white's surface. Eggs come in a number of sizes: jumbo, extra large, large, medium, small, and peewee. Large or extra-large eggs are used in most baking formulas.

Eggs should be refrigerated and the stock rotated as necessary to ensure that only fresh eggs are used. Upon delivery, look for shells that are clean and free of cracks. Discard any eggs with broken shells; they are at a high risk for contamination.

Eggs can be dried and powdered or pasteurized. *Dried eggs* are available in various forms: whole eggs, yolks, or whites. *Pasteurized eggs* are sold as whole eggs (which may be fortified), yolks, or whites. They can be purchased in refrigerated or frozen liquid form, as well as dried and powdered. Once thawed, frozen pasteurized eggs are perishable and must be stored and handled like fresh eggs.

Separating an Egg

Eggs separate most easily when they are cold. When separating eggs, you should have four clean containers ready: one to catch the white as the egg is separated, one to hold the clean whites, one for the yolks, and one for any whites containing some yolk.

Crack the egg's shell and pull it apart into two halves over one of the containers. Pour the egg from one half to the other, allowing the white to fall into the container. When all of the white has separated from the yolk, drop the yolk into a

separate container. Examine the white in the bowl, and drop it into another container. If the white has any bits of yolk in it, add only other whites with bits of yolk to it; these whites can be used in other dishes, where the whites need not be beaten to a foam. Keep the clean whites in a separate container.

Keep the eggs chilled as you work, and refrigerate the whites and yolks, labeled and dated, as soon as you have finished if you do not plan to use them immediately.

Egg substitutes may be entirely egg-free or they may be made with egg whites, with dairy or vegetable products substituted for the yolks. Egg substitutes are used for specific types of dietary baking and cooking.

Oils, Shortenings, and Other Fats

OILS AND SHORTENINGS

Vegetable and other similar oils are produced by pressing a high-oil-content food, such as olives, nuts, corn, avocados, or soybeans. The oil may then be filtered, clarified, or hydrogenated, depending on its intended use. The hydrogenation process causes the oil to remain solid at room temperature; in this state, it is known as shortening. All oils and shortenings should be stored in a dry place away from light and extremes of heat.

Vegetable oils are often neutral in flavor and color and have relatively high smoking points. If the label does not specify a source, the oil is usually a blend of oils. *Canola oil* (or rapeseed oil) is a light, golden-colored oil extracted from rapeseeds and is low in saturated fat. *Corn oil* is a mild-flavored refined oil, medium yellow in color, inexpensive, and versatile. *Soybean oil* has a pronounced flavor and aroma; it is found primarily in blended vegetable oils and margarines.

Olive oils vary in heaviness and may be pale yellow to deep green depending on the particular fruit and the processing method. Cold-pressed olive oil is superior in flavor to thermally refined oil. The finest olive oil available is *extra virgin olive oil.* It has a naturally low level of acid, typically less than 1 percent. *Virgin olive oil,* also known as *pure olive oil,* is the next best grade. Both extra virgin and virgin olive oils are prized for their flavor. For this reason they are often used in preparations where the oil is not cooked and in or on products after they have been cooked or baked to preserve and take advantage of their flavor. A blend of *refined olive oil* (virgin oil that has been thermally treated to remove its undesirable characteristics) and virgin olive oil is commonly used for baking and cooking.

Most **nut oils** have rich aromas. They are usually more perishable than vegetable or olive oils. Store them under refrigeration to keep them fresh, and use them within a few weeks of opening for the best flavor. Most *peanut oils* are a pale yellow refined oil, with a very subtle scent and flavor, but some less-refined types are darker and have a more pronounced peanut flavor.

Oil sprays are vegetable oils (usually blended) packaged in pump or aerosol spray containers. They are used for lightly coating pans and griddles.

Hydrogenated shortenings are produced from liquid fats that have been chemically altered under pressure with purified hydrogen to make them solid at room temperature. Shortening may contain some animal fats unless specifically labeled as vegetable shortening.

Emulsifying shortening or **high-ratio shortening** is a hydrogenated shortening that contains monoglycerides and other agents so that it better absorbs and retains moisture in baked goods. Emulsifying shortening is used in recipes where the amount of sugar and liquids is proportionally greater than the flour.

OTHER FATS

Margarine is a solid fat made with hydrogenated vegetable oils and milk, either liquid or milk solids. Regular margarines contain 80 percent fat. Margarine can also contain salt, artificial flavorings, and preservatives. A wide variety of margarines are available, from regular to whipped to reduced-fat and cholesterol-lowering blends, in sticks, blocks, or tubs.

Lard is made from rendered pork fat. It is processed and hydrogenated to make it solid. It may also be treated to neutralize its flavor.

Chocolate

The extraction and processing of chocolate from cacao beans is a lengthy and complex process. The first stage involves crushing the kernels into a paste; at this point it is completely unsweetened and is called *chocolate liquor.* The liquor is then further ground to give it a smoother, finer texture, and sweeteners and other ingredients may be added. The liquor may also be pressed to force out most of the *cocoa butter.* The solids that are left are ground into cocoa powder. Cocoa butter is combined with chocolate liquor to make baking and eating chocolates, or it may simply be flavored and sweetened to make white chocolate. Cocoa butter also has numerous pharmaceutical and cosmetic uses.

Chocolate keeps for several months if wrapped and stored in a cool, dry, ventilated area away from sunlight. Ordinarily it should not be refrigerated, since this could cause moisture to condense on the surface of the chocolate. Under particularly hot and humid kitchen conditions, however, it may be preferable to refrigerate or freeze chocolate to prevent loss of flavor. Sometimes stored chocolate develops a white "bloom." Bloom merely indicates that some of the cocoa butter has melted and then recrystallized on the surface, and chocolate with a bloom can still be safely used. Cocoa powder should be stored in tightly sealed containers in a dry place. It will keep almost indefinitely.

TYPES OF CHOCOLATE

Cocoa powder is a powdered chocolate product with a cocoa butter content ranging from 10 to 25 percent. *Dutch-process cocoa powder,* which is 22 to 24 percent cocoa butter, has been treated with an alkali to reduce its acidity. Dutch-process cocoa powder is darker in color than regular cocoa powder.

Unsweetened chocolate (also known as bitter or baking chocolate) contains no sugar. It is approximately 95 percent chocolate liquor and 5 percent cocoa butter.

Bittersweet chocolate typically contains at least 50 percent chocolate liquor, 15 percent cocoa butter, and 35 to 50 percent sugar. **Semisweet chocolate** usually contains at least 35 percent chocolate liquor, 15 percent cocoa butter, and 40 percent sugar. These chocolates may be used interchangeably in most recipes.

Couverture chocolate contains 15 percent chocolate liquor, 35 percent cocoa butter, and 50 percent sugar. Its high fat content makes it ideal for coating candy, pastries, and cakes.

Milk chocolate is 10 percent chocolate liquor, 20 percent cocoa butter, 50 percent sugar, and 15 percent milk solids. **Sweet chocolate** is 15 percent chocolate liquor, 15 percent cocoa butter, and 70 percent sugar. These chocolates often contain other added ingredients and flavors.

White chocolate is made from cocoa butter, sugar, flavorings, and milk. Since it does not contain chocolate liquor, it is not legally considered true chocolate.

Confectionery coating is a chocolate product containing no cocoa butter. Confectionery coating is made with vegetable fats and requires no tempering prior to use. It is also referred to as summer coating or compound chocolate. Confectionery coating is available in a range of flavors such as milk chocolate and bittersweet chocolate.

LEAVENERS

There are many different ways in which a baked product may be leavened. Some are leavened through the use of a technique or method, others by the addition of an ingre-

BACK ROW:
Milk chocolate, Dutch-process cocoa powder, couverture, white chocolate, milk chocolate

FRONT ROW:
Cocoa powder, semisweet chocolate, bittersweet chocolate, unsweetened chocolate

dient, and others still by a combination of the two. (For more information on leavening see pages 79–82.) Ingredients that are added to provide leavening fall into one of two categories, biological (yeast) or chemical (baking soda or baking powder).

YEAST

Active dry yeast is dehydrated, dormant yeast granules. It requires a warm liquid to activate it. Active dry yeast should be stored in an airtight container in the refrigerator or freezer.

Rapid rise yeast is a type of dehydrated yeast formulated to provide a quick rise. It is extremely active once rehydrated and dies quickly. Rapid rise yeast should be stored in an airtight container in the refrigerator or freezer.

Instant dry yeast is derived from cultures that can ferment using both beet sugar and malt sugar, guaranteeing fermentation activity through all phases of the dough. It can be used without rehydration. When working with instant dry yeast, very cold or icy water should be used in the mixing process.

Compressed fresh yeast is a highly perishable yeast product. It should have a moist, firm texture and show no discoloration or dry, crumbly spots. Store it under refrigeration.

CHEMICAL LEAVENERS

Baking powder is a mixture of bicarbonate of soda and an acid (the leavening agents) and a starch. It may be double- or single-acting. (For more information on baking powder, see page 81.)

Baking soda is sodium bicarbonate. It requires both an acid and moisture in order to leaven a product. (For more information on baking soda, see page 80.)

Salt

Table salt may be *iodized,* meaning it contains added iodine, a preventive against goiter, or *noniodized.* Its small, dense, grains adhere poorly to food, dissolve slowly in solution, and are difficult to blend.

Kosher salt is a coarse salt that weighs less by volume than table salt. It dissolves more readily and adheres to food better.

Sea salt is collected through the evaporation of natural saltwater. The salt's thin, flaky layers adhere well to food and dissolve quickly. Sea salt also contains various trace minerals that occur naturally in the waters from which they are collected. As a result, sea salt from different areas of the world taste different. All are generally more complex in flavor than table and kosher salt. Sea salt can be purchased in fine-grain and coarser crystal forms.

Rock salt, also known as **bay salt,** is a very coarse salt used in crank ice cream makers. It may have a gray tint from the impurities it contains. Rock salt is generally not manufactured for consumption.

Herbs, Spices, and Flavorings

HERBS

Fresh herbs should be examined carefully for quality. They should appear fresh and firm, with no evidence of wilting or bruising. Fresh herbs are perishable; store them under refrigeration, loosely wrapped in dampened paper towels and then plastic. Some herbs, such as basil and mint whose leaves are easily bruised, are best stored, if space permits, as if they were bouquets of flowers, with the stems in cool water.

Basil is an herb belonging to the mint family and has green pointed leaves and a pungent licorice flavor. It may be used fresh or dried.

Chive is an herb belonging to the onion family and has a mild onion flavor. It has long, slender light green stems and lavender-colored flowers, both of which are edible and used commonly in culinary applications. It is available fresh or dried but is most commonly used as a fresh herb.

CLOCKWISE FROM TOP LEFT: Chives, flat-leaf parsley, curly parsley, mint, oregano, rosemary, dill, basil (in center)

Dill is an herb with blue-green, thread-like foliage and yellow feathery flowers that produce small brown seeds, all of which are edible; the seeds have the most pungent flavor.

There are many varieties of **mint.** *Peppermint* has a strong flavor. It is available fresh, dried, or as an extract. *Spearmint* has gray-green leaves and a milder flavor than peppermint.

Oregano is an herb belonging to the mint family; it has small oval leaves. Oregano and **marjoram** are similar in flavor, but oregano is stronger. Both may be used fresh or dried.

Parsley has a mild, peppery flavor. Its leaves may be curly or flat (also called Italian parsley), depending on the variety. It is available fresh or dried, but is primarily used as a fresh herb.

Rosemary is another herb in the mint family, with leaves shaped like pine needles. It has a resin-like aroma and flavor and is available fresh, dried, or ground.

SPICES

Allspice is the dried berry of the pimiento tree. Its flavor is reminiscent of cinnamon, nutmeg, and cloves. It is available whole or ground.

Caraway and **anise seed** are both derived from herbs in the parsley family. Anise seeds have a distinct licorice flavor. Anise is available as whole seeds, ground, or as an extract. Caraway seeds are sometimes labeled "kimmel"; they are available whole or ground.

Cardamom is a plant in the ginger family. Each of its pods contains 15 to 20 small seeds. Cardamom has a pungent aroma and a sweet and spicy flavor. It is available as whole pods or ground.

Cinnamon is the stripped dried bark of an evergreen in the laurel family. It is sold whole, in sticks, or ground.

Cloves are the dried unopened buds of a tropical evergreen tree. They have a strong flavor. Cloves are available whole or ground.

Nutmeg is the seed of the nutmeg tree. It has a sweet and spicy flavor and is available either whole or ground. **Mace** is the lacy membrane covering the nutmeg seed. It has a pungent nutmeg flavor and is available ground or whole.

Peppercorns may be black, white, green, or pink. *Black peppercorns* are picked when not quite ripe and then dried; the Tellicherry peppercorn is one of the most prized black peppercorns. *White peppercorns* are allowed to ripen before they are picked, then the husks are removed and they are dried. Black and white pepper is available as whole berries, cracked, or ground. *Mignonette,* or *shot pepper,* is a combination of coarsely ground or crushed black and white peppercorns. *Green peppercorns* are picked when underripe, then packed in vinegar or brine or freeze-dried. Drain and rinse brine-packed peppercorns before using; reconstitute freeze-dried peppercorns in water before use. *Pink peppercorns* are the dried berries of the *Baies* rose plant, not a true peppercorn. They are usually available freeze-dried.

Vanilla beans are the pod of a delicate orchid flower. Vanilla has a distinct aromatic flavor. Vanilla is available as whole beans and as an extract.

Garlic is the bulb of the garlic plant; each bulb is made up of 7 to 12 cloves. It is available fresh, powdered, or granulated.

Ginger is the rhizome of the ginger plant. It has a pungent, hot flavor. It is available fresh, in dried pieces, ground, or crystallized.

Nuts

With the exception of the peanut, which grows underground in the root system of a leguminous plant and is actually a legume, nuts are the fruits of certain trees. They are available in various forms: in the shell, shelled, roasted, blanched, sliced, slivered, or chopped, and as nut butter.

Nuts have a number of uses, adding flavor and texture to many dishes. They are fairly expensive and should be stored carefully to keep them from becoming rancid. Nuts that have not been roasted or shelled will keep longer than those that have been. Shelled nuts can be stored in the freezer or refrigerator if space allows. In any case, they should be stored in a cool, dry, well-ventilated area and checked periodically to be sure they are still fresh.

The **almond** is a teardrop-shaped nut that is part of a fruit that resembles an apricot. It has a pale tan, woody shell. *Sweet almonds* are sold whole, in the shell or shelled, blanched or unblanched, roasted, sliced, or slivered, and as almond paste and other products. The sale of *bitter almonds* is illegal in the United States; however, once processed, they are used to flavor extracts and liquors that are readily available.

Brazil nuts are among the largest nuts. They grow in segmented clusters; each segment contains a hard, wrinkled, three-sided brown seed. Brazil nuts are sold whole, in the shell or shelled.

Cashews are kidney-shaped nuts that grow as the appendage of an apple-like fruit (the fruit is not eaten). The shell of the cashew contains toxic oils, so cashews are always sold shelled, raw or toasted, whole or in pieces.

Chestnuts have hard glossy brown shells covering the round- or teardrop-shaped nuts. There are sold whole, in the shell or shelled, canned, packed in syrup or water, candied, frozen, in vacuum-sealed packages, or as purée.

Coconuts are the fruits of a type of palm tree. The "nut" is composed of a woody brown outer shell covered with hairy fibers surrounding a layer of rich white nut meat. Coconuts are sold whole, and coconut meat is sold shredded or in flakes (sweetened or unsweetened). Coconut milk, coconut cream, and other coconut-based products are also available.

Hazelnuts (also called filberts) are small, nearly round nuts, rich and delicately flavored. Their shiny, hard shells have a matte spot where they were attached to the tree. Hazelnuts are sold whole, in the shell or shelled, or chopped.

Macadamia nuts are extremely rich, sweet nuts native to Australia. They are pale in color and nearly round. Macadamia nuts are sold shelled and roasted in coconut oil.

Peanuts are sold in the shell or shelled, raw (or natural), roasted, or dry-roasted, or as a butter.

Pecans have two lobes and a rich flavor. The shell is medium-brown, smooth, and glossy. They are sold in the shell or shelled, as halves or pieces.

Natural **pistachio nuts** have cream-colored shells; the nutmeat is green with a distinctive sweet flavor. Pistachios are usually sold whole in the shell, raw or roasted (usually salted), natural or dyed red. Occasionally they are sold shelled, whole or chopped.

Walnuts are mild, tender, oily nuts. They grow in two segments inside a hard shell and are typically light brown with deep ridges patterning the surface. *White walnuts* (or *butternuts*) and *black walnuts* are two North American varieties. Butternuts are richer, while black walnuts have a stronger flavor. Walnuts are sold whole in the shell or shelled, as halves or pieces, or pickled.

CLOCKWISE FROM TOP LEFT: Whole coconut, peanuts, chestnuts packed in water, whole blanched almonds, whole unblanched almonds, slivered almonds, pine nuts, cashews, sliced almonds, pistachios, macadamia nuts, flaked coconut, walnuts, pecans (in center)

Seeds

Some of the seeds used in the kitchen are considered spices (celery or fennel seed, for example), but others, including sunflower and pumpkin seeds, are treated more like nuts. These seeds, or the pastes made from them, should be stored in the same manner as nuts.

Anise seeds are small gray to gray-green almond-shaped seeds that have an intense licorice flavor. They are used whole or ground.

Caraway seeds are small, light brown, crescent-shaped seeds with an intense flavor. They are commonly used in rye bread.

Poppy seeds are tiny, round, blue-black seeds with a rich, slightly musty flavor. They are sold whole and as a paste.

CLOCKWISE FROM TOP RIGHT: Sesame seeds, poppy seeds, pumpkin seeds, sunflower seeds

Pumpkin seeds are flat, oval, cream-colored seeds. They have a semihard hull and a soft, oily interior. They are sold whole in the shell (raw or roasted) and shelled (raw or roasted).

Sesame seeds are tiny flat oval seeds. They may be black (or unhulled) or tan (hulled). They are somewhat oily, with a rich, nutty flavor. Sesame seeds are sold whole, shelled or unshelled, toasted, and as a paste (also known as *tahini*).

Sunflower seeds are flat, teardrop-shaped, light tan, oily seeds with a woody black-and-white shell. Sunflower seeds are sold whole in the shell or shelled.

Selecting and Handling Fresh Produce

Fruits and vegetables should be free of bruises, mold, brown or soft spots, and pest damage. Any attached leaves should be unwilted. They should be plump, not shriveled. Specific information on particular types of produce is given in the sections below.

Since it is usually not possible to examine produce until it has been delivered to the restaurant or bakery, one way to help ensure quality is to buy according to grade. Grading is based on U.S. Department of Agriculture standards. Lower-grade items, particularly fruits, may be used successfully in preparations such as baked pies and puddings, where appearance is not a factor.

Most produce has a noticeably better quality and flavor the closer it is to its source. Fruits that have been shipped, such as apricots, peaches, and strawberries, for example, may require special handling, which can drive up their cost, despite continued efforts to develop strains that combine good shipping qualities with superior flavor.

More and more vegetables are being grown hydroponically, that is, in nutrient-enriched water rather than soil. Hydroponic growing takes place indoors under regulated temperature and lighting conditions, so any growing season may be duplicated. Hydroponically grown lettuces, spinach, herbs, and tomatoes are all readily available. Although they have the advantage of being easy to clean, these products may have less flavor than conventionally grown fruits and vegetables.

With a few exceptions (including bananas, potatoes, and dry onions), ripe fruits and vegetables should be refrigerated. Unless otherwise specified, produce should be kept at a temperature of 40° to 45°F/4° to 7°C, with a relative humidity of 80 to 90 percent.

Keep fresh produce dry; excess moisture can promote spoilage. Likewise, most produce should not be peeled, washed, or trimmed until just before use. The outer leaves of lettuce, for example, should be left intact; carrots should remain unpeeled. The exceptions to this rule are the leafy tops on vegetables such as beets, turnips, carrots, and radishes. They should be removed, and either discarded or used as soon as possible, because even after harvesting, these leaves absorb nutrients from the vegetable and increase moisture loss.

Fruits and vegetables that need further ripening, notably peaches and pears, should be stored at room temperature, 65° to 70°F/18° to 21°C. Once the produce is ripe, refrigerate it to keep it from overripening.

CLOCKWISE FROM TOP LEFT: Asian pears, Bosc pears, red pears, Red Delicious apples, D'Anjou pears, Comice pears, Red D'Anjou pears (cut), Forelle pears, Bartlett pears, Fuji apples, lady apples, McIntosh apples, Golden Delicious apples, Rome Beauty apples, Granny Smith apples (in bag in center), Bosc pear (leaning against cutting board)

APPLES

The most commonly available apple varieties include *Golden* and *Red Delicious, McIntosh, Granny Smith, Rome Beauty, Fuji,* and *Gala.* There are, however, hundreds of other varieties grown in orchards throughout the country. A little searching might result in a find that makes your apple tart uniquely flavorful.

Different varieties of apples have particular characteristics. Some are best for eating out of hand or for preparations where they are left fresh and uncooked. Other types are best for pies and baking; they tend to retain a recognizable shape and some texture even when baked. Still others are notable for their ability to cook down into a rich, smooth purée. For cider, a blend of apples is usually best to give the finished drink a full, well-balanced flavor.

Fresh apples can be held in climate-controlled cold storage for many months without significant loss of quality. This makes it possible to get good fresh apples throughout the year. Dried apples, prepared applesauce, apple juice (bottled or frozen concentrate), cider, spiced or plain pie fillings, and a host of other prepared items made from apples are also available.

The flesh of many apples begins to turn brown once it is cut and comes into contact with air. Dousing the cut-up apples in water that has had a little lemon juice added will help prevent browning but may not be desirable when a pure apple taste is important.

Multipurpose apple varieties, good as table fruit, in baking, for sauces, and for freezing, include Red and Golden Delicious (firm, sweet, and aromatic), Granny Smith (tart, extremely crisp, and fine-textured), McIntosh (sweet and very juicy, with a crisp texture), Rome Beauty (firm flesh with a mild tart-sweet flavor), and Winesap (firm, tart-sweet, and aromatic).

Baking varieties include Greening (mild, sweet-tart flavor; good for pies and sauces; and also freezes well), Jonathan (tender, semitart flesh), and Northern Spy (crisp, firm-textured, and juicy with a sweet-tart taste).

There are many varieties of apples that are available only in certain areas of the country. If you have any questions, ask your purveyor or another reputable source for the best use of a particular variety.

BERRIES

Strawberries, raspberries, blueberries, and blackberries are so seasonal that for most people, seeing a particular berry in the market means that spring has arrived or summer is at its height. Some varieties can be found at virtually any time of the year, but even with improved handling and shipping methods, some specialty berries are still only available fresh in season and from local purveyors.

Berries (with the exception of cranberries) are highly perishable and are susceptible to bruising, mold, and overripening in fairly short order. Inspect all berries and their packaging carefully before you accept them. Jui-stained cartons or juice leaking through the carton is a clear indication that the fruit has been mishandled or is old. Once one or two berries begin to turn moldy, the entire batch goes quickly.

The season for fresh berries varies from region to region, though many berries are widely available as imports from other regions or countries. A variety of processed forms are also available: frozen (individually quick frozen, or IQF, with or without sugar), purées, concentrates, and dried.

Berries (except for cranberries) can be eaten fresh or used in baked items, syrups, purées and sauces, cordials, jellies, jams, and syrups. Some classic berry preparations include strawberry shortcake, fresh berry cobblers, pies, jams, jellies, and ice creams.

Strawberries are red, shiny, heart-shaped berries with their tiny seeds on the exterior. They are available year-round, but their peak season is late spring to early summer. Generally speaking, small berries have a sweeter more intense flavor than the larger berries.

Raspberries are actually clusters of tiny fruits (drupes), each containing a seed; red, black, and yellow (golden) or white varieties are available.

Dewberries are a type of raspberry.

Mulberries resemble raspberries but are in fact unrelated. They are juicy, with a slightly musty aroma.

Boysenberries are a hybrid of the raspberry, blackberry, and loganberry.

Blackberries, also known as **bramble berries,** resemble raspberries in form, but are deep purple in color. Their peak season is mid- to late summer.

FROM LEFT TO RIGHT: Blackberries, strawberries, raspberries, blueberries

Blueberries are bluish-purple berries with a dusty silver-blue bloom. Typically, the smaller berries have a sweeter, more intense flavor than the larger berries.

Currants are small round berries that may be red, black, or white. The red are generally the sweetest.

Elderberries are small and purple-black. They are typically used in cooked applications as they have a very sour flavor.

Gooseberries have a smooth skin and a papery husk that may still be attached when they are sold. They can be green, golden, red, purple, or white. Some have fuzzy skins.

Grapes are shiny, smooth skinned, and range in color from green to deep purple and in flavor from very sweet to sour. Dried, they are known as raisins. Dried seedless Zante grapes are known as dried currants.

Cranberries are shiny red (some have a white blush), firm, and sour.

CITRUS FRUITS

Citrus fruits are characterized by their extremely juicy, segmented flesh and skins that contain aromatic oils. Grapefruits, lemons, limes, and oranges are the most common citrus fruits. They range in flavor from very sweet (oranges) to very tart (lemons).

There are four basic types of **oranges:** juice, eating, bitter, and mandarin. *Juice oranges* have smooth skin that is somewhat difficult to peel. They are usually plump and sweet, which makes them ideal for juicing. *Eating oranges* include the navel, which is large, seedless, and easy to peel. They may or may not have seeds. *Blood oranges* have orange skin with a blush of red. They are aromatic and have pockets of dark red or maroon flesh and are used for both juice and eating. *Bitter oranges* are used almost exclusively to make marmalade. *Mandarin oranges*, a category that includes mandarins, tangerines, and clementines, have skins thinner than those of oranges that are loose and peel very easily. Mandarins are seedless. Tangerines are juicy with a sweet-tart flavor and usually have many seeds. Clementines have less acid than most oranges and are as fragrant as they are flavorful. Because of their dainty size, they are often featured as a garnish.

All **grapefruits** have yellow skin, sometimes with a rosy blush where the sun hit them. The skin of white grapefruits may have a green blush, and the flesh is pale yellow; seedless varieties are available. Pink grapefruits have yellow skin with a pink blush; the flesh is pink. The skin of red grapefruits has a red blush, and the flesh is deep red with a mellow sweet-tart flavor. Both the pink and red are juiced or eaten fresh.

Lemons have yellow-green to deep yellow skin and extremely tart flesh; they always have seeds. Meyer lemons are not true lemons; they are a hybrid that was imported from China. They are most likely a cross between an orange and a lemon and are about the size of a large lemon, with smooth skin. The flesh is a light orange-yellow color, and the juice is sweeter than regular lemon juice.

Persian limes have dark green, smooth skin, and flesh that is tart and seedless. **Key limes** have light green skin. Their most famous use is in Key lime pie.

Kumquats are small oblong fruits with a golden-orange peel. The flesh contains small white seeds. With a sweet-tart peel and tart juicy flesh, kumquats are entirely edible.

MELONS

Melons are fragrant, succulent fruits related to squashes and cucumbers. They come in many varieties and range in size from the acor cantaloupe, which is only 1 to 2 lb/454 to 907 g, to the watermelon. The four major types of melons are cantaloupes, muskmelons, watermelons, and winter melons (including honeydew, casaba, and crenshaw).

The ability to determine when a melon is ripe is one that eludes some people. Depending upon the type, you should look for a number of different signs. Cantaloupes should have a "full slip"—this means that the melon ripened on the vine and grew away from the stem, leaving no rough edges at the stem end; underripe cantaloupes usually have a scarred or rough stem end. Some melons become slightly soft at the stem end when properly ripened, but for certain varieties this indicates that they are over the hill. Aroma and heaviness for size are the best general keys to determining ripeness, regardless of variety.

CLOCKWISE FROM TOP LEFT:
White grapefruit, lemon, mandarin oranges, navel orange, Key limes (in mesh bag), pink grapefruit, pomelo (cut), blood oranges (cut), Meyer lemons, Persian limes (cut and whole), tangerines (peeled), kumquats, white grapefruit (cut), navel oranges

FROM LEFT TO RIGHT: Gallia (halved, with seeds removed), honeydew (halved, with seeds), cantaloupe wedge, carlencas (whole and halved), watermelon wedge, cantaloupe (halved)

Cantaloupes have coarse netting or veining over their surface and a yellow to buff background color; the stem end should have a smooth mark to show that the melon ripened on the vine. Their flesh is smooth, orange, juicy, and fragrant.

Muskmelons resemble cantaloupes except that they are deeply ridged.

The most popular and well-known **watermelon** is the large oval variety (15 to 30 lb/6.80 to 13.61 kg) with a light and dark green-striped rind and pink flesh. Watermelons, however, come in many different varieties with flesh that may be white, yellow, or pink. All varieties have a thick hard rind and crisp, granular, juicy (or watery) flesh. They are available in seedless varieties.

Winter melons are a group of melons characterized by their late harvest, which comes in late fall due to the extended ripening time they require. *Casaba melons* have a light to yellow-green skin that becomes smooth and velvety as the melons ripen. Casabas have a rich melon aroma when ripe. *Crenshaw melons* have very fragrant, salmon-colored flesh and, when they are ripe, a slight softening near the stem. *Honeydew melons* are juicy with vivid green flesh; their skin loses any greenish cast and develops a velvety and slightly tacky feel when they are ripe. *Persian melons* have dark green skin with yellow markings and yellow-orange flesh. When ripe, they feel heavy for their size and yield slightly when pressed.

PEARS

Pears, like apples, are grown in many varieties, with the most common being Bartlett, Bosc, Comice, d'Anjou, and Seckel. Because the flesh of pears is extremely fragile, they are picked for shipping before they have fully ripened. The fruit continues to soften at room temperature. In addition to being eaten out of hand, pears are often poached whole or used in sorbet.

The **Asian pear** is an apple-shaped fruit with a smooth skin that ranges in color from green to yellow-brown. The white flesh has a juicy, mildly sweet flavor.

Bartlett pears, also known as **Williams pears,** have green skin that turns yellow as the fruit ripens. Red Bartlett pears have a brilliant scarlet-colored skin.

Bosc pears have a long neck and dark, russeted skin that turns brown when the fruit is ripe.

Comice pears are round with a short neck and stem and a greenish-yellow skin, sometimes with a reddish blush. They are very sweet and juicy.

D'Anjou pears have green skin that becomes yellow as they ripen and may have brown scarring.

Seckel pears are small and crisp, with green skin and a red blush. They are usually eaten fresh.

STONE FRUITS

Peaches, nectarines, apricots, plums, and cherries are often referred to as stone fruits because they have one large central pit, or stone. In North America, they typically come into peak season through the late spring and into summer. Stone fruits need to be handled delicately because their flesh has a tendency to bruise easily. Stone fruits are used in preserves, shortcakes, pies, and cobblers, as well as in savory dishes. In addition to their fresh form, they are commonly available canned, frozen, and dried. Fruit brandies, wines, and cordials flavored with peaches, cherries, and plums are produced in many countries.

Peaches are sweet and juicy, with a distinctive fuzzy skin. They come in many varieties, but all peaches fall into one of two categories: *clingstone* or *freestone.* Clingstone peaches have flesh that clings to the pit, whereas the flesh of freestone peaches separates easily. Depending on the variety, peach flesh ranges from white to creamy yellow to yellow-orange to red, with a whole host of combinations possible.

Nectarines are similar in shape, color, and flavor to peaches, but they have smooth skin. Like peaches, they are classified as either clingstone or freestone; some varieties have flesh with a texture similar to that of plums.

Apricots have slightly fuzzy skin, like peaches, but are smaller, with somewhat drier flesh. The skin ranges in color from yellow to golden orange, and some have rosy patches.

Plums can be as small as an apricot or as large as a peach. When ripe, they are sweet and juicy, and some have tart skins that contrast nicely with their succulent flesh. *Greengage plums,* with green skin and flesh, are a popular dessert variety. *Santa Rosa plums* are red with light yellow flesh. *Black Friar plums* have dark purple skins with a silvery bloom and deep red to purple flesh. *Damson plums,* the most well-known cooking plums, have purple skin with a silver-blue bloom. *Prune plums,* also called Italian plums, are small, with purple skin and green flesh that is relatively dry and separates cleanly from the pit; they are eaten fresh and dried as prunes, now sometimes called dried plums.

CLOCKWISE FROM TOP RIGHT: Assortment of stone fruits in basket, nectarine, purple plum, red plum, apricots, nectarines, peach

There are numerous varieties of **cherries,** and they come in many shades of red, from the light crimson *Queen Anne* to the almost black *Bing* and some are yellow/golden, such as *Royal Ann.* They vary in texture from firm and crisp to soft and juicy, and flavors run the gamut from sweet to sour. Cherries can be found fresh throughout their growing season, and they are also sold canned, dried, candied, or frozen and as prepared fillings for Danish, pies, and other pastries. Cherry syrups and cherry-flavored cordials are also available; kirschwasser, a clear cherry cordial, is often used in bakeshops and kitchens.

EXOTIC OR TROPICAL FRUITS

A wide variety of fruits fall into this category, most of which are grown in tropical regions: figs, guavas, kiwis, mangoes, papayas, pineapples, plantains, pomegranates, passion fruit, and star fruit. An ever-increasing number of exotic fruits are available through regular and specialty outlets.

Unlike most fruits, **bananas** are usually picked green and allowed to ripen en route to the buyer. When ripe, they have a firm yellow skin and a few black spots. The flesh is soft and creamy white.

Guavas are round to oblong-shaped fruits with light green to yellow edible skin. The flesh usually ranges in color from white to yellow but may even be salmon or red. It contains tiny edible seeds.

Kiwis, or kiwifruits, are small oval fruits with brownish hairy skin. The flesh is bright green, with small edible black seeds and a citrus-like flavor.

Lychees are small round fruits with a thin, bumpy red to brown skin and a single large seed. The flesh is gray-white and translucent with a grape-like texture and a sweet grape-cherry flavor.

Mangoes are round to oval fruits with red to orange-yellow skin that may be tinged with green. They are very juicy and sweet, with an intense and aromatic aroma. The yellow-orange flesh surrounds a large flat seed.

Papayas are pear-shaped fruits with smooth yellow-orange to green skin. The juicy, yellow-orange flesh, which has a melon-peach flavor, surrounds a cluster of small black seeds in the center of the fruit.

Passion fruits are round or egg-shaped fruits with leathery, purple-brown skin. The pulp has a jelly-like consistency and contains many seeds. The pulp and crunchy edible seeds have a sweet-tart, lemony flavor.

There are two types of common **persimmon,** both about the size of a baseball. The *Fuyu persimmon* has a round, slightly flattened shape with pale orange to brilliant red-orange skin. Its orange flesh is crisp, with a sweet, mild flavor. The *Hachiya persimmon* is heart shaped with brilliant orange-red skin. Its soft, orange flesh has a sweet, spicy flavor. The Hachiya is very astringent when not completely ripe.

Pomegranates (sometimes called Chinese apples) are round and about the size of a grapefruit. The red skin has a leathery texture. Under the skin, thin white membranes encase edible crimson-colored seeds that have a crisp texture and tangy-sweet flavor.

Star fruits (or carambola) are egg-shaped fruits with deep chevron ridges that result in a star shape when the fruit is sliced crosswise. The skin is yellow, smooth, and edible. The juicy, crisp pale yellow flesh has a sweet-tart flavor and contains only a few seeds.

RHUBARB

Although rhubarb is technically a vegetable, it is classified here as a fruit because of the way it is used. Often known as pie plant, it grows in long stalks with broad, somewhat curly leaves. Only the reddish green stalks are eaten; the leaves should never be used, because they contain large quantities of oxalic acid, a toxic compound. Rhubarb is crisp and very sour, so it is usually cooked and sweetened.

Extracts

The pastry chef and baker use a variety of flavoring extracts for cooking and baking. Many different herbs, spices, nuts, and fruits are used to prepare extracts, which are alcohol based. Common extracts include *vanilla, lemon, mint,* and *almond.*

Extracts can lose their potency if they are exposed to air, heat, or light. To preserve their flavor, store in tightly capped dark glass jars or bottles away from heat or direct light.

Wines, Cordials, and Liqueurs

A general rule of thumb for selecting wines, cordials, and liqueurs for use in cooking and baking is that if it is not suitable for drinking, it is not suitable for cooking.

Brandies, including fruit brandies and cognac, Champagne, dry red and white wines, port, Sauternes, sherry, stout, ale, beer, and sweet and dry vermouth, as well as liquors and liqueurs such as bourbon, crème de cassis, kirschwasser, gin, Kahlúa, rum, and Scotch are all useful in the bakeshop.

Purchase wines and liqueurs that are affordably priced and of good quality. Table wines lose their flavor and become acidic once they are opened, especially if subjected to heat, light, and air. To preserve flavor, keep them in sealed bottles or bottles fitted with pouring spouts, and refrigerate them when not needed. Fortified wines (Madeira, sherry, and port, for example) are more stable than table wines and can be held in dry storage if there is not enough room to refrigerate them.

CLOCKWISE FROM UPPER LEFT: Bananas, fingerling bananas, pineapple (whole and cut), mangoes, passion fruit (whole and cut), star fruit (whole and cut), kiwi, papaya (whole and cut)

Coffee and Tea

Coffee and tea may be used to infuse flavor in countless pastry and confection preparations. Tea is most often used to infuse its flavor into a warm liquid that will be added to the item, whereas coffee may be used in its many forms to add its flavor. Coffee beans, ground or whole, may be used to infuse their flavor as is done with tea. Powdered or instant coffee is often dissolved in a small amount of water or other liquid to form a paste that is then added directly to the formula.

CHAPTER 3

Equipment Identification

JUST AS AN ARTIST LEARNS TO MASTER ALL THE INSTRUMENTS NECESSARY FOR PAINTING, SCULPTING, OR DRAWING, BAKERS AND PASTRY CHEFS LEARN TO MASTER A VARIETY OF SMALL TOOLS AND LARGE EQUIPMENT. THESE DEVICES ARE AS IMPORTANT AS YOUR OWN FINGERS—QUITE LITERALLY AN EXTENSION OF YOUR HANDS. TOOLS AND EQUIPMENT OF ALL SORTS REPRESENT ONE OF THE BIGGEST INVESTMENTS IN THE PROFESSIONAL BAKESHOP AND PASTRY KITCHEN.

Scaling and Measuring Tools

In baking, even more so than in cooking, precise measurement of ingredients is vital to the success of the product. Precise measurements are crucial both to keep costs in line and to ensure consistency of quality and quantity. Measurements are taken of weight, volume, temperature, distance or length, and density.

SCALES

Scales must be used correctly to be effective. You want the weight of only the ingredient, not the ingredient and the container holding it. Before using any scale, you must take certain steps to account for the weight of containers. This process is known as setting a scale to tare or setting it to zero.

A **beam balance** (or **baker's balance**) has two platforms attached on either end of a beam. The point where the beam and the base meet is the fulcrum. At the front of the scale, a weight hangs from a bar notched at 1-oz/28-g increments. To weigh an ingredient, slide the hanging weight to the correct amount. To find an ingredient's weight, move the hanging weight until the platforms are level. To set the scale to zero, make sure that the two platforms are level. Beam balances can measure quantities far greater than the maximum weight shown on the scale if counterweights (typically available in weights of 1 lb/454 g, 2 lb/907 g, and 4 lb/1.81 kg) are used. To use a counterweight, set the weight on the right platform, then add enough of the ingredient to the left platform to make the two platforms level.

Spring scales have a platform set on top of a pedestal that contains a spring mechanism for weighing and a dial indicator on the front. To tare a spring scale, place the container for measuring the ingredients on the scale and turn the dial so that the pointer or arrow is aligned with zero. Spring scales are designed to read in any number of increments. Some are very sensitive and can measure small amounts, while others are made so that they only measure in large increments.

Digital scales have a stainless-steel platform set on an electronic base with digital display. Scales capable of measuring very small amounts typically have a smaller total capacity. Scales capable of weighing large amounts (more than 4 lb/1.81 kg) are less sensitive when measuring small amounts. To tare a digital scale, you press a button to reset the scale to zero. Most digital scales can switch between metric and U.S. standard measuring systems.

VOLUME MEASURES

Graduated pitchers or beakers and **measuring cups and spoons** are commonly used in the bakeshop to measure liquids and pourable ingredients (eggs, molasses, or corn syrup, for example). Pitchers and cups are scaled off with lines or markings to show varying measures. Clear pitchers and cups are easy to fill accurately. For the most accurate results, use the smallest measure possible to measure ingredients, place the vessel on a level surface and bend down to take the reading at eye level. Measuring spoons should be filled to the rim. Don't fill them over the batter or other mixture, in case you accidentally overpour.

Dry measuring cups are commonly used in recipes written for the home baker. In the bakeshop, they are used to measure small amounts of certain dry ingredients, such as salt, spices, and baking soda. To use measuring cups and spoons for dry ingredients, overfill the measure, then use a straightedge, such as the side of a metal spatula, to scrape the excess away; the ingredient should fill the measure evenly up to the rim.

THERMOMETERS

When a **mercury thermometer** is immersed in a liquid, the mercury inside the glass tube rises or falls, and the reading is taken from calibrated markings on the stem. Some mercury thermometers are enclosed in wire cages. Many have adjustable hooks or clips so they can be attached to a pan.

Stem-type thermometers are excellent for checking the internal temperature of products such as doughs or custards; they can also be used to check the temperature of liquids. These thermometers consist of a long stem with a digital or dial head that indicates the temperature.

Probe thermometers consist of a plastic digital-read base with a metal probe on the end of a cord; some have an alarm setting to indicate that a specific temperature has been reached.

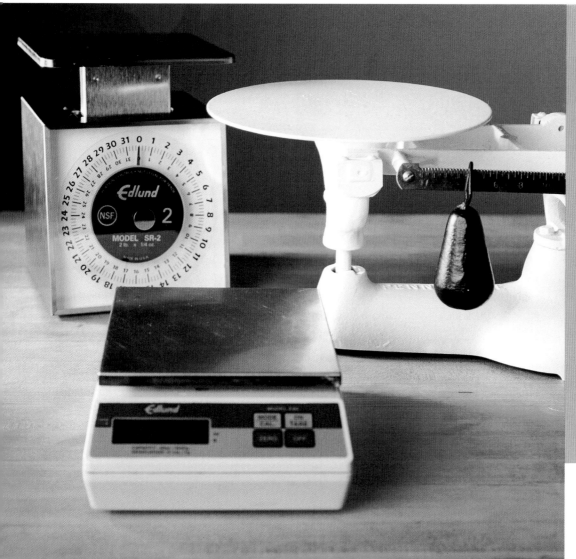

The digital scale (foreground), beam balance or baker's balance, and spring scale (background) are the three basic types of scales used in bakeshops and pastry kitchens.

Any bakeshop should have thermometers capable of measuring accurately over a wide range of temperatures. Standard **instant-read thermometers** are available with both dial and digital readouts. Digital thermometers typically measure a wider range of temperatures than dial-type thermometers can, and they are usually more accurate when measuring shallow liquids.

Some **candy (or sugar or deep fat) thermometers** are calibrated in degrees only; others also indicate the most commonly used temperatures for sugar cooking (such as thread, soft ball, and hard crack). Candy thermometers should register from 100° to 400°F/38° to 204°C and should be able to withstand temperatures up to 500°F/260°C. To check a thermometer's accuracy, let it stand for 10 minutes in boiling water. It should read 212°F/100°C. If there is any discrepancy, subtract or add the correct number of degrees to make up for the difference when using the thermometer.

Cutting Tools

KNIVES

A basic knife collection includes four essential knives, a chef's or French knife, a utility knife, a paring knife, and a slicer, as well as a number of special knives and cutting tools for specific purposes.

All cutting tools work best when they are properly maintained. A sharp tool not only performs better but is safer to use, because less pressure is required to cut through the ingredient. Learn to sharpen knives with a stone and a steel so that you can maintain them yourself. Have severely dulled or damaged tools professionally reground to restore the edge if possible. Some tools cannot be sharpened. Handle them carefully to extend their useful lives, and replace them when they become difficult to use safely.

Keep knives properly stored when not in use. There are a number of safe, practical ways to store knives, including knife kits or rolls for one's personal collection and slots, racks, and magnetized holders in the kitchen. Storage arrangements should be kept just as clean as knives. Cloth or vinyl rolls should be washed and sanitized periodically. To keep knives organized and at hand in your work area, arrange them on a clean side towel, along with your steel. (For more information on care and maintenance of knives see *The Professional Chef's Knife Kit* by The Culinary Institute of America.)

Always use an appropriate cutting surface. Wooden or composition cutting boards are best. Cutting on metal, glass, or marble surfaces will dull and eventually damage the blade of a knife.

Keeping knives clean helps to extend their lives. Clean knives thoroughly immediately after using them with soap and hot water. Sanitize the entire knife, including the handle, bolster, and blade, as necessary, so that it will not cross contaminate food. Dry knives carefully before storing them or using them again.

To pass a knife safely to someone, present it with the handle toward the other person. Whenever you carry a knife from one area of the kitchen to another, hold the blade point down, with the sharpened edge facing you, and let people know you are passing by with something sharp. Ideally, you should sheathe or wrap the knife before walking anywhere with it, or put it in a carrier.

When you lay a knife down on a work surface, be sure that no part of it extends over the edge of the cutting board or worktable. That will prevent anyone walking by from brushing against it or knocking it onto the floor. Also, be sure the blade is facing away from the edge of the work surface. Finally, never try to catch a falling knife.

Types of Knives

Chef's, or **French, knives** are all-purpose knives used for a variety of chopping, slicing, and mincing tasks. The blade is usually 8 to 14 in/20 to 36 cm long with a straight edge. Look for a high-carbon stainless-steel blade, a full tang (the continuation of the blade that extends into the knife's handle), good balance, and a handle that fits your hand comfortably.

Utility knives are similar to chef's knives except that they are smaller and lighter, for light cutting chores. Their blades are generally 5 to 7 in/13 to 18 cm long.

A **paring knife** is a short knife used for paring and trimming vegetables and fruits. The blades are 2 to 4 in/5 to 10 cm long, and they come in a number of shapes: pointed, bird beak, tourné, and sheep's foot.

Slicers are used to slice breads, cakes, and pastries. Their blades are long and thin and can range in length from 8 to 12 in/20 to 30 cm. They also have a variety of edges. Bread knives and other serrated slicers are excellent for slicing foods with a relatively spongy texture, such as most breads and some cakes; the "teeth" saw through the crumb without tearing or pulling. Slicing blades with straight edges are used to slice delicate pastries and cakes. Straight-edge slicing knives (typically 10 to 12 in/25 to 30 cm long) are also useful for icing and decorating. Some slicers have offset handles.

A **mandoline** can cut large amounts of food quickly into uniform slices or strips of varying thickness. This manually operated slicing device is made of nickel-plated stainless steel with blades of high-carbon steel. Levers adjust the blades to achieve the cut and thickness desired. A mandoline can be used to make such cuts as slices, julienne, gaufrettes, and bâtonnets. As with electric food slicers, be sure to use the guard—the carrier that holds the food—to prevent injury.

TOP ROW:
Mandoline, box graters, nested cutters

MIDDLE ROW:
Rasp *or* Microplane, serrated slicer, straight slicer, chef's knife, paring knife, lame, melon baller, bench knife

BOTTOM ROW:
Assorted cookie cutters, portion scoops of various sizes

Kitchen scissors or **shears** should be made of heavy-duty stainless steel and come apart easily for cleaning. They are used in décor for sugar work, in confections for making hard candies, and in bread making to score and shape loaves.

Other Small Tools

GRATERS, ZESTERS, AND RASPS

Graters, zesters, and rasps may be used for a variety of tasks such as shaving fine flakes of citrus zest, chocolate, nutmeg, or grating cheeses. **Graters** are made of metal perforated with openings that shred away pieces of an ingredient. The openings range in size from very small, for grating nutmeg, to large, for grating moister foods that might otherwise fall apart. Some graters are flat, others have a curved surface. A box grater has at least two grating faces and can usually perform a variety of grating and, often, some slicing tasks.

A **citrus zester** is a small hand tool consisting of a metal head attached to a handle. As the head is passed over the citrus fruit, the cutting edges remove the outer layer of colored zest but leave behind the bitter white pith. You can also use a swivel-bladed peeler (cuts away thin slices from the skin) or a grater with small openings instead of a zester. A **rasp** is a long (approximately 12 in/30 cm) flat piece of stainless steel with small perforations; some have handles well suited for zesting as well as finely grating chocolate and hard cheeses.

PEELERS, REAMERS, AND CORERS

Swivel-bladed peelers remove thin layers of skin (or zest) from fruits and vegetables. They are available in a number of different styles.

A **lemon reamer** is a conical shaped tool (6 to 6½ in/15 to 17 cm long) with deep ridges and a handle and is used for extracting the juice from small citrus fruits such as lemons. Reamers are traditionally made of nonporous wood, but they are now also available in metal or plastic.

An **apple corer** may be a hand tool or a mechanical device. A manual corer has a stainless-steel cylinder ⅝ in/1.6 cm in diameter with a sawtooth end for cutting into the fruit. Corers are usually 6½ in/17 cm long. A mechanical corer offers greater efficiency and speed. This device has an arm with three prongs that are inserted into the apple, fixing it on a crank handle that drills it into a cylindrical blade that extracts the core. These corers can simultaneously peel the apples as they are rotated, with a small sharp blade.

SPOONS AND TONGS

Spoons for use in the kitchen may be made of metal, wood, or composite materials. Some spoons have deep bowls, others are flat, more like a paddle. *Slotted* or *perforated spoons* are used to lift foods out of liquids.

Wooden spoons and paddles are made of unfinished tight-grained woods. Wood does not conduct or transfer heat well, so there is no threat of burning your fingers or

changing critical temperatures of mixtures. Hardwoods are less likely to pick up flavors and stains from food; they are also less likely to split or crack.

Spiders and **skimmers** operate on a similar principle as spoons but are very wide and quite flat and have a very long handle.

Paddles are used in chocolate and confection work. They scrape clean easily, making it easier to work with mixtures that require careful blending and temperature control, such as chocolate.

Tongs act as an extension of your thumb and forefinger to lift, turn, and transfer hot food or other objects. They have two metal arms that are hinged together and spring-loaded. Some versions can be locked closed. Tongs range in size from 8 to 18 in/20 to 46 cm long.

WHIPS

Whips, also called whisks, are made from a number of thin wires bound together with a handle. In most whips, the wires are bent to make a closed loop. Whips are used to blend or whisk ingredients, to loosen and evenly distribute ingredients, and to make foams such as whipped cream or meringue. Handheld whips may have as few as two wires or as many as twenty. *Balloon whips* are sphere shaped and have thin wires to incorporate air for making foams. *Flat whips* often have thicker wires. The thickness of the wires on a whip determines its flexibility and function. Whips range from 10 to 16 in/25 to 41 cm in length.

SPATULAS AND SCRAPERS

Rubber spatulas are used to scrape mixtures from bowls and into baking pans, to push foods through sieves, to fold ingredients together, and to spread batters and fillings into even layers. These hand tools have a flexible head of synthetic rubber, silicone, or similar material on the end of a handle. The head is shaped for a specific function and may be narrow or broad, with a pointed, angled, or blunt tip; some have a notch on one side for cleaning the rims of bowls. Spatulas made from high-temperature resistant synthetic rubber or silicone can be used to stir and blend ingredients over direct heat, up to 600°F/316°C. Spatulas range in length from about 10 in/25 cm to slightly longer than 20 in/51 cm.

Metal spatulas look something like knives. They have long metal blades, although the edge of the blade is not sharp, and typically have blunt, rounded ends. Baking spatulas have blunt ends and are made of thinner metal than knives. The handles can be made of polypropylene or wood. The length of the spatulas may range from 4 to 14 in/10 to 36 cm and the handle can be straight or offset. The offset handle is angled so that the blade is about ½ in/1 cm below the handle.

Plastic bowl scrapers are like the head of a rubber scraper, without a handle. They may be rounded on one side and are efficient at scraping bowls completely clean, leaving no waste. Clean, sanitize, and air-dry rubber spatulas and bowl scrapers, either in a ware-washing machine or by hand.

Fondant funnel, apple corer, apple peeler, bain-marie with assorted wire whips, ladles, lemon reamer, bowl scraper, peeler, assorted pastry tips, small palette knives (straight and offset), spider, pastry cutters, turntable, assorted pastry bags, large metal décor spatulas (tapered, straight, and offset)

SCOOPS AND LADLES

Scoops and ladles are used as portioning tools. **Scoops** have bowls of varying sizes attached to a handle. Some scoops have a spring-operated mechanism that pushes batters, ice creams, or other preparations cleanly from the bowl, making it easy to scale them consistently during production or service.

Melon ballers, also called Parisian scoops, may be round or oval, with straight or fluted edges. The scoop is twisted into the food to make a perfect ball or oval. They are most typically used to portion melon or other ingredients, such as ganache, that are soft enough to scoop but firm enough to hold their shape.

Ladles are used for portioning as well as for measuring pourable ingredients or mixtures such as sauces. The bowl of the ladle holds a specific volume, ranging from 1 to 12 fl oz/30 to 360 mL. The bowl is attached to a long handle; some ladles are one piece, while the handles of others are a separate piece of metal attached to the bowl. Ladles with a 45-degree angle between the bowl and the handle work best in most instances.

Hand Tools for Sifting, Straining, and Puréeing

Sieves and strainers are used to sift and aerate dry ingredients, as well as to remove any large impurities from them. They are also used to drain or purée cooked or raw foods. The delicate mesh of some strainers is highly vulnerable to damage. To keep sieves and strainers in good condition, wash them as soon as you are finished with them, and dry them completely before storing them. Sieves and strainers are produced in a range of sizes to accommodate a variety of tasks. Some are small enough to dust a napoleon with confectioners' sugar, others are large enough to strain several quarts of ice cream base. Strainers should be made of a heat-resistant material so that hot liquids can be strained immediately upon removal from the stovetop.

A **food mill** has a curved blade that is rotated over a disk by a hand-operated crank. Most professional models have interchangeable disks with holes of varying fineness. An exception is the Foley food mill, which has a fixed mesh disk. (Note: Many mixing machines can be used as food mills, using attachments that allow them to strain and purée foods.)

A **drum sieve** (or **tamis**) consists of a tinned-steel, nylon, or stainless-steel screen stretched over an aluminum or wood frame. Drum sieves are used for sifting or puréeing. A *champignon* (mushroom-shaped pestle) or a rigid plastic scraper is used to push the food through the screen.

Conical sieves are used for straining and/or puréeing foods. The openings in the cone can be various sizes, from very large to very small, and depending on the size of the openings can be made of either perforated metal or a mesh screen. A fine-mesh conical sieve is also known as a bouillon strainer. A pointed pestle is effective for pushing the ingredient or product through the mesh.

Colanders are stainless-steel, aluminum, or plastic bowls pierced with holes and are used for straining or draining foods. Colanders are available in a variety of sizes. Some have loop handles and others have single handles; they may have feet or a round base.

Cheesecloth is a light, fine-mesh gauze frequently used along with or in place of a fine conical sieve to strain very fine sauces and similar items. It is also used for making sachets. Before use, cheesecloth should be rinsed thoroughly in hot and then cold water to remove any loose fibers. Cheesecloth also clings better to the sides of bowls, sieves, and the like when it is wet. Drape the wet cheesecloth in the bowl or colander and pour the liquid through it.

Tools for Bread Baking

A **lame** is a thin-arced razor blade clamped into a small-stainless steel, wooden, or plastic handle. (*Lame* is the French word for razor.) This specialized tool is used to score proofed yeast breads and rolls before they are baked to create patterns and designs on the crust. The blade must be very sharp and used in swift angled motions to create clean slices without pulling or tearing the dough.

A **bench knife** has a thin, stiff, rectangular steel blade set in a wooden or plastic handle to make it easier to grip and use. The blade, which is usually 6 in/15 cm wide, has no sharpened edges, making it useful for scraping, lifting, folding, and cutting dough.

Fine-mesh strainer, drum sieve, cheesecloth; rolling pins, left to right: rod-and-bearing, textured aluminum French-style, springerle, aluminum French-style with a different texture, straight wood, ball-bearing, paper French, and small straight wooden; mixing bowls, hotel pans, cutting boards

A **couche,** or heavy linen cloth, is used for proofing baguettes. The shaped dough is arranged in the folds of the cloth and left to proof; the folds and the fabric itself help to preserve the shape of the dough and keep it moist.

Loaf pans, or tins, are oblong or rectangular pans used to bake pound cakes, other loaf cakes, and quick breads, as well as loaves of yeast-raised bread. They are made of glass or metal, with or without a nonstick coating. They are available in a wide range of sizes from large to mini. A *Pullman loaf pan* has a sliding cover and is used to prepare perfectly square, finely grained slicing loaves (also known as *pain de mie*). The pans are typically made of tinned steel. A pan for a 1½-lb/680-g loaf is 13 in/33 cm long, 4¼ in/11 cm wide, and 4 in/10 cm deep; and a pan for a 2-lb/907-g loaf is 16 in/41 cm long, 4 in/10 cm wide, and 4 in/10 cm deep.

Bannetons, or dough-rising baskets (or *brotformen*) are round or oblong straw or willow baskets used for proofing, molding, and shaping bread. Some are lined with linen.

Peels are large flat wooden paddles designed for transferring doughs onto the deck of an oven. To use a peel, sprinkle it with cornmeal before loading the dough onto the peel. Use a quick jerking motion to slide the dough off the peel onto the deck of the oven.

Tools for Pastries and Cookies

Rolling pins are used to flatten and thin doughs such as yeasted bread, pastry, tart, and cookie doughs and puff pastry, as well as marzipan. They may be made of wood, metal, marble, or synthetic materials. Some pins have a smooth surface; others are textured or engraved to leave an impression of a pattern or picture on the dough. The task at hand will dictate the type of pin best suited for the job.

Clean and dry rolling pins thoroughly, immediately after use. Don't soak wooden pins for extended periods. Pins made of porous materials such as wood may absorb the taste of soaps and detergents and transfer them to delicate doughs, so use only warm water and rub with a soft cloth to clean them.

Rod-and-bearing rolling pins consist of a cylinder made of hard wood with a steel rod inserted through the middle, which is fixed with ball bearings and handles at either end, inserted through the center. These heavy pins are used to roll large amounts of dough and stiff doughs. They are available in lengths up to 18 in/46 cm. Pins of this style are also available with a cylinder made of stainless steel, or marble. These materials remain cool during rolling, which helps to keep pastry doughs at the proper working temperature.

Straight (or French) *rolling pins* are straight, thick dowels. They were traditionally made of hardwood and now are also available in nylon. These pins are typically 1¼ in/3 cm to 2 in/5 cm in diameter and 18 to 20 in/46 to 51 cm long. Because they don't have handles, they allow the baker or pastry chef to more easily feel the evenness and thickness of the dough while rolling it out.

Tapered rolling pins are thicker in the center, tapering evenly to both ends. They are usually about 2¾ in/7 cm in diameter at the center and 22 in/56 cm long. Their tapered design makes them most useful for rolling circles of dough to line pie and tart pans.

Marzipan and *basket-weave rolling pins* have a patterned surface to create impressions on marzipan used for décor. These pins are made as rod-and-bearing pins or simply of plain cylinders made of nylon or plastic.

Springerle rolling pins are made of wood or plastic resin. They have ornate and intricate pictures or designs in relief, which are traditionally used to imprint springerle or gingerbread cookie doughs before baking. Springerle plaques are also available; the plaque is simply pressed into the rolled dough to imprint it before baking.

Cookie cutters are used to stamp out individual cookies from rolled doughs. They are made of thin sheet metal (tin, stainless steel, or copper) or plastic that has been molded or formed into shapes (circles, squares, hearts, animals, and so on). The cutting edges must be even and sharp enough to slice through the dough cleanly, and the cutters should be easy to grip.

A *dough docker* has a handle attached to a roller studded with rounded spikes of metal or plastic 1 to 2 in/3 to 5 cm long. The docker is used to quickly and cleanly pierce airholes in rolled sheets of dough before baking blind (see page 511).

Pastry brushes may be made of soft, flexible nylon or unbleached hog bristles. The bristles are blunt cut and 2½ in/6 cm long, and the brushes come in a variety of widths for various tasks. They should be washed and air-dried after each use.

A *pastry wheel* has a very sharp, round, nickel-plated blade attached to a handle; the wheel rotates as it is pushed over rolled dough, making long, smooth, continuous cuts. The diameter of the wheel can range from 2 in/5 cm (for cutting thinner doughs) up to 5 in/13 cm (for very thick doughs). The wheels may have straight or fluted edges.

Tools for Décor Work

Pastry bags and tips and parchment paper cones are used for décor work and to portion, apply, and shape meringues, icings, jams, and soft batters and doughs.

Pastry bags are available in various sizes. Many bakeshops and pastry kitchens have turned to disposable bags to prevent cross contamination or food-borne illness. Wash reusable bags, which are usually made of nylon, or plastic-coated fabric, with plenty of hot water and enough soap to thoroughly degrease them. Rinse them well and air-dry completely before using again or storing.

Piping tips are generally made of nickel-plated metal and are stamped with a numerical identification code. Although there are no industry-wide standards when it comes to numbering conventions for pastry tips, the numbers do have a relationship to the diameter of the tip's opening: the bigger the number, the larger the opening. Tips may have round, oval, star, or other-shaped openings. The differences in shape and diameter permit the pastry chef to apply a wide range of both simple and complex décor to cakes and pastries.

Parchment paper cones may be used in the same way as pastry bags and tips. Parchment paper can be purchased in ready-cut triangles for rolling into cones, or pastry chefs may cut their own from sheets of parchment. The size of the cone depends on the size of the parchment triangle. Cones may be rolled leaving the desired size of opening for piping, or the opening may be cut with scissors after the cone is tightly rolled. Different sizes and shapes of openings may be cut to yield a wide range of décor.

Cake and decorating combs are used to make designs by creating a pattern of lines in the icing coating a cake or pastry. They have teeth with different shapes and sizes. A cake comb is a thin triangle of stainless steel with different size tooth grooves on each side. Rubber decorating combs have stainless-steel frames to which the combs are attached for use.

Wire cooling racks are grates made of heavy-gauge chrome-plated steel wire. They have feet that raise them above the counter so that moisture does not collect under cooling baked goods. These racks can also be used for glazing and confectionery work, as they allow the excess glaze or chocolate to run off freely rather than pooling around the base of the confection, pastry, or cake.

Turntables for cake decorating consist of a pedestal topped with a round platform 12 in/30 cm in diameter to hold the cake or pastry as you work. The turntable can be rotated around the rod in the center of the pedestal. Some chefs prefer instead to set cakes on cardboard circles (also called cake circles), which they balance on their fingertips and then gently rotate as they work; this method allows them to keep the cake at eye level while they work, but it does require a bit of coordination.

Tools for Confectionery and Décor Work

CONFECTIONERY TOOLS

A **heavy copper pot** with a pour spout is very useful for sugar cooking. These pots are available in several diameters: 5 in/13 cm (holding 24 fl oz/720 mL), 6½ in/16 cm (holding 50 fl oz/1.50 L), and 8 in/20 cm (holding 3 qt/2.88 L). Copper is preferred for sugar cooking because it conducts heat evenly.

A **fondant funnel** is a metal or plastic funnel with a manually operated valve at the small opening. These funnels generally have a capacity of 1 or 2 qt/960 mL or 1.92 L. They are useful for filling chocolates, making candies, and portioning sauces.

Chocolate molds are used for making figures, such as an Easter bunny, and for making filled chocolates. Clear, rigid, polycarbonate plastic molds are easier to care for and use than vacuum plastic molds or tin chocolate molds. However, vacuum plastic molds are relatively inexpensive. Tin molds may be both more elaborate and durable, but they must be thoroughly cleaned and dried to prevent rusting.

Dipping tools include a variety of hand tools consisting of stainless- or nickel-plated steel prongs or loops fastened into wooden or plastic handles. They are designed for dipping any nut, fruit, or ganache or candy into a chocolate, syrup, or fondant coating.

Chocolate cutters are made of strong tinned steel or a fiberglass and plastic composite. They range from ¼ to 1½ in/6 mm to 4 cm in diameter and up to 1 in/3 cm in height. The cutting edges are very sharp. Cutters are often crafted into animal, geometric, and floral shapes, and more. They are sold individually or in sets that can include as many as seventy-four pieces.

Caramel rulers, also called confectioners' bars, are metal bars used for framing ganache and caramel while it is in "liquid" form so that it sets to a specific thickness and dimensions for cutting into individual pieces. They are made of nickel-plated steel and are available in lengths of 20 or 30 in/51 or 76 cm. The bars weigh 6 lb/2.72 kg each, giving them enough weight to contain the liquid confection, and range in height from ⅜ to ½ in/1 to 1.3 cm.

A **guitar** is a stainless-steel cutter that is used to precisely cut multiple squares, rectangles, triangles, or diamonds out of slabs of a number of different semisoft confections, such as ganache, caramel, and gelées. Each set comes with at least three interchangeable cutting frames. It consists of a stainless-steel square or rectangular platform with linear spaces that adjust to fit different size, interchangeable cutting frames, which are threaded with stainless-steel wire that cuts through the confections.

Transfer sheets are acetate sheets with designs imprinted on them in plain or colored cocoa butter. They are used to imprint designs on chocolate.

Chocolate cutters (oval, round, and diamond shapes), cake and decorating combs, caramel bars, chocolate molds, transfer sheet with hearts, more chocolate cutters, PVC rolling pin, palette knife for décor work, ball roller, assorted cutters and stylus, blown sugar pump, silicone leaf mold

DÉCOR TOOLS

Marzipan and gum paste modeling tools are small hand tools with tips made from high-quality plastic or stainless steel so they maintain their fine detailing. They come in a variety of shapes for crafting decorations and textures. They are sold individually or in sets of up to twelve.

An **airbrush** is used to spray food colors onto confections and cakes. It enables the decorator to create a wide range of shades and patterns, as well as blend colors to produce special effects.

Acetate sheets are shiny, flexible nonstick sheets used for chocolate work, as well as for molding various pastries and cakes. They are sold ten sheets to a box, 15⅞ by 24 in/40 by 61 cm each, as well as in rolls of varying lengths and widths.

To keep sugar soft and malleable so that it can be molded, formed, or blown, the pastry chef applies heat using various tools. A **heat gun** looks somewhat like a blow dryer, but it doesn't blow the air with as much force or produce as much heat. It can also be used to heat a bowl of chocolate to keep it in temper.

Sugar lamps have a 24-in/61-cm neck on a weighted base, with an infrared heat bulb.

A **blow dryer** can also be used to heat sugar and keep it soft. The best ones come with a stand so that they can be operated hands-free.

A **blown sugar pump** is a rubber squeeze ball that fits in the palm of your hand attached to an aluminum tip. It is squeezed to blow air into sugar to create a "balloon" that may be shaped and molded by hand as it is expanded. Sugar pumps are approximately 10½ in/27 cm long. A double-bulb pump has an extra air chamber in the rubber squeeze tube to better control the flow of air into the sugar.

Bakeware

BAKING PANS

Hotel pans are stainless-steel pans that come in a number of standard sizes. These pans have a lip that allows them to hang on storage shelves or steam tables that are made specifically to the same measurements. They are deeper than sheet pans, making them well suited for use as a hot water bath for baking custards and other preparations that require a hot water bath.

Sheet pans are flat-rimmed baking pans ranging in size from 17¾ by 25¾ in/45 by 65 cm (full-size sheet pan) to 12⅞ by 17¾ in/31 by 45 cm (half-size sheet pan) to 9½ by 13 in/24 by 33 cm (quarter-size sheet pan), with sides of 1 in/2 cm. Sheet pans are made of aluminum, with or without a nonstick coating. In the pastry kitchen or bakery, they are used for baking cookies and sheet cakes, among other things.

Cake pans are made in various materials, including glass, silicone, tinned steel, and aluminum (with or without a nonstick coating). They are available in diameters ranging from 2 to 24 in/5 to 61 cm and depths ranging from ¾ to 4 in/2 to 10 cm. Aluminum conducts heat and thus bakes evenly, making it the most common material for cake pans.

TOP SHELF: Assorted cake pans, parchment paper, madeleine molds, rolled silicone baking mats, tube pan, paisley-shaped ejection molds with a cutter, half sheet pans

MIDDLE SHELF: Copper sugar-cooking pots, flexible silicone pyramid-shaped mold, banneton, linen couche, tart and tartlet pans, aluminum pie pans

BOTTOM SHELF: Sauce pots and sauté pans, loaf pans, cake rings, hotel pans, cooling or glazing racks, full sheet pans

Springform pans are available in diameters from 6 to 12 in/15 to 30 cm, with depths ranging from 2½ to 3 in/6 to 8 cm. The ring of a springform pan is joined with a clip closure that creates tension when closed and holds the removable bottom in place. These pans are used for baking cakes that have a delicate structure, making it difficult to unmold them from a traditional rigid cake pan without damaging them. Most springform pans are aluminum.

Tube pans have a center tube, so they conduct heat through the center of the batter as well as from the sides and bottom. They are useful for evenly baking heavy batters without overbrowning the outside of the cake. Tube pans also work well for batters that need to bake quickly, such as angel food cake. They are usually made of thin aluminum, with or without a nonstick coating. They come in a range of sizes and may have fluted, molded, or straight sides.

Pie pans (tins) are round pans with sloping sides, commonly made from glass, earthenware, or metal (with or without nonstick coating). They range from 8 to 10 in/20 to 25 cm in diameter and from 1½ to 3 in/4 to 8 cm deep.

Tart pans have fluted sides and removable bottoms. They may be round, square, or rectangular. They are made of tinned steel, with or without a nonstick coating. Round pans range from 4 to 13 in/10 to 33 cm in diameter and ¾ to 2¼ in/2 to 6 cm deep. Square pans are usually 9 in/23 cm across and 1 in/3 cm deep. Rectangular tart pans are 8 by 11 in/20 by 28 cm or 4½ by 14¾ in/11 by 37 cm and 1 in/3 cm deep.

Tartlet pans are most commonly made of tinned steel, with or without a nonstick coating. They come in various shapes and may have removable or fixed bottoms. They range from 1⅛ to 4 in/3 to 10 cm in size (measured across the base). The sides, which may be plain or fluted, are from ½ to ⅝ in/1 to 1.6 cm high.

RINGS AND MOLDS

Cake rings are stainless-steel rings available in diameters ranging from 2¾ to 12 in/7 to 30 cm and heights from 1⅓ to 3 in/3 to 8 cm. They are used for molding cakes and individual pastries.

Flan rings are straight-sided stainless-steel rings with rounded edges. They are used for baking and molding tarts and European-style flans. They are available in diameters ranging from 2½ to 11 in/6 to 28 cm and are ¾ in/2 cm high.

A **madeleine mold** is a tinned-steel or aluminum sheet with scalloped impressions used for molding the small cakes called madeleines. They are available with or without a nonstick coating and have from 12 to 40 cavities per mold. The impressions are available in two sizes—large and small.

Flexible silicone molds are made of silicone-coated fiberglass. They come in many different sizes and shapes for making individual or multiserve desserts and pastries. They can be used for molding chocolate or frozen desserts, as well as for baking pastries and cakes.

Modular ejection molds are acrylic molds available in different shapes and sizes; each mold comes with an extractor of matching shape and size. They are used to mold frozen, cold, or warm individual pastries that are made with ice creams, or stabilized mousses and/or creams.

Flexible silicone mats are able to withstand oven temperatures up to 500°F/260°C. They are used for lining sheet pans to give them a nonstick baking surface. They also provide a nonstick heat-resistant surface for candy making. The mats are about ⅛ in/3 mm thick and come in full sheet pan and half sheet pan sizes. They should be stored flat to prevent them from splitting.

Parchment paper is grease-resistant, nonstick, heatproof, quick-release coated paper. It has endless uses in the bakeshop and pastry shop, such as lining baking pans and making piping cones for décor work. The paper can be reused until it becomes dark and brittle. It comes in large (full sheet pan size) sheets, in rolls, or precut for special uses such as piping cones or cake pan liners.

Stovetop Pots and Pans

A variety of pots and pans are used in the bakeshop and pastry kitchen. **Sauté pans** (sometimes referred to as skillets) are shallow pans, wider than they are tall. The sides may be sloping (*sauteuse*) or straight (*sautoir*). The different materials used for these pans determine how a particular pan behaves over direct heat. Cast iron heats slowly but maintains an even heat. Stainless steel conducts heat quickly, making it more responsive to temperature changes. Sauté pans are made in a wide range of sizes, with or without nonstick surfaces. **Crêpe** and **omelet pans** are similar in construction, though they have a smaller diameter (usually 7 or 8 in/18 or 20 cm in diameter) than sauté pans. **Saucepots** are deeper than they are wide, and they may have straight or flared sides. They come in a number of standard sizes and are a versatile pot, used for preparing anything from a reduction to a sauce or filling.

Large Equipment

When working with large equipment such as mixers and sheeters, safety precautions must always be observed. Proper maintenance and cleaning should also be performed consistently in order to keep this equipment in good working order and to prevent injury.

If a machine is unfamiliar to you, ask for instruction in operating it safely; ask for help if you need it, and, if possible, run it while someone familiar with the machine can supervise you.

Many large machines have built-in safety features—always use them. Make sure that the machine is stable, lids are secure, and hand guards are used.

MIXING, CHOPPING, AND PURÉEING EQUIPMENT

Mixing, chopping, and puréeing equipment has the potential to be extremely dangerous. The importance of observing all the necessary safety precautions cannot be overemphasized.

A **blender** consists of a base, which houses the motor, and a removable lidded jar with a propeller-like blade set in the bottom. The speed settings for the motor, of which there may be as many as eighteen or as few as two, are in the base. Jars are made of stainless steel, plastic, or glass and come in several sizes. Blenders are excellent for puréeing, liquefying, and emulsifying foods because the tall narrow shape of the jar keeps the food circulating and in close contact with the blade.

An **immersion blender** (also known as a hand blender, stick blender, or burr mixer) is a long, slender one-piece machine that works like an inverted countertop blender. The top part of the machine houses the motor, which generally runs at just one speed, and a plastic handhold with an on/off button extends above the motor. On professional/commercial models, a stainless-steel driveshaft, which varies in length depending on the model, extends from the motor and is attached to the blade that is immersed in the food being puréed. An immersion blender serves the same functions as a regular blender, but the advantage of an immersion blender is that even large batches of food can be puréed directly in the cooking vessel.

Planetary mixer (20 qt/19.20 L), food processor, immersion (stick or burr) blender

Vertical chopping machines (VCMs) operate on the same principle as a blender. A motor at the base is permanently attached to a bowl with integral blades. As a safety precaution, the hinged lid must be locked in place before the unit will operate. A VCM is used to grind, whip, emulsify, blend, or crush foods.

In a **food chopper** (buffalo chopper) food is placed in a bowl that rotates when the machine is turned on; the food passes under a hood where blades chop the food. Some units have hoppers or feed tubes and interchangeable disks for slicing and grating. Food choppers are available in floor and tabletop models. They are generally made of aluminum, with stainless-steel bowls.

A **food processor** houses the motor in its base. The work bowl is fitted over a stem and locked into place, along with the appropriate blade or disk. Foods are placed in the bowl, the lid placed on top and closed, and the motor turns the stem and the blade rapidly to grind, purée, blend, emulsify, crush, or knead or, with special disks, slice, julienne, or shred foods.

MIXERS

Planetary mixers are also known as vertical mixers. They get their name from the motion of the mixing attachment, which moves in a path like that of a planet orbiting the sun inside the stationary mixing bowl. These mixers come with three standard attachments—a paddle, a whip, and a dough hook—and have multiple uses.

Spiral mixers are stationary mixers, meaning that the bowl, rather than the mixing attachment, rotates. These mixers have bowls that tilt and only one attachment, a spiral-shaped hook. They are used exclusively for mixing bread doughs. They work the dough quickly but gently enough to control the amount of friction.

Oblique mixers, also known as fork mixers, are similar in construction to spiral mixers except that their attachment is a fork rather than a spiral. They are also used exclusively for bread doughs because they work the dough gently to minimize the amount of friction in the same mannner as spiral mixers.

OVENS

Ovens cook foods by surrounding them with hot air, a gentler and more even source of heat than the direct heat of a burner. Although many types of dishes are prepared in ovens, they are most commonly used for roasting and baking. There are different ovens to suit a variety of needs, depending on an establishment's menu or bakeshop's needs and the available space.

Conventional ovens can be located below a range top. **Deck ovens** normally consist of two to four wide flat decks stacked one above another, though single-deck models are available. Food is placed directly on the floor of a deck oven rather than on a wire rack as in a conventional oven. Some deck ovens have ceramic or firebrick bases; these are used for breads and pastries that require direct intense bottom heat to develop the crust. Deck ovens usually are gas or electric, although charcoal- and wood-burning units are also available. The heat source for conventional and deck ovens is located at the bottom, underneath the deck, or floor, of the oven, and heat is conducted through the deck.

Steam-injection ovens vent steam into the oven as breads and rolls bake. The steam helps to develop the crust and ensures that yeast-raised breads stay moist long enough to expand properly during baking.

In a **convection oven,** fans force hot air to circulate around the food, cooking it evenly and quickly. Convection ovens are available in gas or electric models in a range of sizes.

Combi ovens, either gas or electric, combine the advantages of steaming and convection ovens. They can be used in steam mode, hot-air convection mode, or heat/steam (combi) mode. Combi ovens are available in a number of different configurations.

A **microwave oven** uses electricity to generate microwave radiation, which cooks or reheats foods very quickly. Microwave ovens are available in a variety of sizes and power ratings. Some models have a convection function.

PROOFER

For professional bread bakers in a high-volume operation, a **proofer** is an essential piece of equipment. Proofers maintain the most desirable environment for yeast growth. In this way they help to maintain production schedules and ensure that items are of uniform quality. Some proofers have refrigeration capabilities, making them able to retard yeast growth. Proofers like this are known as proofer/retarders. **Retarders** also help with production in the same ways, as does a proofer, by maintaining production schedules and quality standards. They are available as stationary walk-ins or as mobile boxes.

REFRIGERATION EQUIPMENT

Adequate refrigeration storage is crucial to any food-service operation. All units should be maintained properly through regular, thorough cleaning (including the door gaskets). Such precautions will help reduce spoilage and thus reduce food costs. Placing the units so that unnecessary steps are eliminated will save time and labor. Several types of refrigeration units are available. A **walk-in refrigerator** is the largest type. It usually has shelves arranged around the walls, and some walk-ins are large enough to accommodate rolling carts for additional storage. Some units have pass-through or reach-in doors to facilitate access to frequently required items. It is possible to zone a walk-in to maintain different temperature and humidity levels for storing various foods. Walk-ins may be situated in the kitchen or outside the facility. If space allows, walk-ins located outside the kitchen can prove advantageous, because deliveries can be made at any time without disrupting service.

A **reach-in refrigerator** may be a single unit or part of a bank of units. Reach-ins are available in many sizes. Units with pass-through doors are especially helpful for the pantry area, so that salads, desserts, and other cold items can be retrieved by the wait staff as needed.

On-site refrigeration units include refrigerated drawers or undercounter reach-ins, which hold foods on the line at the proper temperature. They eliminate unnecessary travel, which can create a hazard during peak production periods.

Portable refrigeration is provided by refrigerated carts that can be stationed as needed in the kitchen. Display refrigeration cases are generally used to showcase dessert items or pastries in a restaurant dining room or cakes and pastries for sale in a shop.

ICE CREAM MACHINES

Simple **hand-cranked** or **electric ice cream machines** have a motor that either turns the paddle within the cooling chamber or rotates the chamber around the paddle. The bowl is usually removable and must be frozen for at least 12 hours before use. Bowls range from 6 to 9 in/15 to 23 cm in diameter and up to 6½ in/17 cm tall. These machines can produce up to a quart/liter of ice cream per batch.

Commercial ice cream makers have built-in refrigeration units to make large-scale production of ice cream and other frozen confections possible. There are two basic types: continuous and batch. With a *continuous ice cream freezer*, the ice cream base is fed continuously into the machine at a high rate of speed. This type of machine allows for control of overrun, viscosity, and temperature of the finished product.

Batch ice cream freezers churn a specific amount of ice cream base at one time. Batch ice cream freezers are available in two basic configurations: horizontal and vertical. *Horizontal machines* have a cylinder that lies horizontally within the unit. They incorporate a considerable amount of air into the product. *Vertical machines* have a vertical cylinder within the unit for churning and freezing the ice cream base. They incorporate the least amount of air into the product as the mix is scraped and blended.

Professionals and Their Tools

Most equipment is manufactured by a number of different companies. There will be differences in quality, the number of additional features, shape, size, and cost. Quality tools are often more expensive, but they last longer and perform better than poorly made tools. Over time, you will want to accumulate both the basic and more specialized tools of your trade for your own kit or, perhaps, outfit a shop or kitchen of your own. You can read about tools of all sorts in a variety of industry publications and learn about them at trade shows. Consult the Appendixes for a list of recommended readings and other resources for equipment.

Some of the tools and equipment used in professional kitchens and bakeshops today are the same as those used centuries ago. Others are recent innovations and rely on advanced technology such as computer chips or infrared. The ability to select, use, and safely maintain all equipment is fundamental to the smooth and efficient operation of a kitchen or bakeshop. As new pieces of equipment are developed and introduced, it is your responsibility to learn how they might benefit your operation and your development as a baking and pastry arts professional.

Baking Science and Food Safety

THERE ARE DOZENS OF SCIENTIFIC PRINCIPLES AT WORK IN BAKING. AS AN INTRODUCTION TO THE TOPIC OF FOOD SCIENCE, THIS SECTION PROVIDES AN OVERVIEW OF THE MOST BASIC OF THESE PRINCIPLES.

Baking Science

Food science is an exacting study, dedicated to discovering and clarifying the complex reactions involved in food preparation. A general knowledge of how basic ingredients can be changed through the effects of temperature, agitation, and/or acids or alkalis gives the baker or pastry chef the freedom to develop new items. It also aids the chef in problem solving, such as changing a formula's original cooking method, finding a suitable shortcut for a long or complex recipe, or substituting one ingredient for another. These challenges may be inspired by a need to liven up or update a menu, cut costs, streamline production, or introduce a new technique or ingredient.

Books and articles on these topics should be part of every baker's or pastry chef's professional reading (see Appendix C).

Five Basic Baking Ingredients

Flour, eggs, water, fat, and/or sugar are necessary in all baking and pastry goods. The ways in which these ingredients interact with one another and other ingredients during mixing and baking dictate the quality of the end product. For the purpose of understanding how these ingredients influence a finished product, they can be divided into two categories: stabilizers and liquefiers.

Proteins in Flour and Their Functions in Baking

Gluten is formed by the proteins present in wheat flour (wheat is the only grain that forms measurable amounts of gluten, making it an indispensable grain in the kitchen or bakeshop). Flour gives strength to and acts to absorb the bulk of the moisture in most baked goods. As the flour takes up water, gluten strands begin to form. To further develop these strands and make them more cohesive and elastic, the mixture is agitated (mixed). Gluten development is essential for certain baked goods, such as breads, in which a somewhat chewy texture is desirable; in other baked goods, however, such as cakes that should be tender and moist, excessive gluten development is a flaw. The differences among desired outcomes for the textures of different types of baked goods led to the development of flours with varying gluten levels.

While the gluten level of the flour has a very significant role in the final texture of a product, the amount of mixing a dough or batter undergoes, particularly if the flour has a moderate to high percentage of gluten, will also have a marked impact. Gluten is composed of two distinct proteins: glutenin and gliadin. When flour is mixed with water, the glutenin and gliadin begin to join together (with the water intermingled) to form strands or sheets of gluten. The glutenin provides the elasticity; the gliadin, the extensibility. The formation of these strands provides the structure for many baked goods. If a flour with too little or no gluten is used in bread making, the bread will not rise. Yeast is the catalyst for risen bread, but it is also necessary to have well-developed gluten to trap the gases produced by the fermenting yeast for bread to rise.

STABILIZERS

A stabilizer is any ingredient that helps to develop the solid structure, or "framework," of a finished product. Of the five basic baking ingredients, flour and eggs act as stabilizers. Flour and eggs both lend structure and nutritional value to a finished product, but the way each of these ingredients acts is different.

Flour represents the bulk of most of the formulas made in any bakeshop. It acts as a binding and absorbing agent, and it may be thought of as the "backbone" of the majority of bakeshop formulas. It is the gluten (the protein component in flour) that builds structure and strength in baked goods. Different types of flours have different gluten-to-starch ratios that can create vastly different results in the texture, appearance, and flavor of the final product if used in the same formula. A flour with a higher gluten content will result in a tougher crumb, whereas a flour with a lower gluten content will result in a more tender crumb.

Eggs lend additional stability during baking. They influence the texture and grain as well; by facilitating the incorporation and distribution of air, they promote an even-grained and fine texture. Eggs also have leavening power. As eggs (whole, yolks, or whites) are whipped, they trap air that expands when heated, resulting in a larger and lighter product.

In addition, eggs help to develop flavor and aroma in a product, mostly from the fat and nutrients contained in the yolk. Egg yolks also contribute to a drier finished product, and egg whites add volume and moisture.

LIQUEFIERS

The remaining three of the five basic baking ingredients—water (as well as milk and other liquids), fats, and sugar—act as liquefiers; that is, they help to loosen or liquefy a dough or batter. Some liquefiers, such as sugar, may actually tighten or bind a dough when first added, but their interaction with other ingredients ultimately tenderizes, or loosens, the dough or batter.

Water acts to dilute or liquefy water-soluble ingredients such as sugar and salt. It also facilitates the even distribution of sugar, salt, and yeast in a dough if these ingre-

Hydration of a Dough or Batter

In the baking process, liquid provides the moisture necessary for hydration of the ingredients. The moisture aids in the development of the gluten in the flour, in gelatinization of starches, and in dissolving other ingredients to achieve even distribution and consistency. Typically, the liquid used in baking and pastry formulas is water or milk, or a combination of the two.

Products made with water are less expensive and have a longer shelf life. Those made with milk contain more nutrients and are more flavorful. The sugars present in milk also help these products develop a golden brown color in the oven.

dients are mixed thoroughly with the water before introducing the remaining ingredients in the formula. In bread making, water is typically the primary liquefier. A bread formula with a higher percentage of water results in a more open grain and softer crumb. In addition, water helps to develop the proteins in flour, necessary for proper leavening. Water also acts as a leavener when it changes to steam and expands.

Milk performs many of the same functions as water, but because of its additional components (fat, sugar, minerals, and protein), it also serves a number of other functions and adds flavor as well. As the sugar (lactose) in milk caramelizes, it gives a rich color to the product's surface, and it can also aid in development of a firm crust. The lactic acid in milk has a tightening effect on the proteins in flour that serves to increase stability, resulting in a product with a fine grain and texture.

Fats fall into the category of liquefiers. If the total amount of fat added to a dough or batter equals no more than 3 percent of the weight of the finished dough or product, it acts to increase the elasticity of the proteins in the flour, thereby helping the bread or other product expand during baking. In baking, fats and oils are also classified as shortening agents, a term derived from their ability to split the long, elastic gluten strands that can toughen doughs and batters. This tenderizing effect renders the strands more susceptible to breaking, or shortening, resulting in a more tender and less dense crumb.

Sugar has a tendency to tighten up a mixture when it is first incorporated. By its nature, however, it attracts moisture, a characteristic that causes it to ultimately loosen, or liquefy, a batter or dough. For the gluten in flour to develop, it needs moisture. Because sugar attracts moisture, it acts to inhibit gluten development in the bat-

Shortening Agents

BUTTER

Butter is made from cow's milk. It is approximately 80 percent fat, 10 to 15 percent water, and 5 percent milk solids. The advantages of using butter in baking are its flavor and lower melting point.

LARD

Lard is rendered pork fat. It is most often used in conjunction with other fats.

OILS

Most baking formulas require solid fats because they are necessary for creaming and other mixing processes, so oils are not often used.

SHORTENINGS

Solid shortenings are hydrogenated vegetable fats created for baking. They are made by injecting hydrogen gas into purified oil as it is heated. Hydrogenated fats will have varied melting temperatures depending on the purpose for which they were manufactured. Most are designed to cream well, and thus have a higher melting point.

To create emulsified shortening, mono- and diglycerides are added to shortening, resulting in increased absorption and retention of moisture. Recipes using emulsified shortening have higher ratios of milk, sugar, fat, and eggs to flour, resulting in richer cakes that are less prone to drying out. Emulsified shortening is typically used when the quantity of sugar in a recipe is equal to or greater than the amount of flour.

Additional Functions of Sugar in Baking

- **IT AIDS IN THE CREAMING PROCESS.** The crystalline structure of granulated sugar makes it an effective agent for the incorporation of air into batters mixed by the creaming method. The incorporated air is then held by the shortening agent, the other main ingredient in any creaming-method formula.

- **IT RETAINS MOISTURE AND PROLONGS FRESHNESS.** Sugar absorbs moisture from other ingredients as well as from the atmosphere, thereby helping to keep finished products moist and delay drying out or staling.

- **IT IMPARTS COLOR TO CRUSTS.** Through caramelization and the Maillard reaction (for more information on browning reactions see page 84), sugar aids in the development of deep golden crust color during baking, which also adds flavor.

- **IT CONTRIBUTES FOOD VALUE.** Sugar in moderate amounts can supply some of the carbohydrate requirements of a normal diet.

ter or dough, preventing it from becoming too tough or elastic. Furthermore, when used in the correct proportion, sugar can help to maintain the elasticity of the gluten strands present in a dough or batter. With maximum elasticity, the gluten can expand more easily so the item is more efficiently leavened, allowing for the proper development of volume and the creation of a moist and tender crumb. During baking, sugar also interacts with the starch component of flour to delay its gelatinization, enabling batters and doughs to stay softer longer, allowing greater spread and rise before setting.

Leaveners

To leaven is to raise, or to make lighter. There are several ways to accomplish this in baking: with yeasts (also known as organic leaveners), with chemical agents such as baking powder or baking soda, or with steam through mechanical leavening. Each method is best suited for specific applications and produces very different results. The different leavening methods may be used alone or in conjunction with one another (as in croissants, for example) to yield different effects.

YEAST

Yeast is a living organism that needs suitable conditions to thrive. Commercially-sold baker's yeast is of the strain *Saccharomyces cerevisiae,* which has been determined to be the best suited for bread baking.

Yeast needs warmth, moisture, and food (carbohydrates) to begin fermenting. By definition, fermentation is the anaerobic respiration of microorganisms. The process converts carbohydrates into alcohol and carbon dioxide. The carbon dioxide acts to leaven a dough or batter as the gas is trapped in the web of protein (gluten) strands that developed during the mixing process. The alcohol acts to tenderize the gluten strands, improving the overall texture of the product; it cooks out during baking, leaving no undesirable flavor.

The fermentation process is important in building the internal structure and flavor of the dough. Given the proper environment, yeast cells will continue to ferment until they either run out of food or the by-products of fermentation begin to poison them and they die. For these reasons, as well as the necessity of maintaining production schedules, it is easy to see why time is an important element in making quality yeast-raised products. Consequently, it is important to understand how the fermentation of yeast can be controlled.

Yeast cells are sensitive to the temperature of the environment. The ideal temperature for fermentation is between 80° and 90°F/27° and 32°C. Lower temperatures will retard or arrest yeast development. Temperatures at or above 105°F/41°C will also slow fermentation. Yeast dies at 138°F/59°C.

While sugar provides an immediate food source for yeast to begin fermentation, too much sugar can act to slow the fermentation process. High concentrations of sugar can have the same dehydrating effect as salt, causing yeast cells to die.

Salt plays many roles in baking, but its contributions are most evident in bread baking. It helps to slow yeast growth and, when used in the correct proportions, will help to control the rate of fermentation. However, too much salt can damage or kill the yeast by dehydrating the cells, resulting in a heavier, denser product. For this reason, salt should never come in direct contact with yeast.

CHEMICAL LEAVENERS

Baking soda and baking powder are the primary chemical leaveners. With these leaveners, an alkaline ingredient—the baking soda or baking powder (which also contains an acid and a starch)—interacts with an acid. The alkali and acid, when combined with a liquid, react to produce carbon dioxide that expands during baking, leavening the dough or batter.

Baking soda, or sodium bicarbonate, is a common leavening agent for cakes, quick breads, and cookies. Sodium bicarbonate is an alkali and is, therefore, positive-

Other Functions of Salt in Bread Baking

- **IT STRENGTHENS THE GLUTEN STRANDS.**

- **IT CONTRIBUTES TO ELASTICITY,** which in turn acts to improve the texture of the final product.

- **IT IS AN IMPORTANT FLAVOR COMPONENT IN BREADS.** It enhances both the subtle flavors in the other ingredients and those that result from the fermentation process. Without salt, bread tastes flat.

Acid, Alkali, and pH

The pH of a solution is the measure of its acidity or alkalinity. A pH of 7 denotes a neutral solution, which indicates a balance between the negative and positive ions within the solution. If a solution has a pH higher than 7, it is alkaline or base and has a positive charge. If a solution has a pH lower than 7, it is acidic and has a negative charge. Compounds that are charged are unstable, meaning that they have a natural affinity to become neutral. They may break down on their own when heat is applied, or they may break down in reaction to the presence of a compound or element that has the opposite charge.

ly charged and seeks to be in a neutral state. (For more information on alkalis, see the sidebar above.) When sodium bicarbonate reacts with an acid, it breaks down and releases carbon dioxide, which is captured in the dough or batter and causes it to rise (leaven) as it is baked. To break down and be relieved of its charge, sodium bicarbonate requires the presence of an acidic ingredient, such as chocolate, vinegar, a cultured dairy product, fruit juice, or molasses.

Baking powder is a mixture of sodium bicarbonate, an acid, and cornstarch. The sodium bicarbonate and soda will react with the acid to create carbon dioxide when combined with a liquid, and the carbon dioxide acts to leaven the product. The cornstarch in baking powder absorbs moisture and keeps the acid and alkaline components from reacting with each other before they are mixed into a dough or batter.

There are two types of baking powder: single-acting and double-acting. Single-acting baking powder contains sodium bicarbonate and cream of tartar (called a dry acid). Because cream of tartar is easily dissolved, this type of baking powder only needs to be combined with a liquid for the two substances to react and release the carbon dioxide that will leaven the dough or batter. Double-acting baking powder combines sodium bicarbonate with dry acids that have different solubility rates. One of the acids is easily soluble and will begin to react with the sodium bicarbonate when wet. The other needs heat in order to completely dissolve, thus delaying its reaction until the product is in the oven.

MECHANICAL LEAVENING

Mechanical leavening occurs when air and/or moisture, trapped during the mixing process, expands as it is heated during baking, creating pockets trapped by cooking proteins causing "balloon-like" expansion that aids in the leavening process. This method of leavening occurs when one of three distinct methods is used: foaming, creaming, or lamination.

In the foaming mixing method, eggs, eggs yolks, and/or egg whites are beaten to incorporate air until they form a foam. This foam is then added to the remaining batter, folded in so as to disrupt as few of the air pockets as possible and maintain the volume of the foam. The air trapped in these bubbles then expands during baking and causes the product to rise.

The creaming mixing method blends fat and sugar together to incorporate air. The creamed mixture is then combined with the remaining ingredients, and as the product bakes, the air trapped during the creaming process expands and leavens the product.

In lamination, alternating layers of fat and dough are created through different folding and rolling techniques (for more information on lamination techniques see page 261). When the dough is baked, the fat melts, releasing water in the form of steam, which acts to leaven the dough. The steam fills the pockets left by the melting fat and expands, causing the product to rise; the fat then "fries" the dough so that the spaces are retained.

Sweeteners

MONOSACCHARIDES AND OLIGOSACCHARIDES

A monosaccharide, or single sugar, is the basic building block of all sugars and starches. Fructose and dextrose are both monosaccharides. These are the simplest sugars. When fructose and dextrose are bonded together, they form a disaccharide, or double sugar, called sucrose—that is, table sugar. Many monosaccharides linked together in long chains are called polysaccharides. Starches such as cornstarch are made up of such chains, thousands of saccharides long. Although starches are also made up of sugar molecules, they do not taste sweet, and they do not dissolve in water when they are in long chains.

Oligosaccharides lie somewhere in between table sugar and the starches present in cornstarch and flour that we are so familiar with. They are chains of sugar molecules—not so long as those in starches but longer than those in sugars. Like starches, they do not taste sweet; unlike starches, they dissolve in water. All of these terms are vital to understanding corn syrup and glucose, because they are the ingredients in our humble bucket of glucose syrup.

Crystallization of Sugar

Crystallization is a process that occurs when sugar is deposited from a solution. This type of deposition allows the sugar molecules to assume their characteristic geometric form. Sugar crystallization is influenced by many things: saturation levels, agitation, temperature, cooling, seeding, invert sugar, and acid. Through manipulation of these factors, the process of crystallization may be controlled to create the typical crystalline and noncrystalline structures used in the bakeshop or pastry kitchen, such as fondant, rock candy, hard candies, and caramel.

In order for sugars to crystallize out of solution, the solution must be sufficiently saturated for precipitation to occur. Typically, in a bakeshop or pastry kitchen, sugar will be dissolved in water through the introduction of heat, which facilitates the dissolving and incorporation of more sugar. The solution may then be heated to a specific temperature, thereby evaporating water and serving to further increase the den-

Saturated and Supersaturated Sugar Solutions

Saturation and supersaturation are vital concepts for the confectioner, as they are directly linked with the process of crystallization. At a given temperature, a specific quantity of water can dissolve only a finite quantity of sugar. The warmer the water, the more sugar it can dissolve. When no more sugar can be dissolved in a certain amount of water at a certain temperature, the solution is said to be saturated. When a saturated solution is heated to evaporate some of the water, the solution becomes supersaturated. Supersaturated solutions are created by dissolving sugar in water, then cooking them to evaporate a portion of the water, leaving behind a solution that contains a higher concentration of sugar in solution than could have been initially dissolved in the same amount of water. Supersaturated solutions are delicate systems. Sugar molecules are attracted to each other, and with so many of them in such a small amount of liquid, they are quite likely to join together. This action results in the formation of crystals.

Invert Sugar

The term *invert sugar* refers to a sugar (sucrose or table sugar) whose optical or refractory properties have been altered. This altering occurs when it is boiled together with a dilute acid such as cream of tartar (in solution), lemon juice, or vinegar. In the presence of the acid, the sucrose breaks down into its two components, dextrose and fructose. There are also naturally occurring invert sugars, such as honey. However, many, if not most, of these natural invert sugars contain other components or impurities that make them ill suited for use in the sugar-cooking and candy-making processes, as the impurities typically burn at a much lower temperature than is required to cook the sugar.

sity, or saturation, of the solution. The more saturated, or "densely packed," a solution, the more likely and more easily it will begin to crystallize. Crystallization occurs as the particles in solution collide with one another; hence agitation is a key contributor to the process. If agitation is initiated while the solution is still hot, large crystals will form as molecules become attached at a slower rate. As the mixture cools, crystals form more readily, promoting rapid growth of many tiny crystals when it is stirred or otherwise agitated. If the mixture is allowed to cool without agitation and is then stirred, it will crystallize rapidly but will form small crystals rather than large ones.

The introduction of a "seed" will cause crystallization. A seed is anything from whole sugar crystals to air bubbles to a skewer (as when making rock candy) that will act as a surface for the sugar crystals to adhere to and grow on.

Controlling or delaying crystallization allows the sugar solution to be manipulated or pulled without graining. It allows the confectioner to make chewy caramels that will not crystallize.

Benefits of Glucose Syrup

- **IT MAKES COOKED CONFECTIONS SOFTER AND EASIER TO WORK WITH.** Added to cooked sugar in the proper amount, it will increase its elasticity.

- **IT IS A HUMECTANT.** That is, when it is added to baked goods, it helps to retain moisture, resulting in a moister product and a longer shelf life.

- **IT IS USUALLY LESS SWEET THAN SUGAR.** For example, 42 DE corn syrup is only about 60 percent as sweet as cane sugar. By substituting this syrup for a percentage of the sugar in a formula, the sweetness of baked goods or frozen desserts can be decreased without sacrificing the textural advantages afforded by sugar.

Certain ingredients may be introduced into a sugar solution to inhibit crystallization. A small amount of glucose syrup or another invert sugar is often added to the solution. The molecular structure of glucose and other invert sugars is different from that of sucrose. This difference means the invert sugar will inhibit crystallization by getting in the way of the sucrose molecules that start to attach to each other as they begin to crystallize out of the solution. A second way to inhibit crystallization is to introduce a small amount of an acid into the solution. When sucrose (table sugar) is boiled with dilute acids, the acids will cause the inversion of some of the sucrose molecules. The resultant invert sugars will interfere with the crystallization process just as glucose syrup does.

Hygroscopic Properties of Sugar and Salt

Sugar and salt are both hygroscopic, meaning they will readily take up water under certain conditions of humidity. In baked products, they act to retain moisture, extending shelf life. In items such as hard candies, however, this attraction of moisture acts to begin to break down the structure of the candy or other item, causing it to become soft and sticky.

Browning Reactions

There are two types of processes that create browning in food: caramelization and the Maillard reaction. Browning occurring from either of these processes results in a rich color and enhances both the flavor and aroma of the food. Caramelization occurs when sucrose is present, and only at high temperatures. As sugar is heated, it melts and then begins to break down. As the temperature continues to increase, different compounds will form and then break down, creating different flavors and colors throughout the cooking process. The Maillard reaction (for example, the browning of bread crust in the oven) occurs between reducing sugars and proteins and can occur at low temperatures more slowly and at high temperatures over short periods of time. It is a complex browning reaction that results in the particular flavor and color of foods that do not contain much sugar.

Thickeners

Sauces, puddings, fillings, mousses, and creams can be thickened and/or stabilized by many ingredients, including starches, such as flour, cornstarch, tapioca, and arrowroot, gelatin, and eggs. These thickeners may be used to lightly thicken a mixture, such as a sauce, or to produce something that is firmly set, such as Bavarian cream.

The quantity and type of thickener, as well as how it is stirred or otherwise manipulated, will determine the properties of the finished product. For example, if a custard is cooked over direct heat and stirred constantly, the result will be a sauce that pours easily. Baked in a water bath, with no stirring at all, the same custard base will set into firm custard.

GELATINIZATION OF STARCHES

When starch granules suspended in water are heated, they begin to absorb liquid and swell, causing an increase in the viscosity of the mixture. This reaction, known as gelatinization, allows starches to be used as thickening agents.

POLYSACCHARIDES

Polysaccharides are starches that are commonly used as thickening agents in preparations such as sauces and fillings. They are complex carbohydrates that are composed of two types of starch molecules, both of which are made of long chains of dextrose. However, one, known as amylose, exists in long linear chains, and the other, known as amylopectin, exists in dendritic (branched) patterns. The ratio in which the two types of starch molecules, amylose and amylopectin, occur in a starch will dictate the starch's use. The higher the percentage of amylose, the more prone the starch is to gel. When more amylopectin is present, the starch will act to increase viscosity or thicken to a greater extent without causing a gel to form. Starches high in amylose are derived from grain sources such as wheat and corn, while starches with a high percentage of amylopectin are derived from roots and tubers, such as tapioca.

It is only after a starch in liquid is heated that the granules can absorb liquid and begin to thicken the liquid. As the starch is heated, the molecules within each granule begin to move faster and their bonds begin to loosen, allowing liquid to work its way into the normally tightly bound granules. As the granules absorb liquid, they swell, making it easier for more liquid to be absorbed. All starches have different temperatures at which they begin to thicken.

RETROGRADATION

Starches high in amylose that have been gelatinized and then undergo freezing, refrigeration, or aging may begin to retrograde, or revert to their insoluble form. This reaction causes changes in food texture and appearance (staling in breads and similar products or cloudiness or graininess in sauces, puddings, and creams). But all starches do not have the same tendency toward retrogradation. It is important to choose the correct starch for the necessary application. For example, when making pies to be frozen, it is best to use modified food starch to thicken the filling, rather than cornstarch (see table below).

Gelling and/or Thickening Agents and Their Uses

STARCH	SOURCE	CHARACTERISTICS	USES
MODIFIED FOOD STARCHES	Various	Flavorless; freezes well	Fruit fillings
CORNSTARCH	Grain	Prone to retrogradation; must be heated to a boil to remove flavor	Sauces, puddings, and fruit fillings
FLOUR	Grain	Prone to retrogradation; must be heated to a boil to remove flavor	Puddings, fruit fillings
ARROWROOT	Tuber	Flavorless; makes a translucent paste that will set to a gel; if overagitated, overcooked, or used in too large a quantity, may make the product stringy and gooey	Soups, sauces
TAPIOCA/CASSAVA	Root	Doesn't set to a gel; doesn't retrograde	Puddings, fruit fillings
POTATO	Tuber	If overagitated, overcooked, or used in too large a quantity, may make the product stringy and gooey	Kosher baking
AGAR-AGAR	Sea vegetable	Strong thickening properties; sets to a firm gel; has a very high melting point	Gelées and vegetarian desserts
PECTIN	Citrus skins, apples, and other high-pectin fruits	Requires a low pH and high sugar content to form a gel	Jellies, jams, preserves, and gelées
GELATIN	Animal	Melts below body temperature; boiling may reduce its strength; enzymatic reactions with certain fruits will prevent setting	Mousses, aspics, and gelées
EGGS	Animal	If not used in conjunction with a starch, will curdle when overcooked; yolks create a soft velvety set, whites create a resilient set	Custards, custard sauces, and puddings

PECTIN

Pectin is a carbohydrate derived from the cell walls of certain fruits. Some common sources of pectin are apples, cranberries, currants, quince, and the skins of citrus fruits, all of which are high in pectin. Pectin may be used as a gelling agent or as a thickener. To gel, it requires the correct balance of sugar and an acid. Pectin molecules have a natural attraction for water molecules; when pectin is put in solution alone, the molecules will become surrounded by water molecules and will not gel the solution. The addition of an acid interrupts this attraction, and sugar further acts to draw the water away from the pectin molecules, allowing them to connect together and form a three-dimensional network.

GELATIN

Gelatin is typically used to produce light, delicate foams (such as Bavarian creams, mousses, and stabilized whipped cream) that set so they may be molded and/or sliced. Available in both granulated and sheet form, gelatin must first be rehydrated, or "bloomed," in a cool liquid. Once it has absorbed the liquid, it is then gently heated to melt the crystals, either by adding the softened gelatin to a hot mixture, such as a custard sauce, or by gently heating it over simmering water.

Gelatin, a protein derived from the bones and connective tissue of animals, is composed of molecules that attract water. When they first come in contact with water, they swell; then, as they are heated, they completely dissolve. As the mixture cools, the proteins join together to form a three-dimensional web (much as in coagulation) that holds in the moisture. This system is called a gel. When used in making a mousse or Bavarian cream, the gelatin solution is beaten into a mixture containing many air pockets. The proteins are thus stretched to hold the air as well as the moisture, creating a stabilized product. Gelatin is also used commercially in the production of ice cream, as it interferes with formation of ice crystals.

EGGS AS THICKENERS

Whole eggs, egg yolks, or whites may be used, alone or in conjunction with other thickeners, to thicken a food. Eggs act to thicken through the coagulation of proteins. As their proteins begin to coagulate, liquid is trapped in the network of set proteins, resulting in a smooth, rather thick texture. This is known as a partial coagulation,

Enzymes and Gelatin

When working with gelatin, it is important to remember that there are a few types of fruits that contain proteases—enzymes that will break down the collagen in gelatin and not allow it to set, or gel. Among these fruits are kiwi, pineapple, papaya, honeydew melon, and banana. To use these fruits in any gelatin-based application, you must first allow the fruit or fruit purée to simmer for 2 to 3 minutes, to destroy all of the poretease enzymes, before adding the gelatin.

where the proteins hold moisture; if the mixture were cooked or baked further, the proteins would fully coagulate and expel water, causing the product to curdle.

At the molecular level, natural proteins are shaped like coils or springs. When natural proteins are exposed to heat, salt, or acid, they denature—that is, their coils unwind. When proteins denature, they tend to bond together, or coagulate, and form solid clumps. An example of this is a cooked egg white, which changes from a transparent fluid to an opaque solid. As proteins coagulate, they lose some of their capacity to hold water, which is why protein-rich foods give off moisture as they cook, even if steamed or poached. Denatured proteins are easier to digest than natural proteins.

Most commonly, proteins are denatured through the application of an acid, agitation, or heat. The addition of one or more of these elements will act to alter the structure of the protein by disrupting the bonds that shape its molecules. This change in structure permits the protein to behave in a different manner. For example, the proteins will extend in length, so that they are more likely to come in contact with one another and bond, forming a web (or coagulating). In this way proteins become useful as a thickening agent that can be used in many applications where starches may not be appropriate, such as in frozen desserts.

Emulsions

An emulsion is a system of two immiscible liquids (liquids that are unable to be mixed together to form a true solution) that appears to be a completely homogenous mixture but is in fact a two-phase system, having a dispersed phase and a continuous phase. When mixed to combine, one of the liquids breaks up into minute droplets (dispersed phase) and the other remains as a matrix in which droplets are dispersed (continuous phase). There are two types of emulsions: temporary and permanent.

A temporary emulsion is one that will separate into two distinct layers in a short period of time. In a permanent emulsion, the two liquids do not separate as easily, because of the presence of a third element, known as an emulsifier. Emulsifiers are naturally occurring substances that are attracted to both fat and water and thus facilitate maintaining a stable emulsion between two immiscible liquids.

Tempering Chocolate

Tempered chocolate has a glossy finish, snap, and creamy texture. All chocolate you buy is tempered, if it has been properly stored since its time of manufacture, but if you are going to dip centers, mold it, or use it for other confectionery or décor work, you will need to melt it and then temper it. Cocoa butter, the fat found in chocolate, may set into one of four types of crystals: beta, gamma, alpha, or beta prime. Only the beta crystals are stable and yield the gloss, snap, and proper texture. To temper chocolate, all of the crystals must first be fully melted. For the chocolate to maintain gloss and snap, as it is cooling, it must form stable beta crystals. They can be caused to form by gradually reducing the temperature of the melted chocolate until it is at 80°F/27°C, while applying constant agitation. To encourage the formation of the beta crystals, some additional, already tempered chocolate (known as a "seed") may be added to the mixture.

Food Safety

The importance of storing and preparing food properly cannot be overemphasized. Practicing and monitoring safe procedures will keep both your employees and customers safe from injury or food-borne illness.

Food-Borne Illness

FOOD CONTAMINANTS

Foods can serve as carriers of many different illnesses. The most common symptoms of food-borne illnesses include abdominal cramps, nausea, vomiting, and diarrhea, possibly accompanied by fever. The symptoms may appear within a matter of hours after consumption of the affected food, but in some cases several days may elapse before onset. In order for food-borne illness to be officially declared an outbreak, it must involve two or more people who have eaten the same food and it must be confirmed by health officials.

Food-borne illnesses are caused by *adulterated foods* (foods unfit for human consumption). The severity of the illness depends on the amount of adulterated food ingested and, to a great extent, the individual's susceptibility. Children, the elderly, and anyone whose immune system is already under siege generally will have much more difficulty than a healthy adult in combating a food-borne illness.

The source of the contamination affecting the food can be chemical, physical, or biological. Insecticides and cleaning compounds are examples of *chemical contaminants* that may accidentally find their way into foods. *Physical contaminants* include such things as bits of glass, rodent hairs, and paint chips, which might cause injury as well as illness. Careless food handling can mean that a plastic bandage or an earring could fall into the food and result in illness or injury.

Biological contaminants account for the majority of food-borne illnesses. These include naturally occurring poisons, known as toxins, found in certain wild mushrooms, rhubarb leaves, and green potatoes, among other plants. The predominant biological agents, however, are disease-causing microorganisms known as *pathogens,* which are responsible for up to 95 percent of all food-borne illnesses. Microorganisms of many kinds are present virtually everywhere, and most are helpful, even essential, or harmless; only about 1 percent of microorganisms are actually pathogenic.

Food-borne illnesses caused by biological contaminants fall into two subcategories: intoxication and infection. *Intoxication* occurs when a person consumes food containing toxins from bacteria, molds, or certain plants and animals. Once in the body, these toxins act as poison. Botulism is an example of an intoxication. In the case of an *infection,* the food eaten by an individual contains large numbers of living pathogens. These pathogens multiply in the body and usually attack the gastrointestinal lining. Salmonellosis is an example of an infection. Some food-borne illnesses have characteristics of both an intoxication and an infection. *E. coli* 0157:H7 is an agent that causes such an illness.

The specific types of pathogens responsible for food-borne illnesses are fungi, viruses, parasites, and bacteria. *Fungi,* which include molds and yeast, are more adaptable than other microorganisms and have a high tolerance for acidic conditions. They are more often responsible for food spoilage than for food-borne illness. Fungi are important to the food industry, in the production of cheese, bread, and wine and beer.

Viruses do not actually multiply in food, but if through poor sanitation practice a virus contaminates food, consumption of that food may result in illness. Infectious hepatitis, caused by eating shellfish harvested from polluted waters (an illegal practice) or poor hand-washing practices after using the bathroom, are examples. Once in the body, viruses invade a cell (called the host cell) and essentially reprogram it to produce more copies of the virus. The copies leave the dead host cells behind and invade still more cells. The best defenses against food-borne viruses are purchasing shellfish only from certified waters and maintaining good personal hygiene.

Parasites are pathogens that feed on and take shelter in another organism, called a host. The host receives no benefit from the parasite and, in fact, suffers harm, or even death, as a result. Amoebas and various worms, such as *Trichinella spiralis,* which is associated with pork, are among the parasites that contaminate foods. Different parasites reproduce in different ways. An example is the parasitic worm that exists in the larva stage in muscle meats. Even after it is consumed by a human being or another animal, its life and reproductive cycles continue. When the larvae reach adult stage, the fertilized female releases more eggs, which hatch and travel to the muscle tissue of the host, and the cycle continues.

Bacteria are responsible for a significant percentage of biologically caused food-borne illnesses. In order to better protect food during storage, preparation, and service, it is important to understand the classifications and patterns of bacterial growth. Bacteria are classified by their requirement for oxygen, by the temperatures at which they grow best, and by their spore-forming abilities. *Aerobic bacteria* require the presence of oxygen. *Anaerobic bacteria* do not require oxygen and may even die when exposed to it. *Facultative bacteria* are able to function with or without oxygen.

In terms of sensitivity to temperature, bacteria fall into the following categories:

1. **Mesophilic bacteria** grow best between 60° and 100°F/16° and 38°C. Because the temperature of the human body as well as of commercial kitchens fall within that range, mesophilic bacteria tend to be the most abundant and the most dangerous.

2. **Thermophilic bacteria** grow most rapidly between 110° and 171°F/ 43° and 77°C.

3. **Psychrophilic bacteria** prefer cooler temperatures, between 32° and 60°F/ 0° and 16°C.

BACTERIAL GROWTH AND HAZARDOUS FOODS

Bacteria reproduce by means of fission: one bacterium grows and then splits into two bacteria of equal size. These bacteria divide to form four, the four form eight, and so on. Under ideal circumstances, bacteria will reproduce every 20 minutes or so. In about 12 hours, one bacterium can multiply into sixty-eight billion bacteria, more than enough to cause illness.

Certain bacteria are able to form endospores, which protect them against adverse circumstances such as high temperatures or dehydration. Endospores allow an individual bacterium to resume its life cycle if favorable conditions should resume.

Bacteria require three basic conditions for growth and reproduction: a protein source, readily available moisture, and a moderate pH level. The higher the amount of protein in a food, the greater its potential as a carrier of a food-borne illness. The amount of moisture available in a food is measured on the water activity (Aw) scale; this scale runs from 0 to 1, with 1 representing the Aw of water. Foods with a water activity above 0.85 can support bacterial growth.

A food's relative acidity or alkalinity is measured on the scale known as pH. A moderate pH—a value between 4.6 and 10 on a scale that ranges from 1 to 14—is best for bacterial growth, and most foods fall within that range. Adding a highly acidic ingredient, such as vinegar or citrus juice, to a food can lower its pH and extend its shelf life, making it less susceptible to bacterial growth.

Many foods meet the three conditions necessary for bacterial growth and are therefore considered to be potentially hazardous. Meats, poultry, seafood, tofu, and dairy products (with the exception of some hard cheeses) are all categorized as potentially hazardous foods. Foods do not have to be animal-based to contain protein, and cooked rice, beans, pasta, and potatoes are also potentially hazardous, as are sliced melons, sprouts, and garlic-and-oil mixtures.

Food that contains pathogens in great enough numbers to cause illness may look and smell normal. Disease-causing microorganisms are too small to be seen with the naked eye, so it is usually impossible to ascertain visually that food is adulterated. And because the microorganisms, particularly the bacteria, that cause food to spoil are different from the ones that cause food-borne illness, food may be adulterated and still have no "off" odor.

Although cooking will destroy many of the harmful microorganisms that may be present, careless food handling after cooking can reintroduce pathogens that will grow even more quickly, without competition for food and space from the microorganisms that cause spoilage. Although shortcuts and carelessness do not always result in food-borne illness, inattention to detail increases the risk of an outbreak that may cause serious illness or even death. The various expenses that a restaurant can incur as the result of an outbreak of food-borne illness can be staggering. In addition, negative publicity and loss of prestige are blows from which many restaurants can simply never recover.

Avoiding Cross Contamination

Many food-borne illnesses are a result of unsanitary handling procedures in the kitchen. Cross contamination occurs when disease-causing elements or harmful substances are transferred from a contaminated surface to a heretofore uncontaminated one. To avoid cross contamination, adhere to the following practices.

Good personal hygiene is one of the best defenses against cross contamination. The employee who reports for work when he or she has a contagious illness or an infected cut on his or her hand puts every customer and other employees at risk. Anytime your hands come in contact with a possible source of contamination, especially your face, hair, eyes, and mouth, they should be thoroughly washed before continuing work.

Food is at greatest risk of cross contamination during the preparation stage. Ideally, separate work areas and cutting boards should be used for raw and cooked foods. Equipment and cutting boards should always be cleaned and thoroughly sanitized between uses. For example, before cutting a piece of pork on the same surface you used to cut chicken, it is important to clean and sanitize not only the cutting surface, but also your hands, the knife, and the sharpening steel. Wiping cloths for this purpose should be held in a double-strength sanitizing solution and placed near each workstation to encourage use.

Proper Hand Washing

To cut down on cross contamination and avoid spreading illness, wash your hands as often as you need to, and wash them correctly. The 1999 FDA Food Code states that hands and forearms should be washed using soap and 110°F/43°C water for 20 seconds. Wash your hands at the beginning of each shift and each new task, after handling raw foods, after going to the bathroom, and after handling money or other nonfood items, to mention just a few points in the workday.

First wet your hands, then apply soap. Use enough soap to work up a good lather. Use a nail brush to clean under your nails and around the cuticles if necessary, and scrub well. (It takes about 10 seconds to sing "Happy Birthday"; in order to be sure you have lathered for 20 seconds, try singing this song to yourself twice while washing your hands.) Rinse your hands thoroughly in warm water, and dry them completely using paper towels.

All food must be stored carefully to prevent contact between raw and cooked items. Place drip pans beneath raw foods to catch drips and prevent splashing. Do not handle ready-to-eat foods with bare hands. Instead, use a suitable utensil (deli tissue, spatula, tongs, or the like) or single-use food-handling gloves (intended to be used only for a single task and replaced before beginning a new task).

Keeping Foods Out of the Danger Zone

An important weapon against pathogens is the observance of strict time and temperature controls. Generally, the disease-causing microorganisms found in foods need to be present in significant quantities in order to make someone ill. (There are exceptions, however, E. coli 0157:H7 being one.) Once pathogens have established themselves in a food source, they will either thrive or be destroyed, depending upon how long foods are in the so-called danger zone.

There are pathogens that can live at all temperature ranges. For most of those capable of causing food-borne illness, however, the friendliest environment is one with temperatures from 41° to 140°F/5° to 60°C—the danger zone. Most pathogens are either destroyed or will not reproduce at temperatures above 140°F/60°C. Storing food at temperatures below 41°F/5°C will slow or interrupt the cycle of reproduction. (It should be noted that intoxicating pathogens may be destroyed during cooking, but any toxins they have produced are still there.)

When conditions are favorable, pathogens can reproduce at an astonishing rate. Therefore, controlling the time during which foods remain in the danger zone is critical to the prevention of food-borne illness. Foods left in the danger zone for longer than 4 hours are considered adulterated. Additionally, one should be fully aware that the 4-hour period does not have to be continuous, but is in fact cumulative—which means that the meter starts running again each time the food enters the danger zone. Once the 4-hour period has been exceeded, foods cannot be recovered by heating, cooling, or any other method.

RECEIVE AND STORE FOODS SAFELY

It is not unheard of for foods to be delivered to a food-service operation already contaminated. To prevent this from happening to you, inspect all goods to be sure they arrive in sanitary conditions. Make a habit of checking delivery trucks for signs of unsanitary conditions, such as dirt or pests. If the truck is a refrigerated or freezer unit, check the ambient temperature inside to see that it is adequate. Use a thermometer to check the temperature of the product as well. Check expiration dates, and verify that foods have the required government inspection and certification stamps or tags. Randomly sample bulk items, as well as individual packages within cases. Reject any goods that do not meet your standards.

Once you have accepted a delivery, move the items immediately into proper storage conditions. Break down and discard cardboard boxes as soon as possible, because they provide nesting areas for insects, especially cockroaches.

Refrigeration and freezing units should be regularly cleaned. They should be equipped with thermometers to make sure that the temperature remains within a safe range. Although in most cases chilling will not actually kill pathogens, it does drasti-

cally slow down reproduction. In general, refrigerators should be kept between 36°
and 40°F/2° and 4°C, but quality is better served if certain foods can be stored at specific temperatures:

Meat and poultry: 32° to 36°F/0° to 2°C

Fish and shellfish: 30° to 34°F/–1° to 1°C

Eggs: 38° to 40°F/3° to 4°C

Dairy products: 36° to 40°F/2° to 4°C

Produce: 40° to 45°F/4° to 7°C

Separate refrigerators for each of the above categories are ideal, but if necessary, a single unit can be divided into sections. The front of the box will be the warmest area,
the back the coldest.

Reach-in and walk-in refrigerators should be put in order at the end of every
shift. Before it is put in the refrigerator, food should be properly cooled, stored in
clean containers, wrapped, and labeled clearly with the contents and date. Store raw
products below and away from cooked foods to prevent cross contamination by drip-
ping. Because air circulation is essential for effective cooling, avoid overcrowding the
box, and make sure the fan is not blocked.

Do not stack trays directly on top of food; this will reduce the amount of air that
can circulate and may also result in cross contamination. Use the principle of "first in,
first out" (FIFO) when arranging food, so that older items are in the front.

Dry storage is used for foods such as canned goods, spices, condiments, cereals,
and staples such as flour and sugar, as well as for some fruits and vegetables that do not
require refrigeration and have low perishability. As with all storage, the area must be
clean, with proper ventilation and air circulation. Foods should not be stored on the
floor or near the walls, and there must be adequate shelving to prevent overcrowding.
The FIFO system should be practiced here as well, and all containers should be labeled
with a date. Cleaning supplies should be stored in a separate place from foods.

HOLD COOKED OR READY-TO-SERVE FOODS SAFELY

Keep hot foods hot and cold foods cold. Use hot-holding equipment (steam tables,
double boilers, bain-maries, heated cabinets or drawers, chafing dishes, and so on) to
keep hot foods at or above 140°F/60°C. Do not use hot-holding equipment for cooking or reheating; it cannot be counted on to raise the temperature of the food through
the danger zone quickly enough.

Use cold-holding equipment (ice or refrigeration) to keep cold foods at or below
41°F/5°C. If using ice, the foods should be in a container of some sort, not directly on the
ice. Use a perforated insert and drip pan to allow melting ice to drain away from foods.

COOLING FOODS SAFELY

One of the leading causes of food-borne illness is improperly cooled foods. Cooked
foods that are to be stored need to be cooled down to below 41°F/5°C as quickly as
possible. Cooling to below 41°F/5°C should be completed within 4 hours or less,
unless you use the two-stage cooling method endorsed by the Food and Drug

Administration in its 1999 Food Code. In the first stage of this method, foods should be cooled down to 70°F/21°C within 2 hours; in the second stage, foods should reach 41°F/5°C or below within an additional 4 hours, for a total cooling time of 6 hours.

The proper way to cool hot liquids is to transfer them to a metal container (plastic containers insulate rather than conduct heat), then place the container in an ice water bath that reaches the same level as the liquid inside the container. Bricks or a rack set under the container will allow the cold water to circulate better. Stir the liquid in the container frequently so that the warmer liquid at the center mixes with the cooler liquid at the edges of the container, bringing the overall temperature down more rapidly. Stirring also discourages potentially dangerous anaerobic bacteria from multiplying at the center of the mixture.

Semisolid and solid foods should be refrigerated in single layers in shallow containers, to allow greater surface exposure to the cold air and thus quicker chilling. For the same reason, large cuts of meat or other foods should be cut into smaller portions, cooled to room temperature, and wrapped before refrigerating.

REHEATING FOODS SAFELY

Improperly reheated foods are another frequent cause of food-borne illness. When foods are prepared ahead and then reheated before serving, they should move through the danger zone as rapidly as possible and be reheated to at least 165°F/74°C for at least 15 seconds. As long as proper cooling and reheating procedures are followed each time, foods may be cooled and reheated more than once.

Food handlers must use the proper methods and equipment for reheating potentially hazardous foods, which should be brought to the proper temperature over direct heat (burner, flattop, grill, or conventional oven) or in a microwave oven. A steam table will adequately hold reheated foods above 140°F/60°C, but it will not bring foods through the danger zone quickly enough to be used for reheating them. An instant-read thermometer should always be used to check temperatures; the thermometer should be carefully cleaned and sanitized after each use.

THAWING FROZEN FOODS SAFELY

Frozen foods can be safely thawed in several ways. Once thawed, they should be used as soon as possible, and, for optimal quality and flavor, they should not be refrozen. The best—though slowest—method is to allow the food to thaw under refrigeration. The food, still wrapped, should be placed in a shallow container on a bottom shelf to prevent any drips from contaminating other items stored nearby or below.

If there isn't time to thaw foods in the refrigerator, covered or wrapped food can be placed in a container under running water approximately 70°F/21°C or below. Use a stream of water strong enough to wash loose particles of ice off the food, but do not allow the water to splash on other food or surfaces. Be sure to clean and sanitize the sink both before and after thawing.

Individual portions that are to be cooked immediately can be thawed in a microwave oven. Liquids, small items, or individual portions can be cooked without thawing, but larger pieces of solid or semisolid foods that are cooked while still frozen become overcooked on the outside before they are thoroughly done throughout.

Do not thaw food at room temperature; it is an invitation to pathogens.

The potential for transmitting food-borne illness does not end when the food leaves the kitchen. Restaurant servers should also be instructed in good hygiene and safe food-handling practices. They should wash their hands properly after using the bathroom, eating, smoking, touching their face or hair, and handling money, dirty dishes, or soiled table linens (particularly napkins).

Ideally, there should be some servers who are designated to serve foods and others who are responsible for clearing used dishes and linens. Servers should touch only the edges and bottoms of plates as they transport them from kitchen to dining room. When setting tables, they should never touch the parts of flatware that will come in contact with food, and they should handle glassware by the stems or bases only. Servers should clean side stands, trays, and tray stands before the start of each shift and as necessary during service. They should handle napkins as little as possible and always fold them on a clean surface, and table linens should only be used once. And they should serve all foods using the proper utensils; ice and rolls should be handled with tongs, never with fingers.

Hazard Analysis Critical Control Points (HACCP)

HACCP is an acronym that is fast becoming commonly used in food service and food safety. It stands for Hazard Analysis Critical Control Points, which is a scientific state-of-the-art food safety program originally developed for astronauts. HACCP takes a systematic and preventive approach to the conditions that are responsible for most food-borne illnesses. It is preventative in nature; it attempts to anticipate how food-safety problems are most likely to occur and then takes steps to prevent them from occurring.

The HACCP system has been adopted by both food processors and restaurants, as well as by the FDA and USDA. At this time, there is no mandate that HACCP must be used by food-service establishments. However, instituting such a plan may prove to be advantageous on a variety of levels.

If you decide to begin instituting HACCP procedures in your restaurant or bakeshop, you should know that an initial investment of time and human resources is required. It is becoming obvious, however, that this system can ultimately save money and time, as well as improve the quality of food you are able to provide your customers.

The heart of HACCP lies in the following seven principles:

1. **Assess the hazards.** The first step in an HACCP program is a hazard analysis of each menu item or recipe. It requires a close look at the process of putting that menu item together, beginning with the delivery of the starting ingredients. Every step in the process must be looked at by designing a flowchart that covers the period from "dock to dish." In addition, it is best to have all persons involved in the flow of the food present when setting up an HACCP program, for the person receiving the food on the loading dock may have an important bit of information that can help set up the program and identify the true flow of food.

The types of hazards you should be concerned with are the biological, chemical, or physical conditions that could cause a food to be unsafe for consumption. The biological hazards are typically microbiological, though the possibility of toxicity (such as from poisonous mushrooms) should not be ignored. Microbiological hazards include bacteria, viruses, and parasites.

2. **Identify the critical control points.** After you have established a flow diagram and identified the potential hazards, the next step is to identify the critical control points (CCPs). From the moment food is received—and throughout production—you have the ability to control what happens to that food (including not accepting it from your vendor if it does not meet your specifications). You must decide which of the different control points (steps) are critical ones. One of the most difficult aspects of putting together an HACCP program is making sure not to overidentify these critical control points, because that could lead to a cumbersome amount of paperwork. In addition, a profusion of CCPs could obscure the real control issues. A critical control point is one at which you have the ability to eliminate or reduce an existing hazard or to prevent or minimize the likelihood that a hazard will occur. According to the 1999 FDA Food Code, a critical control point is "a point or procedure in a specific food system where loss of control may result in an unacceptable health risk."

The cooking step, as a rule, is a critical control point. Other critical control points are usually associated with time/temperature relationships (thawing, hot-holding, cold-holding, cooling, and reheating). Some other considerations that should be addressed in identifying a critical control point are as follows: At this step, can food be contaminated? Can the contaminants increase or survive? Can this hazard be prevented through some kind of intervention (commonly referred to as "corrective action")? Can hazards be prevented, eliminated, or reduced by steps taken earlier or later in the flow? And, can you monitor, measure, and document the CCP?

3. **Establish critical limits and control measures.** Critical limits are generally standards for control measures at each critical control point. Many will have already been established by local health departments, but you may want to establish new critical limits for your food operation that exceed the regulatory standard, or establish a new standard that meets with health department approval. (The 1999 FDA Food Code refers to these possibilities as "variances.")

By way of example, an established critical limit for the cooking step in preparing a chicken dish is a 165°F/74°C final internal temperature. This critical limit prevents the possibility of a patron contracting salmonellosis. If you were to hold this chicken on the line before actual service, it would have to be kept at 140°F/60°C to prevent any proliferation of pathogenic microbes. Holding would be a step in the process that would be considered critical.

Control measures are what you can do ahead of time to facilitate the achievement of your critical limit. For example, when preparing to cook chicken to 165°F/74°C, you should make sure your equipment is working well. Before you roast chicken, you should preheat the oven. If you are going to monitor the temperature of the chicken with a thermometer, you should make sure it is accurately calibrated. You also have to know how to cook and to take internal temperatures. Therefore, training is often a control measure too.

4. **Establish procedures for monitoring CCPs.** The critical limits for each critical control point must identify what is to be monitored. You must also establish how the CCP will be monitored and who will do it. For example, one employee may be designated to monitor the temperature of the roasting chicken. For each batch, the employee should be instructed to check the internal temperature of the largest chicken and the one in the middle of the pan.

   Monitoring helps improve the system by allowing for the identification of problems or faults at any particular point in the process. This allows for more control or improvement in the system because it provides an opportunity to take corrective action if a critical limit was not met. Monitoring lets you know if the desired results were achieved. In the example of the chicken, was it indeed cooked to an acceptable temperature?

5. **Establish corrective action plans.** If a deviation or substandard level occurs for any step in the process, a plan of action must be identified. For example, if the roasted chicken was held at an incorrect temperature (120°F/49°C) for too long in a steam table, the corrective action would be to discard it. If frozen fish arrives from the purveyor with a buildup of ice, indicating that it has been defrosted and refrozen again, the fish should be rejected. Specific corrective actions must be developed for each CCP, because the handling of each food item and its preparation can vary greatly from one kitchen to the next.

6. **Set up a record-keeping system.** Keep documentation on hand to demonstrate whether or not the system is working. Recording events at CCPs ensures that critical limits are met and preventive monitoring is occurring. Documentation typically consists of time/temperature logs, checklists, and forms.

   It's important to keep the forms readily accessible and easy to fill out. Having a temperature log on a clipboard at a grill station for the cook to record internal temperatures of one out of every ten orders that goes out to customers would be a realistic responsibility for a line cook. Having reliable and accurately calibrated thermometers on hand is also necessary. Do not make the logs or forms too complicated or cumbersome; this could encourage "dry lab," that is, falsification of records.

7. **Develop a verification system.** This step is essentially establishing procedures to ensure that the HACCP plan is working correctly. Have a supervisor, executive chef, or outside party verify that the plan is working. If procedures are not being followed, try to find out what modifications you can make so the plan works better. The most difficult part of putting an

HACCP plan together is going through it the first time. After the initial paperwork, it essentially involves monitoring and recording. As your employees become accustomed to filling out the forms correctly, they will be establishing positive behaviors that promote food safety. These new behaviors will naturally spill over into the preparation of other recipes, making the development of an HACCP plan for each new dish easier.

The way in which an individual operation may apply these principles will vary. Adapt the system as necessary to fit your establishment's style. Chain restaurants, for example, receive and process foods differently than à la carte restaurants.

Cleaning and Sanitizing

Cleaning refers to the removal of soil or food particles, whereas *sanitizing* involves using moist heat or chemical agents to kill pathogenic microorganisms. For equipment that cannot be immersed in a sink, or for equipment such as knives and cutting boards used during food preparation, use a wiping cloth, soaked in a double-strength sanitizing solution and then wrung out, to clean and sanitize between uses. Iodine, chlorine, or quaternary ammonium compounds are common sanitizing agents. Check the manufacturer's instructions for procedures for use.

Small equipment, tools, pots, and tableware should be run through a ware-washing machine or washed manually in a three-compartment sink. The many kinds of ware-washing machines all use some sanitation method, such as very hot water (usually 180° to 195°F/82° to 91°C) or chemical agents.

Hard water, which contains high levels of iron, calcium, or magnesium, may interfere with the effectiveness of detergents and sanitizing agents and may also cause deposits that can clog machinery. Water-softening additives can prevent these problems.

After sanitizing, equipment and tableware should be allowed to air-dry completely; using paper or cloth toweling could result in cross contamination.

Keeping Pests Out

Careful sanitation procedures, proper handling of foods, and a well-maintained facility all work together to prevent a pest infestation. Besides being destructive and unpleasant, rats, mice, roaches, and flies may also harbor various pathogens. Take the following steps to prevent infestation:

Clean all areas and surfaces thoroughly.

Wipe up spills immediately and sweep up crumbs.

Cover garbage, and remove it every 4 hours.

Elevate garbage containers on concrete blocks.

Keep food covered or refrigerated.

Check all incoming boxes for pests and remove boxes as soon as items are unpacked.

Store food away from walls and floors, and maintain cool temperatures and good ventilation.

Prevent pests from entering the facility by installing screened windows and screened self-closing doors.

Fill in all crevices and cracks, repair weak masonry, and screen off any openings to buildings, including vents, basement windows, and drains.

If necessary, consult a professional exterminator.

Kitchen Safety

In addition to the precautions necessary to guard against food-borne illness, care must also be taken to avoid accidents involving staff or guests. The following safety measures should be practiced.

HEALTH AND HYGIENE

Maintain good general health; have regular physical and dental checkups. Do not handle food when ill. Cover your face with a tissue when coughing or sneezing, and wash your hands afterward. Attend to cuts or burns immediately. Keep any burn or break in your skin covered with a clean waterproof bandage, and change it as necessary.

Observe the fundamentals of good personal hygiene. Keep hair clean and neat, and contain it if necessary. Keep fingernails short and well maintained, without polish. Keep your hands away from your hair and face when working with food. Do not smoke or chew gum when working with food.

Begin each shift in a clean, neat uniform. Do not wear your uniform to or from work or school. Store the uniform and all clothing in a clean locker. Do not wear jewelry other than a watch and/or a plain ring, to reduce risk of personal injury and/or cross contamination.

WORKING SAFELY

Clean up grease and other spills as they occur. Use salt or cornmeal to absorb grease, then clean the area.

Warn coworkers when you are coming up behind them with something hot or sharp.

Alert the pot washer when pots, pans, and handles are especially hot.

Beware of grill fires. If one occurs, do not attempt to put it out with water. Removing excess fat and letting any marinades drain completely from foods to be grilled will help prevent flare-ups.

Keep fire extinguishers in proper working order and place them in areas of the kitchen where they are most likely to be needed.

Remove lids from pots in such a manner that the steam vents away from your face, to avoid steam burns.

Bend at the knees, not the waist, to lift heavy objects.

Pick up anything on the floor that might trip someone.

Learn about first aid, CPR, and mouth-to-mouth resuscitation. Have well-stocked first-aid kits on hand (see page 105).

Make sure that all dining room and kitchen staff know how to perform the Heimlich maneuver on a choking person. Post instructions in readily visible areas of the kitchen and dining room.

Handle equipment carefully, especially knives, mandolines, slicers, grinders, band saws, and other equipment with sharp edges.

Observe care and caution when operating mixers. Always keep your hands away from an operating mixer.

Use separate cutting boards for cooked and raw foods, and sanitize after using.

Wash hands thoroughly after working with raw foods.

Use tasting spoons, and use them only once—do not "double-dip." Do not use your fingers or kitchen utensils when tasting food.

Store any toxic chemicals (cleaning compounds and pesticides, for example) away from food to avoid cross contamination.

Use only dry side towels for handling hot items.

Use instant-read thermometers (and sanitize them after using) to ensure that adequate temperatures are reached.

Post emergency phone numbers near every phone.

FIRE SAFETY

It takes only a few seconds for a simple flare-up on the grill or in a pan to turn into a full-scale fire. Grease fires, electrical fires, or even a waste container full of paper going up when a match is carelessly tossed into it are easy to imagine happening in any busy kitchen. A comprehensive fire-safety plan should be in place and a standard part of all employee training.

The first step in avoiding fires is to make sure that the entire staff, both kitchen and dining room, is fully aware of the potential dangers of fire everywhere in a restaurant. If you see someone handling a situation improperly, first get the situation under control, then take the time to explain what your concern is and how to avoid the situation in the future.

Next, be sure that all equipment is up to code. Frayed or exposed wires and faulty plugs can all too easily be the cause of a fire. Overburdened outlets are another common culprit. Any equipment that has a heating element or coil must also be maintained carefully, both to be sure that workers are not likely to be burned and to prevent fires.

Thorough training is another key element in any good fire-safety program. Everyone should know what to do in case of a fire. Having frequent fire drills is a good idea. Instruct your kitchen staff in the correct way to handle a grill fire and grease fire.

There should also be fire extinguishers in easily accessible areas. Check each extinguisher to see what type of fire it is meant to control, and make sure you and your staff understand when and how to operate each type.

Proper maintenance of extinguishers and timely inspections by your local fire department are vital. Fire-control systems, such as an Ansul system, also need to be serviced and monitored so that they will perform correctly if you need them. Above all, make sure you never try to put out a grease, chemical, or electrical fire by throwing water on the flames.

Everyone should know where the fire department number is posted and who is responsible for calling the department if necessary.

The exits from any area of the building should be easy to find, clear of any obstructions, and fully operational. Your guests will have to rely on you and other staff to get them safely out of the building if necessary. Identify one spot outside the building, at a safe distance, where everyone should assemble when they've exited safely. Then you will be able to tell immediately who may still be inside the building and need to be rescued by firefighters.

The main rule for fire is to be prepared for all possibilities. You cannot assume it won't happen to you.

DRESSING FOR SAFETY

More than simply completing the look of the chef, the parts of the typical chef's uniform play important roles in keeping workers safe as they operate in a potentially dangerous environment. The chef's jacket is double-breasted, which creates a two-layer cloth barrier against steam burns, splashes, and spills. The design also means that the jacket can easily be rebuttoned on the opposite side to cover up spills. The jacket sleeves are long, to protect against burns and scalding splashes, and they should not be rolled up. The same is true of pants. Shorts, while they may seem like a good idea for a hot environment, are inappropriate because they offer no protection. Pants should be worn without cuffs, which can trap hot liquids and debris. Ideally, pants should have a snap fly and be worn without a belt; if hot grease is spilled on the legs, this allows for fast removal of the pants, which could lessen the severity of the burn.

Be it a tall white toque or a favorite baseball cap, chefs wear hats to contain their hair, preventing it from falling into the food. Hats also help absorb sweat. Neckerchiefs serve a similar sweat-absorbing role. The apron protects the jacket and pants from excessive staining.

Most chefs use side towels to protect their hands when working with hot pans, dishes, or other equipment. They are not meant to be used as wiping cloths—side towels used to lift hot items must be dry in order to provide protection; once they become even slightly damp, they can no longer insulate properly.

While athletic shoes are very comfortable, they are not ideal for working in a kitchen. If a knife should fall from a work surface, most athletic shoes would offer very little protection. Hard leather shoes with slip-resistant soles are recommended, because of the protection they offer and the support they give your feet.

Jackets, pants, side towels, aprons, and shoes can harbor bacteria, molds, parasites, and even viruses. Because these pathogens can be transmitted with ease from your uniform to foods, a sanitary uniform is important. Wear your uniform at work only, not when traveling to and from the job, when you can pick up pathogens along the way.

Proper laundering can sanitize your uniform to make it safe and clean. If you don't use a laundry/uniform service, use hot water, a good detergent, and a sanitizer, such as borax or chlorine bleach, to remove bacteria and grime. Automatic dish-washing soap (used in household machines) contains an enzyme to help break up stuck-on food. These same enzymes can help to release food stains on uniforms. Add 4 oz/113 g of coarse dishwasher detergent to the wash water.

Regulations, Inspection, and Certification

Federal, state, and local government regulations work to ensure the wholesomeness of food that reaches the public. Any new food-service business should contact the local health department well in advance of opening to ascertain the necessary legal requirements. A professional pastry chef moving to a new area to work should contact local authorities for ordinances specific to that area. Some states and local jurisdictions offer sanitation certification programs. Certification is often available through certain academic institutions.

THE OCCUPATIONAL SAFETY AND HEALTH ADMINISTRATION (OSHA)

OSHA is a federal organization that was instituted in 1970 and falls under the purview of the Health and Human Services Administration. Its goal is helping employers and workers to establish and maintain a safe, healthy work environment.

Among OSHA's regulations is the mandate that all places of employment have an adequate and easily accessible first-aid kit on the premises. In addition, any organization that has more than ten employees must keep records of all accidents and injuries to employees that require medical treatment. Any employee requests for improvements in the safety of the workplace, including repair or maintenance of the physical plant and equipment necessary to perform one's job, must be attended to by the organization.

As money for many health and human service organizations has dwindled, OSHA's ability to make on-site inspection has also been reduced. It now concentrates its efforts on providing services where the risk to worker safety is greatest. This does not mean that small businesses can operate with impunity, however, for any employee can call OSHA's offices and report violations.

Americans with Disabilities Act (ADA)

This act is intended to make public places accessible and safe for those with a variety of disabilities. Any new construction or remodeling done to a restaurant must meet ADA standards. They include, for example, providing wheelchair-accessible telephones and toilets with handrails. Most contractors will have the necessary information, but if you are unsure, contact a local agency.

A Special Note about Smokers

Many restaurants have banned smoking, voluntarily, as a result of public pressure, or because of legislative mandates. While this may improve the air quality within the restaurant itself and provide a more pleasant dining experience for nonsmoking guests, there is one thing that should be kept in mind: Simply banning smoking in the dining room and the bar may not ban smoking from the entire premises. Common sense will tell you that smokers will very likely smoke cigarettes up to the moment they walk in the door, and light up as soon as they step back outside. One carelessly flung match or a single smoldering cigarette butt can spell ruin.

Place sand-filled buckets or urns near the areas where you expect or prefer to have smokers take their cigarette breaks. If you do allow smoking in your restaurant, make sure that bartenders, bus people, and wait staff have a safe way to dispose of the contents of ashtrays.

Of course, smoking should never be allowed in the kitchen area.

Drugs and Alcohol in the Workplace

One final topic that is of great importance in the workplace is the right of all workers to be free from the hazards imposed by a coworker who comes to work under the influence of drugs or alcohol. The abuse of any substance that can alter or impair one's ability to perform his or her job is a serious concern. Reaction times may be slowed, and the ability to concentrate and to comprehend instructions reduced. Inhibitions are often lowered, and judgment is generally impaired. As a result, people's safety or even their lives can be at stake. A poorly judged effort when emptying the hot oil from the deep fryer could result in permanent disability. A playful attempt at passing a knife could literally put out an eye. Forgetting to take the time to properly store and reheat foods could lead to an outbreak of a food-borne illness that could kill someone.

The responsibilities of a professional working in any kitchen are too great to allow someone suffering from a substance-abuse problem to diminish the respect and trust you have built with your customers and staff.

First-Aid Supplies

Adhesive strips in assorted sizes

Bandage compresses

Sterile gauze dressings, individually wrapped

Rolled gauze bandage

First-aid adhesive tape

Cotton swabs (for applying antiseptic or removing particles from eyes)

Tourniquet

Tongue depressors (for small splints)

Scissors

Tweezers

Needle (for removing splinters)

Rubbing alcohol (for sterilizing instruments such as tweezers and needles)

Mild antiseptic (for wounds)

Antibiotic cream

Syrup of ipecac (to induce vomiting)

Petroleum jelly

CHAPTER 5

Baking Formulas and Bakers' Percentages

Scaling flour
accurately for
bread on a beam
balance scale

Standardized Formulas

The formulas used in a professional baking and pastry setting must be standardized. Unlike published recipes meant to work in a variety of settings for a wide audience, standardized formulas suit the specific needs of an individual pastry kitchen or bakeshop. Preparing well-written and accurate standardized formulas is a big part of the professional pastry chef or baker's work, as these are records that include much more than just ingredient names and preparation steps. Standardized formulas establish overall yields, portion sizes, holding and serving practices, and plating information. They set standards for equipment as well as temperatures and times for cooking and baking. These standards help to ensure consistent quality and quantity, and they permit pastry chefs and bakers to gauge the efficiency of their work and reduce costs by eliminating waste as appropriate.

In addition, the wait staff must be familiar enough with an item or plated dessert to be able to answer any questions a customer might have. For example, the type of nuts used in an item may matter very much to an individual who has an allergy to peanuts.

Standardized formulas can be handwritten or stored on computer, using a recipe management program or other such database or software program. The formulas should be written in a consistent, clear, easy-to-follow format and readily accessible to the entire staff. The pastry chef or baker should instruct pastry kitchen or bakeshop staff to follow standardized formulas to the letter unless otherwise instructed, as well as encourage service staff to refer to standardized formulas when a question arises about ingredients or preparation methods.

As you prepare a standardized formula, be as precise and consistent as possible. Include as many of the following elements as necessary:

Name/title of the food item or dish

Yield for the formula, expressed as one or more of the following: total weight, total volume, or total number of portions

Portion information for each serving, expressed as one or more of the following: number of items (count), volume, or weight

Ingredient names, expressed in appropriate detail (specifying variety or brand as necessary)

Ingredient measures, expressed as one or more of the following: count, volume, or weight

Ingredient preparation instructions, sometimes included in the ingredient name, sometimes included in the method as a separate step

Equipment information for preparation, cooking, storing, holding, and serving

Preparation steps detailing mise en place, mixing, cooking and/or baking, and temperatures for safe food handling (see also Hazard Analysis Critical Control Points (HACCP), page 96)

Service information, including how to finish and plate a dessert, sauces and garnishes, if any, and proper service temperatures

Holding and reheating procedures, including equipment and times and temperatures for safe storage

Critical control points (CCPs) (to learn more about CCPs see page 97) at appropriate stages in the formula, to indicate temperatures and times for safe food-handling procedures during storage, preparation, holding, and reheating.

Formula Calculations

Often you will need to modify a recipe. Sometimes the yield must be increased or decreased. You may be adapting a recipe from another source to a standardized format, or you may be adjusting a standardized formula for a special event, such as a banquet or a reception. You may need to convert from volume measures to weight, or from metric measurements to the U.S. system. Or you may want to determine how much the ingredients in a particular formula cost.

THE FORMULA CONVERSION FACTOR

To increase or decrease the yield of a formula, you need to determine the formula conversion factor. Once you know that factor, you then multiply all the ingredient amounts by it and convert the new measurements into appropriate formula units for your pastry kitchen or bakeshop. This may require converting items listed by count into weight or volume measurements, or rounding measurements to reasonable quantities. And in some cases you will have to make a judgment call about those ingredients that do not scale up or down exactly, such as spices, salt, thickeners, and leaveners.

$$\frac{\text{Desired yield}}{\text{Original yield}} = \text{Formula conversion factor (FCF)}$$

The desired yield and the original yield must be expressed in the same way before you can use the formula; that is, both must be in the same unit of measure. For example, if the original formula gives the yield in ounces and you want to make 2 qt of the sauce, you will need to convert quarts into fluid ounces. Or, if your original formula says that it makes five portions and does not list the size of each portion, you may need to test the formula to determine portion size.

CONVERTING TO A COMMON UNIT OF MEASURE

To convert measurements to a common unit (by weight or volume), use the following chart. This information can be used both to convert scaled measurements into practical and easy-to-use formula measures and to determine costs.

For some ingredients, straightforward multiplication or division is all that is needed. To increase a formula for poached pears from 5 servings to 50, for example, you would simply multiply 5 pears by 10; no further adjustments are necessary. But

FORMULA MEASURE	COMMON CONVERSION TO VOLUME	COMMON UNIT (U.S.)	COMMON UNIT (METRIC)
1 pound	N/A	16 ounces	454 grams
1 tablespoon	3 teaspoons	$^1/_2$ fluid ounce	30 milliliters
1 cup	16 tablespoons	8 fluid ounces	240 milliliters
1 pint	2 cups	16 fluid ounces	480 milliliters
1 quart	2 pints	32 fluid ounces	960 milliliters
1 gallon	4 quarts	128 fluid ounces	3.75 liters

once you have converted them, some other ingredient amounts may need some fine-tuning. You may need to round off a result or convert it to the most logical unit of measure. Measures for ingredients such as thickeners, spices, seasonings, and leavenings, for example, should not always be simply multiplied or divided. If a formula that makes six 6-in/15-cm cakes requires ½ oz/14 g of baking powder, it is not necessarily true that you will need 4 oz/113 g of baking powder to leaven six times the amount of the same batter, if you are mixing it all in one batch. In such cases, the only way to be sure is to test the new formula and adjust it until you are satisfied with the result.

Other considerations when converting formula yields include the equipment you have, the production issues you face, and the skill level of your staff. Rewrite steps as necessary to suit the realities of your establishment at this point. It is important to do this now, so you can discover any further changes to the ingredients or methods that the new yield might cause. For instance, to mix enough bread dough to make ten 1-lb/454-g loaves of bread requires a large mixer, but if you only want to make two 1-lb/454-g loaves, you need a much smaller mixing bowl. The smaller batch of dough would fit in the large mixing bowl, but there would not be enough dough for the mixer to be able to mix and develop the structure for the bread properly.

CONVERTING NUMBER OF PORTIONS

Sometimes you need to modify the portion size of a formula as well as the total yield. For instance, you may have a sauce formula that makes four 2-fl-oz/60-mL portions, but you want to make forty 2-fl-oz/60-mL portions. To make the conversion:

First, determine the total original yield of the formula and the total desired yield.

$$\text{Number of portions} \times \text{Portion size} = \text{Total yield}$$
$$4 \times 2 \text{ fl oz} = 8 \text{ fl oz (total original yield)}$$
$$40 \times 2 \text{ fl oz} = 80 \text{ fl oz (total desired yield)}$$

Then, determine the formula conversion factor and modify the formula as described above.

$$\frac{80 \text{ fl oz}}{8 \text{ fl oz}} = 10 \text{ (formula conversion factor)}$$

Volume versus Weight Measure

CONVERTING VOLUME MEASURES TO WEIGHT

Confusion often arises between weight and volume measures when ounces are the unit of measure. It is important to remember that weight is measured in ounces and volume is measured in *fluid* ounces. A standard volume measuring cup is equal to 8 fl oz/ 240 mL, but the contents of the cup may not always weigh 8 oz/227 g. One cup (8 fl oz/ 240 mL) of shredded coconut weighs only 2½ oz/71 g, but one cup (8 fl oz/240 mL) of peanut butter weighs 9 oz/255 g. However, since measuring dry ingredients by weight is much more accurate, it is the preferred and most common method used for measuring dry ingredients in professional kitchens and bakeshops.

Water is the only substance for which it can be safely assumed that 1 fl oz (a volume measure) equals 1 oz by weight. But you can convert a volume measure of another ingredient into a weight if you know how much a cup of the ingredient (prepared as required by the formula) weighs. This information is available in a number of charts or ingredients databases.

A variety of volume measuring tools is useful when adapting formulas originally written in common household measures.

First, record a description of the ingredient, the way it is received (whole, frozen, chopped, canned, etc.)

Next, prepare the ingredient as directed by the formula (sift flour, roast nuts, chop or melt chocolate, drain items packed in syrup). Record this advance preparation too.

Then measure the ingredient carefully according to the formula, using nested measures for dry ingredients or liquid cups or pitchers for liquid ingredients (see page 52 for measuring techniques).

Then set up your scale and set it to tare (see page 52).

Then weigh the ingredient.

Finally, record the weight of the ingredient, noting all the advance preparation steps involved (sifting, melting, chopping, and so forth).

CONVERTING BETWEEN U.S. AND METRIC MEASUREMENT SYSTEMS

The metric system, used throughout most of the world, is a decimal system, meaning that it is based on multiples of 10. The gram is the basic unit of weight, the liter the basic unit of volume, and the meter the basic unit of length. Prefixes added to the basic units indicate larger or smaller units.

The U.S. system uses ounces and pounds to measure weight and teaspoons, tablespoons, fluid ounces, cups, pints, quarts, and gallons to measure volume. Unlike the metric system, the U.S. system is not based on multiples of a particular number, so it is not as simple to increase or decrease quantities. Rather, the equivalencies of the different units of measure must be memorized or derived from a chart.

Most modern measuring equipment is capable of measuring in both U.S. and metric units. If, however, a formula is written in a system of measurement for which you do not have the proper measuring equipment, you will need to convert to the other system.

To convert ounces and pounds to grams: Multiply ounces by 28.35 to determine grams; divide pounds by 2.2 to determine kilograms

To convert grams to ounces or pounds: Divide grams by 28.35 to determine ounces; divide grams by 454 to determine pounds

To convert fluid ounces to milliliters: Multiply fluid ounces by 30 to determine milliliters

To convert milliliters to fluid ounces: Divide milliliters by 30 to determine fluid ounces

To convert Celsius to Fahrenheit: Multiply the degrees Celsius by 1.8 and add 32 to get the Fahrenheit equivalent (C x 1.8 + 32 = F)

To convert Fahrenheit to Celsius: Subtract 32 from the degrees Fahrenheit; divide the result by 1.8 to get the Celsius equivalent (F − 32 ÷ 1.8 = C)

Metric Prefixes

kilo = 1,000	**deci** = 1/10
hecto = 100	**centi** = 1/100
deka = 10	**milli** = 1/1000

Calculating Cost per Formula Unit of Measure

Most food items purchased from suppliers are packed and priced by wholesale bulk sizes (crate, case, bag, carton, and so on). In kitchen production, the packed amount is generally broken down and often used for several different items. Therefore, in order to assign the correct prices to the formula being prepared, it is necessary to convert purchase pack prices to unit prices, expressed as price per pound, per single unit, per dozen, per quart, and the like.

To find the cost of a unit in a pack with multiple units, divide the as-purchased cost of the pack by the number of units in the pack.

$$\frac{\text{Total cost}}{\text{Number of units}} = \text{Cost per unit}$$

$$\text{Number of units} \times \text{Cost per unit} = \text{Total cost}$$

Calculating the Yield of Fresh Fruits and Vegetables

For many food items, trimming is required before the items are used. In order to determine an accurate cost for such items, trim loss must be taken into account. The yield percentage is important in determining the quantity to order.

$$\frac{\text{Edible-portion quantity}}{\text{As-purchased quantity}} = \text{Yield percentage}$$

First, record the as-purchased quantity (APQ).

$$\text{APQ} = 5 \text{ lb lemons}$$

Trim the item(s), saving unusable trim and edible-portion quantity in separate containers. Weigh each separately and record their weights on a costing form.

$$\text{EPQ} = 36.5 \text{ oz lemon juice}$$
$$\text{Trim loss} = 43.5 \text{ oz}$$

Divide the EPQ by the APQ to determine the yield percentage.

$$\frac{36.5}{80} = 0.456 \times 100 = 45.6\%$$

$$\text{Yield percentage} = 45.6\%$$

Calculating the As-Purchased Quantity (APQ)

Because many formulas assume the ingredients listed are ready to cook, it is necessary to consider trim loss when purchasing items. In such cases, the edible-portion quantity must be converted to the as-purchased quantity that will yield the desired edible-portion quantity.

$$\frac{EPQ}{\text{Yield percentage}} = APQ$$

Example

A formula requires 20 lb of peeled and diced potatoes. The yield percentage for potatoes is 85 percent. Therefore, 20 lb divided by 85 percent will equal the amount to purchase.

Generally, the as-purchased quantity obtained by this method is rounded up, since the yield percentage is, by its nature, an estimate.

It should be kept in mind that not all foods, of course, have trim loss. Many pastry and bakeshop ingredients, such as sugar, flour, and spices, are processed or refined foods that have 100 percent yield. Other foods have a yield percentage that depends on how they are to be served. If, for example, the ingredient is to be served by the piece (a poached pear), or if a formula calls for it by count (15 strawberries), there is no need to consider the yield percentage; the correct number of items is simply purchased to create the desired number of servings. However, if you are making fruit tartlets and the formula calls for 2 oz/57 g of sliced pineapple and 1 oz/28 g of sliced strawberries per serving, you must consider the yield percentage when ordering.

Calculating the Edible-Portion Quantity (EPQ)

Sometimes it is necessary to determine how many portions can be obtained from raw product. For example, if you have a case of fresh kiwis that weighs 10 lb and you want to know how many 4-oz servings the case will yield, you need to determine the yield percentage, either by referring to a list of yield percentages or by performing a yield test. Once you know the yield percentage, you can compute the weight of the kiwis after trimming.

$$APQ \times \text{Yield percentage} = EPQ$$
$$10\text{ lb} \times 0.85 = 8.5\text{ lb}$$

The second step is to compute how many 4-oz servings the edible-portion quantity, 8.5 lb, will yield.

$$\frac{EPQ}{\text{Portion size}} = \text{Number of servings}$$

$$4\text{ oz} = \tfrac{1}{4}\text{ lb }(0.25\text{ lb})$$
$$\frac{8.5\text{ lb}}{0.25\text{ lb}} = 34$$

Thus, you would be able to obtain 34 servings from the case of kiwi fruit. (If it is necessary to round off your result from a similar calculation, you should round down the number of portions, since it would not be possible to serve a partial portion.)

Calculating the Edible-Portion Cost

As discussed earlier, formulas often assume that ingredients are ready to cook. When it comes to costing a formula, the edible-portion cost (EPC) per unit can be calculated from the as-purchased cost (APC) per unit, as long as the two are expressed in the same unit of measure.

$$\frac{APC}{Yield\ percentage} = EPC$$

$$EPQ \times EPC = Total\ cost$$

Bakers' Percentages

Bakers' percentages have two basic functions. First, when a formula is expressed in bakers' percentages, it is easy to see and evaluate the relationship between the different ingredients. This facilitates a deeper understanding of the formula than just a listing of the specific weight and/or volume measures for the individual ingredients. An understanding of the relationships between ingredients will help the baker or pastry chef to recognize a faulty formula and to prepare basic products, if necessary, without the aid of written formulas. The second function of bakers' percentages is to make it easy to use a formula in the bakeshop or pastry kitchen. When a formula is expressed in bakers' percentages, it is easy to scale it up or down.

A percentage is a part of a whole (100 percent). In bakers' percentages, the whole is always the flour; *that is, the flour is always 100 percent.* If there are two or more types of flour, their sum must equal 100 percent. The percentages for all other ingredients are derived from the flour. Because the whole is equal to the flour, and not the sum total of all the ingredients, the sum of all the ingredients will always exceed 100 percent. Occasionally the percentage of another ingredient may exceed 100 percent, if it is required in a greater amount than the flour.

CALCULATING THE PERCENTAGE VALUE
FOR AN INGREDIENT

To determine the percentage value for each ingredient in a formula, simply divide the weight of the ingredient by the weight of the flour and then multiply the result by 100.

Example

A bread formula calls for 5 lb of flour and 3 lb of diced potato. To calculate the percentage value for the diced potato, divide its weight by the weight of the flour (which is always 100 percent) and then multiply the result by 100.

$$\frac{Total\ weight\ of\ ingredient}{Total\ weight\ of\ flour} = Decimal\ value \times 100 = Percentage\ value\ of\ ingredient$$

$$\frac{3\ lb\ diced\ potato}{5\ lb\ flour} = 0.6 \times 100 = 60$$

The resulting percentage value is 60 percent.

Note: *Remember that when making any calculations, numerical values must be expressed in the same unit of measure (e.g., pounds, ounces, grams, kilograms); if necessary, convert any values before beginning the calculation.*

Multiply the percentage value by 100, then multiply by the weight of the flour.

Example

A bread formula lists the ingredient values only in percentages. You want to make a batch of dough using 5 lb of flour, and you need to calculate the weight for the potatoes, which are valued at 60 percent, so you can prep them for making the dough the next day.

$$\begin{array}{c} \text{Total weight} \\ \text{of flour} \end{array} \times \begin{array}{c} \text{Decimal value} \\ \text{of ingredient} \end{array} = \begin{array}{c} \text{Total weight} \\ \text{of ingredient} \end{array}$$

$$\text{5 lb flour} \times 0.6 = \text{3 lb potatoes}$$

Desired Dough Temperature

The desired dough temperature (DDT) is the ideal average temperature of a dough while you are working with it. For lean doughs, this temperature is typically 75° to 80°F/24° to 27°C. Working with a lean dough at this temperature will help to keep the gluten strands relaxed. The ideal DDT for enriched doughs is slightly higher, as it is important to keep the fats that have been added to the dough soft while it is being worked. (To learn more about DDT, see pages 126–127.)

The DDT, the total temperature factor (TTF), and the sum of the known temperatures that influence the DDT are used to calculate the temperature of the water.

To make this calculation, first calculate the TTF. To find the TTF, multiply the DDT by the number of temperature factors to be considered. For a straight mix dough, there are three factors to be considered. For a sourdough or a dough that uses a pre-ferment, there are four, or sometimes five, factors, depending on the number of elements that are going to be added.

After you have found the TTF, you then subtract the sum of the known temperatures from it to give the ideal temperature for the water. The known temperatures are the temperature of the flour and the room and the amount of friction the dough will undergo in the mixer. Here the number 2 is used as an example for friction factor, but this number may be higher or lower depending on batch size, speed, and type of mixer.

The flour's temperature is one of the known elements in calculating DDT (desired dough temperature).

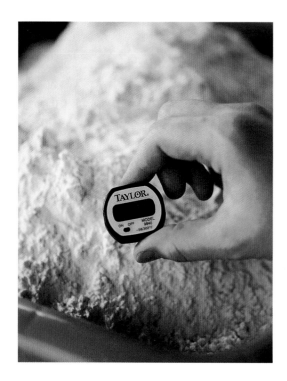

Example

You are making an enriched straight mix dough. The flour temperature is 65°F, the room temperature is 75°F, and the dough will be mixed for a total of 12 minutes.

First, calculate the TTF.

$$\text{DDT} \times \text{Number of TTF factors} = \text{TTF}$$
$$80 \times 3 = 240$$

Then, find the value for the mixer friction.

$$\text{Number of minutes mixing} \times 2 = \text{Mixer friction}$$
$$12 \times 2 = 24$$

Then find the sum of all the known temperature factors.

$$\frac{\text{Flour}}{\text{temperature}} + \frac{\text{Room}}{\text{temperature}} + \frac{\text{Mixer}}{\text{friction}} = \frac{\text{Sum of known}}{\text{temperature factors}}$$
$$65 + 75 + 24 = 164$$

Finally, find the water temperature.

$$\text{TTF} - \text{Sum of known temperature factors} = \text{Water temperature}$$
$$240 - 164 = 76°F$$

In warmer climates, it may be advisable to have a colder DDT. If necessary, ice can be used to lower the temperature of the water.

For example, if the calculated water temperature for 40 lb of water is 45°F, but the temperature of the water is 60°F, ice can be used to lower the temperature of the water. To calculate how much ice to use, an "ice Btu factor" must be determined using the following equation:

$$\frac{\left(\begin{array}{c} \text{Total weight} \\ \text{of water} \end{array} \right) \left(\begin{array}{c} \text{Water} \\ \text{temperature} \end{array} - \begin{array}{c} \text{Desired water} \\ \text{temperature} \end{array} \right)}{144} = \text{Weight of ice}$$

First subtract the actual water temperature from the desired water temperature to find the "degree difference."

$$60°F - 45°F = 15°F$$

Next, multiply the total number of pounds of water by the "degree difference."

$$40 \text{ lb} \times 15 = 600$$

Finally, divide the result by 144, the Btu factor (the number of British thermal units it takes to melt 1 lb of ice).

$$\frac{600}{144} = 4.16$$

The result is the number of pounds of ice needed to achieve the desired water temperature and, ultimately, the DDT. Subtract the number of pounds of ice needed from the total amount of water needed to see how much water you need when adding ice to the formula.

$$40 - 4.16 = 35.9$$

In this formula, you will need to reduce the water to 35.9 lb, to compensate for the 4.16 lb of ice. If you round the numbers, so they can be measured easily, you will need 36 lb of water and 4 lb of ice.

CHAPTER 6

Yeast Doughs

WHEN FLOUR, WATER, YEAST, AND SALT ARE WORKED TOGETHER IN THE CORRECT PROPORTIONS FOR THE APPROPRIATE AMOUNT OF TIME, A STRONG AND ELASTIC DOUGH DEVELOPS. THE BREAD BAKER KNOWS THAT THE INGREDIENTS PLAY A KEY ROLE IN THE QUALITY OF THE DOUGH, AS DO THE MIXING AND FERMENTATION METHODS. THE TECHNIQUES IN THIS CHAPTER TAKE THE BREAD-BAKING PROCESS UP THROUGH A FINISHED DOUGH. IN CHAPTER 7, THESE DOUGHS ARE SHAPED AND BAKED INTO A VARIETY OF LOAVES, CAKES, AND ROLLS.

Direct Fermentation

The simplest and fastest method for producing a lean dough is direct fermentation: Commercially produced yeast is combined with flour, water, and salt and mixed until the dough is supple and elastic, with well-developed gluten.

Flour, as a main component, provides the structure and crumb in breads through the action of the proteins and starches it contains. The amount of water or other liquids also has an impact on the finished loaf. As the amount of liquid in a dough increases, the bread's structure changes.

Some breads are meant to have a more delicate texture, with a softer crust and crumb. In these formulas, sugars and fats, in the form of butter, oil, eggs, and/or syrups, control or affect how well the gluten develops, how long and elastic the gluten strands become, how the yeast behaves, and how open or closed the crumb is after baking.

Yeast is directly related to not only the texture of the bread but also to its flavor. The way in which yeast is introduced into the dough—by either direct or indirect fermentation—gives the bread baker the range of techniques necessary to create simple lean dough quickly and efficiently and to create hearty, complex breads using such indirect fermentation methods as sponges, poolishes, bigas, and sourdoughs. The direct fermentation method of bread making requires fewer steps and less advance preparation than indirect fermentation methods; however, the lack of a pre-ferment limits the quality of the finished product by limiting fermentation time. The processes occurring during fermentation further develop the structure and flavor of the dough—the more time allotted for fermentation, the better the development of the internal structure and flavor of the dough. (For more about gluten development, starch gelatinization, and fermentation, see pages 76–88.)

White Wheat Lean Dough

Makes 8 lb 7¾ oz/3.85 kg dough   DDT: 75°F/24°C

BREAD FLOUR	100%	5 lb	2.27 kg
INSTANT DRY YEAST	0.83%	⅔ oz	19 g
WATER	66.9%	53½ fl oz	1.61 L
SALT	2.2%	1¾ oz	50 g

1. Combine the flour and yeast. Add the water and salt and mix on low speed for 2 minutes. Mix on medium speed for about 3 minutes. The dough should be smooth and elastic.

2. Bulk ferment the dough until nearly doubled, about 30 minutes. Fold the dough gently. Ferment for another 30 minutes, and fold again. Allow the dough to ferment for another 15 minutes before dividing.

3. See pages 184 and 207 for shaping, proofing, and baking options suitable for this dough.

THE STRAIGHT MIXING METHOD

The straight mixing method is most often used with formulas that rely on direct fermentation. For this mixing method, the ingredients are added in different order depending on the type of yeast used. If instant dry yeast is used, the yeast should be first blended with the flour and then all other ingredients should be placed in the bowl on top of the flour-yeast mixture. If active dry or compressed fresh yeast is used, the yeast should be first blended with the water and allowed to fully dissolve. Next the flour should be added and all remaining ingredients should be placed on top of the flour.

After all the ingredients are in the mixing bowl, they should be blended together on low speed until just combined. Then turn the mixer to medium speed and blend the dough to full development.

Stages of Mixing Bread Dough

In bread making, as with any baked item, the proper execution of mixing is crucial to the quality of the end product. When mixing bread dough there are four identifiable stages that signal a change in structure and the stage of development of the dough.

Stage 1: Pickup Period

During the pickup period the ingredients are blended on low speed, until just combined. The dough is a wet, sticky, rough mass at this point.

Stage 2: Cleanup Period or Preliminary Development

The cleanup period is the preliminary development of the dough. At this point the dough is mixing at a moderate speed and will appear somewhat rough.

Stage 3: Initial Development Period

During the initial development period the elasticity of the gluten begins to develop and the dough starts to pull away from the sides of the mixing bowl. At this point the mixer should be running at a medium speed; a high speed would work the dough too roughly at this point, breaking the structure of the gluten rather than promoting its development.

Stage 4: Final Development Period

At this point the gluten is fully developed. The dough is smooth and elastic and leaves the sides of the bowl completely clean as the mixer is running. To test for full gluten development, remove a piece of dough from the mixer and stretch it. If the dough stretches to form a thin membrane, allowing light to filter through, then the gluten has been properly and sufficiently developed.

When dough is overmixed it will be very sticky and wet and will have little or no elasticity. This occurs because the gluten strands have been broken down; the resulting product will not rise or bake properly.

Advantages of Proper Mixing

Optimum absorption

Proper gluten development

Slightly shorter fermentation time

1 The pickup stage of dough development

2 The cleanup stage

3 Initial dough development

4 Final dough development

5 The gluten window

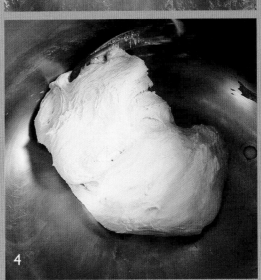

Substituting One Yeast for Another

Each of the formulas in this chapter was developed using instant dry yeast. In the past, fresh compressed yeast was the standard variety used by commercial bakers. However, today it is becoming more common for bakeshops to use dry varieties of yeast because they produce excellent results, are easier to store, and have a much longer shelf life. Generally, it is best to follow the manufacturer's instructions for use, as all dry yeast products are not alike.

The most common ratio of yeast to flour is approximately ½ oz/14 g fresh yeast to 18 oz/510 g flour, although this ratio can vary according to the type of bread, the techniques used in production, the retarding, and/or the ingredients in the formula. Too little yeast will not raise dough sufficiently, while too much will give the bread an overly strong yeast flavor. The bakers' percentages included in the formulas in this chapter indicate the ratios for that dough and can be used as a guide for modification of these and other formulas.

Use the following table to convert from one type of yeast to another.

TYPE OF YEAST	PERCENTAGE	EXAMPLE
FRESH YEAST	100%	10 oz/284 g
ACTIVE DRY YEAST	40%	4 oz/113 g
INSTANT DRY YEAST	33%	3⅓ oz/94 g

Active dry yeast should be reactivated in twice its volume amount of water at 105°F/41°C for 3 to 5 minutes before blending them with the remaining ingredients in the formula. Combine fresh yeast with some of the milk or water in the formula to blend evenly before adding the remaining ingredients. Instant dry yeast does not have to be activated, but it should not come in direct contact with ice-cold liquids or ice. When converting a formula from fresh yeast to instant or active dry, most manufacturers suggest that the difference in weight be made up with additional water. The additional water will maintain the yield and hydration level of the dough.

Desired Dough Temperature and British Thermal Units

Dough temperature is important because it directly affects fermentation. Suggested temperatures for certain ingredients are based upon the desired dough temperature (DDT). (The DDT is included in each formula.) The colder the final temperature of a dough is, the longer the fermentation time will be; the warmer the final dough temperature is, the more quickly a dough will ferment. The fermentation time directly affects the quality and consistency of the finished product, and impacts production schedules as well, making the desired dough temperature a very important factor in bread baking.

The temperature of a directly fermented dough immediately after mixing is influenced by three factors: the temperature of the ingredients when added, the ambient temperature, and the friction created by the mixer during mixing. For a dough produced using the indirect fermentation method, all of these factors apply, along with the temperature of all pre-ferments added to the dough. The sum of all the factors affecting the temperature of a dough are known as the total temperature factor (TTF).

The typical desired dough temperature for most yeast doughs is 75°F/24°C; however, an acceptable temperature for a finished dough may be from 65° to 85°F/18° to 29°C.

To produce a dough within this temperature range, the temperature of the water is critical because it is the easiest factor to control with precision. It is common to use ice water when it is necessary to cool a dough. Cooling a dough by this method is useful, for example, when a long mixing time is predicted, when fermentation needs to be slowed, or when the ambient temperature is high and cannot be controlled. To calculate the quantity of ice, British thermal units or Btu's are used. If a pre-ferment is added that has been stored under refrigeration, it may be necessary to use slightly warm water. See page 119 for instructions on calculating the DDT, TTF, and ice Btu factor.

Bulk Fermentation

The first fermentation period, known as bulk fermentation, develops the flavor of the bread. Bulk fermentation is especially important when using the direct fermentation method; without the addition of pre-ferments, this is the only time to develop the flavors of fermentation. Regulating the temperature may extend the time of rate of fermentation during this period. Keeping the dough at cooler temperatures will result in a longer fermentation period and thus more flavor development.

The alcohol produced during fermentation tenderizes the gluten strands, making them more elastic so they expand, allowing the bread to rise properly. More tender gluten strands produce a loaf with a tender and chewy crumb. Gluten is also further developed during this time through the process of folding.

The properly mixed dough is transferred to a bowl or tub (stiff or firm doughs can be placed on a lightly floured tabletop). Cover the dough with cloth or plastic wrap to prevent a skin from forming on the surface and let it rest at the appropriate temperature until it has doubled in size. The times suggested in our formulas are based on fermentation at room temperature (75°F/24°C).

RETARDING DOUGH

Retarding dough means to purposely cool the dough, typically at temperatures of around 40°F/4°C in order to slow the fermentation process. Retarding permits bakers to organize their work to meet production and employee schedules. It also allows the gluten to relax further, since the fermentation is prolonged. This results in dough that is easier to shape. A prolonged fermentation also gives dough time to develop a more pronounced sour flavor, so retarding dough can effectively enhance the quality of doughs made using direct fermentation.

The extended time at lower temperatures during bulk fermentation also means that you can properly ferment dough with a smaller amount of yeast. In fact, adding the full amount of yeast called for in a formula, usually allowed to ferment at around 65°F/18°C, would cause the dough to overferment if it were retarded and would produce a flatter loaf with a coarse grain and crumb.

Gluten is further developed during folding.

FOLDING OVER THE DOUGH

Dough is folded over to redistribute the available food supply for the yeast, equalize the temperature of the dough, expel the built-up fermentation gases (carbon dioxide and ethyl alcohol), and further develop the gluten in the dough.

Doughs that have a typical hydration of around 67 percent or less should be treated gently during the folding process. It is more difficult for the gases resulting from the fermentation process to leaven the bread because of its density and the tightness of the gluten. For these reasons it is important to fold carefully to preserve the already developed structure. A slack dough, such as that for ciabatta, requires more aggressive treatment when folding over. It is more difficult to develop the gluten in slack doughs and they require more gluten development to hold their shape and retain their inner structure.

Bagel Dough

Makes 8 lb ½ oz/3.64 kg dough   DDT: 78°F/26°C

HIGH-GLUTEN FLOUR	100%	5 lb	2.27 kg
INSTANT DRY YEAST	0.4%	⅓ oz	9 g
WATER	57.5%	46 fl oz	1.38 L
SALT	2.1%	1¾ oz	50 g
DIASTATIC MALT SYRUP	0.94%	¾ oz	21 g

1. Combine the flour and yeast. Add the water, salt, and malt syrup and mix on low speed for 4 minutes. Mix on medium speed for 5 minutes. The dough should be stiff, dry, and elastic and have strong gluten development.

2. See pages 210 and 212 for shaping, proofing, and baking options suitable for this dough.

Bagel dough has a consistency referred to as *bucky*.

Whole Wheat Lean Dough

Makes 8 lb 10½ oz/3.93 kg dough   DDT: 75°F/24°C

BREAD FLOUR	60%	3 lb	1.36 kg
WHOLE WHEAT FLOUR	40%	2 lb	907 g
INSTANT DRY YEAST	0.75%	⅔ oz	19 g
WATER	70%	56 fl oz	1.68 L
SALT	2.2%	1¾ oz	50 g

1. Combine the flours and yeast. Add the water and salt and mix on low speed for 3 minutes. Mix on medium speed for 3 minutes. The dough should be soft but with sufficient gluten development.

2. Bulk ferment the dough until nearly doubled, about 30 minutes. Fold gently and ferment for another 30 minutes. Fold again. Allow the dough to ferment for another 15 minutes before dividing.

3. See page 197 for shaping, proofing, and baking options suitable for this dough.

Fiber-Enriched Doughs

Whole wheat flour and flour made from grains such as rye, barley, buckwheat, rice, oats, millet, corn, and soy all contribute distinctive tastes and textures, as well as nutrition, to breads, and they also make them heavier and denser. Typically, some measure of white wheat flour is included in formulas calling for whole wheat or nonwheat flours in order to develop a light, open crumb.

The bran in whole-grain flours interferes with the development of gluten. Bran cuts the strands of gluten, inhibiting their development and reducing their ability to trap the carbon dioxide produced by the yeast. The higher the percentage is of whole wheat or nonwheat flour in a formula, the more pronounced its effect will be on the characteristics of the finished loaf.

One of the ways bread bakers aid the development of gluten in formulas containing these flours is known as autolyse (see the sidebar on page 131).

AUTOLYSE

An autolyse step may be used in any bread formula, and it is especially useful when making fiber-enriched dough. It means that the flour and water are briefly combined, just enough for a rough mixture to form. Then the mixture is left to rest for a period of 10 to 30 minutes, allowing the flour to absorb enough water for gluten development to begin. The gluten relaxes, since mixing is not agitating it. The dough has rested sufficiently when it appears very smooth.

One advantage of the autolyse step is that mixing times are shortened, and shorter mixing times produce gluten that has greater extensibility. Another advantage is the development of a sweet aroma and flavor in the baked loaf.

The salt and yeast are added to the dough after the autolyse is complete. Added earlier, the salt would tighten the gluten and the yeast would begin fermenting. The alcohol produced by the yeast would have an undesirable effect on the gluten as well. The dough is mixed until the gluten is properly developed and it is ready for bulk fermentation.

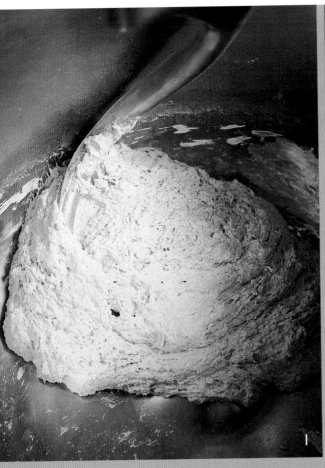

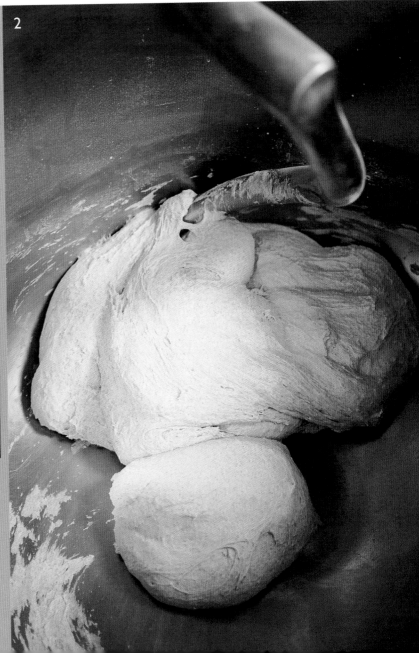

1 In the initial stage of an autolyse, the dough is very coarse.

2 A finished dough made with an autolyse becomes very smooth.

Durum Rosemary Dough

Makes 15 lb 9 oz/7.06 kg dough   DDT: 78°F/26°C

DURUM FLOUR	74.1%	6 lb 10 oz	3.01 kg
BREAD FLOUR	25.9%	2 lb 5 oz	1.05 kg
INSTANT DRY YEAST	0.45%	¾ oz	21 g
WATER	70%	100 fl oz	3 L
SALT	2.1%	3 oz	85 g
ROSEMARY, coarsely chopped	0.7%	1 oz	28 g

1. Combine the flours and yeast. Add the water, salt, and rosemary and mix on low speed for 3 minutes. Mix on medium speed for 4 minutes. The dough should be slightly stiff with sufficient gluten development.

2. Bulk ferment the dough until nearly doubled, about 40 minutes. Fold gently. Allow the dough to ferment for another 40 minutes before dividing.

3. See page 186 for shaping, proofing, and baking options suitable for this dough.

Soft Roll Dough

Makes 9 lb 4 oz/4.20 kg dough   DDT: 75°F/24°C

BREAD FLOUR	100%	5 lb	2.27 kg
INSTANT DRY YEAST	1.66%	1¼ oz	35 g
WHOLE MILK, room temperature	50%	40 fl oz	1.20 L
BUTTER, soft	10%	8 oz	227 g
EGGS (55°F/13°C)	10%	8 oz	227 g
SUGAR	10%	8 oz	227 g
SALT	2.5%	2 oz	57 g

1. Combine the flour and yeast. Add the milk, butter, eggs, sugar, and salt. Mix on low speed for 4 minutes and on medium speed for 3 minutes. The dough should be firm but elastic.

2. Bulk ferment the dough until nearly doubled, about 1 hour. Fold gently.

3. See pages 218-219 for shaping, proofing, and baking options suitable for this dough.

Enriched Doughs

The term *enriching* indicates that ingredients containing fat are added to the dough. Many different ingredients, such as milk, oil, and butter, may be used to enrich a dough. Often, enriched breads also contain some measure of sugar that as been introduced through either the addition of ingredients that contain some type of sugar (i.e., lactose through the use of milk), or simply by the addition of a granulated or syrup form of sugar.

The addition of fat and/or sugar dramatically affects the finished product. The additional fat acts to shorten the gluten strands and increase the elasticity of the gluten in a dough. This will have a tenderizing effect on the finished product, yielding a more tender crumb and the development of a soft crust. Additional sugars promote quick fermentation and browning of the crust during baking.

Grissini Dough

Makes 8 lb 8 oz/3.86 kg dough   DDT: 78°F/26°C

HIGH-GLUTEN FLOUR	100%	5 lb	2.27 kg
INSTANT DRY YEAST	1.66%	1¼ oz	35 g
WHOLE MILK, room temperature	45%	36 fl oz	1.08 L
BUTTER, soft	15%	12 oz	340 g
OLIVE OIL	3.75%	3 oz	85 g
SALT	2.5%	2 oz	57 g
MALT SYRUP	1.9%	1½ oz	43 g

1. Combine the flour and yeast. Add the milk, butter, olive oil, salt, and malt. Mix on low speed for 4 minutes and on medium speed for 3 minutes. The dough should be very stiff. Let the dough rest for 15 minutes.

2. Bulk ferment the dough until nearly doubled, about 30 minutes.

3. See page 203 for shaping, proofing, and baking options suitable for this dough.

Pain de Mie Dough

Makes 15 lb 5¾ oz/6.97 kg dough   DDT: 77°F/25°C

BREAD FLOUR	100%	8 lb 9 oz	3.88 kg
INSTANT DRY YEAST	0.75%	1 oz	28 g
WHOLE MILK, room temperature	68.6%	94 fl oz	2.82 L
BUTTER soft	5.5%	7½ oz	213 g
SUGAR	2.75%	3¾ oz	106 g
SALT	2.2%	3 oz	85 g

1. Combine the flour and yeast. Add the milk, butter, sugar, and salt. Mix on low speed for 4 minutes and on medium speed for 4 minutes. The dough should be slightly soft but elastic.

2. Bulk ferment the dough until nearly doubled, about 1 hour 15 minutes. Fold gently. Allow the dough to ferment for another 15 minutes before dividing.

3. See pages 134 and 222 for shaping, proofing, and baking options suitable for this dough.

Wheat Dough for Pullman Loaves

Makes 25 lb 7¼ oz /11.55 kg dough   DDT: 75°F/24°C

BREAD FLOUR	70%	10 lb 8 oz	4.76 kg
WHOLE WHEAT FLOUR	30%	4 lb 8 oz	2.04 kg
INSTANT DRY YEAST	0.63%	1½ oz	43 g
WHOLE MILK, warm	58.75%	141 fl oz	4.23 L
VEGETABLE OIL	5.63%	13½ oz	383 g
SUGAR	2.82%	6¾ oz	191 g
SALT	2.2%	5¼ oz	149 g

1. Combine the flours and yeast. Add the milk, oil, sugar, and salt. Mix on low speed for 2 minutes and on medium speed for 5 minutes. The dough should be slightly dry and have sufficient gluten development.

2. Bulk ferment the dough until nearly doubled, about 1 hour. Divide.

3. See page 224 for shaping, proofing, and baking options suitable for this dough.

Rye Dough with Caraway Seeds for Pullman Loaves

Makes 25 lb 11 oz/11.65 kg dough   DDT: 75°F/24°C

BREAD FLOUR	76.25%	11 lb 7 oz	5.19 kg
MEDIUM RYE FLOUR	23.75%	3 lb 9 oz	1.62 kg
INSTANT DRY YEAST	0.6%	1½ oz	43 g
WATER	61.25%	147 fl oz	4.41 L
SUGAR	1.9%	4½ oz	128 g
SALT	2.2%	5¼ oz	149 g
VEGETABLE OIL	1.9%	4½ oz	128 g
MOLASSES	1.9%	4½ oz	128 g
CARAWAY SEED	1.25%	3 oz	85 g

1. Combine the flours and yeast. Add the water, sugar, salt, oil, and molasses. Mix on low speed for 4 minutes and on medium speed for 3 minutes. The dough should be firm but elastic. Blend in the caraway seeds.

2. Bulk ferment the dough until nearly doubled, about 45 minutes. Fold gently. Allow the dough to ferment for another 15 minutes before dividing.

3. See page 224 for shaping, proofing, and baking options suitable for this dough.

Sunflower Seed Dough

Makes 14 lb 11 oz/6.66 kg dough   DDT: 79°F/26°C

BREAD FLOUR	100%	6 lb 8 oz	2.95 kg
INSTANT DRY YEAST	0.65%	⅔ oz	19 g
WHOLE MILK, room temperature	86.5%	90 fl oz	2.70 L
WHEAT BRAN	11.5%	12 oz	340 g
HONEY	7.7%	8 oz	227 g
SUNFLOWER OIL	5.75%	6 oz	170 g
SALT	2.4%	2½ oz	71 g
SUNFLOWER SEEDS, lightly toasted	11.5%	12 oz	340 g

1. Combine the flour and yeast. Add the milk, bran, honey, oil, and salt. Mix on low speed for 4 minutes and on medium speed for 4½ minutes. The dough should be slightly soft but with full gluten development. It will tighten up during bulk fermentation. Add the sunflower seeds after 4 minutes on medium speed.

2. Bulk ferment the dough until nearly doubled, about 1 hour. Divide.

3. See pages 186 and 208 for shaping, proofing, and baking options suitable for this dough.

Note   You can substitute lightly toasted pumpkin seeds for the sunflower seeds.

Beer Bread Dough

Makes 15 lb 10½ oz/7.10 kg dough   DDT: 75°F/24°C

BREAD FLOUR	85.6%	6 lb 9¾ oz	3 kg
MEDIUM RYE FLOUR	14.4%	1 lb 1¾ oz	503 g
INSTANT DRY YEAST	0.4%	½ oz	14 g
DARK BEER	57.1%	70½ fl oz	2.12 L
PÂTE FERMENTÉE (page 149)	28.5%	2 lb 3¼ oz	1 kg
COTTAGE CHEESE	14.4%	1 lb 1¾ oz	503 g
SALT	2.4%	3 oz	85 g

1. Combine the flours and yeast. Add the beer, pâte fermentée, cottage cheese, and salt. Mix on low speed for 3 minutes and on medium speed for 4 to 5 minutes. The dough should be sticky but have sufficient gluten development.

2. Bulk ferment the dough until nearly doubled, about 45 minutes. Fold gently. Allow the dough to ferment for another 15 minutes before dividing.

3. See pages 198 and 209 for shaping, proofing, and baking options suitable for this dough.

Belgian Apple Cider Dough

Makes 18 lb 15½ oz/8.60 kg dough   DDT: 75°F/24°C

BREAD FLOUR	66.7%	4 lb 6½ oz	2 kg
MEDIUM RYE FLOUR	33.3%	2 lb 3¼ oz	9.99 kg
INSTANT DRY YEAST	0.33%	⅓ oz	9 g
APPLE CIDER	66.7%	70½ fl oz	2.12 L
SOUR CREAM	33.3%	2 lb 3¼ oz	9.99 kg
PÂTE FERMENTÉE (page 149)	83.5%	5 lb 8¼ oz	2.50 kg
SALT	2.25%	2⅓ oz	66 g

1. Combine the flours and yeast. Add the cider, sour cream, pâte fermentée, and salt. Mix on low speed for 4 minutes and on medium speed for 3 minutes. The dough should be sticky but have sufficient gluten development.

2. Bulk ferment the dough until nearly doubled, about 30 minutes. Fold gently. Allow the dough to ferment for another 30 minutes before dividing.

3. See page 193 for shaping, proofing, and baking options suitable for this dough.

Prosciutto and Provolone Dough

Makes 14 lb 14½ oz/6.76 kg dough   DDT: 76°F/24°C

BREAD FLOUR	100%	6 lb 4 oz	2.84 kg
INSTANT DRY YEAST	1%	1 oz	28 g
WATER	58%	58 fl oz	1.74 L
OLIVE OIL	10%	10 oz	284 g
BUTTER, soft	2.75%	2¾ oz	78 g
SALT	2.2%	2¼ oz	64 g
PROSCIUTTO, medium dice	32%	2 lb	907 g
PROVOLONE, medium dice	32%	2 lb	907 g

1. Combine the flour and yeast. Add the water, olive oil, butter, and salt. Mix on low speed for 4 minutes and on medium speed for 2 minutes. Add the prosciutto and provolone and mix on medium speed for an additional minute. The dough should be slightly moist but have sufficient gluten development.

2. Bulk ferment the dough until nearly doubled, about 30 minutes. Fold gently. Allow the dough to ferment for another 30 minutes before dividing.

3. See page 186 for shaping, proofing, and baking options suitable for this dough.

Cheddar and Onion Rye Dough

Makes 11 lb/4.99 kg dough   DDT: 78°F/26°C

BREAD FLOUR	76.25%	3 lb 13 oz	1.73 kg
MEDIUM RYE FLOUR	23.75%	1 lb 3 oz	539 g
INSTANT DRY YEAST	0.63%	½ oz	14 g
WATER	71.25%	57 fl oz	1.71 L
SALT	2.5%	2 oz	57 g
SUGAR	1.9%	1½ oz	43 g
MOLASSES	1.9%	1½ oz	43 g
VEGETABLE OIL	1.9%	1½ oz	43 g
CHEDDAR CHEESE, large dice	20%	1 lb	454 g
YELLOW ONIONS, large dice	20%	1 lb	454 g

1. Combine the flours and yeast. Add the water, salt, sugar, molasses, and oil. Mix on low speed for 4 minutes and on medium speed for 2 minutes. Add the cheese and onions and mix on medium speed for an additional minute. The dough should be tight with strong gluten development.

2. Bulk ferment the dough until nearly doubled, about 1 hour 15 minutes. Fold gently.

3. See pages 186 and 208 for shaping, proofing, and baking options suitable for this dough.

Rustic Raisin Dough

Makes 14 lb 14½ oz/6.76 kg dough   DDT: 75°F/24°C

BREAD FLOUR	100%	6 lb 4 oz	2.83 kg
INSTANT DRY YEAST	1.5%	1½ oz	43 g
WHOLE MILK, room temperature	80%	80 fl oz	2.40 L
HONEY	3%	3 oz	85 g
SALT	2%	2 oz	57 g
RAISINS	52%	3 lb 4 oz	1.47 kg

1. Combine the flour and yeast. Add the milk, honey, and salt. Mix on low speed for 4 minutes and on medium speed for 4 minutes. The dough should have good gluten development but also be soft and slightly moist. Blend in the raisins.

2. Bulk ferment the dough until nearly doubled, about 1 hour. Fold gently.

3. See page 186 for shaping, proofing, and baking options suitable for this dough.

Note   You can substitute currants for the raisins. You can substitute walnuts for half of the raisins.

Raisin Bread with Cinnamon Swirl Dough

Makes 16 lb 5¾ oz/7.42 kg dough   DDT: 78°F/26°C

BREAD FLOUR	100%	8 lb 1 oz	3.66 kg
INSTANT DRY YEAST	0.78%	1 oz	28 g
WHOLE MILK, room temperature	52.7%	68 fl oz	2.04 L
BUTTER, soft	9.1%	11¾ oz	333 g
SUGAR	9.1%	11¾ oz	333 g
EGGS	9.1%	11¾ oz	333 g
SALT	2.3%	3 oz	85 g
RAISINS	18.6%	1 lb 8 oz	680 g
GROUND CINNAMON	1.2%	1½ oz	43 g

1. Combine the flour and yeast. Add the milk, butter, sugar, eggs, and salt. Mix on low speed for 4 minutes and on medium speed for 4 minutes; in the last minute of mixing, add the raisins, and in the last 30 seconds of mixing, add the cinnamon, mixing just long enough to create a swirl. The dough should be slightly soft.

2. Bulk ferment the dough until nearly doubled, about 1 hour. Fold gently.

3. See page 223 for shaping, proofing, and baking options suitable for this dough.

Challah Dough

Makes 9 lb 6½ oz/4.27 kg dough   DDT: 78°F/26°C

BREAD FLOUR	100%	5 lb 4 oz	2.38 kg
INSTANT DRY YEAST	1.2%	1 oz	28 g
WATER	38%	32 fl oz	960 mL
EGG YOLKS	19%	1 lb	454 g
VEGETABLE OIL	9.5%	8 oz	227 g
SUGAR	9.5%	8 oz	227 g
SALT	1.8%	1½ oz	43 g

1. Combine the flour and yeast. Add the water, egg yolks, oil, sugar, and salt. Mix on low speed for 4 minutes and on medium speed for 4 minutes. The dough should be slightly firm and smooth, not sticky.

2. Bulk ferment the dough until nearly doubled, about 1 hour. Fold gently.

3. See pages 227 and 228 for shaping, proofing, and baking options suitable for this dough.

Sweet Dough

Makes 12 lb 4½ oz/5.57 kg dough   DDT: 75°F/24°C

BREAD FLOUR	100%	7 lb 8 oz	3.40 kg
INSTANT DRY YEAST	1.25%	1½ oz	43 g
WHOLE MILK	26.6%	32 fl oz	960 mL
EGGS	15%	1 lb 2 oz	510 g
SUGAR	10%	12 oz	340 g
BUTTER, soft	10%	12 oz	340 g
SALT	2%	2½ oz	71 g

1. Combine the flour and yeast. Add the milk, eggs, sugar, butter, and salt. Mix on low speed for 4 minutes and on medium speed for 4 minutes. The dough should be slightly soft but elastic.

2. Bulk ferment the dough until nearly doubled, about 1 hour 15 minutes. Fold gently.

3. Divide the dough and place on two greased sheet pans. Cover and refrigerate overnight.

4. See pages 230 and 231 for shaping, proofing, and baking options suitable for this dough.

Brioche Dough

Makes 11 lb 10¾ oz/5.29 kg dough   DDT: 75°F/24°C

BREAD FLOUR	100%	5 lb	2.27 kg
INSTANT DRY YEAST	1.7%	1⅓ oz	38 g
EGGS	40%	2 lb	907 g
WHOLE MILK, room temperature	20%	16 fl oz	480 mL
SUGAR	10%	8 oz	227 g
SALT	2%	1½ oz	43 g
BUTTER, softened but still pliable	60%	3 lb	1.36 kg

1. Combine the flour and yeast. Add the eggs, milk, sugar, and salt and mix on low speed for 4 minutes.

2. Gradually add the butter, with the mixer running on medium speed, scraping down the sides of the bowl as necessary. After the butter has been fully incorporated, mix on medium speed for 15 minutes, or until the dough begins to pull away from the sides of the bowl.

3. Place the dough on a sheet pan that has been lined with parchment and greased. Cover tightly with plastic wrap and refrigerate overnight.

4. See pages 220 and 225 for shaping, proofing, and baking options suitable for this dough.

Variation   **Orange Brioche Dough** Add 1 oz/28 g finely grated orange zest tot he brioche dough in Step 2 with the butter.

1 The consistency of brioche dough when it is ready for the butter to be added

2 The consistency of properly mixed brioche dough after adding the butter

Craquelin Dough

Makes 6 lb 4 oz/2.84 kg dough   DDT: 45°F/7°C

BRIOCHE DOUGH (page 142)	80%	5 lb	2.27 kg
SUGAR CUBES	20%	1 lb 4 oz	567 g
LEMON ZEST, grated (optional)		1¼ oz	35 g

1. Mix the dough and sugar cubes (and lemon zest, if desired) on low speed for 1 to 2 minutes, or until the sugar cubes are just incorporated.

2. See page 226 for shaping, proofing, and baking options suitable for this dough.

Crescia al Formaggio Dough

Makes 12 lb 11½ oz/5.77 kg dough   DDT: 80°F/27°C

BREAD FLOUR	100%	5 lb	2.27 kg
INSTANT DRY YEAST	1.53%	3½ oz	99 g
PARMESAN, finely grated	54.6%	2 lb 11¾ oz	1.24 kg
WATER	18.2%	14½ fl oz	435 mL
EGGS	31.8%	1 lb 9½ oz	723 g
BUTTER, soft	27.3%	1 lb 5¾ oz	617 g
EGG YOLKS	13.7%	11 oz	312 g
SUGAR	2.3%	1¾ oz	50 g
SALT	2.3%	1¾ oz	50 g

1. Combine the flour and yeast. Add the cheese, water, eggs, butter, egg yolks, sugar, and salt. Mix on low speed for 2 minutes and on medium speed for 5 minutes. The dough should have sufficient gluten development but still be soft.

2. Bulk ferment the dough until nearly doubled, about 1 hour. Fold gently.

3. See page 186 for shaping, proofing, and baking options suitable for this dough.

Soft Pretzel Dough

Makes 8 lb 13¾ oz/4.02 kg dough   DDT: 75°F/24°C

BREAD FLOUR	100%	5 lb 8 oz	2.49 kg
INSTANT DRY YEAST	1.7%	1½ oz	43 g
WATER	50%	44 fl oz	1.32 L
BUTTER, soft, cubed	5.1%	4½ oz	128 g
MALT SYRUP	2.25%	2 oz	57 g
SALT	2%	1¾ oz	50 g

1. Combine the flour and yeast. Add the water, butter, malt syrup, and salt. Mix on low speed for 2 minutes and on medium speed for 8 minutes. The dough should be stiff, with strong gluten development.

2. Bulk ferment the dough until nearly doubled, about 50 minutes.

3. See page 232 for shaping, proofing, and baking options suitable for this dough.

Semolina Pizza Dough

Makes 15 lb 11¼ oz/7.12 kg dough   DDT: 75°F/24°C

BREAD FLOUR	57.8%	5 lb 5 oz	2.41 kg
DURUM FLOUR	42.2%	3 lb 14 oz	1.76 kg
INSTANT DRY YEAST	0.51%	¾ oz	21 g
WATER	63.9%	94 fl oz	2.82 L
OLIVE OIL	3.75%	5½ oz	156 g
SALT	2.7%	4 oz	113 g

1. Combine the flours and yeast. Add the water, olive oil, and salt. Mix on low speed for 2 minutes and on medium speed for 4 minutes. The dough should have good gluten development but still be a little sticky.

2. Bulk ferment the dough until nearly doubled, about 50 minutes. Fold gently. Allow the dough to ferment for another 15 minutes before dividing. Refrigerate overnight. Take out 1 hour prior to use.

3. See pages 234-236 for shaping, proofing, and baking options suitable for this dough.

Lavash Dough

Makes 11 lb 5¼ oz/5.14 kg dough DDT: *78°F/26°C*

BREAD FLOUR	46%	2 lb 14 oz	1.30 kg
DURUM FLOUR	20%	1 lb 4 oz	567 g
CAKE FLOUR	17%	1 lb 1 oz	482 g
WHOLE WHEAT FLOUR	17%	1 lb 1 oz	482 g
INSTANT DRY YEAST	0.5%	½ oz	14 g
WHOLE MILK, room temperature	42.5%	42½ fl oz	1.28 L
WATER	29.25%	29¼ fl oz	878 mL
MOLASSES	3.25%	3¼ oz	92 g
HONEY	3.25%	3¼ oz	92 g
SALT	2.5%	2½ oz	71 g

1. Combine the flours and yeast. Add the milk, water, molasses, honey, and salt. Mix on low speed for 10 minutes. The dough should pull cleanly away from the sides of the bowl but still be wet and soft.

2. Bulk ferment the dough until nearly doubled, about 30 minutes. Fold gently. Scale and retard overnight.

3. See page 239 for shaping, proofing, and baking options suitable for this dough.

Naan Dough

Makes 1 lb 11¼ oz/773 g dough   DDT: 74°F/23°C

ALL-PURPOSE FLOUR	100%	14 oz	397 g
INSTANT DRY YEAST	2.4%	⅓ oz	9 g
WATER	42.9%	6 fl oz	180 mL
CLARIFIED BUTTER	14.3%	2 oz	57 g
PLAIN YOGURT	14.3%	2 oz	57 g
EGGS	12.5%	2 oz	57 g
SUGAR	7.2%	1 oz	28 g
SALT	1.8%	1½ tsp	7.5 g

1. Combine the flour and yeast. Add the water, butter, yogurt, eggs, sugar, and salt and mix on low speed for 4 minutes. The dough should be very elastic but still wet.

2. Bulk ferment the dough until nearly doubled, about 1 hour. Fold gently.

3. See pages 238 and 240 for shaping, proofing, and baking options suitable for this dough.

Pita Dough

Makes 3 lb 5¾ oz/1.52 kg dough   DDT: 78°F/26°C

BREAD FLOUR	50%	1 lb	454 g
WHOLE WHEAT FLOUR	50%	1 lb	454 g
INSTANT DRY YEAST	0.78%	¼ oz	7 g
WATER	62.5%	20 fl oz	600 mL
OLIVE OIL	3.2%	1 oz	28 g
SALT	2.3%	¾ oz	21 g
SUGAR	0.4%	¾ tsp	3.75 g

1. Combine the flours and yeast. Add the water, olive oil, salt, and sugar. Mix on low speed for 4 minutes and on medium speed for 3 minutes. The dough should be slightly moist but with strong gluten development.

2. Bulk ferment the dough until nearly doubled, about 30 minutes. Fold gently.

3. See page 237 for shaping, proofing, and baking options suitable for this dough.

Yeast-Raised Doughnut Dough

Makes 5 lb 5½ oz/2.42 kg dough   DDT: 80°F/27°C

BREAD FLOUR	62.4%	1 lb 10½ oz	751 g
PASTRY FLOUR	37.6%	1 lb	454 g
INSTANT DRY YEAST	3.2%	1⅓ oz	38 g
WATER	50%	21¼ fl oz	638 mL
EGGS	12.4%	5¼ oz	149 g
SUGAR	6.5%	2¾ oz	78 g
NONFAT DRY MILK	6.5%	2¾ oz	78 g
BAKING POWDER	1.75%	¾ oz	21 g
SALT	1.75%	¾ oz	21 g
GROUND NUTMEG	0.35%	1 tsp	2 g
EMULSIFIED SHORTENING	18.8%	8 oz	227 g

1. Combine the flours and yeast. Add the water, eggs, sugar, dry milk, baking powder, salt, and nutmeg and mix on low speed for 2 minutes, or until the ingredients are well incorporated. Add the shortening and mix on medium speed for 8 minutes.

2. Mix on high speed for 3 minutes, or until the dough pulls away from the sides of the bowl. The dough should have sufficient gluten development but still be soft.

3. Bulk ferment the dough until nearly doubled, about 30 minutes. Fold gently. Allow the dough to ferment for another 30 minutes before dividing.

4. See page 243 for shaping, proofing, and baking options suitable for this dough.

Berliner Dough

Makes 4 lb 8 oz/2.04 kg dough   DDT: 68°F/20°C

BREAD FLOUR	100%	2 lb 4 oz	1.02 kg
INSTANT DRY YEAST	2.8%	1 oz	28 g
WHOLE MILK	45.4%	16 fl oz	480 mL
BUTTER, soft	14.9%	5¼ oz	149 g
SUGAR	14.9%	5¼ oz	149 g
EGGS	14.9%	5¼ oz	149 g
EGG YOLKS	5.7%	2 oz	57 g
SALT	0.7%	1½ tsp	7.5 g
LEMON ZEST, grated	1.4%	½ oz	14 g
VANILLA EXTRACT	1.4%	1 tsp	15 mL

1. Combine the flour and yeast. Add the milk, butter, sugar, eggs, egg yolks, salt, lemon zest, and vanilla extract. Mix on low speed for 8 to 12 minutes. The dough should have very strong gluten development and be very tight but smooth.

2. Bulk ferment the dough until nearly doubled, about 30 minutes. Fold gently. Allow the dough to ferment for another 30 minutes before dividing.

3. See pages 241 and 242 for shaping, proofing, and baking options suitable for this dough.

Lean Dough with Pâte Fermentée

Makes 10 lb/4.54 kg dough   DDT: 78°F/26°C

BREAD FLOUR	100%	5 lb	2.27 kg
INSTANT DRY YEAST	0.63%	½ oz	14 g
WATER	67.2%	53¾ fl oz	1.61 L
PÂTE FERMENTÉE (page 149)	30%	1 lb 8 oz	680 g
SALT	2.2%	1¾ oz	50 g

1. Combine the flour and yeast. Add the water, pâte fermentée, and salt. Mix on low speed for 4 minutes and on medium speed for 2 minutes. The dough should be slightly soft but very smooth, with sufficient gluten development.

2. Bulk ferment the dough until nearly doubled, about 40 minutes. Fold gently, and ferment for another 30 minutes. Fold again. Allow the dough to ferment for another 20 minutes before dividing.

3. See page 148 for shaping, proofing, and baking options suitable for this dough.

Indirect Fermentation and Pre-Ferments

The longer the yeast in a dough remains active, the better the flavor and texture of the finished bread will be. Indirect fermentation means that some portion of the dough is allowed to ferment on its own before being mixed with the remainder of the formula's ingredients. This portion, often referred to as a pre-ferment, typically includes only flour, water (or milk), and some or all of the yeast called for in the final dough.

It is important to plan for pre-ferments in a production schedule. The time requirement for each type of pre-ferment is slightly different, as noted below.

Pâte fermentée, or "old dough," is nothing more exotic than a piece of a Wheat Lean Dough reserved from the previous day's production. The dough is wrapped and refrigerated until needed, then added along with the other ingredients to make a batch of dough, as in the Lean Dough formula on page 123. The yeast in the pâte fermentée has undergone an extended fermentation and has developed a rich, appealing "sour" flavor.

The *sponge method* combines one-third to one-half of the formula's total liquid with all the yeast and enough flour to make a very loose dough. The sponge can be made directly in the mixing bowl, as the fermentation period is typically less than 1 hour. When the sponge has doubled in size, the remaining ingredients are mixed in to make the final dough.

A *poolish* combines equal parts flour and water (by weight) with some yeast (the amount varies according to the expected length of fermentation time, using less for longer, slower fermentations). The poolish is fermented at room temperature long enough to double in volume and start to recede, or decrease in volume. This may take anywhere from 3 to 15 hours. The poolish should be mixed in a plastic or other non-reactive container large enough to hold the mixture comfortably as it ferments.

A *biga* is the stiffest of the pre-ferments. It contains flour and enough water to equal 50 to 60 percent of the flour's weight as well as 0.33 to 0.5 percent of the formula's total yeast. After the biga has properly fermented, it must be loosened with a portion of the formula's liquid to make it easier to blend into the dough.

Sourdoughs are established by capturing wild yeast in a flour and water dough. For more about these special pre-ferments, see page 149.

Multigrain Dough

Makes 14 lb 5 oz/6.49 kg dough   DDT: 75°F/24°C

SOAKER			
9-GRAIN MIXTURE	37.2%	1 lb	454 g
SUNFLOWER SEEDS	8.2%	3½ oz	99 g
FLAX SEEDS	5.2%	2¼ oz	64 g
WATER (90°F/32°C)	49.4%	21 fl oz	630 mL
FINAL DOUGH			
BREAD FLOUR	57.5%	2 lb 14 oz	1.30 kg
WHOLE WHEAT FLOUR	42.5%	2 lb 2 oz	964 g
INSTANT DRY YEAST	.94%	¾ oz	21 g
WATER	58.4%	47 fl oz	1.4 L
SALT	3.1%	2½ oz	71 g
PÂTE FERMENTÉE (page 149)	70%	3 lb 8 oz	1.59 kg
SOAKER (above)	53.75%	2 lb 11 oz	1.22 kg

1. To prepare the soaker, combine the 9-grain mixture, sunflower seeds, and flax seeds with the water in a plastic tub and cover. Soak at room temperature until the soaker has absorbed the water and is slightly dry, 8 to 12 hours.

2. To prepare the final dough, combine the flours and yeast. Add the water and salt and mix on low speed for 4 minutes. Add the soaker and mix on low speed for 2 minutes, or until the gluten is fully developed and the dough is a little dry and soft with good elasticity.

3. Bulk ferment the dough until nearly doubled, about 30 minutes. Fold gently. Allow the dough to ferment for another 20 minutes before dividing.

4. See pages 198 and 208 for shaping, proofing, and baking options suitable for this dough.

Soakers

When adding a significant quantity of grains, or adding any amount of large, whole grains such as wheat berries, it is best to soak the grains first before incorporating them into the final dough. Whole grains tend to deprive the dough of moisture and will also damage the developing gluten network.

A soaker can be made using one of two methods: hot or cold. A hot soaker pregelatinizes the starch of the soaker's grain, which can improve the crust and decrease baking time of some whole-grain breads. Hot soakers work faster, but some chefs feel that there is some loss of flavor and quality. A cold soaker must be prepared at least a day in advance. For a cold soaker, the grains and liquid are incorporated slightly, covered, and allowed to soak overnight. A hot soaker is produced by bringing the liquid to a boil and then incorporating the grains. Continue to cook the mixture for about 5 minutes over low heat. Set the soaker aside for at least 1 hour to allow it to cool before adding it to the dough.

Soakers are added to the dough after it has started to develop and are mixed into the dough on medium speed for a few minutes, just until they are fully and evenly incorporated.

Panettone Dough

Makes 10 lb 4½ oz/4.66 kg dough   DDT: 78°F/26°C

SPONGE			
BREAD FLOUR	100%	1 lb 5 oz	595 g
WHOLE MILK (80°F/27°C)	66.7%	14 fl oz	420 mL
INSTANT DRY YEAST	6%	1¼ oz	35 g
FINAL DOUGH			
SPONGE (above)	57%	2 lb 4¼ oz	1.03 kg
BREAD FLOUR	67%	2 lb 10½ oz	1.20 kg
EGGS	25.2%	1 lb	454 g
WHOLE MILK	18.9%	12 fl oz	360 mL
SUGAR	14.6%	9¼ oz	262 g
CANDIED ORANGE PEEL	12.75%	8 oz	227 g
CANDIED LEMON PEEL	12.75%	8 oz	227 g
RAISINS	12.6%	8 oz	227 g
GOLDEN RAISINS	12.6%	8 oz	227 g
SALT	2.75%	1¾ oz	50 g
GLUCOSE SYRUP	2%	1¼ oz	35 g
ORANGE ZEST, grated	0.75%	½ oz	14 g
LEMON ZEST, grated	0.75%	½ oz	14 g
INSTANT DRY YEAST	0.75%	½ oz	14 g
BUTTER (55°F/13°C)	18.9%	12 oz	340 g

1. To prepare the sponge, mix the flour, milk, and yeast on low speed until blended, about 2 minutes. Cover and ferment until the sponge has risen and just begun to recede, about 45 minutes at 75°F/24°C.

2. To prepare the final dough, combine the sponge, flour, eggs, milk, sugar, orange and lemon peel, raisins, salt, glucose, orange and lemon zest, and yeast. Mix on low speed for 4 minutes and on medium speed for 2 minutes. Gradually add the butter, then mix on medium speed for 10 minutes. The dough should be soft but very elastic.

3. Bulk ferment the dough until nearly doubled, about 1 hour 15 minutes. Fold gently. Allow the dough to ferment for another 15 minutes before dividing.

4. See pages 186 and 217 for shaping, proofing, and baking options suitable for this dough.

Gugelhopf Dough

Makes 15 lb 8¼ oz/7.04 kg dough   DDT: 79°F/26°C

SPONGE			
BREAD FLOUR	100%	2 lb 4 oz	1.02 kg
WHOLE MILK (75°F/24°C)	100%	36 fl oz	1.08 L
INSTANT DRY YEAST	7.6%	2¾ oz	78 g
VANILLA BEANS, scraped		4 each	4 each
FINAL DOUGH			
SUGAR	20.75%	1 lb 6 oz	624 g
SALT	1.4%	1½ oz	43 g
BUTTER, soft	20.75%	1 lb 6 oz	624 g
EGGS	13.2%	2 lb	907 g
BREAD FLOUR	66%	4 lb 6 oz	1.98 kg
SPONGE (above)	70.5%	4 lb 10¾ oz	2.12 kg
RAISINS	20.75%	1 lb 6 oz	624 g
ALMONDS, chopped	3.75%	4 oz	113 g

1. To prepare the sponge, mix the flour, milk, yeast, and vanilla bean seeds on low speed until blended, about 2 minutes. Cover and ferment until the sponge has risen and just begun to recede, about 20 minutes at 75°F/24°C.

2. To prepare the final dough, cream the sugar, salt, and butter on medium speed, scraping down the bowl periodically until smooth, fluffy, and lighter in color, about 5 minutes. Gradually add the eggs, scraping down the bowl periodically.

3. Add the bread flour and the sponge. Mix on low speed for 5 minutes and on medium speed for 5 minutes, until the dough is completely smooth.

4. Add the raisins and almonds. Mix on low speed for about 20 minutes, or until the mixture pulls away from the side of the bowl. The dough should be moist but have strong gluten development.

5. Bulk ferment the dough until nearly doubled in size, about 20 minutes.

6. See page 216 for shaping, proofing, and baking options suitable for this dough.

Christmas Stollen Dough

Makes 9 lb 10¾ oz/4.39 kg dough   DDT: 80°F/27°C

FRUIT AND NUT MIXTURE			
GOLDEN RAISINS	53.2%	2 lb 3¼ oz	9.99 kg
CANDIED LEMON PEEL	15.5%	10½ oz	298 g
CANDIED ORANGE PEEL	6.6%	4½ oz	128 g
DARK RUM	5.2%	3½ fl oz	105 mL
WHOLE ALMONDS, blanched	19.5%	13¼ oz	376 g
SPONGE			
BREAD FLOUR	100%	1 lb 6 oz	624 g
WHOLE MILK (50°F/10°C)	60.3%	13¼ fl oz	398 mL
INSTANT DRY YEAST	4.5%	1 oz	28 g
FINAL DOUGH			
SPONGE (above)	88%	2 lb 4¼ oz	1.03 kg
BREAD FLOUR	50%	1 lb 6 oz	624 g
BUTTER	54.5%	1 lb 8 oz	680 g
ALMOND PASTE	4.5%	2 oz	57 g
SUGAR	4.5%	2 oz	57 g
SALT	2.25%	1 oz	28 g
LEMON ZEST, grated	0.57%	1¼ tsp	6.75 g
GROUND CLOVES	0.15%	pinch	pinch
GROUND GINGER	0.15%	pinch	pinch
GROUND ALLSPICE	0.15%	pinch	pinch
GROUND CINNAMON	0.15%	pinch	pinch
FRUIT AND NUT MIXTURE (above)	154.5%	4 lb 3 oz	1.90 kg

1. To prepare the fruit and nut mixture, rinse the raisins and lemon and orange peel with warm water and combine them with the rum in a plastic container. Cover and let the mixture soak at room temperature for at least 8 and up to 24 hours. Just before folding the garnish into the dough in Step 4, add the nuts.

2. To prepare the sponge, mix the flour, milk, and yeast on low speed until blended, about 2 minutes. Cover and ferment until the sponge has risen and just begun to recede, 30 to 40 minutes at 75°F/24°C.

3. To prepare the final dough, mix the sponge, flour, butter, almond paste, sugar, salt, lemon zest, cloves, ginger, allspice, and cinnamon on medium speed for 3 minutes. The dough should be sticky but have sufficient gluten development.

4. Bulk ferment the dough until nearly doubled, about 35 minutes. Very carefully fold in the fruit and nut mixture (see Adding Flavorings and Garnishes, page 171). Bulk ferment the dough until nearly doubled again, about 15 minutes.

5. See page 215 for shaping, proofing, and baking options suitable for this dough.

Whole Wheat Dough with Poolish
Makes 15 lb 9¼ oz/7.07 kg dough   DDT: 79°F/26°C

POOLISH			
WHOLE WHEAT FLOUR	100%	3 lb	1.36 kg
WATER (55°F/13°C)	100%	48 fl oz	1.44 L
INSTANT DRY YEAST	0.08%	pinch	pinch
FINAL DOUGH			
BREAD FLOUR	33.3%	3 lb	1.36 kg
WHOLE WHEAT FLOUR	33.3%	3 lb	1.36 kg
INSTANT DRY YEAST	0.35%	½ oz	14 g
POOLISH (above)	66.6%	6 lb	2.72 kg
WATER	37.5%	54 fl oz	1.62 L
SALT	2%	2¾ oz	78 g

1. To prepare the poolish, mix the flour, water, and yeast together by hand until well incorporated. Cover and ferment at 75°F/24°C until bubbly, frothy, and just starting to recede, 10 to 15 hours at 75°F/24°C.

2. To prepare the final dough, combine the flours and yeast. Add the poolish, water, and salt. Mix on low speed for 4 minutes and on medium speed for 4 minutes. The dough should be moist but with strong gluten development.

3. Bulk ferment the dough until nearly doubled, about 30 minutes. Fold gently. Allow the dough to ferment for another 30 minutes before dividing.

4. See page 198 for shaping, proofing, and baking options suitable for this dough.

Lean Dough with Poolish

Makes 8 lb 8 oz/3.86 kg dough   DDT: 78°F/26°C

POOLISH			
BREAD FLOUR	100%	1 lb 8 oz	680 g
WATER (55°F/13°C)	100%	24 fl oz	720 mL
INSTANT DRY YEAST	0.04%	pinch	pinch
FINAL DOUGH			
BREAD FLOUR	70%	3 lb 8 oz	1.59 kg
INSTANT DRY YEAST	0.63%	½ oz	14 g
POOLISH (above)	60%	3 lb	1.36 kg
WATER	37.2%	29¾ fl oz	893 mL
SALT	2.2%	1¾ oz	50 g

1. To prepare the poolish, mix the flour, water, and yeast together by hand until well incorporated. Cover and ferment at 75°F/24°C for 10 to 15 hours, until it has risen and just begun to recede; it will be bubbly and frothy on top.

2. To prepare the final dough, combine the flour and yeast. Add the poolish, water, and salt. Mix on low speed for 4 minutes and on medium speed for 2 minutes. The dough should be soft and smooth with good gluten development.

3. Bulk ferment the dough until nearly doubled, about 40 minutes. Fold gently and ferment for another 30 minutes. Fold once more. Allow to ferment for another 20 minutes before dividing.

4. See pages 200, 202, 205 and 206 for shaping, proofing, and baking options suitable for this dough.

Tomato Dough

Makes 9 lb 9¾ oz/4.36 kg dough   DDT: 75°F/24°C

POOLISH			
BREAD FLOUR	100%	1 lb 1 oz	482 g
WATER (55°F/13°C)	100%	17 fl oz	510 mL
INSTANT DRY YEAST	0.03%	pinch	pinch
ROASTED TOMATOES			
TOMATOES, cut in half	43.75%	2 lb 6½ oz	1.09 kg
OLIVE OIL		as needed	as needed
BASIL, chopped	0.85%	¾ oz	21 g
GARLIC, roughly chopped	0.55%	½ oz	14 g
SALT		as needed	as needed
CRACKED BLACK PEPPER		as needed	as needed
FINAL DOUGH			
BREAD FLOUR	71.5%	3 lb 15 oz	1.79 kg
WHOLE WHEAT FLOUR	9%	8 oz	227 g
INSTANT DRY YEAST	0.85%	¾ oz	21 g
POOLISH (above)	38.6%	2 lb 2 oz	964 g
WATER	1.7%	1½ fl oz	45 mL
SUGAR	2.8%	2½ oz	71 g
BUTTER (75°F/24°C)	2.8%	2½ oz	71 g
SALT	2%	1¾ oz	50 g

1. To prepare the poolish, mix the flour, water, and yeast together by hand until well incorporated. Cover and ferment at 75°F/24°C for 10 to 15 hours, until it has risen and just begun to recede; it will be bubbly and frothy on top.

2. To prepare the tomatoes, place the tomatoes on a baking sheet, cut side up. Drizzle with olive oil and scatter with the basil, garlic, salt, and pepper. Roast in a 300°F/149°C oven until slightly dried, about 1 hour.

3. When the tomatoes are cool enough to handle, remove the skins; reserve the garlic. Drain off excess juice and oil from tomatoes; roughly chop.

4. To prepare the final dough, combine the flours and yeast. Add the roasted tomatoes and reserved garlic, poolish, water, sugar, butter, and salt. Mix on low speed for 3 minutes and on medium speed for 2 minutes. The dough should be soft and smooth with good gluten development.

5. Bulk ferment the dough until nearly doubled, about 45 minutes. Fold gently. Allow the dough to ferment for another 30 minutes before dividing.

6. See page 186 for shaping, proofing, and baking options suitable for this dough.

Semolina Dough

Makes 15 lb 13½ oz/7.19 kg dough   DDT: 76°F/24°C

POOLISH			
DURUM FLOUR	100%	3 lb	1.36 kg
WATER (55°F/13°C)	100%	48 fl oz	1.44 L
INSTANT DRY YEAST	0.08%	pinch	pinch
FINAL DOUGH			
DURUM FLOUR	33.3%	3 lb	1.36 kg
BREAD FLOUR	33.3%	3 lb	1.36 kg
INSTANT DRY YEAST	0.5%	¾ oz	21 g
POOLISH (above)	66.7%	6 lb	2.72 kg
WATER	40.3%	58 fl oz	1.74 L
SALT	1.9%	2¾ oz	78 g

1. To prepare the poolish, mix the flour, water, and yeast together by hand until well incorporated. Cover and ferment at 75°F/24°C for 10 to 15 hours, until it has risen and begun to recede; it will be bubbly and frothy on top.

2. To prepare the final dough, combine the flours and yeast. Add the poolish, water, and salt. Mix on low speed for 5 minutes and on medium speed for 2 minutes. The dough should be strong and very elastic.

3. Bulk ferment the dough until nearly doubled, about 30 minutes. Fold gently. Allow the dough to ferment for another 30 minutes before dividing.

4. See page 198 for shaping, proofing, and baking options suitable for this dough.

Lean Dough with Biga

Makes 8 lb 8 oz/3.86 kg dough   *DDT: 78°F/26°C*

BIGA			
BREAD FLOUR	100%	1 lb 8 oz	680 g
WATER (60°F/16°C)	55%	13¼ fl oz	398 mL
INSTANT DRY YEAST	0.03%	pinch	pinch
FINAL DOUGH			
BREAD FLOUR	70%	3 lb 8 oz	1.59 kg
INSTANT DRY YEAST	0.63%	½ oz	14 g
WATER	50.6%	40½ fl oz	1.22 L
BIGA (above)	46.6%	2 lb 5¼ oz	1.06 kg
SALT	2.2%	1¾ oz	50 g

1. To prepare the biga, combine the flour, water, and yeast. Mix on low speed for 3 minutes, or until thoroughly combined. Transfer to a container, cover, and ferment at 75°F/24°C for 18 to 24 hours, until the biga has risen and begun to recede; it should still be bubbly and airy.

2. To prepare the final dough, combine the flour and yeast. Add the water, biga, and salt. Mix on low speed for 4 minutes and on medium speed for 2 minutes. The dough should still be slightly soft but very smooth, with sufficient gluten development.

3. Bulk ferment the dough until nearly doubled, about 40 minutes. Fold gently and ferment for another 30 minutes. Fold again. Allow the dough to ferment for another 20 minutes before dividing.

4. See page 159 for shaping, proofing, and baking options suitable for this dough.

Roasted Potato Dough

Makes 11 lb 6 oz/5.16 kg dough   DDT: 75°F/24°C

SOAKER			
CRACKED WHEAT	100%	3¼ oz	92 g
WATER (90°F/32°C)	100%	3¼ fl oz	98 mL
WHOLE WHEAT BIGA			
BREAD FLOUR	50%	9¼ oz	262 g
WHOLE WHEAT FLOUR	50%	9¼ oz	262 g
WATER (60°F/16°C)	68%	12½ fl oz	375 mL
INSTANT DRY YEAST	0.03%	pinch	pinch
ROASTED POTATOES			
YUKON GOLD POTATOES	50%	2 lb 8¼ oz	1.14 kg
OLIVE OIL		as needed	as needed
SALT		as needed	as needed
PEPPER		as needed	as needed
FINAL DOUGH			
BREAD FLOUR	70.5%	3 lb 8½ oz	1.60 kg
WHOLE WHEAT FLOUR	2.5%	2 oz	57 g
MEDIUM RYE FLOUR	4%	3¼ oz	92 g
INSTANT DRY YEAST	0.3%	¼ oz	7 g
WATER	50%	24¼ fl oz	728 mL
WHOLE WHEAT BIGA (above)	38.6%	1 lb 15 oz	879 g
SOAKER (above)	8%	6½ oz	184 g
SALT	2.5%	2 oz	57 g

1. To prepare the soaker, combine the cracked wheat and water in a plastic tub. Cover and soak under refrigeration for at least 8 and up to 12 hours.

2. To prepare the biga, combine the flours, water, and yeast. Mix on low speed for 3 minutes, or until thoroughly combined. Transfer to a container, cover, and ferment at 75°F/ 24°C for 18 to 24 hours, until the biga has risen and begun to recede; it should still be bubbly and airy.

3. To prepare the potatoes, toss them with olive oil to coat lightly. Season with salt and pepper. Roast in a 400°F/204°C convection oven until soft in the center, about 25 minutes. Cool the potatoes completely.

4. To prepare the final dough, combine the flours and yeast. Add the water, biga, soaker, and salt and mix on low speed for 4 minutes. Add the roasted potatoes and mix on medium speed for 2 minutes. The dough should be slightly stiff and the potatoes evenly distributed.

5. Bulk ferment the dough until nearly doubled, about 30 minutes. Fold gently and ferment for another 30 minutes. Fold again. Allow the dough to ferment for another 15 minutes before dividing.

6. See page 191 for shaping, proofing, and baking options suitable for this dough.

Rosemary Dough

Makes 10 lb 3¼ oz/4.63 kg dough   DDT: 75°F/24°C

BIGA			
BREAD FLOUR	100%	1 lb	454 g
WATER (60°F/16°C)	55%	8½ fl oz	255 mL
INSTANT DRY YEAST	0.08%	pinch	pinch
FINAL DOUGH			
BREAD FLOUR	83.3%	5 lb	2.27 kg
INSTANT DRY YEAST	0.25%	¼ oz	7 g
WATER	50%	48 fl oz	1.44 L
BIGA (above)	25%	1 lb 8 oz	680 g
WHOLE MILK	6.75%	6½ fl oz	195 mL
OLIVE OIL	2.6%	2½ oz	71 g
SALT	1.6%	1½ oz	43 g
ROSEMARY, coarsely chopped	0.5%	½ oz	14 g

1. To prepare the biga, combine the flour, water, and yeast. Mix on low speed for 3 minutes, or until thoroughly combined. Transfer to a container, cover, and ferment at 75°F/24°C for 18 to 24 hours, until the biga has risen and begun to recede; it should still be bubbly and airy.

2. To prepare the final dough, combine the flour and yeast. Add the water, biga, milk, olive oil, salt, and rosemary. Mix on low speed for 4 minutes and on medium speed for 3 minutes. The dough should still be slightly soft, with good gluten development.

3. Bulk ferment the dough until nearly doubled, about 30 minutes. Fold gently, and ferment for another 30 minutes. Fold again. Allow the dough to ferment for another 15 minutes before dividing.

4. See page 192 for shaping, proofing, and baking options suitable for this dough.

Ciabatta Dough

Makes 9 lb/4.08 kg dough   DDT: 75°F/24°C

BIGA			
BREAD FLOUR	100%	1 lb 10 oz	737 g
WATER (60°F/16°C)	50%	13¼ fl oz	398 mL
INSTANT DRY YEAST	0.03%	pinch	pinch
FINAL DOUGH			
BREAD FLOUR	67.1%	3 lb 5¾ oz	1.52 kg
INSTANT DRY YEAST	0.3%	¼ oz	7 g
WATER	56.6%	45¼ fl oz	1.36 L
BIGA (above)	50%	2 lb 7¼ oz	1.11 kg
SALT	2.3%	2 oz	57 g

1. To prepare the biga, combine the flour, water, and yeast. Mix on low speed for 3 minutes, or until thoroughly combined. Transfer to a container, cover, and ferment at 75°F/24°C for 18 to 24 hours, until the biga has risen and begun to recede; it should still be bubbly and airy.

2. To prepare the final dough, combine the flour and yeast. Add the water, biga, and salt. Mix on low speed for 4 minutes and on medium speed for 1 minute. The dough should be blended but not too elastic (ciabatta dough is a wet, slack dough).

3. Bulk ferment the dough in a tub or bowl until nearly doubled, about 30 minutes. Fold gently in half four times (the dough should feel like jelly). Ferment for another 30 minutes. Fold in half again, gently, two times. Allow the dough to ferment for another 15 minutes before dividing.

4. See page 213 for shaping, proofing, and baking options suitable for this dough.

Pouring ciabatta dough out of a tub

Working with Wet Doughs

The gluten development of any dough is a very important aspect of the bread-making process. After proper mixing, a wet or slack dough is still very loose compared to a basic lean dough. It should be transferred to a tub or bucket for bulk fermentation. The dough is left to rise, then folded. For wet doughs, the folding step is crucial if the dough is to develop a good structure. Gently stretching the dough as you fold strengthens the gluten enough to create a good texture and crumb.

Wet doughs are likely to collapse. They should be handled as little and as gently as possible after bulk fermentation and during scaling and shaping to retain their structure. They are often shaped into free-form or relatively flat loaves that are simply scaled and stretched (see page 213 for more about shaping ciabatta). Wet doughs do not require slashing or scoring before baking.

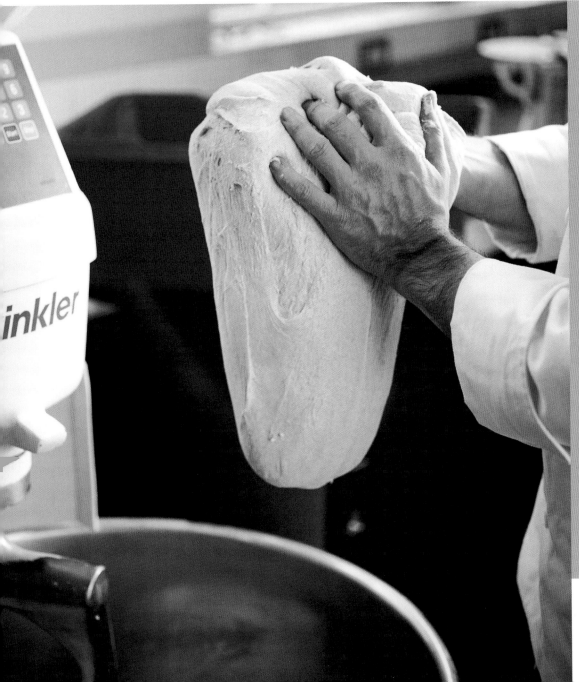

Use care when handling soft, wet doughs.

Focaccia Dough

Makes 11 lb 6¼ oz/5.17 kg dough DDT: 75°F/24°C

BIGA			
BREAD FLOUR	100%	1 lb 8 oz	680 g
WATER (60°F/16°C)	55.2%	13¼ fl oz	398 mL
INSTANT DRY YEAST	0.03%	pinch	pinch
FINAL DOUGH			
BREAD FLOUR	76.9%	5 lb	2.27 kg
INSTANT DRY YEAST	0.5%	½ oz	14 g
WATER	53.8%	56 fl oz	1.68 L
BIGA (above)	35.8%	2 lb 5¼ oz	1.06 kg
OLIVE OIL	6.25%	6½ oz	184 g
SALT	1.9%	2 oz	57 g

1. To prepare the biga, combine the flour, water, and yeast. Mix on low speed for 3 minutes, or until thoroughly combined. Transfer to a container, cover, and ferment at 75°F/24°C for about 8 hours, until the biga has risen and begun to recede; it should still be slightly bubbly and airy.

2. To prepare the final dough, combine the flour and yeast. Add the water, biga, and olive oil and mix on low speed for 4 minutes. Add the salt and mix on medium speed for 30 seconds. The dough should be very loose.

3. Bulk ferment the dough until nearly doubled, about 45 minutes. Fold gently. Allow the dough to ferment for another 45 minutes before dividing.

4. See page 214 for shaping, proofing, and baking options suitable for this dough.

White Wheat Sourdough

Makes 15 lb 4 oz/6.92 kg dough   *DDT: 79°F/26°C*

BREAD FLOUR	92.8%	6 lb 10½ oz	3.02 kg
WATER	68%	78 fl oz	2.34 L
WHEAT SOURDOUGH STARTER (page 168)	41.8%	3 lb	1.36 kg
ORGANIC WHOLE WHEAT FLOUR	7.2%	8¼ oz	234 g
SALT	2.8%	3¼ oz	92 g

1. Combine the flour, water, and sourdough and mix on low speed for 4 minutes. Allow the dough to rest for 15 minutes. Add the salt and mix on medium speed for 2 minutes. The dough should be slightly soft but elastic.

2. Bulk ferment the dough until nearly doubled, about 1 hour. Fold gently and ferment for another hour. Fold again. Allow the dough to ferment for another 20 minutes before dividing.

3. See page 198 for shaping, proofing, and baking options suitable for this dough.

Sourdough Starters

Sourdough starters add flavor to breads, and in some formulas that may be their primary function. But sourdough is a true leavener. Although it is time-consuming to prepare and maintain a sourdough starter to be used as a primary leavener, breads made with sourdough have a deep, complex flavor and a good texture. A sourdough is acidic enough to enhance the shelf life of breads and rolls. A strong, vigorous sourdough can be maintained indefinitely with proper feedings.

Each sourdough has its own characteristics, dependent upon both the ingredients selected and the type of wild yeasts in any given environment. Both wheat and rye flours are used in sourdough starters. Wheat flours generate lactic acid; rye develops acetic acid. These acids influence the flavor of the finished bread. Organic flours are easiest to use for starters since they are minimally processed and do not contain the additives found in nonorganic flours.

The initial stage of establishing a sourdough calls for mixing flour and water. The dough is then left to rest. As it rests, it attracts the ambient yeasts in the air. Grapes, potatoes, onions, and apples contain a high percentage of the natural yeasts desirable for creating a starter. Adding them to the flour and water mixture will speed the process of creating a starter. When the yeast starts to feed, grow, and reproduce in the mixture, it ferments the dough, making it bubbly and airy and giving it a tangy or sour aroma. The dough will expand to double its original volume, start to fall when the yeast activity peaks, and then begin to decline as the yeast consumes the food source.

Left unattended, the yeast will die. To keep the starter alive, or to maintain or build up an established starter, it should be given additional feedings of flour and water. These feedings should be done on a fairly regular schedule, usually once a day. It is important that the ratio of flour to water used for feeding is the same one used to establish the sour. New starters benefit from at least three and up to five feedings prior to their first use.

Once a starter is established it should be replenished once or more daily until the desired amount is achieved. After it is built up it should be replenished to maintain a par level. The starter can be replenished after it has risen and begins to fall. This is the signal that the culture has digested enough nutrients, in turn causing the collapse of the mixture. Replenishing at least three to five times is usually sufficient. The amount of replenishing can vary as long as the temperature and flour to water ratio is correct.

When a balanced, vigorous culture is established, it will provide leavening and flavor to bread and the presence of organic acids from the sourdough and the higher acidity of the bread will give it a better shelf life. Another benefit of a well-balanced and well-maintained culture is that it can be maintained indefinitely.

A sourdough starter that has been stored under refrigeration needs to come to room temperature before it can be used in a bread formula. To replenish a starter, use the following procedure: Remove the starter from refrigeration and let it rest at 75°F/24°C for 6 to 8 hours. Then feed it with a mixture of flour and water; add as much of this mixture as necessary to produce the amount of starter required for your formula. Wheat starters should be fed with a mixture of flour and water that is at 66 percent hydration; for example, for every 1 lb/454 g of flour you add to the starter, add about 10½ oz/315 mL of water. Rye starters should be fed with a mixture that is at 100 percent hydration; add equal amounts of rye flour and water (by weight) to the starter. Feed the starter once more on the following day at the same hydration level and allow it to ferment for 4 hours at 75°F/24°C before using it in a bread formula. Sourdough starters that are held under refrigeration and not used frequently must be fed at least every 3 weeks if they are to remain active.

Wheat or Durum Sourdough Starter

Makes 1 lb 8 oz/680 g starter

INITIAL SOUR (DAYS 1 AND 2)			
WATER (80°F/27°C)	100%	4 fl oz	120 mL
ORGANIC WHEAT OR DURUM FLOUR	100%	4 oz	113 g
FIRST FEEDING (DAY 3)			
INITIAL SOUR (above)	100%	4 oz	113 g
WATER (80°F/27°C)	100%	4 fl oz	120 mL
ORGANIC WHEAT OR DURUM FLOUR	100%	4 oz	113 g
SECOND FEEDING (DAY 4)			
SOUR AFTER FIRST FEEDING (above)	200%	8 oz	227 g
WATER (80°F/27°C)	100%	4 fl oz	120 mL
ORGANIC WHEAT OR DURUM FLOUR	100%	4 oz	113 g
THIRD FEEDING (DAY 5)			
SOUR AFTER SECOND FEEDING (above)	33%	4 oz	113 g
WATER (60°F/16°C)	66%	8 fl oz	240 mL
ORGANIC WHEAT OR DURUM FLOUR	100%	12 oz	340 g

1. Mix the ingredients for the initial sour. Cover and let rest at room temperature for 24 hours. The flour and water tend to separate overnight; recombine on the second day. Let rest for another 24 hours at 75°F/24°C.

2. On the third day, combine 4 oz/113 g of the initial sour mixture with the water for the first feeding and blend to fully combine; discard excess sour. Blend in the flour for the first feeding. Cover and let rest at 75°F/24°C for 24 hours.

3. On the fourth day, combine 8 oz/227 g of the sour mixture from Step 2 with the water for the second feeding and blend to fully combine; discard excess sour. Blend in the flour for the second feeding. Cover and let rest at 75°F/24°C for 24 hours.

4. On the final day, combine 4 oz/113 g of the sour from Step 3 with the water for the third feeding and blend to fully combine; discard excess sour. Blend in the flour for the third feeding. Let the starter rest covered at 75°F/24°C for 4 hours before using in a bread formula.

Rye Sourdough Starter

Makes 19.5 oz/553 g starter

INITIAL SOUR (DAYS 1 AND 2)			
WATER (80°F/27°C)	100%	4 fl oz	120 mL
ORGANIC RYE	100%	4 oz	113 g
FIRST FEEDING (DAY 3)			
INITIAL SOUR (above)	100%	4 oz	113 g
WATER (80°F/27°C)	100%	4 fl oz	120 mL
ORGANIC RYE	100%	4 oz	113 g
SECOND FEEDING (DAY 4)			
SOUR AFTER FIRST FEEDING (above)	200%	8 oz	227 g
WATER (80°F/27°C)	100%	4 fl oz	120 mL
ORGANIC RYE	100%	4 oz	113 g
THIRD FEEDING (DAY 5)			
SOUR AFTER SECOND FEEDING (above)	33%	4 oz	113 g
WATER (60°F/16°C)	66%	8 fl oz	240 mL
ORGANIC RYE	100%	8 oz	227 g

Follow the method used for Wheat or Durum Sourdough Starter on page 168. Note the different hydration level for the Rye Sourdough Starter.

Whole Wheat Sourdough

Makes 16 lb 5¼ oz/7.41 kg dough   DDT: 76°F/24°C

BREAD FLOUR	50%	3 lb 12 oz	1.70 kg
WHOLE WHEAT FLOUR	50%	3 lb 12 oz	1.70 kg
WATER	75%	90 fl oz	2.70 L
WHEAT SOURDOUGH STARTER (page 168)	40%	3 lb	1.36 kg
SALT	2.7%	3¼ oz	92 g

1. Combine the flours, water, and sourdough and mix on low speed for 4 minutes. Allow the dough to rest for 15 minutes. Add the salt and mix on medium speed for 2 minutes. The dough should be slightly soft but elastic.

2. Bulk ferment the dough until nearly doubled, about 1 hour. Fold gently and ferment for another hour. Fold again. Allow the dough to ferment for another 20 minutes before dividing.

3. See page 198 for shaping, proofing and baking options suitable for this dough.

Walnut Fig Dough

Makes 7 lb 8 oz/3.40 kg dough   DDT: 75°F/24°C

WHOLE WHEAT LEAN DOUGH (page 130)	80%	6 lb	2.72 kg
WALNUTS, toasted and chopped	8.3%	10 oz	284 g
FIGS, coarsely chopped	8.3%	10 oz	284 g
HONEY	3.3%	4 oz	113 g

1. Combine the walnuts, figs, and honey. Fold the mixture into the dough halfway through bulk fermentation time.

2. Ferment the dough until nearly doubled, about 30 minutes, and fold gently. After another 30 minutes, fold again. Allow the dough to ferment for another 15 minutes before dividing.

3. See page 198 for shaping, proofing, and baking options suitable for this dough.

Adding Flavorings and Garnishes

Fresh herbs, roasted garlic, ground or whole spices, grated cheeses, dried fruits, and nuts are some of the ingredients added to bread doughs for flavor or as a garnish. Formulas calling for salty or acidic ingredients may require modification so that these ingredients do not interfere dramatically with yeast activity or the desired flavor for that bread. Finely ground or dry ingredients may be added at the beginning of the mixing time. In other cases, it may be easier to work a garnish into the dough halfway through bulk fermentation time. The dough can be put back in the mixer and the garnish mixed in on low speed just until evenly blended, or the garnish may be folded by hand into the dough.

Generally the folding method is best for hard ingredients, such as nuts, that can damage the gluten strands, or for soft ingredients, such as olives, that you do not want to break.

Spread or flatten the dough on a lightly floured work surface. Sprinkle the garnish ingredients evenly over the dough and fold it over gently. Continue to fold until the garnish ingredients are evenly distributed throughout the dough.

Adding a garnish to a dough by folding it in

Variations

Roasted Garlic Lean Dough:

For every 3 lb 4¾ oz/1.50 kg flour or 5 lb 9¾ oz/ 2.54 kg dough, add 2 oz/57 g roasted garlic. This is 3.8% garlic added.

Herb Lean Dough:

For every 1 lb/454 g flour or 1 lb 11¼ oz/773 g dough, add 21 rosemary needles, 1 sprig thyme (picked) and 1 sprig oregano (picked).

Olives:

For every 3 lb 4¾ oz/1.50 kg flour or 5 lb 9¾ oz/2.54 kg dough, add 8 oz/227 g rinsed and drained olives. (This is 15% olives added.) Rinsing the olives reduces their salt content, to keep the salt and water levels in the dough in balance; drain well before adding to the dough.

Apple and Walnut Sourdough

Makes 15 lb 13¾ oz/7.19 kg dough   DDT: 77°F/25°C

BREAD FLOUR	83.1%	6 lb 5 oz	2.86 kg
WHOLE WHEAT FLOUR	16.9%	14 oz	397 g
WATER	84.3%	70 fl oz	2.10 L
WHEAT SOURDOUGH STARTER (page 168)	49.4%	2 lb 9 oz	1.16 kg
SALT	3.3%	2¾ oz	78 g
GRANNY SMITH APPLES, coarsely chopped	14.5%	12 oz	340 g
WALNUTS, lightly toasted and coarsely chopped	14.5%	12 oz	340 g
GROUND CINNAMON	1.2%	1 oz	28 g

1. Combine the flours, water, and sourdough and mix on low speed for 4 minutes. Allow the dough to rest for 15 minutes. Add the salt and mix on medium speed for 3 minutes. The dough should be slightly soft but elastic.

2. Bulk ferment the dough until nearly doubled, about 1 hour. Fold gently and ferment for another hour. Fold again. Allow the dough to ferment for another 20 minutes before folding in the apples and walnuts (see Adding Flavorings and Garnishes, page 171).

3. See page 198 for shaping, proofing, and baking options suitable for this dough.

Sourdough with Rye Flour

Makes 15 lb 9¾ oz/7.08 kg dough   DDT: 76°F/24°C

BREAD FLOUR	60%	4 lb 8 oz	2.04 kg
MEDIUM RYE FLOUR	40%	3 lb	1.36 kg
WATER	65%	78½ fl oz	2.36 L
WHEAT SOURDOUGH STARTER (page 168)	40%	3 lb	1.36 kg
SALT	2.7%	3¼ oz	92 g

1. Combine the flours, water, and sourdough and mix on low speed for 3 minutes. Allow the dough to rest for 15 minutes. Add the salt and mix on medium speed for 3 minutes, or until the dough is slightly soft but elastic.

2. Bulk ferment the dough until nearly doubled, about 1 hour. Fold gently and ferment for another hour. Fold again. Allow the dough to ferment for another 20 minutes.

3. See page 198 for shaping, proofing, and baking options suitable for this dough.

Multigrain Sourdough

Makes 12 lb 5 oz/5.58 kg dough   DDT: 75°F/24°C

SOAKER			
9-GRAIN CEREAL	30.33%	1 lb	454 g
SUNFLOWER SEEDS	12.32%	6½ oz	184 g
OATS	12.32%	6½ oz	184 g
WATER	60.66%	32 fl oz	960 mL
FINAL DOUGH			
BREAD FLOUR	100%	3 lb 5 oz	1.50 kg
INSTANT DRY YEAST	1.23%	¼ oz	7 g
WATER	45.5%	24 fl oz	720 mL
PÂTE FERMENTÉE (page 149)	75.83%	2 lb 8 oz	1.13 kg
WHEAT SOURDOUGH STARTER (page 168)	30.33%	1 lb	454 g
MOLASSES	2.37%	1¼ oz	35 g
SOAKER (above)	115%	3 lb 13 oz	1.73 kg
SALT	2.84%	1½ oz	43 g

1. To prepare the soaker, combine the 9-grain cereal mix, sunflower seeds, and oats with the water in a plastic tub and cover. Soak at room temperature until the soaker has absorbed the water and is slightly dry, 8 to 12 hours.

2. To prepare the final dough, combine the flour and yeast. Add the water, pâte fermentée, sourdough, molasses, soaker, and salt and mix on low speed for 4 minutes. Allow the dough to rest for 15 minutes. Add the salt and mix on medium speed for 3 minutes, or until the dough is slightly stiff.

3. Bulk ferment the dough until nearly doubled, about 30 minutes. Fold gently and ferment for another 30 minutes. Fold again. Allow the dough to ferment for another 30 minutes before dividing.

4. See page 186 for shaping, proofing, and baking options suitable for this dough.

Chocolate Cherry Sourdough

Makes 19 lb 6½ oz/8.80 kg dough   DDT: 75°F/24°C

ESPRESSO GRANULES, not instant	5.3%	4¼ oz	120 g
WATER	81.25%	65 fl oz	1.95 L
WHEAT SOURDOUGH STARTER (page 168)	63.2%	3 lb 2½ oz	1.43 kg
PÂTE FERMENTÉE (page 149)	40%	2 lb	907 g
BREAD FLOUR	100%	5 lb	2.27 kg
COCOA POWDER	10.6%	8½ oz	241 g
INSTANT DRY YEAST	0.95%	¾ oz	21 g
SALT	3.2%	2½ oz	71 g
CHOCOLATE CHUNKS	41.9%	2 lb 1½ oz	950 g
DRIED CHERRIES	41.9%	2 lb 1½ oz	950 g

1. Line a fine strainer with cheesecloth and place the espresso ground beans in it. Pour 26½ fl oz/795 mL boiling water over the espresso granules. Cool to room temperature.

2. Combine the cooled espresso, the remaining water, the sourdough, and pâte fermentée and mix on low speed just until blended, about 1 minute. Add the flour, cocoa powder, yeast, and salt and mix on low speed for 4 minutes and then on medium speed for 3 minutes. Add the chocolate chunks and dried cherries and mix on low speed until well combined, about 1 minute. The dough should be slightly loose.

3. Bulk ferment the dough until nearly doubled, about 45 minutes. Fold gently. Allow the dough to ferment for another 45 minutes before dividing.

4. See page 186 for shaping, proofing, and baking options suitable for this dough.

Durum Sourdough

Makes 22 lb ½ oz/9.99 kg dough   DDT: 75°F/24°C

DURUM FLOUR	50%	5 lb	2.27 kg
BREAD FLOUR	50%	5 lb	2.27 kg
INSTANT DRY YEAST	0.32%	½ oz	14 g
WATER	82.5%	132 fl oz	3.96 L
DURUM SOURDOUGH STARTER (page 168)	35%	3 lb 8 oz	1.59 kg
SALT	2.5%	4 oz	113 g

1. Combine the flours and yeast. Add the water and sourdough and mix on low speed for 4 minutes. Allow the dough to rest for 15 minutes. Add the salt and mix on low speed for 4 minutes. The dough should be fairly loose.

2. Bulk ferment the dough until nearly doubled, about 2 hours, folding the dough gently every 30 minutes, for a total of three folds.

3. See page 186 for shaping, proofing, and baking options suitable for this dough.

Rustic Rye Sourdough

Makes 12 lb 4 oz/5.556 kg dough   DDT: 78°F/26°C

MEDIUM RYE FLOUR	56.25%	2 lb 13 oz	1.28 kg
BREAD FLOUR	43.75%	2 lb 3 oz	992 g
INSTANT DRY YEAST	0.63%	½ oz	14 g
WATER	75%	60 fl oz	1.80 L
RYE SOURDOUGH STARTER (page 169)	41.9%	2 lb 1½ oz	950 g
SUNFLOWER SEEDS, lightly toasted	25%	1 lb 4 oz	567 g
SALT	2.5%	2 oz	57 g

1. Combine the flours and yeast. Add the water and sourdough and mix on low speed for 4 minutes. Allow the dough to rest for 15 minutes. Add the sunflower seeds and salt and mix on medium speed for 3 minutes. The dough should be slightly wet but elastic.

2. Bulk ferment the dough until nearly doubled, about 1 hour. Fold gently and ferment for another hour. Fold again. Allow the dough to ferment for another 30 minutes before dividing.

3. See page 198 for shaping, proofing, and baking options suitable for this dough.

Multigrain Rye Sourdough

Makes 15 lb/6.80 kg dough   DDT: 79°F/26°C

SOAKER			
9-GRAIN MIXTURE	21.5%	18¾ fl oz	563 mL
FLAXSEEDS	13.8%	12 oz	340 g
SUNFLOWER SEEDS	7.8%	7 oz	198 g
WATER (90°F/32°C)	56.9%	49½ fl oz	1.49 L
FINAL DOUGH			
BREAD FLOUR	61.6%	3 lb 2½ oz	1.43 kg
MEDIUM RYE FLOUR	38.4%	1 lb 15½ oz	893 g
INSTANT DRY YEAST	1.2%	1 oz	28 g
RYE SOURDOUGH STARTER (page 169)	42.5%	2 lb 5 oz	1.05 kg
WATER	36.9%	30¼ fl oz	908 mL
SOAKER (ABOVE)	106%	5 lb 7 oz	2.47 kg
SALT	3.4%	2¾ oz	78 g

1. To prepare the soaker, combine the 9-grain mixture, flaxseeds, and sunflower seeds with the water in a plastic tub. Soak at room temperature until the soaker has absorbed the water and is slightly dry, 8 to 12 hours.

2. To prepare the final dough, combine all ingredients. Mix on low speed for 4 minutes. Mix on medium speed for 30 seconds.

3. Bulk ferment the dough until nearly doubled, about 30 minutes. Divide.

4. See page 198 for shaping, proofing, and baking options suitable for this dough.

Whole-Grain Carrot Dough

Makes 13 lb 13¾ oz/6.29 kg dough   DDT: 80°F/27°C

SOAKER			
9-GRAIN MIXTURE	46.3%	2 lb 12 oz	1.25 kg
ROLLED OATS	7.4%	9 oz	255 g
WATER	46.3%	44 fl oz	1.32 L
FINAL DOUGH			
HIGH-GLUTEN FLOUR	52.6%	2 lb 3¼ oz	999 g
MEDIUM RYE FLOUR	47.4%	1 lb 15¾ oz	900 g
INSTANT DRY YEAST	1.5%	1 oz	28 g
RYE SOURDOUGH STARTER (page 169)	63%	2 lb 10¼ oz	1.20 kg
WATER	47.7%	32 fl oz	960 mL
SOAKER (above)	144.7%	6 lb 1 oz	2.75 kg
PUMPKIN SEEDS, lightly toasted	10.5%	7 oz	198 g
CARROTS, grated	6.7%	4½ oz	128 g
SALT	3%	2 oz	57 g
MALT SYRUP	1.5%	1 oz	28 g

1. To prepare the soaker, combine the 9-grain mixture and rolled oats with the water in a plastic tub. Soak under refrigeration until the soaker has absorbed the water and is slightly dry, 8 to 12 hours.

2. To prepare the final dough, combine the flours and yeast. Add the sourdough and water and mix on low speed for 4 minutes. Allow the dough to rest for 15 minutes. Add the soaker, pumpkin seeds, carrots, salt, and malt and mix on medium speed for 3 minutes. The dough should be slightly sticky but have sufficient gluten development.

3. Bulk ferment the dough until nearly doubled, about 30 minutes.

4. See page 198 for shaping, proofing, and baking options suitable for this dough.

100% Rye Dough

Makes 10 lb 14 oz/4.93 kg dough   DDT: 80°F/27°C

MEDIUM RYE FLOUR	100%	3 lb 13¾ oz	1.75 kg
INSTANT DRY YEAST	0.8%	½ oz	14 g
RYE SOURDOUGH STARTER (page 169)	92.7%	3 lb 9¼ oz	1.62 kg
WATER	85.4%	52¾ fl oz	1.58 L
SALT	2.8%	1¾ oz	50 g

1. Combine the flour and yeast. Add the sourdough, water, and salt and mix on low speed for 5 to 6 minutes. The dough should be loose and clay-like, with no elasticity or gluten development.

2. Bulk ferment the dough until nearly doubled, 55 to 60 minutes.

3. See page 222 for shaping, proofing, and baking options suitable for this dough.

Vollkornbrot (European Pumpernickel) Dough

Makes 19 lb 8 oz/8.85 kg dough   DDT: 80°F/27°C

CRACKED RYE SOURDOUGH STARTER			
RYE SOURDOUGH STARTER (page 169)	10%	6½ oz	184 g
STEEL-CUT CRACKED RYE	100%	3 lb 13¾ oz	1.75 kg
WATER	100%	61¾ fl oz	1.85 L
SOAKER			
STEEL-CUT CRACKED RYE	52.75%	1 lb 10½ oz	751 g
WATER, boiling	47.25%	23¾ fl oz	713 mL
FINAL DOUGH			
CRACKED RYE SOURDOUGH STARTER (above)	162.2%	8 lb 1¾ oz	3.68 kg
INSTANT DRY YEAST	1.25%	1 oz	28 g
STEEL-CUT CRACKED RYE	100%	5 lb	2.27 kg
SOAKER (above)	62.8%	3 lb 2¼ oz	1.42 kg
WATER	60%	48 fl oz	1.44 L
SALT	3.75%	3 oz	85 g

1. To prepare the cracked rye sourdough starter, mix the rye sourdough starter, cracked rye, and water in a plastic tub. Cover and ferment for 18 to 20 hours at 75°F/24°C; the starter should be bubbly and have a light alcohol aroma.

2. To prepare the soaker, combine the cracked rye with the water in a plastic tub. Soak at room temperature until the rye has absorbed the water and is slightly dry, 8 to 12 hours.

3. To prepare the final dough, combine the cracked rye sourdough starter, yeast, cracked rye, soaker, water, and salt. Mix on low speed for 8 minutes and on medium speed for 5 minutes. The dough should be very loose and very sticky.

4. Bulk ferment the dough in the mixing bowl until nearly doubled, 45 to 50 minutes.

5. After the dough has fermented, mix on low speed for 15 seconds to expel the carbon dioxide that has built up.

6. See page 224 for shaping, proofing, and baking options suitable for this dough.

CHAPTER 7

Yeast-Raised Breads and Rolls

THE STAGES AFTER MIXING AND BULK FERMENTATION (SHAPING AND BAKING AS WELL AS HANDLING, COOLING, AND STORAGE) ALSO HAVE A GREAT DEAL TO DO WITH THE QUALITY OF YEAST-RAISED BREADS, ROLLS, AND CAKES. BREAD DOUGHS CAN BE GIVEN A VARIETY OF SHAPES, RANGING FROM SIMPLE BOULES AND ROUND ROLLS TO INTRICATELY BRAIDED LOAVES. PROOFING THE DOUGH AFTER IT HAS BEEN SHAPED GIVES IT ADDITIONAL TIME TO DEVELOP. SIMPLE RUSTIC SHAPES, SUCH AS BAGUETTES AND BATARDS, ARE OFTEN USED FOR LEAN DOUGHS. ENRICHED DOUGHS ARE SOFT ENOUGH TO TWIST AND BRAID.

Boule

Makes 1 loaf   DDT: 75°F/24°C

WHITE WHEAT LEAN DOUGH (page 123)	1 lb	454 g

1. Preshape the dough into a round piece (for preshaping instructions see page 189). Let the dough rest, covered, until relaxed, 15 to 20 minutes. (Note: When making multiple loaves, work sequentially, starting with the first piece of dough you divided and rounded.)

2. Cup both hands around the dough. Using your thumbs, push the dough away from you in an arc to the right, keeping a small piece of dough between the table and the edges of your palms. Using the edges of your palms as a guide, pull the dough toward you in an arc to the left. There should still be a small piece of dough that is squeezed between the table and the edges of your palms. Repeat this circular motion two or three more times, applying gentle pressure while rounding the dough, to create a tight, smooth outer skin. Place the boule seam side up in a round basket or on a board dusted with cornmeal seam side down.

3. Proof until the dough springs back slowly to the touch, 1 to 1½ hours. Flip the dough seam side down onto a peel. Score the boule with an arc.

4. Presteam a 460°F/238°C deck oven. Load the bread into the oven and steam for 3 seconds. Bake until the crust is golden brown and the bread sounds hollow when thumped on the bottom, 25 to 30 minutes. Vent during the final 10 minutes of baking. Cool completely on a rack.

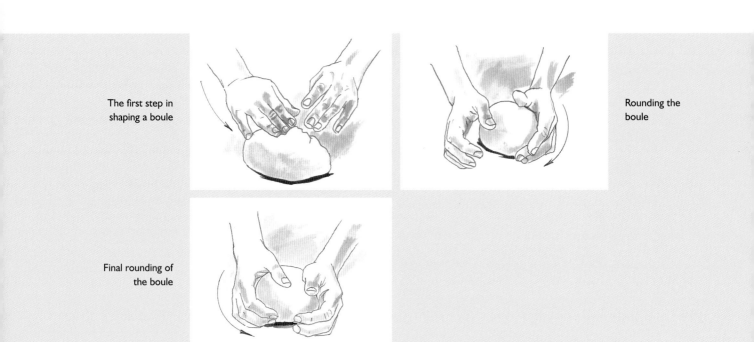

The first step in shaping a boule

Rounding the boule

Final rounding of the boule

Scaling and Preshaping

Accurate scaling guarantees the correct weight of the dough pieces when dividing. However, scaling should be done quickly, so as not to overage the dough. Scaling time should not exceed 15 to 20 minutes. Proper scaling will also allow for uniformity in proofing and baking times. Dough is usually divided either entirely by hand, using a scale, or first divided into large portions by hand and then divided into smaller pieces with a dough divider.

After scaling, the dough is given a gentle first shaping, or "preshaping." Always lay the shaped pieces on the bench in the order they are shaped, in regular rows, so that you can start with the first piece when giving the dough the final shaping. The objective of preshaping is to get a smooth, tight skin that will help to trap the gases that develop during fermentation.

During scaling and preshaping, two things happen to the dough: First, because it is cut, the carbon dioxide trapped inside begins to escape, which causes the structure of the dough to begin to collapse; and second, the gluten strands are worked, which causes them to contract, making the dough tighter and tougher to work with.

For Large Rounds *(from 6 oz to 4½ lb/170 g to 2.04 kg)*:

1. Position the dough so one long edge is parallel to the edge of the work surface.

2. Fold the top edge of the dough down to the bottom edge. Using the heel of your hand, seal the two edges together. Rotate the dough 90 degrees.

3. Fold the top edge of the dough down to the bottom edge. Using the heel of your hand, seal the two edges together.

4. Cup both hands around the dough and pull it toward you until the seam is on the bottom.

For Small Rounds *(from 2 to 6 oz/57 to 170 g)*:

1. Position the dough so one long edge is parallel to the edge of the work surface.

2. Fold the top edge of the dough down to the bottom edge. Using the heel of your hand, seal the two edges together. Rotate the dough 90 degrees.

3. Fold the top edge of the dough down to the bottom edge. Using the heel of your hand, seal the two edges together.

4. Place your hand over the ball of dough and curl your fingers so that the first knuckles of your fingers are touching the table. Your fingertips should almost be touching the palm of your hand, and your thumb should be out to the side and touching the table; the heel of your hand should also be touching the table. The dough should be sitting near the top of your palm, near your thumb, forefinger, and middle finger.

5. Using your palm, push the dough away from you in an arc to the right. Using your fingertips, pull the dough toward you in an arc to the left. Repeat this circular motion, applying gentle pressure while rounding the dough, to create a tight, smooth ball.

For Large Oblongs *(from 12 oz to 1¾ lb/340 to 794 g)*:

1. Position the dough so one long edge is parallel to the edge of the work surface.
2. Stretch the dough into a rectangle 10 in/25 cm long. Fold the left and right edges of the rectangle into the center of the dough, pressing the dough lightly with your fingertips.

3. Fold the top edge of the dough down to the center of the dough, pressing lightly with your fingertips. Fold the top of the dough down to the bottom edge. Seal the two edges together, using the heel of your hand.

4. Roll the dough into an even cylinder 6 in/15 cm long.

After dough is preshaped into rounds or oblongs, it is ready to rest; this period is known as resting or intermediate fermentation. Covering the dough prevents a crust from forming.

For Small Oblongs *(from 3 to 6 oz/85 to 170 g)*:

1. Turn the dough so one long edge is parallel to the edge of the work surface.

2. Stretch the dough into a rectangle 3 in/8 cm long. Fold the left and right edges of the rectangle into the center of the dough, pressing the dough lightly with your fingertips.

3. Fold the top edge of the dough down to the center of the dough, pressing lightly with your fingertips. Fold the top of the dough down to the bottom edge. Seal the two edges together, using the heel of your hand.

4. Roll the dough into an even cylinder 3 in/8 cm long.

DOUGH NAME	DIVIDING WEIGHT	GARNISH	APPROXIMATE PROOFING TIME
CHEDDAR AND ONION RYE BREAD (page 138)	1 lb 8 oz/680 g	N/A	1 hour 10 minutes
CHOCOLATE CHERRY SOURDOUGH (page 174)	1 lb 8 oz/680 g	N/A	45 minutes to 1 hour
CRESCIA AL FORMAGGIO (page 143)	1 lb/454 g	N/A	50 to 65 minutes
DURUM ROSEMARY BREAD (page 132)	1 lb 6 oz/624 g	N/A	55 minutes
DURUM SOURDOUGH (page 175)	2 lb 6 oz/1.08 kg	Top rolled in durum flour	1 to 1½ hours
MULTIGRAIN SOURDOUGH (page 173)	1 lb 4 oz/567 g	N/A	35 to 45 minutes
PANETTONE (page 152)	1 lb 4 oz/567 g	Do not egg wash	1 hour 40 minutes (in greased paper wrapper)
PROSCIUTTO AND PROVOLONE BREAD (page 138)	1 lb 4 oz/567 g	N/A	1½ hours (¾ proof)
RUSTIC RAISIN BREAD (page 139)	1 lb 8 oz/680 g	N/A	1½ hours
SUNFLOWER SEED BREAD (page 136)	1 lb 8 oz/680 g	Top with sunflower seeds	1 hour
TOMATO BREAD (page 157)	1 lb 4 oz/567 g	N/A	45 minutes

Resting or Intermediate Fermentation

Bulk fermentation is the first fermentation the dough undergoes. After dividing and preshaping, the dough is allowed to ferment again. This period has various names: bench rest, table rest, or secondary or intermediate fermentation. This stage allows the dough to relax and recover from the dividing and preshaping process in preparation for final shaping; it allows the gluten to relax, so the dough will become somewhat slack and easier to manipulate into its final shape, and it allows the yeast cells to recover, rebuilding the carbon dioxide and therefore the internal structure of the dough. Normally this stage lasts from 10 to 20 minutes. It is important to keep the loaves covered with plastic wrap or a linen cloth to prevent the formation of a skin or dry crust.

SCORING	STEAMING	BAKING TEMPERATURE/ TIME	VENTING TIME (before end of bake)
3 parallel horizontal lines	Presteam/ steam 3 seconds	425°F/218°C/35 minutes	5 minutes
An X	Presteam/ steam 3 seconds	400°F/204°C/30 minutes	10 minutes
An X	Presteam/ steam 3 seconds	385°F/196°C/25 to 35 minutes	10 minutes
A slash down the center	Presteam/ steam 4 to 5 seconds	465°F/241°C/30 minutes	10 minutes
Stalk of wheat pattern	Presteam/ steam 3 seconds	450°F/232°C/45 to 50 minutes	25 minutes
Arc	Presteam/ steam 3 seconds	435°F/224°C/45 to 50 minutes	15 minutes
An X (insert a pat of butter inside of X)	Presteam/ steam 3 seconds	350°F/177°C/35 minutes	N/A
An X	Presteam/ steam 3 seconds	435°F/224°C/35 minutes	5 minutes
4 parallel horizontal lines	Presteam/ steam 3 seconds	400°F/204°C/40 minutes	10 minutes
Square	Presteam/ steam 3 seconds	450°F/232°C/40 minutes	10 minutes
Spiral	Presteam/ steam 3 seconds	435°F/224°C/45 to 50 minutes	10 minutes

Final Shaping

After the secondary fermentation, the dough is given its final shape. A boule is re-shaped using the same method as for preshaping. The various formulas in this chapter illustrate the most common shaping techniques used for lean and enriched yeast doughs. Brush the dough with egg wash or water, if using, after it is shaped so that the dough can be evenly coated without affecting it after its final rise (see also Washes, page 189). Any simple garnishes such as seeds or coarse salt can be applied once the crust is brushed with egg wash or water; the wash will hold them in place.

Final Fermentation (Proofing)

After shaping, the dough undergoes one more fermentation. Some doughs, such as the lean dough used to prepare boules, can simply be placed on a worktable or a board that has been dusted with flour or cornmeal. Other doughs or shapes may be placed on a linen cloth (couche) or sheet pans, in loaf pans, or in baskets (bannetons), wooden molds, or other molds. During this final rise, it is again important to ensure that a skin does not form on the surface of the dough. If you are not using a proof box for this final proof, the dough should be covered. Using the temperature and humidity controls in a proof box will prevent this from happening without the dough being covered.

A temperature- and humidity-controlled proof box can provide the necessary relative humidity of approximately 80 percent so the surface of the dough does not dry out. (Conversely, if the humidity is too high, the loaves will become too sticky for proper crust formation.) The ambient temperature for the final proof should be from 90° to 100°F/32° to 38°C for maximum yeast activity; the ideal temperature is 98°F/37°C. If the temperature during this final proof is too high, insufficient yeast activity will result in poor grain and loss of flavor, and the shelf life of the bread will be shorter. A temperature that is too low will result in a longer proofing time.

Small items, such as rolls, must be allowed to fully ferment during final proofing because they bake quickly, leaving less time for fermentation in the ovens. Large items, such as loaves, should be proofed to a slightly less developed state than small items, as they require longer baking times and will continue to ferment (or proof) for a longer time in the oven. Lean doughs should be proofed less than enriched doughs, as they will develop a crust quickly in the oven that will stop their expansion, while the fat in enriched doughs will prevent crust formation, allowing for more expansion in the oven.

Finishing Techniques

SCORING

Many breads are scored with a razor, sharp knife, scissors, or *lame* before loading them into the oven. Scoring helps develop a good-quality loaf with an even appearance and crumb. It allows the bread to release steam and continue to expand until the structure is set. By scoring the dough, the baker can control the final shape of the bread by determining where the product expands during baking. Baking an unscored bread results in an unevenly shaped loaf. The crust forms too early to permit full expansion and, consequently, the full development of the internal structure of the loaf.

Some breads, such as baguettes, are scored with traditional scoring patterns that are used as a way to label the breads, making it easy for both clients and staff to identify them.

WASHES

Water is often brushed or sprayed on shaped breads before baking to ensure a crispy crust and promote the gelatinization of the starch on the surface of the bread. Use beaten eggs as a wash to create a glossy, shiny crust and seal in the moisture in the bread. Typically whole eggs are used. A wash of only yolks would burn more quickly, especially at the higher temperatures required for baking most breads.

Milk or cream is often used for breads baked at lower temperatures. Because the lactose in milk (or cream) caramelizes at 170°F/77°C, it gives breads a darker crust than water. In addition, the bread will bake a little faster because the milk fat acts to conduct heat.

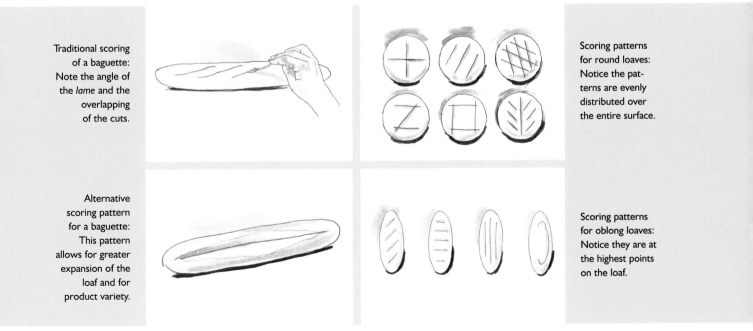

Traditional scoring of a baguette: Note the angle of the *lame* and the overlapping of the cuts.

Alternative scoring pattern for a baguette: This pattern allows for greater expansion of the loaf and for product variety.

Scoring patterns for round loaves: Notice the patterns are evenly distributed over the entire surface.

Scoring patterns for oblong loaves: Notice they are at the highest points on the loaf.

Baking

After it is placed in the oven, the dough continues to rise for a brief period. This is known as *oven spring,* and it continues during the first few minutes of baking, until the dough reaches an internal temperature of 140°F/60°C, at which point the yeast dies.

Most breads, except those that have been brushed with egg wash, are steamed at the outset of the baking process. The steam gives a final boost of volume, allows for maximum expansion of the dough, adds sheen and color to the crust, and improves the flavor of the bread. Venting the bread as it bakes releases the steam or moisture from the oven and facilitates crust formation. Steam is typically used in baking lean doughs. It helps develop texture and keeps the surface of the dough soft so that it can expand during the beginning stages of baking. It also acts to gelatinize the starches on the surface of the dough to facilitate crust formation. After the steam evaporates or is vented from the oven, the browning of the crust takes place. The moisture from the steam still remaining on the dough conducts heat rapidly and the surface of the bread sets quickly, thus ending the expansion of the loaf and beginning the development of a crisp, brown crust.

The length of time bread bakes is determined by a number of factors, including the weight of the loaf, the type of oven (hearth, rotating, convection, etc.), oven temperature, and humidity, among other factors.

Lean doughs should be baked in a hot oven (400° to 465°F/204° to 241°C) with steam; enriched doughs should be baked at a slightly lower temperature (approximately 350° to 375°F/177° to 191°C). Beyond this, other things that may affect the specific baking temperature are the type of oven, the size and shape of the product, the desired crust and color development, or other characteristics, such as the length of the pan proofing.

During baking, carbon dioxide and steam are released in the bread and expand to further leaven the bread. The gluten (and eggs, if used) stretches and coagulates to develop the internal structure of the bread. The starches gelatinize to form the crust, and flavor and color develop as sugar caramelizes.

Once the loaves are baked, it is important that they be cooled properly in order to preserve the crust and structure of the bread, as well as to allow for final development of flavor. All breads, but especially those made with lean doughs, should be cooled on wire racks to maintain air circulation around the entire loaf. This will prevent moisture from collecting on the bread as it cools.

Horseshoe

Makes 1 loaf   DDT: 75°F/24°C

ROASTED POTATO DOUGH (page 160)	1 lb 2 oz	510 g
WHITE RYE FLOUR, for dusting	as needed	as needed
POTATO SLICES	1	1
OLIVE OIL, for brushing	as needed	as needed

1. Preshape the dough into an oblong piece (for preshaping instructions see page 184). Let the dough rest, covered, until relaxed, 15 to 20 minutes. (Note: When making multiple loaves, work sequentially, starting with the first piece of dough you divided and rounded.)

2. Dust the work surface with rye flour. Position the dough lengthwise, parallel to the edge of the work surface with the seam side up. Fold the dough lengthwise in half and seal the two edges together by pressing firmly with the heel of your hand, keeping the seam straight. Roll the dough under your palms into an even cylinder 12 in/30 cm long with tapered ends.

3. Dust a small rolling pin and use it to make a depression 3 in/8 cm wide down the center of the dough; the dough at the bottom of the hollow should be only 1/4 in/6 mm thick.

4. Roll the two long edges of the dough toward each other until they meet in the middle. Place the dough seam side up in a couronne basket, forming a horseshoe shape.

5. Proof, covered, until the dough springs back slowly to the touch, 45 minutes to 1 hour.

6. Flip the dough seam side down onto a peel. Score it with one long slash from end to end and place a potato slice in the center of the dough at the top of the horseshoe. Brush the dough lightly with olive oil.

7. Presteam a 435°F/224°C deck oven. Load the bread into the oven and steam for 3 seconds. Bake until the crust is golden brown and the bread sounds hollow when thumped on the bottom, 45 to 60 minutes. Vent the bread once it starts to brown. Cool completely on a rack.

Rectangular Loaf

Makes 1 loaf   DDT: 75°F/24°C

ROSEMARY DOUGH (page 161)	1 lb 4 oz	567 g

1. Preshape the dough into an oblong piece (for preshaping instructions see page 184). Let the dough rest, covered, until relaxed, 15 to 20 minutes. (Note: When making multiple loaves, work sequentially, starting with the first piece of dough you divided and rounded.)

2. Using the backs of your hands, stretch the dough gently and evenly into a rough rectangle 6 by 8 in/15 by 20 cm. It is very important to keep the thickness of the dough even.

3. Proof, covered, until the dough springs back slowly to the touch but does not collapse, 30 to 40 minutes.

4. Starting at one corner of the dough, score the dough three times, scoring from that same corner to each of the other three corners. Then score the dough two more times in between the first three slashes, radiating out from the same corner to the corresponding side.

5. Presteam a 450°F/232°C deck oven. Load the bread into the oven and steam for 3 seconds. Bake until the crust is golden brown and the bread sounds hollow when thumped on the bottom, 25 to 30 minutes. Vent during the final 10 minutes. Cool completely on a rack.

Triangular Loaf

Makes 1 loaf   DDT: 75°F/24°C

BELGIAN APPLE CIDER DOUGH (page 137)	18 lb	8.16 kg
APPLE CIDER PASTE		
MEDIUM RYE FLOUR	14 oz	397 g
INSTANT DRY YEAST	1 oz	28 g
APPLE CIDER	1 lb 8¾ oz	702 g
SALT	½ oz	14 g
WHITE RYE FLOUR, for dusting	as needed	as needed

1. Preshape the dough into a round piece (for preshaping instructions see page 184). Let the dough rest, covered, until relaxed, 15 to 20 minutes. (Note: When making multiple loaves, work sequentially, starting with the first piece of dough you divided and rounded.)

2. To prepare the apple cider paste, combine the flour and yeast. Blend the apple cider with the salt and then mix into the flour-yeast mixture and combine thoroughly. (Note: This makes enough for 12 loaves of bread.)

3. Dust the work surface with rye flour. Turn the dough seam side down. Dust a small rolling pin. Work the rolling pin from one edge of the dough outward, creating a flap ¼ in/6 mm thick. Repeat this process two more times to create three evenly spaced flaps that are at 120-degree angles to each other around the edges of the dough to form a triangle.

4. Turn the dough seam side up. Fold each flap toward the center of the dough to make a triangle, and flip the dough over again.

5. Spread 3¼ oz/92 g apple cider paste over the top of the loaf in an even layer about ¼ in/6 mm thick. Dust the top of the loaf with medium rye flour.

6. Proof, uncovered, until the dough springs back slowly to the touch, 45 minutes to 1 hour.

7. Presteam a 450°F/232°C deck oven. Load the bread into the oven and steam for 3 seconds. Bake until the crust is golden brown and the bread sounds hollow when thumped on the bottom, 35 to 40 minutes. Vent during the final 10 minutes. Cool completely on a rack.

LEFT TO RIGHT:
White Wheat
Sourdough and
Chocolate Cherry
Sourdough (on
rack), Cheddar
Onion Rye Rolls,
Focaccia, Roasted
Potato Horseshoe,
Pita Bread,
Baguettes, Grissini;
(front) Pretzels

Split Loaf

Makes 1 loaf   DDT: 75°F/24°C

LEAN DOUGH WITH PÂTE FERMENTÉE (page 148)	1 lb	454 g

1. Preshape the dough into a round piece (for preshaping instructions see page 184). Let the dough rest, covered, until relaxed, 15 to 20 minutes. (Note: When making multiple loaves, work sequentially, starting with the first piece of dough you divided and rounded.)

2. Working with the dough seam side down, dust lightly with medium rye flour and use a rolling pin to create a split in the dough 2 in/5 cm wide and 2 in/5 cm deep. Turn the dough, split side down, into a lightly floured banneton or couche.

3. Proof, covered, until the dough springs back slowly to the touch but does not collapse, 1 to 1½ hours.

4. Flip the dough split side up onto a peel.

5. Presteam a 460°F/238°C deck oven. Load the bread into the oven and steam for 3 seconds. Bake until the crust is golden brown and the bread sounds hollow when thumped on the bottom, 25 to 30 minutes. Vent during the final 10 minutes. Cool completely on a rack.

Variation   **Boule with a Cross** After the boule has proofed, make two hollows the same size as the one in the Split Loaf to form a cross in the center of the loaf. The baking instructions are the same.

Shaping a split loaf with a rolling pin and rye flour (not included in process)

Bâtard

Makes 1 loaf   DDT: 75°F/24°C

WHOLE WHEAT LEAN DOUGH (page 130)	1 lb 4 oz	567 g

1. Preshape the dough into an oblong piece (for preshaping instructions see page 184). Let the dough rest, covered, until relaxed, 15 to 20 minutes. (Note: When making multiple loaves, work sequentially, starting with the first piece of dough you divided and rounded.)

2. Position the dough lengthwise, parallel to the edge of the work surface with the seam side up, and press lightly with your fingertips. Fold the top edge of the dough down to the center of the dough, pressing lightly with your fingertips to tighten.

3. Fold the dough lengthwise in half and use the heel of your hand to seal the two edges, keeping the seam straight. Roll the dough under your palms into a cylinder 8 in/20 cm long, moving your hands outward from the center of the cylinder toward the ends and slightly increasing the pressure as you move outward, until both ends have an even, gentle taper. Then increase the pressure at the ends of the loaf to seal.

4. Proof, covered, until the dough springs back slowly to the touch but does not collapse, 45 minutes.

5. Score the bâtard straight down the center, under the skin.

6. Presteam a 460°F/238°C deck oven as others. Load the bread into the oven and steam for 3 seconds. Bake until the crust is golden brown and the bread sounds hollow when thumped on the bottom, 25 to 30 minutes. Vent during the final 10 minutes. Cool completely on a rack.

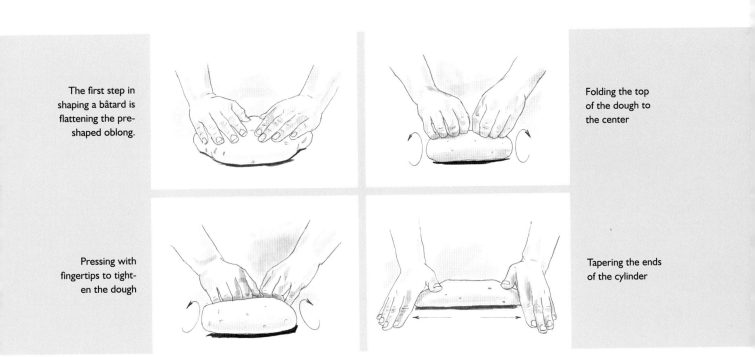

The first step in shaping a bâtard is flattening the preshaped oblong.

Folding the top of the dough to the center

Pressing with fingertips to tighten the dough

Tapering the ends of the cylinder

DOUGH NAME	DIVIDING WEIGHT	GARNISH	APPROXIMATE PROOFING TIME
APPLE AND WALNUT SOURDOUGH (page 172)	1 lb 4 oz/567 g	N/A	30 minutes (room temp.)/ 18 hours (refrigerated)/ 2 hours (room temp.)
BEER BREAD DOUGH (page 137)	1 lb/454 g	Top rolled in malt powder	40 to 50 minutes
WHOLE-GRAIN CARROT DOUGH (page 177)	1 lb/454 g	Top rolled in rolled oats	30 minutes (¾ proof)
LEAN DOUGH WITH BIGA (page 159)	14 oz/397 g	N/A	1 to 1½ hours
MULTIGRAIN DOUGH (page 150)	1 lb/454 g	Top rolled in your choice of seeds	45 minutes to 1 hour
MULTIGRAIN RYE SOURDOUGH (page 176)	1 lb 8 oz/680 g	Top rolled in sesame seeds	35 minutes (¾ proof)
RUSTIC RYE SOURDOUGH (page 175)	1 lb 8 oz/680 g	N/A	30 minutes (¾ proof)
SEMOLINA DOUGH (page 158)	1 lb 4 oz/567 g	N/A	50 minutes
SOURDOUGH WITH RYE FLOUR (page 172)	1 lb 8 oz/680 g	N/A	30 minutes (room temp.)/ 18 hours (refrigerated)/ 2 hours (room temp.)
WALNUT FIG DOUGH (page 170)	15 oz/425 g	N/A	1 hour 20 minutes
WHITE WHEAT SOURDOUGH (page 165)	1 lb 8 oz/680 g	N/A	30 minutes (room temp.)/ 18 hours (refrigerated)/ 2 hours (room temp.)
WHOLE WHEAT DOUGH WITH POOLISH (page 155)	1 lb 4 oz/567 g	N/A	1 hour
WHOLE WHEAT SOURDOUGH (page 170)	1 lb 8 oz/680 g	N/A	30 minutes (room temp.)/ 18 hours (refrigerated)/ 2 hours (room temp.)

SCORING	STEAMING	BAKING TEMPERATURE/ TIME	VENTING TIME (before end of bake)
A slash down the center	Presteam/ steam 3 seconds	470°F/243°C/35 minutes	10 minutes
5 or 6 parallel diagonal scores	Presteam/ steam 3 seconds	450°F/232°C/25 minutes	10 minutes
N/A	Presteam/ steam 3 seconds	450°F/232°C/35 to 40 minutes	15 minutes
3 parallel diagonal lines	Presteam/ steam 3 seconds	450°F/232°C/30 minutes	10 minutes
5 or 6 parallel diagonal scores	Presteam/ steam 3 seconds	475°F/246°C/30 minutes	10 minutes
3 parallel diagonal lines	Presteam/ steam 3 seconds	470°F/243°C/45 minutes	10 minutes
A slash down the center	Presteam/	470°F/243°C/40 minutes	10 minutes
Arc	Presteam/ steam 3 seconds	475°F/246°C/40 minutes	10 minutes
Arc	Presteam/ steam 3 seconds	470°F/243°C/40 minutes	10 minutes
2 parallel diagonal lines	Presteam/ steam 3 seconds	450°F/232°C/35 to 40 minutes	15 minutes
Arc	Presteam/ steam 3 seconds	470°F/243°C/40 minutes	10 minutes
3 parallel diagonal lines	Presteam/ steam 3 seconds	470°F/243°C/35 minutes	10 minutes
Arc	Presteam/ steam 3 seconds	470°F/243°C/40 minutes	10 minutes

Baguette

Makes 1 loaf   DDT: 75°F/24°C

LEAN DOUGH WITH POOLISH (page 156)	14 oz	397 g

1. Preshape the dough into an oblong piece (for preshaping instructions see page 184). Let the dough rest, covered, until relaxed, 15 to 20 minutes. (Note: When making multiple loaves, work sequentially, starting with the first piece of dough you divided and rounded.)

2. Position the dough lengthwise, parallel to the edge of the work surface with the seam side up. Press lightly with your fingertips to stretch it into a rectangle 10 in/25 cm long, using as little flour as possible. Fold the top edge of the dough down to the center of the dough, pressing lightly with your fingertips to tighten the dough. Fold the dough lengthwise in half and use the heel of your hand to seal the two edges together, keeping the seam straight. Roll the dough under your palms into a cylinder 20 in/51 cm long. Keep the pressure even and hold your hands flat and parallel to the work surface. Move your hands outward from the center of the cylinder toward the ends and slightly increase the pressure as you move outward, until both ends have an even, gentle taper. Then increase the pressure at the ends of the loaf to seal them.

3. Place the loaf seam side down on the linen. Proof, covered, until the dough springs back very slowly to the touch, 30 to 45 minutes. (Note: Baguettes should be slightly under-proofed when loaded into the oven.)

4. Score the dough with five or seven diagonal lines down the center third of the loaf, overlapping each cut by ½ in/1 cm.

5. Presteam a 475°F/246°C deck oven. Load the bread into the oven and steam for 3 seconds. Bake until the crust is golden brown and the bread sounds hollow when thumped on the bottom and you hear a crackle when you hold it next to your ear, 20 to 25 minutes. Vent during the final 10 minutes. Cool completely on a rack.

1 To start shaping a baguette, fold the top edge of the dough to the center, pressing lightly with your fingertips to tighten the dough.

2 Seal the edges together using the heel of your hand.

3 Taper each end, using increased pressure and tapering the ends evenly.

Ficelle

Makes 1 loaf   DDT: 75°F/24°C

LEAN DOUGH WITH POOLISH (page 156)	6 oz	170 g

1. Preshape the dough into an oblong piece (for preshaping instructions see page 184). Let the dough rest, covered, until relaxed, 15 to 20 minutes. (Note: When making multiple loaves, work sequentially, starting with the first piece of dough you divided and rounded.)

2. Position the dough lengthwise, parallel to the edge of the work surface, with the seam side up. Press lightly with your fingertips to stretch it into a rectangle 10 in/25 cm long, using as little flour as possible. Fold the top edge of the dough down to the center of the dough, pressing lightly with your fingertips to tighten the dough. Fold the dough lengthwise in half and use the heel of your hand to seal the two edges together, keeping the seam straight. Roll the dough under your palms into a cylinder 20 in/51 cm long, keeping the pressure even and holding your hands flat and parallel to the work surface to create a smooth, even loaf. Then taper the final 2 in/5 cm of each end by using increased pressure, tapering the ends evenly.

3. Place the ficelle seam side down on linen. Proof, covered, until the dough springs back very slowly to the touch, 30 to 45 minutes. (Note: Ficelles are often slightly underproofed when loaded into the oven.)

4. Score the dough with five or seven diagonal lines down the center third of the loaf, overlapping each cut by ½ in/1 cm.

5. Presteam a 475°F/246°C deck oven. Load the bread into the oven and steam for 3 seconds. Bake until the crust is golden brown and the bread sounds hollow when thumped on the bottom and you hear a crackle when you hold it next to your ear, 25 to 30 minutes. Vent during the final 5 minutes. Cool completely on a rack.

Grissini

Makes 3 dozen grissini (³⁄₈ oz/10.6 g each)   DDT: 75°F/24°C

GRISSINI DOUGH (page 133)	13¾ oz	390 g
OLIVE OIL, for brushing	as needed	as needed
OPTIONAL GARNISHES: coarse salt, poppy seeds, and/or sesame seeds	as needed	as needed

1. Line sheet pans with parchment paper.

2. Using a rolling pin, roll the dough into a rectangle 12 in/30 cm long and the width of the rollers on a pasta machine. Trim one short edge to even it; this is the edge that should be fed into the pasta machine.

3. Starting with the rollers at the widest opening and resetting them to the next setting after each complete pass, roll the dough through the pasta machine until it is the desired thickness, about ¼ in/6 mm or setting number 5 on most pasta machines.

4. Using the fettuccine cutter attachment, cut the dough lengthwise into strips ¼ in/6 mm wide, or cut it by hand. Lay the strips crosswise on the parchment-lined sheet pans, making sure they do not touch. Brush the strips lightly with olive oil.

5. Proof, covered, until the dough rises slightly, about 15 minutes. Brush the grissini lightly with olive oil and scatter with any optional garnishes.

6. Bake in a 385°F/196°C deck oven until the grissini are golden brown, 8 to 12 minutes. Cool completely on racks.

Feeding grissini dough through a pasta machine

Epi

Makes 1 loaf   DDT: 75°F/24°C

LEAN DOUGH WITH POOLISH (page 156)	14 oz	397 g

1. Preshape the dough into an oblong piece (for preshaping instructions see page 184). Let the dough rest, covered, until relaxed, 15 to 20 minutes. (Note: When making multiple loaves, work sequentially, starting with the first piece of dough you divided and rounded.)

2. Position the dough lengthwise, parallel to the edge of the work surface with the seam side up. Press lightly with your fingertips to stretch it into a rectangle 10 in/25 cm long, using as little flour as possible. Fold the top edge of the dough down to the center of the dough, pressing lightly with your fingertips to tighten the dough. Fold the dough lengthwise in half and use the heel of your hand to seal the two edges together, keeping the seam straight. Roll the dough under your palms into a cylinder 20 in/51 cm long, keeping the pressure even and holding your hands flat and parallel to the work surface to create a smooth, even loaf. Then taper the final 2 in/5 cm of each end by using increased pressure, tapering the ends evenly.

3. Place the dough seam side down on the linen. Proof, covered, until the dough springs back very slowly to the touch, 30 to 45 minutes. (Note: Epi are often slightly underproofed when loaded into the oven.)

4. Transfer the dough to a peel. Using scissors held at a 45-degree angle, starting 2½ in/6 cm from one end of the loaf, make diagonal cuts down the center of the loaf, placing each cut piece to the side as you cut, alternating sides to create the look of a stalk of wheat.

5. Presteam a 475°F/246°C deck oven. Load the bread into the oven and steam for 3 seconds. Bake until the crust is golden brown and the bread sounds hollow when thumped on the bottom and you hear a crackle when you hold it next to your ear. Vent during the final 5 minutes. Cool completely on a rack.

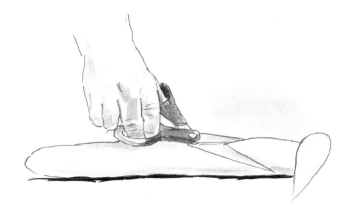

Cutting and spreading epi

Double Epi

Makes 1 loaf   DDT: 75°F/24°C

LEAN DOUGH WITH POOLISH (page 156)	14 oz	397 g

1. Preshape the dough into an oblong piece (for preshaping instructions see page 184). Let the dough rest, covered, until relaxed, 15 to 20 minutes. (Note: When making multiple loaves, work sequentially, starting with the first piece of dough you divided and rounded.)

2. Position the dough lengthwise, parallel to the edge of the work surface with the seam side up. Press lightly with your fingertips to stretch the dough into a rectangle 10 in/25 cm long, using as little flour as possible. Fold the top edge of the dough down to the center of the dough, pressing lightly with your fingertips to tighten the dough. Fold the dough lengthwise in half and use the heel of your hand to seal the two edges together, keeping the seam straight. Roll the dough under your palms into a cylinder 20 in/51 cm long, keeping the pressure even and holding your hands flat and parallel to the work surface to create a smooth, even loaf. Then taper the final 2 in/5 cm of each end by using increased pressure, tapering the ends evenly.

3. Place the dough seam side down on the linen. Proof, covered, until the dough springs back very slowly to the touch, 30 to 45 minutes. (Note: Epi are often slightly underproofed when loaded into the oven.)

4. Transfer the dough to a peel. Make a cut lengthwise down the center of the loaf, leaving ½ in/1 cm at each end uncut. Gently pull the two halves of the loaf apart.

5. Each half of the loaf is shaped separately, as follows: Fold the cut piece of dough over to the opposite side of where it was cut. Cut another piece of dough 2½ in/6 cm from where you made the first cut, cutting from the opposite side this time. Fold the cut piece of dough over to the opposite side of where it was cut. Continue cutting and folding the dough in alternating directions, keep the cuts on the same side of the loaf parallel and uniformly spaced. The finished loaf will look like a stalk of wheat.

6. Presteam a 475°F/246°C deck oven. Load the bread into the oven and steam for 3 seconds. Bake until the crust is golden brown and the bread sounds hollow when thumped on the bottom and you hear a crackle when you hold it next to your ear, 10 to 15 minutes. Vent during the final 10 minutes. Cool completely on a rack.

Boule with Flap/Tabatière

Makes 1 loaf   DDT: 75°F/24°C

WHITE WHEAT LEAN DOUGH (page 123)	1 lb	454 g
VEGETABLE OIL, for brushing	as needed	as needed

1. Preshape the dough into a round piece (for preshaping instructions see page 184). Let the dough rest, covered, until relaxed, 15 to 20 minutes. (Note: When making multiple loaves, work sequentially, starting with the first piece of dough you divided and rounded.)

2. Roll half of the round using a small rolling pin dusted with medium rye flour and working from the center of the round out, into a half-circle flap 1/4 in/6 mm thick and 1 1/2 times longer than the other half of the dough. Brush the edge of the flap lightly with vegetable oil and fold it over the other half of the dough. Place the boule flap side down in a round basket or on a board dusted with flour.

3. Proof, covered, until the dough springs back slowly to the touch but does not collapse, 1 to 1 1/2 hours.

4. Flip the boule seam side down onto a peel.

5. Presteam a 460°F/238°C deck oven. Load the bread into the oven and steam for 3 seconds. Bake until the crust is golden brown and the bread sounds hollow when thumped on the bottom, 25 to 30 minutes. Vent during the final 10 minutes. Cool completely on a rack.

Round Rolls

Makes 3 dozen rolls (1⅓ oz/38 g each)   DDT: 75°F/24°C

MULTIGRAIN DOUGH WITH PÂTE FERMENTÉE (page 150)	3 lb	1.36 kg

1. Preshape the dough into a round (for preshaping instructions see page 184). Let the dough rest, covered, until relaxed, 15 to 20 minutes.

2. Divide the dough by hand or using a dough divider into 36 pieces (1⅓ oz/38 g each). Press each piece lightly with your fingertips to flatten. Fold the top edge of the dough down to the center of the dough, pressing lightly with your fingertips to tighten the dough. Rotate the dough 90 degrees, fold the dough in half, and use the heel of your hand to seal the two edges together. Cup the roll in your hand and re-round the dough, applying gentle pressure to create a tight, smooth ball.

3. Proof, covered, until the dough springs back slowly to the touch but does not collapse, about 30 minutes.

4. Score the rolls with a straight cut down the center of each one.

5. Presteam a 450°F/232°C deck oven. Load the rolls into the oven and steam for 3 seconds. Bake until the rolls have a golden brown crust and sound hollow when thumped on the bottom, about 15 minutes. Vent the rolls when they start to brown. Cool completely on racks.

DOUGH NAME	DIVIDING WEIGHT	GARNISH	APPROXIMATE PROOFING TIME
CHEDDAR AND ONION RYE BREAD (page 138)	3 lb/1.36 kg	N/A	45 to 50 minutes
SUNFLOWER SEED BREAD (page 136)	3 lb/1.36 kg	N/A	35 to 40 minutes

Bâtard-Style Rolls

Makes 3 dozen rolls (1⅓ oz/38 g each)   DDT: 75°F/24°C

BEER BREAD DOUGH (page 137)	3 lb	1.36 kg
MALT POWDER, for topping (optional)	as needed	as needed

1. Preshape the dough into a round (for preshaping instructions see page 184). Let the dough rest, covered, until relaxed, 15 to 20 minutes.

2. Divide the dough by hand or using a dough divider into 36 pieces (1⅓ oz/38 g each). Press each piece lightly with your fingertips to flatten. Fold the top edge of the dough down to the center of the dough, pressing lightly with your fingertips to tighten the dough. Fold the dough in half again and use the heel of your hand to seal the two edges together, keeping the seam straight.

3. Roll a piece of dough under your palms into a cylinder 3 in/8 cm long, keeping the pressure even and holding your hands flat and parallel to the work surface to create a smooth, even roll. Using your palms, gently taper the ends of the dough by increasing the pressure as you roll outward to the ends of the dough. Mist the rolls with water.

4. Proof, covered, until the dough springs back slowly to the touch but does not collapse, about 30 minutes.

5. Score the rolls with a straight cut down the center of each one.

6. Presteam a 460°F/238°C deck oven. Load the rolls into the oven and steam for 3 seconds. Bake until the rolls have a golden brown crust and sound hollow when thumped on the bottom, about 15 minutes. Vent the rolls when they start to brown. Cool completely on racks.

SCORING	STEAMING	BAKING TEMPERATURE/ TIME	VENTING TIME (before end of bake)
A slash down the center	Presteam/ steam 3 seconds	425°F/218°C/12 to 15 minutes	3 minutes
A slash down the center	Presteam/ steam 3 seconds	435°F/224°C/12 to 15 minutes	3 minutes

Bagels

Makes 25 bagels (6 oz/170 g each)   DDT: 78°F/26°C

BAGEL DOUGH (page 129)	9 lb 6 oz	4.25 kg
MALT SYRUP (per 5 gal/ 18.75 L water)	8 oz	227 g

1. Divide the dough into 6-oz/170-g pieces.

2. Preshape each piece of dough into an oblong piece (for preshaping instructions see page 184). Allow them to rest, covered, for 10 minutes.

3. Start with the first piece of dough that you shaped and work sequentially. Roll each piece of dough under your palms into a cylinder 6 in/15 cm long; begin rolling with your palms near the center of the dough and use even pressure from the center to the ends. Taper the ends very slightly.

4. Shape each cylinder into a ring, overlapping the ends by 1 in/3 cm; make sure the seams are aligned with the rest of the ring. Place two or three of your fingers in the center of the bagel and roll the overlapped ends gently against the worktable until they are the same diameter as the rest of the bagel. (Note: As you are working, it may become necessary to moisten your hands or the table to prevent sticking.) After rolling, the bagels should be 4 in/10 cm wide with a hole 2 in/5 cm in diameter.

5. Place the bagels seam side down on cornmeal-dusted sheet pans. Cover the bagels and proof under refrigeration for 8 hours or overnight.

6. Just before simmering them in the malt solution, let the proofed bagels rest at room temperature, covered, for 15 minutes.

7. Line sheet pans with parchment paper. Bring 5 gal/18.75 L of water to a boil and add the malt. Add a few bagels at a time to the water, stir once or twice to keep them from sticking together, and simmer until they rise to the top, about 20 seconds. Transfer the bagels to an ice bath until cool, 2 to 3 seconds, then lift from the ice water and place on the parchment-lined sheet pans. Garnish the bagels while still wet. Let the bagels air-dry slightly. Place the bagels onto parchment-lined upside-down sheet pans and allow them to dry slightly.

8. Transfer the bagels to a peel and load them into a 500°F/260°C deck oven. Bake until golden brown but still soft and slightly springy to the touch, 10 to 15 minutes. Cool completely on racks.

Bagels

To make bagels successfully, it's important to keep a few guidelines in mind. It is important to use high-gluten flour and malt syrup in the dough. The high-gluten flour helps to develop the characteristic chewiness of a bagel. And the malt syrup contains enzymes that help to break down the carbohydrates in the flour into sugars, further developing the texture and flavor of the bagels.

Bagel dough is often described as *bucky*, meaning that it is very tight and dry. The dough should be mixed until it is very, very smooth. This extensive mixing will make the dough slightly tacky even though it contains little water. Unlike most other breads, bagels should be shaped immediately after the dough is mixed. Then the bagels should be retarded overnight to develop flavor and relax the gluten. The following day, they are poached in a mixture of water and malt. The poaching activates the yeast, and the water that remains on the bagels results in the sheen on the surface of the bagels, as the starches are gelatinized before going into the oven. The bagels must first dry slightly before they are put directly on the deck, or they will stick.

1 Roll the bagel under the palm of your hand to seal the seam and even out its diameter.

2 Poach the bagels in a malt water bath just until they float to the surface.

Bialys

Makes 25 bialys (5 oz/142 g each)   DDT: 78°F/26°C

BAGEL DOUGH (page 129)	7 lb 13 oz	3.54 kg
ONIONS, caramelized	2 lb 4 oz	1.02 kg
POPPY SEEDS	1½ oz	43 g

1. Divide the dough into 5-oz/142-g pieces. Preshape the dough into flattened round pieces. Allow them to rest, covered, for 10 minutes. Start with the first piece of dough that you shaped and work sequentially.

2. Dust each piece of dough lightly with flour. Flatten each piece slightly, using the palm of your hand. Using the heel of your hand, press each piece of dough into a disk that is 3 in/8 cm in diameter and 1 to 1½ in/3 to 4 cm thick. Using your fingertips, make a depression in the center of the disk that is 1½ in/4 cm in diameter and ½ in/1 cm deep.

3. Place the bialys seam side down on the cornmeal-dusted sheet pans. Proof, covered, until the dough springs back slowly to the touch but does not collapse, about 30 minutes. Combine the onions and poppy seeds.

4. Redefine the depression in the center of the dough using your fingertips. Fill each bialy with 1½ oz/43 g onion and poppy seed filling.

5. Transfer the bialys to a peel and load them into a 475°F/246°C deck oven. Bake until golden brown but still soft and slightly springy to the touch, 10 to 15 minutes. Cool completely on racks.

Ciabatta

Makes 8 loaves (1 lb 2 oz/510 g each)   DDT: 75°F/24°C

CIABATTA DOUGH (page 162)	9 lb	4.08 kg

1. Place the dough on the table and dust the top of it with flour. (Note: Keep the work surface well floured when working with ciabatta dough.) Using the palms of your hands, gently stretch the dough into a rectangle 16 in/41 cm long and 1½ in/4 cm thick. Be careful to avoid tearing or puncturing the dough with your fingertips. Using a floured bench scraper, divide the dough into two rectangles 4½ by 8 in/11 by 20 cm.

2. Let the dough rest, covered, 15 to 20 minutes.

3. Gently free the dough from the table with a bench scraper, trying not to tear it. Flip the dough over onto floured linens. Gently stretch each piece into a rough rectangle about 4½ by 10 in/11 by 25 cm.

4. Proof, covered, until the dough springs back slowly to the touch but does not collapse, 30 to 45 minutes.

5. Lightly flour the top of the dough. Flip each ciabatta over onto a small floured board, then slide each one onto a floured peel.

6. Presteam a 460°F/238°C deck oven. Load the ciabatta into the oven and steam for 3 seconds. Bake until the crust is golden brown and the ciabatta sounds hollow when thumped on the bottom, 25 to 30 minutes. Vent during the final 10 minutes. Cool completely on racks.

1 Cut pieces of uniform weight without using a scale to minimize the handling of this wet dough.

2 Stretch the dough out on a couche for intermediate fermentation.

Focaccia

Makes 1 loaf   DDT: 75°F/24°C

FOCACCIA DOUGH (page 164)	1 lb	454 g
OLIVE OIL, for brushing	as needed	as needed
OPTIONAL GARNISHES		
FRESH HERBS	as needed	as needed
GARLIC, sliced and sautéed	as needed	as needed
ROASTED TOMATO SLICES	as needed	as needed
ONIONS, sliced and sautéed	as needed	as needed
SALT, coarsely ground	as needed	as needed

1. Preshape the dough lightly into a round piece (for preshaping instructions see page 184). Rest the dough, covered, until relaxed, 15 to 20 minutes. (Note: When making multiple loaves, work sequentially, starting with the first piece of dough you divided and rounded.)

2. Brush the dough lightly with olive oil. Using only your fingertips, gently press the dough down, and then stretch it into a circle 10 in/25 cm in diameter, keeping the thickness of the dough even.

3. Proof, covered, until the dough springs back slowly to the touch but does not collapse, 30 to 45 minutes.

4. Brush the dough lightly with olive oil again. Gently stipple the dough, creating random indentations with your fingertips, stretching the circle to 10 in/25 cm in diameter. Scatter with any optional toppings, if desired.

5. Presteam a 460°F/238°C deck oven. Load the focaccia into the oven and steam for 3 seconds. Bake until the crust is golden brown and the focaccia sounds hollow when thumped on the bottom, 25 to 30 minutes. Vent during the final 10 minutes. Brush lightly with olive oil and sprinkle with salt. Cool completely on a rack.

Dimple the proofed focaccia dough with your fingertips.

Stollen

Makes 1 loaf   DDT: 80°F/27°C

CHRISTMAS STOLLEN DOUGH (page 154)	1 lb	454 g
CLARIFIED BUTTER, for brushing	as needed	as needed
VANILLA SUGAR, for coating (page 827)	as needed	as needed
CONFECTIONERS' SUGAR, for dusting	as needed	as needed

1. Preshape the dough into a round piece (for preshaping instructions see page 184). Let the dough rest, covered, until relaxed, 15 to 20 minutes. (Note: When making multiple loaves, work sequentially, starting with the first piece of dough you divided and rounded.)

2. Gently flatten the dough with your fingertips. Working with the seam side up, fold the dough in half. Seal the two edges by pressing firmly with the heel of your hand, keeping the seam straight. Roll the dough under your palms into a cylinder 8 in/20 cm long, keeping the pressure even and holding your hands flat and parallel to the work surface to create a smooth, even roll.

3. Turn the dough lengthwise, parallel to the edge of the worktable with the seam side down. Roll half of the dough into a flap 1/4 in/6 mm thick in the shape of a semicircle. The edges of the flap should be 1/2 in/1 cm thick.

4. Fold 1/2 in/1 cm of the left and right sides of the dough toward the center of the dough. Roll the folded left and right edges of the dough so that they are the same thickness as the rest of the flap of dough.

5. Make an indentation lengthwise down the center of the thicker half of the dough with a straight rolling pin. Fold the flap over and insert the thicker edge of the flap into the indentation. Press into place by gently rolling with the rolling pin.

6. Proof, covered, until the dough relaxes slightly, about 30 minutes.

7. Bake in a 350°F/177°C deck oven until the stollen is golden brown and sounds hollow when thumped on the bottom, 30 to 35 minutes. Cool on a rack just until the bread can be handled; it should still be warm.

8. While the bread is still hot, remove any burnt fruit or nuts from the outside of the bread. Brush the sides, top, and bottom of the bread with clarified butter and roll in the vanilla sugar. Cool completely on a rack.

9. Dust the stollen with sifted confectioners' sugar just before wrapping or slicing.

Crown

Makes 1 loaf   DDT: 79°F/26°C

GUGELHOPF DOUGH (page 153)	1 lb 4 oz	567 g
BLANCHED WHOLE ALMONDS, for garnish mold	8 oz	227 g

1. Preshape the dough into a round (for preshaping instructions see page 184). Let the dough rest, covered, until relaxed, 15 to 20 minutes. (Note: When making multiple loaves, work sequentially, starting with the first piece of dough you divided and rounded.)

2. Coat the Gugelhopf mold with a light film of oil. Arrange the almonds in the bottom of the pan in a single layer.

3. Make a hole in the center of the dough using the end of a floured rolling pin. Holding the dough between your thumbs and forefingers, gently expand the hole by rotating the dough, keeping the hole directly in the center, until the opening is 3 in/8 cm across. Gently place the dough seam side up in the pan.

4. Proof, covered, until the dough has risen to the top of the pan, 1 to 1½ hours.

5. Presteam a 375°F/191°C deck oven. Load the bread into the oven and steam for 4 seconds. Bake until the crust is golden brown and the top of the bread springs back fully to the touch, another 30 minutes. Vent the bread when it starts to brown. Cool completely on a rack.

Panettone

Makes 1 loaf   DDT: 78°F/26°C

PANETTONE DOUGH (page 152)	1 lb 4 oz	567 g
EGG WASH, for brushing (page 825)	as needed	as needed
UNSALTED BUTTER	as needed	as needed

1. Preshape the dough into a round (for preshaping instructions see page 184). Let the dough rest, covered, until relaxed, 15 to 20 minutes. (Note: When making multiple loaves, work sequentially, starting with the first piece of dough you divided and rounded.)

2. Grease a large paper panettone wrapper. Re-round the dough to create a tight, smooth boule. Place the dough seam side down in the panettone wrapper. Lightly brush the top of the loaf with egg wash.

3. Proof, covered, until the dough springs back slowly to the touch but does not collapse, about 1 hour 40 minutes.

4. Lightly brush the bread with egg wash again. Score the bread with an X in the center. Insert a small pat of unsalted butter in the center of the cut.

5. Bake in a 385°F/196°C convection oven with steam until the panettone is golden brown and the sides spring back fully when touched through the wrapper, 35 to 40 minutes. Cool completely on a rack.

Parker House Rolls

Makes 3 dozen rolls (1¾ oz/50 g each)   DDT: 75°F/24°C

SOFT ROLL DOUGH (page 132)	4 lb	1.81 kg
CLARIFIED BUTTER, for brushing	as needed	as needed

1. Preshape the dough into a round (for preshaping instructions see page 184). Line sheet pans with parchment. Let the dough rest, covered, until relaxed, 15 to 20 minutes.

2. Divide the dough into 36 pieces by hand or using a dough divider (1¾ oz/50 g each). Re-round each piece and let rest, covered, for10 minutes.

3. Roll each piece of dough into an oval 5 in/13 cm long and 2½ in/6 cm wide; the dough will be about ⅛ in/3 mm thick. Brush any excess flour off the dough as you work. Fold each oval in half so that they are now 2½ in/6 cm long, 2½ in/6 cm wide, and ¼ in/6 mm thick. Turn the dough so that the folded edge is facing toward you. Roll the bottom 2 in/5 cm of the dough until it is ⅛ in/3 mm thick. The remaining ½ in/1 cm of dough at the top should still be ¼ in/6 mm thick.

4. Arrange the rolls in rows on the lined sheet pans, spacing them 4 in/10 cm apart. Brush with clarified butter. Proof until the dough springs back slowly to the touch, 30 to 40 minutes.

5. Bake in a 375°F/191°C convection oven until the rolls are golden brown and shiny, about 20 minutes. Brush the rolls with clarified butter as soon as they are removed from the oven. Cool completely on the pans.

Shaping Parker House rolls

Knot Rolls

Makes 3 dozen rolls (1¾ oz/50 g each)   DDT: 75°F/24°C

SOFT ROLL DOUGH (page 132)	4 lb	1.81 kg
EGG WASH, for brushing (page 825)	as needed	as needed

1. Preshape the dough into a round (for preshaping instructions see page 184). Line sheet pans with parchment. Let the dough rest, covered, until relaxed, 15 to 20 minutes.

2. Divide the dough into 36 pieces (1¾ oz/50 g each) by hand or using a dough divider. Starting with the first piece of dough that you shaped and working sequentially, flatten a piece of dough slightly with your fingertips. Fold the top edge of the dough down to the center of the dough, pressing lightly with your fingertips to tighten the dough. Fold the dough in half again and use the heel of your hand to seal the two edges together, keeping the seam straight. Roll the dough under your palms into an even rope 6 in/15 cm long.

3. Lay 2 in/5 cm of one end of the rope over your forefinger and middle finger. There should be ½ in/1 cm of dough hanging over your fingers; bring it under your fingers and cross it over the dough sitting on your fingers.

4. Bring the longer piece of dough underneath the dough sitting on your fingers. This will be the base of the knot; there should be ½ in/1 cm of dough to the left of the knot and 2 in/5 cm of dough to the right of it. There should be one side of the roll where the knot is formed and one side of the roll that is smooth.

5. Bring the longer piece of dough around the smooth side of the dough, and pinch the ends of the dough together. Turn the roll so that the pinched ends are on the bottom.

6. Arrange the rolls in rows on the lined sheet pans, spacing them 4 in/10 cm apart. Brush the rolls with egg wash. Proof, covered, until the dough springs back slowly to the touch but does not collapse, 30 to 50 minutes.

7. Lightly brush the rolls again with egg wash. Bake in a 375°F/191°C convection oven until the rolls are golden brown and shiny, about 20 minutes. Cool completely on the pans.

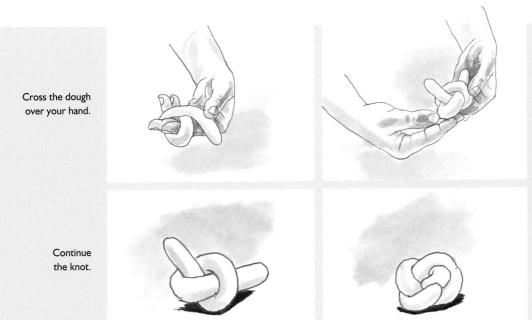

Cross the dough over your hand.

Bring the longer piece of dough underneath the piece of dough sitting on your fingers.

Continue the knot.

Pinch the two ends together.

Brioche à Tête

Makes 25 brioches (1¾ oz/50 g each)   DDT: 75°F/24°C

BRIOCHE DOUGH (page 142)	2 lb 11¾ oz	1.24 kg
EGG WASH, for brushing (page 825)	as needed	as needed

1. Lightly oil brioche tins.

2. Remove the dough from the refrigerator and divide it by hand into 25 pieces (1¾ oz/50 g each). Preshape each piece into a round, lightly flouring the work surface as needed. Refrigerate until cool, 15 minutes.

3. Start with the first piece of dough that you shaped and work sequentially. The remainder of the dough may need to be refrigerated during shaping to keep it cool and workable. Roll each piece of dough into a ball. Lightly coat the side of your hand with flour. Make a head (*tête*) by pinching one-quarter of the dough ball with the side of your hand and rolling it back and forth on the worktable, making a depression in the dough to pinch but not detach one-quarter of the ball; the larger piece of dough should be about 2¾ in/7 cm long and the *tête* ¾ in/2 cm long.

4. Flour your fingertips lightly and gently press a hole all the way through the center of the larger piece of dough. Place the *tête* into the center of the larger piece of dough and push it through the hole. Place each brioche into a greased brioche tin, with the *tête* on top.

5. Brush the brioches lightly with egg wash, brushing away any excess that accumulates in the crevices. Proof, covered, until the dough springs back slowly to the touch but does not collapse, 1½ to 2 hours.

6. Gently brush the brioches again with egg wash. Bake in a 385°F/196°C deck oven until a rich golden brown, 12 to 15 minutes. Cool for 10 minutes in the tins, then promptly remove and finish cooling on racks.

Note   Orange Brioche Dough may be substituted for Brioche Dough.

1 Make a head (*tête*) by pinching one-quarter of the dough ball with the side of your hand and rolling back and forth on the worktable.

2 Use your fingertips to make a hole in the center of the larger piece of dough.

3 Push the head of the dough into the hole.

Pan Bread (Lean Version)

Makes 1 loaf   DDT: 80°F/27°C

100% RYE DOUGH (page 178)	2 lb	907 g

1. Preshape the dough into an oblong (for preshaping instructions see page 184). Lightly grease a 2-lb/907-g loaf pan (8 in/20 cm long, 4½ in/11 cm wide, and 3 in/8 cm deep). Let the dough rest, covered, until relaxed, 15 to 20 minutes. (Note: When making multiple loaves, work sequentially, starting with the first piece of dough you divided and rounded.)

2. Place the dough lengthwise parallel to the edge of the worktable with the seam side up. Press lightly with your fingertips to stretch it into a rectangle 8 in/20 cm long, using as little flour as possible. Fold the top edge of the dough down to the center of the dough, pressing lightly with your fingertips to tighten the dough.

3. Fold the dough lengthwise in half and use the heel of your hand to seal the two edges together, keeping the seam straight. Roll the dough under your palms into a cylinder 10 in/25 cm long, keeping the pressure even and holding your hands flat and parallel to the work surface to create a smooth, even loaf.

4. Place the dough seam side down in a greased loaf pan. Proof, covered, until the dough fills the pan and starts to crack at the surface, 30 to 40 minutes.

5. Presteam a 450°F/232°C deck oven. Load the bread into the oven and steam for 5 seconds. Bake until the crust is a deep golden brown and the sides of the bread spring back when pressed, about 1 hour. Vent during the final 20 minutes. Remove the bread from the pan and cool completely on a rack.

Pan Bread (Enriched Version)

Makes 1 loaf   DDT: 77°F/25°C

PAIN DE MIE DOUGH (page 134)	1 lb 4 oz	567 g
EGG WASH, for brushing (page 825)	as needed	as needed

1. Preshape the dough into an oblong (for preshaping instructions see page 184). Lightly grease a 2-lb/907-g loaf pan (8 in/20 cm long, 4½ in/11 cm wide, and 3 in/8 cm deep). Let the dough rest, covered, until relaxed, 15 to 20 minutes. (Note: When making multiple loaves, work sequentially, starting with the first piece of dough you divided and rounded.)

2. Place the dough lengthwise with the seam side up. Press lightly with your fingertips to stretch it into a rectangle 8 in/20 cm long, using as little flour as possible. Fold the top edge of the dough down to the center of the dough, pressing lightly with your fingertips to tighten the dough.

3. Fold the dough lengthwise in half and use the heel of your hand to seal the two edges together, keeping the seam straight. Roll the dough under your palms into a cylinder 10 in/25 cm long, keeping the pressure even and holding your hands flat and parallel to the work surface to create a smooth, even loaf.

4. Place the dough seam side down in a greased loaf pan. The dough will spring back on itself slightly and fit snugly in the pan. Brush the loaf lightly with egg wash. Proof, covered, until the dough fills the pan and springs back slowly to the touch but does not collapse, 1½ to 2 hours.

5. Gently brush the bread again with egg wash. Bake in a 375°F/191°C deck oven until the crust is a rich golden brown and the sides of the bread spring back when pressed, 25 to 30 minutes. Remove the bread from the pan and cool completely on a rack.

Pan Bread (Rolled Up)

Makes 1 loaf   DDT: 78°F/26°C

RAISIN BREAD WITH CINNAMON SWIRL DOUGH (page 140)	1 lb 4 oz	567 g
EGG WASH, for brushing (page 825)	as needed	as needed
CINNAMON SUGAR		
SUGAR	12 oz	340 g
CINNAMON AND BROWN SUGAR (page 826)	1 oz	28 g

1. Preshape the dough into an oblong (for preshaping instructions see page 184). Lightly grease a 2-lb/907-g loaf pan (8 in/20 cm long, 4½ in/11 cm wide, and 3 in/8 cm deep). Let the dough rest, covered, until relaxed, 15 to 20 minutes. (Note: When making multiple loaves, work sequentially, starting with the first piece of dough you divided and rounded.)

2. Roll the dough into an even rectangle 8 by 12 in/20 by 30 cm. Brush the dough lightly with egg wash and sprinkle 1 oz/28 g cinnamon sugar evenly over the surface. Roll the dough up along the 12-in/30-cm side under your palms into a cylinder 8 in/25 cm long, keeping the pressure even and holding your hands flat and parallel to the work surface to create a smooth, even loaf.

3. Place the dough seam side down in a greased loaf pan. The dough will spring back on itself slightly and fit snugly in the pan. Brush the loaf lightly with egg wash. Proof, covered, until the dough fills the pan and springs back slowly to the touch but does not collapse, 1½ to 2 hours.

4. Gently brush the bread again with egg wash. Presteam a 375°F/191°C deck oven. Load the bread into the oven and steam for 3 seconds. Bake until the crust is brown and the sides spring back when pressed, 25 to 30 minutes. Vent during the final 10 minutes. Remove the bread from the pan and cool completely on a rack.

Pullman Bread

Makes 1 loaf   DDT: 75°F/24°C

RYE DOUGH WITH CARAWAY SEEDS (page 135)	3 lb	1.36 kg

1. Grease a 3-lb/1.36-kg Pullman loaf pan and lid generously. Preshape the dough into a round (for preshaping instructions see page 184). Let the dough rest, covered, until relaxed, 15 to 20 minutes. (Note: When making multiple loaves, work sequentially, starting with the first piece of dough you divided and rounded.)

2. Place the dough lengthwise with the seam side up. Press lightly with your fingertips to stretch it into a rectangle 8 in/20 cm long, using as little flour as possible. Fold the top edge of the dough down to the center of the dough, pressing lightly with your fingertips to tighten the dough.

3. Fold the dough lengthwise in half and use the heel of your hand to seal the two edges together, keeping the seam straight. Roll the dough under your palms into a cylinder 10 in/25 cm long, keeping the pressure even and holding your hands flat and parallel to the work surface to create a smooth, even loaf.

4. Let the dough rest, covered, until relaxed, 15 to 20 minutes.

5. Turn the dough seam side up and position it so that a long side is parallel to the edge of the work surface. Work the dough lightly with your fingertips to release some of the gas, then gently stretch it into a rectangle 16 in/41 cm long and 2½ in/6 cm wide. Fold 1 in/2 cm of each short end in toward the center of the dough. Fold the long sides into the center, overlapping them slightly, and use the heel of your hand to seal the two edges together, keeping the seam straight. Fold the dough lengthwise in half and use your fingertips to seal the edges together, keeping the seam straight.

6. Roll the dough under your palms into a cylinder 18 in/46 cm long, keeping the pressure even and holding your hands flat and parallel to the work surface to create a smooth, even loaf. Push the ends of the loaf toward the center until the cylinder is 16 in/41 cm long. Place the dough seam side down in the greased loaf pan. The dough will spring back on itself slightly and fit snugly in the pan. Proof, uncovered, until the pan is three-quarters full and the dough springs back slowly to the touch, about 1 hour.

DOUGH NAME	DIVIDING WEIGHT	APPROXIMATE PROOFING TIME	SCORING
VOLLKORNBROT (page 179)	2 lb/907 g	1 hour; spray with water after proofing	N/A
WHEAT PULLMAN BREAD (page 134)	3 lb/1.36 kg	1 hour	N/A

7. Place the lid on the pan and allow the dough to proof for 15 additional minutes, or until it is ¼ in/6 mm from the top of the pan.

8. Bake in a 400°F/204°C deck oven until the crust is a rich golden brown and the sides of the bread spring back when pressed, 40 to 50 minutes. Remove the bread from the pan and cool completely on a rack.

Brioche Loaf

Makes 1 loaf   DDT: 75°F/24°C

BRIOCHE DOUGH (page 142)	1 lb	454 g
EGG WASH, for brushing (page 825)	as needed	as needed

1. Lightly grease a 2-lb/907-g loaf pan (8 in/20 cm long, 4½ in/11 cm wide, and 3 in/8 cm deep).

2. Remove the dough from the refrigerator and divide it by hand into 2-oz/57-g pieces. Preshape each piece into a round, lightly flouring the work surface as needed. (Note: Refrigerate the dough as necessary during shaping to keep it cool and workable.) Refrigerate the rolls until cool, about 15 minutes.

3. Place the pieces of dough in the loaf pan in 2 rows of 4. Brush lightly with egg wash, brushing away any excess that accumulates in the crevices. Proof, covered, until the dough is almost double in size and springs back slowly to the touch but does not collapse, 1 to 2 hours.

4. Gently brush the dough again with egg wash. Bake in a 375°F/191°C deck oven until the crust is a rich golden brown and the sides of the bread spring back fully when pressed, 30 to 35 minutes. Remove from the pan and cool completely on a rack.

STEAMING	BAKING TEMPERATURE/TIME	VENTING TIME (before end of bake)
Presteam/ steam 5 seconds	425°F/218°C/1 hour 15 minutes to 1 hour 20 minutes	N/A
N/A	400°F/204°C/40 to 50 minutes	N/A

Craquelin

Makes 1 loaf   DDT: 82°F/28°C

CRAQUELIN DOUGH (page 143)	12 oz	340 g
BRIOCHE DOUGH (page 142)	3 oz	85 g

1. Coat a panettone wrapper (5 in/13 cm in diameter and 6 in/15 cm high) with a light film of fat. Preshape the craquelin into a round (for preshaping instructions see page 184). Let the craquelin dough rest, covered, until relaxed, about 45 minutes. Meanwhile, pre-shape the brioche dough into a round and let it rest, covered and under refrigeration, until relaxed, about 30 minutes. (Note: When making multiple loaves, work sequentially, starting with the first pieces of dough you divided and rounded.)

2. Roll the brioche dough into a 6-in/15-cm circle. Wrap it around the craquelin dough to enclose it completely, and gather the edges together at the bottom to form a boule. Place the loaf seam side down in the prepared paper wrapper.

3. Proof, covered, until the dough springs back slowly to the touch but does not collapse, 2 to 3 hours.

4. Score the loaf with an X in the center or snip the entire surface with scissors.

5. Presteam a 375°F/191°C deck oven. Load the bread into the oven and steam for 5 seconds. Bake until the crust is golden brown and the sides of the bread spring back fully when pressed through the wrapper, 25 to 30 minutes. Cool completely on a rack.

Wrapping a thin sheet of brioche around the craquelin dough

Challah (3-Braid)

Makes 1 loaf   DDT: *78°F/26°C*

CHALLAH DOUGH (page 141)	1 lb	454 g
EGG WASH MADE WITH YOLKS ONLY, for brushing (page 825)	as needed	as needed

1. Divide the dough into 5½-oz/156-g pieces. Preshape the dough into oblong pieces (for preshaping instructions see page 184). Allow the dough to rest, covered, 15 to 20 minutes.

2. Start with the first piece of dough that you shaped and work sequentially. Starting at the center of the dough, roll each piece outward, applying gentle pressure with your palms. Apply very little pressure at the center of the dough, but increase the pressure as you roll toward the ends of the dough. Roll each piece of dough into an evenly tapered strand 12 in/30 cm long. It is imperative that all of the strands be the same length. If they are not, the finished braid will be uneven.

3. Dust the top of the strands very lightly with white rye flour. (This will keep the dough dry as you braid and help maintain the overall definition of the braid.)

4. Lay three strands of dough vertically parallel to each other. Begin braiding in the center of the strands. Place the left strand over the center strand, then place the right strand over the center strand. Repeat this process until you reach the end of the dough. Pinch the ends together tightly.

5. Turn the braid around and flip it over so that the unbraided strands are facing you. Starting again from the left, repeat the braiding process until you reach the end of the dough. Pinch the ends together tightly.

6. Brush the dough lightly with egg wash made solely from egg yolks. Allow the dough to proof, covered, until the dough springs back lightly to the touch but does not collapse, about 1 hour. There should be a small indentation left in the dough. Make sure that the egg wash is dry before you apply a second coat. Egg wash the dough again very gently before baking.

7. Bake in a 350°F/177°C convection oven until the braids are dark golden brown and shiny, 20 to 25 minutes. Cool completely on a rack.

Challah (6-Braid)

Makes 1 loaf   DDT: 78°F/26°C

CHALLAH DOUGH (page 141)	1 lb	454 g
EGG WASH MADE WITH YOLKS ONLY, for brushing (page 825)	as needed	as needed

1. Divide the dough into 2¾-oz/78-g pieces. Preshape the dough into oblong pieces (for preshaping instructions see page 184). Allow the dough to rest, covered, 15 to 20 minutes.

2. Start with the first piece of dough that you shaped and work sequentially. Starting at the center of the dough, roll each piece outward, applying gentle pressure with your palms. Apply very little pressure at the center of the dough, but increase the pressure as you roll toward the ends of the dough. Roll each piece of dough into an evenly tapered strand 12 in/30 cm long. It is imperative that all of the strands be the same length. If they are not, the finished braid will be uneven.

3. Dust the top of the strands very lightly with white rye flour. This will keep the dough dry as you braid and help maintain the overall definition of the braid.

4. Lay six strands of dough vertically parallel to each other. Pinch together the top ends of the strands of dough. You may need to place a weight on top of the pinched ends to make sure that they do not come undone. Keep the braiding tight as you proceed down the length of the strands.

5. Place the second strand from the right over the strand that is on the far left. Place the strand on the far right in the center of the strands. This will be over the third strand from the right. Place the second strand from the left over the strand that is on the far right. Place the strand on the far left in the center of the strands. This will be over the third strand from the left. Repeat this process down the entire length of the strands. Pinch the ends together tightly.

6. Brush the dough lightly with egg wash made solely from egg yolks. Allow the dough to proof, covered, until the dough springs back lightly to the touch but does not collapse, about 1 hour. There should be a small indentation left in the dough. Make sure that the egg wash is dry before you apply a second coat. Egg wash the dough again very gently before baking.

7. Bake in a 350°F/177°C convection oven until the braids are dark golden brown and shiny, 20 to 25 minutes. Cool completely on a rack.

Pinch the strands together at one end.

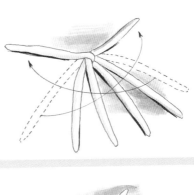

Lay strand 1 to the far right and strand 6 to the far left.

Lay strand 6 between strands 3 and 4.

Lay strand 2 to the far right over all the strands.

Lay strand 1 between strands 3 and 4.

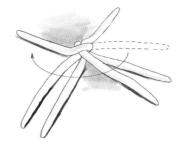

Lay strand 5 to the far left over all the strands. Then begin the process again from Figure 2 and repeat until the loaf is complete.

Pinch the ends of the strands together.

Coffee Cake (Braided)

Makes 1 cake   DDT: 75°F/24°C

SWEET DOUGH (page 141)	1 lb	454 g
CHERRY FILLING (page 506)	4 oz	113 g
CREAM CHEESE FILLING (page 830)	4 oz	113 g
EGG WASH, for brushing (page 825)	as needed	as needed
COARSE SUGAR, for garnish	as needed	as needed
APRICOT GLAZE, warm (Appendix A)	2 oz	57 g
FONDANT	as needed	as needed

1. Preshape the dough into an oblong (for preshaping instructions see page 184). Let the dough rest, covered, until relaxed, 15 to 20 minutes. (Note: When making multiple cakes, work sequentially, starting with the first piece of dough you divided and rounded.)

2. Position the dough lengthwise, parallel to the edge of the work surface with the seam side up. Roll the dough into a rectangle 10 by 12 in/25 by 30 cm; the dough should be about ¼ in/6 mm thick. Turn the dough so that a short side is facing you.

3. Using a large plain pastry tip, pipe the cherry filling down the center of the dough and then pipe a strip of the cream cheese filling on either side.

4. Make parallel diagonal cuts at a 45-degree angle evenly down both sides of the dough, spacing the cuts about 1 in/2 cm apart. Fold the top left strip diagonally over the filling and press it gently into the dough on the opposite side. Fold the strip on the opposite side over and press into place. Continue, alternating sides, for a braided effect. Trim any excess dough.

5. Transfer to a parchment-lined sheet pan. Brush the dough lightly with egg wash. Proof, covered, until the dough springs back slowly to the touch but does not collapse, 1 to 1½ hours.

6. Brush the dough very lightly again with egg wash. Sprinkle with coarse sugar. Bake in a 350°F/177°C convection oven until dark golden brown and shiny, about 30 minutes.

7. Brush the warm coffee cake with warmed apricot glaze. Drizzle with fondant icing, if desired. Cool completely on a rack.

Coffee Cake (Twisted)

Makes 1 cake   *DDT: 75°F/24°C*

SWEET DOUGH (page 141)	1 lb	454 g
FRANGIPANE FILLING (Appendix A)	3 oz	85 g
EGG WASH, for brushing (page 825)	as needed	as needed
APRICOT GLAZE, warm (Appendix A)	as needed	as needed

1. Preshape the dough into an oblong (for preshaping instructions see page 184). Let the dough rest, covered, until relaxed, 15 to 20 minutes. (Note: When making multiple cakes, work sequentially, starting with the first piece of dough you divided and rounded.)

2. Position the dough lengthwise, parallel to the edge of the work surface with the seam side up. Roll the dough into a rectangle 11 by 14 in/28 by 36 cm; the dough should be about 1/8 in/3 mm thick. Turn the dough so that a short side is facing you.

3. Spread the frangipane filling over the dough, leaving a 1-in/2-cm strip of dough exposed along the side closest to you. Moisten the exposed strip of dough lightly with water. Starting at the top, roll up the dough tightly and evenly toward you to make a compact cylinder 11 in/28 cm long.

4. Using a bench scraper or a sharp knife, cut the cylinder lengthwise in half. Twist the two pieces of dough together, making sure to keep the cut sides facing up.

5. Brush the dough very lightly with egg wash. Place on a parchment-lined sheet pan. Proof until the dough springs back slowly to the touch, 1 to 1 1/2 hours.

6. Brush the dough again very lightly with egg wash. Bake in a 350°F/177°C convection oven until the coffee cake springs back fully to the touch and is dark golden brown and shiny, about 30 minutes.

7. Brush the warm coffee cake with warmed apricot glaze. Cool completely on a rack.

Soft Pretzels

Makes 25 pretzels (5½ oz/156 g each)   DDT: 75°F/24°C

SOFT PRETZEL DOUGH (page 144)	8 lb 9½ oz	3.90 kg
LYE SOLUTION		
WATER (105°F/41°C)	32 fl oz	960 mL
SODIUM HYDROXIDE PELLETS	1¼ oz	35 g
COARSE SALT, for garnish	as needed	as needed

1. Divide the dough into 5½-oz/156-g pieces. Preshape the dough into oblong pieces (for preshaping instructions see page 184). Let the dough rest, covered, until relaxed, 5 to 10 minutes. Work sequentially, starting with the first piece of dough you divided and rounded.

2. One at a time, stretch each piece of dough into a rectangle 10 in/25 cm long. Fold the top edge of the dough down to the center of the dough, pressing lightly with your fingertips. Fold the top edge of the dough to the bottom edge. Using the heel of your hand, seal the two edges together.

3. Turn the dough seam side down. Starting with each of your hands 2 in/5 cm from the center of the dough, roll the dough under your palms until it is 30 in/76 cm long, with a thicker portion 4 in/10 cm long in the center.

4. Lay the dough on the table and cross the ends over each other, leaving 3 in/8 cm of dough on each side of the crossing point (the thicker center of the dough should be clos-

Lay the dough on the table in a U shape and cross the ends over each other.

Twist the ends together once.

Bring the ends down and attach them to either side of the thicker center of the dough, pressing them to seal.

est to you). Twist the ends together once. Bring the ends of the dough over and attach them to either side of the thicker center of the dough, pressing gently to seal them. Transfer to a parchment-lined sheet pan.

5. Proof, covered, until the dough gives slightly when touched, about 30 minutes.

6. Relax the dough under refrigeration until it forms a skin, about 25 minutes.

7. To prepare the lye solution, combine the water and sodium hydroxide pellets, stirring until the pellets are completely dissolved. (Note: Wear protective gloves and goggles; be careful not to get any of the solution on your skin.)

8. Remove the pretzels from the refrigerator and allow them to stand for 5 to 10 minutes. (Note: If you dip the pretzels right away, the water temperature will drop and the sodium hydroxide will be less likely to stay in solution.)

9. Using tongs, dip the pretzels in the lye solution and then place them on screens to drain. Discard the lye solution once you have finished removing the pretzels by pouring it down the drain; it cannot be reused. Sprinkle the pretzels immediately with coarse salt. Make an incision 3 in/8 cm long and 1/4 in/6 mm deep in the thicker part of each pretzel.

10. Place the pretzels onto sheet pans lined with a silicone mat or lightly oiled parchment and bake in a 475°F/246°C deck oven (with the vent open) until deep golden brown, 12 to 15 minutes. Cool completely on racks.

Working with Lye

After pretzels are shaped and proofed, they are dipped in a solution of water and sodium hydroxide (no more than 4 percent) before baking. This caustic solution, known as lye, gives the surface of the pretzels their characteristic color, shine, and tangy, salty flavor. When the pretzels are baked, the sodium hydroxide is transformed into inert salts. Use caution when working with a lye solution. Wear goggles and rubber gloves to prevent contact with the solution. As the pretzels are dipped, they should be placed directly on screens to drain and then on silicone- or parchment-lined sheet pans. Once they are all dipped, they should go directly into the oven.

Semolina Pizza

Makes 25 pizza rounds (6 oz/170 g each)   DDT: 75°F/24°C

SEMOLINA PIZZA DOUGH (page 144)	9 lb 6 oz	4.25 kg
SEMOLINA FLOUR, for dusting	as needed	as needed

1. Divide the dough into 6-oz/170-g pieces. Preshape the dough into round pieces (for pre-shaping instructions see page 184). Let the dough rest, covered and, under refrigeration, until relaxed, 1 hour. Work sequentially, starting with the first piece of dough you divided and rounded.

2. Using a rolling pin, roll each piece of dough into a round 9 in/23 cm in diameter. Transfer the dough to parchment-lined sheet pans that have been dusted with semolina flour, or place each round on a peel before you add any topping.

3. Top the dough as desired (see topping formulas below), leaving a 1-in/3-cm crust border ungarnished.

4. Load the pizzas into a 500°F/260°C deck oven and bake until golden brown around the edges, 3 to 4 minutes. Serve at once.

Spinach Pizza

Makes 25 pizza rounds

SPINACH	3 lb 12 oz	1.70 kg
OLIVE OIL	2 oz	57 g
SEMOLINA PIZZA (above)	25 rounds	25 rounds
BASIL PESTO (Appendix A)	13 oz	369 g
RICOTTA CHEESE	2 lb 6 oz	1.08 kg
RICOTTA SALATA, grated	1 lb 9 oz	709 g

1. Sauté the spinach in the olive oil until slightly wilted and bright green in color. Drain and reserve.

2. For each pizza, place a dough round on an oven peel or sheet pan that has been dusted with semolina flour.

3. Spread 1½ oz/43 g of the pesto on the dough. Top with 1½ oz/43 g of the spinach, 1½ oz/43 g of the ricotta cheese, and 1 oz/28 g of the ricotta salata.

4. Bake in a 500°F/260°C deck oven until golden brown around the edges, 3 to 4 minutes. Serve at once.

Margherita Pizza

Makes 25 pizza rounds

GARLIC, minced	2½ oz	71 g
EXTRA VIRGIN OLIVE OIL	1 lb 4 oz	567 g
CANNED CRUSHED TOMATOES	3 lb 12 oz	1.70 kg
SALT	2 tsp	10 g
BLACK PEPPER	2 tsp	4 g
ROSEMARY, chopped	2 tbsp	6 g
SEMOLINA PIZZA (page 234)	25 rounds	25 rounds
MOZZARELLA CHEESE, grated	3 lb 2 oz	1.42 kg
PARMESAN CHEESE, grated	12½ oz	354 g

1. Sweat the garlic in the olive oil over low heat until translucent, about 6 minutes.

2. Add the tomatoes, salt, and pepper. Cook, covered, over medium heat until the sauce has thickened slightly and has a good aroma, about 30 minutes.

3. Add the rosemary and cook for 15 minutes.

4. For each pizza, place a dough round on an oven peel or sheet pan that has been dusted with semolina flour. Cover the dough with 3 oz/85 g of the sauce, leaving a ½-in/1-cm border. Top with 2 oz/57 g of the mozzarella cheese and ½ oz/14 g of the Parmesan.

5. Bake in a 500°F/260°C deck oven until golden brown around the edges, 3 to 4 minutes. Serve at once.

Wild Mushroom Pizza

Makes 25 pizza rounds

BUTTER	4 oz	113 g
ALL-PURPOSE FLOUR	2½ oz	71 g
MILK	48 fl oz	1.44 L
EXTRA VIRGIN OLIVE OIL	10 oz	284 g
OYSTER MUSHROOMS, stems removed	2 lb 8 oz	1.13 kg
BUTTON MUSHROOMS, sliced	1 lb 4 oz	567 g
SHIITAKE MUSHROOMS, stems removed	1 lb 4 oz	567 g
DRIED MORELS, reconstituted	1¼ oz	35 g
DRIED PORCINI, reconstituted and chopped	1¼ oz	35 g
SHALLOTS, minced	1¼ oz	35 g
GARLIC, chopped	1 oz	28 g
PORT WINE	24 fl oz	720 mL
PARSLEY, chopped	1¼ oz	35 g
THYME, chopped	1¼ tsp	1.25 g
TARRAGON, chopped	1¼ tsp	1.25 g
GROUND NUTMEG	1 tsp	2 g
SALT	1 tbsp	15 g
BLACK PEPPER	1 tbsp	6 g
MASCARPONE CHEESE	6½ oz	184 g
SEMOLINA PIZZA (page 234)	25 rounds	25 rounds
AGED MONTEREY JACK CHEESE, grated	2 lb 6 oz	1.08 kg
PARMESAN CHEESE, grated	1 lb 3 oz	539 g
CHIVES, snipped	1 oz	28 g

1. Melt ½ oz/14 g of the butter in a saucepot. Add the flour, stirring to incorporate, and cook, stirring constantly, over medium heat for 5 minutes. Do not let the roux develop any color.

2. Gradually add the milk, whisking constantly. Cook, stirring constantly, until the sauce coats the back of a spoon. Remove from the heat.

3. Heat the remaining 3½ oz/99 g butter and the olive oil in a saucepan over medium heat. Add all the mushrooms and sauté until lightly browned, approximately 10 minutes.

4. Add the shallots and garlic and sauté until aromatic. Deglaze the pan with the port and reduce for several minutes, until most of the liquid has evaporated. Add the parsley, thyme, tarragon, nutmeg, salt, and pepper.

5. Add the mushroom mixture to the cream sauce base, stirring until well mixed. Stir in the mascarpone cheese.

6. For each pizza, place a dough round on an oven peel or sheet pan that has been dusted with semolina flour. Spread 5 oz/142 g of the mushroom sauce on the dough. Top with 1½ oz/43 g of the Jack cheese, ¾ oz/21 g of the Parmesan cheese, and about 1 tsp/1 g of the snipped chives.

7. Bake in a 500°F/260°C deck oven until golden brown around the edges, 3 to 4 minutes. Serve at once.

Pita Bread

Makes 11 pitas (4½ oz/128 g each)   DDT: 78°F/26°C

PITA DOUGH (page 146)	3 lb 1½ oz	1.40 kg

1. Divide the dough into 4½-oz/128-g pieces. Preshape the dough into round pieces (for preshaping instructions see page 184). Let the dough rest, covered, until relaxed, 15 to 20 minutes. Work sequentially, starting with the first piece of dough you divided and rounded.

2. Using a rolling pin, roll each piece of dough into a round 7 in/18 cm in diameter. Transfer to parchment-lined sheet pans, cover, and let relax for 10 minutes.

3. Load the pitas into a 500°F/260°C deck oven and bake until puffed but not browned, 3 to 4 minutes. Stack the pitas five high and wrap each stack in a cloth. Cool before serving.

Naan Bread

Makes 8 flatbreads (3 oz/85 g each)   DDT: 74°F/23°C

NAAN DOUGH (page 146)	1 lb 8 oz	680 g
GARNISH		
CLARIFIED BUTTER, melted	as needed	as needed
POPPY SEEDS OR BLACK ONION SEEDS	2 tbsp	12 g

1. Divide the dough into 3-oz/85-g pieces. Preshape the dough into round pieces (for pre-shaping instructions see page 184). Let the dough rest, covered, until relaxed, 15 to 20 minutes. Work sequentially, starting with the first piece of dough you divided and rounded.

2. Gently stretch each piece of dough into a round 7 in/18 cm in diameter, so that the center is ¼ in/6 mm thick and there is a border ½ in/1 cm wide all around. Pull one edge out to elongate each round slightly, creating a teardrop shape.

3. Place the breads on parchment-lined sheet pans, brush them with clarified butter, and sprinkle the seeds on top.

4. Bake the naan in a 425°F/218°C deck oven until golden brown and puffed, about 10 minutes. Cool completely on racks.

Stretching the naan dough into a teardrop shape

Lavash

Makes 11 sheets (1 lb/454 g each)   DDT: 78°F/26°C

LAVASH DOUGH (page 145)	11 lb	4.99 kg
OLIVE OIL, for garnish	as needed	as needed
SESAME SEEDS, for garnish	as needed	as needed
POPPY SEEDS, for garnish	as needed	as needed

1. Divide the dough into 1-lb/454-g pieces. Preshape the dough into round pieces (for pre-shaping instructions see page 184). Lightly brush sheet pans with olive oil. Let the dough rest, covered, until relaxed, 15 to 20 minutes. Work sequentially, starting with the first piece of dough you divided and rounded.

2. Roll each piece of dough to $\frac{1}{16}$ in/1.5 mm thick on a dough sheeter, flouring the dough periodically as you roll it. The dough should be $16\frac{1}{2}$ by $24\frac{1}{2}$ in/42 by 62 cm. (Note: You can also stretch the dough using the backs of your hands, similar to the way you stretch strudel dough—for information on strudel dough see page 258. If you shape the dough by hand, it is important to keep the dough even; if it is stretched unevenly, it will bake unevenly.)

3. Place each sheet of dough on one of the greased sheet pans. If the dough is not big enough to cover the entire pan, have another person help stretch it to fit the sheet pan; use the backs of your hands to gently stretch the dough.

4. Brush the top of the dough lightly with olive oil and sprinkle with seeds of your choice.

5. Allow the dough to relax for 15 to 20 minutes.

6. Bake in a 400°F/204°C convection oven until light golden brown, about 7 minutes. Cool completely on racks, then wrap well.

Notes   You can bake the lavash 70 percent of the way, until it is baked but not yet golden brown, and then reheat before use in a 400°F/204°C oven.

Allowing the dough to rest covered under refrigeration overnight, rather than for only 15 to 20 minutes (as stated in Step 1), provides for better development of flavor characteristics.

Filled Flatbread

Makes 8 flatbreads (9 oz/255 g each)   DDT: 75°F/24°C

OLIVE OIL	2 oz	57 g
GARLIC, minced	1 oz	28 g
GREEN PEPPERS, minced	11 oz	312 g
CANNED PLUM TOMATOES, drained, seeded, and coarsely chopped	1 lb 1½ oz	496 g
GREEN ONIONS, minced	2 oz	57 g
SALT	1 tsp	5 g
RED PEPPER FLAKES	1 tsp	2 g
GROUND CARAWAY	¼ tsp	0.50 g
GROUND CORIANDER	¼ tsp	0.50 g
GROUND CUMIN	¼ tsp	0.50 g
FLAT-LEAF PARSLEY, minced	2 oz	57 g
NAAN DOUGH (page 146)	3 lb 5½ oz	1.52 kg
OLIVE OIL, for frying	as needed	as needed

1. To prepare the filling, heat the olive oil in a skillet. Add the garlic and cook over medium heat until it just begins to lightly brown. Add the peppers and cook for 2 minutes, or until they soften, stirring occasionally. Add the tomatoes and simmer for 15 minutes, or until the mixture thickens, stirring occasionally.

2. Add the green onions and seasonings and simmer for 1 minute. Stir in the parsley. Transfer the filling to a stainless-steel bowl and allow to cool to room temperature.

3. Divide the dough into 3¼-oz/92-g pieces. Preshape the dough into round pieces (for pre-shaping instructions see page 184). Let the dough rest, covered, until relaxed, 10 to 15 minutes. Work sequentially, starting with the first piece of dough you divided and rounded.

4. Using a rolling pin, roll each piece of dough into a round 6 in/15 cm in diameter. Spread 3 oz/85 g filling in the center of each of the eight rounds, leaving a 1-in/3-cm border all around. Brush the exposed border with water.

5. Place one of the remaining eight rounds on top of each of the filled pieces of dough. Pinch the edges of each bread together and then stretch the dough gently into a round 9 in/23 cm in diameter.

6. Heat a small amount of olive oil in a skillet until it is almost smoking. Add one bread and cook for 1 minute, then flip it over. Fry for another 2 to 2½ minutes, or until there are light brown specks on the bottom. Flip the bread over once again and fry for another minute, or until lightly browned. Fry the remaining breads, adding more oil as necessary.

7. Keep the breads warm by wrapping them in a cotton cloth and shingling them in a basket.

Apple Fritters

Makes 20 fritters (4 oz/113 g each)   DDT: 68°F/20°C

BERLINER DOUGH (page 148)	3 lb	1.36 kg
PÂTE À CHOUX (page 255)	8¾ oz	248 g
GOLDEN DELICIOUS APPLES, cut into brunoise	1 lb 2¾ oz	532 g
CINNAMON SUGAR (Appendix A)	¾ oz, plus as needed for dusting	21 g, plus as needed for dusting
OIL, for deep frying	as needed	as needed

1. Line sheet pans with parchment paper and grease lightly.

2. Roll the dough into a rectangle 12 by 16 in/30 by 41 cm; the dough should be ¼ in/6 mm thick.

3. With an offset spatula, spread the pâte à choux in an even layer (⅛ in/3 mm) over the Berliner dough, leaving a 1-in/3-cm strip of dough exposed along one long side. Toss the apples with the cinnamon sugar and scatter evenly over the pâte à choux. Brush the exposed strip of dough lightly with water.

(continued)

Frying apple fritters

4. Starting with the side opposite the exposed strip of dough, roll the dough up into a tight, even cylinder, keeping the dough tight and the diameter of the cylinder even. Then roll the cylinder gently back and forth to seal the seam.

5. Using a serrated knife, slice the cylinder into pieces ¾ in/2 cm wide. Lay the slices on the prepared sheet pans, leaving 1 in/3 cm between them to allow them to expand.

6. Proof, covered, until the dough springs back slowly to the touch but does not collapse, about 45 minutes.

7. Using a paring knife, cut the parchment paper around the fritters into individual squares.

8. Carefully flip the fritter into a deep fryer (350°F/177°C), quickly peel off the parchment, and fry until golden brown on the first side, 2 to 3 minutes. Turn and fry until the second side is golden and the fritter is cooked through, 2 to 3 minutes longer.

9. Lift the fritters from the hot oil with a spider or basket, allowing the oil to drain away over the fryer. Drain on paper towels briefly before rolling in cinnamon sugar.

Berliners (Jelly Doughnuts)

Makes 3 dozen Berliners (2 oz/57 g each)   DDT: 68°F/20°C

BERLINER DOUGH, preshaped into a round (page 148)	4 lb 8 oz	2.04 kg
OIL, for frying	as needed	as needed
RASPBERRY JAM	2 lb 4 oz	1.02 kg
SUGAR, for coating	as needed	as needed
CONFECTIONERS' SUGAR, for dusting	as needed	as needed

1. Divide the dough by hand or with a dough divider into 36 pieces (2 oz/57 g each). Shape each one into a tight round and press lightly with the palm of your hand to flatten slighlty. Transfer, seam side down, to a sheet pan lined with a piece of greased parchment paper.

2. Proof, covered, until the dough springs back slowly to the touch but does not collapse, about 1 hour.

3. Carefully transfer the proofed Berliners, a few at a time, seam side up, to the deep fryer (350°F/177°C) and fry, covered, until golden brown on the first side, 1 minute. Turn and fry, uncovered, another 1½ minutes. Turn once more and fry until the top is deep golden brown, 20 to 30 seconds.

4. Lift the Berliners from the hot oil with a spider or basket, allowing the oil to drain away over the fryer. Drain on paper towels just until cool enough to handle.

5. Fill a pastry bag fitted with a small plain pastry tip and inject 1 oz/28 g of the raspberry jam into each Berliner. Dip both sides of each one in granulated sugar, place them seam side down on racks, and sift confectioners' sugar over them.

Yeast-Raised Doughnuts

Makes 57 doughnuts (1½ oz/43 g each)   DDT: 80°F/27°C

YEAST-RAISED DOUGHNUT DOUGH (page 147)	5 lb 5½ oz	2.42 kg
OIL, for frying	as needed	as needed
TOPPINGS AND/OR COATINGS	See sidebar below	

1. Roll the dough to ½ in/1 cm thick. Let the dough rest, covered, until relaxed, 10 minutes.

2. Cut the doughnuts with a doughnut cutter or with two round cutters (use a 3-in/8-cm cutter for the doughnuts and a 1-in/3-cm cutter for the holes; keep the holes evenly centered so the doughnuts fry evenly.)

3. Proof, covered, until the dough springs back slowly to the touch but does not collapse, 15 minutes.

4. Carefully transfer the proofed doughnuts, a few at a time to a deep fryer (350°F/177°C) and fry until golden brown on the first side, 2 minutes. Turn and fry until the second side is golden and the doughnuts are cooked through, 2 to 4 minutes.

5. Lift the doughnuts from the hot oil with a spider or basket, allowing the oil to drain away directly over the fryer. Drain on paper towels before coating or topping.

Finishing and Garnishing Doughnuts

Roll still-warm doughnuts in confectioners' sugar, vanilla sugar, or cinnamon sugar. Or, warm plain or flavored fondant to 110°F/43°C. After the doughnuts have cooled completely, transfer them to glazing racks and coat with an even layer of fondant. Garnish with sprinkles, plain or toasted coconut, or decorating sugars.

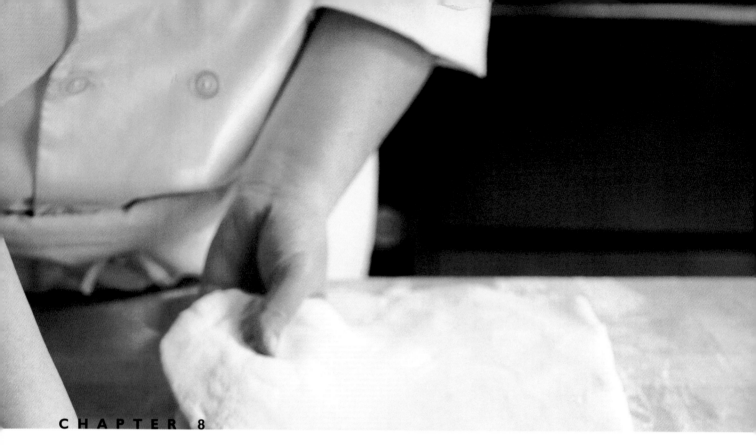

CHAPTER 8

Pastry Doughs and Batters

PASTRY DOUGHS ARE THE FOUNDATION FOR A WIDE RANGE OF PREPARATIONS. PIE DOUGH, SHORT DOUGH, AND PUFF PASTRY ARE ONLY A FEW EXAMPLES. ALL ARE MADE OF THE SAME BASIC INGREDIENTS, BUT DIFFERENT PREPARATION TECHNIQUES GIVE THEM VASTLY DIFFERENT CHARACTERISTICS, MAKING EACH SUITABLE FOR DIFFERENT APPLICATIONS. PASTRY BATTERS SUCH AS CRÊPE BATTER OR PÂTE À CHOUX ALSO SERVE AS ELEMENTAL PREPARATIONS AND ARE USED IN COUNTLESS CLASSICAL AND CONTEMPORARY DESSERTS AND PASTRIES.

Basic Pie Dough

Makes 6 lb 6 oz/2.89 kg

ALL-PURPOSE FLOUR	3 lb	1.36 kg
SALT	½ oz	14 g
BUTTER, cut into pieces and chilled	1 lb	454 g
SHORTENING, cut into pieces and chilled	1 lb	454 g
COLD WATER	16 fl oz	480 mL

1. Combine the flour and salt in the bowl of a stand mixer. Add the butter and shortening and blend using a dough hook attachment until pea-size nuggets form, about 3 minutes. Add the water all at once and continue to mix until the dough just comes together.

2. Turn the dough out onto a lightly floured work surface. Scale the dough as desired. Wrap tightly and refrigerate for at least 1 hour before rolling. (The dough can be held under refrigeration or frozen.)

Rubbed Doughs

The characteristic flaky texture of rubbed doughs is developed by rubbing together the fat and the flour, leaving flakes of fat visible. The larger the flakes of fat in the mixture, the flakier the baked dough will be.

Pastry and all-purpose flours are, in general, ideal for the rubbed dough method. Cake flour is too high in starch, so it will not absorb enough water and will produce a dough with a pasty consistency. Bread flour, because of its high protein content, will absorb water quickly and in comparatively great quantities, developing gluten readily and in great amounts. This will make a dough that is tough and elastic. On the other hand, pastry flour and all-purpose flour have the proper balance of starch and protein, with the desired amount of water absorption and gluten development to produce a dough that is both flaky and tender.

Fat contributes to the development of a flaky texture in pastry doughs. The amount of fat and the way it is added to the other ingredients in a formula have a significant impact on the finished baked good. Leaving the fat in pieces or chunks, rather than combining it thoroughly, gives doughs a flaky texture. When a rubbed dough is baked, the pieces of fat melt to create pockets in the interior of the dough. As the fat melts, steam is released from the moisture held in the fat. This steam expands the pockets, which then become set as the dough continues to bake, thus creating a flaky, textured baked good. Butter, lard, hydrogenated shortening and other fats may be used in the production of rubbed doughs. All of these fats are solid at room temperature, and when cold have a firm consistency that makes it possible to use them for this method. Of all the fats, butter alone will yield the most flavor, but it is difficult to handle because it has a lower melting point than shortening and lard. Water is the most common liquid in rubbed dough formulas, but milk or cream may also be used. When substituting milk or cream for water in a rubbed dough formula, decrease the amount of fat to adjust for the fat present in the milk or cream.

Always keep rubbed doughs cool during mixing and when working with them. The ideal working temperature is 60°F/16°C. If the dough becomes too warm, the fat may become too soft and absorb into the dough, destroying the layers in the dough.

To make a rubbed dough, first flake the firm cold fat into the flour. This can be done by hand, using your fingertips, or in an electric mixer or a food processor (use the metal blade, not the plastic dough blade). Next, add all the liquid at once to the flour-fat mixture and blend the dough quickly but thoroughly.

Turn the dough out onto a lightly floured work surface. Gather and press it together into a disk or flat rectangle. Wrap the dough tightly in plastic wrap and chill it under refrigeration until firm enough to work. The period of rest and cooling before working and rolling is vital to ensure that the fat does not become too soft nor the flour overworked.

There are two basic types of rubbed doughs: flaky and mealy. The larger the flakes of fat are before the liquid is added, the flakier and crisper the baked crust will be. If the flakes of butter or shortening are rubbed into the dough just until they are about the size of peas, the dough will be what is often referred to as "flaky" pie dough. When the liquid is added, the dough is worked just enough to allow the moisture to be absorbed by the flour and just until the ingredients to come together, at which point the dough should be allowed to rest and cool under refrigeration.

Adding water to a dough

A cross section of flaky dough shows layers of fat interspersed throughout the dough.

Flaky pie dough is best for pies, tarts, and other preparations where the filling is baked in the crust. It is not well suited for preparations where the crust is completely prebaked and allowed to cool and then a liquid filling is added that must set under refrigeration. After baking, the pockets that lend the flaky texture in this type of dough easily allow juices and/or liquids to leak from the crust.

If the butter or shortening is more thoroughly worked into the dough, until the mixture resembles coarse meal, the result will be what is sometimes referred to as a "mealy" dough. Mealy pie doughs have a finer, more tender texture than do flaky pie doughs. With the fat more evenly interspersed in the flour, its ability to shorten gluten strands present in the dough becomes more apparent, as the resulting dough is very tender. As with flaky pastry dough, mealy dough should be wrapped in plastic wrap and allowed to rest under refrigeration so the butter or other fat will firm and the gluten will relax before the dough is worked and rolled.

Mealy doughs are well suited for all types of pies and tarts, but most particularly for formulas that require a fully baked shell (see Baking Blind, page 511) filled with a precooked filling, such as a cream, that will have to set under refrigeration before it can be sliced and served.

Pâte Brisée

Makes 4 lb/1.81 kg

CAKE FLOUR	2 lb 4 oz	1.02 kg
SALT	¾ oz	21 g
BUTTER, cubed	1 lb 2 oz	510 g
WATER	8 fl oz	240 mL
EGGS	4 oz	113 g

1. Combine the flour and salt in the bowl of an electric mixer. Add the cubed butter and blend using a dough hook attachment until a paste forms, about 4 minutes.

2. Combine the water and eggs. Add the egg and water mixture gradually to the flour while mixing on low speed, just until a shaggy mass forms. Tightly cover the mixture with plastic wrap and allow it to rest under refrigeration for 1 hour.

3. Turn the dough out onto a lightly floured work surface. Gather and press it together. Scale the dough as desired. Wrap tightly and refrigerate for at least 1 hour before rolling. (The dough can be held under refrigeration or frozen.)

Variation   **Whole Wheat Pâte Brisée** Substitute 4 oz/113 g whole wheat flour for 8 oz/227 g of the cake flour.

1-2-3 Cookie Dough
Makes 6 lb/2.72 kg

BUTTER, soft	2 lb	907 g
SUGAR	1 lb	454 g
VANILLA EXTRACT	1 tbsp	15 mL
EGGS	8 oz	227 g
CAKE FLOUR, sifted	3 lb	1.36 kg

1. Cream together the butter, sugar, and vanilla on medium speed using a paddle attachment, scraping down the bowl periodically, until smooth and light in color. Add the eggs gradually, a few at a time, scraping down the bowl and blending until smooth after each addition. Add the flour all at once and mix on low speed until just blended.

2. Turn the dough out onto a lightly floured work surface. Scale the dough as desired. Wrap tightly and refrigerate for at least 1 hour before rolling. (The dough can be held under refrigeration or frozen.)

Variations   **Lemon Cookie Dough** Add 1 tbsp/9 g finely grated lemon zest in Step 1.

1-2-3 Cookie Dough with Graham Cracker Crumbs Replace 8 oz/227 g of the cake flour with an equal amount of graham cracker crumbs and add in Step 1 with the flour.

Rich Short Dough

Makes 6 lb 6 oz/2.90 kg

BUTTER, soft	2 lb	907 kg
CONFECTIONERS' SUGAR, sifted	1 lb	454 kg
VANILLA EXTRACT	1 tsp	5 mL
LEMON ZEST, grated	1 tsp	3 g
EGG YOLKS	1 lb	454 g
CAKE FLOUR, sifted	3 lb	1.36 kg

1. Cream together the butter, sugar, vanilla extract, and lemon zest on medium speed using a paddle attachment, scraping down the bowl periodically, until smooth and light in color. Add the egg yolks gradually, a few at a time, scraping down the bowl and blending until smooth after each addition. Add the flour all at once and mix on low speed until just blended.

2. Turn the dough out onto a lightly floured work surface. Scale the dough as desired. Wrap tightly and refrigerate for at least 1 hour before rolling. (The dough can be held under refrigeration or frozen.)

Short Dough

Short dough contains a high percentage of fat, which produces a very tender and crumbly crust. If worked excessively, however, a short dough will become tough. Cake flour is the preferred choice for short doughs because of its ability to absorb moisture. Short doughs include eggs, either whole eggs or yolks, which contribute to the flavor and color of the dough, as well as to its tender texture.

To make a short dough, combine the sugar and butter and mix only until it forms a smooth paste to ensure even blending; do not mix vigorously so that air is incorporated. To prevent the mixture from breaking or curdling, have the eggs and any other liquid ingredients at room temperature, and blend them in carefully.

Add the flour and mix at low speed only until just combined; overmixing will make the dough tough. If the dough appears to be somewhat rough or coarse when it is removed from the mixer, work it gently by hand just until it comes together and shape it into a disk or flat rectangle and wrap tightly in plastic wrap. Refrigerate before using to allow the dough to firm up and the gluten to relax. The butter becomes soft during the mixing process, making short dough difficult to work with immediately after mixing.

Chocolate Short Dough

Makes 5 lb/2.27 kg

ALL-PURPOSE FLOUR	2 lb 3 oz	992 g
DUTCH-PROCESS COCOA POWDER	3 oz	85 g
BUTTER, soft	1 lb 8 oz	680 g
SUGAR	12 oz	340 g
VANILLA EXTRACT	1 tsp	5 mL
EGGS	6 oz	170 g

1. Sift the flour and cocoa powder together.

2. Cream the butter, sugar, and vanilla on medium speed using a paddle attachment, scraping down the bowl periodically, until smooth and light in color, about 5 minutes. Add the eggs gradually, a few at a time, scraping down the bowl and blending until smooth after each addition. Add the dry ingredients all at once, mixing on low speed until just blended.

3. Turn the dough out onto a lightly floured work surface. Scale the dough as desired. Wrap tightly and refrigerate for at least 1 hour before rolling. (The dough can be held under refrigeration or frozen.)

Savory Short Dough

Makes 4 lb/1.81 kg

CAKE FLOUR, sifted	2 lb	907 kg
BUTTER, soft	1 lb 4 oz	567 g
SALT	¾ oz	21 g
EGGS	10 oz	284 g

1. Combine the cake flour, butter, and salt and mix on medium speed using a paddle attachment until combined, about 5 minutes.

2. Add the eggs gradually, a few at a time, and mix until the dough is fully blended.

3. Turn the dough out onto a lightly floured work surface. Scale the dough as desired. Wrap tightly and refrigerate for at least 1 hour before rolling. (The dough can be held under refrigeration or frozen.)

Cornmeal Short Dough

Makes 8 lb 6 oz/3.80 kg

ALL-PURPOSE FLOUR, sifted	2 lb 4 oz	1.02 kg
CORNMEAL	1 lb 4 oz	567 g
SALT	1½ tsp	7.5 g
BUTTER, soft	2 lb	907 g
SUGAR	1 lb 4 oz	567 g
EGG YOLKS	12 oz	340 g
WATER	4 fl oz	120 mL

1. Combine the flour, cornmeal, and salt.

2. Cream together the butter and sugar on medium speed using a paddle attachment, scraping down the bowl periodically, until smooth and light in color, about 5 minutes. Add the egg yolks gradually, a few at a time, scraping down the bowl and blending until smooth after each addition. Add the dry ingredients all at once and mix on low speed until just blended. Add the water and blend just until incorporated.

3. Turn the dough out onto a lightly floured work surface. Scale the dough as desired. Wrap tightly and refrigerate for at least 1 hour before rolling. (The dough can be held under refrigeration or frozen.)

Almond Paste Short Dough

Makes 4 lb/1.81 kg

ALMOND PASTE, broken into pieces	1 lb 4 oz	567 g
BUTTER	1 lb	454 g
EGGS	6 oz	170 g
CAKE FLOUR, sifted	1 lb 4 oz	567 g

1. Cream together the almond paste and butter on medium speed using a paddle attachment, scraping down the bowl periodically, until smooth and light in color, about 5 minutes. Add the eggs gradually, a few at a time, scraping down the bowl and blending until smooth after each addition. Add the flour all at once and mix on low speed until just blended.

2. Turn the dough out onto a lightly floured work surface. Scale the dough as desired. Wrap tightly and refrigerate for at least 1 hour before rolling. (The dough can be held under refrigeration or frozen.)

Almond Dough

Makes 5 lb/2.27 kg

PASTRY FLOUR	1 lb 6 oz	624 g
BAKING POWDER	½ oz	14 g
BUTTER, soft	1 lb 2 oz	510 g
SUGAR	1 lb 2 oz	510 g
VANILLA EXTRACT	1½ tsp	7.50 mL
EGGS	6 oz	170 g
ALMONDS, finely crushed	1 lb 2 oz	510 g

1. Sift the flour and baking powder together.

2. Cream together the butter, sugar, and vanilla extract on medium speed using a paddle attachment, scraping down the bowl periodically, until smooth and light in color, about 5 minutes. Add the eggs one at a time, scraping down the bowl and blending until smooth after each addition. Add the flour mixture and the almonds all at once and mix on low speed until just blended.

3. Turn the dough out onto a lightly floured work surface. Scale the dough as desired. Wrap tightly and refrigerate for at least 1 hour before rolling. (The dough can be held under refrigeration or frozen.)

Linzer Dough

Makes 3 lb/1.36 kg

CAKE FLOUR	15 oz	425 g
BAKING POWDER	2½ tsp	7.50 g
GROUND CINNAMON	1 tsp	2 g
BUTTER, soft	12½ oz	354 g
SUGAR	9 oz	255 g
VANILLA EXTRACT	1 tbsp	15 mL
EGGS	6 oz	170 g
CAKE CRUMBS, finely ground	2 oz	57 g
HAZELNUTS, finely ground and lightly toasted	6 oz	170 g

1. Sift the flour, baking powder, and cinnamon together.

2. Cream together the butter, sugar, and vanilla extract on medium speed using a paddle attachment, scraping down the bowl periodically, until smooth and light in color, about 5 minutes. Add the eggs gradually, a few at a time, scraping down the bowl and blending until smooth after each addition. Add the dry ingredients, cake crumbs, and hazelnuts and mix on low speed until just blended.

3. Turn the dough out onto a lightly floured work surface. Scale the dough as desired. Wrap tightly and refrigerate for at least 1 hour before rolling. (The dough can be held under refrigeration or frozen.)

Graham Cracker Crust

Makes 1 lb 4 oz/567 g

GRAHAM CRACKER CRUMBS	10 oz	284 g
BROWN SUGAR	4 oz	113 g
BUTTER, melted	6 oz	170 g

1. Process the graham cracker crumbs, brown sugar, and butter in a food processor just until crumbly, about 5 minutes.

2. The crust is ready to be pressed into prepared pans and baked.

Crumb Crusts

Crumb crusts are simple, flavorful, quick-to-make crusts. They are typically used in two types of preparations: pudding or cream pies and cheesecakes. Graham crackers are most commonly used as the base for crumb crusts, but other types of cookies may be used for different flavors.

The crumbs are sweetened as necessary and blended with butter; sometimes a small amount of egg white is added to help make the crust hold together after baking. The crumb mixture is then pressed into an even layer into the pie or other baking pan and prebaked to evaporate some moisture and make the crust more flavorful and crisp. Scale the crust into prepared pans and press into an even layer, about ¼ in/6 mm thick. (Scaling notes: Use about 3 oz/85 g per 6-in/15-cm pan; 5 oz/142 g per 8-in/20-cm pan.) Crumb crusts should be baked at 350°F/177°C until set and light golden brown, about 7 minutes. Cool the crust completely before filling.

For pudding and cream pies, the filling is cooked, then poured into the cooled baked crust, and refrigerated until set. For cheesecakes, the batter is poured into the cooled baked crust and then baked until set.

Pâte à Choux

Makes 6 lb/2.72 kg

MILK	32 fl oz	960 mL
BUTTER	1 lb	454 g
SUGAR	1½ tsp	7.50 g
SALT	1½ tsp	7.50 g
BREAD FLOUR	1 lb	454 g
EGGS	2 lb	907 g

1. Bring the milk, butter, sugar, and salt to a boil over medium heat, stirring constantly. Remove from the heat, add the flour all at once, and stir vigorously to combine. Return the pan to medium heat and cook, stirring constantly, until the mixture pulls away from the sides of the pan, about 3 minutes.

2. Transfer the mixture to the bowl of a stand mixer and beat briefly on medium speed with a paddle attachment. Add the eggs two at a time, beating until smooth after each addition.

3. The pâte à choux is ready to be piped and baked (see Piped Pastries pages 628-630).

Notes   For a drier and deeper blond pâte à choux, substitute an equal part of water for the milk. For a shiny finish, egg wash pâte à choux prior to baking.

Variations **Chocolate Pâte à Choux** Substitute cocoa powder for 2 oz/57 g of the flour and increase the amount of sugar by 1½ oz/43 g.

Gougères Add ¼ tsp/0.50 g cayenne pepper and 1 lb/454 g grated Gruyère to the batter in Step 2, just before adding the eggs. Pipe into domes approximately ¾ in/2 cm in diameter, weighing about ⅓ oz/9 g each. Bake for about 35 minutes at 350°F/177°C.

Herb Tomato Gougères Substitute 12 oz/340 g olive oil for the butter. Increase the salt to ¾ oz/21 g. Add the following garnish to the finished pâte à choux in Step 2: ½ tsp/1 g ground black pepper, 3 oz/85 g finely chopped oil-packed sun-dried tomatoes, ½ oz/14 g finely chopped basil, and 2 tbsp/6 g finely chopped thyme. Pipe into domes approximately ¾ in/2 cm in diameter weighing about ⅓ oz/9 g each. Bake for about 35 minutes at 350°F/177°C.

Pâte à Choux

Pâte à choux is a cooked batter made by combining a liquid, butter, flour, and eggs. The batter can be piped into various shapes and sizes, and as it bakes, it expands and dries into crisp, hollow pastry shells or crusts.

Usually either water or milk is used as the liquid in the batter, and the two yield very different results. Milk will cause the pastry to darken more quickly in the oven, before it has dried out enough to become crisp; that, along with the solids present in the milk, will produce more tender, flavorful pastry. When water is used, the temperature of the oven can be manipulated, starting with a very high temperature to encourage full expansion and then lowering the temperature to dry out the pastries, creating a fully dried pastry that will be very crisp and light.

As pâte à choux is stirred and cooked, a film starts to develop on the bottom of the pot.

The type of flour is also important. Flours with a higher percentage of protein are able to absorb more liquid and will allow for the addition of a greater amount of eggs, yielding a lighter finished product. Additionally, a flour with a higher protein content will develop more gluten strands, making a more elastic dough, which will also help create a lighter finished product. For these reasons, bread flour, which has a protein content of 12 to 13 percent, is best.

All of the flour must be added to the boiling liquid at once and blended in very quickly to ensure the full hydration of the starch granules in the flour and the formation of a smooth paste. The mixture should be stirred quickly and vigorously. The pre-cooking and agitation of the batter allows for greater moisture absorption as well as the development of the gluten in the flour, which creates light, crisp pastry.

COOKING AND BAKING PÂTE À CHOUX

To make pâte à choux, bring the liquid and fat to a rolling boil, and then add the flour all at once. Stir constantly to prevent lumps from forming and continue to cook until the mixture pulls away from the sides of the pan.

Transfer the mixture to the bowl of an electric mixer and, using the paddle attachment, mix for a few moments to cool the batter slightly. Add the eggs gradually, in three or four additions, mixing the dough until it is smooth again each time. Scrape the sides and bottom of the bowl as necessary. The dough should have a pearl-like sheen and be firm enough to just hold its shape when piped.

Strudel Dough

Makes 1 lb 11¾ oz/787 g

BREAD FLOUR	1 lb	454 g
SALT	1½ tsp	7.50 g
WATER	13 fl oz	390 mL
VEGETABLE OIL	2½ oz	71 g

1. Sift the flour and salt together. Transfer to the bowl of an electric mixer. Add the water and oil and blend on low speed using a dough hook attachment until just blended. Then mix on high speed until the dough is smooth, satiny, and very elastic, about 10 minutes.

2. Turn the dough out onto a work surface and gather it into a ball. Rub it with oil and wrap in plastic wrap. Let the dough rest at room temperature for 1 hour, or refrigerate it overnight before using. Allow the dough to come to room temperature before stretching. (See Apple Strudel, page 539.)

Strudel Dough

Strudel dough is a slightly enriched soft dough. Bread flour is used for strudel dough because of its higher protein content, which accounts for the development of the elasticity of the dough that allows it to be stretched to make thin layers of pastry. The dough is mixed well to develop the gluten and then allowed to rest in a warm place (cold dough has less elasticity and is therefore more difficult to work with). The dough is then stretched until extremely thin and transparent. Commercially made phyllo dough, another thin flaky dough, is often used in place of strudel dough.

Cannoli Dough

Makes 3 lb/1.36 kg

BREAD FLOUR	2 lb	907 g
SUGAR	2½ oz	71 g
WATER	9 fl oz	270 mL
CIDER VINEGAR	6 fl oz	180 mL
EGGS	1 oz	28 g
BUTTER, soft	4 oz	113 g

1. Combine all the ingredients in the bowl of an electric mixer. Using a dough hook attachment, mix on high speed until the dough is well developed but slack, or loose, about 8 minutes.

2. Turn the dough out onto a lightly floured work surface. Roll out into a rectangle 12 by 24 in/30 by 61 cm. Give the dough one three-fold (for instructions on administering a three-fold see page 263).

3. Wrap the dough tightly in plastic wrap and allow it to rest for at least 2 hours and up to 2 days under refrigeration before shaping.

Crêpe Batter

Makes 20 oz/567 g

MILK	10 fl oz	300 mL
EGGS	6 oz	170 g
OIL	1 oz	28 g
SUGAR	½ oz	14 g
SALT	1½ tsp	7.50 g
BREAD FLOUR, sifted	4 oz	113 g

1. Blend the milk, eggs, oil, sugar, and salt in a bowl. Add the flour and whisk until evenly blended.

2. Strain the batter through a fine-mesh sieve. Let the batter rest under refrigeration for at least 30 minutes and up to 8 hours. (See Crêpes, page 653, for cooking and filling information.)

Butter Puff Pastry Dough

Makes 8 lb 12 oz/3.97 kg

DOUGH		
BREAD FLOUR	1 lb 10 oz	737 g
CAKE FLOUR	6 oz	170 g
BUTTER, soft	4 oz	113 g
WATER	20 fl oz	600 mL
SALT	¾ oz	21 g
ROLL-IN		
BUTTER, pliable (60°F/16°C)	2 lb 4 oz	1.02 kg
BREAD FLOUR	4 oz	113 g

1. To prepare the dough, sift together the flours. Blend in the butter on low speed with a dough hook attachment until pea-size nuggets form. Combine the water and salt; add all at once to the dough, and mix on low speed until smooth about 3 minutes. Shape the dough into a rough rectangle. Transfer to a sheet pan lined with parchment, wrap the dough in plastic wrap, and allow it to relax under refrigeration for 30 to 60 minutes.

2. To prepare the roll-in, blend the butter, bread flour, and cake flour on low speed with a paddle attachment until smooth, about 2 minutes. Transfer to a sheet of parchment paper. Cover with a second sheet and roll into a rectangle 8 by 12 in/20 by 30 cm. Square off the edges, cover with plastic wrap, and refrigerate until firm but still pliable. Do not allow the roll-in to become cold.

3. To lock the roll-in into the dough, turn the dough out onto a lightly floured work surface and roll it into a rectangle 16 by 24 in/41 by 61 cm, keeping the edges straight and the corners square. Set the roll-in on half of the dough and fold the remaining half of the dough over the roll-in. Seal the edges, turn the dough 90 degrees, and roll into a rectangle 16 by 24 in/41 by 61 cm, making sure the edges are straight and the corners are square.

4. Administer a four-fold (for instructions see page 263). Cover the dough in plastic wrap and allow it to rest for 30 minutes under refrigeration.

5. Turn the dough 90 degrees from its position before it was refrigerated and roll out into a rectangle 16 by 24 in/41 by 61 cm, making sure the edges are straight and the corners are square. Administer a second four-fold. Cover the dough in plastic wrap and allow it to rest for 30 minutes under refrigeration. Repeat this process two more times for a total of 4 four-folds, turning the dough 90 degrees each time before rolling and allowing the dough to rest, covered in plastic wrap, under refrigeration for 30 minutes between each fold.

6. After completing the final fold, wrap the dough in plastic wrap and allow it to rest under refrigeration for 30 minutes before using.

Variations   **Chocolate Puff Pastry** Substitute Dutch-process cocoa powder for 2 oz/57 g of the flour for the roll-in.

Garlic Puff Pastry Add the following to the roll-in: 1 oz/28 g chopped garlic, 1½ oz/43 g chopped shallot, ¾ oz/21 g chopped parsley, and ½ oz/14 g salt.

Laminated Doughs

Laminated doughs include croissant, puff pastry, and Danish. To make a laminated dough, a previously prepared dough (the initial dough) is folded and rolled together with a block of fat called a roll-in. Through a series of folds or turns, multiple layers of dough and fat are created that both leaven the doughs and contribute to their crispness, tenderness, and lightness. The fat, which separates the layers of this "final dough," melts during baking and releases steam. The melting fat leaves spaces between the fine layers of dough and the steam acts to expand these spaces (or pockets), which are set as the dough continues to bake, creating flaky crisp layers of pastry. Creating the proper number of fat and dough layers in the dough is critical to the success of laminated doughs. With too few layers, the steam will escape and the pastry will not rise. Folding the dough too many times can be a problem because the layers of fat and dough merge together as the fat begins to become incorporated into the dough, rather than remaining as separate layers, preventing the dough from rising.

Dough that is to be laminated must be mixed carefully. Overmixing can result in too much gluten formation, making the dough elastic and difficult to roll out. After the dough is mixed, it should be allowed to rest for a minimum of 20 minutes under refrigeration to chill it and fully relax the gluten. The dough should be gently rolled into the desired shape for the lock-in before it is refrigerated to reduce the amount of manipulation necessary during lock-in and lamination. While the dough is resting, the roll-in fat should be prepared.

A number of different types of fats may be used in lamination. However, butter lends the best flavor and mouth feel. The butter should be worked, either by hand or carefully using a stand mixer, until it is smooth and malleable but not overly soft. A small amount of flour may be added to the butter to make it easier to work with and to absorb excess moisture in the butter. It is important that the fat be completely smooth, as any lumps will tear the dough as it is rolled in, preventing proper layering. The temperature of the roll-in is also very important. It should be the same consistency as the dough when the two are rolled together. The butter must not be allowed to become so soft that it begins to ooze from the dough as it is rolled, nor should it be so firm that it could tear the dough or break into bits during rolling. After the roll-in fat is prepared, it should be refrigerated until it is firm but still malleable.

Folding may be the most important factor in making a laminated dough, as the distinct layers of fat and dough must be maintained throughout the process. The dough must be rolled out evenly and the corners kept square throughout the lock-in and all subsequent folds to ensure proper layering.

It is easy to see the layers in this chocolate puff pastry.

LOCK-IN

The lock-in is the first fold and the step that introduces the roll-in (or lamination fat) to the dough. The roll-in fat and the dough must be the same consistency. Let the roll-in stand at room temperature for a few minutes if it is too hard, or refrigerate it if it is too soft. The roll-in fat can be added to the dough using one of several methods: envelope, single-fold, or three-fold.

For the *envelope method,* the dough is rolled into a square, or a rectangle. The roll-in is rolled into a smaller square, or rectangle, and placed diagonally in the center of the dough so that each corner points to the center of a side of the dough square. The corners of the dough are then folded over the fat envelope-style so that they meet in the center. In the *single-fold method,* the roll-in is rolled into a rectangle that is half the size of the dough square, or rectangle, and placed on one half of the dough, then the other half of the dough is folded over it and the edges are sealed to completely encase the roll-in fat. In the *three-fold method,* the fat is rolled into a rectangle that covers two-thirds of the dough. The third of the dough not covered with the roll-in fat is folded over to cover half of the roll-in, or the center of the rectangle, and then the remaining side (or third) is folded over that. The edges are then sealed to completely encase the roll-in fat. After the lock-in is complete, the dough is turned 90 degrees, rolled out to its original dimensions, the first laminating fold is administered, and the dough is wrapped and refrigerated so the gluten will relax and the fat will chill before it is further manipulated.

After the roll-in is added to the dough, each subsequent fold is usually either a three-fold or a four-fold (which is also known as a book-fold). Each time, before folding and rolling the dough, brush any excess flour from its surface. When you fold the dough, the corners should squarely meet and the edges should be straight and perfectly aligned. After each fold, the dough should be refrigerated to allow it to relax and the butter to chill; the length of time the dough will need to rest will depend in large part on the temperature of the kitchen. For each fold, the dough is turned 90 degrees from the previous one to ensure that the gluten is stretched equally in all directions. Too much stress in one direction will make the dough difficult to roll and rise unevenly and misshapen during baking as the gluten contracts.

SINGLE-FOLD

To administer a single-fold, divide the sheet of dough visually in half, and fold the dough over itself to form two layers. This type of fold doubles the number of layers in the pastry.

LOCK-IN

The first step of a lock-in

The second step of a lock-in

THREE-FOLD

For a three-fold, divide the sheet of pastry visually into thirds, and fold one of the outer thirds of the dough over the middle third of the pastry. Fold the remaining outer third of the dough over the folded dough. This fold triples the number of layers in the dough each time.

FOUR-FOLD

For a four-fold, or book-fold, divide the sheet of pastry visually into quarters, and fold the outer quarters into the middle so that their edges meet. Then fold the dough over as if closing a book. This type of fold quadruples the number of layers in the dough each time.

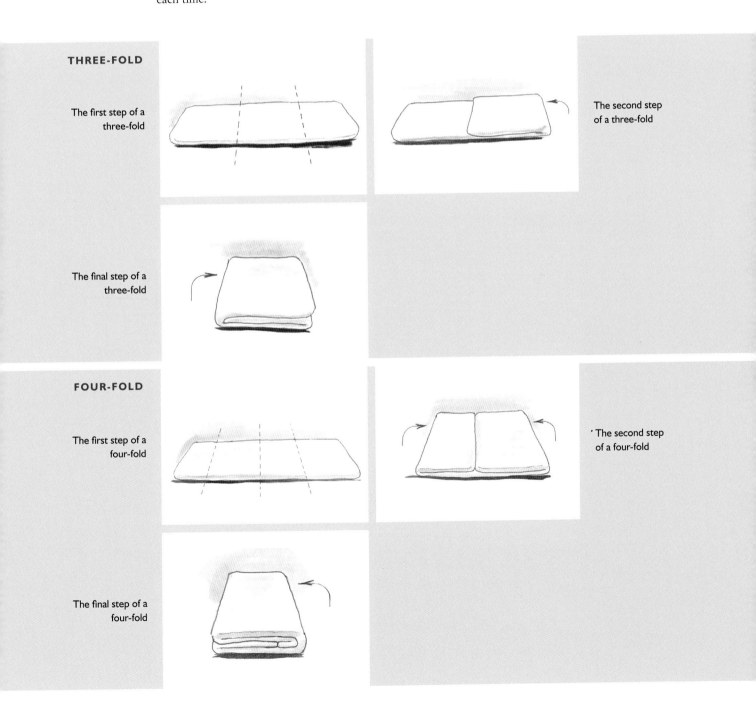

THREE-FOLD

The first step of a three-fold

The second step of a three-fold

The final step of a three-fold

FOUR-FOLD

The first step of a four-fold

The second step of a four-fold

The final step of a four-fold

INVERTED PUFF PASTRY

For inverted puff pastry the same rules apply as for all other laminated doughs. For inverted puff pastry, the butter layer, rather than the dough, is the outer layer. The dough is worked less when preparing inverse dough, for a more tender result.

STORAGE OF LAMINATED DOUGH

To prepare puff pastry and other laminated doughs for freezing, and to ease their use when frozen, follow this simple procedure.

Roll the dough approximately ¼ in/6 mm thick. If necessary, cut the dough into smaller sheets; sheets the size of a sheet pan (16 by 48 in/41 by 122 cm) or half sheet pan (16 by 24 in/41 by 61 cm) are often the most practical. Layer the sheets on a sheet pan, placing a sheet of appropriately sized parchment paper between each one. Wrap the pan tightly in plastic wrap and place in the freezer. (Use the same method for refrigerated storage.)

As you cut puff pastry, you may create scraps, or trim. They can be reserved to be rerolled and used in pastries where a dramatic high straight rise is not critical. Layer the scraps on top of each other, keeping them flat to preserve the layers of fat and dough. Then the dough may be rolled and stored under refrigeration or frozen. Recommendations for the use of these scraps are the same as for blitz puff pastry; they should not be used for items that require a high and even rise.

Inverse Puff Pastry

Makes 11 lb 13 oz/5.36 kg

WATER DOUGH		
BREAD FLOUR	3 lb	1.36 kg
SALT	1½ oz	43 g
WATER	28 fl oz	840 mL
BUTTER, soft	8 oz	227 g
BUTTER DOUGH		
BUTTER, cold	4 lb 8 oz	2.04 kg
CAKE FLOUR	2 lb	907 g

1. To prepare the water dough, combine the bread flour, salt, water, and softened butter on medium speed with a dough hook attachment until completely blended, about 8 minutes.

2. Form the dough into a rough rectangle 8 by 12 in/20 by 30 cm and transfer it to a parchment-lined sheet pan. Press the dough into the sheet pan, wrap it tightly in plastic wrap, and let it relax under refrigeration for 30 to 60 minutes.

3. To prepare the butter dough, blend the butter and flour on high speed with a dough hook attachment until smooth, about 2 minutes. Transfer the dough to a sheet of parchment paper. Cover with a second sheet and roll into a rectangle 16 by 24 in/41 by 61 cm. Square off the edges using your hands or the rolling pin, cover with plastic wrap, and refrigerate until firm but still pliable.

4. To lock the water dough into the butter dough, turn the butter dough out onto a lightly floured work surface. Place the water dough on half of the butter dough rectangle and fold the butter dough over to encase the water dough. Press the edges together to seal. Turn the dough 90 degrees and roll out into a rectangle 16 by 48 in/41 by 122 cm, making sure the edges are straight and the corners are square.

5. Administer a four-fold (for instructions on how to make a four-fold see page 263) and roll out to the same dimensions as before.

6. Administer a second four-fold and roll out to the same dimensions as before. Cover the dough in plastic wrap and allow it to rest for 1 hour under refrigeration.

7. Repeat this process two more times for a total of 4 four-folds, refrigerating and turning the dough 90 degrees each time before rolling. After completing the final fold, wrap the dough in plastic wrap and allow it to firm under refrigeration for at least 2 hours. (The dough can be held under refrigeration or frozen.)

Blitz Puff Pastry

Makes 5 lb/2.27 kg

CAKE FLOUR	1 lb	454 g
BREAD FLOUR	1 lb	454 g
BUTTER, cubed and chilled	2 lb	907 g
SALT	¾ oz	21 g
WATER, cold	18 fl oz	540 mL

1. Combine the cake and bread flour in the bowl of a stand mixer. Add the butter and toss with your fingertips until the butter is coated with flour. Combine the salt and water and add to the flour all at once. Mix on low speed with a dough hook attachment until the dough forms a shaggy mass.

2. Tightly cover the mixture with plastic wrap and allow it to rest under refrigeration, until the butter is firm but not brittle, about 20 minutes.

3. Place the shaggy mass on a lightly floured work surface and roll out into a rectangle that is ½ in/1 cm thick and approximately 12 by 30 in/30 by 76 cm.

4. Administer a four-fold (for instructions on how to make a four-fold see page 263), roll out the dough to the same dimensions, and administer a second four-fold. Tightly wrap the dough in plastic wrap and allow it to rest under refrigeration for 30 minutes.

5. Repeat this process two more times for a total of 4 four-folds, refrigerating and turning the dough 90 degrees each time before rolling. After completing the final fold, wrap the dough in plastic wrap and allow it to firm under refrigeration for at least 1 hour. (The dough can be held under refrigeration or frozen.)

Blitz Puff Pastry

When rolling out blitz dough, it is more important to maintain the ½-in/1-cm thickness of the dough than to maintain the precise dimensions of the rectangle. It is very important that the dough be rolled thin enough to flatten the butter sufficiently to achieve the "puff" effect when the dough is baked.

Because there is no roll-in, blitz puff pastry is easier and faster to make than traditional puff dough. However, the flavor and quality of blitz puff dough should be just as good as that of the traditionally made dough, and a well-made blitz dough will have no significant textural differences from the traditional dough. The only time blitz puff pastry should not be substituted for traditionally made puff pastry is in an application such as vol-au-vents, where a very high, even rise is required.

Croissant Dough

Makes 10 lb 8 oz/4.76 kg

DOUGH		
BREAD FLOUR	4 lb 8 oz	2.04 kg
SUGAR	7 oz	198 g
INSTANT DRY YEAST	¾ oz	21 g
SALT	1¾ oz	50 g
MILK	60 fl oz	1.80 L
BUTTER, soft	7 oz	198 g
ROLL-IN		
BUTTER, cold	2 lb 8 oz	1.13 kg

1. To prepare the dough, blend the flour, sugar, yeast, and salt on low speed with a dough hook attachment. Add the milk and butter and mix until just incorporated.

2. Turn the dough out onto a lightly floured surface. Cover and allow to ferment until doubled in volume, about 2 hours.

3. Fold over the dough and spread it out to a rectangle approximately 12 by 16 in/30 by 41 cm on a parchment-lined sheet pan. Wrap the dough tightly with plastic wrap and let it rest overnight under refrigeration.

4. Using a rolling pin, pound out the roll-in butter to make it pliable. Shape it into a rectangle 8 by 12 in/20 by 30 cm. Chill the butter slightly.

5. To lock the roll-in into the dough, turn the dough out onto a lightly floured work surface and roll it into a rectangle 16 by 24 in/41 by 61 cm, keeping the edges straight and the corners square. Place the roll-in on half of the dough rectangle. Fold the remaining half of the dough over the roll-in. Seal the edges, turn the dough 90 degrees, and roll into a rectangle 16 by 24 in/41 by 61 cm, making sure the edges are straight and the corners are square.

6. Administer a four-fold (for instructions on a four fold see page 263). Cover the dough in plastic wrap and allow it to rest for 30 minutes under refrigeration.

7. Turn the dough 90 degrees from its position before it was refrigerated and roll into a rectangle 16 by 24 in/41 by 61 cm, making sure the edges are straight and the corners are square. Administer a three-fold (for instructions on how to make a three-fold see page 263). Cover the dough in plastic wrap and allow it to rest for 30 minutes under refrigeration. Repeat this process one more time for a total of 2 three-folds.

8. After completing the final fold, wrap the dough in plastic wrap and allow it to rest under refrigeration for at least another 30 minutes before using. (The dough can be held under refrigeration or frozen.)

Both croissant dough and Danish dough are laminated using the same principles that apply when making puff pastry. The only difference is that these two doughs have the additional leavening power of yeast. The addition of yeast to a laminated dough results in pastry that is tender and soft, rather than crisp like puff pastry.

Danish Dough

Makes 10 lb 8 oz/4.76 kg

DOUGH		
BREAD FLOUR	4 lb	1.81 kg
SUGAR	7¼ oz	206 g
INSTANT DRY YEAST	1 oz	28 g
SALT	1 oz	28 g
BUTTER, soft	6 oz	170 g
EGGS	13 oz	369 g
MILK	28 fl oz	840 mL
ROLL-IN		
BUTTER, cold	3 lb	1.36 kg

1. To prepare the dough, blend the flour, sugar, yeast, salt, butter, eggs, and milk on low speed with a dough hook attachment, about 2 minutes. Increase to medium speed and mix for an additional 4 minutes.

2. Turn the dough out onto a lightly floured surface. Cover the dough and allow it to ferment until doubled in volume, about 2 hours.

3. Fold over the dough and spread it into a rectangle 12 by 16 in/30 by 41 cm on a parchment-lined sheet pan. Wrap the dough tightly with plastic wrap and let it rest overnight under refrigeration.

4. Using a rolling pin, pound out the roll-in butter to make it pliable. Shape it into a rectangle 8 by 12 in/20 by 30 cm. Chill the butter slightly.

5. To lock the roll-in into the dough, turn the dough out onto a lightly floured work surface and roll it into a rectangle 16 by 24 in/41 by 61 cm, keeping the edges straight and

the corners square. Place the roll-in on half of the dough rectangle. Fold the remaining half of the dough over the roll-in. Seal the edges, turn the dough 90 degrees, and roll into a rectangle 16 by 24 in/41 by 61 cm, making sure the edges are straight and the corners are square.

6. Administer a four-fold (for instructions on a four-fold see page 263). Cover the dough in plastic wrap and allow it to rest for 30 minutes under refrigeration.

7. Turn the dough 90 degrees from its position before it was refrigerated and roll into a rectangle 16 by 24 in/41 by 61 cm, making sure the edges are straight and the corners are square. Administer a three-fold (for instructions on how to make a three-fold see page 263). Cover the dough in plastic wrap and allow it to rest for 30 minutes under refrigeration. Repeat this process one more time for a total of 2 three-folds.

8. After completing the final fold, wrap the dough in plastic wrap and allow it to rest under refrigeration for at least another 30 minutes before using. (The dough can be held under refrigeration or frozen.)

CHAPTER 9

Quick Breads and Cakes

QUICK BREADS AND CAKES ARE SERVED AS BREAKFAST PASTRIES OR SIMPLE DESSERTS. THEY ARE ALSO "FOUNDATION PREPARATIONS" USED FOR ASSEMBLED CAKES AND TORTES, INCLUDING WEDDING AND OTHER SPECIAL-OCCASION CAKES. THE PASTRY CHEF USES SEVEN BASIC MIXING METHODS—BLENDING; CREAMING; TWO-STAGE; COLD, WARM, AND SEPARATED FOAMING; AND COMBINATION—TO PREPARE ALL OF THESE.

CLOCKWISE FROM LEFT: Pumpkin Bread, Morning Glory Muffins, Cranberry Orange Muffins, Raisin Scones

Basic Principles of Quick Breads and Cakes

There are certain rules that apply to the preparation of any quick bread or cake regardless of the mixing method used. For all quick breads and cakes it is important to sift the dry ingredients together both to remove lumps and blend the dry ingredients evenly, which will in turn help to ensure a fully combined batter with minimal mixing time. A short mixing time is an important factor, as gluten development is undesirable. Another asset of sifting the dry ingredients is that it will evenly distribute the leavener. Chemical leaveners, which are often used in quick breads and cakes, must be evenly distributed to ensure uniform texture and crumb.

All ingredients should be at room temperature before they are combined. Ingredients that are too cold may cause the batter to separate. Usually liquids should be added incrementally to a batter to ensure full hydration and complete incorporation of the dry ingredients.

In nearly all mixing methods used for quick breads and cakes the development or introduction of air cells into the batter is very important to the process. In creamed batters this is achieved as the fat and sugar are creamed together, while in a foamed cake the air cells are developed as the eggs are beaten and folded into the batter. Regardless of the method of development and incorporation, air cells facilitate the leavening of a product and are important to the proper development of structure and crumb during baking. If air cells are not fully developed, the resulting product will lack leavening and have a dense, coarse crumb.

Pan Preparation

Pans are lined with parchment paper to ease the process of removing a baked product from the pan. For creamed or foamed batters that must be spread rather than poured, it is important to apply a thin film of butter or other fat to the pan before placing the parchment in the base of the pan. The fat will keep the paper stationary while the batter is spread. This is particularly important when using large pans. The sides of the pan should also be greased and lightly floured, or greased with pan grease, which already contains a measure of flour. Pans being used for sponge cakes should be lined with parchment, but the sides of the pans should remain untreated.

Angel food cakes require no pan preparation. The full rise of this cake is partially dependent on the batter being able to cling to the side of the pan as it rises during baking. Angel food cakes should also have no treatment to the bottom of the pans, as they are cooled upside down to facilitate removal and to help retain their height and inner structure after cooling.

Pans should be filled approximately three-quarters full with batter, unless otherwise specified in the formula's method. This should allow for sufficient room for the product to rise during baking. Pans filled with batters made by the creaming, chiffon, and two-stage mixing methods should be gently tapped on a counter to help to remove any large air bubbles that may have developed as the batter was scaled into the pan.

Cooling Quick Breads and Cakes

After removal from the oven, quick breads and cakes should be allowed to cool slightly in the pan before unmolding. To remove a cake or quick bread from the pan, run a small knife or metal spatula between the cake and the pan. Press the tool to the pan so as not to cut or damage the item in any way. Invert the pan onto a wire rack, tap lightly, and lift gently to release. Peel the parchment paper from the bottom of the cake to allow steam to escape. Items must cool completely before they are filled, iced, glazed, or otherwise decorated.

The pans for angel food cakes recieve no treatment, which could make the cakes difficult to unmold. However, this type of cake is cooled upside down, allowing steam to build between the pan and the cake, making it easier to release.

Cheesecakes should cool completely in the pan at room temperature and then be wrapped tightly and refrigerated until the custard has completely set, typically overnight. To unmold a cheesecake, remove the plastic wrap and run a small knife or metal spatula between the pan and the cake. Press the tool to the pan to ensure the item to be unmolded is not cut or damaged in any way. Warm the bottom of the pan gently over an open burner, place a cake round that has been tightly wrapped in plastic on top of the cake, invert, and gently tap to release. Remove the pan and invert the cake to set it right side up.

Storing Quick Breads and Cakes

Quick breads and cakes are items that stale quickly when left exposed to the air. Cakes and quick breads may be stored tightly wrapped in plastic wrap and frozen for up to three weeks without adverse effects. They may be left to thaw at room temperature before use.

Removing the parchment liners from cakes after they have cooled; patterned Joconde Sponge (page 316) shown here.

Cream Scones

Makes 5 dozen scones (4 oz/113 g each)

BREAD FLOUR	5 lb 10 oz	2.55 kg
SUGAR	1 lb 5 oz	595 g
BAKING POWDER	5¼ oz	149 g
SALT	2¼ oz	64 g
HEAVY CREAM, chilled	72 fl oz	2.16 L
MILK	6 fl oz	180 mL
COARSE SUGAR	6 oz	170 g

1. Combine the bread flour, sugar, baking powder, and salt and mix on medium speed with a paddle attachment until well blended, about 5 minutes. Add the cream and mix until just combined.

2. Scale the dough into 2 lb 5 oz/1.05 kg portions and pat each portion by hand into a cake pan or ring 10 in/25 cm in diameter. Remove the dough from the ring, place on a parchment-lined sheet pan, and freeze thoroughly.

3. Cut each disk into 10 equal wedges and place the individual wedges on parchment-lined sheet pans. Brush with the milk and sprinkle with the coarse sugar.

4. Bake at 350°F/177°C until golden brown, 20 to 25 minutes.

5. Cool the scones on the pans for a few minutes, then transfer to racks to cool completely.

Variations **Raisin Scones** Add 3 lb/1.36 kg raisins to the dough in Step 1 just before blending in the wet ingredients. Follow the remaining method as stated above.

Dried Cherry Scones Add 3 lb/1.36 kg dried cherries to the dough in Step 1 just before blending in the wet ingredients. Follow the remaining method as stated above.

Apricot Almond Ginger Scones Add 1 lb/454 g sliced almonds, 2 lb/907 g chopped dried apricots, and 5 oz/142 g minced crystallized ginger to the dough in Step 1 just before blending in the wet ingredients. Follow the remaining method as stated above.

Ham and Cheddar Scones Omit the milk and coarse sugar. Add 3 lb/1.36 kg diced ham, 3 bunches chopped green onion, and 1 lb 8 oz/680 g diced cheddar cheese in Step 1 just before blending in the wet ingredients. Follow the remaining method as stated above.

The Blending Mixing Method

The blending method consists of making two mixtures, one with the wet ingredients and one with the dry, and then combining the two together. Any garnish ingredients are typically added last. The key to a successful blending method is not to overmix the batter. The wet and dry ingredient mixtures should be blended only until just combined. Overmixing will produce too much gluten, resulting in a coarser grain and tougher crumb in the baked product.

All-purpose or pastry flour is used for most items made by this method because of the moderate protein content. Special flours, such as cornmeal or whole wheat flour, may replace some or all of the white wheat flour in a given formula to add flavor and develop a different texture. The flour(s) should be sifted together with the other dry ingredients, such as baking soda and/or powder, sugar, salt, cocoa, or ground spices.

Cream, milk, buttermilk, water, and even watery vegetables like zucchini all add moisture to a baking formula. Fats shorten developing gluten strands, which helps to create a tender texture in the baked good. Solid fats like butter or shortening are most often melted for this method so they can be blended with the other liquid ingredients.

When adding the wet ingredients to the dry ingredients, add them all at once and blend, using a mixer or by hand, just until the dry ingredients are evenly moistened. Scrape the bowl down once or twice to mix the batter evenly. Mixing these batters as briefly as possible ensures a light, delicate texture. Overmixed batters may develop too much gluten and the resulting item will not have the desired fine, delicate texture.

Specific formulas may call for adding such ingredients as fresh or dried fruit (see Dried Fruits, page 295), nuts, or chocolate. Typically, they are folded into the batter just before scaling and baking. However, they may also be incorporated along with the dry ingredients.

Ginger Cake

Makes 35 cakes (2 oz/57 g each)

BUTTER	8 oz	227 g
DARK BROWN SUGAR	7 oz	198 g
LIGHT CORN SYRUP	10½ oz	298 g
MOLASSES	10½ oz	298 g
FRESH GINGER, finely minced	1 tbsp	15 g
GROUND CINNAMON	1½ tsp	3 g
BAKING SODA	1 tbsp	9 g
MILK	13 fl oz	390 mL
EGGS	6 oz	170 g
ALL-PURPOSE FLOUR, sifted	1 lb	454 g

1. Lightly butter and dust with flour 35 baking pans (3 in/8 cm in diameter and 1½ in/4 cm high).

2. Melt the butter, add the brown sugar, corn syrup, molasses, ginger, and cinnamon and blend well. Remove from the heat.

3. Blend the baking soda with the milk, add the eggs, and add to the sugar mixture.

4. Add the sifted flour and blend well. Pour 2 oz/57 g of the batter into each prepared pan.

5. Bake in a 375°F/191°C oven until a skewer inserted in the center of a cake comes out clean. Be careful not to overbake; the cake should be very moist yet baked through.

6. Cool completely and unmold.

Buttermilk Biscuits

Makes 40 biscuits (1½ oz/43 g each)

BREAD FLOUR	1 lb 8 oz	680 g
ALL-PURPOSE FLOUR	1 lb 8 oz	680 g
SUGAR	4 oz	113 g
BAKING POWDER	3 oz	85 g
SALT	¾ oz	21 g
BUTTER, cold	1 lb	454 g
EGGS	8 oz	227 g
BUTTERMILK	24 fl oz	720 mL
EGG WASH (page 825)	as needed	as needed

1. Line a sheet pan with parchment paper.

2. Combine the flours, sugar, baking powder, and salt.

3. Add the butter and rub together until the mixture has the appearance of a coarse meal.

4. Combine the eggs and buttermilk. Add to the flour mixture, tossing to combine.

5. Roll out the dough on a lightly floured work surface to a thickness of 1 in/3 cm and, using a 2-in/5-cm cutter, cut out the biscuits.

6. Place the biscuits on the prepared pans and lightly brush with egg wash.

7. Bake at 425°F/218°C until golden brown, about 15 minutes

8. Transfer the biscuits to racks and allow to cool completely.

Pumpkin Quick Bread

Makes 10 loaves (1 lb 14 oz/851 g each)

RAISINS	2 lb	907 g
WATER	28 fl oz	840 mL
BREAD FLOUR	3 lb	1.36 kg
ALL-PURPOSE FLOUR	8 oz	227 g
BAKING POWDER	1¼ oz	35 g
BAKING SODA	¾ oz	21 g
GROUND CLOVES	1 tbsp	6 g
GROUND NUTMEG	1 tbsp	6 g
GROUND CINNAMON	1 tbsp	6 g
SALT	1 oz	28 g
SUGAR	4 lb 8 oz	2.04 kg
PUMPKIN PURÉE	3 lb 5 oz	1.50 kg
EGGS	1 lb 8 oz	680 g
VEGETABLE OIL	23 fl oz	690 mL

1. Coat the pans with a light film of fat or use appropriate paper liners. Plump the raisins in the water.

2. Sift together the flours, baking powder, baking soda, cloves, nutmeg, cinnamon, and salt.

3. Combine the sugar, pumpkin, eggs, and oil and mix on medium speed with a paddle attachment until blended. Scrape the bowl as needed.

4. Add the sifted dry ingredients and mix until a rough batter forms. Add the raisins and water and mix until the batter is evenly moistened.

5. Scale 1 lb 14 oz/851 g batter into each prepared loaf pan. Gently tap the filled pans to burst any air bubbles.

6. Bake at 350°F/177°C until the bread springs back when pressed and a tester inserted near the center comes out clean, about 45 minutes.

7. Cool the loaves in the pans for a few minutes, then transfer to racks and cool completely.

Banana Bread

Makes 6 loaves (1 lb 14 oz/851 g each)

ALL-PURPOSE FLOUR	2 lb 13 oz	1.28 kg
BAKING POWDER	2½ tsp	7.50 g
BAKING SODA	¾ oz	21 g
SALT	1½ tsp	7.50 g
BANANAS, very ripe	4 lb 4 oz	1.93 kg
LEMON JUICE	½ fl oz	15 mL
SUGAR	2 lb 13 oz	1.28 kg
EGGS	12 oz	340 g
VEGETABLE OIL	14 fl oz	420 mL
PECANS, coarsely chopped	8 oz	227 g

1. Coat the loaf pans with a light film of fat.

2. Sift together the flour, baking powder, baking soda, and salt.

3. Purée the bananas and lemon juice together.

4. Combine the sugar, banana purée, eggs, and oil and mix on medium speed with a paddle attachment until blended. Scrape the bowl as needed.

5. Add the sifted dry ingredients and mix until just combined. Mix in the pecans.

6. Scale 1 lb 14 oz/851 g batter into each prepared loaf pan. Gently tap the filled pans to burst any air bubbles.

7. Bake at 350°F/177°C until the bread springs back when pressed and a tester inserted near the center comes out clean, about 55 minutes.

8. Cool the loaves in the pans for a few minutes, then transfer to racks and cool completely.

Zucchini Bread

Makes 7 loaves (1 lb 12 oz/794 g each)

ALL-PURPOSE FLOUR	2 lb 5 oz	1.05 kg
BAKING POWDER	½ oz	14 g
BAKING SODA	½ oz	14 g
SALT	1 oz	28 g
GROUND CINNAMON	1 oz	28 g
GROUND NUTMEG	1 tbsp	6 g
GRANULATED SUGAR	1 lb 8 oz	680 g
BROWN SUGAR	1 lb 8 oz	680 g
VEGETABLE OIL	29 fl oz	870 mL
EGGS	1 lb 2 oz	510 g
ZUCCHINI, grated	2 lb 4 oz	1.02 kg
WHOLE WHEAT FLOUR	7 oz	198 g
PECANS, coarsely chopped	1 lb	454 g

1. Coat the loaf pans with a light film of fat.

2. Sift together 1 lb 14 oz/851 g of the all-purpose flour with the baking powder, baking soda, salt, cinnamon, and nutmeg.

3. Combine the sugar, brown sugar, oil, and eggs and mix on medium speed with a paddle attachment until blended. Scrape the bowl as needed.

4. Add the sifted dry ingredients and mix until just combined.

5. Combine the zucchini with the remaining 7 oz/198 g all-purpose flour and the whole wheat flour. Blend the zucchini mixture and the pecans into the batter. Mix in the pecans.

6. Scale 1 lb 12 oz/794 g batter into each prepared loaf pan. Gently tap the filled pans to burst any air bubbles.

7. Bake at 350°F/177°C until the bread springs back when pressed and a tester inserted near the center comes out clean, about 55 minutes.

8. Cool the loaves in the pans for a few minutes, then transfer to racks and cool completely.

Cranberry Orange Muffins

Makes 1 dozen muffins (3½ oz/99 g each)

ALL-PURPOSE FLOUR	13 oz	369 g
BAKING POWDER	1 tbsp	9 g
SUGAR	10½ oz	298 g
BUTTER, soft	2¾ oz	78 g
SALT	1½ tsp	7.50 g
EGGS	5 oz	142 g
BUTTERMILK	5 fl oz	150 mL
VANILLA EXTRACT	½ fl oz	15 mL
VEGETABLE OIL	2¾ fl oz	83 mL
CRANBERRIES (fresh or frozen)	11 oz	312 g
ORANGE ZEST, grated	1½ oz	43 g
COARSE SUGAR	2 oz	57 g

1. Coat the muffin tins with a light film of fat or use appropriate paper liners.

2. Sift together the flours and baking powder.

3. Cream together the sugar, butter, and salt on medium speed with the paddle attachment, scraping down the bowl periodically, until the mixture is smooth and light in color, about 5 minutes.

4. Whisk the eggs, buttermilk, vanilla, and oil together. Add to the butter-sugar mixture in two to three additions, mixing until fully incorporated after each addition and scraping down the bowl as needed.

5. Add the sifted dry ingredients and mix on low speed until evenly moistened. Fold in the cranberries and orange zest.

6. Scale 3½ oz/99 g batter into the prepared muffin tins, filling them three-quarters full. Gently tap the filled tins to release any air bubbles and sprinkle with coarse sugar.

7. Bake at 375°F/191°C for 30 minutes, or until a skewer inserted near the center of a muffin comes out clean.

8. Cool the muffins in the tins for a few minutes, then transfer to racks to cool completely.

Note   Replace the coarse sugar with Streusel Topping (page 829) for an alternative.

Variation   **Blueberry Muffins** Omit the cranberries and orange zest and fold in 12 oz/340 g blueberries (fresh or frozen) in Step 5 after adding the dry ingredients. Follow the remaining method as stated above.

The Creaming Mixing Method

Muffins, cakes, quick breads, cookies, and other baked goods made with the creaming method develop their light and airy structure through the incorporation of air during mixing and by use of chemical leaveners. For the creaming method, first the fat and sugar are "creamed," or blended, until very smooth and light. Then the eggs are added and, finally, the sifted dry ingredients are added in two or three additions; if there is any liquid, the dry ingredients and liquid are added alternately, starting and ending with the dry ingredients. It is important that ingredients for a creamed batter or dough are at room temperature and the fat (butter, shortening, nut paste, etc.) is soft before beginning to mix.

Cream together the fat and sugar with the paddle attachment on medium speed, scraping down the sides and bottom of the bowl occasionally as you work to ensure all the fat is blended evenly, until the mixture is pale in color and light and smooth in texture. When the butter and sugar have this appearance, it indicates that a sufficient amount of air has been incorporated into the mixture. If the ingredients are not sufficiently creamed, the final product will be dense and lack the light, tender qualities characteristic of creamed baked goods. There are formulas made by the creaming

Note the difference in texture and color between butter and sugar that are just combined (on left) and fully creamed butter and sugar (on right).

method, however, such as some cookies, where minimum air incorporation is desirable. In these cases the butter and sugar are blended for a shorter amount of time, just until the mixture is smooth.

Once the butter and the sugar are properly creamed, the eggs should be added gradually and in stages, mixing until fully incorporated and scraping down the bowl after each addition. Scraping down the bowl is important to develop a completely smooth batter. Adding the eggs in batches will help to prevent the batter from separating. Blending eggs into the butter-sugar mixture creates an emulsion (for more about emulsions see page 88). The more eggs added, the more difficult it becomes to sustain the emulsion and the mixture can begin to separate, developing a curdled or broken appearance. Using eggs at room temperature or warming the eggs slightly (not above 80°F/27°C) when an unusually large amount is to be added will help to emulsify and fully blend the mixture. If the mixture should separate, continue to mix until it becomes smooth again. However, sometimes this curdled appearance is unavoidable because of the ratio of eggs to fat. In these instances, blend in the eggs to create as smooth a mixture as possible, and when the dry ingredients are added make sure to blend to a smooth consistency.

The sifted dry ingredients are generally added in one of two ways: all at once, or alternating with the liquid ingredient (milk, juice, etc.). Regardless of the method of addition, after adding the dry ingredients the dough or batter should be mixed minimally, or just until incorporated. Excessive mixing would act to develop gluten, which would toughen the dough or batter and, therefore, the final product.

The liquid ingredients are also commonly added in one of two ways: alternating with the dry ingredients, or all at once after the dry ingredients are combined. When adding the dry and liquid ingredients alternately, add one-third of the dry ingredients, then about one-half of the liquid ingredients, mixing until smooth and scraping down the bowl after each addition. Repeat this sequence until all of the dry and liquid ingredients have been added. Increase the speed and beat the batter just until it is evenly blended and smooth. Sometimes, but not often, the liquid may be added to the creamed mixture immediately after the eggs. This is done only when the amount of liquid is very small, as it is likely to cause the creamed mixture to begin to separate. It is difficult to get a creamed mixture to accept a large amount of liquid.

Lastly, add any remaining flavoring or garnishing ingredients, such as nuts, chocolate chips, or dried fruit, mixing or folding until just incorporated.

Lemon Poppy Seed Muffins

Makes 1 dozen muffins (4 oz/113 g each)

ALL-PURPOSE FLOUR	13 oz	369 g
BAKING POWDER	1 tbsp	9 g
SUGAR	10⅓ oz	293 g
BUTTER	8¾ oz	248 g
CRÈME FRAÎCHE	5 oz	142 g
EGGS	9 oz	255 g
VEGETABLE OIL	2 fl oz	60 mL
LEMON JUICE	1 fl oz	30 mL
LEMON ZEST, grated	1½ oz	43 g
POPPY SEEDS	1¾ oz	50 g

1. Coat the muffin tins with a light film of fat or use appropriate paper liners.

2. Sift together the flour and baking powder.

3. Cream together the sugar, butter, and salt on medium speed using the paddle attachment, scraping down the bowl periodically, until the mixture is smooth and light in color, about 5 minutes. Blend in the crème fraîche.

4. Whisk the eggs, oil, and lemon juice together. Add to the butter-sugar mixture in three additions, mixing until fully incorporated after each addition and scraping down the bowl as needed. Blend in the lemon zest and poppy seeds.

5. Add the sifted dry ingredients and mix on low speed until evenly moistened.

6. Scale 4 oz/113 g batter into the prepared muffin tins, filling them three-quarters full. Gently tap the filled tins to release any air bubbles.

7. Bake at 375°F/191°C for 30 minutes, or until a skewer inserted near the center of a muffin comes out clean.

8. Cool the muffins in the tins for a few minutes, then transfer to racks to cool completely.

Morning Glory Muffins

Makes 1 dozen muffins (4½ oz/128 g each)

ALL-PURPOSE FLOUR	14 oz	397 g
SUGAR	12¼ oz	347 g
GROUND CINNAMON	1 tsp	2 g
BAKING SODA	2¼ tsp	9 g
SALT	¼ tsp	1.25 g
COCONUT, shredded	3½ oz	99 g
RAISINS	5½ oz	156 g
CARROTS, grated	5½ oz	156 g
APPLE, grated	7 oz	198 g
PINEAPPLE, crushed, drained	5½ oz	155 g
WALNUTS, chopped, toasted	2¾ oz	78 g
EGGS	8 oz	227 g
VEGETABLE OIL	7½ fl oz	225 g
VANILLA EXTRACT	1 tsp	5 mL
ROLLED OATS	as needed	as needed

1. Coat the muffin tins with a light film of fat or use appropriate paper liners.

2. Sift together the flour, sugar, cinnamon, baking soda, and salt. Blend the coconut, raisins, carrots, apple, pineapple, and walnuts into the sifted dry ingredients.

3. Combine the eggs, oil, and vanilla together.

4. Blend the dry ingredient mixture into the egg mixture.

5. Scale 4½ oz/128 g batter inot the prepared muffin tins, filling them three-quarters full. Gently tap the filled tins to release any air bubbles. Sprinkle rolled oats over the top of each muffin.

6. Bake at 375°F/191°C for 30 minutes, or until a skewer inserted near the center of a muffin comes out clean.

7. Cool the muffins in the tins for a few minutes, then transfer to racks to cool completely.

Strawberry Rhubarb Streusel Muffins

Makes 1 dozen (3½ oz/99 g each)

RHUBARB, medium dice	11 oz	312 g
BUTTER	3¾ oz	106 g
ALL-PURPOSE FLOUR	13 oz	369 g
BAKING POWDER	1 tbsp	9 g
SUGAR	10½ oz	298 g
SALT	½ tsp	2.50 g
EGGS	5 oz	142 g
BUTTERMILK	5 fl oz	150 mL
VEGETABLE OIL	2¾ fl oz	83 mL
VANILLA EXTRACT	1 tbsp	15 mL
STRAWBERRIES, medium dice	11 oz	312 g
STREUSEL TOPPING (page 829)	12 oz	340 g

1. Sauté the rhubarb in 1 oz/28 g of the butter until soft. Remove from the heat and cool.

2. Coat the muffin tins with a light film of fat or use appropriate paper liners.

3. Sift together the flour and baking powder.

4. Cream together the sugar, the remaining 2¾ oz/78 g butter, and salt on medium speed using the paddle attachment, scraping down the bowl periodically, until the mixture is smooth and light in color, about 5 minutes.

5. Whisk the eggs, buttermilk, oil, and vanilla extract together. Add to the butter-sugar mixture in two to three additions, mixing until fully incorporated after each addition and scraping down the bowl as needed.

6. Add the sifted dry ingredients and mix on low speed until evenly moistened. Fold in the sautéed rhubarb and strawberries.

7. Scale 3½ oz/99 g batter into the prepared muffin tins, filling them three-quarters full. Gently tap the filled tins to release any air bubbles. Sprinkle the top of each muffin with Streusel topping.

8. Bake at 375°F/191°C for 30 minutes, or until a skewer inserted near the center of a muffin comes out clean.

9. Cool the muffins in the tins for a few minutes, then transfer to racks to cool completely.

Bran Muffins

Makes 1 dozen muffins (3½ oz/99 g each)

BREAD FLOUR	6 oz	170 g
BAKING POWDER	½ oz	14 g
SUGAR	4 oz	113 g
BUTTER, soft	2 oz	57 g
SALT	¾ tsp	3.75 g
EGGS	4 oz	113 g
MILK	4 fl oz	120 mL
HONEY	1 oz	28 g
MOLASSES	1 oz	28 g
WHEAT BRAN	2 oz	57 g

1. Coat the muffin tins with a light film of fat or use appropriate paper liners.

2. Sift together the flour and the baking powder.

3. Cream together the sugar, butter, and salt on medium speed with the paddle attachment, scraping down the bowl periodically, until the mixture is smooth and light in color, about 5 minutes.

4. Combine the eggs and milk and add to the butter mixture in three additions, mixing until fully incorporated after each addition and scraping down the bowl as needed. Add the honey and molasses and blend until just incorporated.

5. Add the sifted dry ingredients and the bran and mix on low speed until evenly moistened.

6. Scale 3½ oz/99 g batter into the prepared muffin tins, filling them three-quarters full. Gently tap the filled tins to release any air bubbles.

7. Bake at 375°F/191°C for 30 minutes, or until a skewer inserted near the center of a muffin comes out clean.

8. Cool the muffins in the tins for a few minutes, then transfer to racks to cool completely.

Old-Fashioned Pound Cake

Makes 6 large cakes (2 lb/907 g each)

CAKE FLOUR	3 lb 4½ oz	1.49 kg
BAKING POWDER	1½ oz	43 g
BUTTER, soft	2 lb 5½ oz	1.06 kg
SUGAR	2 lb 5½ oz	1.06 kg
SALT	½ oz	14 g
EGGS	3 lb 12 oz	1.70 kg

1. Coat the loaf pans with a light film of fat or use appropriate pan liners.

2. Sift together the flour and baking powder.

3. Cream together the butter, sugar, and salt on medium speed with the paddle attachment, scraping down the bowl as needed, until the mixture is smooth and light in color, about 5 minutes.

4. Blend the eggs and add in three additions.

5. Add the sifted dry ingredients, mixing on low speed until just blended and scraping down the bowl as needed.

4. Scale 2 lb/907 g batter into each prepared loaf pan.

5. Bake at 350°F/177°C until a skewer inserted near the center of a cake comes out clean, about 50 minutes.

6. Cool the cakes in the pans for a few minutes, then transfer to racks to cool completely.

Variations   **Marble Pound Cake** Add 12 oz/340 g melted and cooled bittersweet chocolate: After blending the batter, transfer one-third of the batter to a separate bowl and add the melted chocolate, folding it in thoroughly using a rubber spatula. Gently pour the chocolate batter into the plain batter. Using the handle of a wooden spoon, gently swirl the batters together with 3 to 4 strokes. Do not overblend. Scale and bake as directed above.

Lemon Pound Cake Add the grated zest and juice of three lemons to the butter and sugar before creaming them together. Scale and bake as directed above.

Sour Cream Streusel Pound Cake

Makes 6 bundt cakes (9 in/23 cm each)

LIGHT BROWN SUGAR	1 lb 2 oz	510 g
WALNUTS, finely chopped	6 oz	170 g
CHOCOLATE CHIPS	6 oz	170 g
GROUND CINNAMON	1 tbsp	6 g
COCOA POWDER, sifted	2½ tsp	7.50 g
CAKE FLOUR	2 lb 4 oz	1.02 kg
BAKING POWDER	½ oz	14 g
BAKING SODA	1¾ tsp	7 g
BUTTER, soft	1 lb 8 oz	680 g
SUGAR	1 lb 8 oz	680 g
SALT	1¾ tsp	8.75 g
EGGS	1 lb 8 oz	680 g
SOUR CREAM	1 lb 8 oz	680 g
VANILLA EXTRACT	½ fl oz	15 mL

1. Coat the bundt pans with a light film of fat.

2. To prepare the streusel, toss together the brown sugar, walnuts, chocolate chips, cinnamon, and cocoa until evenly blended.

3. To prepare the batter, sift together the flour, baking powder, and baking soda.

4. Cream together the butter, sugar, and salt on medium speed with the paddle attachment, scraping down the bowl as needed, until the mixture is smooth and light in color, about 5 minutes.

5. Blend the eggs, sour cream, and vanilla. Add the egg mixture in three additions, alternating with the sifted dry ingredients and mixing on low speed until just blended, scraping down the bowl as needed.

6. Scale 11 oz/312 g batter into each prepared pan. Scatter 5 oz/142 g of the streusel filling evenly over the batter in each pan, swirl with a skewer to incorporate slightly, and cover with an additional 11 oz/312 g batter.

7. Bake at 350°F/177°C until a skewer inserted near the center of a cake comes out clean, about 50 minutes.

8. Cool the cakes in the pans for a few minutes, then transfer to racks to cool completely.

Rum Cake

Makes 6 bundt cakes (9 in/23 cm each)

CAKE		
CAKE FLOUR	3 lb	1.36 kg
BAKING POWDER	1½ oz	43 g
BUTTER, soft	2 lb	907 g
SUGAR	3 lb 8 oz	1.59 kg
SALT	1 tbsp	15 g
ORANGE ZEST, grated	1 oz	28 g
LEMON ZEST, grated	1 oz	28 mL
EGGS	1 lb 6 oz	624 g
EGG YOLKS	1 lb 6 oz	624 g
MILK	24 fl oz	720 mL
RUM SYRUP		
SUGAR	3 lb	1.36 kg
WATER	24 fl oz	720 mL
CORN SYRUP	1 lb	454 g
DARK RUM	12 fl oz	360 mL

1. Coat the bundt pans with a light film of fat.

2. Sift together the flour and baking powder.

3. Cream together the butter, sugar, salt, and zests on medium speed with the paddle attachment, scraping down the bowl as needed, until the mixture is smooth and light in color, about 5 minutes.

4. Blend the eggs and yolks and add in three additions, mixing until fully incorporated after each addition and scraping down the bowl as needed.

5. Add the sifted dry ingredients alternately with the milk on low speed in three additions, mixing until smooth and fully incorporated after each addition.

6. Scale 2 lb/907 g batter into each prepared cake pan.

7. Bake at 350°F/177°C until a skewer inserted near the center of the cake comes out clean, about 30 minutes.

8. To prepare the syrup, combine all ingredients except the rum and bring to a boil. Remove from the heat and let cool, then stir in the rum.

9. Cool the cakes in the pans for a few minutes, then invert onto a wire rack. Brush the warm cakes with the rum syrup.

Lemon Buttermilk Cake

Makes 6 bundt cakes (8 in/20 cm each)

BREAD FLOUR	3 lb 13 oz	1.73 kg
BAKING SODA	2 tsp	8 g
SALT	2 tsp	10 g
BUTTER, soft	2 lb	907 g
SUGAR	3 lb 6 oz	1.53 kg
LEMON ZEST, grated	1¼ oz	35 g
EGGS	1 lb 8 oz	680 g
BUTTERMILK	32 fl oz	960 mL
LEMON JUICE	6 fl oz	180 mL

1. Coat the bundt pans with a light film of fat.

2. Sift together the flour, baking soda, and salt.

3. Cream the butter, sugar, and lemon zest together on medium speed with the paddle attachment, scraping down the bowl as needed, until the mixture is smooth and light in color, about 5 minutes.

4. Blend the eggs and add in three additions, mixing until fully incorporated after each addition and scraping down the bowl as needed.

5. Add the sifted dry ingredients alternately with the buttermilk in three additions, mixing on low speed until just incorporated. Add the lemon juice and blend.

6. Scale 2 lb 6 oz/1.08 kg batter into each prepared pan.

7. Bake at 350°F/177°C until the cakes spring back when lightly touched and a skewer inserted near the center comes out clean, about 60 minutes.

8. Cool the cakes in the pans for a few minutes, then transfer to racks to cool completely.

Polenta Cake

Makes 6 cakes (8 in/20 cm each)

ALL-PURPOSE FLOUR	1 lb 5 oz	595 g
BAKING POWDER	1 oz	28 g
SALT	¾ oz	21 g
BUTTER, soft	2 lb 13 oz	1.28 kg
SUGAR	3 lb 3 oz	1.45 kg
EGGS	2 lb 4 oz	1.02 kg
EGG YOLKS	2 lb 4 oz	1.02 kg
VANILLA EXTRACT	½ fl oz	15 mL
CORNMEAL	1 lb 5 oz	595 g

1. Coat the pans with a light film of fat and line them with parchment circles.

2. Sift together the flour, baking powder, and salt.

3. Cream together the butter and sugar on medium speed with the paddle attachment, scraping down the bowl as needed, until the mixture is smooth and light in color, about 5 minutes.

4. Whisk together the eggs, egg yolks, and vanilla. Gradually add to the egg mixture, mixing on low speed and scraping down the bowl periodically, until evenly blended.

5. Add the sifted dry ingredients and the cornmeal, mixing on low speed until evenly moistened.

6. Scale 1 lb 14 oz/851 g batter into each prepared pan. Gently tap the pans to release any air bubbles.

7. Bake at 350°F/177°C until a skewer inserted near the center of a cake comes out clean, 50 to 60 minutes.

8. Cool the cakes in the pans for a few minutes, then transfer to racks to cool completely.

Variation   **Almond Polenta Cake** Substitute almond extract for the vanilla extract.

Marjolaine

Makes two full sheet pans (16 by 24 in/41 by 61 cm each)

HAZELNUTS, finely ground	1 lb 6 oz	624 g
ALMONDS, finely ground	1 lb 6 oz	624 g
ALL-PURPOSE FLOUR	6 oz	170 g
SUGAR	2 lb 4 oz	1.02 kg
EGG WHITES	2 lb	907 g

1. Line sheet pans with parchment paper.

2. Combine the hazelnuts, almonds, flour, and 1 lb 8 oz/680 g of the sugar.

3. Whip the egg whites to soft peaks using the whip attachment on medium speed. Add the remaining 12 oz/340 g sugar gradually to the egg whites and beat to medium peaks.

4. Fold the dry ingredients into the beaten egg whites.

5. Spread the meringue evenly on the parchment-lined sheet pans.

6. Bake at 370°F/188°C until light golden brown, about 20 minutes.

7. Immediately remove the marjolaine from the hot pans to prevent it from drying out by inverting onto cooling racks. Peel off the parchment and allow to cool completely.

Dried Fruits

Plumping dried fruits by macerating them in a liquid will make them tender and juicy, eliminating any possibility of the undesirable leathery texture they can sometimes have in finished baked goods. Plumping dried fruits also serves to keep the amount of liquid in the formula balanced, as dried fruits can absorb moisture from the dough or batter if they are not first plumped. Furthermore, the liquid used for plumping the fruit can add its own flavor. Fruit can be plumped in liquor, such as brandy or rum, or in fruit juices or apple cider. Choose a liquid that complements the other flavors in the formula.

To plump fruit, place it in a bowl, add enough liquid to cover, and allow it to stand until rehydrated and softened. Soaking time will depend on the fruits, their age, and/or the particular drying process used. However, overnight is usually sufficient.

For quicker maceration, combine the dried fruit and liquid in a saucepan and bring to a simmer over medium heat. Remove from the heat and let the fruit stand in the liquid, covered, until plumped.

When dried fruit is added to a formula, whether plumped or not, it is often first tossed in a small measure of flour, which will help to prevent the fruit from sinking to the bottom of the pan during baking.

Christmas Fruitcake

Makes 6 loaves (1½ qt/1.44 L each)

GOLDEN RAISINS	2 lb 4 oz	1.02 kg
DARK RAISINS	2 lb 4 oz	1.02 kg
CANDIED FRUIT, diced	4 lb 8 oz	2.04 kg
CANDIED CHERRIES	12 oz	340 g
HONEY	12 oz	340 g
DRY SHERRY	16 fl oz	480 mL
BREAD FLOUR	1 lb 8 oz	680 g
SALT	1½ oz	43 g
GROUND GINGER	1 tbsp	6 g
GROUND CLOVES	2 tsp	4 g
GROUND CINNAMON	1 tbsp	6 g
SUGAR	1 lb 3½ oz	553 g
BUTTER, soft	1 lb 8 oz	680 g
EGGS	1 lb 8 oz	680 g
WALNUTS	12 oz	340 g

1. Combine the light and dark raisins, candied fruit, candied cherries, honey, and dry sherry and let soak overnight.

2. Coat the loaf pans with a light film of fat and dust with flour.

3. Sift the flour, salt, and spices together.

4. Cream together the sugar and butter on medium speed with the paddle attachment, scraping down the bowl as needed, until the mixture is smooth and light in color, about 5 minutes.

5. Add the eggs gradually, a few at a time, mixing on low speed until fully incorporated and scraping down the bowl as needed.

6. Add the sifted dry ingredients to the butter mixture, mixing until smooth. Fold in the walnuts and the fruit mixture.

7. Scale 3 lb/1.36 kg batter into each prepared pan.

8. Bake at 275°F/135°C until a skewer inserted near the center of the cake comes out with a few moist crumbs, 2 to 2½ hours.

9. Cool the cakes in the pans for a few minutes, then transfer to racks to cool completely.

Note Cake may be finished with a coating of apricot glaze (page 429) or a dusting of confectioners' sugar after it has cooled completely.

High-Ratio White Cake

Makes 6 cakes (8 in/20 cm each)

SUGAR	2 lb 10 oz	1.19 kg
CAKE FLOUR	2 lb 8 oz	1.13 kg
BAKING POWDER	1½ oz	43 g
SALT	1 oz	28 g
MILK	18 fl oz	540 mL
EGGS	10½ oz	298 g
EGG WHITES	13½ oz	383 g
VANILLA EXTRACT	1½ fl oz	45 mL
BUTTER, soft	1 lb 8 oz	680 g

1. Coat the pans with a light film of fat and line them with parchment circles.

2. Combine the sugar, flour, baking powder, and salt.

3. Combine the milk, eggs, egg whites, and vanilla.

4. Blend the butter with the dry ingredients and half of the milk mixture and mix on medium speed with the paddle attachment for 4 minutes, scraping down the bowl periodically, until smooth.

5. Add the remaining milk mixture in three additions, mixing for 2 minutes after each addition.

6. Scale 1 lb 8 oz/680 g batter into each prepared pan.

7. Bake at 350°F/177°C until the cake springs back when lightly touched in the center, about 35 minutes.

8. Cool the cakes in the pans for a few minutes, then transfer to racks to cool completely.

Variation   **High-Ratio Yellow Cake** Increase the quantity of whole eggs to 13½ oz/383 g and substitute 10½ oz/298 g egg yolks for the egg whites. Follow the method as stated above.

The Two-Stage Mixing Method

The two-stage mixing method was designed for use with high-ratio cakes. This type of batter contains a higher proportion of sugar and emulsifiers than other cakes. High-ratio cakes are typically made using an emulsified shortening, but the emulsifiers in the formula may also be boosted with additional eggs.

A high-ratio cake is one in which the weight of the sugar is equal to or greater than the weight of the flour and the weight of the eggs is equal to or greater than the weight of the fat. High-ratio shortening and/or additional egg yolks act as emulsifiers. The combination of these emulsifiers (shortening and/or egg yolks) and the two-stage mixing method results in a smooth batter. This method relies in part on specific and longer mixing times than those used in other mixing methods to develop the flavor and texture.

The first step in this method is to combine or sift together all the dry ingredients and then to combine all the wet ingredients, including the eggs.

In the first stage of mixing, combine the dry ingredient mixture with all of the fat and half of the liquid mixture and mix for 4 minutes on medium speed, scraping down the bowl periodically to ensure the batter is mixed evenly.

In the second stage, blend the remaining liquid into the batter in three equal parts, mixing for 2 minutes after each addition, for a total of 6 minutes. Scrape the bowl periodically to make certain that the batter is blended evenly.

1 The first stage in the two-stage mixing method

2 The second stage

High-Ratio Chocolate Cake

Makes 6 cakes (8 in/20 cm each)

SUGAR	2 lb 2½ oz	978 g
CAKE FLOUR	13½ oz	383 g
COCOA POWDER, sifted	7½ oz	213 g
BAKING POWDER	1½ oz	43 g
BAKING SODA	1½ oz	43 g
SALT	1½ tsp	7.50 g
MILK	18 fl oz	540 mL
EGGS	1 lb 6½ oz	638 g
CORN SYRUP	6 oz	170 g
VANILLA EXTRACT	1½ fl oz	45 mL
BUTTER, soft	1 lb 6½ oz	638 g

1. Coat the pans with a light film of fat and line them with parchment circles.

2. Combine the sugar, flour, cocoa powder, baking powder, baking soda, and salt.

3. Combine the milk, eggs, corn syrup, and vanilla.

4. Blend the butter with the dry ingredients and half of the milk mixture and mix on medium speed with the paddle attachment for 4 minutes, scraping down the bowl periodically, until smooth.

5. Add the remaining milk mixture in three additions, mixing for 2 minutes after each addition.

6. Scale 1 lb 8 oz/680 g batter into each prepared pan.

7. Bake at 350°F/177°C until the cake springs back when lightly touched in the center, about 35 minutes.

8. Cool the cakes in the pans for a few minutes, then transfer to racks to cool completely.

Devil's Food Cake

Makes 6 cakes (8 in/20 cm each)

SUGAR	3 lb 13 oz	1.72 kg
CAKE FLOUR	2 lb 5 oz	1.05 kg
BAKING SODA	1¼ oz	35 g
BAKING POWDER	2½ tsp	7.50 g
EGGS	1 lb 8 oz	680 g
BUTTER, melted and kept warm	1 lb 9 oz	709 g
WATER, warm	50 fl oz	1.50 L
VANILLA EXTRACT	1 fl oz	30 mL
COCOA POWDER, sifted	15 oz	425 g

1. Coat the pans with a light film of fat and line them with parchment circles.

2. Combine the sugar, flour, baking soda, and baking powder.

3. Blend the eggs and add in three additions, using the paddle attachment on medium speed, mixing until fully incorporated after each addition and scraping down the bowl as needed.

4. Add the butter and mix until evenly blended. Add the water and vanilla and mix, scraping down the bowl periodically, until a smooth batter forms. Add the cocoa powder and mix until evenly blended.

5. Scale 2 lb 3 oz/992 g batter into each prepared pan.

6. Bake at 350°F/177°C until a skewer inserted near the center of a cake comes out clean, about 45 minutes.

7. Cool the cakes in the pans for a few minutes, then transfer to racks to cool completely

Angel Food Cake

Makes 5 tube cakes (8 in/20 cm each)

SUGAR	2 lb 8 oz	1.13 kg
CREAM OF TARTAR	½ oz	14 g
CAKE FLOUR	15½ oz	439 g
SALT	1½ tsp	7.50 g
EGG WHITES	2 lb 8 oz	1.13 kg
VANILLA EXTRACT	½ fl oz	15 mL

1. Sprinkle the insides of five 8-in/20-cm tube pans lightly with water.

2. Combine 1 lb 4 oz/567 g of the sugar with the cream of tartar. Sift together the remaining 1 lb 4 oz/567 g sugar with the flour and salt.

3. Whip the egg whites and vanilla to soft peaks using the whip attachment on medium speed.

4. Gradually add the sugar and cream of tartar mixture to the egg whites, whipping on medium speed until medium peaks form.

5. Gently fold the sifted sugar and flour mixture into the egg whites until just incorporated.

6. Scale 15 oz/425 g batter into each prepared tube pan.

7. Bake at 350°F/177°C until a cake springs back when lightly touched, about 35 minutes.

8. Invert each tube pan onto a funnel or long-necked bottle on a wire rack to cool. Alternatively, for each cake, invert a small ramekin on top of a wire rack and prop the cake pan upside down and at an angle on the ramekin. Allow the cakes to cool completely upside down.

9. Carefully run a palette knife around the sides of each pan and around the center tube to release the cake. Shake the pan gently to invert the cake onto the wire rack.

Angel Food Mixing Method

Angel food cake is a light, spongy cake based on beaten egg whites and sugar (a meringue) that is stabilized with flour. All of the leavening in an angel food cake is supplied by the air that is whipped into the meringue. It is drier than sponge or chiffon cakes because it does not contain any fat. These cakes have good structure, but because they contain no fat, they have a unique texture, which makes them less desirable for use in layer cakes or as a component of any layered, sliced dessert or pastry.

For this method, it is important to assemble all equipment and ingredients and sift the flour and sugar before beginning to mix. Organized advance preparation will ensure the batter goes from mixer to oven in the shortest amount of time, reducing the loss of volume from the batter and, therefore, maintaining the volume of the finished cake.

After all advance preparation is done, beat the whites until they form soft peaks. Continue whipping and add the sugar, streaming it in gradually with the machine running. Once the meringue has medium, glossy peaks, fold in the sifted dry ingredients by hand, working quickly to reduce the deflation of the beaten egg whites.

Sprinkling the tube pan with a small amount of water before adding the batter will help develop a thin crisp crust on the cake.

Vanilla Sponge Cake

Makes 6 cakes (8 in/20 cm each)

BUTTER, melted	9 oz	255 g
VANILLA EXTRACT	1 fl oz	30 mL
EGGS	1 lb 11 oz	765 g
EGG YOLKS	9 oz	255 g
SUGAR	1 lb 11 oz	765 g
CAKE FLOUR, sifted	1 lb 11 oz	765 g

1. Coat the pans with a light film of fat and line them with parchment circles.

2. Blend the melted butter with the vanilla.

3. Combine the eggs, egg yolks, and sugar in an electric mixer bowl. Set over a pan of barely simmering water and whisk constantly until the mixture reaches 110°F/43°C.

4. Put the bowl on the mixer and whip with the whip attachment on high speed until the foam is three times its original volume and no longer increasing in volume.

5. Fold in the flour. Fold the melted butter into the batter.

6. Scale 16 oz/454 g batter into each prepared cake pan.

7. Bake at 375°F/190°C until the tops of the cakes spring back when lightly touched, about 30 minutes.

8. Cool the cakes in the pans for a few minutes, then transfer to racks to cool completely.

Variation   **Chocolate Sponge Cake** Replace 4 oz/113 g of the flour with Dutch process cocoa powder. Sift the cocoa powder together with the flour. Follow the remaining method as stated above.

Cold and Warm Foaming Methods

A foaming method is any method in which the eggs are whipped or beaten to incorporate air before they are incorporated into the batter. The air incorporated into the eggs creates a light and airy batter and help to leaven the baked item. When using any foaming method it is vital that all ingredients and equipment be assembled and receive any preliminary treatment before beginning to mix the batter. The flour and any other dry ingredients should be sifted thoroughly to ensure full aeration. Butter, if called for in the ingredient list, should be melted and allowed to cool slightly. For the cold and warm foaming methods, whole eggs are used.

For the cold foaming method, place the eggs and sugar into the bowl of an electric mixer, large enough to accommodate the volume of the fully beaten eggs. Using a wire whip attachment, whip the mixture to maximum volume on high speed. To determine when the eggs have reached maximum volume, watch as they are beaten; when the aerated mixture just begins to recede, maximum volume has been achieved. At this time remove the bowl from the mixer.

For the warm foaming method, place the eggs and sugar in the bowl of an electric mixer, but before beating place the bowl over a pan of barely simmering water and stir the mixture with a wire whip until it reaches 110°F/43°C. Heating the eggs with the sugar before beating allows the mixture to achieve maximum volume faster and creates a more stable foam because the sugar has been dissolved and the protein in the eggs becomes more elastic.

After the egg mixture has reached maximum volume, reduce the mixer speed to medium and continue to blend for 5 additional minutes. Whipping at high speed creates large air bubbles; continuing to mix at a lower speed divides the bubbles, reducing their size and creating a more stable foam, thereby stabilizing the batter.

Fold the sifted dry ingredients into the beaten eggs gently and gradually, but quickly, to prevent excessive loss of volume. For folding, use a large spatula or other implement with a large, broad, flat surface. This will allow for a larger amount of batter to be lifted with each fold, facilitating the rapid incorporation of ingredients without breaking down the fragile aerated structure. Fold the melted fat into the batter last. You may want to temper in the butter; some chefs feel this eases the fat's full incorporation and lessens any deflating effects on the batter. To do this, first lighten the butter by incorporating a small amount of batter. Then fold this mixture into the remaining batter. Immediately after mixing, scale the batter into each prepared pan and bake.

1 Proper folding technique

2 Tempering butter before adding it to a sponge batter

Flourless Chocolate Cake

Makes 6 cakes (9 in/23 cm each)

EGGS	3 lb	1.36 kg
EGG YOLKS	1 lb 2 oz	510 g
GRANULATED SUGAR	1 lb 6 oz	624 g
SEMISWEET CHOCOLATE, melted and kept warm	3 lb 12 oz	1.70 kg
SALT	½ oz	14 g
VANILLA EXTRACT	1 fl oz	30 mL
HEAVY CREAM, chilled	64 fl oz	1.92 L
CONFECTIONERS' SUGAR	as needed	as needed

1. Lightly butter six 9-in/23-cm cake pans and line them with parchment circles.

2. Combine the eggs, egg yolks, and sugar and whisk over a double boiler until the mixture reaches 110°F/43°C. Transfer to the bowl of an electric mixer.

3. Add the chocolate, salt, and vanilla to the egg mixture and whip with the whip attachment on medium speed until the mixture cools.

4. Meanwhile, in a separate bowl, whip the heavy cream to medium peaks.

5. Using a rubber spatula, fold the whipped cream into the chocolate mixture in two additions.

6. Scale 2 lb/907 g batter into each prepared pan.

7. Bake in a water bath at 400°F/204°C until the cakes are firm to the touch in the center and have formed a crust, about 25 minutes.

8. Allow the cakes to cool completely in the pans. Unmold and dust with confectioners' sugar before serving.

Chocolate XS

Makes 6 cakes (8 in/20 cm each)

BUTTER	as needed	as needed
WATER	24 fl oz	720 mL
SUGAR	2 lb 11½ oz	1.23 kg
SEMISWEET DARK CHOCOLATE, chopped	1 lb 13 oz	822 g
BITTERSWEET CHOCOLATE, chopped	2 lb 2 oz	964 g
BUTTER, melted	2 lb 11 oz	1.22 kg
EGGS	3 lb 10 oz	1.64 kg
VANILLA EXTRACT	1 fl oz	30 mL

1. Brush the insides of six 8-in/20-cm cake pans with the softened butter and line with parchment circles.

2. Combine the water and 1 lb 13 oz/822 g of the sugar in a heavy-bottomed saucepan and bring to a boil. Remove from the heat and add both chocolates; stir until the chocolate is melted. Stir in the melted butter. Let cool to room temperature.

3. Whip the eggs, the remaining 14½ oz/411 g sugar, and the vanilla using the whip attachment on high speed until light and fluffy, about 4½ minutes.

4. Gently fold the melted chocolate mixture into the egg mixture.

5. Scale 2 lb 5 oz/1.05 kg batter into each prepared pan.

6. Bake in a water bath at 350°F/177°C until the tops of the cakes feel firm, about 1 hour.

7. Cool, then wrap in plastic wrap and refrigerate overnight in the pans before unmolding.

Carrot Cake

Makes 6 cakes (8 in/20 cm each)

SUGAR	4 lb 4 oz	1.93 kg
SALT	1¼ oz	35 g
BREAD FLOUR	2 lb 2 oz	964 g
GROUND CINNAMON	1¼ oz	35 g
BAKING POWDER	½ oz	14 g
BAKING SODA	1¼ tsp	5 g
EGGS	2 lb 6 oz	1.08 kg
VEGETABLE OIL	30 fl oz	900 mL
CARROTS, grated	2 lb 8 oz	1.13 kg
WALNUTS, chopped	12 oz	340 g

1. Coat the pans with a light film of fat and line them with parchment circles.

2. Combine the sugar and salt. Sift together the flour, cinnamon, baking powder, and baking soda.

3. Whip the eggs using the whip attachment on medium speed until thick, about 8 minutes. Increase the mixer speed to high and continue whipping until the eggs thicken to the ribbon stage, about 8 minutes.

4. Gradually add the oil, whipping on high speed until evenly blended.

5. Gradually add the sugar mixture, whipping at medium speed. Add the sifted flour mixture, mixing on low speed until just incorporated.

6. Fold in the grated carrots and chopped walnuts.

7. Scale 1 lb 3 oz/539 g batter into each prepared cake pan.

8. Bake at 350°F/177°C until a skewer inserted near the center of a cake comes out clean, about 50 minutes.

9. Cool the cakes in the pans for a few minutes, then transfer to racks to cool completely.

Roulade

Makes 1 sheet pan (16 by 24 in/41 by 61 cm)

EGG YOLKS	1 lb	454 g
SUGAR	6 oz	170 g
VANILLA EXTRACT	½ fl oz	15 mL
EGG WHITES	8 oz	227 g
BREAD FLOUR, sifted	6 oz	170 g

1. Line a sheet pan with parchment paper.

2. Whip together the egg yolks, 3 oz/85 g of the sugar, and the vanilla with the whip attachment on medium speed until thick and light in color, about 10 minutes.

3. Whip the egg whites with a clean whip attachment on medium speed until frothy. Gradually add the remaining 3 oz/85 g sugar while continuing to whip, then whip until medium peaks form.

4. Gently blend one-third of the beaten egg whites into the egg yolk mixture to lighten it. Gently fold in the remaining egg whites.

5. Gradually fold in the sifted flour.

6. Spread the batter in the prepared sheet pan.

7. Bake at 400°F/204°C until the cake springs back when touched, 7 to 10 minutes.

8. Immediately unmold the cake onto a clean sheet pan. Cool completely.

Variation **Chocolate Roulade** Reduce the flour to 4½ oz/128 g and add 1½ oz/43 g Dutch process cocoa powder. Sift the flour and cocoa powder together. Follow the remaining method as stated above.

Separated Foam Mixing Method

In this variation on a standard cold foam mixing method, the whole eggs are separated and beaten separately into two foams. These foams are then folded together. The separated foam mixing method is slightly more difficult than the cold foaming method because egg whites, which are whipped alone, will rapidly lose volume. For this reason it is important when using this mixing method that all ingredients and equipment are assembled and receive any preliminary treatment before beginning to mix the batter (e.g., lining pans, sifting dry ingredients, melting the fat, etc.).

First, whip the egg yolks with a portion of the sugar to the ribbon stage, or until the mixture has thickened enough to fall in ribbons from the whip and is pale yellow in color. Set this foam aside. Whipped egg yolks are stable and won't lose volume.

Next, whip the whites until soft peaks form. Gradually add the remaining sugar with the mixer running on medium speed, and continue whipping on medium or high speed until the whites form medium peaks. The point to which the whites are beaten is important. If the whites are beaten to stiff peaks, the additional agitation they undergo during folding will cause them to become overbeaten. Overbeaten eggs are less elastic, more difficult to incorporate, will break down more easily, will not develop a stable internal structure, and have less leavening power.

Immediately after the whites reach their desired peak they should be gently folded into the foamed egg yolks. To fully blend these two components, first combine a small measure of the whites with the yolks to lighten them and make their consistency more akin to that of the whites. Fold the remaining whites into the yolk mixture. Fold in the remaining ingredients as in the cold and warm foaming methods.

Fold about one-third of the whites into the yolks to lighten them. Gently but thoroughly fold in the remaining whites until the batter is smooth and there are no visible pockets of egg whites.

Fold the sifted dry ingredients into the beaten egg mixture gently and gradually, but quickly, to prevent excessive loss of volume. For folding, use a large spatula or other implement with a large, broad, flat surface. This will allow for a larger amount of batter to be lifted with each fold, facilitating the rapid incorporation of ingredients without breaking down the fragile aerated structure. Fold the melted fat into the batter last. Immediately after mixing, scale the batter into each prepared pan and bake.

Chocolate Soufflé Cake

Makes 6 cakes (9 in/23 cm each)

BITTERSWEET CHOCOLATE, finely chopped	5 lb 7 oz	2.47 kg
BUTTER	2 lb 7 oz	1.11 kg
VANILLA EXTRACT	1 fl oz	30 mL
SALT	½ oz	14 g
EGG YOLKS	3 lb 6 oz	1.53 kg
EGGS	12 oz	340 g
SUGAR	1 lb 14 oz	851 g
GRAND MARNIER	12 fl oz	360 mL
EGG WHITES	3 lb 6 oz	1.53 kg

1. Line the bottoms of the cake pans with buttered parchment paper. Line the sides of the cake pans with buttered parchment strips that extend 3 in/8 cm above the top of each pan to form a collar.

2. Melt the chocolate and butter together over a double boiler, whisking gently to blend. Allow to cool completely. Stir in the vanilla and salt.

3. Whip the egg yolks, eggs, and 15 oz/425 g of the sugar with the whip attachment on medium speed, scraping down the bowl as needed, until light, about 5 minutes.

4. Add the Grand Marnier and whip until incorporated.

5. In a separate bowl, whip the egg whites with a clean whip attachment on medium speed until frothy. Gradually add the remaining 15 oz/425 g sugar and continue to whip until medium peaks form.

6. Fold one-third of the beaten egg whites into the yolk mixture to lighten it. Fold in the chocolate mixture, then fold in the remaining egg whites.

7. Pour the batter into the prepared pans.

8. Bake at 375°F/191°C until set, about 35 minutes.

9. Cool the cakes in the pans completely before unmolding.

Dobos Sponge

Makes 48 layers (8 in/20 cm each)

EGG YOLKS	2 lb 8 oz	1.13 kg
SUGAR	2 lb	907 g
VANILLA EXTRACT	½ fl oz	15 mL
EGG WHITES	3 lb 8 oz	1.59 kg
CAKE FLOUR, sifted	2 lb	907 g
BUTTER, melted	10 oz	284 g

1. Draw forty-eight 8-in/20-cm circles on sheets of parchment, using a cake circle or pan as a guide. Place the parchment with the ink/pencil side down so it does not come in contact with the batter.

2. Beat the egg yolks, 1 lb/454 g of the sugar, and the vanilla with the whip attachment on high speed until pale and thick, about 10 minutes.

3. Beat the egg whites to soft peaks on medium speed using a clean whip attachment. Add the remaining 1 lb/454 g sugar gradually to the beating whites. Continue to beat until medium peaks form.

4. Fold the beaten egg whites one-third at a time into the yolk mixture. Gradually fold in the flour.

5. Fold in the melted butter.

6. Using an offset spatula, spread 3½ oz/99 g batter evenly inside each of the traced circles.

7. Bake at 425°F/218°C until light golden brown, 5 to 7 minutes.

8. Immediately transfer the sponge circles to cooling racks. Cool completely.

Hazelnut Sponge Cake

Makes 6 cakes (8 in/20 cm each)

CAKE FLOUR	11 oz	312 g
BREAD FLOUR	4 oz	113 g
GROUND CINNAMON	1 tsp	3 g
HAZELNUTS, finely ground and toasted	11 oz	312 g
EGG YOLKS	1 lb 14 oz	851 g
CONFECTIONERS' SUGAR, sifted	9 oz	255 g
VANILLA EXTRACT	2 tsp	10 mL
LEMON ZEST, grated	1 tbsp	9 g
SALT	½ oz	14 g
EGG WHITES	1 lb 14 oz	851 g
SUGAR	9 oz	255 g

1. Coat the pans with a light film of fat and line them with parchment circles.

2. Sift the cake flour, bread flour, and cinnamon together. Combine the hazelnuts with the sifted dry ingredients.

3. Whip together the egg yolks, confectioners' sugar, vanilla, lemon zest, and salt with the whip attachment on medium speed until thick and light in color, about 10 minutes.

4. Whip the egg whites with a clean whip attachment on medium speed until soft peaks form. Gradually add the sugar while beating and continue to whip to medium peaks.

5. Gently blend one-third of the beaten egg whites into the egg yolk mixture to lighten it. Gently fold in the remaining egg whites.

6. Gradually fold in the dry ingredients.

7. Scale 1 lb/454 g batter into each prepared cake pan.

8. Bake at 350°F/177°C until the center of a cake is firm to the touch, 25 to 30 minutes.

9. Cool the cakes in the pans for a few minutes, then transfer to racks to cool completely.

Havana Cake

Makes 6 cakes (8 in/20 cm each)

NUT BATTER		
BREAD FLOUR	9 oz	255 g
HAZELNUTS, finely ground and toasted	1 lb 1 oz	482 g
ALMOND PASTE	15 oz	425 g
SUGAR	15 oz	425 g
BUTTER, soft	13 oz	369 g
SALT	½ tsp	2.50 g
VANILLA EXTRACT	½ fl oz	15 mL
EGGS	1 lb 3 oz	539 g
CHOCOLATE BATTER		
COCOA POWDER, sifted	5½ oz	156 g
GROUND CINNAMON	½ oz	14 g
HAZELNUTS, finely ground and toasted	1 lb 7 oz	652 g
SALT	½ tsp	2.50 g
EGG WHITES	1 lb 12 oz	794 g
SUGAR	1 lb 9 oz	709 g
VANILLA EXTRACT	½ fl oz	15 mL

1. Lightly butter the cake pans and line them with parchment circles.

2. To make the nut batter, sift the flour into a bowl. Blend in the ground hazelnuts.

3. Cream together the almond paste, sugar, butter, salt, and vanilla using the paddle attachment on medium speed, scraping down the bowl as needed, until the mixture is smooth and light in color, about 5 minutes. Blend the eggs and add in three additions, mixing until fully incorporated after each addition and scraping down the bowl as needed. Add the dry ingredients, mixing on low speed until just incorporated.

4. To make the chocolate batter, sift together the cocoa powder and cinnamon. Blend in the ground hazelnuts. Stir in the salt.

5. Whip the egg whites with the whip attachment on medium speed until soft peaks form. Gradually add the sugar while continuing to whip, then whip until stiff peaks form.

6. Fold the dry ingredients gradually into the whipped egg whites. Fold in the vanilla.

7. Spread 6¾ oz/191 g of the chocolate batter in an even layer at the bottom of each pan. Pipe 14½ oz/411 g of the nut batter through a pastry bag fitted with a large plain tip in

a spiral on top of the chocolate batter, and spread into an even layer. Spread another 6¾ oz/191 g of the chocolate batter on top, and smooth the top.

8. Bake at 350°F/177°C until a skewer inserted near the center of a cake comes out clean, about 45 minutes.

9. Cool the cakes in the pans for a few minutes, then transfer to racks to cool completely.

Spanish Vanilla Cake

Makes 6 cakes (8 in/20 cm each)

BREAD FLOUR	1 lb 14 oz	851 g
ALMONDS, ground and toasted	1 lb 14 oz	851 g
CHOCOLATE SHAVINGS (page 769)	12 oz	340 g
ALMOND PASTE	2 lb 7 oz	1.11 kg
LEMON ZEST, grated	1 oz	28 g
VANILLA EXTRACT	3 fl oz	90 mL
SALT	1½ tsp	7.50 g
EGG YOLKS	1 lb 8 oz	680 g
EGG WHITES	2 lb 10 oz	1.19 kg
SUGAR	2 lb 4 oz	1.02 kg
BUTTER, melted and kept warm	15 oz	425 g

1. Lightly butter six 8-in/20-cm cake pans and line them with parchment circles.

2. Mix together the bread flour, toasted almonds, and chocolate shavings.

3. Cream together the almond paste, lemon zest, vanilla, and salt using the paddle attachment on medium speed, scraping down the bowl as needed, until smooth, about 5 minutes.

4. Blend the egg yolks and add in three additions, scraping down the bowl as needed.

5. Whip the egg whites with the whip attachment on medium speed until soft peaks form. Gradually add the sugar while continuing to whip, whipping until medium-soft peaks form.

6. Gently blend one-third of the beaten egg whites into the almond paste mixture to lighten it. Gently fold in the remaining egg whites.

7. Gradually fold in the flour mixture until just incorporated. Fold in the melted butter.

8. Scale 1 lb 15 oz/879 g batter into each prepared cake pan.

9. Bake at 350°F/177°C until the center of a cake springs back when touched, 35 to 40 minutes.

10. Cool the cakes in the pans for a few minutes, then transfer to racks to cool completely.

Chocolate Almond Cake

Makes 6 cakes (8 in/20 cm each)

BREAD FLOUR	10 oz	284 g
ALMONDS, **finely ground and toasted**	1 lb 12 oz	794 g
BUTTER, **soft**	1 lb 12 oz	794 g
CONFECTIONERS' **SUGAR**	1 lb 12 oz	794 g
EGG YOLKS	1 lb 5 oz	595 g
EGGS	13 oz	369 g
BITTERSWEET CHOCOLATE, **melted**	2 lb 1 oz	936 g
EGG WHITES	1 lb 12 oz	794 g

1. Coat the pans with a light film of fat and line them with parchment circles.

2. Combine the flour and the almonds.

3. Cream together the butter and 1 lb 4 oz/567 g of the confectioners' sugar using the paddle attachment on medium speed, scraping down the bowl as needed, until the mixture is smooth and light in color, about 5 minutes.

4. Whisk together the egg yolks and eggs and warm them over a hot water bath, whisking constantly, to 85°F/29°C. Gradually add the warm eggs to the creamed mixture, mixing on low speed and scraping down the bowl as needed, until evenly blended.

5. Add the chocolate all at once and mix, scraping down the bowl periodically, until evenly blended.

6. Whip the egg whites with the whip attachment on medium speed until soft peaks form. Gradually add the remaining 8 oz/227 g confectioners' sugar while beating and continue to whip to medium peaks.

7. Fold the egg whites into the chocolate mixture. Fold in the dry ingredients.

8. Scale 2 lb 8 oz/1.13 kg batter into each prepared cake pan.

9. Bake at 375°F/191°C until the center of a cake is firm to the touch, about 45 to 50 minutes.

10. Cool the cakes in the pans for a few minutes, then transfer to racks to cool completely.

Combination Mixing Method

The combination mixing method combines the creaming mixing method (see page 283) and the foaming method (see page 308), giving the cake some of the qualities of both: the rich moist crumb of a creamed cake and some of the lightness of a batter that has the additional leavening power of beaten egg whites. For this method, a creamed mixture is made. Then beaten egg whites are folded in, and finally the dry ingredients are folded into the batter. When making anything using this method, as with other foamed batters (see cold and warm foaming methods, page 302), advance preparation (e.g., pan preparation, sifting, ingredients assembly, etc.) is critical to successful completion.

The first step in the combination mixing method, after all advance preparation is done, is the same as that for a creamed batter: The butter and some of the sugar are creamed together, and the whole eggs and yolks from the formula are blended into the mixture. Next, beat the egg whites until soft peaks form and then stream in the sugar gradually with the mixer running on medium speed and beat the whites until medium peaks form.

The beaten whites are then folded into the creamed mixture. To incorporate the meringue into the creamed mixture while keeping as much volume as possible, first add about one-third of the beaten egg whites, blending them in gently but thoroughly, to lighten the creamed mixture. After that, the batter will accept the remaining beaten egg whites more easily and with less vigorous mixing, allowing for less loss of volume. Gently fold in the remaining meringue just until evenly blended.

Fold in the sifted dry ingredients and any garnish, such as chopped nuts, working quickly but gently. The dry ingredients are added last because if they were added to the creamed mixture before the meringue, the batter would be much too stiff to accept the light, airy meringue.

Adding the meringue to the creamed butter mixture in the combination mixing method

Patterned Joconde Sponge

Makes 2 sheet cakes (16 by 24 in/41 by 61 cm each)

STENCIL BATTER		
BUTTER, soft	3 oz	85 g
CONFECTIONERS' SUGAR, sifted	3 oz	85 g
EGG WHITES	3 oz	85 g
CAKE FLOUR, sifted	3 oz	85 g
SPONGE CAKE		
CAKE FLOUR, sifted	3 oz	85 g
BLANCHED ALMOND FLOUR	10 oz	284 g
EGGS	12 oz	340 g
CONFECTIONERS' SUGAR	10 oz	284 g
EGG WHITES	8 oz	227 g
SUGAR	1 oz	28 g
BUTTER, melted and cooled	2 oz	57 g

1. To prepare the stencil batter, cream the butter and confectioners' sugar together in a food processor fitted with a metal chopping blade.

2. Add the egg whites gradually to the mixture with the food processor running.

3. Blend the flour into the egg white mixture.

4. Place a stencil on a silicone pad or parchment paper. Spread the batter in a thin layer over the stencil, scrape the batter off, and remove the stencil, leaving behind the batter-stenciled pattern. Transfer the silicone pad or parchment paper to a flat sheet pan and freeze.

5. To prepare the joconde sponge, combine the cake flour with the almond flour.

6. Whip the eggs and confectioners' sugar on medium speed until very light, 15 to 20 minutes.

7. Whip the egg whites with the whip attachment on medium speed until frothy. Slowly add the granulated sugar, then continue to whip until medium peaks form.

8. Fold one-third of the beaten egg whites into the yolk mixture to lighten it. Gradually fold in the flour mixture. Gently but thoroughly fold in the remaining beaten egg whites.

9. Fold in the cool melted butter. Run a wire whip through the batter several times to deflate it slightly.

Spreading the batter evenly for a joconde sponge

10. Divide the batter evenly between the prepared pans, spreading it quickly, before the stencils melt, but gently to avoid losing volume.

11. Bake at 400°F/204°C until the cakes are a light golden brown, 5 to 7 minutes.

12. Cool the cakes in the pans for a few minutes, then transfer to racks to cool completely.

Chiffon Cake

Makes 6 cakes (8 in/20 cm each)

CAKE FLOUR	3 lb	1.36 kg
BAKING POWDER	2 tbsp	18 g
SUGAR	2 lb	907 g
EGG YOLKS	10 oz	284 g
VEGETABLE OIL	24 fl oz	720 mL
WATER	24 fl oz	720 mL
VANILLA EXTRACT	½ fl oz	15 mL
EGG WHITES	1 lb 4 oz	567 g

1. Coat the cake pans with a light film of fat and line them with parchment circles.

2. Sift the flour and baking powder together. Combine with 1 lb/454 g of the sugar.

3. Combine the egg yolks, oil, water, and vanilla.

4. Add the egg yolk mixture gradually to the dry ingredients using the whip attachment on medium speed. After a paste has formed, scrape down the sides of the bowl. Continue adding the yolk mixture until all is incorporated. Beat for an additional 2 minutes on medium speed.

5. Whip the egg whites with a clean whip attachment on medium speed until soft peaks form. Gradually add the remaining 1 lb/454 g sugar while beating the whites and continue to beat until medium peaks form.

6. Gently blend one-third of the meringue into the egg yolk mixture to lighten it. Gently fold in the remaining egg whites.

7. Scale 1 lb 8 oz/680 g batter into each prepared pan.

8. Bake at 375°F/191°C until the top of a cake springs back to the touch, about 35 minutes.

9. Cool in the pans for a few minutes, then transfer to racks to cool completely.

Variations **Chocolate Chiffon Cake** Substitute 9 oz/255 g sifted cocoa powder for the same amount of flour. Follow the method as stated above.

Orange Chiffon Cake Add the grated zest of one orange in Step 3 and substitute orange juice for the water; add in Step 4 after all the dry ingredients have been added. Follow the remaining method as stated above.

Lemon Chiffon Cake Add the grated zest of two lemons in Step 3 and substitute lemon juice for the water; add in Step 4 after all the dry ingredients have been added. Follow the remaining method as stated above.

Lime Chiffon Cake Add the grated zest of three limes in Step 3 and substitute lime juice for the water; add in Step 4 after all the dry ingredients have been added. Follow the remaining method as stated above.

Chiffon Mixing Method

The chiffon mixing method is simple to execute and produces a beautiful cake with a tender, moist crumb with ample structure and stability, making it a good choice for building tiered cakes. All advance preparation (pan preparation, etc.) is important for chiffon cakes, as it is for other foamed cakes (for more information on advance preparation for foamed cakes see page 302); however, it is less critical here, as batters made by the chiffon mixing method are more stable than batters in which beaten (foamed) egg whites are used.

To make a chiffon cake, sift together the dry ingredients and mix in a portion of the sugar. Blend all the wet ingredients together except for the egg whites. Next, blend the wet ingredients into the sifted dry ingredients. Beat the egg whites until soft peaks form, then stream in the remaining sugar gradually with the mixer running on medium speed. Continue beating the egg whites until medium peaks form.

Finally, fold the meringue into the batter. To do this, first lighten the batter by incorporating approximately one-third of the egg whites. Then gently fold in the remaining two-thirds of the beaten egg whites.

Lemon Cake

Makes 6 cakes (8 in/20 cm each)

ALL-PURPOSE FLOUR	2 lb 13 oz	1.28 kg
CORNSTARCH	12 oz	340 g
BAKING POWDER	1 oz	28 g
BUTTER, soft	3 lb 10½ oz	1.66 kg
CONFECTIONERS' SUGAR	2 lb 13 oz	1.28 kg
LEMON ZEST, grated	4 oz	113 g
EGG YOLKS	2 lb	907 g
EGG WHITES	2 lb	907 g
SUGAR	12½ oz	354 g
LEMON SYRUP		
LEMON JUICE	6 fl oz	180 mL
CONFECTIONERS' SUGAR	2 lb	907 g

1. Coat the cake pans with a light film of fat and line them with parchment circles.

2. Sift together the flour, cornstarch, and baking powder.

3. Cream the butter, confectioners' sugar, and lemon zest using the paddle attachment on medium speed, scraping down the bowl as needed, until the mixture is smooth and light in color, about 5 minutes. *(continued)*

4. Gradually add the egg yolks, a few at a time mixing on low speed until fully incorporated after each addition and scraping down the bowl as needed.

5. Whip the egg whites with the whip attachment until soft peaks form. Gradually add the granulated sugar, and continue to whip until medium peaks form.

6. Fold one-third of the beaten egg whites into the egg yolk mixture to lighten it. Gently fold in the remaining egg whites.

7. Fold the sifted dry ingredients gradually into the mixture.

8. Scale 2 lb 4 oz/1.02 kg batter into each prepared cake pan. Gently tap the pans to release any air bubbles.

9. Bake at 350°F/177°C until a skewer inserted near the center of a cake comes out clean, about 1 hour.

10. To prepare the syrup, whisk together the lemon juice and confectioners' sugar in a stainless steel bowl until smooth.

11. Cool the cakes in the pans for a few minutes, then unmold the cakes onto racks.

12. Brush the cakes with the lemon glaze while they are still warm.

Cheesecake

Makes 6 cheesecakes (8 in/20 cm each)

GRAHAM CRACKER CRUST (page 254)	15 oz	425 g
CREAM CHEESE	7 lb 8 oz	3.40 kg
SUGAR	2 lb 4 oz	1.02 kg
SALT	½ oz	14 g
EGGS	1 lb 14 oz	851 g
EGG YOLKS	3 oz	85 g
HEAVY CREAM	15 fl oz	450 mL
VANILLA EXTRACT	1½ fl oz	45 mL

1. Coat the cake pans with a light film of fat and line them with parchment circles.

2. Press 2½ oz/71 g of the crust mixture evenly into the bottom of each pan.

3. Combine the cream cheese, sugar, and salt and mix on medium speed with the paddle attachment, occasionally scraping down the bowl, until the mixture is completely smooth, about 3 minutes.

4. Whisk the eggs and egg yolks together. Add the eggs to the cream cheese mixture in four additions, mixing until fully incorporated after each addition and scraping down the bowl as needed.

5. Add the heavy cream and vanilla and mix until fully incorporated.

6. Scale 2 lb 8 oz/1.13 kg batter into each prepared pan. Gently tap the pans to release any air bubbles.

7. Bake in a hot water bath at 325°F/163°C until the centers of the cakes are set, about 1 hour 15 minutes.

8. Cool the cakes completely in the pans on wire racks. Wrap the cakes, in the pans, in plastic wrap and refrigerate overnight to fully set.

9. To unmold, apply the gentle heat of a low open flame to the bottom and sides of each cake pan. Run a knife around the side of the pan. Place a plastic wrap–covered cake circle on top of the cake, invert, and tap the bottom of the pan to release the cake if necessary. Remove the pan, peel off the paper from the bottom of the cake, and turn onto a cake circle or serving plate.

1 Run a knife around the sides of the cheesecake to release it from the pan.

2 Invert the cake out of the pan onto the cardboard circle.

Marbleizing
batters

Variations   **Chocolate Cheesecake** To 2 lb 8 oz/1.13 kg batter for one 8-in/20-cm cake, add 2½ oz/71 g sifted cocoa powder and blend well. Proceed as directed above.

White Chocolate Cheesecake To 2 lb 8 oz/1.13 kg batter for one 8-in/20-cm cake, add 5 oz/142 g melted white chocolate and blend well. Proceed as directed above.

Marble Cheesecake To 8 oz/227 g batter for one 8-in/20-cm cake, add 2 oz/57 g melted bittersweet chocolate: Pour the chocolate batter into 2 lb/907 g plain batter and gently swirl three or four times with the end of a wooden spoon. Do not overmix. Pour the marbleized batter into the prepared pan and proceed as directed above.

Lemon Cheesecake To 2 lb 8 oz/1.13 kg batter for one 8-in/20-cm cake, add 2 fl oz/60 mL lemon juice and the grated zest of one lemon and blend well. Proceed as directed above.

Pumpkin Cheesecake To 23 oz/652 g batter for one 8-in/20-cm cake, add 10 oz/284 g pumpkin purée and blend well. Proceed as directed above.

Note   Cheesecakes are often served just as they are out of the oven, chilled and unmolded. However, toppings are commonly added that reflect the flavor profile of the cake after it is removed from the pan. For example, a chocolate or marble cheesecake can be glazed with ganache, a thin layer of curd can top a lemon cheese cake, or a pumpkin cheesecake could be lightly dusted with cinnamon or confectioners' sugar. The most common topping for a cheesecake is fresh seasonal fruit.

Walnut Cheesecake

Makes 6 cheesecakes (8 in/20 cm each)

GRAHAM CRACKER CRUST (page 254)	15 oz	425 g
CONFECTIONERS' SUGAR, sifted	10½ oz	298 g
CREAM CHEESE	6 lb 10½ oz	3.02 kg
MAPLE SYRUP	1 lb 6 oz	624 g
EGGS	1 lb 6 oz	624 g
SOUR CREAM	1 lb	454 g
WALNUT PRALINE PASTE (page 830)	3 lb 5½ oz	1.52 kg
VANILLA EXTRACT	1 fl oz	30 mL
WHITE CHOCOLATE, melted and cooled	1lb 6 oz	624 g
WALNUTS, toasted roughly chopped (page xxx)	9 oz	255 g

1. Lightly butter six 8-in/20-cm cake pans and line them with parchment circles.

2. Press 2½ oz/71 g of the crust mixture evenly into the bottom of each pan.

3. Cream the sugar, cream cheese, and maple syrup on medium speed with the paddle attachment, scraping down the bowl periodically, until smooth, fluffy, and lighter in color, about 5 minutes.

4. Gradually add the eggs and sour cream, scraping down the bowl periodically. Add the walnut praline paste and vanilla and blend thoroughly.

5. Transfer 2 lb/907 g of the cheesecake batter to another bowl and blend in the white chocolate. Blend the white chocolate mixture into the remaining cheesecake batter.

6. Scale 2 lb 8 oz/1.13 kg batter into each prepared pan. Sprinkle 1½ oz/43 g chopped dragée walnuts over each cheesecake. Gently tap the pans to release any air bubbles.

7. Bake in a hot water bath at 325°F/163°C until the centers of the cakes are set, about 1 hour 15 minutes.

8. Allow the cakes to cool completely in the pans on wire racks. Tightly wrap the cakes in the pans and refrigerate overnight to fully set.

9. To unmold, apply the gentle heat of a low open flame to the bottom and sides of each cake pan. Place a plastic wrap–covered cake circle on top of the cake, invert, and tap the bottom of the pan to release the cake if necessary. Remove the pan, peel off the paper from the bottom of the cake, and turn onto a cake circle or serving plate.

Cookies

THE WORD *COOKIE* DERIVES FROM A DUTCH WORD THAT MEANS "SMALL CAKE."

USING THIS AS THE CONTEMPORARY DEFINITION, THE TERM *COOKIE* CAN

INCLUDE ANYTHING FROM THE CLASSIC CHOCOLATE CHUNK TO TWICE-BAKED

BISCOTTI TO GLAZED AND FILIGREED PETITS FOURS. EACH TYPE OF COOKIE

REQUIRES DIFFERENT SHAPING TECHNIQUES SUCH AS ROLLING, STAMPING, AND

MOLDING. MANY ARE FILLED, GLAZED, OR OTHERWISE FINISHED AFTER BAKING.

Chocolate Chunk Cookies

Makes 12 dozen cookies

ALL-PURPOSE FLOUR	4 lb 5 oz	1.96 kg
SALT	1½ oz	43 g
BAKING SODA	1 oz	28 g
BUTTER, soft	2 lb 14 oz	1.30 kg
SUGAR	1 lb 14 oz	851 g
LIGHT BROWN SUGAR	1 lb 6 oz	624 g
EGGS	1 lb 2 oz	510 g
VANILLA EXTRACT	1¼ fl oz	38 mL
SEMISWEET CHOCOLATE CHUNKS	4 lb 5 oz	1.96 kg

1. Line sheet pans with parchment.

2. Sift together the flour, salt, and baking soda.

3. Cream the butter and sugars on medium speed with a paddle attachment, scraping down the bowl periodically, until the mixture is smooth and light in color, about 5 minutes.

4. Combine the eggs and vanilla. Add to the butter-sugar mixture in three additions, mixing until fully incorporated after each addition and scraping down the bowl as needed. On low speed, mix in the sifted dry ingredients and the chocolate chunks until just incorporated.

5. Scale the dough into 1½-oz/43-g portions and place on the prepared pans. Alternatively, the dough may be scaled into 2-lb/907-g units, shaped into logs 16 in/41 cm long, wrapped tightly in parchment paper, and refrigerated until firm enough to slice. Slice each log into 16 pieces and arrange on the prepared sheet pans in even rows.

6. Bake at 375°F/191°C until golden brown around the edges, 12 to 14 minutes. Cool completely on the pans.

Variation   **Chocolate Cherry Chunk Cookies** Add 2 lb/907 g chopped dried cherries along with the chocolate in Step 4.

CLOCKWISE FROM
UPPER RIGHT:
Almond Spritz
Cookies, Vanilla
Kipferl, Sugar
Cookies (star shapes),
Shortbread Cookies,
Swedish Oatmeal
Cookies, Sugar
Cookies
(moon shapes)

Drop Cookies

Cookies that are made from doughs and batters firm enough to hold their shape on a sheet pan are referred to as drop cookies. Most of these doughs are prepared by either the creaming or the foaming method. For the professional baker or chef there are a variety of scoop sizes commonly used to portion cookie dough. To portion drop cookies, fill a scoop of the appropriate size with dough and level it off, then release it onto the parchment-lined sheet pan. If indicated in the formula, flatten the mounded dough for a more even spread. The dough for most drop cookies can also be portioned by slicing rather than scooping, a method that is very efficient for volume production. To portion dough by this method, scale the dough into manageable portions and shape each one into a log. Wrap the dough in parchment paper or plastic wrap, using it to compress the dough into a compact cylinder, and refrigerate or freeze until firm. Slice the dough into uniform slices.

When portioning cookies using either method, arrange them in neat rows on the pan and leave enough room between for them to spread out as they bake. Most drop cookies are golden brown around the edges and on the bottom when properly baked. For many of these cookies, the upper surface should still look moist but not wet. Cool completely before storing in airtight containers at room temperature or freezing.

General Pan Preparation for Cookies

To ensure proper baking and even spread, use only flat pans. Pans should usually be lined with either parchment paper or silicone mats.

Some cookies, such as tuiles, bake best on silicone baking mats. If these are not available, butter and flour the pans for such cookies (see page 350 for pan preparation for tuile cookies). Generally, however, flouring pans for baking cookies is not desirable, as the flour could prevent the full spread of a cookie. Greasing pans for cookies is also not commonly recommended, as the fat may cause excessive spreading and browning of the bottoms.

For cookies with a particularly high fat content, which tend to brown easily, it is good practice to use two stacked sheet pans. Double-panning will create an air pocket that insulates the cookies, allowing for gentle heating of the bottoms.

Place cookies in orderly rows on the prepared pans, leaving room enough to spread.

General Cooling Instructions for Cookies

Most cookies should be removed from the pan as quickly as possible after baking to prevent further browning. Some cookies, however, are too soft to be removed immediately and should be allowed to cool briefly on the baking pan just until they have set enough to be transferred to a wire cooling rack. Certain cookies, such as tuiles, may be molded as soon as they are removed from the oven.

Mudslide Cookies

Makes 12½ dozen cookies

CAKE FLOUR	10½ oz	298 g
BAKING POWDER	1 oz	28 g
SALT	1¾ tsp	8.75 g
ESPRESSO, brewed	4 fl oz	120 mL
VANILLA EXTRACT	½ fl oz	15 mL
UNSWEETENED CHOCOLATE, chopped	1 lb 4 oz	567 g
BITTERSWEET CHOCOLATE, chopped	4 lb	1.81 kg
BUTTER, soft	10½ oz	298 g
EGGS	2 lb 12 oz	1.25 kg
SUGAR	4 lb	1.81 kg
WALNUTS, chopped	1 lb 5 oz	595 g
SEMISWEET CHOCOLATE CHIPS	4 lb 8 oz	2.04 kg

1. Line sheet pans with parchment.

2. Sift together the flour, baking powder, and salt.

3. Blend the espresso and vanilla extract.

4. Melt the unsweetened and bittersweet chocolate together with the butter. Stir to blend.

5. Beat the eggs, sugar, and coffee mixture with a whip attachment on high speed until light and thick, 6 to 8 minutes. Blend in the chocolate mixture on medium speed. On low speed, mix in the dry ingredients until just blended. Blend in the walnuts and chocolate chips just until incorporated.

6. Scale the dough into 2-oz/57-g portions and arrange on the prepared sheet pans in even rows. Alternatively, the dough may be scaled into 2-lb/907-g units, shaped into logs 16 in/41 cm long, wrapped tightly in parchment paper, and refrigerated until firm enough to slice. Slice each log into 16 pieces and arrange on the prepared sheet pans in even rows.

7. Bake at 350°F/177°C until the cookies are cracked on top but still appear slightly moist, about 12 minutes. Allow to cool slightly on the pans. Transfer to racks and cool completely.

Oatmeal Raisin Cookies

Makes 12 dozen cookies

ALL-PURPOSE FLOUR	2 lb 4 oz	1.02 kg
BAKING SODA	1 oz	28 g
GROUND CINNAMON	½ oz	14 g
SALT	½ oz	14 g
BUTTER, soft	3 lb	1.36 kg
SUGAR	1 lb 3 oz	539 g
LIGHT BROWN SUGAR	3 lb 8 oz	1.59 kg
EGGS	1 lb 4 oz	567 g
VANILLA EXTRACT	1 fl oz	30 mL
ROLLED OATS	3 lb 3 oz	1.45 kg
DARK RAISINS	1 lb 8 oz	680 g

1. Line sheet pans with parchment.

2. Sift together the flour, baking soda, cinnamon, and salt.

3. Cream the butter and sugars on medium speed with a paddle attachment, scraping down the bowl periodically, until the mixture is smooth and light in color, about 10 minutes. Blend the eggs and vanilla and add to the butter-sugar mixture in three additions, mixing until fully incorporated after each addition and scraping down the bowl as needed. On low speed, mix in the sifted dry ingredients and the oats and raisins until just incorporated.

4. Scale the dough into 2-oz/57-g portions and arrange on the prepared sheet pans in even rows. Alternatively, the dough may be scaled into 2-lb/907-g units, shaped into logs 16 in/41 cm long, wrapped tightly in parchment paper, and refrigerated until firm enough to slice. Slice each log into 16 pieces and arrange on the prepared sheet pans in even rows.

5. Bake at 375°F/191°C until the cookies are light golden brown, about 12 minutes. Allow to cool slightly on the pans. Transfer to racks and cool completely.

Varitation　**Oatmeal Fruit Cookies** Omit the raisins. Add 8 oz/227 g chopped dried pears, 8 oz/227 g chopped dried apricots, 8 oz/227 g dried blueberries, 8 oz/227 g chopped dried strawberries, 1 lb/454 g dried cranberries, and 8 oz/227 g toasted sliced almonds along with the oats in Step 3.

Swedish Oatmeal Cookies

Makes 12 dozen cookies

CAKE FLOUR	2 lb	907 g
BAKING SODA	⅔ oz	19 g
BUTTER, soft	2 lb 8 oz	1.13 kg
SUGAR	1 lb 10 oz	737 g
ROLLED OATS	1 lb 8 oz	680 g
DARK RAISINS	10 oz	284 g
GOLDEN RAISINS	10 oz	284 g

1. Line sheet pans with parchment.

2. Sift together the cake flour and baking soda.

3. Cream the butter and sugar on medium speed with a paddle attachment, scraping down the bowl periodically, until the mixture is smooth and light in color, about 5 minutes. On low speed, mix in the sifted dry ingredients and oats and raisins until just incorporated.

4. Scale the dough into 1 lb 4 oz/567 g portions. Shape each portion into a log 16 in/41 cm long. Wrap tightly in plastic wrap and chill until firm enough to slice.

5. Slice each log into 20 slices and arrange on the prepared sheet pans in even rows.

6. Bake at 375°F/191°C until light golden brown, about 15 minutes. Transfer to racks and cool completely.

Hermit Bars

Makes 12 dozen cookies

CAKE FLOUR	4 lb	1.81 kg
BAKING SODA	1¼ oz	35 g
SUGAR	2 lb 4 oz	1.02 kg
BUTTER, soft	1 lb 4 oz	567 g
MOLASSES	9½ oz	269 g
GROUND ALLSPICE	½ oz	14 g
GROUND CINNAMON	½ oz	14 g
SALT	1½ tsp	7.50 g
EGGS	9½ oz	269 g
WATER, room temperature	8 fl oz	240 mL
RAISINS	1 lb 8 oz	680 g
FONDANT, warmed	4 lb 8 oz	2.04 kg

1. Line sheet pans with parchment.

2. Sift together the flour and baking soda.

3. Cream together the sugar, butter, molasses, allspice, cinnamon, and salt on medium speed with a paddle attachment, scraping down the bowl periodically, until the mixture is smooth and light in color, about 5 minutes.

4. Whisk the eggs and water together. Add to the butter-sugar mixture in three additions, alternating with the sifted dry ingredients, mixing until fully incorporated after each addition and scraping down the bowl as needed. Mix in the raisins until just incorporated. Chill the dough.

5. Scale the dough into 12-oz/340-g portions. Shape into logs 12 in/30 cm long. Place on the prepared sheet pans.

6. Bake at 375°F/191°C, until the logs are light golden brown, 15 to 20 minutes. Transfer to racks and cool completely.

7. Place the logs on a wire rack over a sheet pan. Heat the fondant and thin to a glazing consistency (for instructions on working with fondant, see page 426). Glaze the logs with fondant and allow to set completely. Slice the logs into 1½-in/4-cm cookies.

Sand Cookies

Makes 12 dozen cookies

BUTTER, soft	1 lb 10 oz	737 g
CONFECTIONERS' SUGAR, sifted	9½ oz	269 g
VANILLA EXTRACT	1½ tsp	7.50 mL
ALL-PURPOSE FLOUR, sifted	2 lb 4 oz	1.02 kg
EGG WASH (page 825)	8 oz	227 g
SUGAR	1 lb	454 g

1. Line sheet pans with parchment.

2. Cream the butter, sugar, and vanilla extract on medium speed with a paddle attachment until light and smooth, about 5 minutes. On low speed, mix in the sifted flour. Scrape down the bowl periodically during creaming and mixing to blend evenly.

3. Scale the dough into 12-oz/340-g portions and shape into logs 6 in/15 cm long. Wrap tightly in plastic wrap and refrigerate until firm enough to slice.

4. Brush each log with egg wash and roll in sugar. Slice each log into 12 slices and arrange on the prepared pans in even rows.

5. Bake at 350°F/177°C until the bottoms and edges are pale golden brown, about 12 minutes. Transfer to racks and cool completely. (The cookies can be held in airtight containers at room temperature for up to 5 days or frozen for up to 1 month.)

**ON CAKE PLATE
FROM LEFT:**
Coconut
Macaroons,
Madeleines,
Linzer Cookies;
Rugelach (in front)

Coconut Macaroons

Makes 20 dozen cookies

SUGAR	2 lb	907 g
LIGHT CORN SYRUP	4 oz	113 g
EGG WHITES	1 lb	454 g
SHREDDED UNSWEETENED COCONUT	3 lb	1.36 g
CAKE FLOUR, sifted	2 oz	57 g

1. Line sheet pans with parchment.

2. Heat the sugar, corn syrup, and egg whites over simmering water until the mixture reaches 140°F/60°C, whipping constantly. Remove the pan from the heat and mix in the coconut and flour with a wooden spoon until just incorporated.

3. Using a No. 100 scoop, portion the batter, pressing each scoop lightly, and place in even rows on the prepared pans. Air-dry until slightly dry, about 1 hour.

4. Bake at 375°F/191°C until the cookies are a light golden brown, about 12 minutes. Cool completely on the pan.

Orange Coconut Macaroons

Makes 57 cookies

SUGAR	1 lb 2 oz	510 g
ALMOND FLOUR	1¾ oz	50 g
SHREDDED UNSWEETENED COCONUT	10 oz	283 g
EGG WHITES	9 oz	255 g
ORANGE ZEST, grated	3¾ oz	106 g
VANILLA EXTRACT	½ fl oz	15 mL

1. Line sheet pans with parchment.

2. Sift together 9 oz/255 g of the sugar and the almond flour.

3. Heat the remaining 9 oz/255 g sugar, the coconut, and egg whites over simmering water until the mixture reaches 155°F/68°C, whipping constantly. Remove from the heat and stir in the almond-flour mixture, orange zest, and vanilla extract until just incorporated.

4. Using a No. 100 scoop, portion the batter, pressing each scoop lightly, and place in even rows on the prepared pans. Air-dry until slightly dry, about 1 hour.

5. Bake at 375°F/191°C until the cookies are light golden brown, 12 minutes. Cool completely on the pan.

Fudge Brownies

Makes 4½ dozen brownies

UNSWEETENED CHOCOLATE, chopped	1 lb 2 oz	510 g
BUTTER	1 lb 11 oz	765 g
EGGS	1 lb 6½ oz	638 g
SUGAR	3 lb 4 oz	1.47 kg
VANILLA EXTRACT	¾ fl oz	23 mL
CAKE FLOUR, sifted	3 oz	85 g
WALNUTS, coarsely chopped	13 oz	369 g

1. Line a half sheet pan with parchment.

2. Melt the chocolate and butter over a pan of simmering water, blending gently. Remove from the heat.

3. Whip the eggs, sugar, and vanilla extract on high speed until thick and light in color, about 8 minutes.

4. Blend one-third of the egg mixture into the melted chocolate to temper it, then return it to the remaining egg mixture and blend on medium speed, scraping the bowl as needed. On low speed, mix in the flour and nuts until just blended. The batter will be very wet. Pour the batter into the prepared sheet pan and spread evenly.

5. Bake the brownies at 350°F/177°C until a crust forms but they are still moist in the center, about 30 to 40 minutes. Cool completely in the pan.

6. Cut into bars 2 by 3 in/5 by 8 cm.

Note The brownies may be glazed with 2 lb/907 g Hard Ganache (page 425). To glaze the brownies, trim the edges while they are in the pan. Invert the pan of uncut brownies onto the back of another sheet pan and then flip them once more, so they are right side up, onto a wire rack on a sheet pan. Pour warm ganache over the sheet of brownies and spread it evenly. Refrigerate the brownies for about 30 minutes, or until the ganache is firm. Slice the brownies into the dimensions given above using a warm sharp knife.

Bar Cookies

Bar cookies are baked in large sheets and portioned after baking. It is important to spread the batter or dough evenly in the pan to ensure uniform baking. Some bar cookies, such as lemon bars, are made of layers of different components. Each component should be spread carefully and evenly; in some cases, it may be necessary to chill one layer before adding another. (For instructions on lining pans with rolled dough, such as cookie dough or pâte sucrée, see page 503.)

If the bars are to be glazed or iced, allow the sheet to cool completely before adding the glaze or icing.

To ensure clean straight cuts, especially when working with a glazed or iced cookie, chill the full sheet before cutting it, and dip the knife in warm water and wipe it clean before each cut.

Bar cookies generally have a shorter shelf life than other cookies because the exposed sliced edges stale relatively quickly.

Cutting Pecan
Diamonds

Pecan Diamonds

Makes 200 pieces

SHORT DOUGH (page 250)	2 lb 8 oz	1.13 kg
PECAN FILLING		
BUTTER, cubed	2 lb	907 g
LIGHT BROWN SUGAR	2 lb	907 g
SUGAR	8 oz	227 g
HONEY	1 lb 8 oz	680 g
HEAVY CREAM	8 fl oz	240 mL
PECANS, chopped	4 lb	1.81 kg

1. Roll out the dough to a rectangle 18 by 26 in/46 by 66 cm and ⅛ in/3 mm thick. Lay it gently in a sheet pan so that it completely lines the bottom and sides. Dock the dough with a pastry docker or the tines of a fork.

2. Bake at 350°F/177°C until light golden brown, about 10 minutes.

3. To make the filling, cook the butter, both sugars, honey, and heavy cream in a heavy-bottomed saucepan over medium-high heat, stirring constantly, until the mixture reaches 240°F/116°C. Add the nuts and stir until fully incorporated. Immediately pour into the prebaked crust and spread into an even layer.

4. Bake at 350°F/177°C until the filling bubbles or foams evenly across the surface and the crust is golden brown, about 45 minutes. Cool completely in the pan.

5. Using a metal spatula, release the sheet from the sides of the pan and invert the slab onto the back of a sheet pan. Transfer to a cutting board, flipping it over so it is right side up. Trim off the edges. Cut into diamonds with 1-in/3-cm sides.

Florentine Bar Cookies

Makes 115 cookies

SHORT DOUGH, (page 250)	1 lb 4 oz	567 g
FLORENTINE FILLING		
SUGAR	13 oz	369 g
HEAVY CREAM	11 fl oz	330 mL
HONEY	5½ oz	156 g
BUTTER	5½ oz	156 g
SLICED ALMONDS	11 oz	312 g
DRIED CHERRIES, finely chopped	4½ oz	128 g
CANDIED ORANGE PEEL (optional) (page 726)	2½ oz	71 g
CAKE FLOUR, sifted	½ oz	14 g

1. Line a half sheet pan with parchment paper.
2. Roll out the dough to a rectangle 13 by 18 in/33 by 46 cm and ⅛ in/3 mm thick. Lay it gently in a half sheet pan so that it completely lines the bottom and sides. Dock the dough with a pastry docker or the tines of a fork.
3. Bake at 375°F/191°C until the dough is light golden brown, about 10 minutes.
4. To make the filling, cook the sugar, cream, honey, and butter in a heavy-bottomed saucepan over medium heat, stirring constantly, until the mixture reaches 240°F/116°C. Remove from the heat and fold in the almonds, cherries, orange peel (if using), and flour. Pour into the prebaked crust and spread into an even layer.
5. Bake until golden brown, 15 to 20 minutes. Cool. (Note: The cookies may be slightly warm when they are cut.)
6. Using a metal spatula, release the sheet from the sides of the pan. Transfer to a cutting board. Trim off the edges. Cut into 1¼-in/3-cm squares.

Rugelach
Makes 136 cookies

BREAD FLOUR	2 lb 8 oz	1.13 kg
ALL-PURPOSE FLOUR	8 oz	227 g
SALT	¼ tsp	1.25 g
BUTTER, soft	3 lb	1.36 kg
CREAM CHEESE, soft	2 lb 8 oz	1.13 kg
RASPBERRY JAM	2 lb	907 g
PECANS, roughly chopped	1 lb 9 oz	709 g
CINNAMON SUGAR (page 826)	as needed	as needed
EGG WASH, for brushing (page 825)	as needed	as needed

1. Line sheet pans with parchment paper.

2. Sift together the bread flour, flour, and salt.

3. Mix the butter and cream cheese using a paddle attachment on medium speed until smooth, 5 minutes. On low speed, mix in the sifted dry ingredients until just combined. Scrape down the bowl as necessary to blend evenly.

4. Turn the dough out onto a work surface. Roll the dough to an even thickness of ½ in/1 cm in a rectangle approximately 16 by 26 in/41 by 66 cm and give it one three-fold (for information on administering a three-fold, see page 263). Scale the dough into 1-lb/454-g portions and shape into disks.

5. Wrap the dough in plastic wrap and let it rest under refrigeration until cool enough to roll out.

6. Roll out each disk on a lightly floured work surface to a circle ¹⁄₁₆ in/1.5 mm thick and 14 in/36 cm in diameter. Spread the dough with 2½ oz/71 g jam and sprinkle with 3 oz/85 g chopped nuts and ½ oz/14 g cinnamon sugar. Cut into 16 wedges. Roll each

Roll up the cut wedges after spreading the round of dough with filling.

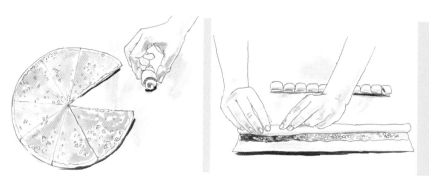

For a different shape, roll the filled round of dough into a cylinder and cut into even pieces.

one into a crescent, beginning at the wide end. Transfer to prepared sheet pans, leaving about 1 in/3 cm between cookies. Lightly brush the cookies with egg wash and sprinkle each with cinnamon sugar.

7. Bake at 375°F/191°C until light golden brown, about 10 minutes. Transfer to racks and cool completely.

Shaping Variation Working with 8-oz/227-g pieces of dough, roll each piece into a rectangle approximately 8 in/20 cm wide and 1/16 in/1.5 mm thick. Spread 5 oz/142 g raspberry jam over the rolled dough and sprinkle with 3 1/2 oz/99 g roughly chopped pecans or walnuts and 1/2 oz/14 g cinnamon sugar. Roll up the dough from the longer side of the rectangle to form a long log. Lightly brush the top of the log with egg wash and sprinkle with 1/2 oz/14 g cinnamon sugar. Cut the log into 1-in/3-cm sections, place on parchment-lined sheet pans, and bake as directed above.

Brandy Snaps
Makes 12 dozen cookies

BUTTER, melted	11 oz	312 g
LIGHT BROWN SUGAR	7 3/4 oz	220 g
DARK CORN SYRUP	14 oz	397 g
BRANDY	3/4 fl oz	23 mL
BREAD FLOUR, sifted	7 oz	198 g
GROUND GINGER	1/2 tsp	1 g

1. Line sheet pans with silicone baking mats. Place butter, sugar, corn syrup, and brandy in a mixing bowl and mix to combine.

2. Add the flour and ginger and mix until smooth.

3. Portion the batter with a No. 100 scoop onto the lined sheet pans, spacing the cookies 4 in/10 cm apart.

4. Bake at 350°F/177°C until light golden brown, about 5 minutes. Remove from the oven and allow to cool slightly. Form into desired shape while warm.

Variation **Sesame Brandy Snaps** Add 1 1/4 oz/35 g sesame seeds to the finished batter.

Sugar Cookies

Makes 10 dozen cookies

ALL-PURPOSE FLOUR	2 lb	907 g
BAKING POWDER	½ oz	14 g
SALT	1½ tsp	7.50 g
BUTTER, soft	1 lb	454 g
SUGAR	1 lb	454 g
EGGS	8 oz	227 g
MILK, room temperature	4 fl oz	120 mL
VANILLA EXTRACT	½ fl oz	15 mL
COARSE SUGAR	12 oz	340 g

1. Line sheet pans with parchment.

2. Sift together the flour, baking powder, and salt.

3. Cream the butter and sugar on medium speed using a paddle attachment until light and fluffy, about 5 minutes. Combine the eggs, milk, and vanilla. Alternately add the sifted dry ingredients and egg mixture in two to three additions, blending until fully incorporated after each addition.

4. Divide the dough into four equal portions, wrap each tightly in plastic wrap, and refrigerate until firm enough to roll. Working with one portion of the dough at a time, on a lightly floured surface roll out the dough to ⅛ in/3 mm thick. Using a 2½-in/6-cm round cutter, cut out cookies. Place the cookies in even rows on the prepared sheet pans and sprinkle with coarse sugar. Collect the scraps of dough, press together, wrap, and refrigerate until firm enough to roll.

5. Bake at 375°F/191°C until golden around the edges, about 12 minutes. Transfer to racks and cool completely.

Traditional Rolled and Cut-Out Cookies

Cookie dough that is to be rolled and cut should usually be refrigerated after mixing to allow the dough to firm up. Line the sheet pans, or prepare them as otherwise directed, before beginning to roll out the dough so that the cut cookies can be transferred directly to a pan.

Divide the dough into manageable portions. Work with one portion at a time and keep the remainder tightly wrapped and refrigerated. Lightly dust the work surface with flour. All-purpose or bread flour is most often used, but for certain types of cookies you may use confectioners' sugar for dusting. Some doughs are particularly soft and delicate and should instead be rolled between two sheets of parchment paper.

Generally cookie doughs should be rolled ⅟₁₆ to ⅛ in/1.5 to 3 mm thick, but the precise thickness depends on the formula.

Rolled and cut cookies generally do not spread much, so they can be placed relatively close together on the sheet pans. The dough will soften as it is rolled and cut; cut cookies should be quickly transferred to the prepared pans so they don't become misshapen when transferred. When using cutters of varying sizes and shapes, bake cookies of like sizes together to ensure even baking.

1 Begin rolling the dough.

2 Turn the dough 90 degrees.

3 Lift the dough and dust the table underneath with flour.

Citrus Crisps

Makes 12 dozen cookies

BUTTER, soft	2 lb	907 g
SUGAR	14½ oz	411 g
SALT	½ oz	14 g
LEMON ZEST, grated	5 oz	142 g
VANILLA EXTRACT	2 tsp	10 mL
ROLLED OATS	1 lb 2 oz	510 g
ALL-PURPOSE FLOUR, sifted	1 lb 1½ oz	496 g
CONFECTIONERS' SUGAR, for dusting	as needed	as needed

1. Line sheet pans with parchment paper.

2. Cream the butter, sugar, salt, lemon zest, and vanilla extract using a paddle attachment on medium speed until light and smooth, about 5 minutes. On low speed, mix in the oats and flour until just combined. Scrape down the bowl periodically during creaming and mixing to blend evenly.

3. Form the dough into 1-in/3-cm balls and place in even rows approximately 3 in/8 cm apart on the prepared sheet pans. Flatten with the palm of your hand.

4. Bake at 350°F/177°C until the edges are light golden, 12 to 15 minutes. Transfer to racks and cool completely.

5. Dust the cookies with confectioners' sugar just before serving.

Linzer Cookies

Makes 65 cookies

LINZER DOUGH (page 254)	3 lb 8 oz	1.59 kg
CONFECTIONER'S SUGAR, for dusting	as needed	as needed
RASPBERRY JAM	4 lb	1.81 kg

1. Line sheet pans with parchment paper.

2. Divide the dough into four equal portions, wrap each tightly in plastic wrap, and refrigerate. Working with one portion of the dough at a time, on a lightly floured surface roll out the dough to ⅛ in/3 mm thick. Using a 1½-in/4-cm fluted cutter, cut out rounds of

dough. Using a 1-in/3-cm plain round cutter, cut out a hole from the center of half of the pieces to make rings. Transfer to the prepared sheet pans, placing the rings and circles on separate pans and arranging them in evenly spaced rows. Collect the scraps of dough, press together, wrap, and refrigerate until firm enough to roll.

3. Bake at 375°F/191°C until light golden brown, 8 to 10 minutes. Transfer to racks and cool completely.

4. Sift confectioners' sugar over the rings. Fill a parchment cone with the jam and pipe a small mound of jam onto the center of each plain cookie. Carefully center the sugar-dusted rings onto the jam-filled bottoms and press gently to secure.

Mirror Cookies

Makes 65 cookies

1-2-3 COOKIE DOUGH (page 249)	3 lb 8 oz	1.59 kg
RASPBERRY JAM	2 lb 12 oz	1.25 kg
WATER	14 fl oz	420 mL
CONFECTIONERS' SUGAR, for dusting	as needed	as needed

1. Line sheet pans with parchment paper.

2. Divide the dough into four equal portions, wrap each tightly in plastic wrap, and refrigerate. Working with one portion of the dough at a time, on a lightly floured surface roll out the cookie dough to ⅛ in/3 mm thick. Using a 1½-in/4-cm plain cutter, cut out rounds of dough. Using a 1-in/3-cm plain round cutter, cut out a hole from the center of half of the pieces to make rings. Transfer the circles and rings to the prepared sheet pans, placing the rings and circles each on separate pans, arranging them in evenly spaced rows. Collect the scraps of dough, press together, wrap, and refrigerate until firm enough to roll.

3. Bake at 350°F/177°C until light golden brown, about 10 minutes. Transfer to racks and cool completely.

4. To prepare the "mirror," heat the raspberry jam with the water in a heavy-bottomed saucepan until translucent, smooth, and slightly reduced, about 10 minutes. Allow to cool slightly.

5. Sift confectioners' sugar over the rings. Carefully center the sugar-dusted rings onto bottoms and pipe the warm jam into the circle using a small plain pastry tip, or a parchment paper cone.

Shortbread Cookies

Makes 3 dozen cookies

ALL-PURPOSE FLOUR	6½ oz	184 g
CORNSTARCH	7 oz	198 g
SALT	pinch	pinch
BUTTER, soft	8 oz	227 g
CONFECTIONERS' SUGAR, sifted	5 oz	142 g

1. Line sheet pans with parchment paper.

2. Sift together the flour, cornstarch, and salt.

3. Cream the butter and sugar on medium speed with a paddle attachment until light and smooth, about 5 minutes. On low speed, mix in the dry ingredients until just blended. Add a little water, a few drops at a time, if necessary, to make a workable dough. Scrape down the bowl as needed during creaming and mixing to blend evenly. Wrap the dough tightly in plastic wrap and refrigerate until firm enough to roll.

Shortbread has a dense, crumbly texture.

4. Roll out the dough on a lightly floured work surface to $1/4$ in/6 mm thick. Cut into rectangles 2 by 3 in/5 by 8 cm and transfer to the prepared sheet pans. Chill for 30 minutes. Collect the scraps of dough, press together, wrap, and refrigerate until firm enough to roll.

5. Bake the shortbread at 350°F/177°C until the edges are a very light gold, about 20 minutes. Transfer to racks and cool completely.

Note Add a small amount of water to the dough trimmings to make a workable dough, reroll, and cut out additional cookies.

Citrus Shortbread Cookies

Makes 3 dozen cookies

BUTTER, soft	10$1/2$ oz	298 g
CONFECTIONERS' SUGAR, sifted	5$1/2$ oz	156 g
EGG YOLKS	1$1/2$ oz	43 g
ORANGE ZEST, grated	2$1/2$ oz	71 g
LEMON ZEST, grated	2$1/2$ oz	71 g
VANILLA BEAN, seeds only	1 each	1 each
VANILLA EXTRACT	1$1/2$ tsp	7.50 mL
CAKE FLOUR, sifted	15 oz	425 g

1. Line sheet pans with parchment paper.

2. Cream the butter and sugar on medium speed with a paddle attachment until light and smooth, about 5 minutes. Blend together the egg yolks, orange and lemon zest, vanilla seeds, and vanilla extract. Add to the butter mixture in two to three additions, mixing until fully incorporated after each addition and scraping the bowl as needed. On low speed, mix in the flour until just blended, scraping the bowl as needed. Wrap the dough tightly in plastic wrap and chill until firm enough to roll.

3. Roll out the dough on a lightly floured work surface to $1/4$ in/6 mm thick. Cut into rectangles 2 by 3 in/5 by 8 cm and transfer to the prepared sheet pans. Collect the scraps of dough, press together, wrap, and refrigerate until firm enough to roll.

4. Bake the shortbread at 350°F/177°C until the edges are a very light gold, about 20 minutes. Transfer to racks and cool completely.

Russian Tea Cookies

Makes 8 dozen cookies

PECANS, toasted	12 oz	340 g
SUGAR	5 oz	142 g
BUTTER, soft	1 lb	454 g
VANILLA EXTRACT	¾ tsp	3.75 mL
SALT	1½ tsp	7.50 g
ALL-PURPOSE FLOUR	1 lb 2 oz	510 g
CONFECTIONERS' SUGAR, for dusting	as needed	as needed

1. Line sheet pans with parchment paper.

2. Grind the pecans with 1¾ oz/50 g of the sugar in a food processor to a fine meal.

3. Cream the butter, the remaining 3¼ oz/92 g sugar, the vanilla, and salt on medium speed with a paddle attachment until light and smooth, 5 to 6 minutes. On low speed, mix in the flour and ground nuts until just blended. Scrape down the bowl as needed during creaming and mixing to blend evenly.

4. Roll the dough into ¾-in/2-cm balls and flatten slightly, or scoop the dough using a No. 50 scoop, and place on the prepared sheet pans. Chill for at least 1 hour.

5. Bake the cookies at 325°F/163°C until light golden brown, about 20 minutes.

6. While the cookies are still warm, transfer to racks and dust generously with confectioners' sugar. Cool to room temperature. Dust again with confectioner's sugar.

Zedern Brot

Makes 80 cookies

ALMOND PASTE	1 lb	454 g
CONFECTIONERS' SUGAR	5 oz	142 g
ALMONDS, toasted and finely ground	5 oz	142 g
CANDIED FRUIT, finely chopped	1 oz	28 g
BREAD FLOUR	½ oz	14 g
EGG WHITES	2 oz	57 g
ROYAL ICING (page 770)	as needed	as needed

1. Line sheet pans with parchment paper.

2. Combine the almond paste, confectioners' sugar, almonds, candied fruit, flour, and egg whites and blend on low speed with a paddle attachment to form a stiff paste, about 10 minutes.

3. Roll out the dough on a lightly floured work surface to a sheet $\frac{1}{2}$ in/1 cm thick. Spread a thin layer (about $\frac{1}{16}$ in/1.5 mm) of medium stiff royal icing across the surface. Place the glazed sheet in the freezer until firm.

4. Using a $1\frac{1}{4}$-in/3-cm round cutter that has been lightly moistened, cut into crescent shapes. Place 1 in/3 cm apart on the prepared sheet pans. Collect the scraps of dough, press together, wrap, and refrigerate until firm enough to roll.

5. Bake at 275°F/135°C until light golden brown around the edges, about 25 minutes. Transfer to racks and cool completely.

Vanilla Kipferl

Makes 12 dozen cookies

BUTTER, soft	1 lb	454 g
VANILLA CONFECTIONERS' SUGAR, sifted (page 827)	6⅓ oz	180 g
VANILLA EXTRACT	2 tsp	10 mL
GROUND CINNAMON	1 tsp	2 g
SALT	pinch	pinch
EGG YOLK	¾ oz	21 g
CAKE FLOUR, sifted	1 lb	454 g
HAZELNUTS, finely ground	4½ oz	128 g
VANILLA CONFECTIONERS' SUGAR	as needed	as needed

1. Cream the butter, vanilla sugar, vanilla extract, cinnamon, and salt on medium speed with a paddle attachment until light and smooth, about 8 minutes. Add the egg yolk and mix until smooth and evenly blended. On low speed, mix in the flour and hazelnuts until just blended. Scrape down the bowl as needed during creaming and mixing to blend evenly.

2. Wrap the dough well and chill until firm enough to roll out, about 1 hour.

3. Line sheet pans with parchment paper. Shape the dough into ropes $\frac{1}{2}$ in/1 cm in diameter. Cut each rope into $2\frac{1}{2}$-in/6-cm lengths and gently form into tapered crescent shapes. Place in even rows on the prepared sheet pans.

4. Bake at 350°F/177°C until light golden brown, about 8 minutes.

5. While the cookies are still warm, toss gently in vanilla confectioners' sugar to coat. Cool completely and repeat when cold.

Nut Tuile Cookies

Makes 25 cookies

ALMONDS	2 oz	57 g
HAZELNUTS	3 oz	85 g
SUGAR	6 oz	170 g
ALL-PURPOSE FLOUR	2½ oz	71 g
SALT	pinch	pinch
EGG WHITES	4 each	4 each

1. Line sheet pans with parchment paper or silicone baking mats. Have stencils and an off-set spatula, as well as shaping implements such as cups, dowels, or rolling pins, depending on the desired shapes, assembled.

2. Combine the almonds, hazelnuts, and sugar in a food processor and pulse to grind to a fine powder. Add the flour and salt and pulse several times to combine. Transfer to a large bowl.

3. Whip the egg whites on high speed using a whip attachment until medium peaks form. Using a rubber spatula, fold gently into the nut mixture in three additions.

4. Using the offset spatula and desired stencil, spread the batter on the prepared sheet pans.

5. Bake at 375°F/191°C until an even light brown, about 10 minutes. Remove from the oven and immediately shape the cookies.

Stenciled Cookies

Stenciled cookies are made using batters that can be spread very thin and baked without loosing their detailed shape. Batters that can be used in this way may be spread in a thin layer to create a variety of shapes using stencils. Additionally, cookies of this type may be shaped further immediately after baking by laying the still-warm cookie over a form such as a rolling pin, dowel, or cup.

Pans that are to be used for stenciled cookies may be lined with silicone baking mats. If baking mats are unavailable, grease and flour inverted sheet pans and freeze them before using; freezing will solidify the fat and flour coating so it will not come off during the stenciling process.

Place the stencil on the prepared pan and use a small offset metal spatula to spread a thin, even layer of batter over it; it is important to spread the batter evenly so the cookies bake uniformly. Carefully lift the stencil, and repeat.

Stenciled cookies bake quickly and should be watched almost constantly. To shape stenciled cookies, they may be draped over a rolling pin to create the classic "tuile" shape, twisted around a dowel to create a spiral, or draped over a cup or ramekin to make a container, to name only a few variations. The cookies must be warm and pliable enough to mold without cracking; if necessary, return the pan of baked cookies to the oven to rewarm them briefly. For this reason, stenciled cookies should be made in small batches; if the pan must be returned to the oven too many times, the last cookies on the pan may burn.

Spread the batter over the stencil with a spatula. Use a variety of different stencils to create cookie garnishes.

Lace Nut Tuiles

Makes 100 cookies

WALNUTS, PECANS, HAZELNUTS, OR ALMONDS, ground	10 oz	284 g
SUGAR	10 oz	284 g
BUTTER, soft	8 oz	227 g
ORANGE ZEST, grated	1 oz	28 g
LIGHT CORN SYRUP	10 oz	284 g
ALL-PURPOSE FLOUR, sifted	3 oz	85 g

1. Line sheet pans with silicone baking mats. Have shaping implements such as cups, dowels, or rolling pins, depending on the desired shapes, assembled. Grind the nuts to a coarse meal.

2. Cream the sugar, butter, and orange zest on medium speed with a paddle attachment until light and smooth, about 5 minutes. Gradually add the corn syrup, mixing until smooth and evenly blended. On low speed, mix in the flour. Fold in the nuts by hand, or mix on low speed until just combined. Scrape down the bowl as needed during creaming and mixing to blend evenly.

3. Roll the dough into 1-in/3-cm balls. Place 4 in/10 cm apart on the prepared sheet pans and flatten slightly.

4. Bake at 350°F/177°C until an even light brown, 5 minutes. Remove from the oven and shape while still warm. Or leave the cookies flat, and cool in the pans on racks.

Nougatine Tuiles

Makes 100 cookies

GLUCOSE SYRUP	8 oz	227 g
SUGAR	8 oz	227 g
ALMONDS, finely ground	8 oz	227 g
BUTTER	6 oz	170 g

1. Line a half sheet pan with a silicone baking mat.

2. Heat the glucose syrup and sugar in a heavy-bottomed saucepan over medium heat until the sugar dissolves. Add the almonds and butter and bring to a boil. Remove from the heat.

3. Spread onto the lined sheet pan while it is still warm. As it starts to cool, cover with parchment and roll out to an even thickness.

4. Bake at 325°F/163°C until golden brown, about 15 minutes.

5. Flip the sheet of nougatine onto a sheet of parchment paper and cut into desired shapes, then bend to shape if desired. (Note: Briefly rewarm the tuiles in a warm oven if they are too cool to bend.)

Honey Tuiles
Makes 150 cookies

ALL-PURPOSE FLOUR	13 oz	369 g
CONFECTIONERS' SUGAR	10 oz	284 g
BUTTER, soft	10½ oz	298 g
HONEY	6 oz	170 g
EGG WHITES	5 oz	142 g

1. Sift together the flour and confectioners' sugar.

2. Cream the butter, sugar, and honey on medium speed with a paddle attachment until smooth, about 5 minutes. Add honey and add the egg whites, blending until fully incorporated. Scrape the bowl. On low speed, mix in the flour. Scrape down the bowl as needed during creaming and mixing to blend evenly.

3. Transfer the batter to a storage container, cover, and chill until firm enough to work with.

4. Line sheet pans with silicone baking mats. Have stencils and an offset spatula, as well as shaping implements such as cups, dowels, or rolling pins, depending on the desired shapes, assembled. Using the offset spatula and desired stencil, spread the batter on the prepared sheet pans.

5. Bake at 325°F/163°C until golden brown, about 10 minutes. Remove from the oven and shape while still warm. Or leave the cookies flat, and cool in pans on racks.

Variation   **Chocolate Tuiles** Substitute cocoa powder for 2 oz/57 g of the all-purpose flour and sift the two together with the confectioners' sugar.

Checkerboard Cookies
Makes 80 cookies

VANILLA DOUGH		
BUTTER, soft	4 oz	113 g
CONFECTIONERS' SUGAR	2½ oz	71 g
LEMON ZEST	1 tbsp	9 g
EGG WHITES	2½ oz	71 g
VANILLA EXTRACT	1 tsp	5 mL
CAKE FLOUR, sifted	6 oz	170 g
CHOCOLATE DOUGH		
BUTTER, soft	4 oz	113 g
CONFECTIONERS' SUGAR	2½ oz	71 g
CAKE FLOUR	6 oz	170 g
COCOA POWDER	1 oz	28 g
EGG WHITES	2½ oz	71 g
VANILLA EXTRACT	1 tsp	5 mL

1. To make the vanilla dough, cream together the butter, sugar, and lemon zest on medium speed with a paddle attachment until smooth, about 8 minutes. Gradually add the egg whites and vanilla, mixing until fully incorporated after each addition and scraping down the bowl as needed. On low speed, mix in the sifted flour just until incorporated.

2. Divide the dough in half. Form each piece into a square 5 by 5 in/13 by 13 cm and ½ in/1 cm thick, wrap in plastic, and refrigerate until firm enough to roll.

3. Meanwhile, make the chocolate dough: Cream together the butter and sugar on medium speed with a paddle attachment until smooth and light in color, 6 to 8 minutes. Sift together the flour and cocoa powder. Gradually add the egg whites and vanilla to the butter-sugar mixture, mixing until fully incorporated after each addition and scraping down the bowl as needed. On low speed, mix in the sifted dry ingredients just until incorporated.

4. Divide the chocolate dough in half. Form each piece into a square 5 by 5 in/13 by 13 cm and ½ in/1 cm thick, wrap in plastic wrap, and refrigerate until firm enough to roll.

5. Working on a lightly floured work surface, roll out one piece of the vanilla dough into a square 6 by 6 in/15 by 15 cm and ¼ in/6 mm thick and set aside. Roll out a piece of the chocolate dough to the same dimensions. Brush the vanilla dough lightly with water and gently press the chocolate dough on top. Roll out the remaining piece of vanilla dough to the same dimensions, brush the chocolate layer lightly with water, and gently press

the vanilla dough on top. Roll out the remaining piece of chocolate dough to the same dimensions, brush the vanilla layer lightly with water, and gently press the chocolate dough on top. Wrap the layered dough in plastic wrap and refrigerate or freeze until firm enough to cut.

6. Trim the edges of the vanilla and chocolate layered dough square to make them even. Cut the square into twelve 1/4-in/6-mm strips. Form four logs of four strips each, stacking them so the chocolate and vanilla doughs alternate to form a checkerboard.

7. Roll out one piece of the remaining vanilla dough on a lightly floured work surface into a strip 1/8 in/3 mm thick, 6 in/15 cm wide, and 10 in/25 cm long. Brush the vanilla dough lightly with water, place one of logs on the strip, and roll up, gently pressing each side on the counter to adhere the vanilla dough "casing." Repeat the process with the remaining 1/8 by 5 by 6 in/3 mm by 13 cm by 15 cm strip of rolled vanilla dough and another checkerboard log.

8. Repeat the process, rolling out the remaining piece of vanilla dough to a strip 1/8 by 6 by 10 in/3 mm by 15 cm by 25 cm,. and covering the remaining two logs.

9. Wrap the logs in plastic wrap and refrigerate until firm enough to cut.

10. Trim one end of each log and cut 20 cookies, each 1/4 in/6 mm thick, from each log.

11. Place on parchment-lined sheet pans.

12. Bake at 350°F/177°C until lightly brown on the edges, 15 minutes. Transfer to racks and cool completely.

Note   This recipe can be used to make ribbon and pinwheel cookies.

Madeleines

Makes 200 small (1 in/3 cm) madeleines

ALL-PURPOSE FLOUR	14 oz	397 g
BAKING POWDER	2½ tsp	7.50 g
BUTTER, soft	9 oz	255 g
SUGAR	14 oz	397 g
LEMON ZEST, grated	1 tbsp	9 g
EGGS	11 oz	312 g
MILK	5 fl oz	150 mL
VANILLA EXTRACT	½ fl oz	15 mL

1. Sift together the flour and baking powder.

2. Cream the butter, sugar, and lemon zest on medium speed with a paddle attachment until light and fluffy, about 5 minutes. Combine the eggs, milk, and vanilla. Add in two or three additions, mixing until fully incorporated after each addition. On low speed, mix in the sifted dry ingredients. Scrape down the bowl as needed during creaming and mixing to blend evenly.

3. Cover the batter tightly with plastic wrap and allow it to rest overnight under refrigeration.

4. Coat madeleine pans with softened butter and dust with flour. Fill a pastry bag fitted with a No. 4 plain tip with the cold batter and pipe into the prepared madeleine pans, filling the molds three-quarters full.

5. Bake at 400°F/204°C until the edges are a medium golden brown, about 10 minutes.

6. Transfer the pans to racks and cool slightly before unmolding and serving.

Chocolate Madeleines

Makes 10 dozen small (1 in/3 cm) madeleines

BUTTER	5 oz	142 g
SEMISWEET CHOCOLATE, finely chopped	3 oz	85 g
COCOA POWDER, sifted	2 tbsp	18 g
SUGAR	6 oz	170 g
ALL-PURPOSE FLOUR, sifted	9 oz	255 g
SALT	pinch	pinch
EGGS	6 oz	170 g
EGG YOLKS	1 oz	28 g
VANILLA EXTRACT	1 tsp	5 mL

1. Lightly coat madeleine pans with softened butter and dust with flour.

2. Melt the butter and chocolate over a pan of barely simmering water, whisking gently to blend. Remove from the heat.

3. Whisk together the cocoa powder, sugar, flour, and salt. Stir into the melted chocolate mixture. Blend the eggs, egg yolks, and vanilla extract, add to the batter, and stir until just combined.

4. Place the batter over a pan of barely simmering water and heat, stirring constantly, just until warm, about 2 minutes. Remove from the heat.

5. Fill a pastry bag fitted with a No. 2 plain tip with the batter and pipe into the prepared madeleine pans, filling each mold half full.

6. Bake at 375°F/191°C until firm to the touch and lightly crisp along the edges, about 12 minutes.

7. Transfer the pans to racks and cool slightly before unmolding and serving.

Springerle

Makes 12 dozen cookies

ANISE SEEDS, toasted	1 to 2 oz	28 to 57 g
CAKE FLOUR	2 lb 8 oz	1.13 kg
BREAD FLOUR	2 lb 8 oz	1.13 kg
BAKING SODA	1 tsp	4 g
ANISE SEEDS, finely chopped	1 oz	28 g
CONFECTIONERS' SUGAR (10X SUGAR)	5 lb	2.27 kg
EGGS	2 lb	907 g
SALT	1 tsp	5 g

1. Sprinkle sheet pans with the toasted anise seeds. Have springerle molds or rolling pin ready.

2. Sift together the flours, baking soda, and finely chopped anise seeds into a large bowl and make a well in the center.

3. Whip together the confectioners' sugar, eggs, and salt using a whip attachment on high speed, until thick and light in color, 3 to 5 minutes. Pour the egg mixture into the well and knead the ingredients into a smooth dough.

4. Roll the dough out on a floured surface to ½ in/1 cm thick, and press with springerle molds. Or roll with a springerle rolling pin and cut into cookies. (The yield above is based on rectangular molds 1 by 2 in/3 by 5 cm.) Place the cookies on the prepared sheet pans.

5. Air-dry the cookies for a minimum of 6 hours, or until a slight crust forms.

6. Bake at 300°F/149°C until dry and set but still white, with no hint of browning, about 25 minutes. Transfer to racks and cool completely.

Molded Cookies

Molded cookies may be formed by hand, stamped or pressed, or piped into carved or cast molds to create an intricate design.

Cookie dough that is to be molded must be firm enough to hold its shape. If the dough is too soft, it should be refrigerated until it is firm enough to work with. To ensure that the cookies are clearly imprinted with the design and unmold easily, molds should be impeccably clean. Some molded cookies are made from foamed batters; in that case, the molds should be sprayed with nonstick baking spray or coated with a light film of butter and dusted with flour.

Most molded cookies are baked immediately after they are formed. However, springerle must be allowed to air-dry for several hours to ensure that they retain their intricate patterns. Drying springerle allows a crust to form on the top surface of the cookies, which will preserve the impression during baking by preventing the surface from rising or cracking. Because the cookies are leavened, they will expand from the bottom.

Pressing springerle dough with a mold

Almond Anise Biscotti

Makes 32 biscotti

BREAD FLOUR	10 oz	284 g
BAKING SODA	1 tsp	4 g
EGGS	6 oz	170 g
SUGAR	6½ oz	184 g
SALT	1¼ tsp	1.25 g
ANISE EXTRACT	1 tsp	5 mL
WHOLE ALMONDS	7 oz	198 g
ANISE SEEDS	2 tbsp	12 g

1. Line a sheet pan with parchment paper.

2. Sift together the flour and baking soda.

3. Whip the eggs, sugar, salt, and anise extract using a wire whip attachment on high speed until thick and light in color, about 5 minutes. On low speed, mix in the dry ingredients until just incorporated. Add the almonds and anise seeds by hand and blend until evenly combined.

4. Form the dough into a log 16 in/39 cm long and 4 in/10 cm wide and place on the prepared sheet pan.

5. Bake at 300°F/149°C until light golden brown and set firm, about 1 hour. Remove the pans from the oven and cool for 10 minutes. Lower the oven temperature to 275°F/135°C.

6. Using a serrated knife, cut each strip crosswise into slices ½ in/1 cm thick. Place on sheet pans and bake, turning the biscotti once halfway through the baking time, until golden brown and crisp, 20 to 25 minutes. Transfer to racks and cool completely.

Twice-Baked Cookies

The doughs for twice-baked cookies may be prepared by the creaming or foaming methods. They are piped or formed into logs or loaves and baked until the internal structure is fully set but the color is not fully developed. Generally the logs are allowed to cool briefly but not completely, so they won't be too brittle when sliced. A serrated blade is less likely to chip and fray the edges of the cookies as they are sliced. The cookies are then further baked at a lower temperature to dry them fully and develop more flavor and color; any seeds and nuts will toast at this point and the sugars in the dough will caramelize.

Slicing biscotti
before it is baked
a second time

Orange Biscotti

Makes 4 dozen biscotti

BREAD FLOUR	10 oz	284 g
BAKING POWDER	1 tsp	3 g
EGGS	6 oz	170 g
SUGAR	6½ oz	184 g
ORANGE ZEST	1 oz	28 g
VANILLA EXTRACT	1 tsp	5 mL
ALMOND EXTRACT	¼ tsp	1.25 mL
SALT	¼ tsp	1.25 g
SLIVERED ALMONDS	7 oz	198 g
CANDIED ORANGE, peel, minced (page 726)	6 oz	170 g

1. Line a sheet pan with parchment paper.

2. Sift together the flour and baking powder.

3. Whip the eggs, sugar, orange zest, vanilla and almond extracts, and salt using a wire whip attachment on high speed until thick and light in color, about 5 minutes. On low speed, mix in the dry ingredients until just incorporated. Scrape down the bowl as needed to blend evenly. Using a rubber spatula, fold in the almonds and candied orange peel.

4. Form the dough into a strip 24in/61cm long strip on the prepared sheet pan.

5. Bake at 300°F/149°C until light golden brown, about 1 hour. Remove the pans from the oven and cool for 10 minutes. Lower the oven temperature to 275°F/135°C.

6. Using a serrated knife, cut each strip crosswise into slices ½ in/1 cm thick. Place on prepared sheet pans and bake, turning the biscotti once halfway through the baking time, until golden brown and crisp, 20 to 25 minutes. Transfer to racks and cool completely.

Chocolate Biscotti

Makes 4 dozen biscotti

CAKE FLOUR	8¾ oz	248 g
BAKING SODA	1 tsp	4 g
COCOA POWDER	1¼ oz	35 g
EGGS	6 oz	170 g
SUGAR	5½ oz	156 g
INSTANT ESPRESSO POWDER	1 tbsp	7 g
VANILLA EXTRACT	1 tsp	5 mL
ALMOND EXTRACT	¼ tsp	1.25 mL
SALT	¼ tsp	2 g
BITTERSWEET CHOCOLATE CHUNKS	5 oz	142 g

1. Line a sheet pan with parchment paper.

2. Sift together the flour, baking soda, and cocoa powder.

3. Whip the eggs, sugar, espresso powder, vanilla and almond extracts, and salt using a wire whip attachment on high speed until thick and light in color, 6 to 8 minutes. On low speed, mix in the sifted dry ingredients until just incorporated. Using a rubber spatula, fold in the chocolate.

4. Form the dough into a strip 24in/61cm long on the prepared sheet pan.

5. Bake at 300°F/149°C until a skewer inserted in the center of the strip comes out clean, about 1 hour. Remove from the oven and cool for 5 to 10 minutes. Lower the oven temperature to 275°F/135°C.

6. Using a serrated knife, cut each strip into slices ½ in/1 cm thick. Place on prepared sheet pans and bake for 12 minutes. Flip the biscotti over and continue baking until completely dried and crisp, 12 to 15 minutes. Transfer to racks and cool completely.

Zwiebach

Makes 12 dozen zwiebach

BREAD FLOUR	1 lb 9½ oz	723 g
BAKING POWDER	¾ oz	21 g
EGGS	1 lb 10 oz	737 g
SUGAR	1 lb 3 oz	539 g
ALMOND PASTE	3¼ oz	92 g
VANILLA EXTRACT	½ fl oz	15 mL

1. Line sheet pans with parchment paper.

2. Sift together the bread flour and baking powder.

3. Blend the eggs, sugar, and almond paste in the bowl of the mixer and heat over a pan of simmering water, whisking constantly, until the mixture reaches 110°F/43°C. Remove from the heat and stir in the vanilla extract.

4. Whip the egg mixture using a whip attachment on medium speed, about 5 minutes. Gently fold in the sifted dry ingredients by hand until just incorporated.

5. Fit a pastry bag with a No. 9 plain tip and fill with the batter. Pipe 12 strips 6 in/15 cm long and 4 in/10 cm wide (forming them by piping out strips 6 in/15 cm long side by side so they touch one another and form a strip 4 in/10 cm wide down the center of the prepared sheet pans).

6. Bake at 325°F/163°C until lightly golden brown (the logs will have fused together), 15 to 17 minutes. Remove from the oven and cool slightly. Lower the oven temperature to 275°F/135°C.

7. Cut each log into slices ½ in/1 cm thick. Place on sheet pans and bake until lightly golden brown around the edges, about 10 minutes. Transfer to racks and cool completely.

Almond Spritz Cookies

Makes 12 dozen cookies

ALMOND PASTE	10 oz	284 g
EGG WHITES	7 oz	198 g
BUTTER, soft	1 lb 4 oz	567 g
SUGAR	10 oz	284 g
SALT	1½ tsp	7.50 g
RUM	1½ tsp	7.50 mL
VANILLA EXTRACT	½ fl oz	15 mL
CAKE FLOUR, sifted	1 lb 7 oz	652 g
RASPBERRY JAM	6 oz	170 g

1. Line sheet pans with parchment paper.

2. Blend the almond paste with 1 oz/28 g of the egg whites (about one white) on low speed with a paddle attachment until smooth. Add the butter, sugar, and salt and cream together on medium speed until light and fluffy, 5 minutes. Add the remaining 6 oz/170 g egg whites, the rum, and vanilla extract and mix until completely blended. On low speed, mix in the flour until just blended.

3. Using a pastry bag fitted with a No. 4 star tip, pipe the dough onto the prepared sheet pans into cookies 1½ in/4 cm in diameter. Make a small indent in the center of each cookie using a skewer. Using a parchment cone, pipe a little raspberry jam into each indentation.

4. Bake at 375°F/191°C until light golden brown, about 10 minutes. Transfer to racks and cool completely.

Note   If desired, dip half of each cookie in tempered chocolate after they have completely cooled.

Piping Cookies

For piped cookie batters or doughs made with meringue or beaten egg whites, it's especially important to have the pans prepared and the piping bag and pastry tip assembled before mixing the batter.

To fill a piping bag with batter, fold the top of the bag down to make a cuff, and use a rubber spatula to fill the bag. Twist the top of the bag to seal and squeeze to release any air in the tip of the bag.

To pipe, use constant, even pressure. To finish each cookie, release the pressure and then lift the tip away; if the tip is lifted away before the pressure is released, the batter or dough will form a "tail" at the top of the cookie, which is likely to become dark or burn during baking.

Piping spritz cookies; note the angle of the bag and the uniformity of the piped cookies.

Anise Cookies

Makes 5 dozen cookies

CAKE FLOUR	6 oz	170 g
BREAD FLOUR	3 oz	85 g
CONFECTIONER'S SUGAR, sifted	8½ oz	241 g
EGGS	4½ oz	128 g
EGG YOLKS	1 oz	28 g
ANISE SEEDS, crushed	1 tbsp	6 g
ANISE EXTRACT	1 tsp	5 mL

1. Line sheet pans with parchment paper.

2. Sift together the cake and bread flours.

3. Blend the sugar, eggs, and egg yolks in the bowl of the mixer and heat over a pan of barely simmering water until the mixture reaches 110°F/43°C, whisking constantly. Remove from the heat. Whip at high speed to ribbon stage using a whip attachment and fold in the sifted dry ingredients with a rubber spatula. Fold in the anise seeds and extract just until incorporated.

4. Using a pastry bag fitted with a No. 5 plain tip, pipe the batter into drops 1 in/3 cm in diameter on the parchment-lined sheet pans.

5. Bake at 375°F/191°C until light golden brown, about 10 minutes. Transfer to racks and cool completely.

Vanilla Pretzels

Makes 12 dozen cookies

BUTTER, soft	9 oz	255 g
CONFECTIONERS' SUGAR, sifted	4½ oz	128 g
EGGS	4½ oz	128 g
MILK	2 fl oz	60 mL
CAKE FLOUR, sifted	14 oz	397 g
DARK CHOCOLATE, melted, tempered	3 lb	1.36 kg
COARSE SUGAR, for coating	1 lb 8 oz	680 g

1. Trace pretzel shapes onto parchment paper and line sheet pans with the parchment, inverting it so the pencil markings are on the underside of the paper.

2. Cream the butter and confectioners' sugar on medium speed with a paddle attachment until smooth, about 5 minutes. Blend the eggs and milk and add in two or three additions, blending completely and scraping down the bowl after each addition. On low speed, mix in the flour until just blended.

3. Fit a pastry bag with a No. 2 plain tip and fill it with the batter. Pipe pretzel shapes using the traced patterns on the prepared sheet pans.

4. Bake at 375°F/191°C until light golden brown, about 8 minutes. Transfer to racks and cool completely.

5. Dip the pretzels into tempered chocolate and transfer to racks set over sheet pans. Sprinkle with coarse sugar once the chocolate is lightly set.

Hazelnut Cookies

Makes 12 dozen cookies

BUTTER, soft	6 lb 12 oz	3.06 kg
SUGAR	3 lb 6 oz	1.53 kg
SALT	1¾ tsp	8.75 g
VANILLA EXTRACT	1 fl oz	30 mL
EGGS	1 lb 2 oz	510 g
CAKE FLOUR, sifted	10 lb 2 oz	4.59 kg
HAZELNUTS, toasted and coarsely ground	3 lb 6 oz	1.53 kg
EGG WASH (page 825)	as needed	as needed
COARSE SUGAR	1 lb 8 oz	680 g

1. Line sheet pans with parchment paper.

2. Cream the butter, sugar, salt, and vanilla extract on medium speed with a paddle attachment until smooth, about 5 minutes. Blend the eggs and add in two or three additions, blending completely and scraping down the bowl after each addition. On low speed, mix in the flour and hazelnuts until just blended.

3. Scale the dough into three equal portions and roll into cylinders 2 in/5 cm in diameter and 12 in/30 cm long. Wrap tightly in plastic wrap and refrigerate until firm enough to slice. Brush the cylinders with egg wash and roll in coarse sugar.

4. Slice each cylinder into ¼-in/6-mm slices and place the cookies 2 in/5 cm apart on the prepared sheet pans.

5. Bake at 350°F/177°C until very light gold, 12 to 15 minutes. Transfer to racks and cool completely.

Note   If desired, dip half of each cookie in tempered chocolate and transfer to racks set over sheet pans.

Ladyfingers

Makes 170 ladyfingers

EGG YOLKS	10 oz	284 g
SUGAR	13 oz	369 g
VANILLA EXTRACT	1 tbsp	15 mL
EGG WHITES	13 oz	369 g
CAKE FLOUR, sifted	12 oz	340 g
CONFECTIONERS' SUGAR, for dusting	as needed	as needed

1. Line sheet pans with parchment paper.

2. Whip the egg yolks with 9 oz/255 g of the sugar and the vanilla extract with a whip attachment on high speed until thick and light, about 8 minutes.

3. Whip the egg whites with a clean whip attachment on medium speed until soft peaks form. Add the remaining 4 oz/114 g sugar to the whites in a steady stream, then increase to high speed and whip until medium peaks form.

4. Working quickly but gently, fold the egg whites into the yolks. Fold in the sifted cake flour.

5. Fill a pastry bag fitted with a No. 4 plain tip with the batter and pipe into 3-in/8-cm lengths on the parchment-lined sheet pans. Dust generously with confectioners' sugar.

6. Bake at 400°F/204°C until the edges turn a light golden brown, about 15 minutes. Transfer to racks and cool completely.

Variation **Chocolate Ladyfingers** Substitute 2 oz/57 g cocoa powder for 2 oz/57 g of the cake flour and sift it with the flour before proceeding as directed above.

Langues-de-Chat Sandwiches

Makes 116 sandwiched cookies

CAKE FLOUR	12 oz	340 g
BREAD FLOUR	4 oz	113 g
BUTTER, soft	14 oz	397 g
SUPERFINE SUGAR	7 oz	198 g
CONFECTIONERS' SUGAR	7 oz	198 g
VANILLA EXTRACT	1½ tsp	7.50 mL
EGG WHITES	10 oz	284 g
HARD GANACHE (page 425)	1 lb 13 oz	822 g
CONFECTIONERS' SUGAR, for dusting	as needed	as needed

1. Sift together the cake and bread flours.

2. Cream together the butter, both sugars, and vanilla extract on medium speed with a paddle, attachment scraping down the bowl often, until smooth and light, about 5 minutes. Blend the egg whites and add in two or three additions, fully incorporating and scraping down the bowl after each addition.

3. Fill a pastry bag fitted with a No. 4 plain tip with the batter and pipe into strips 3 in/8 cm long on the parchment-lined sheet pans, leaving a 2-in/5-cm space between cookies.

4. Bake at 375°F/191°C until golden brown around the edges, 12 to 15 minutes. Transfer to racks and cool completely.

5. Sandwich two cookies together with 2 tsp ganache or other fillings. Dust the tops lightly with confectioners' sugar.

Frangipane Cake

One sheet 13½ by 17½ in/34 by 44 cm (or 50 pieces 1 in/3 cm square)

ALMOND PASTE	7 oz	198 g
BUTTER, soft	7 oz	198 g
SUGAR	7 oz	198 g
EGGS	9 oz	255 g
CAKE FLOUR, sifted	3 oz	85 g

1. Line a half sheet pan with parchment paper.

2. Cream the almond paste, butter, and sugar on medium speed with a paddle attachment until light and fluffy, about 10 minutes. Blend the eggs and add in two or three additions, fully incorporating and scraping down the bowl after each addition. On low speed, mix in the flour until just blended.

3. Spread the batter evenly in the parchment-lined sheet pan.

4. Bake at 375°F/191°C until golden brown, about 20 minutes. Cool completely in the pan.

5. Wrap tightly in plastic wrap while in the pan and refrigerate or freeze until needed, up to three weeks. (To assemble Petits Fours, see below.)

Glazed Petits Fours

The term *petit four* refers to a small sweet item that can be consumed in one or two bites. This category, also called *mignardises,* includes a wide variety of pastries. Classic glazed petits fours are just one type. Frangipane is the cake of choice for glazed petits fours not just because of its flavor, but because its dense, moist crumb makes it suitable for dipping in fondant without causing the cake to crumble.

The cake must first be chilled before unmolding, cutting, or assembling the petits fours. After the cake has cooled, invert it onto a rack and remove the parchment. Cut the cake crosswise into three equal pieces. Spread the top of the first layer with a very thin coating of apricot jam. Top with the second layer of cake, putting the top of the cake down, spread with jam, and top with the third layer. Spread the last layer with a very thin coating of jam (each finished petit four should be no higher than 1 in/3 cm). Roll out 8 oz/227 g marzipan to ⅛ in/3 mm thick and cover the top of the frangipane. Trim off any excess marzipan and invert the layered cake onto a parchment-lined sheet pan so the marzipan is on the bottom.

Tightly wrap the layered sheet in plastic wrap and refrigerate or freeze until firm. Cut the petits fours into rectangles, squares, or diamonds with a knife or into a variety of shapes (circles, ovals, flowers, etc.) using different cutters.

To dip and glaze the cut petits fours, heat and thin fondant (see page 426) in a bowl that is deep enough to accommodate the petits fours. One at a time, place a petit four upside down in the fondant and gently press it down until the bottom of the cake is level with the surface of the fondant. Remove the glazed cake using two forks (one at the top and one at the base) and place it on an icing screen to allow the fondant to set completely before adding any décor.

The classical décor for glazed petits fours is piped filigree, but there are other contemporary décor options; see page Appendix D.

ABOVE:
Dipping petits fours in warmed fondant

RIGHT:
Piping a filigree design on petits fours for décor

CHAPTER 11

Custards, Creams, Mousses, and Soufflés

WHEN THE PASTRY CHEF COMBINES EGGS, MILK, AND SUGAR AND BAKES THEM, THE RESULT MAY BE A SMOOTH AND CREAMY CRÈME BRÛLÉE OR A SILKY CRÈME CARAMEL. WHEN THESE SAME INGREDIENTS ARE STIRRED TOGETHER OVER GENTLE HEAT, VANILLA SAUCE, OR CRÈME ANGLAISE, IS THE RESULT. STARCHES OR GELATIN CAN BE INCLUDED TO PRODUCE TEXTURES THAT RANGE FROM THICK BUT SPOONABLE TO A SLICEABLE CREAM. FOLDING IN MERINGUE OR WHIPPED CREAM PRODUCES MOUSSE, BAVARIAN CREAM, DIPLOMAT CREAM, CHIBOUSTE, OR A SOUFFLÉ.

Crème Brûlée

Makes 10 portions (5 fl oz/150 mL each)

HEAVY CREAM	32 fl oz	960 mL
SUGAR	6 oz	170 g
SALT	pinch	pinch
VANILLA BEAN	1 each	1 each
EGG YOLKS, beaten	5½ oz	156 g
BRÛLÉE SUGAR (page 824)	5 oz	142 g
CONFECTIONERS' SUGAR, for dusting	4½ oz	128 g

1. Combine the cream, 4 oz/113 g of the sugar, and the salt and bring to a simmer over medium heat, stirring gently with a wooden spoon. Remove from the heat. Split the vanilla bean, scrape the seeds from the pod, add both the pod and scrapings to the pan, cover, and steep for 15 minutes.

2. Bring the cream to a boil.

3. Meanwhile, blend the egg yolks with the remaining 2 oz/57 g sugar. Temper by gradually adding about one-third of the hot cream, stirring constantly with a wire whip. Add the remaining hot cream. Strain and ladle into ramekins, filling them three-quarters full.

4. Bake in a water bath at 325°F/163°C until just set, 20 to 25 minutes.

5. Remove the custards from the water bath and wipe the ramekins dry. Refrigerate until fully chilled.

6. To finish the crème brûlée, evenly coat each custard's surface with a thin layer (1/16 in/1.5 mm) of brûlée sugar. Use a propane torch to melt and caramelize the sugar. Lightly dust the surface with confectioners' sugar and serve.

Variations   **Coffee Crème Brûlée** Add 1 oz/28 g dark roast coffee beans to the cream mixture in Step 1. Strain after steeping and proceed as directed above.

Coconut Crème Brûlée Add 2 oz/57 g toasted coconut to the cream mixture in Step 1. Strain after steeping and proceed as directed above.

Cinnamon Crème Brûlée Add 3 cinnamon sticks to the cream mixture in Step 1. Strain after steeping and proceed as directed above.

Note   Vanilla extract can be substituted for the vanilla bean. Blend 1 tbsp/15mL into the custard just before portioning into the ramekins.

Vanilla beans that are used to infuse flavor into preparations such as custards can be rinsed under cold water, dried, and stored for a later use, such as making vanilla sugar.

1   2

1 Temper the eggs by adding some of the hot milk.

2 Caramelize the sugar on top of the crème brûlée with a torch.

Chocolate Crème Brûlée

Makes 10 portions (5 fl oz/150 mL each)

HEAVY CREAM	32 fl oz	960 mL
SUGAR	6 oz	170 g
SALT	pinch	pinch
VANILLA BEAN	1 each	1 each
EGG YOLKS, beaten	5½ oz	156 g
BITTERSWEET CHOCOLATE, melted	6 oz	170 g
BRÛLÉE SUGAR (page 824)	5 oz	142 g
CONFECTIONERS' SUGAR, for dusting	4½ oz	128 g

1. Combine the cream, 4 oz/113 g of the sugar, and the salt and bring to a simmer over medium heat, stirring gently with a wooden spoon. Remove from the heat. Split the vanilla bean, scrape the seeds from the pod, add both the pod and scrapings to the pan, cover, and steep for 15 minutes.

2. Bring the cream to a boil.

3. Meanwhile, blend the egg yolks with the remaining 2 oz/57 g sugar. Temper by gradually adding about one-third of the hot cream, stirring constantly with a wire whip. Add the remaining hot cream. Gradually add about one-third of the hot custard to the chocolate, whipping constantly, then add the remaining hot custard. Strain and ladle into ramekins, filling them three-quarters full.

4. Bake in a water bath at 325°F/163°C until just set, 20 to 25 minutes.

5. Remove the custards from the water bath and wipe the ramekins dry. Refrigerate until fully chilled.

6. To finish the crème brûlée, evenly coat each custard's surface with a thin layer (¹⁄₁₆ in/ 1.5 mm) of brûlée sugar. Use a propane torch to melt and caramelize the sugar. Lightly dust the surface with confectioners' sugar and serve.

Pumpkin Crème Brûlée

Makes 10 portions (5 fl oz/150 mL each)

HEAVY CREAM	24 fl oz	720 mL
PUMPKIN PURÉE	8 oz	227 g
SUGAR	6 oz	170 g
SALT	pinch	pinch
VANILLA BEAN	1 each	1 each
EGG YOLKS, beaten	5½ oz	156 g
BRÛLÉE SUGAR (page 824)	5 oz	142 g
CONFECTIONERS' SUGAR, for dusting	4½ oz	128 g

1. Combine the cream, pumpkin purée, 4 oz/113 g of the sugar, and the salt and bring to a simmer over medium heat, stirring gently with a wooden spoon. Remove from the heat. Split the vanilla bean, scrape the seeds from the pod, add both the pod and scrapings to the pan, cover, and steep for 15 minutes.

2. Bring the cream to a boil.

3. Meanwhile, blend the egg yolks with the remaining 2 oz/57 g sugar. Temper by gradually adding about one-third of the hot cream, stirring constantly with a wire whip. Add the remaining hot cream. Strain and ladle into ramekins, filling them three-quarters full.

4. Bake in a water bath at 325°F/163°C until just set, 20 to 25 minutes.

5. Remove the custards from the water bath and wipe the ramekins dry. Refrigerate until fully chilled.

6. To finish the crème brûlée, evenly coat each custard's surface with a thin layer (1/16 in/1.5 mm) of brûlée sugar. Use a propane torch to melt and caramelize the sugar. Lightly dust the surface with confectioners' sugar and serve.

Baked Custards

A simple baked custard calls for blending eggs, a liquid such as milk or cream, and sugar and baking until set. Milk or cream is the most common base for custard; heavy cream lends a richer flavor and mouth feel than milk. Mascarpone, cream cheese, or another soft fresh cheese may be substituted for part of the cream to yield a richer and firmer result. The proportion of eggs also may be varied, as may the choice of whole eggs, yolks only, or a combination. Use extra yolks along with whole eggs for a softer custard. Use only egg yolks for a richer, creamier mouth feel. Use all whole eggs to give more structure to a custard that is to be unmolded.

There are two basic methods for making a custard base: cold and warm. For the cold method of mixing a custard base, the ingredients are simply stirred together, then poured into molds and baked. While this method is effective for small batches, for larger amounts and a better finished product, the warm method is preferred. It produces a silkier, more even texture in the finished custard, and it also allows you to infuse the milk or cream with flavorings such as vanilla beans, coffee, tea, or spices.

To mix a custard base using the warm method, heat the milk or cream and some of the sugar, stirring with a wooden spoon, until the sugar is completely dissolved. Add the flavorings at this point and allow to steep, if necessary, off the heat and covered, long enough for them to impart a rich, full flavor. Return the mixture to a boil.

Blend the eggs and the remaining sugar to make a liaison. Whisking constantly, slowly add about one-third of the hot milk, a few ladlefuls at a time, to the liaison to temper it. Once the liaison is tempered, you can add the rest of the hot milk more rapidly without scrambling the egg mixture. Pour the mixture through a fine strainer.

Ladle the custard into molds (they can be coated with a light film of softened butter if you intend to unmold the custard) and bake them in a hot water bath (for more information on hot water baths, see below). The water bath keeps the heat constant and gentle, resulting in a smooth texture in the baked custard. To check the custard for doneness, shake the mold gently: when the ripples on the surface move back and forth, rather than in concentric rings, the custard is properly baked.

Remove the molds from the water bath and wipe the ramekins dry. Place on a cool sheet pan, allow them to cool, and then store them under refrigeration. For crème caramel, an overnight resting period (optimally 24 hours) is essential, not only to completely set the custard so it can be unmolded, but also to allow the caramel to liquefy into a sauce.

Hot Water Bath

A hot water bath, or bain-marie, ensures gentle heat at a constant temperature, allowing for even baking or cooking. Using a hot water bath for baking custards also prevents both the formation of a crust and rapid expansion that would lead to cracks on the surface of the custard.

Select a pan with sides at least as high as the sides of the molds. Set the molds in the pan as they are filled, leaving about 1 in/3 cm around each mold so it will be surrounded by hot water. Set the pan securely on the oven deck or rack. Add enough very hot or boiling water to the pan to come to about two-thirds of the height of the molds. Be careful not to splash or pour any water into the custards.

After custards are properly baked and removed from the oven, they should also be removed from the hot water bath. This will stop the cooking process and allow the custards to cool. Custards will continue to cook after they are removed from the oven if they are left in the hot water bath, which may cause them to become overdone. Custards that are overbaked or overcooked will not have as smooth a texture and may have a pronounced "eggy" flavor.

Crème Caramel

Makes 14 portions (4 fl oz/120 mL each)

CARAMEL		
SUGAR	8 oz	227 g
CUSTARD		
MILK	32 fl oz	960 mL
SUGAR	8 oz	227 g
SALT	pinch	pinch
VANILLA EXTRACT	1 tbsp	15 mL
EGGS	12 oz	340 g
EGG YOLKS	2½ oz	71 g

1. To prepare the caramel, add a small amount of the sugar to a medium-hot pan set over medium heat and allow it to melt, then add the remaining sugar in small increments, allowing each addition to fully melt before adding the next. Continue this process until all the sugar has been added to the pan and cook to the desired color. Divide the caramel evenly among the ramekins. Allow to cool completely.

2. To prepare the custard, combine the milk, 4 oz/113 g of the sugar, and the salt and bring to a simmer over medium heat, stirring gently with a wooden spoon. Remove from the heat and add the vanilla.

3. Bring the milk to a boil.

4. Meanwhile, blend the eggs and egg yolks with the remaining 4 oz/113 g sugar. Temper by gradually adding about one-third of the hot milk, whipping constantly. Add the remaining hot milk. Strain and ladle into the caramel-coated ramekins, filling them three-quarters full.

5. Bake in a water bath at 325°F/163°C until fully set, 20 to 25 minutes.

6. Remove the custards from the water bath and wipe the ramekins dry. Cool the custards, then wrap individually and refrigerate for at least 24 hours before unmolding and serving.

7. To unmold the custards, run a small sharp knife between the custard and the ramekin, invert onto a serving plate, and tap lightly to release. Remove the ramekin.

Pan Preparation for Unmolded Baked Custards

Generally, pans or ramekins that are to be used for baked custards do not need any preparation. The one exception is a custard that is to be unmolded, such as crème caramel. In this case, some chefs choose to give the baking containers a very light coating of softened butter or other fat.

UNMOLDING CUSTARDS

Crème caramel is perhaps the most common baked custard that is served unmolded; for this reason the formula must be balanced with enough eggs (whole and/or yolks) so that the custard will keep its shape when unmolded. The custard should be unmolded carefully so that the sides remain smooth. The custard will be smooth, glossy, and creamy white except near the top, where some of the caramel will have baked into the custard, imparting some of its rich flavor and golden color.

It is imperative that the custard be left under refrigeration for a minimum of 24 hours.

To unmold a custard that has been baked in a ramekin, run a knife or metal spatula around the rim, pressing against the side of the ramekin rather than the custard so as to avoiding cutting or marring it. Invert onto a service plate and tap lightly to release. If the custard was baked in an individual aluminum tin, simply invert the mold onto a service plate and puncture the bottom to release the custard.

Run a knife around the edge of the mold and invert the custard onto a plate.

Caramelizing Sugar

When cooking sugar, all your equipment must be clean and free of any grease. The sugar must also be free of impurities, such as flour or other ingredients. Sugar has a very high caramelization point and any impurities in the sugar are likely to burn at a much lower temperature, before the sugar begins to caramelize. A copper or other heavy-bottomed saucepan should be used to ensure constant ,even heat. Sugar may be cooked by one of two methods: wet or dry. The wet method is generally used when sugar must be cooked to a specific stage or temperature. The dry method is used exclusively for caramelizing. The wet method may be used when caramelizing sugar, but the nutty, roasted flavor characteristic of good caramel is better achieved through the dry method.

For the wet method, the sugar is combined in a saucepan with 30 percent or more of its weight in water. Place the pan over high heat and stir constantly until the mixture comes to a boil to ensure all the sugar is melted. Once it has come to a boil, stop

For an even, smooth caramel, melt part of the sugar and then gradually add the remainder.

stirring and skim off any impurities. Using a pastry brush, wash down the sides of the pan with cool water to prevent crystals from forming. Crystallization of the cooking sugar occurs readily on the side of the pan where crystals are deposited from evaporating liquid. These crystals, in turn, can easily act to "seed" the rest of the sugar in the pan, causing it to begin to crystallize, becoming lumpy and granular. Repeat as often as necessary to keep the sides of the pan clean until the sugar has reached the desired temperature, consistency, and/or color.

An alternative to the traditional wet method is to cook the sugar and water over high heat, stirring constantly to dissolve the sugar, until the mixture comes to a boil. Cover the pan and cook for 1 minute; the condensation resulting from covering the pan will wash down the sides of the pan. Remove the cover, reduce the heat to medium, and cook to the desired temperature and/or color.

For the dry method, add a small amount of the sugar to a preheated medium-hot pan set over medium heat and allow it to melt, then add the remaining sugar in small increments, allowing each addition of sugar to fully melt before adding the next. Continue this process until all the sugar has been added to the pan and cook to the desired color. Another option for the dry method is to mix all of the sugar with a small amount of an acid, usually lemon juice, so that it is the consistency of wet sand. Bring the mixture to a boil in a heavy-bottomed saucepan over high heat, stirring constantly to dissolve the sugar. Then cook, without stirring, to the desired color. The dry method requires constant attention, as the sugar cooks rapidly without the water.

When cooking or caramelizing sugar by any method, a small amount of an acid (typically lemon juice at approximately ¼ tsp/1.25 mL for 8 oz/227 g of sugar) can be added to help prevent crystallization from occurring during cooking. (For more information on crystallization, see page 82.)

When caramelizing sugar, regardless of the cooking method, it is important to stop the cooking process by shocking the pan in an ice water bath just as, or just before, it reaches the desired color. Sugar retains heat and can easily become too dark or burn if the cooking process is not arrested.

It is also important to heat any liquids to be added to the caramel and to add them carefully. Caramelized sugar is very hot and will splatter when a colder ingredient is introduced.

Pots de Crème

Makes 12 portions (4 fl oz/120 mL each)

CARAMEL		
SUGAR	5 oz	142 g
CUSTARD		
MILK, warmed	16 fl oz	480 mL
HEAVY CREAM, warmed	16 fl oz	480 mL
EGGS	6 oz	170 g
EGG YOLKS	2 oz	57 g
SUGAR	3 oz	85 g
SEMISWEET CHOCOLATE, melted	4 oz	113 g
VANILLA EXTRACT	1 tbsp	15 mL

1. To prepare the caramel, add a small amount of the sugar to a medium-hot pan set over medium heat and allow it to melt, then add the remaining sugar in small increments, allowing each addition to fully melt before adding the next. Continue this process until all the sugar has been added to the pan and cook to the desired color.

2. To make the custard, carefully add the milk and cream to the caramel over the heat, stirring to incorporate, and bring to a boil.

3. Meanwhile, blend the eggs and egg yolks with the sugar to make the liaison. Temper by adding about one-third of the hot cream mixture, whisking constantly. Add the remaining hot cream mixture. Gradually add about one-third of the hot custard to the chocolate, whisking constantly, then add the remaining hot custard and vanilla. Strain and ladle into ramekins, filling them three-quarters full.

4. Bake in a water bath at 325°F/163°C until fully set, about 30 minutes.

5. Remove the custards from the water bath and wipe the ramekins dry. Refrigerate until fully chilled.

Pastry Cream

Makes 3 lb/1.36 kg

MILK	32 fl oz	960 mL
SUGAR	8 oz	227 g
CORNSTARCH	2½ oz	71 g
EGG YOLKS	10½ oz	298 g
VANILLA EXTRACT	1 tbsp	15 mL

1. Combine 24 fl oz/720 mL of the milk and 4 oz/113 g of the sugar in a saucepan and bring to a boil over medium heat, stirring to dissolve the sugar.

2. Meanwhile, combine the cornstarch with the remaining 4 oz/114 g sugar. Stirring with a wire whip, add the remaining 8 oz/240 mL milk. Add the egg yolks and vanilla extract, stirring with a wire whip until the mixture is completely smooth.

3. Temper the egg mixture by adding about one-third of the hot milk, stirring constantly with a wire whip. Return the mixture to the remaining hot milk in the saucepan. Continue cooking, stirring vigorously with the whip, until the pastry cream comes to a boil and the whip leaves a trail in it.

4. Pour the pastry cream into a large shallow container or bowl. Cover with plastic wrap placed directly on the surface of the cream, and cool over an ice bath.

5. Store the pastry cream, covered, under refrigeration.

Variations　**Honey Pastry Cream**　Omit the 4 oz/113 g of sugar added with the milk. Blend 6 oz/170 g honey and 1 tsp/3 g grated orange zest with 1 lb/454 g of the pastry cream immediately after it is finished cooking.

Liqueur-flavored Pastry Cream　Add 4 fl oz/120 mL liqueur to 1 lb/454 g of the pastry cream immediately after it is finished cooking.

Pastry cream should be brought to a full boil in order to thicken properly.

Creams, curds, and stirred custards must be chilled quickly over ice after cooking.

Stirred Creams and Puddings

Stirred puddings and creams both contain milk (or a similar dairy base), sugar, and a starch, and both are cooked by stirring over direct heat.

Creams and puddings are prepared on the stovetop. They must be cooked, stirring constantly, until they come to a full boil, both so the starch is heated sufficiently to thicken the mixture and to remove any undesirable flavor and mouth feel that uncooked starch would contribute. The starch in the mixture prevents the coagulation of the egg proteins, allowing these products to be cooked to a higher temperature than those made without a starch.

Vanilla Pudding
Makes 2 lb 10 oz/1.19 kg

MILK	32 fl oz	960 mL
SUGAR	6½ oz	184 g
SALT	pinch	pinch
CORNSTARCH	1¾ oz	50 g
EGG YOLKS	2½ oz	71 g
BUTTER	½ oz	14 g
VANILLA EXTRACT	2 tsp	10 mL

1. Combine 24 fl oz/720 mL of the milk, 3½ oz/99 g of the sugar, and the salt in a saucepan and bring to a boil, stirring gently with a wooden spoon.

2. Meanwhile, combine the cornstarch with the remaining 3 oz/85 g sugar. Stirring with a wire whip, add the remaining 8 fl oz/240 mL milk. Add the egg yolks, stirring with a wire whip until the mixture is completely smooth.

3. Temper the egg mixture by adding about one-third of the hot milk, stirring constantly with a wire whip. Return the tempered egg mixture to the remaining hot milk in the saucepan. Continue cooking, stirring constantly with the whip, until the pudding comes to a boil. Remove from the heat and stir in the butter and vanilla extract.

4. Pour into ten 4-oz/113-g serving dishes, or use as desired. Cover and refrigerate until fully chilled.

Variation **Chocolate Pudding** Melt 5 oz/142 g bittersweet chocolate with the butter over a pan of barely simmering water; set aside. In Step 3, after blending in the vanilla, gradually incorporate one-third of the hot pudding into the chocolate mixture, stirring constantly with the whip. Add the chocolate mixture to the remaining pudding and blend to fully combine. Proceed as directed above.

Bread and Butter Pudding

Makes 8 portions (6 oz/170 g each)

DARK RAISINS	3 oz	85 g
RUM	4 fl oz	120 mL
ENRICHED BREAD	9 oz	255 g
BUTTER, melted	3 oz	85 g
MILK	32 fl oz	960 mL
SUGAR	6 oz	170 g
EGGS, beaten	12 oz	340 g
EGG YOLKS, beaten	2¼ oz	64 g
VANILLA EXTRACT	½ tsp	2.50 mL
GROUND CINNAMON	½ tsp	1 g
SALT	½ tsp	2.50 g

1. Place the raisins in a bowl and add the rum. Set aside to plump for 20 minutes, then drain.

2. Cut the bread into ½-in/1-cm cubes. Place on a sheet pan and drizzle with the melted butter. Toast in a 350°F/177°C oven, stirring once or twice, until golden brown.

3. Combine milk and 3 oz/85 g of the sugar in a saucepan and bring to a boil.

4. Meanwhile, blend the eggs, egg yolks, vanilla, and the remaining 3 oz/85 g sugar to make the liaison. Temper by gradually adding about one-third of the hot milk, whipping constantly. Add the remaining hot milk and strain the custard into a bowl.

5. Add the bread, cinnamon, salt, and drained raisins to the custard. Soak over an ice bath for at least 1 hour to allow the bread to absorb the custard. Lightly brush eight ramekins with softened butter.

6. Ladle the mixture into the prepared ramekins, filling them three-quarters full. Bake in a water bath at 350°F/177°C until just set, 45 to 50 minutes.

7. Remove the custards from the water bath and wipe the ramekins dry. Refrigerate until fully chilled.

Variations　**Dried Cherry and Orange Bread Pudding** Substitute dried cherries for the raisins and brandy for the rum. Add the grated zest of 1 large or 2 small oranges to the milk before heating it, and proceed as directed above.

Pumpkin Bread Pudding Whisk 8 oz/227 g pumpkin purée into the hot custard after straining it. Increase the cinnamon to 2½ tsp/5 g and add 1 tsp/ 2 g grated nutmeg along with it. Proceed as directed above.

Chocolate Bread Pudding Omit the raisins and rum. Melt 6 oz/170 g bittersweet chocolate and blend into the hot custard before straining. Proceed as directed above.

Note　The pudding can also be baked in a large hotel pan and portioned for service.

Bread Pudding

Bread pudding is a traditional baked custard that is made with bread and flavorings that are mixed together with a simple custard mixture. Any type of bread can be used, but enriched breads such as brioche and challah impart the best flavor. One of the most important steps in making any bread pudding is allowing the bread sufficient time to absorb some of the custard mixture; if the bread is not allowed to soak in the custard for long enough, the texture of the pudding will suffer.

Rice Pudding

Makes 2 lb 10 oz/1.19 kg

MILK	32 fl oz	960 mL
SUGAR	4 oz	113 g
CINNAMON STICK	1 each	1 each
ORANGE SLICE	1 each	1 each
LONG-GRAIN WHITE RICE, rinsed	3 oz	85 g
CORNSTARCH	¼ oz	7 g
EGGS	3 oz	85 g
VANILLA EXTRACT	1 tsp	5 mL

1. Combine the milk, 2 oz/57 g of the sugar, the cinnamon stick, and orange slice in a saucepan and bring to a boil. Add the rice and simmer over low heat until tender, approximately 30 minutes.

2. Meanwhile, just as the rice is finished cooking, combine the cornstarch with the remaining 2 oz/57 g sugar. Add the eggs, stirring with a wire whip until the mixture is completely smooth.

3. Temper the egg mixture by adding about one-third of the hot milk-rice mixture, stirring constantly with a wire whip. Return the tempered egg mixture to the remaining hot milk in the saucepan. Continue cooking, stirring constantly with the whip, until the pudding comes to a boil. Remove from the heat and remove the cinnamon stick and orange slice. Blend in the vanilla extract.

4. Pour into ten 4 fl oz/120 mL serving dishes, or use as desired. Cover and refrigerate until fully chilled.

Panna Cotta

Makes 19 portions (4 oz/113 g each)

GELATIN	½ oz	14 g
WATER	4 fl oz	120 mL
HEAVY CREAM	32 fl oz	960 mL
SUGAR	12 oz	340 g
SALT	½ tsp	2.50 g
BUTTERMILK	30 fl oz	900 mL

1. Bloom the gelatin in the water and melt.

2. Combine the heavy cream, sugar, and salt in a saucepan and heat, stirring, over medium heat to dissolve the sugar; make sure the mixture does not simmer. Remove from the heat.

3. Add gelatin to the cream mixture, blending well. Allow the mixture to cool to 100°F/38°C and stir in the buttermilk.

4. Pour into ramekins. Cover tightly and refrigerate for several hours or until set.

Variations   **Cinnamon Panna Cotta** Add three cinnamon sticks to the warm cream mixture, cover, and allow to steep for 10 to 15 minutes. Remove the cinnamon sticks and reheat the milk before adding the gelatin. Proceed as directed above.

Lemon Panna Cotta Add 1 tsp/3 g finely grated lemon zest to the cream mixture in Step 2. Proceed as directed above.

Gelatin

Gelatin is used as a stabilizer in many bakeshop preparations. In small amounts, gelatin adds body; in greater amounts, it can set a liquid so firmly that it can be sliced or cut into shapes. Using the precise amount of gelatin is crucial; if too little is used, it will not add enough stabilizing power, while if too much is used, the texture will become rubbery and unpalletable and the flavor undesirable.

Gelatin must be rehydrated, or bloomed, and then melted before use. To bloom, soak in the amount of liquid specified in the formula, which should be approximately 8 fl oz/240 mL of a water-based liquid for every 1 oz/28 g of gelatin. An alternate method commonly used for blooming sheet gelatin is to soak the sheets in enough cold water to completely submerge them. If this method is used, after blooming gently squeeze and wring the sheets to force the excess water out, so as not to add additional liquid to the formula, which would change the consistency and flavor of the finished product.

After it is bloomed the gelatin must be melted. To melt bloomed gelatin, place it in a pan or bowl over low heat or a hot water bath until liquefied. Then stir the melted gelatin into a warm or room-temperature base mixture.

If the base is cold, the gelatin may set up unevenly. If the base is quite warm or hot (at least 105°F/41°C), however, you may opt to add the bloomed gelatin directly to the hot base, rather than melting it separately, and allow the base's heat to melt the gelatin. Be sure to stir gelatin added this way until it is completely blended into the base.

Since the product will begin to set immediately after the gelatin is added, always prepare all molds, service containers, and so forth before beginning preparation.

Some gelatin-stabilized items are served in their molds; others are unmolded before service. To unmold, dip the mold briefly into very hot water, then invert the mold onto a plate and tap it gently to release the item.

Bloomed powdered gelatin (on right), bloomed sheet gelatin (on left)

Lemon Curd

Makes 2 lb 2 oz/964 g

BUTTER, cubed	1 lb 5 oz	595 g
SUGAR	1 lb 2 oz	510 g
LEMON JUICE	18 fl oz	540 mL
LEMON ZEST, grated	1¼ oz	35 g
EGG YOLKS	1 lb 2 oz	510 g

1. Combine 10½ oz/298 g of the butter, 9 oz/255 g of the sugar, and the lemon juice and zest and bring to a boil over medium heat, stirring gently to dissolve the sugar.

2. Meanwhile, blend the egg yolks with the remaining 9 oz/255 g sugar. Temper by gradually adding about one-third of the lemon juice mixture, stirring constantly with a whip. Return the tempered egg mixture to the saucepan. Continue cooking, stirring constantly with the whip, until the mixture comes to a boil.

3. Stir in the remaining butter.

4. Strain the curd into large shallow container or bowl. Cover with plastic wrap placed directly on the surface of the cream. Cool over an ice bath.

5. Store the curd, covered, under refrigeration.

Variations **Orange Curd** Replace the lemon juice with orange juice and the lemon zest with orange zest and reduce the sugar by 4 oz/113 g.

Lime Curd Replace the lemon juice with lime juice and the lemon zest with lime zest.

Grapefruit Curd Replace the lemon juice with grapefruit juice and the lemon zest with grapefruit zest.

Plum Pudding

Makes 2 qt/1.92 L

SUET	8 oz	227 g
BREAD CRUMBS	8 oz	227 g
DRIED CURRANTS	12 oz	340 g
DARK RAISINS	12 oz	340 g
DARK BROWN SUGAR	8 oz	227 g
BLANCHED ALMONDS, chopped	4 oz	113 g
CANDIED ORANGE PEEL, diced	4 oz	113 g
CANDIED CHERRIES, quartered	6 oz	170 g
LEMON ZEST, grated	1 tsp	3 g
EGGS	9 oz	255 g
WHISKEY	2 fl oz	60 mL

1. Line a mold with plastic wrap, leaving enough overhang to cover the pudding.

2. Place the suet and bread crumbs in a food processor and process until smooth. Transfer to the bowl of an electric mixer, add the remaining ingredients, and mix with the paddle attachment until blended.

3. Fill the prepared mold. Cover the pudding with the excess plastic wrap and then cover with foil.

4. Steam the pudding in a steamer until firm, approximately 4 hours. (The pudding can be wrapped in plastic and stored under refrigeration after reaching room temperature. Steam the pudding until warm before service.)

5. Serve warm with hard sauce. (For hard sauce formulas, see page 460.)

Note   The suet should be as clean and white as possible. Be sure to trim off any meat scraps.

Steamed Puddings

Plum pudding (also known as Christmas pudding) is probably the best-known steamed pudding. Steamed puddings are cake-like. Unlike other puddings in this chapter, they contain very little, if any, dairy products such as milk or cream. The traditional base for steamed puddings is a mixture of bread crumbs and suet. Some steamed puddings are based on cake crumbs and butter.

Pudding molds of ceramic or metal (sometimes known as basins) hold the batter as the pudding steams in a hot water bath. Most pudding molds have a center tube and decorative fluted sides. Some have a lid that clamps in place; otherwise, buttered parchment paper, plastic wrap, or foil is used to tightly cover the batter.

To steam a pudding, place a wire rack in a pot large enough to allow the mold to be surrounded by water. Add enough water to the pot so that approximately half the mold will be immersed. Bring the water to a boil and carefully place the mold in the pot, setting it securely on the wire rack. Cover the pot and bring the water to a gentle boil. Check the pot often and add more boiling water as necessary to ensure that the water level remains constant.

Raspberry Mousse
Makes 3 lb 5 oz/1.50 kg

GELATIN	1⅓ oz	38 g
WATER	10 fl oz	300 mL
HEAVY CREAM	14 fl oz	420 mL
RASPBERRY PURÉE	1 lb 8 oz	680 g
EGG WHITES	5 oz	142 g
SUGAR	9 oz	255 g

1. Assemble and prepare the desired pastries, containers, or molds that are to be used in the application of the mousse before beginning preparation.

2. Bloom the gelatin in the water.

3. Whip the heavy cream to medium peaks. Cover and reserve under refrigeration.

4. Warm 12 oz/340 g of the raspberry purée in a saucepan. Remove from the heat. Melt the gelatin. Add the melted gelatin and stir to incorporate. Blend in the remaining 12 oz/340 g purée.

5. Combine the egg whites and sugar in a mixer bowl. Set over a pot of simmering water and heat, stirring constantly with a wire whip, until the mixture reaches 145°F/63°C. Transfer to the mixer and whip at high speed with the whip attachment until stiff peaks form. Continue beating until the meringue has completely cooled.

6. Cool the raspberry purée–gelatin mixture to 70°F/21°C.

7. Gently blend approximately one-third of the meringue into the raspberry purée mixture to lighten it. Fold in the remaining meringue, thoroughly incorporating it. Fold in the reserved whipped cream.

8. Immediately pipe or ladle into prepared pastries or molds. Refrigerate until completely set.

Variations   **Passion Fruit Mousse** Dilute the passion fruit concentrate as directed and substitute it for the raspberry purée.

Mango Mousse Substitute mango purée for the raspberry purée.

Strawberry Mousse Substitute strawberry purée for the raspberry purée.

Coconut Mousse Substitute coconut milk or Coco Lopez purée for the raspberry purée.

Pear Mousse Substitute pear purée for the raspberry purée.

Mousse

The name for this delicate dessert comes from a French word that translates literally as frothy, foamy, or light. To make a mousse, an aerator, such as whipped cream and/or a meringue, is folded into a base such as a fruit purée, vanilla sauce, cream or pudding, curd, sabayon, or pâte à bombe. The base should be light and smooth so the aerator can be incorporated easily.

To make an egg-safe mousse, use pasteurized egg whites or a Swiss or Italian meringue. Stabilizers such as gelatin may be used in varying amounts depending on the desired result. If a mousse is stabilized with gelatin, it will begin to set immediately, so prepare all molds, serving containers, and so forth before beginning preparation.

Folding by hand with a whip

Folding is the technique used to combine a foamy mixture, such as meringue, whipped cream, or beaten egg whites, into a base mixture. The base is usually denser or firmer than the foam and will inevitably collapse the foam somewhat. Proper folding ensures that the foam loses as little volume as possible.

The base should be cooled if necessary before the foam is added. Add the foam to the base, rather than the other way around, and if using more than one foam, add the least stable one last. For example, if you are adding both a meringue and whipped cream, add the meringue first and then the cream.

Working quickly, add a small amount of the foam to the base to lighten it. Some pastry chefs add the foams in thirds for the greatest possible volume. Fold the foam in with a rubber spatula or other tool with a similar broad, flat surface. Using a circular motion, gently run the spatula over the mixture, down and across the bottom of the bowl, and back up to the top again. Rotate the bowl as you work to mix the foam in evenly. Continue to fold the base and foam together until you have an even color and consistency, with no visible pockets of meringue, whipped cream, or the like.

Chocolate Mousse

Makes 4 lb 14½ oz/2.23 kg

HEAVY CREAM	48 fl oz	1.44 L
SUGAR	4 oz	113 g
WATER	3 fl oz	90 mL
EGG YOLKS	1½ oz	43 g
BITTERSWEET CHOCOLATE, melted	1 lb 8 oz	680 g

1. Assemble and prepare the desired pastries, containers, or molds that are to be used in the application of the mousse before beginning preparation.

2. Whip the cream to soft peaks. Cover and reserve under refrigeration.

3. Combine the sugar and water in a heavy-bottomed saucepan and cook over medium heat, stirring to dissolve the sugar. Continue cooking, without stirring, to 248°F/120°C.

4. Meanwhile, beat the egg yolks with the wire whisk attachment until light in texture and color.

5. With the mixer on medium speed, pour the hot sugar syrup into the egg yolks in a fine stream, then continue to beat until the mixture is completely cool.

6. Gently blend approximately one-third of the reserved whipped cream into the egg yolk mixture. Fold in the remaining whipped cream, thoroughly incorporating it.

7. Vigorously whip approximately one-half of the whipped cream mixture into the warm chocolate. Fold in the remaining cream mixture, thoroughly incorporating it.

8. Immediately pipe or spread into prepared pastries or containers. Cover and refrigerate until completely set.

Lemon Mousse
(Lemon Filling for Sheet Cakes)

Makes 2 lb 7 oz/1.11 kg

GELATIN	2½ oz	71 g
WATER	20 fl oz	600 mL
HEAVY CREAM	24 fl oz	720 mL
LEMON CURD (page 394)	12 oz	340 g
SORBET SYRUP (page 480)	3 fl oz	90 mL
LEMON FRUIT COMPOUND	1 tbsp	7 g

1. Assemble and prepare the desired pastries, containers, or molds that are to be used in the application of the mousse before beginning preparation.

2. Bloom the gelatin in the water and melt.

3. Whip the heavy cream to medium peaks. Cover and reserve under refrigeration.

4. Blend together the freshly made, still-warm lemon curd with the sorbet syrup and lemon fruit compound, stirring with a whip. Add the melted gelatin. Strain and cool to 70°F/21°C.

5. Gently blend approximately one-third of the reserved whipped cream into the lemon curd mixture. Fold in the remaining whipped cream, thoroughly incorporating it.

6. Immediately pipe or spread into prepared pastries or containers. Cover and refrigerate until completely set.

Variation   **Grapefruit Mousse** Replace the lemon curd with grapefruit curd (page 394).

White Chocolate Mousse

Makes 3 lb/1.36 kg

GELATIN	½ oz	14 g
WATER	7 fl oz	210 mL
HEAVY CREAM	32 fl oz	960 mL
WHITE CHOCOLATE, chopped	10 oz	284 g
SUGAR	4 oz	113 g
EGG WHITES	6 oz	170 g

1. Assemble and prepare the desired pastries, containers, or molds that are to be used in the application of the mousse before beginning preparation.

2. Bloom the gelatin in 4 fl oz/120 mL of the water.

3. Whip 24 fl oz/720 mL of the cream to soft peaks. Cover and reserve under refrigeration.

4. Melt the gelatin. Melt the white chocolate with the remaining 8 fl oz/240 mL heavy cream in a bowl set over a pan of simmering water, stirring until blended. Remove from the heat and add the melted gelatin.

5. Combine the sugar and remaining 3 fl oz/90 mL water in a heavy-bottomed saucepan and cook over medium heat, stirring to dissolve the sugar. Continue cooking, without stirring, to 248°F/120°C.

6. Meanwhile, place the egg whites in the bowl of an electric mixer fitted with the whip attachment. When the sugar syrup reaches 240°F/116°C, begin whipping the egg whites on high speed until medium peaks form.

7. With the mixer on medium speed, pour the hot sugar syrup into the egg whites in a fine stream, then continue to beat until the meringue is completely cool.

8. Gently blend approximately one-third of the meringue into the white chocolate mixture. Fold in the remaining meringue, thoroughly incorporating it.

9. Gently blend approximately one-third of the reserved whipped cream into the chocolate mixture. Fold in the remaining whipped cream, thoroughly incorporating it.

10. Immediately pipe or spread into prepared pastries or containers. Cover and refrigerate until completely set.

Note This mousse can be prepared without the gelatin and served in individual containers. With the gelatin as a stabilizer, it can be used as a filling for cakes and pastries.

Chocolate Sabayon Mousse

Makes 3 lb 6 oz/1.53 kg

BITTERSWEET CHOCOLATE, chopped	8 oz	227 g
GELATIN	½ oz	14 g
WATER	2 fl oz	60 mL
BRANDY	3 fl oz	90 mL
HEAVY CREAM	24 fl oz	720 mL
VANILLA EXTRACT	1 tbsp	15 mL
EGG YOLKS	6¾ oz	191 g
SUGAR	4 oz	113 g
DRY SHERRY	6 fl oz	180 mL

1. Assemble and prepare the desired pastries, containers, or molds that are to be used in the application of the sabayon before beginning preparation.

2. Melt the chocolate over a pan of barely simmering water. Turn off the heat, and keep the chocolate warm over the hot water.

3. Bloom the gelatin in the water and brandy.

4. Whip the cream with the vanilla to very soft peaks. Cover and reserve under refrigeration.

5. Combine the egg yolks, sugar, and sherry in a stainless steel bowl and whip together until thoroughly blended. Place the bowl over a pan of simmering water and heat, whisking constantly, until the mixture is thick and foamy and has reached at least 165°F/74°C. Remove from the heat. Melt the gelatin.

6. Add the melted gelatin to the egg yolk mixture. Gradually fold in the chocolate. Allow the mixture to cool to 80°F/27°C.

7. Gently blend approximately one-third of the reserved whipped cream into the chocolate mixture. Fold in the remaining whipped cream, thoroughly incorporating it.

8. Immediately pipe or spread into prepared pastries or containers. Cover and refrigerate until completely set.

Varitaion **Mocha Mousse** Replace the Dry Sherry with an equal amount of cold espresso.

Diplomat Cream

Makes 2 lb 2 oz/964 g

HEAVY CREAM	16 fl oz	480 mL
GELATIN	1½ tsp	7 g
WATER	2 fl oz	60 mL
PASTRY CREAM, flavored as desired, warm (page 388)	1 lb	454 g

1. Assemble and prepare the desired pastries, containers, or molds that are to be used in the application of the cream before beginning preparation.

2. Whip the heavy cream to soft peaks. Cover and reserve under refrigeration.

3. Bloom the gelatin in the water and melt.

4. Blend the melted gelatin into the freshly prepared and still-warm pastry cream. Strain, then cool over an ice water bath to 75°F/24°C.

5. Gently blend approximately one-third of the reserved whipped cream into the pastry cream mixture. Fold in the remaining whipped cream, thoroughly incorporating it.

6. Immediately pipe into prepared pastries or containers. Cover and refrigerate until completely set.

Variations   **Orange Diplomat Cream** Replace the pastry cream with an equal amount of orange curd (page 394).

Bavarian Cream

Makes 4 lb 8 oz/2.04 kg

GELATIN	1 oz	28 g
WATER	8 fl oz	240 mL
HEAVY CREAM	32 fl oz	960 mL
VANILLA SAUCE (page 430)	32 fl oz	960 mL

1. Assemble and prepare the desired pastries, containers, or molds that are to be used in the application of the cream before beginning preparation.

2. Bloom the gelatin in the water and melt.

3. Whip the heavy cream to soft peaks. Cover and reserve under refrigeration.

4. Blend the melted gelatin into the freshly prepared and still-warm vanilla sauce. Strain, then cool in an ice water bath to 75°F/24°C, or until it begins to thicken.

5. Gently blend one-third of the vanilla sauce mixture into the reserved whipped cream. Fold into the remaining vanilla sauce mixture, thoroughly incorporating it.

6. Immediately pour into prepared molds. Cover and refrigerate until completely set.

Variations **Chocolate Bavarian Cream** Melt 12 oz/340 g of bittersweet or milk chocolate. Blend approximately one-third of the warm vanilla sauce with the chocolate. Blend the chocolate mixture into the remaining vanilla sauce. Proceed as directed above.

Raspberry Bavarian Cream Reduce the vanilla sauce to 16 fl oz/480 mL, and blend in 16 fl oz/480 mL raspberry purée and 4 oz/113 g sugar. Proceed as directed above.

Praline Bavarian Cream Add 8 oz/227 g praline paste to the vanilla sauce just before the gelatin is added. Proceed as directed above.

Liqueur Bavarian Cream Add 6 fl oz/180 mL orange liqueur to the vanilla sauce just before the gelatin is added. Proceed as directed above.

Lemon Bavarian Cream Reduce the vanilla sauce to 4 fl oz/120 mL and add 8 oz/227 g Lemon Curd (page 394). Blend the vanilla sauce and lemon curd together just before the gelatin is added. Proceed as directed above.

Wine Cream Reduce the vanilla sauce to 16 fl oz/480 mL and add 16 fl oz/480 Chablis. Blend the vanilla sauce and Chablis proceed as directed above.

Bavarian Cream

A Bavarian cream is vanilla sauce that has been stabilized with gelatin and lightened and aerated with an equal proportion, by weight, of whipped cream. Bavarian cream can be used for individual dessert preparations. It can be piped and used in cakes, tortes, and charlottes.

To make a Bavarian cream, whip the cream and reserve under refrigeration so it is ready to be folded into the vanilla sauce mixture. (Since the Bavarian cream will begin to set immediately once it is finished, any molds, service containers, etc. should be prepared before beginning preparation.) The vanilla sauce should be allowed to cool but should not be cold. Blend any flavorings to be added, such as melted chocolate, fruit purée, or liqueur, into the vanilla sauce. The sauce should be intensely flavored, as the whipped cream will dilute its flavor. The finished Bavarian can be molded or used as a filling or topping.

Yogurt Bavarian Cream

Makes 4 lb 8 oz/2.04 kg

GELATIN	1 oz	28 g
WATER	8 fl oz	240 mL
HEAVY CREAM	32 fl oz	960 mL
YOGURT, at room temperature	24 fl oz	720 mL
LEMON VANILLA SAUCE (page 428)	4 fl oz	120 mL
LEMON ZEST, grated	2½ tsp	7.50 g

1. Assemble and prepare the desired pastries, containers, or molds that are to be used in the application of the cream before beginning preparation.

2. Bloom the gelatin in the water and melt.

3. Whip the heavy cream to soft peaks. Cover and reserve under refrigeration.

4. Combine the yogurt with the freshly prepared, still-warm vanilla sauce. Blend in the melted gelatin. Strain, blend in the lemon zest, and cool over an ice water bath to 75°F/24°C.

5. Gently blend one-third of the vanilla sauce mixture into the reserved whipped cream. Fold in the remaining vanilla sauce mixture into the whipped cream mixture, thoroughly incorporating it.

6. Immediately pour into prepared pastries or molds. Cover and refrigerate until completely set.

Tiramisù Cream

Makes 1 lb 8 oz/680 g

HEAVY CREAM	8 fl oz	240 mL
EGG YOLKS	2½ oz	71 g
SUGAR	3 oz	85 g
SWEET MARSALA	3 fl oz	90 mL
MASCARPONE, softened	8 oz	227 g

1. Assemble and prepare the desired pastries, containers, or molds that are to be used in the application of the cream before beginning preparation.

2. Whip the cream to soft peaks. Cover and reserve under refrigeration.

3. Combine the egg yolks, sugar, and Marsala in a stainless steel bowl and whip together until thoroughly blended. Place the bowl over a pan of simmering water and heat, whisking constantly, until the mixture is thick and foamy and has reached at least 165°F/74°C.

4. Remove from the heat and whip, using an electric mixer fitted with the wire whip attachment, on high speed until cool.

5. Fold the egg yolk mixture into the mascarpone. Gently blend in approximately one-third of the reserved whipped cream. Fold in the remaining whipped cream.

6. Immediately pipe or spread into prepared pastries or containers. Cover and refrigerate until completely set.

Note To stabilize Tiramisù cream for use in unmolded or sliced presentations, add 1½ tsp/7 g gelatin, bloomed and melted, to the foam in Step 4.

Variation **Sauternes Creme** Substitute Sauternes for the Sweet Marsala and stabilize with 1½ tsp/ 7 g od gelatin bloomed in 2 fl oz/60 mL of water and melted.

Passion Fruit Chibouste

Makes 4 lb/1.81 kg

GELATIN	½ oz	14 g
WATER	4 fl oz	120 mL
PASSION FRUIT JUICE	32 fl oz	960 mL
SUGAR	1 lb 8 oz	680 g
CORNSTARCH	4 oz	113 g
EGGS	8 oz	227 g
EGG YOLKS	6 oz	170 g
EGG WHITES	1 lb 4 oz	567 g

1. Assemble and prepare the desired pastries, containers, or molds that are to be used in the application of the chibouste before beginning preparation.

2. Bloom the gelatin in the water.

3. Combine 27 fl oz/810 mL of the passion fruit juice and 4 oz/113 g of the sugar in a pot and heat to melt the sugar.

4. Meanwhile, blend the cornstarch with the remaining 5 fl oz/150 mL passion fruit juice. Blend the cornstarch mixture with the eggs, egg yolks, and 4 oz/113 g of the sugar.

5. Temper the egg mixture by gradually adding about one-third of the hot passion fruit juice mixture, stirring constantly with a wire whip. Return the tempered egg mixture to the remaining juice in the saucepan and continue cooking until it comes to a boil. Remove from the heat and add the bloomed gelatin. Cover to keep warm.

6. Place the egg whites in the bowl of an electric mixer fitted with the whip attachment.

7. Combine the remaining 1 lb/454 g sugar and the water and bring to a boil, stirring to dissolve the sugar. Boil without stirring until the mixture reaches 240°F/116°C (soft ball stage).

8. Meanwhile, when the sugar syrup reaches 230°F/110°C, begin beating the egg whites on high speed.

9. When the sugar syrup reaches 240°F/116°C, and the egg whites have reached soft peaks, pour the hot syrup into the whipping egg whites and whip to medium peaks.

10. Fold the meringue into the passion fruit base while still warm.

11. Immediately pour into molds.

Note   Passion fruit juice generally comes in concentrated form. Make sure to reconstitute according to manufacturer's instructions before use.

Variation   **Lemon-Lime Chibouste** Substitute the passion fruit juice with 12 fl oz/360 mL of lemon juice and 20 fl oz/600 mL of lime juice. Follow the remaining steps as stated above.

Chocolate Soufflé

Makes 5 soufflés (4 fl oz/120 mL each)

BUTTER	1½ oz	43 g
BITTERSWEET CHOCOLATE, chopped	5 oz	142 g
PASTRY CREAM FOR SOUFFLÉS, cooled (page 409)	17 oz	482 g
EGG YOLK	1 oz	28 g
EGG WHITES	6 oz	170 g
SUGAR	2½ oz	71 g

1. Coat the inside of the ramekins with a film of softened butter, making sure to coat the rims as well as the insides, and dust with sugar.

2. To prepare the soufflé base, melt the butter and chocolate together in a bowl over a pan of barely simmering water, gently stirring to blend. Blend the chocolate mixture into the pastry cream. Blend in the egg yolk and set aside.

3. To prepare the meringue, whip the egg whites to soft peaks using the whip attachment.

4. Gradually sprinkle in the sugar while continuing to whip, then whip the meringue to medium peaks.

5. Gently blend approximately one-third of the meringue into the chocolate base. Fold in the remaining meringue, thoroughly incorporating it.

6. Portion the soufflé mixture into the prepared ramekins.

7. Bake at 350°F/177°C until fully risen, about 20 minutes.

Variations   **White Chocolate Soufflé** Substitute white chocolate for the bittersweet chocolate.

Grand Marnier, Kahlúa, Frangelico, or Amaretto Soufflé Substitute 1½ fl oz/45mL of the chosen liqueur and two egg yolks for the chocolate. Add them to the pastry cream with the melted butter. Follow the remaining method above.

Praline or Pistachio Soufflé Substitute 2 oz/57 g praline or pistachio paste and two egg yolks for the chocolate. Blend the nut paste and egg yolks into the pastry cream with the melted butter. Follow the remaining method above.

Pumpkin Soufflé Substitute 2 oz/57 g pumpkin purée and two egg yolks for the chocolate. Blend the purée and egg yolks into the pastry cream with the melted butter. Follow the remaining method above.

Lemon or Orange Soufflé When making the pastry cream, infuse the milk with ¼ oz/7 g grated zest of lemons or oranges. Omit the chocolate, and fold the melted butter into the pastry cream. Follow the remaining method above.

Cinnamon Soufflé When making the pastry cream, infuse the milk with three cinnamon sticks. Omit the chocolate, and fold the melted butter into the pastry cream. Follow the remaining method above.

Properly baked
soufflés, ready
for immediate
service

Pastry Cream for Soufflés

Makes 1 lb 10 oz/737 g

MILK	16 fl oz	480 mL
SUGAR	5 oz	142 g
ALL-PURPOSE FLOUR	3 oz	85 g
EGGS	2 oz	57 g
EGG YOLKS	1½ oz	43 g

1. Combine approximately 4 fl oz/120 mL of the milk with 2½ oz/71 g of the sugar in a saucepan and bring to a boil, stirring gently with a wooden spoon.

2. Meanwhile, combine the flour with the remaining 2½ oz/71 g sugar. Stirring with a wire whip, add the remaining 12 fl oz/360 mL milk. Add the eggs and egg yolks, stirring with a wire whip until the mixture is completely smooth.

3. Temper the egg mixture by adding about one-third of the hot milk, stirring constantly with a wire whip. Return the mixture to the remaining hot milk in the saucepan. Continue cooking, vigorously stirring with the whip, until the pastry cream comes to a boil and the whip leaves a trail in it.

4. Pour the pastry cream onto a large shallow container or bowl. Cover with plastic wrap placed directly against the surface of the cream, and cool over an ice bath.

5. Store the pastry cream, covered, under refrigeration.

Hot Soufflés

A hot soufflé is made with a flavored base that is lightened by folding in whipped egg whites, much like a mousse, but rather than being stabilized and chilled, it is baked to further expand the air bubbles trapped in the egg whites and served directly from the oven. Pastry cream and fruit purées are the most common bases for dessert soufflés. Any pastry cream can serve as the base for a soufflé. However, specific formulations of pastry cream can increase the stability of the soufflé by the type and amount of starch used. The formula included here uses flour, but in some cases you may want to combine different starches to achieve specific desired results.

A properly prepared soufflé should rise tall and straight above the rim of the mold. This dramatic dessert demands exacting technique from the pastry chef, including precise timing and execution, and also communication with the waitstaff so that the soufflé can be served straight from the oven, before it begins to deflate.

Before preparing the soufflé mixture, prepare the ramekins. Coat the inside and rim of each ramekin lightly but evenly with softened butter. Dust the molds with granulated or confectioners' sugar. The sugar coating will help the soufflé batter to rise as it bakes.

The base for a soufflé should be as light as possible before folding in the meringue. To lighten a pastry cream that has just been prepared, it should be beaten until cool. One that has been under refrigeration should be beaten until completely smooth. If using a flavored pastry cream, it should have a pronounced flavor, as the meringue will lessen the flavor intensity of the base.

The meringue should be beaten only to soft peaks. Folding the meringue into the flavored base will agitate the meringue, acting to further aerate and bring it to stiffer peaks, and it is important that the foam still have enough elasticity to expand as it bakes. Meringue beaten to stiff peaks will not expand as much during baking, and the soufflé will not rise as high. After the meringue has been folded into the base until evenly mixed, the batter should have a consistency similar to that of a soft peak meringue.

Immediately fill the prepared ramekins. Wipe away any drops of batter, and bake.

Bake the soufflés until they rise about 1 in/3 cm (or more) above the rims of the molds and are lightly set. Serve them immediately, with an appropriately flavored sauce or other garnish.

Raspberry Soufflé

Makes 4 soufflés (4 fl oz/120 mL each)

RASPBERRY PURÉE	7 oz	198 g
SUGAR	9 oz	255 g
EGG WHITES	5 oz	142 g

1. Coat the inside of the ramekins with a film of softened butter, making sure to coat the top rims of the ramekins as well as the insides, and dust with sugar.

2. Combine the purée and sugar in a saucepan and cook over medium heat, stirring to dissolve the sugar, until the mixture reaches 240°F/116°C.

3. Meanwhile, put the egg whites in the bowl of an electric mixer fitted with a wire whip attachment.

4. When the sugar-purée mixture reaches 230°F/110°C, begin whipping the egg whites on medium speed.

5. When the sugar-purée mixture reaches 240°F/116°C, and the egg whites have reached soft peaks, increase the mixer speed to high and carefully pour the hot sugar syrup mixture into the egg whites. Whip only to soft peaks.

6. Immediately put the mixture into a piping bag and fill the prepared ramekins.

7. Bake at 350°F/177°C until fully risen and lightly browned, about 20 minutes.

CHAPTER 12

Icings, Glazes, and Sauces

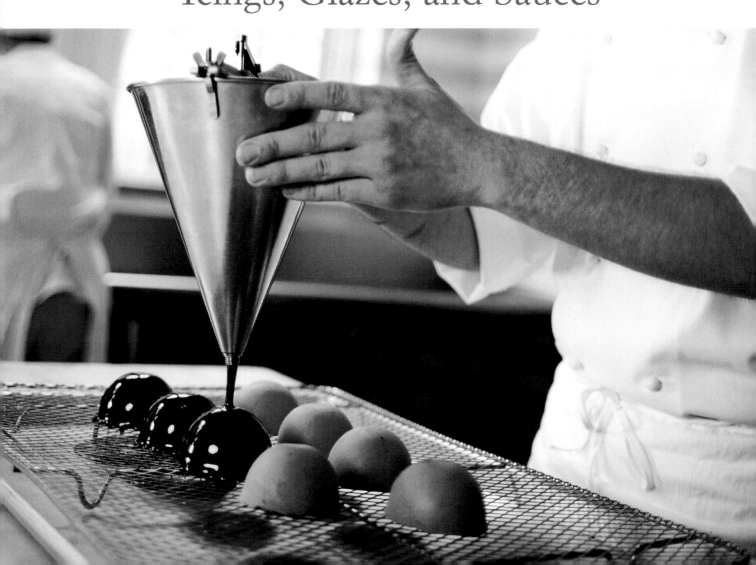

Common Meringue

Makes 1 lb 8 oz/680 g

EGG WHITES	8 oz	227 g
SALT	pinch	pinch
VANILLA EXTRACT	1 tsp	5 mL
SUGAR	1 lb	454 g

1. Place the egg whites, salt, and vanilla in a bowl and whisk until frothy.

2. Gradually add the sugar while continuing to whip, then whip to the desired consistency.

Meringues

Whipping egg whites and sugar together creates the light yet stable aerated mixture known as a meringue. Meringue is commonly used for topping and filling cakes and pastries. It can also be flavored and/or dried in a low oven to make cookies, containers (which can be used to hold fruit, mousse, or sorbet), or layers for cakes. Meringue is also used as an ingredient in mousses and batters to lighten, aerate, and/or leaven them.

A basic ratio for a meringue is 1 part egg whites to 2 parts sugar. As the egg whites are whipped, air is incorporated and the whites break into smaller and smaller globules to form bubbles. When sugar is whipped into the egg whites, the agitation of the mixture and the moisture of the whites begin to dissolve the sugar, which in turn surrounds the air bubbles, coating them and making them more stable.

There are a few basic rules to keep in mind for making a successful meringue. All utensils must be impeccably clean and dry. Make sure that no traces of fat of any kind come in contact with the egg whites, whether in the form of grease on the utensils or other equipment or from traces of egg yolk in the whites themselves. Fat will interfere with the protein strands which will prevent the egg whites from developing into a foam. A small amount of an acid (cream of tartar, lemon juice, or vinegar) will relax the proteins, helping to stabilize the meringue. You can introduce an acid simply by wiping the bowl clean with lemon juice or vinegar before adding the egg whites or by adding a small amount of cream of tartar to the whites just as they begin to foam. Never use cream of tartar when whipping in a copper bowl, as it will cause a toxic reaction, turning the whites slightly green. Room-temperature egg whites will whip up more readily. Be careful to use sugar that is free of impurities such as flour or other ingredients. Whip the egg whites on high speed until they are frothy, then gradually add the sugar while continuing to whip to the desired consistency (soft, medium, or stiff peak). Avoid overwhipping egg whites, as they become dry and lumpy, making them difficult to incorporate into other ingredients. Prepare meringue (especially common meringue) just before you intend to use it, because it will begin to collapse if it stands for any length of time.

THE USE OF AN ICING, GLAZE, OR SAUCE CAN MEAN THE DIFFERENCE BETWEEN A PLAIN BAKED ITEM AND A MORE ELABORATE PASTRY OR DESSERT. THESE PREPARATIONS HAVE A WIDE RANGE OF USES, LIMITED ONLY BY THE IMAGINATION OF THE PASTRY CHEF OR BAKER. THE TECHNIQUES AND APPLICATIONS INVOLVED IN MAKING AND USING THEM ARE IMPORTANT TO MASTER AS THEY ACT TO BALANCE AND ADJUST FLAVORS AND TEXTURES, MAKING THEM AN INTEGRAL PART OF ANY PASTRY OR DESSERT WITH WHICH THEY ARE PAIRED.

TYPES OF MERINGUES

There are three different types of meringue: common (or French), Swiss, and Italian. Simply whipping the egg whites and sugar to the desired consistency makes common meringue. This is the simplest type of meringue to prepare and the least stable. Also, unless pasteurized whites are used, because of the potential danger of salmonella, uncooked or unbaked common meringue should not be eaten. Therefore, it is most often used in batters to provide leavening. It can also be used for making meringue shells, bases or layers for cakes, and for piping simple decorations that are baked.

Swiss meringue is made by stirring the egg whites with sugar using a whip over a hot water bath until they reach a temperature between 115°F and 165°F/46° and 74°C, depending on the intended use. The whites are then whipped in a mixer to the desired peak. The meringue can be piped and baked, or dried, in the oven. Swiss meringue can also be used for the same preparations as common meringue to lighten mousses and creams, to fill various cakes, or to add a delicate piped shell border or other decorative element. Swiss meringue is more stable than common meringue.

Italian meringue is made by whipping the egg whites in a mixer and then adding a cooked sugar syrup. The sugar is cooked to the soft ball stage (240°F/116°C) and added in a thin, steady stream to the whipping egg whites when they have reached the medium peak stage. The whites are then mixed on medium speed to the desired peak. Italian meringue is the most stable of the meringues and is used in various mousses, buttercreams, and for décor work.

STAGES OF MERINGUE (SOFT, MEDIUM, OR STIFF PEAKS)

Each of the various stages of meringue—soft, medium, and stiff peak—is best suited for specific applications. A soft peak meringue will cling to the whip when lifted but will not form pointed peaks. Soft peak meringue is commonly used in soufflés. With medium peak meringue, peaks will form when the whip is lifted from the meringue but will droop slightly. Medium peak meringue is used to lighten mixtures such as creams and batters. When the whip is lifted from a stiff peak meringue, sharp points will form and remain in the meringue. Stiff peak meringue is the best choice for piping and décor work, as it holds its shape. All meringues should be glossy and smooth. If a stiff peak meringue appears dry, dull, or lumpy, it has been overwhipped and will be difficult to work with.

Swiss Meringue

Makes 1 lb 5 oz/595 g

EGG WHITES	8 oz	227 g
VANILLA EXTRACT	1 tsp	5 mL
SALT	pinch	pinch
SUGAR	1 lb	454 g

1. Place the egg whites, vanilla, salt, and sugar in the bowl of an electric mixer and stir until thoroughly combined.

2. Place the bowl over a pot of barely simmering water and slowly stir the mixture until it reaches between 115° and 165°F/46° and 74°C, depending on use.

3. Transfer the mixture to the electric mixer and whip with a wire whip attachment on high speed until the meringue is the desired consistency.

Italian Meringue

Makes 1 lb 8 oz/680 g

SUGAR	1 lb	454 g
WATER	4 fl oz	120 mL
EGG WHITES	8 oz	227 g
SALT	pinch	pinch
VANILLA EXTRACT	1 tsp	5 mL

1. Combine 12 oz/340 g of the sugar with the water in a heavy-bottomed saucepan and bring to a boil over medium-high heat, stirring to dissolve the sugar. Continue cooking, without stirring, until the mixture reaches the soft ball stage (240°F/116°C).

2. Meanwhile, place the egg whites, salt, and vanilla in the bowl of an electric mixer fitted with a wire whip attachment.

3. When the sugar syrup has reached approximately 230°F/110°C, whip the whites on medium speed until frothy. Gradually add the remaining 4 oz/113 g sugar and beat the meringue to medium peaks.

4. When the sugar syrup reaches 240°F/116°C, add it to the meringue in a slow, steady stream while whipping on medium speed. Whip on high speed to stiff peaks. Continue to beat on medium speed until completely cool.

Chocolate Meringue

Makes 1 lb 8¾ oz/702 g

EGG WHITES	8 oz	227 g
SUGAR	13 oz	369 g
CONFECTIONERS' SUGAR	3 oz	85 g
COCOA POWDER	¾ oz	21 g

1. Place the egg whites in a bowl and whisk until frothy.
2. Gradually add the sugar while continuing to whip, then whip to the desired consistency.
3. Sift the confectioners' sugar and cocoa together and fold into the meringue.

1 Adding hot sugar syrup to the egg whites to make an Italian meringue
2 The finished meringue

Italian Buttercream

Makes 3 lb 4 oz/1.47 kg

SUGAR	1 lb	454 g
WATER	4 fl oz	120 mL
EGG WHITES	8 oz	227 g
BUTTER, cut into medium chunks, soft	2 lb	907 g
VANILLA EXTRACT	1 tbsp	15 mL

1. Combine 12 oz/340 g of the sugar with the water in a heavy-bottomed saucepan and bring to a boil over medium-high heat, stirring to dissolve the sugar. Continue cooking, without stirring, to the soft ball stage (240°F/116°C).

2. Meanwhile, place the egg whites in the bowl of an electric mixer fitted with the wire whip attachment.

3. When the sugar syrup has reached approximately 230°F/110°C, whip the egg whites on medium speed until frothy. Gradually add the remaining 4 oz/113 g sugar and beat the meringue to medium peaks.

4. When the sugar syrup reaches 240°F/116°C, add it to the meringue in a slow, steady stream while whipping on medium speed. Whip on high speed until the meringue has cooled to room temperature.

5. Add the soft butter gradually, mixing until fully incorporated after each addition and scraping down the sides of the bowl as necessary. Blend in the vanilla. The buttercream is ready for use or may be tightly covered and stored under refrigeration.

As butter is added to an Italian buttercream, it may look broken (right), but after continued whipping, it develops a very smooth, even consistency (left).

Buttercream

Buttercream is an essential preparation in the pastry shop. Made with fresh sweet butter, natural flavorings, and other top-quality ingredients, it is excellent as a filling and/or icing for many cakes and pastries. There are three types of buttercream: Italian, German, and French. Each of these types of buttercream has different characteristics that make them best suited for different applications.

Italian buttercream is made with meringue, butter, and flavorings. A meringue-based buttercream may be made with either an Italian or Swiss meringue. They are relatively white in color and have a light texture and are ideal for wedding cakes and any pastries where a white buttercream is desired.

German buttercream is a combination of pastry cream, butter, and flavorings. German buttercream has a richer texture than meringue-based buttercreams due to the whole eggs in the pastry cream. However, it has a short shelf life and therefore cannot be made in large quantities and stored. And, because it is yellow in color, it is unsuitable for some purposes where a white icing is desired.

French buttercream is made with either whole eggs or egg yolks, butter, cooked sugar syrup, and flavorings. It is similar to meringue-based Italian buttercream in technique, but the egg yolks make it richer and give it a yellow color.

Layers or coatings of buttercream should be even and thin. It should completely cover the layer or outside of the pastry or cake without being excessively thick. It should add enough moisture, flavor, and texture to complement without overpowering the pastry or cake to which it is applied.

FLAVORING BUTTERCREAM

Many different flavorings are compatible with buttercream. Below is a list of ingredients that are commonly used to flavor buttercream, with a basic amount that can be added to flavor 1 lb/454 g of any type of buttercream. Of course, depending on the intended use, the amount of flavoring can be reduced or increased. Flavors may also be combined.

It is often practical to make a large batch of buttercream and then flavor small portions as desired. Flavorings to be added to buttercream should ideally be at room temperature so they can easily be incorporated.

Before using cold buttercream, allow it to come to room temperature. Then place it in the bowl of an electric mixer fitted with the paddle attachment and mix until smooth and spreadable.

Chocolate Buttercream Add 3 oz/85 g melted and cooled bittersweet chocolate to 1 lb/454 g prepared buttercream.

White Chocolate Buttercream Add 2 oz/57 g melted and cooled white chocolate to 1 lb/454 g prepared buttercream.

Milk Chocolate Buttercream Add 2 oz/57 g melted and cooled milk chocolate to 1 lb/454 g prepared buttercream.

Hazelnut Buttercream Add 2 oz/57 g praline paste, ½ fl oz/15 mL brandy, and 1 tsp/5 mL vanilla extract to 1 lb/454 g prepared buttercream.

Coffee Buttercream Add ½ oz/14 g coffee paste, ½ fl oz/15 mL brandy, and 1tsp/5 mL vanilla extract to 1 lb/454 g prepared buttercream.

Chestnut Buttercream Add 2 oz/57 g chestnut purée, ½ fl oz/15 mL brandy, and 1 tsp/5 mL vanilla extract to 1 lb/454 g prepared buttercream.

French Buttercream
Makes 3 lb/1.36 kg

WHOLE EGGS	8 oz	227 g
EGG YOLKS	8 oz	227 g
SUGAR	1 lb 2 oz	510 g
WATER	4 fl oz	120 mL
BUTTER, cut into medium chunks, soft	1 lb 8 oz	680 g
VANILLA EXTRACT	2 tsp	10 mL

1. Whip the eggs and yolks in an electric mixer fitted with a wire whip attachment on high speed until light and fluffy, about 5 minutes.

2. Combine the sugar and water in a heavy-bottomed saucepan and bring to a boil, stirring to dissolve the sugar. Continue cooking, without stirring, until the mixture reaches 235°F/113°C.

3. Slowly pour the hot sugar syrup into the eggs while whipping on medium speed. Continue to whip until cool.

4. Gradually add the butter, beating until incorporated after each addition and scraping down the sides of the bowl as necessary. Blend in the vanilla.

5. Store, covered, under refrigeration until ready to use.

Swiss Meringue Buttercream

Makes 2 lb 12 oz/1.25 kg

SUGAR	1 lb	454 g
EGG WHITES	8 oz	227 g
BUTTER, cut into medium chunks, soft	1 lb 4 oz	567 g
VANILLA EXTRACT	2 tsp	10 mL

1. Place the sugar and egg whites in a stainless-steel bowl and whisk to combine. Set the bowl over a pan of barely simmering water and heat, whisking constantly, to 165°F/74°C.

2. Transfer the mixture to an electric mixer fitted with a wire whip attachment and whip on high speed until the meringue is the desired consistency.

3. Gradually add the butter to the meringue while whipping on high speed; the buttercream should be light and creamy. Blend in the vanilla.

4. Cover the buttercream with plastic wrap and store under refrigeration.

German Buttercream

Makes 2 lb 4 oz/1.02 kg

BUTTER, soft	1 lb	454 g
CONFECTIONERS' SUGAR, sifted	4 oz	113 g
PASTRY CREAM (page 388)	1 lb	454 g

1. Cream together the butter and sugar until light and fluffy.

2. Gradually add the pastry cream, mixing until fully incorporated after each addition and scraping down the sides of the bowl as necessary.

3. Store, covered, under refrigeration until ready to use.

Cream Cheese Icing

Makes 2 lb/907 g

CREAM CHEESE	1 lb	454 g
BUTTER, soft	8 oz	227 g
CONFECTIONERS' SUGAR, sifted	8 oz	227 g
VANILLA EXTRACT	1 tbsp	15 mL

1. Blend the cream cheese in an electric mixer fitted with a paddle attachment on low speed until smooth.

2. Add the butter, in stages, and blend well. Add the confectioners' sugar and blend on low speed until fully incorporated. Beat on high speed until light and fluffy, about 5 minutes. Blend in the vanilla.

Variation **Lemon Cream Cheese Icing** Add the grated zest of 1 lemon to the icing with the vanilla.

Chantilly Cream

Makes 1 lb 2 oz/510 g

HEAVY CREAM	16 fl oz	480 mL
CONFECTIONERS' SUGAR	2 oz	57 g
VANILLA EXTRACT	1 tbsp	15 mL

1. Whip the cream to very soft peaks.
2. Add the sugar and vanilla and whip to desired peak.

Variations **Cinnamon Chantilly Cream** Add ½ tsp/1 g ground cinnamon before whipping the cream.
Coffee Chantilly Cream Add 1 oz/28 g of Coffee Concentrate (Appendix A) to the Cream before whipping.

Whipping Cream

There are two important considerations when whipping cream: temperature and fat content. Use cold cream (at approximately 40°F/4°C) and a chilled bowl. Whipping cream in a very warm environment can prove difficult. The cold temperature prevents the fat in the cream from melting, which allows for better incorporation of air. Heat causes the fat in the cream to melt, preventing the fat from clinging together, making it impossible to whip.

Cream for whipping must contain at least 30 percent fat. The fat present in cream coats the air as it is incorporated to form stable air bubbles. As whipping continues, more bubbles form, which then cling together, causing the cream to stiffen.

Whipped cream can be flavored in many ways: with extracts, liqueurs or fruit purées. It is used to fill, ice, and/or decorate cakes, tarts, and pastries, and it is served as an accompaniment to endless types of desserts. It is also used to aerate and lighten various creams and mousses.

GUIDELINES FOR WHIPPING CREAM

Use cream with at least a 30 percent fat content.

Use chilled cream and cold equipment, including the bowl.

Work in a cool environment.

Stabilized Whipped Cream

Makes 32 fl oz/960 mL

GELATIN	1 oz	28 g
COLD WATER	16 fl oz	480 mL
HOT WATER	16 fl oz	480 mL
HEAVY CREAM	16 fl oz	480 mL

1. Bloom the gelatin in the cold water.
2. Add the hot water and stir to dissolve the gelatin.
3. Cover tightly and store under refrigeration.
4. To use, melt 3 oz/85 g of the gelatin mixture and add to 16 fl oz/480 mL of heavy cream. Whip to desired peaks.

Soft Ganache

Makes 3 lb 6 oz/1.53 kg

DARK CHOCOLATE, finely chopped	1 lb 4 oz	567 g
HEAVY CREAM	32 fl oz	960 mL

1. Place the chocolate in a stainless-steel bowl.
2. Bring the heavy cream to a simmer.
3. Pour the hot cream over the chocolate. Allow to stand for 1 minute, then gently stir to blend. Strain and cool.
4. Cover with plastic wrap and refrigerate overnight before using.
5. Whip the ganache to desired peaks for use.

Variations **Soft Milk Chocolate Ganache** Substitute milk chocolate for the dark chocolate.

Soft White Chocolate Ganache Substitute white chocolate for the dark chocolate.

Note For a lighter flavored ganache, add an equal amount of cream (by volume) to the chilled ganache before whipping.

Hard Ganache

Makes 5 lb/2.27 kg

DARK CHOCOLATE, finely chopped	4 lb	1.81 kg
HEAVY CREAM	32 fl oz	960 mL

1. Place the chocolate in a stainless-steel bowl.

2. Bring the heavy cream just to a simmer. Pour the hot cream over the chocolate, allow to stand for 1 minute, and stir until the chocolate is thoroughly melted.

3. The ganache can be used immediately, or it can be covered and stored under refrigeration, then rewarmed.

LEFT, TOP TO BOTTOM:
Soft, medium, and hard ganache

RIGHT:
Ganache is an emulsion of chocolate and cream.

Fondant

Fondant is the traditional glaze for petits fours, éclairs, and doughnuts, among other pastries. Most kitchens and bakeshops use purchased fondant. For fondant to have its characteristic glossy finish, it must be warmed until it is liquid enough to flow readily (105°F/41°C). Small items are typically dipped into the fondant, using a dipping fork or similar tool. Larger items are set on racks on sheet pans and the fondant is poured, ladled, spooned, or drizzled over them. Assemble all your equipment before beginning and keep the fondant warm as you work. (See page 562 for more about a glazing setup.)

To prepare the fondant, place it in a stainless-steel bowl and heat over a hot water bath to melt. Do not let the fondant exceed 105°F/41°C. Thin the fondant to the desired consistency with warm water, corn syrup, or another liquid such as a liqueur. Once it has been melted, plain fondant can be flavored and/or colored as desired by adding coloring pastes, purées, concentrates, or chocolate.

To make chocolate fondant, add about 3 oz/85 g melted unsweetened chocolate to 1 lb/454 g warmed fondant. Gradually add the chocolate to the fondant. The amount of chocolate may be adjusted to suit the desired flavor and color.

Glazing with Fondant, Mirror Glazes, or Hard Ganache

To glaze a pastry means to enrobe it in a thin coating of one of many and varied products, including fondant, ganache, and jam- or gelatin-based (or mirror) glazes. Glazing adds visual appeal as well as flavor, and it also helps to increase the shelf life of the finished item by sealing in moisture.

Any glaze should be smooth, fluid, and free of any lumps. A well-applied glaze should always be in a thin, smooth layer.

Ultra Shiny Chocolate Glaze

Makes 32 fl oz/960 mL

GELATIN	1 oz	28 g
BITTERSWEET CHOCOLATE, chopped	2½ oz	71 g
WATER	9½ fl oz	285 mL
SUGAR	1 lb 2 oz	510 g
DUTCH-PROCESS COCOA POWDER	5½ oz	156 g
HEAVY CREAM	5½ fl oz	165 mL

1. Bloom and melt the gelatin. Place the chocolate in a stainless-steel bowl.
2. Bring the water, sugar, cocoa powder, and cream to just below a boil over medium heat.
3. Pour over the bloomed and melted gelatin and chopped chocolate and let stand for 1 minute. Stir to melt and combine. Strain.
4. Use immediately.

Mirror Glaze

Makes 8 fl oz/240 mL

GELATIN	2 oz	57 g
FLAVORED LIQUID OR FRUIT PURÉE, cold	6 fl oz	180 mL
CORN SYRUP	2 oz	57 g

1. Bloom the gelatin in the liquid or purée and melt.
2. Stir in the corn syrup.
3. Cool the glaze to 70°F/21°C before using.

Note Certain fresh fruit juices or purées, such as kiwi, pineapple, and papaya, contain enzymes that will prevent the gelatin from setting if they are not boiled first to destroy the enzymes.

Spiced Mirror Glaze

Makes 30 fl oz/900 mL

WATER	20 fl oz	600 mL
SUGAR	12 oz	340 g
VANILLA BEAN	1 each	1 each
ALLSPICE BERRIES	3 each	3 each
CINNAMON STICKS	2 each	2 each
WHOLE CLOVES	1 each	1 each
GROUND NUTMEG	¼ tsp	0.50 g
GROUND GINGER	¼ tsp	0.50 g
ORANGE ZEST, grated	1 tbsp	9 g
LEMON JUICE	4 fl oz	120 mL
GELATIN	¾ oz	21 g
RUM	1 fl oz	30 mL

1. Combine 15 fl oz/450 mL of the water with the sugar in a saucepan and bring to a boil over medium heat, stirring to dissolve the sugar. Split the vanilla bean, scrape the seeds into the sugar syrup, and add the pod. Add the allspice berries, cinnamon sticks, clove, nutmeg, ginger, orange zest, and lemon juice. Remove from the heat and steep for 15 minutes, then strain.

2. Bloom the gelatin in the rum and remaining 5 fl oz/150 mL water and melt. Blend the melted gelatin with the spiced mixture.

3. Cool the glaze to 70°F/21°C. Use immediately.

Using and Choosing a Sauce

The proper sauce is essential for a successful dessert presentation. Always serve a sauce that will complement or enhance, not overwhelm, the textures and flavors of the dessert. You may want to avoid serving a dessert with a sauce of the same consistency and texture; for example, do not serve creamy vanilla sauce with ice cream. Instead, use a fruit coulis or another sauce that will provide contrast.

The basic types of sauces used in the pastry kitchen include custard (i.e., vanilla sauce or crème anglaise), sabayon, chocolate, fruit (using fresh, frozen, or dried fruit), caramel, and reduction. There are many variations on these basic preparations. By adding or substituting ingredients, you can adapt these sauces to suit any type of dessert item.

Apricot Glaze

Makes 24 fl oz/720 mL

GELATIN	1¼ oz	35 g
WATER	8 fl oz	240 mL
LIGHT CORN SYRUP	12 oz	340 g
LEMON JUICE	4 fl oz	120 mL
APRICOT JAM	6 oz	170 g

1. Bloom the gelatin in the water and melt.
2. Combine the corn syrup, lemon juice, and apricot jam in a saucepan and bring to a boil over medium heat. Blend in the melted gelatin.
3. Cool the glaze to 75°F/24°C. Use immediately.

Thread Glaze

Makes 2 lb/907 g

SUGAR	1 lb 8 oz	680 g
WATER	8 fl oz	240 mL

1. Combine the sugar and water in a heavy-bottomed saucepan and bring to a boil over medium heat, stirring to dissolve the sugar. Boil, without stirring, until the mixture reaches 234°F/112°C.
2. Use the glaze immediately.

Grapefruit Mirror Glaze

Makes 1 lb/454 g

GELATIN	½ oz	14 g
GRAPEFRUIT JUICE, cold	16 fl oz	480 mL

1. Bloom the gelatin in the grapefruit juice in a stainless-steel bowl.
2. Set the bowl over a pan of simmering water and stir to dissolve the gelatin.
3. Cool the glaze to 70°F/21°C before using.

Vanilla Sauce

Makes 48 fl oz/1.44 L

MILK	16 fl oz	480 mL
HEAVY CREAM	16 fl oz	480 mL
SALT	1 tsp	5 g
SUGAR	8 oz	227 g
EGG YOLKS	10 oz	284 g
VANILLA EXTRACT	1 tbsp	15 mL

1. Combine the milk and heavy cream with the salt and 4 oz/113 g of the sugar in a saucepan and bring to a boil, stirring to dissolve the sugar.

2. Meanwhile, blend the egg yolks with the remaining 4 oz/113 g sugar, using a wire whip.

3. Temper the egg yolks by gradually adding one-third of the hot milk, whipping constantly. Return the tempered egg mixture to the remaining hot milk in the saucepan and continue cooking until the mixture thickens enough to coat the back of a spoon.

4. Strain the sauce into a metal container and chill in an ice water bath.

5. Cover tightly with plastic wrap and store under refrigeration.

Variations
Coffee Sauce Add ½ oz/14 g coarsely ground coffee beans to the milk, cream, salt, and sugar and bring to a boil. Cover and allow to steep for 5 to 10 minutes. Strain into a clean saucepan, bring back to a boil, and proceed as directed above.

Cinnamon Sauce Add 1 cinnamon stick to the milk, cream, salt, and sugar and bring to a boil. Cover and allow to steep for 5 to 10 minutes. Strain into a clean saucepan, bring back to a boil, and proceed as directed above.

Peanut Butter Sauce Add 4 oz/113 g peanut butter to 16 fl oz/480 mL Vanilla Sauce. Blend using an immersion blender, cover, and chill.

Lemon Sauce Add ½ oz/14 g grated lemon zest to the milk, cream, salt, and sugar and bring to a boil. Cover and allow to steep for 5 to 10 minutes. Strain into a clean saucepan, bring back to a boil, and proceed as directed above.

Vanilla Sauce

Vanilla sauce, also known as crème anglaise, is one of the fundamental preparations for all pastry shops. It is actually a stirred custard, made with the same ingredients used to prepare a basic baked custard. Because the mixture is stirred constantly as the eggs thicken over heat, the custard stays loose and pourable instead of setting firmly, as it would if baked. Vanilla sauce is used as a sauce accompaniment to many desserts, and also serves as the base for other classical and contemporary applications, such as Bavarian cream and ice cream.

Before you start the sauce, prepare an ice bath. Have a container to hold the finished sauce and a strainer nearby.

After cooking the sauce, immediately pour it through the sieve into the waiting container. Set the container in the ice bath to stop the cooking process, and stir the sauce occasionally as it cools. (Note: If the custard is just slightly overcooked, immediately transfer it to a blender, add a little cold milk or cream, and process until smooth. Blending will rehomogenize the sauce, and the milk or cream will cool it. The rescued sauce will not have quite the same flavor and texture as a properly made sauce, but it should be fine for use as a component in another preparation.)

Once the sauce has cooled, cover the container tightly and refrigerate until you are ready to use it.

Sabayon

Makes 32 fl oz/960 mL

EGG YOLKS	12 oz	340 g
SUGAR	12 oz	340 g
WHITE WINE	12 fl oz	360 mL

1. Combine the egg yolks, sugar, and wine in the bowl of an electric mixer and whip together until thoroughly blended. Place the bowl over a pot of simmering water and heat, whisking constantly, until the mixture is thickened and very foamy and has reached 180°F/82°C.

2. Transfer the bowl to the electric mixer fitted with a wire whip attachment and whip until cool.

3. Transfer the sabayon to a container and cover it with plastic wrap placed directly against the surface to prevent a skin from forming. Sabayon may also be served warm or at room temperature.

Variations   **Zabaglione** Substitute Marsala for the white wine.

Champagne Sabayon Substitute Champagne for the white wine.

Honey Sabayon Substitute honey for the sugar.

Bourbon Sauce Substitute bourbon for the white wine.

Framboise Sabayon Substitute framboise for the white wine.

Calvados Sabayon Substitute calvados for the white wine.

Note   If desired, whip 24 fl oz/720 mL of heavy cream to medium peaks and fold into the cooled sabayon.

Sabayon

Sabayon is a delicate foam of egg yolks, sugar, and wine (Marsala is traditional in the Italian version, zabaglione). The yolks are whipped constantly as they cook over simmering water until a dense, thick foam develops. The mixture should be whipped vigorously. Whipping the mixture serves to incorporate air, developing the foam. Heating the mixture as it is whipped serves a dual purpose. It stabilizes the foam so that the volume is retained (for more about how the proteins in eggs react when cooked, see page 88) and also cooks the eggs sufficiently to make them safe for consumption.

Sabayon is a very rich sauce. For this reason it is traditionally served with lean and/or acidic ingredients such as sliced fresh fruit or berries. Sabayon can be flavored as desired. If chocolate is added, the sauce will lose some of its airiness; the melted chocolate should be stirred in at the very end of the cooking process. This fragile sauce is one of the few dessert sauces that cannot be made ahead and is usually made to order. Sabayon, however, may also serve as the base for a mousse and may be stabilized with gelatin and used as a cake or torte filling.

A properly thickened sabayon "ribbons" off the whisk. Sabayon can be used as a base for mousse, but is also commonly used as a sauce for plated desserts, generally made to order.

Raspberry Sabayon

Makes 32 fl oz/960 mL

EGG YOLKS	9 oz	255 g
SUGAR	9 oz	255 g
RASPBERRY LIQUEUR	6 fl oz	180 mL
HEAVY CREAM	12 fl oz	360 mL

1. Combine the egg yolks, sugar, and liqueur in the bowl of an electric mixer and whip together until thoroughly blended. Place the bowl over a pot of simmering water and whisk constantly until the mixture is thickened and very foamy and has reached approximately 180°F/82°C.

2. Transfer the bowl to the electric mixer fitted with a wire whip attachment and whip on high speed until cool.

3. Whip the heavy cream to soft peaks and gently fold into the sabayon.

4. Serve immediately.

Calvados Sabayon Sauce

Makes 32 fl oz/960 mL

EGG YOLKS	8 oz	227 g
SUGAR	8 oz	227 g
CALVADOS OR OTHER APPLE BRANDY	5½ fl oz	165 mL
HEAVY CREAM	8 fl oz	240 mL

1. Combine the egg yolks, sugar, and Calvados in the bowl of an electric mixer and whip together until thoroughly blended. Place the bowl over a pot of simmering water and heat, whisking constantly, until the mixture is thickened and very foamy and has reached approximately 180°F/82°C.

2. Transfer the bowl to the electric mixer fitted with a wire whip attachment and whip on high speed until cool.

3. Whip the heavy cream to soft peaks and fold into the sabayon.

4. Serve immediately.

Hot Fudge Sauce

Makes 32 fl oz/960 mL

BITTERSWEET CHOCOLATE, melted	13½ oz	383 g
COCOA POWDER	3 oz	85 g
WATER	11 fl oz	330 mL
BUTTER	7 oz	198 g
SUGAR	13 oz	369 g
LIGHT CORN SYRUP	4½ oz	128 g
SALT	½ tsp	2.50 g
VANILLA EXTRACT	1 tbsp	15 mL

1. Place the melted chocolate, cocoa, and water in a saucepan over low heat and stir gently until fully combined. Add the butter, sugar, corn syrup, and salt and simmer over medium heat until thick, about 5 minutes.

2. Remove from the heat and add the vanilla extract.

3. Serve warm.

Chocolate Sauce

The success of any chocolate sauce depends primarily on the quality of the chocolate. Use the best-quality chocolate available to ensure a smooth, richly flavored sauce. The chocolate must also be melted carefully to prevent it from scorching or becoming grainy. Dark chocolate sauces can be made from unsweetened or bittersweet chocolate or a combination of the two. To get the most intense flavor add a measure of cocoa powder, but be sure to adjust the sauce's flavor and sweetness with sugar. Do not dilute ganache to make a chocolate sauce, as the flavor will be reduced too much through thinning; rather, use or develop a chocolate sauce formula that suits the specific needs.

Chocolate Fudge Sauce

Makes 2 lb/907 g

BITTERSWEET CHOCOLATE, finely chopped	6 oz	170 g
BUTTER	2½ oz	71 g
WATER	9 fl oz	270 mL
SUGAR	8 oz	227 g
LIGHT CORN SYRUP	5½ oz	156 g
BRANDY	¾ fl oz	23 mL

1. Melt the chocolate and butter in a stainless-steel bowl set over a pan of barely simmering water, stirring gently to combine.

2. Stir in the water. Stir in the sugar and corn syrup.

3. Transfer the mixture to a saucepan and simmer over low heat until the sugar has melted and all the ingredients are thoroughly combined, about 5 minutes. Remove from the heat and cool slightly.

4. Stir in the brandy.

5. Serve warm.

Chocolate Sauce

Makes 32 fl oz/960 mL

SUGAR	10 oz	284 g
WATER	16 fl oz	480 mL
LIGHT CORN SYRUP	4½ oz	128 g
COCOA POWDER, sifted	4 oz	113 g
BITTERSWEET CHOCOLATE, melted	1 lb	454 g

1. Combine the sugar, water, and corn syrup in a heavy-bottomed saucepan and bring to a boil over medium-high heat. Remove from the heat.

2. Place the cocoa powder in a bowl and add enough of the hot sugar syrup to make a paste, stirring until smooth. Gradually add the remaining syrup and mix until fully incorporated.

3. Add the melted chocolate and blend until fully incorporated.

4. Strain the sauce through a fine-mesh sieve.

5. Serve warm or chilled.

Raspberry Coulis

Makes 32 fl oz/960 mL

RASPBERRIES (fresh or frozen)	2 lb	907 g
SUGAR	1 lb	454 g
LEMON JUICE	2 fl oz	60 mL

1. Combine the raspberries, 8 oz/227 g of the sugar and 1 fl oz/30 mL of the lemon juice in a saucepan over medium heat. Simmer, stirring, until the sugar has dissolved, about 10 minutes.

2. Strain the coulis through a fine-mesh sieve.

3. Add sugar and/or lemon juice to taste, if necessary.

Variations **Strawberry Coulis** Substitute fresh or frozen strawberries for the raspberries.

Kiwi Coulis Substitute kiwi purée for the raspberries.

Mango Coulis Substitute chopped mango for the raspberries.

Note If desired, a slurry made of 2 fl oz/60 mL water and 1 oz/28 g cornstarch (per 32 fl oz/ 960 mL of coulis) can be added to the sauce to thicken it. Bring the coulis to a boil, gradually whisk in the slurry, and bring back to a boil. Cool.

Fruit Sauces

There are two basic categories of fruit sauces: coulis, which is a smooth, puréed mixture made using fresh or frozen fruits; and compotes, which are a chunky mixture made using either dried, fresh, or frozen fruits. Either type of sauce may be cooked or uncooked. However, coulis are typically cooked, or heated only slightly to facilitate the full incorporation of sugar. Compotes, on the other hand, may be simmered for a period of time to infuse flavors, soften dried fruits, or reduce liquids.

Fruit sauces can be made using virtually any type of fruit—fresh, frozen, or dried. It is important to remember to select the highest-quality fruit available. Only the ripest, most flavorful fruits will yield a quality sauce. Fruit must be tasted to be evaluated for flavor and sugar content so that any formula can be adjusted as necessary to achieve the desired sweetness.

Fruit sauces may be used as a base for flourless soufflés. They can also be used to flavor Bavarian cream, buttercream, and other fillings and frostings.

Papaya Coulis

Makes 32 fl oz/960 mL

PAPAYA, peeled, seeded, and cubed	2 each	2 each
PINEAPPLE, peeled, cored, and cubed	½ each	½ each
COCONUT MILK	4 fl oz	120 mL
WHITE CRÈME DE CACAO	2 tbsp	30 mL
RUM	1 tbsp	15 mL
ORANGE JUICE	8 fl oz	240 mL
LEMON JUICE	4 fl oz	120 mL
LIME JUICE	2 fl oz	60 mL
LEMONGRASS, chopped	1 stalk	1 stalk
SUGAR	3 to 6 oz	85 to 170 g

1. Purée the papaya and pineapple in a food processor.
2. Transfer the purée to a saucepan, add the coconut milk, crème de cacao, rum, orange juice, lemon juice, lime juice, lemongrass, and 3oz/85 g sugar and mix well. Bring to a simmer and remove from the heat.
3. Strain the coulis through a fine-mesh sieve.
4. Add sugar to taste, if necessary.
5. Serve warm or cold.

Pineapple Sage Coulis

Makes 32 fl oz/960 mL

MEDIUM PINEAPPLE	1 each	1 each
COCONUT MILK	4 fl oz	120 mL
CUBED PAPAYA, peeled	4 oz	113 g
SUGAR	3 to 5 oz	85 to 142 g
MALIBU RUM	1 fl oz	30 mL
SAGE LEAVES	6 to 8	6 to 8
LIME JUICE	1 fl oz	30 mL
LEMON JUICE	2 fl oz	60 mL

1. Peel and core the pineapple and cut into pieces. Place the pineapple in a saucepan with the coconut milk, papaya, 3 oz/85 g sugar, and the rum. Bring to a simmer and add the sage leaves. Cover, remove from the heat, and cool thoroughly.

2. Remove and discard the sage leaves. Transfer the pineapple mixture to a food processor and purée. Strain through a fine-mesh sieve.

3. Stir the lime and lemon juices into the coulis, blending thoroughly.

4. Add sugar to taste, if necessary.

Plum Röster

Makes 32 fl oz/960 mL

PLUMS, pitted and sliced	3 lb	1.36 kg
SUGAR	5 oz	142 g
WATER	6 fl oz	180 mL
RED WINE (Burgundy)	6 fl oz	180 mL
CINNAMON STICKS	2 each	2 each

1. Combine all the ingredients in a saucepan, bring to a simmer over medium heat, and simmer until the plums are tender, about 30 minutes.

2. Remove the cinnamon stick. Pass the mixture through a food mill or press through a fine-mesh sieve, working as much of the pulp through the mesh as possible.

3. Return the mixture to the saucepan and simmer to reduce by half.

4. Serve warm.

Raspberry Sauce

Makes 32 fl oz/960 mL

RASPBERRY PURÉE	16 fl oz	480 mL
SUGAR	8 oz	227 g
WATER	9 fl oz	270 mL
TAPIOCA STARCH	½ oz	14 g

1. Combine the raspberry purée, sugar, and 8 fl oz/240 mL of the water in a saucepan and bring to a boil.
2. Meanwhile, make a slurry with the tapioca starch and the remaining 1 fl oz/30 mL water.
3. Slowly whisk the slurry into the boiling purée. Return the mixture to a boil, stirring constantly with a whip until thickened.
4. Strain the sauce through a fine-mesh strainer. Cool over an ice bath.

Passion Fruit Sauce

Makes 32 fl oz/960 mL

PASSION FRUIT PURÉE	1 lb 5 oz	595 g
SUGAR	4 to 8 oz	113 to 227 g
WATER	1 fl oz	30 mL
CORNSTARCH	½ oz	14 g
LEMON JUICE	1 fl oz	30 mL

1. Combine the fruit purée and 4 oz/113 g sugar in a saucepan and bring to a boil over medium heat.
2. Meanwhile, make a slurry with the water and cornstarch. Slowly whisk the slurry into the boiling purée and bring back to a boil, whisking until thickened. Remove from the heat.
3. Add sugar and the lemon juice to taste, as necessary. Cool over an ice bath.

Variations **Raspberry Sauce** Substitute raspberry purée for the passion fruit purée.

Papaya Sauce Substitute papaya purée for the passion fruit purée.

Coconut Sauce Substitute coconut purée for the passion fruit purée.

Hot Strawberry Syrup

Makes 32 fl oz/960 mL

STRAWBERRIES (fresh or frozen)	3 lb	1.36 kg
SUGAR	1 lb	454 g
WATER	12 fl oz	360 mL
VANILLA BEAN, split and scraped	1 each	1 each
LEMON JUICE	4 fl oz	120 mL

1. If using frozen strawberries, thaw slightly. Slice the strawberries.

2. Combine the strawberries, sugar, and water in a saucepan, bring to a simmer over medium heat, and simmer until the strawberries are soft, about 15 minutes.

3. Strain the strawberry mixture through a fine-mesh sieve, pressing against the solids with the back of a ladle.

4. Pour the liquid into a saucepan, add the seeds of the vanilla bean and the lemon juice, and simmer until reduced by half, or to the consistency of a syrup, about 30 minutes.

5. Serve hot.

Blood Orange Sauce

Makes 32 fl oz/960 mL

BLOOD ORANGE JUICE	20 fl oz	600 mL
WHITE WINE	6 fl oz	180 mL
SUGAR	6½ oz	184 g
ARROWROOT	1 oz	28 g
WATER	1½ fl oz	45 mL
LEMON JUICE	1 fl oz	30 mL

1. Combine the blood orange juice, wine, and sugar in a heavy-bottomed saucepan and bring to a boil over medium heat, stirring occasionally to dissolve the sugar, and set aside.

2. Make a slurry with the arrowroot and water. Gradually whisk the slurry into the orange juice mixture and return to a boil, whisking constantly.

3. Immediately remove from the heat.

4. Stir in the lemon juice and strain through a fine-mesh sieve. Cool.

Chunky Strawberry Sauce

Makes 20 fl oz/600 mL

STRAWBERRIES	12 oz	340 g
SUGAR	7 to 10 oz	198 to 284 g
WATER	9 fl oz	270 mL
LEMON JUICE	1 tbsp	15 mL
CORNSTARCH	¾ oz	21 g
ORANGE LIQUEUR	2 fl oz	60 mL

1. Chop 12 strawberries into ½-in/1-cm cubes. Reserve.

2. Combine the sugar, the remaining strawberries, 8 fl oz/240 mL of the water, and the lemon juice in a saucepan and bring to a boil. Allow the mixture to simmer for 2 to 3 minutes.

3. Remove from the heat and purée using an immersion blender. Return to the heat and bring back to a boil.

4. Meanwhile, make a slurry with the cornstarch and the remaining 1 fl oz/30 mL water. Gradually whisk the slurry into the sauce and bring back to a boil, whisking until the sauce thickens enough to coat the back of a spoon. Blend in the orange liqueur.

5. Cool the sauce over an ice bath. Refrigerate until needed.

6. Just before serving, fold in the reserved chopped strawberries.

Note   Depending on how ripe the strawberries are, the amount of sugar may need to be adjusted.

Lime Rickey Sauce

Makes 64 fl oz/1.92 L

SUGAR	1 lb 5 oz	595 g
LIME JUICE	10½ fl oz	315 mL
LIGHT RUM	32 fl oz	960 mL

1. Combine all of the ingredients in a saucepan and bring to a boil over medium heat, stirring to dissolve the sugar. Cook, without stirring, until the sauce reaches 220°F/104°C.

2. Remove from the heat and cool completely. Serve chilled or at room temperature.

Coconut Ginger Sauce

Makes 32 fl oz/960 mL

COCONUT MILK	24 fl oz	720 mL
PAPAYA, peeled and cut into small dice	1 each	1 each
LEMONGRASS, finely chopped	2 stalks	2 stalks
GINGER, peeled and thinly sliced	2 oz	57 g
MALIBU RUM	2 fl oz	60 mL
SUGAR	3 to 6 oz	85 to 170 g
LEMON JUICE	1 to 2 fl oz	30 to 60 mL

1. Combine the coconut milk and papaya in a saucepan and simmer over low heat until the papaya is tender, about 15 minutes.

2. Transfer to a food processor and purée. Strain through a fine-mesh sieve and return to the saucepan.

3. Add the lemongrass, ginger, and rum and bring to a simmer. Remove from the heat, cover, and let steep overnight under refrigeration.

4. Strain the sauce. Add the sugar and lemon juice to taste and stir with a whip to combine.

Lemon Verbena Sauce

Makes 24 fl oz/720 mL

LARGE LEMON VERBENA LEAVES	12 each	12 each
WATER	14 fl oz	420 mL
LEMON JUICE	6 fl oz	180 mL
GLUCOSE SYRUP	1 oz	28 g
SUGAR	2 oz	57 g
LEMONGRASS	1 stalk	1 stalk
CORNSTARCH	½ oz	14 g
WHITE WINE	1 fl oz	30 mL

1. Mince 4 of the lemon verbena leaves. Reserve.

2. Combine the water, lemon juice, glucose, sugar, the remaining 8 lemon verbena leaves, and lemongrass in a saucepan and bring to a simmer. Remove from the heat, cover, and allow the mixture to steep for 10 minutes.

3. Cool the mixture, then cover and refrigerate overnight.

4. Strain the lemon verbena mixture through a fine-mesh strainer. Pour into a saucepan and bring to a boil.

5. Meanwhile, make a slurry with the cornstarch and white wine.

6. Gradually whisk the slurry into the sauce and bring back to a boil, whisking until the sauce thickens enough to coat the back of a spoon.

7. Allow the sauce to cool to room temperature.

8. Just before serving, add the reserved minced lemon verbena to the sauce.

Burnt Orange Sauce

Makes 48 fl oz/1.44 mL

ORANGES	1½ each	1½ each
MILK	32 fl oz	960 mL
SUGAR	8 oz	227 g
EGG YOLKS	6 oz	170 g
VANILLA EXTRACT	¼ tsp	1.25 mL

1. Place oranges on a sheet pan and roast in a 375°F/191°C until golden brown. Cut the whole orange into quarters and halve the half.

2. Bring the milk to a boil and add the roasted oranges. Chill over an ice water bath, cover, and refrigerate for 24 hours.

3. Strain the milk and add enough milk to bring it back to 32 fl oz/960 mL.

4. Combine the strained milk with 4 oz/113 g of the sugar in a saucepan and bring to a boil, stirring to dissolve the sugar.

5. Meanwhile, blend the egg yolks with the remaining 4 oz/113 g of sugar, using a whip.

6. Temper the egg yolks by gradually adding one-third of the hot milk, whipping constantly. Return the tempered egg mixture to the remaining hot milk in the saucepan and continue cooking until the mixture thickens enough to coat the back of a spoon.

7. Strain the sauce into a metal container and chill in an ice water bath.

8. Cover with plastic wrap and store under refrigeration.

Fruit Salsa

Makes 1 lb 14 oz/851 g

PAPAYA, cut into small dice	5 oz	142 g
MANGO, cut into small dice	5 oz	142 g
HONEYDEW MELON, cut into small dice	5 oz	142 g
STRAWBERRIES, cut into small dice	5 oz	142 g
PASSION FRUIT JUICE	1 fl oz	30 mL
MINT, finely chopped	1 tbsp	3 g
AMARETTO LIQUEUR	3 fl oz	90 mL
ORANGE JUICE	8 fl oz	240 mL
SUGAR	3 oz	85 g

1. Combine the fruit, passion fruit juice, and mint. Set aside to macerate.
2. Combine the Amaretto, orange juice, and sugar and bring to a boil. Boil until reduced to 7 fl oz/210 mL. Allow to cool to room temperature.
3. Gently blend the reduced liquid into the fruit.
4. Refrigerate until needed.

Orange Marinade

Makes 14 fl oz/420 mL

ORANGE JUICE	4 fl oz	120 mL
HONEY	8 oz	227 g
ORANGE LIQUEUR	4 fl oz	120 mL

1. Combine the orange juice and honey in a saucepan and bring to a simmer.
2. Remove from the heat and stir in the orange liqueur. Allow to cool to room temperature.

Fruit Soaker

Makes 48 fl oz/1.44 L

PORT	8 fl oz	240 mL
ORANGE LIQUEUR	4 fl oz	120 mL
RASPBERRY LIQUEUR	4 fl oz	120 mL
SUGAR	1 oz	28 g
SEASONAL FRUIT, assorted	2 lb 8 oz	1.13 kg

1. Combine the port, orange and raspberry liqueurs, and sugar in a saucepan and bring to a boil over medium heat, stirring to dissolve the sugar.

2. Allow the mixture to cool to room temperature. Clean, peel, and slice the fruit as needed.

3. Pour the port mixture over the fruit, cover, and allow to macerate overnight, tightly covered under refrigeration.

Raisin Sauce

Makes 24 fl oz/720 mL

RAISINS OR CURRANTS	12 oz	340 g
APPLE CIDER	72 fl oz	2.16 L
BROWN SUGAR	4 oz	113 g
GROUND CINNAMON	½ tsp	1 g
GROUND NUTMEG	¼ tsp	0.5 g
VANILLA BEAN	2 each	2 each
APPLE BRANDY	4 fl oz	120 mL

1. Combine the raisins and 8 fl oz/240 mL of the apple cider in a saucepan and bring to a simmer over low heat. Remove from the heat and allow the raisins to plump for at least 30 minutes.

2. Combine the remaining 64 fl oz/1.92 L apple cider, the brown sugar, cinnamon, and nutmeg in a saucepan. Split the vanilla bean and scrape the seeds into the pan. Bring to a simmer and reduce by two-thirds, about 30 minutes.

3. Meanwhile, drain the raisins; set aside.

4. Remove the pan from the heat and stir the apple brandy and plumped raisins into the sauce.

5. Serve warm or chilled.

Dried Cherry Sauce

Makes 1 lb 10 oz/737 g

SUGAR	3 oz	85 g
RED WINE	13 fl oz	390 mL
WATER	6 fl oz	180 mL
ORANGE JUICE	1 fl oz	30 mL
LEMON JUICE	1 fl oz	30 mL
VANILLA BEAN	1 each	1 each
DRIED CHERRIES	4 oz	113 g
CORNSTARCH	½ oz	14 g

1. Combine the sugar, 12 oz/360 mL of the red wine, the water, orange juice, and lemon juice in a saucepan. Split the vanilla bean, scrape the seeds into the pan, add the pod, and bring the mixture to a boil. Remove from the heat and add the cherries.

2. Refrigerate, covered, overnight.

3. Strain the sauce, reserving the cherries. Pour the sauce into a saucepan and bring to a boil.

4. Meanwhile, make a slurry with the cornstarch and the remaining 1 fl oz/30 mL red wine. Gradually whisk the slurry into the sauce and bring back to a boil, whisking until the sauce thickens enough to coat the back of a spoon.

5. Allow the sauce to cool to room temperature.

6. Add the reserved cherries and serve at once.

Candied Cranberry Compote

Makes 32 fl oz/960 mL

SUGAR	1 lb 12 oz	794 g
WATER	24 fl oz	720 mL
CRANBERRIES (fresh or frozen)	1 lb 14 oz	851 g
ORANGE JUICE	4 fl oz	120 mL
CINNAMON STICK	1 each	1 each

1. To prepare the candied cranberries, combine 1 lb 8 oz/680 g of the sugar and 12 fl oz/360 mL of the water in a heavy-bottomed saucepan and bring to a simmer over medium-high heat, stirring until the sugar has dissolved.

2. Add the cranberries and poach until tender; do not allow the syrup to come to a boil. Remove from the heat and allow the cranberries to cool completely in the sugar syrup.

3. Drain the cranberries and spread them on a parchment-lined sheet pan. Dry in a 200°F/93°C oven until they are just slightly sticky, about 1½ hours. Reserve.

4. To prepare the sauce, combine 6 oz/170 g of the cranberries with the remaining 12 fl oz/360 mL water, the orange juice, the remaining 4 oz/113 g sugar, and the cinnamon stick in a saucepan and simmer over medium heat until the cranberries burst and are very soft, about 20 minutes.

5. Remove the cinnamon stick and purée the mixture in a food processor. Transfer to a bowl and gently stir in the remaining candied cranberries.

6. Add sugar to taste, if necessary.

Cranberry Sauce

Makes 20 fl oz/600 mL

FRESH CRANBERRIES	12 oz	340 g
SUGAR	5 oz	142 g
WATER	8 fl oz	240 mL
VANILLA BEAN	1 each	1 each

1. Combine the cranberries, sugar, and water in a saucepan. Split the vanilla bean, scrape the seeds into the pan, add the pod, and bring to a boil over medium heat, whisking to break up the cranberries. Boil until the sauce has reduced slightly and thickened, about 5 minutes.

2. Remove from the heat and cool completely.

Cider Bourbon Sauce

Makes 32 fl oz/960 mL

APPLE CIDER	32 fl oz	960 mL
BOURBON	2 fl oz	60 mL
ARROWROOT	1 oz	28 g

1. Combine 28 fl oz/840 mL of the apple cider with the bourbon in a saucepan and bring to a boil over medium heat.

2. Meanwhile, make a slurry with the arrowroot and the remaining 4 fl oz/120 mL apple cider. Gradually whisk the slurry into the cider mixture and bring back to a boil, whisking constantly until thickened. Immediately remove from the heat.

3. Strain the sauce through a fine-mesh sieve. Cool.

Apple Butter

Makes 32 fl oz/960 mL

APPLES	7 lb	3.18 kg
APPLE CIDER	24 fl oz	720 mL
SUGAR	1 lb	454 g
GROUND CARDAMOM	1 tbsp	6 g
GROUND CINNAMON	2 tsp	4 g
LEMON ZEST, grated	1 tsp	3 g
SALT	¼ tsp	1.25 g

1. Peel, core, and slice the apples. Combine with the apple cider in a large heavy-bottomed saucepan, cover, and bring to a simmer. Simmer until the apples are a soft pulp, about 30 minutes.

2. Pass the apple pulp through a food mill and transfer to a saucepan.

3. Add the sugar, spices, zest, and salt to the apple purée and simmer, stirring frequently, until very thick, about 2 hours.

4. Cool completely.

Variations **Pear Butter** Substitute pears for the apples and pear juice or pear cider for the apple cider.

Peach Butter Substitute peaches for the apples and peach juice or nectar for the apple cider.

Nectarine Butter Substitute nectarines for the apples and apple juice for the apple cider.

Mango Butter Substitute mangoes for the apples and apple juice for the apple cider.

Adding butter to
caramel sauce

Orange Vanilla Bean Sauce

Makes 16 fl oz/480 mL

ORANGE JUICE	16 fl oz	480 mL
WHITE WINE	8 fl oz	240 mL
SUGAR	4 oz	113 g
CINNAMON STICK	1 each	1 each
VANILLA BEAN	1 each	1 each
TAPIOCA STARCH	½ oz	14 g
WATER	1 fl oz	30 mL
ORANGE LIQUEUR	2 fl oz	60 mL

1. Combine the orange juice, white wine, sugar, and cinnamon stick in a saucepan. Split the vanilla bean, scrape the seeds into the pan, add the pod, and bring to a simmer. Stir to dissolve the sugar. Simmer for 15 minutes to reduce and blend the flavors.

2. Make a slurry with the tapioca starch and water. Gradually whisk the slurry into the sauce and cook, whisking, until the sauce thickens enough to coat the back of a spoon.

3. Remove from the heat, strain through a fine strainer, and add the orange liqueur. Cool and serve.

Classic Caramel Sauce

Makes 32 fl oz/960 mL

HEAVY CREAM	24 fl oz	720 mL
SUGAR	13 oz	369 g
GLUCOSE SYRUP	10 oz	284 g
BUTTER, soft, cut into cubes	2¼ oz	64 g

1. Place the cream in a saucepan and bring to a boil over medium heat. Leave over very low heat to keep warm.

2. Prepare an ice bath. Combine the sugar and glucose syrup in a heavy-bottomed saucepan and slowly cook over moderate heat, stirring constantly until all the sugar has dissolved. Stop stirring and continue to cook to a golden caramel. Remove from the heat and shock the saucepan in the ice bath to stop the cooking.

3. Remove from the ice bath and stir in the butter. Carefully stir in the hot cream, mixing until fully blended. Cool.

Caramel Sauce

There are two basic types of caramel sauce: clear and enriched. Clear caramel sauce is made by cooking sugar to a deep, richly flavorful caramel and then adding a liquid. A good standard ratio for making clear caramel sauce is one part by weight of sugar to two parts liquid. The liquid added to the caramel to make the sauce may be anything from water to fruit juices to liqueurs or any combination thereof, depending on the desired flavor profile. Clear caramel sauce does not require that any enrichments be added; however, a small amount of butter is often used to "finish" the sauce by stirring it in after the addition of liquid. Enriched caramel sauces, like their clear counterparts, start with caramelizing sugar, but always have butter and some type of liquid dairy product, usually heavy cream, added as an enrichment. The fat and emulsifiers present in the butter and cream add body and flavor to the sauce. It is important to remember that the liquid (water, fruit juice, liqueur, cream, etc.) which is to be added to caramel must be warmed first to prevent spattering of hot liquid or sugar. Flavors can be infused into clear or enriched caramel sauces by adding ingredients such as spices, teas, or coffee beans to the mixture after liquid has been added. These ingredients should be allowed to steep with the sauce for a few minutes to impart their full flavor and then strained from the sauce before serving. Caramel sauce can be used not only as a sauce accompaniment for a plated dessert but also as the filling for a confection, for décor, or as the base or flavoring for a filling.

Espresso Caramel Sauce
Makes 32 fl oz/960 mL

SUGAR	1 lb	454 g
BREWED COFFEE, warm	20 fl oz	600 mL
ESPRESSO COFFEE BEANS (tied up in cheesecloth)	1 oz	28 g
CINNAMON STICKS	2 each	2 each
VANILLA BEANS	2 each	2 each
HEAVY CREAM	10 fl oz	300 mL
CORNSTARCH	½ oz	14 g
WATER	1 fl oz	30 mL
BUTTER	2 oz	57 g
BRANDY	2 fl oz	60 mL

1. Add a small amount of the sugar to a medium-hot pan set over medium heat and allow it to melt, then add the remaining sugar in small increments, allowing each addition to fully melt before adding the next. Continue this process until all the sugar has been added to the pan and cook to the desired color. Remove from the heat and shock in an ice bath for 10 seconds to stop the cooking process.

2. Carefully add the coffee to the caramel and stir to combine. Add the sachet of espresso and cinnamon sticks. Split the vanilla beans, scrape the seeds into the mixture, add the pods, and simmer until the caramel is infused with the flavoring ingredients, about 15 minutes. Add the heavy cream.

3. Make a slurry with the cornstarch and water. Gradually whisk the slurry into the sauce. Bring the mixture to a boil. Remove the pan from the heat.

4. Stir in the butter and brandy and mix until fully blended.

Clear Apple Caramel Sauce

Makes 48 fl oz/1.44 L

SUGAR	1 lb	454 g
APPLE JUICE, warm	28 fl oz	840 mL
APPLE BRANDY, warm	4 fl oz	120 mL
CINNAMON STICK	1 each	1 each
NUTMEG, cracked	1 each	1 each
BUTTER	2 oz	57 g

1. To prepare the caramel, add a small amount of the sugar to a medium-hot pan set over medium heat and allow it to melt, then add the remaining sugar in small increments, allowing each addition to fully melt before adding the next. Continue this process until all the sugar has been added to the pan and cook to the desired color.

2. Add the apple juice and apple brandy. Stir over medium heat to dissolve the sugar. Add the cinnamon stick and nutmeg and simmer for 20 minutes.

3. Stir in the butter.

Note   Depending on desired consistency the sauce can be thickened before the butter is added with a cornstarch slurry made with 1 tsp/3 g of cornstarch and 2 fl oz/60 mL of apple juice.

Variations   **Clear Pear Caramel Sauce** Replace an equal amount of pear liqueur for the apple brandy and an equal amount of pear cider for the apple juice.

Clear Orange Caramel Sauce Omit the cinnamon and nutmeg. Split and scrape one vanilla bean, adding the seeds and pod to the caramel in Step 2. Replace an equal amount of orange liqueur for the apple brandy and an equal amount of pulp-free orange juice for the apple juice.

Butterscotch Sauce

Makes 48 fl oz/1.44 L

BROWN SUGAR	1 lb 7 oz	652 g
FLOUR	3½ oz	99 g
SALT	1 tsp	5 g
MILK	32 fl oz	960 mL
EGG YOLKS	2½ oz	71 g
BUTTER	2 oz	57 g
VANILLA EXTRACT	½ fl oz	15 mL

1. Combine the brown sugar, flour, and salt in a bowl and place over a pan of barely simmering water. Add the milk gradually, stirring with a whip to combine. Cook for 10 minutes.

2. Place the egg yolks in a bowl and temper with a small amount of the warmed brown sugar mixture, whisking constantly. Add the tempered egg yolk mixture to the remaining brown sugar mixture and cook the sauce over a pan of barely simmering water, stirring constantly with a whisk for 2 minutes.

3. Remove the sauce from the heat and stir in the butter and vanilla.

Milk Chocolate Caramel Fudge Sauce

Makes 32 fl oz/960 mL

SUGAR	1 lb	454 g
WATER	4 fl oz	120 mL
LIGHT CORN SYRUP	4 oz	113 g
HEAVY CREAM, warmed	20 fl oz	600 mL
MILK CHOCOLATE, finely chopped	7 oz	198 g

1. Combine the sugar, water, and corn syrup in a heavy-bottomed saucepan and bring to a boil over medium-high heat, stirring to dissolve the sugar. Cook, without stirring, to a rich golden amber.

2. Carefully blend the warm heavy cream into the caramel. Remove the pan from the heat, add the chocolate, and stir until the chocolate is melted and thoroughly combined.

3. Adjust the consistency with heavy cream, if desired.

4. Serve warm or cold.

Ginger Rum Sauce

Makes 24 fl oz/720 mL

PINEAPPLE JUICE	18 fl oz	540 mL
SUGAR	8 oz	227 g
VANILLA BEAN	1 each	1 each
GINGER, cut into ⅛-in/3-mm slices	1½ oz	43 g
JAMAICAN DARK RUM	3 fl oz	90 mL
CORNSTARCH	½ oz	14 g
WATER	2 fl oz	60 mL
BUTTER	1½ oz	43 g

1. Bring the pineapple juice to a boil. Place over very low heat to keep warm.

2. To prepare the caramel, add a small amount of the sugar to a medium-hot pan set over medium heat and allow it to melt, then add the remaining sugar in small increments, allowing each addition to fully melt before adding the next. Continue this process until all the sugar has been added to the pan and cook to the desired color.

3. Carefully add the warm pineapple juice to the caramel, stirring constantly. Split the vanilla bean, scrape the seeds into the pan, add the pod and ginger, and simmer for 30 minutes to infuse the sauce with their flavors.

4. Add the rum and bring the sauce back to a simmer.

5. Meanwhile, make a slurry with the cornstarch and water. Gradually add the slurry to the sauce, whisking constantly, and cook until the sauce comes back to a boil and coats the back of a spoon.

6. Blend in the butter.

7. Serve warm or chilled.

Honey Cardamom Sauce

Makes 20 fl oz/600 mL

APPLE JUICE	10 fl oz	300 mL
PINEAPPLE JUICE	10 fl oz	300 mL
SUGAR	12 oz	340 g
HONEY	8 oz	227 g
GROUND CARDAMOM	½ tsp	1 g
CORNSTARCH	½ oz	14 g
WATER	2 fl oz	60 mL
BUTTER	½ oz	14 g
ANISE LIQUEUR	1 tbsp	15 mL

1. Bring the apple juice and pineapple juice to a boil. Place over very low heat to keep warm.

2. Place the sugar in a heavy-bottomed saucepan and cook, stirring constantly, over medium heat to a rich golden brown, occasionally washing down the sides of the pan with a wet pastry brush.

3. Add the honey to the caramel and stir until incorporated. Carefully add the warm apple juice mixture, stirring constantly. Add the cardamom and simmer for 15 to 20 minutes to blend the flavors.

4. Make a slurry with the cornstarch and water. Gradually whisk the slurry into the sauce and cook, whisking constantly, until the sauce coats the back of a spoon.

5. Blend in the butter and anise liqueur.

6. Serve warm or cold.

Honey Cognac Sauce

Makes 32 fl oz/960 mL

HONEY	1 lb 3 oz	539 g
GLUCOSE SYRUP	9 oz	255 g
COGNAC	4½ fl oz	135 mL
GROUND CINNAMON	2 tsp	4 g
LEMON JUICE	1 fl oz	30 mL

1. Combine the honey, glucose syrup, and cognac in a heavy-bottomed saucepan and bring to a boil over medium heat. Boil for 2 minutes.

2. Remove the pan from the heat and add the cinnamon and lemon juice.

Vanilla Sauternes Reduction

Makes 20 fl oz/600 mL

SAUTERNES	25 fl oz	750 mL
VANILLA BEANS, split and scraped	4 each	4 each
SUGAR	3 oz	85 g

1. Place the Sauternes in a saucepan, bring to a boil over medium heat, and reduce by one-quarter.

2. Add the vanilla seeds and sugar and heat, stirring, just until the sugar is dissolved, about 2 minutes. Strain through a fine-mesh sieve.

Note Reducing the sauce too far will cause it to discolor.

Reduction sauces have a coating consistency.

Reduction Sauces

Reduction sauces are prepared by simmering juices or wines and other alcoholic beverages over low to moderate heat to thicken and develop their individual characteristic flavors. Reducing liquids to create these types of sauces not only serves to enhance the desired flavor of the ingredient but may also concentrate undesirable characteristics. For this reason, be careful when selecting ingredients for a reduction sauce, as some do not reduce successfully. The reduction will also create the desired consistency, so monitor the sauce as it is cooking for consistency at the required service temperature.

Cherry Sauce

Makes 32 fl oz/960 mL

DRIED CHERRIES	1 lb	454 g
SUGAR	12 oz	340 g
RED WINE	14 fl oz	420 mL
CHERRY LIQUEUR	1 fl oz	30 mL
CINNAMON STICKS	2 each	2 each
LEMON JUICE	1 fl oz	30 mL

1. Combine the cherries, sugar, wine, cherry liqueur, and cinnamon sticks in a saucepan, bring to a simmer over medium heat, and simmer until the cherries are tender, about 30 minutes.

2. Remove the cinnamon sticks, transfer the mixture to a food processor, and purée until smooth.

3. Strain the sauce through a fine-mesh strainer and stir in the lemon juice.

4. Serve warm or cold.

Pineapple Honey Beurre Blanc

Makes 1 lb/454 g

PINEAPPLE JUICE	8 fl oz	240 mL
WHITE WINE	8 fl oz	240 mL
HONEY	2 oz	57 g
GINGER, minced	½ oz	14 g
ALLSPICE BERRIES	8 each	8 each
BUTTER, cut into ½-in/1-cm cubes	1 lb	454 g

1. Combine the pineapple juice, white wine, honey, ginger, and allspice berries in a saucepan, bring to a boil, and boil until reduced to the consistency of a heavy syrup.

2. Reduce the heat to low and whisk in the butter gradually to maintain the emulsion.

3. Keep warm in a bain-marie until ready to serve.

Champagne Sauce

Makes 32 fl oz/960 mL

CHAMPAGNE	16 fl oz	480 mL
ORANGE JUICE	4 fl oz	120 mL
SUGAR	6 oz	170 g
WHITE GRAPES, cut in half	4 oz	113 g
WHITE WINE	1½ fl oz	45 mL
CORNSTARCH	⅔ oz	19 g
ORANGE LIQUEUR	1 tbsp	15 mL

1. Combine the Champagne and orange juice in a saucepan and bring to a boil over medium heat. Add the sugar and grapes and simmer, stirring gently, until the grapes are tender, about 5 minutes.

2. Meanwhile, make a slurry with the white wine and cornstarch. Gradually and constantly whisk the slurry into the sauce and bring back to a boil, whisking constantly.

3. Strain the sauce through a fine-mesh sieve.

4. Stir in the orange liqueur. Cool completely.

Variation   **White Wine Sauce** Substitute white wine for the Champagne.

Orange Hard Sauce

Makes 1 lb 9 oz/709 g

BUTTER, soft	1 lb	454 g
CONFECTIONERS' SUGAR	8½ oz	241 g
ORANGE ZEST, grated	½ oz	14 g
ORANGE JUICE	2 tbsp	30 mL

1. Cream together the butter and sugar in an electric mixer fitted with a paddle attachment on medium speed, scraping down the bowl periodically, until smooth and light in color, about 5 minutes.

2. Add the orange zest and juice and blend until fully incorporated.

3. Fill a pastry bag fitted with a No. 3 star tip with the mixture and pipe rosettes onto parchment paper. Chill well before serving.

Lemon Hard Sauce

Makes 2 lb/907 g

BUTTER, soft	1 lb	454 g
CONFECTIONERS' SUGAR	8½ oz	241 g
DARK RUM	6½ fl oz	195 mL
LEMON JUICE	1 fl oz	30 mL

1. Cream together the butter and sugar in an electric mixer fitted with a paddle attachment on medium speed, scraping down the bowl periodically, until smooth and light in color, about 5 minutes.

2. Add the rum and lemon juice in several additions, blending well after each addition.

3. Fill a pastry bag fitted with a No. 3 star tip with the mixture and pipe rosettes onto parchment paper. Chill well before serving.

Variations   **Honey Hard Sauce** Substitute 2 tbsp/19 g honey for the confectioners' sugar.

Anise Hard Sauce Substitute ½ fl oz/15 mL anise extract for the rum.

Brown Sugar–Butter Rub

Makes 1 lb 4 oz/567 g

BUTTER	4 oz	113 g
BROWN SUGAR	1 lb	454 g

1. Melt the butter in a saucepan over low heat. Add the brown sugar and blend well. Allow the mixture to cool completely before applying to fruit.

CHAPTER 13

Frozen Desserts

SUGAR SYRUPS, DAIRY AND CUSTARD MIXTURES, AND FRUIT PURÉES MAY ALL BE USED AS THE BASE TO MAKE FROZEN DESSERTS. ANY OF THESE BASES MAY THEN BE CHURN- OR STILL-FROZEN. EACH OF THESE TWO METHODS OF PRODUCTION WILL YIELD FROZEN DESSERTS WITH VASTLY DIFFERENT TEXTURES. UNDERSTANDING THE PRINCIPLES OF EACH TYPE OF FROZEN DESSERT WILL GIVE THE CHEF CREATIVE FREEDOM TO EXPLORE DIFFERENT POSSIBILITIES OF FLAVOR, TEXTURE, AND PRESENTATION.

Vanilla Ice Cream

Makes 48 fl oz/1.44 L

MILK	16 fl oz	480 mL
HEAVY CREAM	16 fl oz	480 mL
SUGAR	7 oz	198 g
GLUCOSE SYRUP	1 oz	28 g
SALT	1/4 tsp	1.25 g
VANILLA BEAN	1 each	1 each
EGG YOLKS	10 oz	284 g

1. Combine the milk, heavy cream, 3½ oz/99 g of the sugar, the glucose syrup, and salt in a saucepan. Split the vanilla bean, scrape the seeds into the pan, add the pod, and bring the mixture just to a boil over medium heat. Immediately remove from the heat, cover the pan, and let steep for 5 minutes.

2. Remove the vanilla pod and return the mixture to a simmer.

3. Meanwhile, blend the egg yolks with the remaining 3½ oz/99 g sugar to make the liaison. Temper by gradually adding about one-third of the hot milk mixture, whipping constantly. Return the tempered egg mixture to the remaining hot milk in the saucepan and cook, stirring constantly, until the mixture thickens enough to coat the back of a spoon (180°F/82°C).

4. Strain the ice cream base into a metal container and immediately transfer to an ice bath. Cool to below 40°F/4°C. Cover and refrigerate for a minimum of 12 hours, or overnight.

5. Process in an ice cream machine according to the manufacturer's instructions. Pack into storage containers or molds as desired and freeze for several hours, or overnight, before serving or using in plated desserts.

Variations   **Cinnamon Ice Cream** Replace the vanilla bean with ¼ tsp/1.25 g ground cinnamon in Step 1.

Vanilla, coffee,
and chocolate
ice creams

Churn-Frozen Ice Cream

The basic ingredients for ice cream are milk, cream, sugar, flavorings, and, sometimes, eggs. There are two basic types of ice cream. Custard ice cream, also known as French ice cream, is made with a base of a stirred egg custard (essentially vanilla sauce). The second type does not include eggs. The base is made by simply heating the cream and milk to incorporate the sugar and other ingredients.

Regardless of the type of base, it is good practice to age it under refrigeration (at approximately 40°F/4°C) for several hours before freezing. Aging allows the protein network to absorb more of the moisture present in the base, leaving less water available to form ice crystals, resulting in a smoother ice cream. Churn the chilled base only to "soft-serve" consistency and then extract from the machine, pack into containers, and place in a freezer for several hours to allow it to firm to a servable temperature and consistency.

All the ingredients add flavor to the ice cream, but each one also plays a part in determining consistency and mouth feel. The eggs in custard ice cream make it richer and smoother than its eggless counterpart, both because of the fat and emulsifiers contributed by the egg yolks and because cooking the proteins present in the eggs binds, or holds moisture, interfering with the formation of ice crystals, which results in smaller ice crystals, thus lending a smoother texture to the finished ice cream. (For more about emulsifiers and cooking proteins, see page 88).

Extracting ice cream from the machine

The cream and eggs in ice cream allow for the incorporation of air during freezing. The air incorporated into ice cream, known as "overrun," gives it a smoother mouth feel and lighter body. Too much overrun, however, will diminish the flavor, make the ice cream too soft, and make it melt quickly. Overrun amounts, indicated in percentages, represent the amount of air contained in the ice cream. The legal limit for overrun imposed by the FDA is 100 percent, which would indicate the ice cream increasing in volume by half.

The solids present in milk and cream interfere with the formation of ice crystals, while their emulsifiers help to bind together the liquids and fats. Both of these actions affect mouth feel, as they result in a finer, smoother texture.

Milk powder is often added to ice cream made without eggs. It helps to bind excess liquid in the mixture that would otherwise result in the formation of large ice crystals.

For best results, use a mixture of milk and cream to avoid having too much butterfat in the mix. The butterfat content of ice cream typically ranges from 10 to 14 percent. Butterfat is important, as it contributes both flavor and richness of mouth feel. However, too much fat will result in an undesirable grainy mouth feel. For the same reason, use care in adding ingredients high in butterfat, such as white chocolate, so as not to increase the fat content of the ice cream to an undesirable level.

Sugar both adds sweetness and lowers the freezing point of the base, keeping the ice cream from freezing too hard. Invert sugars, such as corn syrup and glucose syrup, improve texture and help prevent the formation of large ice crystals.

There are a number of methods for adding flavorings to ice cream. Flavorings such as vanilla bean, tea, coffee, or spices can be infused into the milk and cream as they are heating. Then cook the ice cream base as usual, with the flavorings, and strain them out before freezing. Purées can be blended into the custard after it has cooled, or folded into still-soft, just-churned ice cream for a swirled effect. Melted chocolate can be added to the still-warm, just-cooked ice cream base, while nut pastes, such as peanut butter and praline paste, are added to the ice cream base after it is cooked. They may be added while the base is still warm or carefully blended into an aged, chilled base.

Flavoring Ice Cream with Extracts and Compounds

Extracts or compounds such as praline paste and other concentrated, low-moisture flavorings can be added to an ice cream base without affecting the texture of the ice cream.

To use praline paste or other nut pastes, including peanut butter, or melted chocolate, make the ice cream base as directed. As soon as you remove the base from the heat, add the desired flavoring and stir until evenly blended, or add to a base that has been chilled and aged, blending carefully to ensure full incorporation.

Chocolate Ice Cream

Makes 48 fl oz/1.44 L

MILK	16 fl oz	480 mL
HEAVY CREAM	16 fl oz	480 mL
SUGAR	7 oz	198 g
GLUCOSE SYRUP	1 oz	28 g
SALT	¼ tsp	1.25 g
VANILLA BEAN	1 each	1 each
EGG YOLKS	10 oz	284 g
BITTERSWEET CHOCOLATE, melted	6 oz	170 g

1. Combine the milk, heavy cream, 3½ oz/99 g of the sugar, the glucose syrup, salt, and vanilla pod and seeds in a saucepan and bring just to a boil over medium heat. Immediately remove from the heat, cover the pan, and let steep for 5 minutes.

2. Remove the vanilla pod and return the mixture to a simmer.

3. Meanwhile, blend the egg yolks with the remaining 3½ oz/99 g sugar to make the liaison. Temper by gradually adding about one-third of the hot milk mixture, whipping constantly. Return the tempered egg mixture to the remaining hot milk in the saucepan and cook, stirring constantly, until the mixture thickens enough to coat the back of a spoon (180°F/82°C).

4. Remove the pan from the heat and stir in the chocolate until smooth and fully combined. Strain the mixture into a metal container and immediately transfer to an ice bath. Cool to below 40°F/4°C. Cover and refrigerate for a minimum of 12 hours, or overnight.

5. Process in an ice cream machine according to the manufacturer's instructions. Pack into storage containers and freeze for several hours, or overnight, before serving, molding, or using in plated desserts.

Variations   **Milk Chocolate Ice Cream** Reduce the sugar to 4 oz/113 g and replace the bittersweet chocolate with 8 oz/227 g milk chocolate.

White Chocolate Ice Cream Reduce the sugar to 3 oz/85 g and replace the bittersweet chocolate with 8 oz/227 g white chocolate.

Coffee Ice Cream

Makes 48 fl oz/1.44 L

MILK	16 fl oz	480 mL
HEAVY CREAM	16 fl oz	480 mL
SUGAR	7 oz	198 g
GLUCOSE SYRUP	1 oz	28 g
COARSELY GROUND COFFEE BEANS	2 oz	57 g
SALT	1/4 tsp	1.25 g
EGG YOLKS	10 oz	284 g

1. Combine the milk, heavy cream, 3½ oz/99 g of the sugar, the glucose syrup, coffee beans, and salt in a saucepan and bring just to a boil over medium heat. Immediately remove from the heat, cover the pan, and let steep for 5 minutes.

2. Strain the mixture into a clean pan and return to a simmer.

3. Meanwhile, blend the egg yolks with the remaining 3½ oz/99 g sugar to make the liaison. Temper by gradually adding about one-third of the hot milk mixture, whipping constantly. Return the tempered egg mixture to the remaining hot milk in the saucepan and cook, stirring constantly, until the mixture thickens enough to coat the back of a spoon (180°F/82°C).

4. Strain the mixture into a metal container and immediately transfer to an ice bath. Cool to below 40°F/4°C. Cover and refrigerate for a minimum of 12 hours, or overnight.

5. Process in an ice cream machine according to the manufacturer's instructions. Pack into storage containers and freeze for several hours, or overnight, before serving, molding, or using in plated desserts.

Variations   **Green Tea, Earl Grey, or Chai Ice Cream** Replace the coffee beans with ½ oz/14 g of green, Earl Grey, or chai tea leaves.

Star Anise Ice Cream Replace the coffee beans with 1¼ oz/35 g toasted star anise. Do not strain the custard after cooking; leave the anise in the base during refrigeration, then strain before freezing.

Toasted Coconut Ice Cream Replace the coffee beans with 6 oz/170 g lightly toasted unsweetened coconut.

Cardamom Ice Cream Replace the coffee beans with ½ oz/14 g chopped green cardamom pods.

Almond Ice Cream Replace the coffee beans with 4 oz/113 g almond paste.

Praline Ice Cream Replace the coffee beans with 4 oz/113 g praline paste.

Pistachio Ice Cream Replace the coffee beans with 4 oz/113 g pistachio paste.

Peanut Butter Ice Cream Replace the coffee beans with 4 oz/113 g peanut butter.

Raspberry Ice Cream

Makes 48 fl oz/1.44 L

HEAVY CREAM	16 fl oz	480 mL
SUGAR	7 oz	198 g
GLUCOSE SYRUP	1 oz	28 g
SALT	1/4 tsp	1.25 g
EGG YOLKS	10 oz	284 g
RASPBERRY PURÉE	1 lb	454 g

1. Combine the heavy cream, 3½ oz/99 g of the sugar, the glucose syrup, and salt in a saucepan and bring just to a simmer over medium heat.

2. Meanwhile, blend the egg yolks with the remaining 3½ oz/99 g sugar to make the liaison. Temper by gradually adding about one-third of the hot cream mixture, whipping constantly. Return the tempered egg mixture to the remaining hot milk in the saucepan and cook, stirring constantly, until the mixture thickens enough to coat the back of a spoon (180°F/82°C).

3. Strain the mixture into a metal container and immediately transfer to an ice bath. Cool to below 40°F/4°C. Cover and refrigerate for a minimum of 12 hours, or overnight. Blend in the raspberry purée.

4. Process in an ice cream machine according to the manufacturer's instructions. Pack into storage containers or molds and freeze for several hours, or overnight, before serving or using in plated desserts.

Variations **Banana Ice Cream** Replace the raspberry purée with an equal amount of banana purée.

Mango Ice Cream Replace the raspberry purée with an equal amount of mango purée.

Peach Ice Cream Replace the raspberry purée with an equal amount of peach purée.

Passion Fruit Ice Cream Add 8 fl oz/240 mL of milk to the formula in Step 1 with the heavy cream. Replace the raspberry purée with 8 fl oz/240 mL of passion fruit concentrate.

Adding Fruits to Ice Cream

Fresh and puréed fruits are wonderful as garnishes or flavorings for ice creams and other frozen desserts. Depending on the fruit or product, they can be added whole or in chunks, folded in as a swirl, or used as a flavoring for the ice cream base. Whenever you use fresh fruit, taste it to see how sweet it is, then increase or decrease the amount of sweetener you are adding to the base as necessary.

Folding a garnish into ice cream

To use fresh fruit as a garnish in ice cream, poach it in a sugar syrup to prevent it from freezing too hard. For soft fruits, bring the syrup to a boil, then remove from the heat, add the fruit, cover, and allow to stand until cool. Drain the fruit and chill. Fold the poached fruit into the soft ice cream just as it comes from the machine. For harder fruits, use the same technique but leave the fruit in the syrup for approximately 15 minutes, making sure the temperature is maintained between 160° and 180°F/71° and 82°C.

To flavor an ice cream using a fruit purée such as raspberry, peach, mango, or banana, omit the milk when making the base. Age the ice cream as usual, then blend in the desired fruit purée in a quantity equal to the original amount of milk in the formula. Freeze as usual. For very strongly flavored fruits, such as passion fruit or fruit concentrates, replace only half of the milk in the formula with the fruit purée.

Chocolate Swirl Ice Cream

Makes 48 fl oz/1.44 L

MILK	16 fl oz	480 mL
HEAVY CREAM	16 fl oz	480 mL
SUGAR	7 oz	198 g
GLUCOSE SYRUP	1 oz	28 g
SALT	¼ tsp	1.25 g
VANILLA BEAN, split and scraped	1 each	1 each
EGG YOLKS	10 oz	284 g
HARD GANACHE (page 425)	1 lb	454 g

1. Combine the milk, heavy cream, 3½ oz/99 g of the sugar, the glucose syrup, salt, and vanilla pod and seeds in a saucepan and bring just to a boil over medium heat. Immediately remove from the heat, cover the pan, and let steep for 5 minutes.

2. Remove the vanilla pod and return the mixture to a simmer.

3. Meanwhile, blend the egg yolks with the remaining 3½ oz/99 g sugar to make the liaison. Temper by gradually adding about one-third of the hot milk mixture, whipping constantly. Return the tempered egg mixture to the remaining hot milk in the saucepan and cook, stirring constantly, until the mixture thickens enough to coat the back of a spoon (180°F/82°C).

4. Strain the mixture into a metal container and immediately transfer to an ice bath. Cool to below 40°F/4°C. Cover and refrigerate for a minimum of 12 hours, or overnight.

5. Process in an ice cream machine according to the manufacturer's instructions. Transfer to a bowl and fold in the ganache, leaving visible streaks for a marbleized effect. Pack into storage containers and freeze for several hours, or overnight, before serving, molding, or using in plated desserts.

Variations   **Caramel Swirl Ice Cream** Substitute soft caramel for the ganache.

Fruit Swirl Ice Cream Substitute highly reduced fruit purée for the ganache.

Soft Caramel Filling

Makes 1 lb 12 oz/794 g

SUGAR	1 lb	454 g
LEMON JUICE	½ tsp	2.50 mL
HEAVY CREAM, warm	8 fl oz	240 mL
BUTTER	4 oz	113 g

1. To prepare the caramel, combine the sugar and lemon juice in a heavy-bottomed saucepan and bring to a boil over high heat, stirring constantly to dissolve the sugar. Then cook, without stirring, to a rich golden brown.

2. Add the cream slowly over the heat.

3. Whisk in butter over the heat.

4. Allow to cool to room temperature prior to use.

5. Store, covered, at room temperature.

Variegating Ice Creams

To make variegated (swirled) ice creams, fill a pastry bag fitted with a medium-sized plain tip with a room-temperature garnish such as a hard ganache (page 425), marshmallow (page 750), nut paste, jam, preserves, or caramel (formula above) and as the ice cream is extracted from the machine, stream in the garnish. Fold the ice cream mixture just enough to marbleize the ice cream with the ingredients. A good rule for the amount of an ingredient to use for variegation is approximately 20 percent of the total volume of the ice cream.

Variegating ice cream as it is extracted from the batch freezer

Walnut Praline Ice Cream

Makes 48 fl oz/1.44 L

MILK	16 fl oz	480 mL
HEAVY CREAM	16 fl oz	480 mL
SUGAR	7 oz	198 g
GLUCOSE SYRUP	1 oz	28 g
SALT	¼ tsp	1.25 g
WALNUT HALVES	14 oz	397 g
VANILLA BEAN	1 each	1 each
EGG YOLKS	10 oz	284 g
PRALINE		
SUGAR	7 oz	198 g
BROWN SUGAR	2 oz	57 g
CINNAMON	1 tsp	2 g

1. Combine the milk, heavy cream, 3½ oz/99 g of the sugar, the glucose syrup, salt, and walnut halves in a saucepan. Split the vanilla bean, scrape the seeds into the pan, add the pod, and bring the mixture just to a boil over medium heat. Immediately remove from the heat, cover the pan, and let steep for 5 minutes.

2. Remove the vanilla pod and return the mixture to a simmer.

3. Meanwhile, blend the egg yolks with the remaining 3½ oz/99 g sugar to make the liaison. Temper by gradually adding about one-third of the hot milk mixture, whipping constantly. Return the tempered egg mixture to the remaining hot milk in the saucepan and cook, stirring constantly, until the mixture thickens enough to coat the back of a spoon (180°F/82°C).

4. Strain the mixture into a metal container and reserve the walnuts. Immediately transfer the ice cream base to an ice bath. Cool to below 40°F/4°C. Cover and refrigerate for a minimum of 12 hours, or overnight.

5. To prepare the praline, rinse off the walnuts, lightly toast them in a 350°F/177°C oven, and chop them finely.

6. Add a small amount of the sugar to a medium-hot pan set over medium heat and allow it to melt, then add the remaining sugar in small increments, allowing each addition to fully melt before adding the next. Continue this process until all the sugar has been added to the pan and cook to the desired color. Shock the pan in an ice water bath.

7. Sprinkle in the brown sugar and cinnamon, add the toasted chopped walnuts, and stir until mixed.

8. Pour the praline out onto a tray that has been coated with nonstick baking spray. Allow the mixture to cool completely and break it into pea-size pieces.

9. Process the ice cream base in an ice cream machine according to the manufacturer's instructions. Fold in the walnut praline. Pack into storage containers or molds as desired and freeze for several hours, or overnight, before serving or using in plated desserts.

LEFT:
**Green Tea
Ice Cream**

RIGHT:
**Walnut Praline
Ice Cream**

Buttermilk Ice Cream

Makes 48 fl oz/1.44 L

MILK	24 fl oz	720 mL
HEAVY CREAM	8 fl oz	240 mL
SUGAR	8 oz	227 g
SALT	¼ tsp	1.25 g
EGG YOLKS	10 oz	284 g
VANILLA EXTRACT	1 tbsp	15 mL
BUTTERMILK	8 fl oz	240 mL

1. Combine the milk, heavy cream, 4 oz/113 g of the sugar, and salt in a saucepan and bring just to a boil over medium heat.

2. Meanwhile, blend the egg yolks with the remaining 4 oz/113 g sugar to make the liaison. Temper by gradually adding about one-third of the hot milk mixture, whipping constantly. Return the tempered egg mixture to the remaining hot milk in the saucepan and cook, stirring constantly, until the mixture thickens enough to coat the back of a spoon (180°F/82°C).

3. Strain the mixture into a metal container and immediately transfer to an ice bath. Cool to below 40°F/4°C. Blend in the vanilla extract and buttermilk. Cover and refrigerate for a minimum of 12 hours, or overnight.

4. Process in an ice cream machine according to the manufacturer's instructions. Pack into storage containers and freeze for several hours, or overnight, before serving, molding, or using in plated desserts.

Lemon Frozen Yogurt

Makes 32 fl oz/960 mL

PLAIN YOGURT	32 fl oz	960 mL
LEMON JUICE	6 fl oz	180 mL
SUGAR	6 oz	170 g
GLUCOSE SYRUP	1½ oz	43 g

1. Combine the yogurt, lemon juice, sugar, and glucose syrup, stirring until evenly blended.

2. Process in an ice cream machine according to the manufacturer's instructions. Pack into storage containers and freeze for several hours, or overnight, before serving, molding, or using in plated desserts.

Chocolate Frozen Yogurt

Makes 48 fl oz/1.44 L

PLAIN YOGURT (whole-milk or low-fat)	32 fl oz	960 mL
SUGAR	4 oz	113 g
GLUCOSE SYRUP	1 oz	28 g
DARK CHOCOLATE, melted	8 oz	227 g

1. Blend the yogurt, sugar, and glucose syrup, stirring until evenly blended. Temper the melted chocolate by gradually stirring in about one-third of the yogurt mixture. Then blend the chocolate and remaining yogurt mixture together. Cover and refrigerate for a minimum of 12 hours, or overnight.

2. Process in an ice cream machine according to the manufacturer's instructions. Pack into storage containers and freeze for several hours, or overnight, before serving, molding, or using in plated desserts.

Strawberry Frozen Yogurt

Makes 48 fl oz/1.44 L

PLAIN YOGURT (whole-milk or low-fat)	32 fl oz	960 mL
STRAWBERRY PURÉE	12 oz	340 g
SUGAR	8 oz	227 g
GLUCOSE SYRUP	2 oz	57 g

1. Combine the yogurt, strawberry purée, sugar, and glucose syrup, stirring until evenly blended.

2. Process in an ice cream machine according to the manufacturer's instructions. Pack into storage containers and freeze for several hours, or overnight, before serving, molding, or using in plated desserts.

Variation **Raspberry Frozen Yogurt** Replace the strawberry purée with an equal amount of raspberry purée.

Lemon Sorbet

Makes 48 fl oz/1.44 L

SORBET SYRUP (page 480)	1 lb 4 oz	567 g
LEMON JUICE	15 fl oz	450 mL
WATER	13 fl oz	390 mL

1. Combine the sorbet syrup, lemon juice, and water and stir until evenly blended. Cover and chill thoroughly under refrigeration.

2. Process in an ice cream machine according to the manufacturer's instructions. Pack into storage containers and freeze for several hours, or overnight, before serving, molding, or using in plated desserts.

Variations **Lime Sorbet** Replace the lemon juice with an equal amount of lime juice.

Key Lime Sorbet Replace the lemon juice with an equal amount of Key lime juice.

Orange Sorbet

Makes 48 fl oz/1.44 L

SORBET SYRUP (page 480)	14 oz	397 g
ORANGE JUICE	15 fl oz	450 mL
WATER	6 fl oz	180 mL

1. Combine the sorbet syrup, orange juice, and water and stir until evenly blended. Cover and chill thoroughly under refrigeration.

2. Process in an ice cream machine according to the manufacturer's instructions. Pack into storage containers and freeze for several hours, or overnight, before serving, molding, or using in plated desserts.

Variation   **Blood Orange Sorbet** Replace the lemon juice with an equal amount of lime juice.

Sorbet Syrup 65° Brix

Makes 5 lb 8 oz/2.49 kg

SUGAR	3 lb	1.36 kg
WATER	32 fl oz	960 mL
GLUCOSE SYRUP	8 oz	227 g

1. Combine all ingredients and bring to a boil, stirring occasionally.
2. Cool completely. Store, covered, under refrigeration.

Sorbet and Sherbet

Sorbet is a churned frozen dessert that is basically a mixture of sweetened fruit juice or purée and water. Unlike sherbet, sorbet never contains any dairy, but, like sherbet, it may contain added emulsifiers to enhance softness and smoothness of flavor. Sometimes pasteurized egg whites are used in sorbet. They add volume and make a creamier product with a lighter texture. They also act to help prevent the mixture from separating during long-term storage in the freezer. (For 64 fl oz/1.92 L sorbet base, add 1 oz/28 g pasteurized egg whites.)

The sugar content of sorbet is approximately twice that of ice cream. If 10 percent of the sugar in a formula is added in the form of corn syrup, a smoother texture will result. Sorbets made with fruit juice as opposed to purée tend to separate. Juices lack the pulp contained in a purée, which helps to sustain the mixture of water, flavorings, and sugar. To help prevent separation when only fruit juice is used, add a commercial stabilizer or a measure of pasteurized egg whites.

Sorbet, in its simplest form, is a fairly concentrated sugar syrup with added flavoring or flavorings. These flavorings may range from a fresh fruit purée to a fruit juice such as lemon or even to a flavor infusion such as tea, sweet basil, mint, or thyme. A small amount of egg white may be added to the sorbet base to give the final product a smoother texture; it is usually incorporated before the freezing process begins, or added toward the end of the process in the form of a frothy meringue. Purists, however, feel that the addition of egg white to a sorbet masks its clarity and freshness.

When making sorbets and sherbets, as well as granitas, it is essential that the sugar content (or density) of the syrup base be in the proper percentage. If there is too much sugar in the solution, the base will not freeze, because sugar raises the freezing point of a solution. If there is too little sugar, the frozen dessert will be rock hard. The density of a sugar solution is a measure of the amount of sugar dissolved in the liquid. Baumé and Brix are the two most common scales used for measuring sugar density in the pastry shop. A saccharometer is used to measure Baumé (Be), which indicates the specific gravity of the solution. It registers the reading on a scale calibrated from 0° to 40° Be. A refractometer registers the percentage of sugar in a solution. Most sorbets range in density from about 16° to 18° Be, or 30° Brix, depending on the ingredients and desired sweetness. If a saccharometer or refractometer is not at hand, the "floating egg test" can be used. To judge if the solution has the proper sugar density to make a sorbet, float a cleaned raw egg in its shell in the liquid base. If a ring of shell the size of a dime or nickel remains unsubmerged, the solution has the correct concentration of sugar. If a ring larger than the size of a dime or nickel is left exposed, the concentration of sugar is too high; and if the ring is smaller than a dime or nickel, the concentration is too low and should be adjusted before freezing.

Sherbets, which are typically fruit flavored, contain more sugar but less dairy than ice cream. They may be made with milk and/or cream, or with powdered, evaporated, or condensed milk. Emulsifiers such as pectin, gelatin, gums, egg whites, or meringue are often added for a smoother mouth feel. Sherbets like sorbets are usually at approximately 30° Brix, with the dairy adding 1 to 2 percent butterfat, resulting in a richer mouth feel.

When making sorbets or sherbets, remember that the sugar content of most fruits varies according to ripeness. Therefore, it may be necessary to adjust the consistency of the sorbet base by adding more liquid if it is too sweet or more sugar if it is too tart. Let taste be the most important factor.

LEFT:
Check the sugar density of a sorbet syrup with a refractometer.

RIGHT:
Compare the consistency of a sorbet as it comes out of the machine with that of ice cream (shown on page 473).

Grapefruit Sorbet

Makes 48 fl oz/1.44 L

SORBET SYRUP (page 480)	12 oz	340 g
GRAPEFRUIT JUICE	15 fl oz	450 mL
WATER	6 fl oz	180 mL

1. Combine the sorbet syrup, grapefruit juice, and water and stir until evenly blended. Cover and chill thoroughly under refrigeration.

2. Process in an ice cream machine according to the manufacturer's instructions. Pack into storage containers or molds and freeze for several hours, or overnight, before serving or using in plated desserts.

Peach Sorbet

Makes 48 fl oz/1.44 L

SORBET SYRUP (page 480)	10 oz	284 g
PEACH PURÉE	15 oz	425 g
WATER	6 fl oz	180 mL
LEMON JUICE	1 tbsp	15 mL

1. Combine the sorbet syrup, peach purée, water, and lemon juice and stir until evenly blended. Cover and chill thoroughly under refrigeration.

2. Process in an ice cream machine according to the manufacturer's instructions. Pack into storage containers or molds and freeze for several hours, or overnight, before serving or using in plated desserts.

Variations **Mango Sorbet** Replace the peach purée with an equal amount of mango purée.

Kiwi Sorbet Replace the peach purée with an equal amount of kiwi purée.

Pear Sorbet Replace the peach purée with an equal amount of pear purée.

Raspberry Sorbet Replace the peach purée with an equal amount of raspberry purée.

Guava Sorbet Replace the peach purée with an equal amount of guava purée.

Apricot Sorbet Replace the peach purée with an equal amount of apricot purée.

Prickly Pear Sorbet Replace the peach purée with an equal amount of prickly pear purée.

Green Apple Sorbet

Makes 48 fl oz/1.44 L

SORBET SYRUP (page 480)	10 oz	284 g
GREEN APPLE PURÉE	15 oz	425 g
WATER	8 fl oz	240 mL
LEMON JUICE	1 tbsp	15 mL

1. Combine the sorbet syrup, green apple purée, water, and lemon juice and stir until evenly blended. Cover and chill thoroughly under refrigeration.

2. Process in an ice cream machine according to the manufacturer's instructions. Pack into storage containers or molds and freeze for several hours, or overnight, before serving or using in plated desserts.

Banana Sorbet

Makes 48 fl oz/1.44 L

SORBET SYRUP (page 480)	10 oz	284 g
BANANA PURÉE	15 oz	425 g
WATER	10½ fl oz	315 mL

1. Combine the sorbet syrup, banana purée, and water and stir until evenly blended. Cover and chill thoroughly under refrigeration.

2. Process in an ice cream machine according to the manufacturer's instructions. Pack into storage containers or molds and freeze for several hours, or overnight, before serving or using in plated desserts.

Black Currant Sorbet

Makes 48 fl oz/1.44 L

SORBET SYRUP (page 480)	10 oz	284 g
BLACK CURRANT PURÉE	15 oz	425 g
CRÈME DE CASSIS	3 fl oz	90 mL
WATER	10 fl oz	300 mL

1. Combine the sorbet syrup, black currant purée, crème de cassis, and water and stir until evenly blended. Cover and chill thoroughly under refrigeration.

2. Process in an ice cream machine according to the manufacturer's instructions. Pack into storage containers or molds and freeze for several hours, or overnight, before serving or using in plated desserts.

Chocolate Sorbet

Makes 32 fl oz/960 mL

WATER	32 fl oz	960 mL
SUGAR	4 oz	113 g
COCOA POWDER	4 oz	113 g
BITTERSWEET CHOCOLATE, melted	9 oz	255 g

1. Combine the water, sugar, and cocoa powder in a saucepan and bring to a boil over medium heat. Remove the pan from the heat. Blend the mixture into the melted chocolate thoroughly.

2. Strain and refrigerate until chilled.

3. Process in an ice cream machine according to the manufacturer's instructions. Pack into storage containers and freeze for several hours, or overnight, before serving or using in plated desserts.

CLOCKWISE FROM TOP LEFT: Red Wine and Citrus Granita, Green Apple Sorbet, Raspberry Sorbet, Fresh Ginger Granita

Coconut Sorbet

Makes 32 fl oz/960 mL

SORBET SYRUP (page 480)	8 oz	227 g
COCONUT PURÉE	1 lb 5½ oz	610 g
WATER	2 fl oz	60 mL
LIME JUICE	1 fl oz	30 mL

1. Combine the sorbet syrup, coconut purée, water, and lime juice and stir until evenly blended. Cover and chill thoroughly under refrigeration.

2. Process in an ice cream machine according to the manufacturer's instructions. Pack into storage containers or molds and freeze for several hours, or overnight, before serving or using in plated desserts.

Note   Due to the high fat content of the coconut purée, the sorbet will have a smoother finished mouth feel if it is blended in Step 1 using a food processor or stick blender to fully emulsify.

Chocolate Sherbet

Makes 32 fl oz/960 mL

WATER	14 fl oz	420 mL
MILK	4 fl oz	120 mL
SUGAR	5¼ oz	149 g
GLUCOSE SYRUP	1½ oz	43 g
COCOA POWDER	1 oz	28 g
CHOCOLATE-FLAVORED LIQUEUR	4 fl oz	120 mL

1. Combine the water, milk, sugar, glucose syrup, and cocoa powder in a saucepan and bring to a boil over medium heat, stirring to dissolve the sugar. Boil for 3 minutes.

2. Remove from the heat and stir in the chocolate liqueur.

3. Strain through a fine-mesh sieve, transfer to a metal container, and cool in an ice bath. Cover and refrigerate for 6 hours or until fully chilled.

4. Process in an ice cream machine according to the manufacturer's instructions. Pack into storage containers and freeze for several hours, or overnight, before serving, molding, or using in plated desserts.

Vanilla Bean Sherbet

Makes 24 fl oz/720 mL

MILK	15 fl oz	450 mL
HEAVY CREAM	6 fl oz	180 mL
SUGAR	4½ oz	128 g
WATER	3 fl oz	90 mL
LIGHT CORN SYRUP	2¼ oz	64 g
VANILLA EXTRACT	¼ tsp	1.25 mL
VANILLA BEAN	1 each	1 each

1. Combine the milk, cream, sugar, water, corn syrup, and vanilla extract in a saucepan. Split the vanilla bean, scrape the seeds into the pan, and add the pod. Bring the mixture to a boil, stirring to dissolve the sugar.

2. Strain through a fine-mesh sieve, transfer to a metal container, and cool in an ice bath. Cover and refrigerate for a minimum of 12 hours, or overnight.

3. Strain the mixture through a fine-mesh strainer.

4. Process in an ice cream machine according to the manufacturer's instructions. Pack into storage containers and freeze for several hours, or overnight, before serving, molding, or using in plated desserts.

Buttermilk Sherbet

Makes 32 fl oz/960 mL

BUTTERMILK	21 fl oz	630 mL
SUGAR	3½ oz	99 g
HONEY	1¾ oz	50 g
YOGURT	5 fl oz	150 mL
VANILLA BEAN	½ each	½ each

1. Combine the buttermilk, sugar, honey, and yogurt in a saucepan. Split the vanilla bean, scrape the seeds into the pan, and add the pod. Heat the mixture over low heat, stirring to dissolve the sugar.

2. Transfer the mixture to a metal container and cool in an ice bath. Cover and refrigerate until chilled.

3. Strain the sorbet base through a fine-mesh sieve.

4. Process in an ice cream machine according to the manufacturer's instructions. Pack into storage containers and freeze for several hours, or overnight, before serving, molding, or using in plated desserts.

Mango Granita

Makes 32 fl oz/960 mL

WATER	22 fl oz	660 mL
MANGO PURÉE	8 oz	227 g
SUGAR	4 oz	113 g
DARK RUM	1½ fl oz	45 mL
LEMON JUICE	1½ fl oz	45 mL

1. Stir all of the ingredients together until blended and the sugar has dissolved.

2. Pour into a prechilled hotel pan and place in the freezer. Stir the mixture every 15 to 20 minutes with a whisk until it resembles crushed ice.

3. Cover tightly and freeze until needed.

Granita

Like sorbet, granita (also known as granité) is a light and refreshing frozen dessert based on sugar, water, and a flavored liquid such as a fruit juice or liqueur. However, the freezing process for granita, as well as its lower sugar content, makes for a dessert with a very different texture. To freeze granita, use a conventional freezer and a container that allows for large surface area exposure. Stir the mixture every 20 minutes or so with a whisk or a fork, breaking up ice crystals as they begin to form. Continue the process until the granita is completely frozen.

Stirring the mixture only occasionally encourages the formation of large ice crystals, whereas the relatively high sugar-to-liquid ratio and constant churning of sorbet yields a smooth, creamy texture. Alternatively, the base for a granita may be used to make shaved ice; freeze the mixture into a solid block and shave off portions using a metal spoon. Granitas are often served as an intermezzo or as a component of a richer dessert. They may be made sweet or savory. To make a savory granita, infuse the base with dried herbs such as thyme, sage, or rosemary.

Raspberry Granita
Makes 48 fl oz/1.44 L

RASPBERRY PURÉE	1 lb 8 oz	680 g
WATER	24 fl oz	720 mL
SUGAR	8 oz	227 g
LEMON JUICE	1 tbsp	15 mL

1. Stir all of the ingredients together until blended.
2. Pour into a prechilled hotel pan and place in the freezer. Stir the mixture every 15 to 20 minutes with a whisk until it resembles crushed ice.
3. Cover tightly and freeze until needed.

Sour Cherry Granita

Makes 28 fl oz/840 mL

WHITE WINE	4 fl oz	120 mL
HONEY	2 oz	57 g
SUGAR	2 oz	57 g
FRESH CHERRIES, pitted and puréed	1 lb	454 g

1. Stir all of the ingredients together until blended.

2. Pour into a prechilled hotel pan and place in the freezer. Stir the mixture every 15 to 20 minutes with a whisk until it resembles crushed ice.

3. Cover tightly and freeze until needed.

Fresh Ginger Granita

Makes 40 fl oz /1.20 L

FRESH GINGER, peeled	2 oz	57 g
WATER	32 fl oz	960 mL
SUGAR	4 oz	113 g
LEMON JUICE	2 tbsp	30 mL

1. Purée the ginger with 8 fl oz/240 mL of the water.

2. Combine the ginger purée, sugar, and the remaining 24 fl oz/720 mL water in a saucepan and cook over medium heat, stirring to melt the sugar, until the mixture reaches 180°F/82°C.

3. Strain through a fine-mesh sieve and add the lemon juice.

4. Pour into a prechilled hotel pan and place in the freezer. Stir the mixture every 15 to 20 minutes with a whisk until it resembles crushed ice.

5. Cover tightly and freeze until needed.

Green Tea Granita

Makes 32 fl oz/960 mL

SUGAR	6 oz	170 g
WATER	28 fl oz	840 mL
GREEN TEA BAGS	4 each	4 each
LEMON JUICE	2 tbsp	30 mL

1. Combine the sugar and water and bring to a boil, stirring to dissolve the sugar. Add the tea bags, remove from the heat, and steep for 20 minutes.

2. Remove the tea bags and strain the mixture through a fine-mesh sieve if necessary. Add the lemon juice to taste.

3. Pour into a prechilled hotel pan and place in the freezer. Stir the mixture every 15 to 20 minutes with a whisk until it resembles crushed ice.

4. Cover tightly and freeze until needed.

Red Wine and Citrus Granita

Makes 48 fl oz/1.44 L

WATER	24 fl oz	720 mL
RED WINE	14 fl oz	420 mL
SUGAR	10 oz	284 g
ORANGE JUICE	6 fl oz	180 mL
LEMON JUICE	6 fl oz	180 mL
VANILLA BEAN	1 each	1 each

1. Combine the water, red wine, sugar, orange juice, and lemon juice in a saucepan. Split the vanilla bean, scrape the seeds into the pan, and add the pod. Bring the mixture to a boil. Reduce the heat and allow the mixture to simmer for 4 to 5 minutes to blend the flavors.

2. Pour the mixture into a metal container and refrigerate until fully chilled, approximately 6 hours.

3. Pour into a prechilled hotel pan and place in the freezer. Stir the mixture every 20 to 30 minutes with a whisk until it resembles crushed ice.

4. Cover tightly and freeze until needed.

Molded Frozen Desserts

A wide array of molds and containers may be used to mold almost any type of frozen dessert into interesting shapes and forms. Something as simple as a bowl, cake ring, or charlotte mold to the most elaborate specialty pudding and bakeware molds can be used. You can use a single ice cream flavor in a mold lined with a layer of cake, or layer several different complementary flavors and colors in one mold. Add layers of cake or various garnish ingredients, such as chopped nuts or chocolate, or cake or cookie crumbs, to add both flavor and texture.

Regardless of the type of mold, the basic procedure for molding is the same. Line molds with open bottoms, such as cake rings, with plastic wrap to prevent any leakage before the dessert is completely frozen. Lining the base and/or sides of this type of mold with a layer of cake is a common practice. If the sides of the mold are not lined with cake, the molded dessert is often iced before serving.

Whatever type of frozen product you are using, it must be soft enough to spread easily. If possible, use ice cream, frozen yogurt, sorbet, or sherbet directly from the ice cream machine, when it will be the perfect consistency. Working with soft ice cream or the like helps to ensure that no air pockets develop as the mold is filled. If the product you are using is frozen hard, let it stand at room temperature until it is soft and spreadable but not melting.

To fill a mold with one flavor of ice cream or other frozen dessert, fill the mold all at once, spreading the frozen dessert evenly. Periodically tap the mold gently on a counter to get rid of air pockets. Cover the filled mold tightly with plastic wrap and place it in the freezer until it is thoroughly frozen.

To fill a mold with layers of different flavors, add one layer at a time and thoroughly freeze each one before adding another. You can fold garnish ingredients, such as nuts or chopped chocolate, into the softened ice cream (or other frozen dessert) before layering it in the mold, or you can make layers of the garnishes, sprinkling them on top of each layer of ice cream after spreading it into the mold.

Molded frozen desserts must be frozen solid before they can be unmolded, so be sure to allow sufficient time for freezing. To unmold the dessert, immerse the mold briefly in warm water and wipe dry before unmolding, or gently and quickly warm it over an open flame or using a blowtorch or blow-dryer. Invert the dessert onto the plate and gently lift the mold away, being careful not to touch the sides.

Frozen Chocolate Soufflé

Makes 30 portions (4½ fl oz/135 mL each)

EGG WHITES	6 oz	170 g
CREAM OF TARTAR	1 tsp	3 g
SUGAR	12 oz	340 g
GLUCOSE SYRUP	1½ oz	43 g
WATER	4 fl oz	120 mL
DARK CHOCOLATE, melted	12 oz	340 g
HEAVY CREAM, lightly whipped	32 fl oz	960 mL

1. Cut 30 strips (2 by 11 in/5 by 28 cm) of parchment paper or aluminum foil. Wrap each one around a ramekin (4½ fl oz /135 mL) and fasten with tape.

2. Place the egg whites, cream of tartar, and 2 oz/57 g of the sugar in an electric mixer fitted with a wire whisk attachment.

3. Combine the remaining 10 oz/284 g sugar, the glucose syrup, and water in a saucepan and bring to a boil over high heat, stirring to dissolve the sugar. Cook, occasionally brushing down the sides of the pan with a dampened pastry brush, until the syrup reaches 260°F/127°C.

4. Meanwhile, when the sugar syrup reaches 240°F/116°C, begin whipping the egg whites on high speed until soft peaks form.

5. When the sugar syrup reaches 260°F/127°C, carefully pour the hot syrup into the egg whites in a steady stream, while continuing to whip. Then whip the mixture until it reaches room temperature.

6. Gently fold in the melted chocolate. Fold in the heavy cream.

7. Fill the prepared molds to the top and smooth the tops. Freeze for 8 hours, or until firm.

Variations **Frozen Fruit Soufflé** Substitute 1 lb/454 g fruit purée for the chocolate.

Frozen Pistachio, Almond, or Peanut Butter Soufflé Substitute 8 oz/227 g pistachio paste, praline paste, or peanut butter for the chocolate.

Frozen Lemon Soufflé Substitute 8 fl oz/240 mL lemon juice for the chocolate.

Frozen Orange, Hazelnut, or Almond Liqueur Soufflé Replace the chocolate with 16 fl oz/480 mL of the chosen liqueur, prepared as follows: Heat the liqueur and ignite it. When the flames die down, allow to cool completely and add another 2 fl oz/60 mL of the same liqueur.

Frozen Maple Soufflé Replace the sugar and water with 1 lb 9 oz/709 g maple syrup. Omit the chocolate.

Piping a frozen
dessert into an
aluminum foil
collared mold

Still-Frozen Desserts

There are three basic types of still-frozen desserts: frozen soufflés, parfaits, and bombes. Frozen soufflés (also known as soufflés glacés) contain whipped cream, meringue, and a flavoring such as a liqueur, juice, or chocolate. Frozen soufflés are traditionally served in ramekins, as are hot soufflés. To mimic the look of a hot soufflé the ramekins for frozen soufflés are prepared with a collar, a piece of parchment paper or aluminum foil is attached to the ramekin that extends an inch or two above its top. The soufflé mixture is then piped in and leveled off with the top of the collar. The parchment "collar" is removed before service, creating the "look" of a hot soufflé. Parfaits are basically frozen mousse and may be made using almost any method by which a mousse is made. Classically these desserts are served in tall, narrow "parfait" glasses. The American version is layered with fruit and sauces. Bombes are always made using a pâte à bombe (egg yolks cooked over heat as they are beaten with sugar until they are light in color and texture). The pâte à bombe is then incorporated with meringue and/or whipped cream and a flavoring. The term *bombe,* however, has to do with the classic domed shape of this dessert.

The air incorporated into the base of a frozen dessert gives it a light, smooth, spoonable texture. With still-frozen desserts, the air is incorporated before freezing rather than during, as it is for churned frozen desserts. Air is incorporated into these frozen desserts as is done for the preparation of a mousse. Aerated ingredients such as whipped cream, meringue, or beaten egg yolks are folded into a flavored base mixture just before it is deposited into containers and frozen.

Orange Liqueur Soufflé Glacé

Makes 12 portions (4½ fl oz/135 mL each)

EGGS	8 oz	227 g
EGG YOLKS	6 oz	170 g
SUGAR	4½ oz	128 g
ORANGE LIQUEUR	4 fl oz	120 mL
GELATIN	¼ oz	7 g
WATER	1½ fl oz	45 mL
HEAVY CREAM, whipped to soft peaks	16 fl oz	480 mL

1. Cut 12 strips (2 by 11 in/5 by 28 cm) of parchment paper or aluminum foil. Wrap each one around a ramekin (4½ fl oz /135 mL) and fasten with tape. Place the ramekins on a sheet pan and place in the freezer until thoroughly chilled.

2. Combine the eggs, egg yolks, sugar, and orange liqueur in the bowl of an electric mixer and whisk constantly over a pan of simmering water until the mixture reaches 165°F/74°C.

3. Transfer the bowl to the electric mixer fitted with a wire whip attachment. Whip the eggs until three times their original volume and no longer increasing in volume.

4. Meanwhile, bloom the gelatin in the water and melt.

5. Fold the gelatin mixture into the egg mixture. Fold in the whipped cream.

6. Pour the mixture into the prepared molds, level, and freeze.

Chocolate Hazelnut Parfait

Makes 10 portions (4 fl oz/120 mL each)

1-2-3 COOKIE DOUGH (page 249)	1 lb	454 g
GELATIN	1 tsp	5 g
WATER	2 fl oz	60 mL
SUGAR	4½ oz	128 g
EGGS	1½ oz	43 g
EGG YOLKS	3¼ oz	92 g
DARK CHOCOLATE, melted	1¾ oz	50 g
HAZELNUT PASTE	3¼ oz	92 g
BRANDY	1 tbsp	15 mL
VANILLA EXTRACT	2 drops	2 drops
NOUGATINE, finely ground	¾ oz	21 g
HEAVY CREAM, whipped to medium peaks	12 fl oz	360 mL
BRANDIED CHERRIES	20 each	20 each

1. Roll the cookie dough to a thickness of ⅛ inch/3 mm. Cut out 10 rounds using a cutter 3 in/8 cm in diameter and transfer the cookies to a parchment-lined sheet pan. Bake in a 350°F/177°C oven for 10 minutes or until golden brown.

2. Place the 3-in/8-cm dome-shaped, silicone-coated, flexible fiberglass molds in the freezer until thoroughly chilled. Bloom the gelatin in 1 fl oz/30 mL of the water and melt.

3. Cool the gelatin solution to 100°F/38°C. Reserve.

4. Combine the sugar and the remaining 1 fl oz/30 mL water in a heavy-bottomed saucepan and cook over medium heat, stirring to dissolve the sugar. Continue to cook, without stirring, until the mixture reaches 248°F/120°C.

5. Meanwhile, beat the eggs and egg yolks in the bowl of an electric mixer fitted with a wire whip attachment until light in texture and color, about 5 minutes.

6. With the mixer on medium speed, pour the cooked sugar syrup into the egg yolks in a fine stream, then beat until the mixture is completely cool.

7. Blend the reserved gelatin into the egg yolk mixture. Blend in the melted chocolate, hazelnut paste, brandy, vanilla extract, and kroquant. Fold in the whipped cream.

8. Using a pastry bag fitted with a No. 8 plain tip, pipe 3 oz/85 g of the parfait into each of the 10 chilled molds, filling the molds three-quarters full.

9. Place two brandied cherries in the center of each parfait. Place a cookie on top of each parfait; the cookie should be flush with the top of the mold.

10. Cover the parfaits and freeze overnight.

Praline Parfait

Makes 15 portions (6 fl oz/180 mL each)

EGG YOLKS	15 oz	425 g
SUGAR	12 oz	340 g
GLUCOSE SYRUP	1½ oz	43 g
WATER	6 fl oz	180 mL
PRALINE PASTE	8 oz	227 g
HEAVY CREAM, whipped until thickened	32 fl oz	960 mL

1. Place the egg yolks in the bowl of an electric mixer fitted with a wire whip attachment and beat on high speed until light and fluffy, about 5 minutes.

2. Combine the sugar, glucose syrup, and water in a saucepan and bring to a boil over medium-high heat, stirring to dissolve the sugar. Continue to cook, without stirring, until the mixture reaches 260°F/127°C; brush down the sides of the saucepan occasionally with a dampened pastry brush.

3. Carefully pour the hot sugar syrup into the egg yolks in a steady stream, while continuing to whip. Whip until cooled to room temperature.

4. Gently fold the praline paste into the egg yolk mixture. Fold in the heavy cream.

5. Fill the prepared molds to the top and smooth the tops. Freeze until set.

Variation   **Maple Parfait** Replace the sugar and water with 1 lb 9 oz/709 mL maple syrup.

Frozen Lemon Savarin

Makes 10 portions (4 fl oz/120 mL each)

GRANULATED GELATIN	1 tsp	5 g
WATER	1¾ fl oz	53 mL
VANILLA CHIFFON CAKE (⅛ in/3 mm thick)(page 318)	half sheet pan	half sheet pan
LIGHT CORN SYRUP	¾ oz	21 g
SUGAR	4½ oz	128 g
EGG WHITES	2½ oz	71 g
LEMON JUICE	3 fl oz	90 mL
LEMON ZEST, grated	2 tsp	6 g
PLAIN YOGURT	2½ oz	71 g
HEAVY CREAM, whipped to soft peaks	12 fl oz	340 g

1. Place 10 savarin molds on a sheet pan and place in the freezer until thoroughly chilled. Bloom the gelatin in ¾ fl oz/23 mL of the water and melt.

2. Using a 3-in/8-cm round cutter, cut 10 disks out of the cake; reserve.

3. Combine the corn syrup, 3 oz/85 g of the sugar, and the remaining 1 fl oz/30 mL water in a saucepan and bring to a boil, stirring to dissolve the sugar. Continue to cook, without stirring, until the mixture reaches 240°F/116°C.

4. When the sugar syrup has reached approximately 230°F/110°C, whip the egg whites in an electric mixer fitted with a wire whip attachment on medium speed until frothy. Gradually add the remaining 1½ oz/43 g sugar and whip to soft peaks.

5. When the sugar syrup reaches 240°F/116°C, add it to the meringue in a slow, steady stream while whipping on medium speed. Whip on high speed to stiff peaks. Then whip on medium speed until cooled to room temperature.

6. Add the lemon juice and lemon zest to the gelatin mixture. Blend the mixture into the meringue. Fold in the yogurt and then the whipped cream.

7. Using a pastry bag fitted with a No. 4 plain tip, pipe 2¼ fl oz/68 mL of the parfait into each of the 10 chilled savarin molds, filling them nearly full.

8. Place a disk of vanilla chiffon cake over each parfait; the cake should be flush with the top of the mold.

9. Cover the savarins and freeze overnight.

CHAPTER 14

Pies, Tarts, and Fruit Desserts

DESSERTS AND PASTRIES SUCH AS PIES, TARTS, STRUDEL, AND COBBLERS GIVE THE PASTRY CHEF OR BAKER THE OPPORTUNITY TO SHOWCASE NATURAL AND VIBRANT FLAVORS OF FRUITS AND NUTS AS WELL AS THE SWEETNESS AND TEXTURE OF CHEESES AND DAIRY PRODUCTS USED TO MAKE CREAMS AND CUSTARDS. WHEN CREATING DESSERTS OF THIS TYPE, THINK OF WHAT SPICES AND PREPARATION TECHNIQUES WILL ENHANCE AND COMPLEMENT THE TEXTURES SHAPES, AND FLAVORS OF THESE INGREDIENTS.

Apple Pie

Makes 1 pie (9 in/23 cm)

BASIC PIE DOUGH (page 246)	1 lb 4 oz	567 g
GOLDEN DELICIOUS APPLES, peeled, cored, and sliced ⅛ in/3 mm thick	1 lb 8 oz	680 g
SUGAR	5 oz	142 g
TAPIOCA STARCH	½ oz	14 g
CORNSTARCH	¾ oz	21 g
SALT	½ tsp	2.50 g
GROUND NUTMEG	½ tsp	1 g
GROUND CINNAMON	½ tsp	1 g
LEMON JUICE	½ fl oz	15 mL
BUTTER, melted	1 oz	28 g
EGG WASH (page 825)	as needed	as needed

1. Divide the dough in half. Roll out one-half of the dough to ⅛ in/3 mm thick and line the pie pan. Reserve the other half, wrapped tightly, under refrigeration.

2. Combine the sugar, tapioca, cornstarch, salt, nutmeg, cinnamon, lemon juice, and melted butter and toss with the apples.

3. Fill the pie shell with the apple mixture. Brush the rim of the dough with egg wash.

4. Roll out the remaining dough to a thickness of ⅛ in/3 mm and place it over the filling. Crimp the edges to seal, and cut a few vents in the top of the pie.

5. Bake at 375°F/191°C until the filling is bubbling and the crust is a rich golden brown, about 45 minutes.

6. Serve warm, or cool to room temperature before serving.

Note   Other fresh fruit, such as peaches or nectarines, can be substituted for the apples.

Rolling Out Dough and Lining a Pie or Tart Pan

Make sure the dough is chilled before rolling because if the butter or other fat in the crust becomes too soft, the dough will be difficult to handle. If necessary, massage the chilled dough or work it with the rolling pin until it is a malleable consistency. Usually the dough is rolled out directly on a work surface, which is dusted lightly with flour. Bread flour is the best choice for dusting. Because it is lower in starch and has a slightly more granular texture than other types of flour, bread flour dusts a surface more evenly with less clumping. Occasionally confectioners' sugar is used for dusting the work surface, typically for doughs with a higher sugar content.

Dust the work surface very lightly to ensure that very little additional flour or sugar is incorporated into the dough and to avoid clumps of flour that can become imbedded and baked into the dough, preserving its delicate texture and crumb. Lightly dust the dough as well to prevent it from sticking to the rolling pin.

Roll the dough from the center out. Lift and turn the dough as you roll so that you are rolling in all directions. This will keep the dough of even thickness and shape. Lifting and turning the dough will also help to keep it from sticking to the work surface and will reduce the amount of dusting necessary. To lift larger or more delicate pieces of dough, lay the dough over the rolling pin to keep it from tearing.

Work quickly and carefully. Rolling the dough out slowly will allow the fat to become too soft and make it more likely to tear. Particularly delicate or tender doughs may have to be refrigerated intermittently during rolling to prevent that from occurring. This added step is often necessary when making a lattice top, which requires extra handling of the dough. If the dough tears while you are rolling it, simply patch the tear with a small scrap of dough and roll over it so that it becomes incorporated.

Dough for pies and tarts should be rolled to a thickness of ⅛ in/3 mm. If the dough is too thick, it may not bake through, and too much dough can overwhelm the flavors of the filling.

To transfer the rolled dough to the pie or tart pan, carefully roll it around the rolling pin, then gently unroll over the pan. Gently press the dough into the pan, being careful not to tear or stretch the dough. Trim the edge of the dough so that it fits perfectly into the pan. Dock the bottom of the crust when necessary to prevent it from bubbling up.

Scraps of dough can be combined and reused. Stack them, roll into a cohesive mass, and refrigerate until firm before rolling out again.

1 Rolling out dough
   into a round

2 Lining a pie pan
   with dough

Topping Pies and Tarts

The treatment of the top of a pie or tart makes it more interesting and appealing. Typically, toppings of dough or crumb for pies and tarts are used with fruit fillings. Topping a pie or tart helps to prevent the filling from drying during baking by keeping in moisture. Too much moisture, however, can be a bad thing. To prevent excessive moisture buildup and/or retention, cut steam vents into the top of a double-crust pie to allow steam to escape during baking. This will also allow the top crust to develop a crisp, flaky texture. Crumb toppings create less of a moisture barrier, allowing for the release of steam during baking, and therefore do not require vents. Crumb toppings are quick and easy and add a different flavor and texture than crusts made of pastry dough. A pastry top may completely cover the pie or tart or may be cut into strips and woven to create a lattice pattern. Pastry doughs may also be rolled and cut into shapes used to adorn the top or edges of a pie or tart. Crimping the edges of a pie is another way to add a decorative element, and for double-crusted pies and tarts it also serves to seal in the filling and seal the top and bottom crusts together. Many bakers and pastry chefs apply a wash to the top and edges of their pies and tarts to promote the development of a golden brown crust. The wash may be anything from milk or cream to egg wash. For additional sweetness and texture, add a sprinkling of coarse sugar after applying the wash. If you choose to use a wash, use a pastry brush to apply it in a thin, even coat. Some like to apply two coats before baking to promote better shine and browning; apply the first coat of the wash, allow it to dry for 3 to 5 minutes, and then apply the final coat.

Crimping method 1

Crimping method 2

Cherry Pie

Makes 1 pie (9 in/23 cm)

TAPIOCA STARCH	½ oz	14 g
CORNSTARCH	1 oz	28 g
WATER OR FRUIT JUICE	6 fl oz	180 mL
GROUND NUTMEG	½ tsp	1 g
GROUND CINNAMON	½ tsp	1 g
LEMON JUICE	1 tsp	5 mL
SUGAR	5 oz	142 g
SALT	¼ tsp	1.25 g
PITTED CHERRIES	1 lb 8 oz	680 g
BUTTER	1 oz	28 g
BASIC PIE DOUGH (page 246)	1 lb 4 oz	567 g
EGG WASH (page 825)	as needed	as needed

1. Combine the tapioca and cornstarch with just enough of the water or fruit juice to make a slurry.

2. Combine the nutmeg, cinnamon, lemon juice, sugar, salt, and the remaining water and bring to a boil. Add the slurry and return the mixture to a boil, stirring constantly. Add the cherries and bring to a boil once again. Add the butter and gently stir it in until melted. Cool completely.

3. Divide the dough in half. Roll out one portion ⅛ in/3 mm thick and line the pie pan.

4. Spoon the filling into the pie shell. Brush the rim of the dough with egg wash.

5. Roll out the remaining dough ⅛ in/3 mm thick and place it over the filling. Crimp the edges to seal.

6. Bake at 425°F/218°C just until the crust is lightly browned, about 45 minutes. Allow to cool on a wire rack before serving.

Variations   **Blueberry Pie** Substitute an equal amount of blueberries for the cherries.

Apple Pie Substitute an equal amount of peeled, cored, and sliced apples for the cherries.

Peach Pie Substitute an equal amount of peeled, pitted, and sliced peaches for the cherries.

Nectarine Pie Substitute an equal amount of peeled, pitted, and sliced nectarines for the cherries.

Blueberry Pie

Makes 1 pie (9 in/23 cm)

BLUEBERRIES, frozen	1 lb 8 oz	680 g
TAPIOCA STARCH	½ oz	14 g
CORNSTARCH	½ oz	14 g
GROUND NUTMEG	½ tsp	1 g
GROUND CINNAMON	¼ tsp	0.50 g
LEMON ZEST, grated	½ oz	14 g
LEMON JUICE	1 tsp	5 mL
SALT	¼ tsp	1.25 g
SUGAR	5 oz	142 g
BUTTER	1 oz	28 g
BASIC PIE DOUGH (page 246)	1 lb 4 oz	567 g
EGG WASH (page 825)	as needed	as needed

1. Allow the fruit to thaw in a bowl, then drain, reserving the juice.

2. Combine the tapioca and cornstarch with just enough of the juice to make a slurry.

3. Combine the nutmeg, cinnamon, lemon zest, lemon juice, salt, and sugar with the remaining juice and bring to a boil. Add the slurry and return to a boil, then boil, stirring constantly until the mixture thickens, about 2 minutes.

4. Remove from the heat and gently fold in the fruit. Add the butter and gently stir until melted. Cool completely.

5. Divide the dough in half. Roll out one portion ⅛ in/3 mm thick and line the pie pan.

6. Spoon the filling into the pie shell. Brush the rim of the dough with egg wash.

7. Roll out the remaining dough ⅛ in/3 mm thick and place it over the filling. Crimp the edges to seal.

8. Bake at 425°F/218°C just until the crust is lightly browned, about 30 minutes. Allow to cool on a wire rack before serving.

Warm Apple Charlottes

Makes 12 charlottes (4½ fl oz/135 mL)

BUTTER	2 oz	57 g
GRANNY SMITH APPLES, peeled, cored, and sliced ⅛ in/3 mm thick	2 lb	907 g
VANILLA BEAN, seeds	1 each	1 each
LIGHT BROWN SUGAR	4 oz	113 g
GROUND GINGER	1 tsp	2 g
APRICOT JAM	4 oz	113 g
BRANDY	4 fl oz	120 mL
LEMON JUICE	1 fl oz	30 mL
PULLMAN LOAF (page 134)	1 each	1 each
BUTTER, melted	8 oz	227 g

1. Place the butter in a sauté pan over medium-high heat and allow it to melt, but not brown. Add the apples, vanilla bean seeds, brown sugar, and ginger and cook until the apples are just tender, about 5 minutes.

2. Add the apricot jam, brandy, and lemon juice, bring to a simmer, and cook over medium heat until nearly all the liquid has evaporated. Remove from the heat and let cool.

3. Remove the crust from the Pullman loaf and slice it into ¼-in/6-mm slices.

4. Brush each slice of bread with melted butter. Quarter 20 slices.

5. Using 7 to 8 quarters of bread per mold, line the sides of 12 ramekins (4½ fl oz/135 mL each), slightly overlapping the pieces as necessary to completely cover the sides.

6. Using a 3-in/8-cm round cutter, cut 24 circles from the remaining Pullman slices. Place a round in the base of each ramekin.

7. Fill each ramekin with apple filling, pressing it down gently to pack it lightly. Top each filled ramekin with another Pullman round.

8. Bake at 375°F/191°C until golden brown, about 50 minutes. Unmold and serve warm with a sauce of choice and whipped cream.

Tarte Tatin

Makes 1 tart (9 in/23 cm)

SUGAR	8 oz	227 g
LIGHT BROWN SUGAR	4 oz	113 g
GROUND CINNAMON	½ tsp	1 g
GOLDEN DELICIOUS APPLES	6 each	6 each
PÂTE BRISÉE (page 249)	8 oz	227 g
APPLE BRANDY	1 fl oz	30 mL

1. Butter a cake pan 9 in/23 cm in diameter and 2 in/5 cm deep.

2. Melt the granulated sugar in a heavy-bottomed pan, adding it in small increments and stirring after each addition until melted before adding more. Then cook to a rich golden brown caramel.

3. Pour the caramel into the cake pan and cool completely.

4. Sprinkle the brown sugar on top of the caramel and dust with the cinnamon.

5. Peel, core, and halve the apples. Arrange them round side down to completely cover the bottom of the pan.

6. Roll out the pâte brisée ¼ in/6 mm thick and place it over the apples, slightly tucking it in around the edge of the pan.

7. Bake at 400°F/204°C until the crust is golden brown, about 45 minutes.

8. Invert the pan onto a wire rack set over a pan to drain the liquid.

9. Place the liquid in a pan and simmer over medium heat until it begins to thicken. Add the apple brandy and pour over the top of the tart just before serving.

Arranging apples for Tarte Tatin

Strawberry Rhubarb Tart

Makes 1 tart (9 in/23 cm)

SUGAR	6 oz	170 g
CORNSTARCH	1¼ oz	35 g
GROUND CINNAMON	½ tsp	1 g
GROUND CLOVES	⅛ tsp	0.25 g
RHUBARB (fresh or frozen), cut into 1-in/2-cm pieces	8 oz	227 g
STRAWBERRIES (fresh or frozen)	8 oz	227 g
LEMON JUICE	1 fl oz	30 mL
PÂTE BRISÉE (page 249)	1 lb 8 oz	680 g

1. Combine the sugar, cornstarch, cinnamon, and cloves. Toss together with the rhubarb, strawberries, and lemon juice.

2. Divide the pâte brisée in half. Roll out one portion ⅛ in/3 mm thick and line the tart pan. Spoon the filling into the tart shell.

3. Roll out the remaining dough ⅛ in/3 mm thick. Cut it into strips ½ in/1 cm wide. Weave a lattice over the top of the tart, leaving a ½ in/1 cm space between each strip (see the instructions below for weaving a lattice top).

4. Bake at 450°F/232°C for 10 minutes. Reduce the temperature to 350°F/177°C and bake until the crust is golden brown, about 30 minutes more.

Place the strips of dough over the tart in one direction, leaving some space between the strips.

Turn back every other strip to place the crosswise strips. Note that the first crosswise strip is placed in the center of the tart.

Place the last crosswise strip near the edge, on the side of the tart.

Turn the tart 180 degrees to finish placing the crosswise strips.

For blind baking, the shell is lined with parchment and weighted with pie weights, dried beans, or rice.

Blind Baking Pie and Tart Shells

To blind bake means to bake an unfilled pie or tart shell partially or fully before adding the filling. Pastry shells are partially prebaked when the time required to bake the filling will not be long enough to fully bake the crust. Shells are completely prebaked when they are to be filled with a filling that does not require further cooking or baking.

To blind bake a pie or tart shell, line the dough with parchment paper and fill with pie weights, or dry beans or rice. The weights will prevent the bottom of the crust from bubbling up and the sides from collapsing or sliding down the sides of the pan during baking.

Place the pan in the preheated oven. The parchment and weights need only stay in the pan until the crust has baked long enough to set. Once the crust has baked long enough so that it has set and will maintain its form (generally 10 to 12 minutes), remove the parchment and weights to allow for even browning. Return the pan to the oven and bake the crust until the desired color is achieved. If the crust is to be baked again with a filling, bake it just until light golden brown. For a fully baked crust, bake to a deep golden brown, about 20 minutes.

Brush prebaked pastry shells with a light coating of softened butter or melted chocolate and allow to set fully before filling. This will prevent moisture in the filling from seeping into the crust and making it soggy. Apply a thin coating to the shell using a pastry brush. Place the shell in the refrigerator so that the butter or chocolate will harden, then fill the shell.

Sweet Potato Pie

Makes 1 pie (9 in/23 cm)

BASIC PIE DOUGH (page 246)	10 oz	284 g
SWEET POTATO	8 oz	227 g
SUGAR	3⅓ oz	94 g
GROUND CINNAMON	1 tsp	2 g
GROUND ALLSPICE	¼ tsp	0.50 g
SALT	¼ tsp	1.25 g
GROUND MACE	¼ tsp	0.50 g
EGGS, lightly beaten	4 oz	113 g
MILK	8 fl oz	240 mL
BUTTER, melted	1 oz	28 g

1. Roll out the dough ⅛ in/3 mm thick and line the pie pan. Line the pie shell with parchment paper and fill with dry beans or pie weights. Bake the pie shell at 350°F/177°C until very light golden brown, about 15 minutes. Cool completely.

2. Peel the sweet potato and prick with a fork. Lightly oil the potato and place it on a rack in a baking pan.

3. Bake the potato at 350°F/177°C until very tender, about 35 minutes. Cool.

4. Mash the sweet potato until completely smooth. Combine with the remaining ingredients, blending well. Pour into the prebaked pie shell.

5. Bake at 350°F/177°C until the filling is set, about 35 minutes. Cool completely and then refrigerate until the filling is completely set before serving.

Spinach-Feta Quiche

Makes 1 quiche (9 in/23 cm)

PÂTE BRISÉE (page 248)	10 oz	284 g
ONION, chopped	2 oz	57 g
BUTTER	1 oz	28 g
SPINACH, chopped	4 oz	113 g
MILK	6 fl oz	180 mL
CREAM	6 fl oz	180 mL
EGGS	4 oz	113 g
EGG YOLKS	2 oz	57 g
SALT	½ tsp	2.50 g
BLACK PEPPER	½ tsp	1 g
FETA CHEESE, cut into small cubes	3 oz	85 g

1. Roll out the pâte brisée ⅛ in/3 mm thick and line the tart pan. Line the tart shell with parchment paper and fill with dry beans or pie weights. Bake the tart shell at 350°F/177°C until very light golden brown, about 15 minutes. Cool completely.

2. Sauté the onion in the butter until translucent. Add the spinach and cook until wilted. Drain.

3. Combine the milk and cream in a saucepan and bring to a simmer.

4. Meanwhile, combine the eggs, egg yolks, salt, and pepper in a bowl, stirring with a whisk. Add about one-third of the hot milk mixture to the eggs while whisking constantly. Add the remaining hot milk mixture, stirring to incorporate.

5. Spread the spinach mixture in the tart shell and sprinkle the cheese on top. Pour the custard mixture over the top.

6. Bake at 350°F/177°C and bake just until the custard is set, about 45 minutes.

7. Serve warm, at room temperature, or chilled.

Variations **Quiche Lorraine** Omit the spinach, onion, and feta cheese. Use 1 lb/454 g Gruyère, grated, and 1 lb/454 g bacon, diced and rendered. Make the custard as directed above, fill the tart shell, and bake as directed.

Three-Cheese Quiche Omit the spinach, onion, and feta cheese. Use 8 oz/227 g Gruyère, grated, 1 lb/454 g ricotta, and 6 oz/170 g Parmesan, grated. Make the custard as directed above, fill the tart shell, and bake as directed.

Vanilla Cream Pie

Makes 1 pie (9 in/23 cm)

BASIC PIE DOUGH (page 246)	10 oz	284 g
MILK	24 fl oz	720 mL
SUGAR	6 oz	170 g
VANILLA BEAN	1 each	1 each
CORNSTARCH	2 oz	57 g
EGGS	3 oz	85 g
EGG YOLKS	2 oz	57 g
BUTTER	1 oz	28 g

1. Roll out the dough ⅛ in/3 mm thick and line the pie pan. Line the pie shell with parchment paper and fill with dry beans or pie weights. Bake the pie shell at 350°F/177°C until very light golden brown, about 15 minutes. Remove the beans and parchment and continue cooking to a golden brown, about 5 minutes. Cool completely.

2. Combine 18 fl oz/540 mL of the milk with 3 oz/85 g of the sugar in a saucepan. Split the vanilla bean, scrape the seeds into the mixture, and add the pod. Bring the mixture to a boil, stirring to dissolve the sugar.

3. Meanwhile, combine the remaining 3 oz/85 g sugar with the cornstarch, stirring together with a whip. Add the remaining 6 fl oz/180 mL milk, the eggs, and egg yolks and whisk to blend.

4. Temper the egg mixture by gradually adding one-third of the hot milk mixture, whisking constantly. Return the tempered egg mixture to the remaining milk mixture in the saucepan and cook, stirring constantly, just until it reaches a boil. Cook, stirring constantly, for an additional 2 minutes.

5. Remove the pan from the heat and whisk in the butter. Strain through a fine sieve.

6. Pour the hot filling into the prebaked pie shell. Cover the surface of the cream with plastic wrap placed directly against it to prevent a skin from forming. Cool to room temperature.

7. Chill before serving.

Variations **Banana Cream Pie** Spread half of the filling into the pie shell. Cover with a layer of 8 oz/227 g sliced bananas, then top with the remaining filling.

Chocolate Cream Pie Add 3 oz/85 g melted bittersweet chocolate to the cream with the butter immediately after boiling.

Coconut Cream Pie Add 2 oz/57 g lightly toasted unsweetened coconut to the milk before heating it.

Working with Puff Pastry

When working with puff pastry, keep it as cold as possible. Work in manageable batches, so that the dough won't sit at room temperature for too long. If the butter is allowed to soften, it will cause the layering to collapse and prevent the full rise of the dough.

Lightly dust the work surface with flour (preferably bread flour) to prevent the dough from sticking. Roll the dough from the center out in all directions, lifting and turning the dough as you work to prevent the gluten from being overworked in any one direction. Uneven rolling will cause the pastry to misshapen during baking.

When using puff pastry to line a tart pan, it should be rolled very thin and docked well to inhibit excessive rising during baking. When blind baking puff pastry for items such as napoleons, it should be weighted down to prevent it from fully rising. If allowed to fully rise, it would be too flaky to cut into smaller portions or for building pastries.

Puff pastry is always baked at a relatively high temperature (400° to 425°F/204° to 218°C) to encourage the full rise. Lower temperatures would not create enough steam or set the structure of the pastry quickly enough, and it would either never rise or collapse.

Puff Pastry Apple Tart

Makes 1 tart (9 in/23 cm)

PUFF PASTRY (page 260)	10 oz	284 g
APRICOT JAM	2 oz	57 g
APPLE, peeled, cored, and finely chopped	1 each	1 each
APPLES, peeled, cored, and sliced	4 each	4 each
SUGAR	2 oz	57 g
APRICOT GLAZE, warm (page 429)	1 oz	28 g

1. Roll out the puff pastry ¼ in/6 mm thick. Cut a 10-in/25-cm circle from the dough.

2. Place the round of dough on a sheet pan lined with parchment paper. Spread a thin layer of apricot jam over the circle of dough, leaving a ½-in/1-cm border of dough around the entire tart. Spread the chopped apple over the jam. Arrange the sliced apples on top of the chopped apple in a fanned spiral, starting from the center and working out to the edges. Sprinkle the sugar on top of the apples.

3. Bake at 400°F/204°C until golden brown, about 20 minutes.

4. Using a pastry brush, glaze the tart with the apricot glaze.

Rustic Peach Tart

Makes 1 tart (9 in/23 cm)

BLITZ PUFF PASTRY (page 266)	10 oz	283 g
PEACHES, peeled, pitted, and cut into ¼-in/6-mm slices	1 lb	454 g
GROUND NUTMEG	¼ tsp	0.50 g
SUGAR	2 oz	57 g
EGG WASH (page 825)	as needed	as needed
CAKE CRUMBS	1½ oz	43 g
ALMONDS, slivered (optional)	1½ oz	43 g
COARSE SUGAR	2 oz	57 g

1. Roll out the puff pastry ⅛ in/3 mm thick. Cut a 10-in/25-cm circle from the dough and place it on a parchment-lined sheet pan.

2. Toss the peaches with the nutmeg and sugar.

3. Brush the outside 1-in/3-cm perimeter of the puff pastry circle lightly with egg wash. Sprinkle the cake crumbs on top of the pastry, leaving a 2-in/5-cm border. Mound the peaches on top of the cake crumbs. Sprinkle the almonds, if using, on top of the fruit.

4. Fold the edges of the puff pastry over the fruit, pleating the dough as necessary. Brush the pleated edge of the pastry lightly with egg wash and sprinkle with the coarse sugar.

5. Bake at 400°F/204°C until golden brown, about 1 hour.

Note   Substitute apples, sour cherries, apricots, or pears for the peaches.

Working with Fresh Fruit

For the most flavor, choose fruit that is in season. The best way to select fruit is to taste it. When tasting is not possible, select fruit with the desired color, aroma, and firmness (see Chapter 2: Ingredient Identification for more information on fruit). Combine fruits and berries to create different and more complex flavor profiles and textures: for example, strawberry and rhubarb, or pears and cranberries. Using different varieties of the same fruit can also have the same effect: for example, Granny Smith and Golden Delicious apples. High-moisture fruits such as peaches and cherries generally benefit from precooking with a starch before assembling into a pie, while lower-moisture fruits such as apples and pears can simply be tossed with sugar, starch, and flavorings and placed directly into a shell for baking.

Cutting Citrus Suprêmes

To cut citrus fruit into suprêmes (segments), slice off the top and bottom of the fruit, and slice the skin and white pith completely away. Then slice between the connective membranes on either side of each citrus segment to release it; twist the knife and use a scooping motion to cut out the suprême.

Peeling and Slicing a Mango

To peel and slice a mango, first remove the skin with as little of the edible flesh as possible. Cut off the flesh from the broad sides of the pit in two large sections, cutting as close to the pit as possible. Then cut the flesh from the two narrow sides, following the curve of the pit. Cube or slice the flesh as desired.

Peeling a Kiwi

To peel a kiwi, slice off one end of the fruit. Work the tip of a spoon down between the flesh and the skin and carefully slide it all the way around the fruit, then pop out the flesh. Cube or slice as desired.

CLOCKWISE FROM LEFT: Cutting orange segments, also referred to as suprêmes

Cutting a mango

Peeling a kiwi

Peeling and Seeding a Melon

To peel and seed a melon, use a chef's knife to peel off the skin, following the natural curve of the melon. Cut the melon in half and scoop out the seeds and strings with a spoon. Cube or slice the melon as desired.

To use a melon baller or Parisian scoop to cut melon balls or ovals, halve the unpeeled melon and scoop out the seeds and strings. Scoop out the melon flesh, rotating the baller as you work to create spheres or ovals.

Peeling and Cutting a Pineapple

To peel and cut a pineapple, use a chef's knife to cut off the top and bottom of the fruit. Moving the blade of the knife with the contours of the fruit, cut away the skin, being careful to remove the "eyes" without removing too much of the edible flesh. To dice or cube the pineapple, slice the fruit from the core in four sections, make the slices the desired width, and then dice or cube. To cut the pineapple into rings, lay the peeled fruit on its side and cut into slices of the desired thickness. Remove the core from each slice using a small round cutter.

Pitting and Coring Fruit

To remove the pit from a stone fruit, cut around the circumference of the fruit, down to the pit, using the seam as a guide. Twist the two sections of the fruit in opposite directions to release the flesh from the seed.

To core apples and pears, either use a special coring tool or cut the fruit from the core in four segments. Then cube or slice as desired.

Peeled apples, pears, and other fruits that oxidize quickly when their flesh comes in contact with the air may be tossed in a small amount of lemon juice to prevent browning during preparation.

LEFT TO RIGHT:
Peeling a pineapple; pitting stone fruit

Florida Sunshine Tart

Makes 1 tart (9 in/23 cm)

PUFF PASTRY (page 260)	10 oz	284 g
EGG WASH (page 825)	as needed	as needed
CLASSIC CARAMEL SAUCE (page 451)	4 oz	113 g
PASTRY CREAM (page 388)	6 oz	170 g
ORANGES, peeled	8 each	8 each
APRICOT GLAZE, warm (page 429)	2 oz	57 g

1. Roll out the puff pastry ¼ in/6 mm thick. Cut a 10-in/25-cm circle from the pastry. Cut a 9-in/23-cm circle from the center of the circle, creating a ring ½ in/1 cm wide.

2. Brush the puff pastry circle with egg wash. Cut the puff pastry to open it and place it on top of the circle to create a border around its edge. Cut off any excess so the ends of the border ring do not overlap. Brush the top of the ring with egg wash. Dock the bottom of the circle and place on a parchment-lined sheet pan.

3. Bake at 350°F/177°C until lightly browned, 15 to 20 minutes. Reduce the oven temperature to 300°F/149°C and bake until the shell is dry and golden brown, about 10 minutes longer.

4. Pour the caramel sauce into the shell while it is still warm and spread it evenly. Allow the caramel to cool completely and chill.

5. Using a pastry bag fitted with a No. 5 plain tip, pipe the pastry cream into the bottom of the shell in concentric circles.

6. Cut the oranges into suprêmes. Arrange the segments in a spiral in the shell, overlapping the segments and completely covering the pastry cream.

7. Brush the oranges with a thin layer of apricot glaze. Refrigerate until ready to serve.

Lemon Fantasy Tart

Makes 1 tart (9 in/23 cm)

1-2-3 COOKIE DOUGH (page 249)	10 oz	284 g
EGGS	8 oz	227 g
SUGAR	6¾ oz	191 g
HEAVY CREAM	5 fl oz	150 mL
LEMON ZEST, grated	1 tsp	3 g
LEMON JUICE	4 fl oz	120 mL

1. Roll out the dough ⅛ in/3 mm thick and line the tart pan.

2. Blind bake the tart shell at 325°F/163°C until very light golden brown, 10 to 12 minutes. Cool completely.

3. Whisk together the eggs and sugar.

4. Whip the cream to soft peaks.

5. Add the lemon zest and juice to the egg mixture. Fold in the cream.

6. Pour the filling into the tart shell. Bake at 350°F/177°C until just set, about 45 minutes. Cool completely.

7. Chill for several hours, or until fully set.

Raspberry Mascarpone Tart

Makes 1 tart (9 in/23 cm)

1-2-3 COOKIE DOUGH (page 249)	10 oz	284 g
MASCARPONE	4 oz	113 g
HONEY	2 oz	57 g
VANILLA EXTRACT	1 tsp	5 mL
LEMON JUICE	2 fl oz	60 mL
HEAVY CREAM	6 fl oz	180 mL
RASPBERRIES	8 oz	227 g
APRICOT GLAZE, warm (page 429)	2 oz	57 g

1. Roll out the dough ⅛ in/3 mm thick and line the tart pan. Line the tart shell with parchment paper and fill with dry beans or pie weights. Bake the tart shell at 350°F/177°C until very light golden brown, about 15 minutes. Remove the beans and parchment and continue cooking to a golden brown, about 5 minutes. Cool completely.

2. Mix the mascarpone, honey, vanilla, and lemon juice until well blended.

3. Whip the heavy cream to soft peaks. Fold the cream into the mascarpone mixture.

4. Pour the filling into the cooled tart shell and spread it evenly. Arrange the raspberries on top of the tart. Brush the berries with the warm glaze.

Lemon Mousse Tart

Makes 1 tart (9 in/23 cm)

RICH SHORT DOUGH (page 250)	10 oz	284 g
GELATIN	2 tsp	10 g
WATER	1 fl oz	30 mL
HEAVY CREAM	8 fl oz	240 mL
HALF-AND-HALF	4 fl oz	120 mL
SUGAR	3 oz	85 g
EGG YOLKS	2 oz	57 g
VANILLA EXTRACT	1 tsp	5 mL
LEMON JUICE	1 fl oz	30 mL

1. Roll out the dough ⅛ in/3 mm thick and line the tart pan. Line the tart shell with parchment paper and fill with dry beans or pie weights. Bake the tart shell at 350°F/177°C until very light golden brown, about 15 minutes. Remove the beans and parchment and continue cooking to a golden brown, about 5 minutes. Cool completely.

2. Bloom the gelatin in the water.

3. Whip the heavy cream to soft peaks. Cover and reserve under refrigeration.

4. Combine the half-and-half and 1½ oz/43 g of the sugar in a saucepan and bring to a simmer over medium heat, stirring to dissolve the sugar.

5. Meanwhile, blend the egg yolks with the remaining 1½ oz/43 g sugar to make the liaison. Temper by gradually adding about one-third of the hot half-and-half, whipping constantly. Return the tempered egg mixture to the hot half-and-half in the saucepan and cook, stirring gently, until the custard thickens enough to coat the back of a spoon. Strain.

6. Add the bloomed gelatin to the warm custard, blending well. Allow the mixture to cool slightly, then blend in the vanilla and lemon juice.

7. Gently blend one-third of the lemon custard mixture into the reserved whipped cream. Fold in the remaining lemon mixture.

8. Pour into the prepared tart shell and spread evenly.

9. Refrigerate for 1 hour before serving.

Pecan Pie

Makes 1 pie (9 in/23 cm)

BASIC PIE DOUGH (page 246)	10 oz	284 g
SUGAR	½ oz	14 g
BREAD FLOUR	½ oz	14 g
DARK CORN SYRUP	10½ oz	298 g
EGGS, beaten	3½ oz	99 g
VANILLA EXTRACT	1 tsp	5 mL
SALT	1 tsp	5 g
BUTTER, melted	1 oz	28 g
PECAN HALVES, toasted	4 oz	113 g

1. Roll out the dough ⅛ in/3 mm thick and line the pie pan.

2. Combine the sugar and flour in a bowl and whisk together. Add the corn syrup and blend thoroughly. Add the eggs, vanilla, and salt and mix until incorporated. Stir in the melted butter.

3. Spread the pecans evenly in the pie shell and pour the corn syrup mixture on top.

4. Bake at 450°F/232°C until the crust begins to brown, about 15 minutes. Reduce the oven temperature to 325°F/163°C and bake until the filling is set, about 25 minutes longer.

Variations **Pecan Cranberry Pie** Add 5 oz/142 g fresh or frozen cranberries along with the pecans.

Chocolate Pecan Pie Add 6 oz/170 g chocolate chunks along with the pecans.

Almond and Pine Nut Tart

Makes 1 tart (9 in/23 cm)

1-2-3 COOKIE DOUGH (page 249)	10 oz	284 g
ALMOND PASTE	6 oz	170 g
SUGAR	2½ oz	71 g
EGGS	3 each	3 each
VANILLA EXTRACT	1 tsp	5 mL
ALL-PURPOSE FLOUR	1½ oz	43 g
PINE NUTS	2 oz	57 g
CONFECTIONERS' SUGAR	as needed	as needed

1. Roll out the dough ⅛ in/3 mm thick and line the tart pan.
2. Combine the almond paste, sugar, and 1 egg, blending until smooth. Add the remaining eggs one at a time, mixing until fully incorporated after each addition. Blend in the vanilla. Add the flour and mix until incorporated.
3. Pour the filling into the tart shell. Scatter the pine nuts over the top.
4. Bake at 350°F/177°C until the filling is set, about 35 minutes. Cool completely.
5. To serve, remove from the tart pan and dust with confectioners' sugar.

Caramel Orange Tart

Makes 1 tart (9 in/23 cm)

1-2-3 COOKIE DOUGH (page 249)	10 oz	284 g
HEAVY CREAM	10 fl oz	300 mL
VANILLA BEAN, split	½ each	½ each
ORANGE JUICE	8 fl oz	240 mL
SUGAR	3½ oz	99 g
EGG YOLKS, beaten	4 oz	113 g

1. Roll out the dough ⅛ in/3 mm thick and line the tart pan. Line the tart shell with parchment paper and fill with dry beans or pie weights. Bake the pie shell at 350°F/177°C until very light golden brown, about 15 minutes. Cool completely.

2. Pour the cream into a saucepan. Scrape the seeds from the vanilla bean into the cream and bring the cream to a simmer. Remove from the heat, cover, and allow to steep for 15 minutes.

3. Combine the orange juice and sugar in a small saucepan over high heat and stir constantly until the mixture comes to a boil to ensure all the sugar is melted. Once it has come to a boil, stop stirring. Using a pastry brush, wash down the sides of the pan with cool water to prevent crystals from forming. Repeat as often as necessary to keep the sides of the pan clean until the sugar has reached a rich golden brown. Slowly add the cream, stirring until fully incorporated. Cool.

4. Blend the egg yolks into the caramel mixture.

5. Fill the tart shell with the caramel custard. Bake at 325°F/163°C until the filling is set, about 40 minutes.

6. Cool completely before serving.

Zesty Lime Tart

Makes 1 tart (9 in/23 cm)

1-2-3 COOKIE DOUGH (page 249)	10 oz	283 g
BUTTER	5½ oz	156 g
SUGAR	4½ oz	128 g
LIME ZEST, grated	¾ oz	21 g
LIME JUICE	4½ fl oz	135 mL
EGG YOLKS	2 oz	57 g
CANDIED LIME PEEL (page 726)	2 oz	57 g

1. Roll out the dough ⅛ in/3 mm thick and line the tart pan. Line the tart shell with parchment paper and fill with dry beans or pie weights. Bake the tart shell at 350°F/177°C until very light golden brown, about 15 minutes. Remove the beans and parchment and continue cooking to a golden brown, about 5 minutes. Cool completely.

2. Combine the butter, 2¼ oz/64 g of the sugar, the lime zest, and juice in a saucepan and bring to a boil, stirring frequently to dissolve the sugar.

3. Meanwhile, blend the egg yolks with the remaining 2¼ oz/64 g sugar to make the liaison. Temper by gradually adding about one-third of the hot butter mixture, whipping constantly. Return to the saucepan and cook until thickened enough to evenly coat a spoon.

4. Strain the mixture into the tart shell. Chill thoroughly.

5. To serve, garnish with the candied lime peel.

Apple Custard Tart

Makes 1 tart (9 in/23 cm)

1-2-3 COOKIE DOUGH (page 249)	10 oz	284 g
APRICOT JAM	2²⁄₃ oz	75 g
APPLES, peeled, cored, and cut into ¼-in/6-mm slices	3 each	3 each
BUTTER, melted	1 oz	28 g
CINNAMON SUGAR (page 826)	1 tsp	4 g
EGGS	6 oz	170 g
SUGAR	4 oz	113 g
SOUR CREAM	8 oz	227 g
MILK	6 fl oz	180 mL
VANILLA EXTRACT	½ tsp	2.50 mL
APRICOT GLAZE, warm (page 429)	5 oz	142 g
SLICED ALMONDS, toasted and coarsely chopped	1 oz	28 g

1. Roll out the dough ⅛ in/3 mm thick and line the tart pan. Line the tart shell with parchment paper and fill with dry beans or pie weights. Bake the tart shell at 350°F/177°C until very light golden brown, about 15 minutes. Cool completely.

2. Spread the apricot jam over the bottom of the tart shell. Arrange the sliced apples in concentric circles on top of the jam. Using a pastry brush, brush the melted butter over the apples. Sprinkle with the cinnamon sugar.

3. Bake at 375°F/191°C until the apples are tender and the crust is golden brown, about 40 minutes.

4. Whisk together the eggs, sugar, sour cream, and milk. Remove the tart from the oven and pour the sour cream mixture over the cooked apples, filling the tart shell to the top.

5. Reduce the oven temperature to 300°F/149°C and bake until the custard is set, about 35 minutes longer. Cool to room temperature.

6. Brush the top of the tart with the apricot glaze. Press the almonds around the edge of the tart.

Apple-Almond Tart

Makes 1 tart (9 in/23 cm)

PÂTE BRISÉE (page 249)	10 oz	283 g
FRANGIPANE FOR FILLINGS (Appendix A)	12 oz	340 g
PASTRY CREAM (page 388)	8 oz	227 g
APPLES, peeled, cored, and cut into ¼-in/6-mm slices	3 each	3 each
CINNAMON SUGAR (page 826)	2 oz	57 g
APRICOT GLAZE, warm (page 429)	3 oz	85 g
SLICED ALMONDS, toasted and coarsely chopped	2 oz	57 g

1. Roll out the pâte brisée ⅛ in/3 mm thick and line the tart pan.

2. Combine the frangipane and pastry cream in an electric mixer fitted with a paddle attachment and mix on medium speed, scraping down the bowl periodically, until well blended, about 3 minutes.

3. Pour the mixture into the tart shell and spread evenly.

4. Arrange the sliced apples on top of the pastry cream mixture in a fanned spiral, working from the center out. Sprinkle the apples with the cinnamon sugar.

5. Bake at 375°F/191°C until the filling is golden brown, about 40 minutes.

6. Using a pastry brush, brush the tart with the apricot glaze. Sprinkle the toasted almonds around the edge of the tart.

Note This tart can also be made with plums, peaches, apricots, nectarines, or other sliced fruit of choice.

Cheese Tart

Makes 1 tart (9 in/23 cm)

1-2-3 COOKIE DOUGH (page 249)	10 oz	284 g
CREAM CHEESE	2 oz	57 g
SUGAR	2²/₃ oz	75 g
EGGS	6 oz	170 g
HEAVY CREAM	4 fl oz	120 mL
ORANGE ZEST, grated	1 tbsp	9 g
RASPBERRIES (fresh or frozen)	8 oz	227 g

1. Roll out the dough ¹/₈ in/3 mm thick and line the tart pan. Line the tart shell with parchment paper and fill with dry beans or pie weights. Bake the tart shell at 350°F/177°C until very light golden brown, about 15 minutes. Cool completely.

2. Combine the cream cheese and sugar in the bowl of an electric mixer fitted with the paddle attachment and mix until smooth. Gradually add the eggs, mixing until fully incorporated after each addition and scraping down the sides of the bowl periodically. Add the cream and orange zest and blend well.

3. Place the raspberries in the tart shell so they cover the bottom evenly. Pour the filling over the raspberries and spread it evenly.

4. Bake at 350°F/177°C until the filling is set, about 45 minutes.

5. Serve warm or chilled.

Clafoutis

Makes 10 portions (4 fl oz/120 mL each)

MILK	12 fl oz	360 mL
SUGAR	4 oz	113 g
SALT	pinch	pinch
VANILLA BEAN, split	¹/₂ each	¹/₂ each
EGGS	3 each	3 each
ALL-PURPOSE FLOUR	1¹/₂ oz	43 g
TART CHERRIES, pitted	12 oz	340 g
CONFECTIONERS' SUGAR, for dusting	as needed	as needed

1. Coat 10 ramekins (4 fl oz /120 mL each) with a thin film of butter and dust them lightly with sugar.

2. Combine the milk, 2 oz/57 g of the sugar, the salt, and the vanilla bean and seeds in a saucepan and bring to boil, stirring to dissolve the sugar.

3. Meanwhile, blend the eggs with the flour and the remaining 2 oz/57 g sugar to make the liaison. Temper by gradually adding about one-third of the hot milk, whipping constantly, then add the remaining hot milk. Strain.

4. Divide the cherries equally among the prepared ramekins. Divide the custard mixture among the ramekins, pouring it over the cherries.

5. Bake in a hot water bath at 350°F/177°C until the custard is set, about 20 minutes.

6. Lighly dust with confectioners' sugar. Serve warm.

Apricot Clafoutis

Makes 1 tart (9 in/23 cm)

1-2-3 COOKIE DOUGH (page 249)	10 oz	284 g
APRICOTS, halved	6 each	6 each
CAKE FLOUR	1¼ oz	35 g
SUGAR	1¾ oz	50 g
BUTTER, melted	1¾ oz	50 g
MILK	6 fl oz	180 mL
HEAVY CREAM	6 fl oz	180 mL
CRÈME FRAÎCHE	½ oz	14 g
EGG YOLK	1 each	1 each
CONFECTIONERS' SUGAR, for dusting	as needed	as needed

1. Roll out the dough ⅛ in/3 mm thick and line the tart pan. Line the tart shell with parchment paper and fill with dry beans or pie weights. Bake the tart shell at 350°F/177°C until very light golden brown, about 15 minutes. Cool completely.

2. Arrange the apricot halves in the tart shell in concentric circles with the cut side down.

3. Whisk together the flour and sugar. Blend in the butter, milk, cream, and crème fraiche. Blend in the egg yolk.

4. Pour the filling over the apricots.

5. Bake at 350°F/177°C until the filling is set, about 45 minutes.

6. Lighlty dust with confectioners' sugar. Serve warm.

Belgian Chocolate Rice Tart

Makes 1 tart (9 in/23 cm)

PÂTE BRISÉE (page 249)	10 oz	284 g
BASMATI RICE	3½ oz	99 g
WATER	6 fl oz	180 mL
MILK	4 fl oz	120 mL
BUTTER	2 oz	57 g
SUGAR	3½ oz	99 g
DARK CHOCOLATE, finely chopped	5⅔ oz	160 g
EGG YOLKS	5⅔ oz	160 g
HEAVY CREAM	2⅔ fl oz	80 mL
COCOA POWDER	as needed	as needed
CHANTILLY CREAM (page 422)	as needed	as needed

1. Roll out the pâte brisée ⅛ in/3 mm thick and line the tart pan. Line the tart shell with parchment paper and fill with dry beans or pie weights. Bake the shell at 350°F/177°C until very light golden brown, about 15 minutes. Cool completely.

2. Meanwhile, combine the rice and water in a saucepan and bring to a boil. Cover and simmer until the rice is tender, about 30 minutes. Remove from the heat.

3. Combine the milk, butter, and sugar in a saucepan and bring to a boil. Remove from the heat. Blend in the rice and chocolate, and cool until just warm.

4. Add the yolks and heavy cream to the rice mixture, blending well.

5. Pour the mixture into the tart shell and spread it evenly.

6. Bake at 375°F/191°C until the custard has set, about 15 minutes. Cool completely and then refrigerate until chilled.

7. Just before serving, dust the tart lightly with cocoa powder and garnish with Chantilly cream.

Walnut Tart

Makes 1 tart (9 in/23 cm)

1-2-3 COOKIE DOUGH (page 249)	10 oz	284 g
WALNUTS	7 oz	198 g
EGGS	6 oz	170 g
MAPLE SYRUP	5 oz	142 g
SUGAR	4 oz	113 g
BUTTER, melted	1 oz	28 g
BRANDY	1 fl oz	30 mL
CONFECTIONERS' SUGAR, for dusting	as needed	as needed

1. Roll out the dough ⅛ in/3 mm thick and line the tart pan. Line the tart shell with parchment paper and fill with dry beans or pie weights. Bake the tart shell at 350°F/177°C until very light golden brown, about 15 minutes. Cool completely.

2. Spread the walnuts evenly in the tart shell.

3. Combine the eggs, maple syrup, sugar, butter, and brandy, blending well. Pour into the tart shell.

4. Bake at 350°F/177°C until the filling is set, about 35 minutes. Allow to cool completely.

5. Just before serving, dust lightly with confectioners' sugar.

Cranberry Pecan Tart

Makes 1 tart (9 in/23 cm)

1-2-3 COOKIE DOUGH (page 249)	12 oz	340 g
BUTTER	4½ oz	128 g
LIGHT CORN SYRUP	10 oz	284 g
LIGHT BROWN SUGAR	6 oz	170 g
EGGS	5 oz	142 g
VANILLA EXTRACT	1½ tsp	7.50 mL
CRANBERRIES	2 oz	57 g
PECANS, chopped	4 oz	113 g
PECAN HALVES	10 oz	284 g

1. Roll out the pâte sucrée ⅛ in/3 mm thick and line the tart pan. Line the tart shell with parchment paper and fill with dry beans or pie weights. Bake the tart shell at 350°F/177°C until very light golden brown, about 15 minutes. Cool completely.

2. Combine the butter, corn syrup, and sugar in a saucepan and heat, stirring, until the sugar has dissolved. Remove from the heat.

3. Whip the eggs in the bowl of an electric mixer fitted with the wire whip attachment until pale in color and light in texture, about 5 minutes. Blend in the sugar mixture. Blend in the vanilla extract.

4. Spread the cranberries and chopped pecans evenly in the tart shell. Pour the filling evenly over them. Arrange the pecan halves on top of the filling in concentric circles.

5. Bake at 350°F/177°C until the filling is set, about 40 minutes. Allow to cool completely and serve, or refrigerate until fully chilled and then serve.

Chocolate Macadamia Nut Tart

Makes 1 tart (9 in/23 cm)

CHOCOLATE SHORT DOUGH (page 257)	12 oz	340 g
BITTERSWEET CHOCOLATE, finely chopped	2 oz	57 g
HEAVY CREAM	3 fl oz	90 mL
INSTANT ESPRESSO POWDER	1 tsp	3 g
SUGAR	4 oz	213 g
HEAVY CREAM, hot	4 fl oz	120 mL
BUTTER	1 oz	28 g
MACADAMIA NUTS, lightly toasted	2 oz	57 g

1. Roll out the dough ⅛ in/3 mm thick and line the tart pan. Line the tart shell with parchment paper and fill with dry beans or pie weights. Bake the tart shell at 350°F/177°C until very light golden brown, about 15 minutes. Remove the beans and parchment and continue cooking to a golden brown, about 5 minutes. Cool completely.

2. Put the chocolate in a bowl. Bring the cream to a simmer, add the espresso, and stir until dissolved. Pour the cream over the chocolate, allow to stand for 5 minutes, and stir until melted and smooth. Allow to cool.

3. Heat a heavy-bottomed pan. Add the sugar in small increments, stirring after each addition and making sure all the sugar is melted before adding more. Cook to a rich golden brown.

4. Remove the pan from the heat. Slowly stir in the hot cream, then stir in the butter. Allow to cool slightly.

5. Pour approximately 2 oz/57 g of the caramel into the tart shell and spread it evenly over the bottom. Scatter half the macadamia nuts evenly over the caramel. Pour the ganache over the nuts and spread it evenly.

6. Freeze the tart for 1 hour.

7. Pour the remaining caramel onto the center of the tart and spread it evenly over the ganache. Arrange the remaining macadamia nuts on top of the tart. Refrigerate until fully chilled.

Spiced Apple and Dried Fig Cobblers

Makes 20 cobblers (12 fl oz/360 mL each)

GRANNY SMITH APPLES	15 each	15 each
BROWN SUGAR	8 oz	227 g
GROUND CINNAMON	1¼ tsp	2.50 g
GROUND NUTMEG	½ tsp	1 g
PORT	14 fl oz	420 mL
RED WINE	14 fl oz	420 mL
WATER	14 fl oz	420 mL
SUGAR	10 oz	284 g
LEMON JUICE	1 fl oz	30 mL
ORANGES, cut into sixths (with peel)	2 each	2 each
CINNAMON STICKS	2 each	2 each
CLOVES	3 each	3 each
BLACK PEPPERCORNS, cracked	1 tbsp	8.50 g
STAR ANISE, cracked	1 each	1 each
DRIED FIGS, stem ends removed	1 lb 10 oz	737 g
BASIC PIE DOUGH (page 246)	1 lb 6 oz	624 g
EGG WASH (page 825)	as needed	as needed

1. Peel and core the apples. Cut into slices ¼ in/6 mm thick and toss with the sugar, cinnamon, and nutmeg.

2. Combine the port, red wine, water, sugar, lemon juice, oranges, cinnamon sticks, cloves, peppercorns, and star anise in a pot and simmer gently for 20 minutes.

3. Strain the liquid into another pot. Add the figs and simmer until the figs are tender, about 20 minutes. Drain. (The liquid can be reserved for poaching other fruit.)

4. Cut the figs into quarters. Combine the figs with the apple mixture.

5. Divide the filling mixture evenly among 20 ramekins (12 fl oz/360 mL each).

6. Roll out the pie dough ¼ in/6 mm thick. Cut into 20 rounds big enough to cover the tops of the ramekins, approximately 4 in/10 cm in diameter.

7. Top the filled ramekins with the dough rounds. Lightly brush with egg wash.

8. Bake at 325°F/163°C until the tops are golden brown, about 20 minutes.

9. Serve warm.

Three-Berry Cobblers

Makes 20 cobblers (12 fl oz/360 mL each)

STRAWBERRIES, hulled and halved	2 lb	907 g
RASPBERRIES	1 lb 10 oz	737 g
BLUEBERRIES	2 lb	907 g
SUGAR	8 oz	227 g
CORNSTARCH	2½ oz	71 g
BASIC PIE DOUGH (page 246)	1 lb 6 oz	624 g
EGG WASH (page 825)	as needed	as needed

1. Combine all the berries in a bowl and toss with the sugar and cornstarch.

2. Divide the mixture evenly among 20 ramekins (12 oz/360 mL each).

3. Roll out the pie dough ¼ in/6 mm thick. Cut dough into 20 rounds big enough to cover the ramekins, approximately 4 in/10 cm in diameter.

4. Top the filled ramekins with the pie dough rounds. Lightlty brush with egg wash.

5. Bake at 325°F/163°C until the tops are golden brown, about 20 minutes.

6. Serve warm.

Apple Crisp

Makes 20 portions (4 fl oz/120 mL each)

CRISP TOPPING		
QUICK-COOKING OATMEAL	14 oz	397 g
WHOLE WHEAT FLOUR	6⅓ oz	179 g
DARK BROWN SUGAR	1 lb	454 g
SLICED ALMONDS, coarsely chopped	3⅓ oz	94 g
GROUND CINNAMON	1½ tbsp	9 g
BUTTER, cut into small cubes, chilled	12 oz	340 g
APPLE FILLING		
GOLDEN DELICIOUS APPLES, peeled, cored, and sliced ⅛ in/3 mm thick	36 each	36 each
BUTTER, cubed	8 oz	227 g
LIGHT BROWN SUGAR	1 lb	454 g
GROUND CINNAMON	2 tsp	4 g
RAISINS	4 oz	113 g
GOLDEN RAISINS	4 oz	113 g
SALT	½ tsp	2.50 g
LEMON JUICE	as needed	as needed

1. To prepare the topping, combine all the ingredients except the butter and toss together. Rub the butter into the mixture so that it resembles coarse meal.

2. Spread the topping mixture on a parchment-lined sheet pan and bake at 325°F/163°C until golden brown, 15 to 20 minutes. Allow to cool.

3. To prepare the filling, sweat the apples in the butter in a large pan, stirring occasionally until they are just beginning to soften, about 5 minutes. Add the brown sugar and cinnamon, stirring to coat, and continue cooking until the apples are tender, about 5 minutes. Stir in the raisins and salt. Add lemon juice to taste. Allow to cool completely.

4. Divide the apple mixture evenly among 20 ramekins (4 fl oz/120 mL each). Top with the crisp topping.

5. Bake at 375°F/191°C until heated through, about 15 minutes.

6. Serve warm.

Note You can substitute other seasonal fruits for the apples.

Strudel

As versatile as pie, strudel can be savory or sweet, providing the filling is low in moisture.

Vent the top of the strudel to allow excess moisture to escape to prevent the filling and dough from becoming too soft. Strudel dough is stretched to create a paper-thin sheet. The high-gluten content of bread flour and a resting time after mixing allows this dough to be stretched paper thin. During assembly, strudel dough is brushed with butter and rolled up to encase a filling. This creates a flaky pastry with many layers, just as are created by the lamination of puff pastry or by the layering of phyllo dough.

Rolling filling up in strudel dough

Apple Strudel

Makes 2 strudels (24 in/61 cm each), or 24 portions

GRANNY SMITH APPLES	5 lb	2.27 kg
RAISINS	4 oz	113 g
CINNAMON SUGAR (page 826)	8 oz	227 g
DRIED BREAD CRUMBS	6 oz	170 g
BUTTER, melted	8 oz	227 g
STRUDEL DOUGH	1 lb 12 oz	794 g

1. Peel and core the apples. Cut into slices ¼ in/6 mm thick and toss with the raisins and cinnamon sugar.

2. Toss the bread crumbs with 2 oz/57 g of the butter.

3. Cover a work surface with a large linen cloth and dust the cloth with bread flour. Divide the dough in half, set one portion aside, and cover. Roll the other portion into a rectangle 12 by 18 in/30 by 46 cm on the floured cloth and allow the dough to relax for 15 minutes.

4. To stretch the dough, work with two people on opposite sides of the table. Place your hands under the dough and begin to lift and stretch it from the center out. Continue stretching until the dough is very thin and almost transparent.

5. Brush the dough with 4 oz/113 g of the remaining melted butter. Sprinkle half the bread crumbs evenly over the entire surface of the stretched dough and then place half of the sliced apples in a strip along one of the edges of the dough. Roll up the dough, starting by lifting up one edge of the linen, then continuing to use the linen to help you roll so that the pastry forms a tight log. Transfer the strudel to a sheet pan and repeat with the remaining dough and filling.

6. Brush the tops of the strudels with the rest of the melted butter. Vent the top of the strudel by making a 1-in/3-cm cut in the dough at 2-in/5-cm intervals.

7. Bake at 350°F/177°C until light golden brown, about 25 minutes.

8. Serve immediately.

Cranberry Pear Strudel

Makes 2 strudels (24-in/61-cm each), or 24 portions

DRIED CRANBERRIES	4 oz	113 g
WHITE RUM	4 fl oz	120 mL
DRIED BREAD CRUMBS	4 oz	113 g
BUTTER	6½ oz	184 g
BARTLETT PEARS	5 lb	2.27 kg
CINNAMON SUGAR (page 826)	6 oz	170 g
LEMON JUICE	2 fl oz	60 mL
STRUDEL DOUGH	1 lb 12 oz	794 g

1. Soak the cranberries in the rum for 30 minutes, or until fully plumped; drain.

2. Sauté the bread crumbs in ½ oz/14 g of the butter until golden brown.

3. Peel and core the pears. Cut into slices ¼ in/6 mm thick and combine with the cranberries and cinnamon sugar.

4. Cover a work surface with a large linen cloth and dust the cloth with flour. Divide the dough in half; set one portion aside and cover. Roll the remaining portion into a rectangle 12 by 18 in/30 by 46 cm on the floured cloth and allow the dough to relax for 15 minutes. Melt the remaining butter.

5. To stretch the dough, work with two people on opposite sides of the table. Place your hands under the dough and begin to lift and stretch the dough from the center out. Continue stretching until the dough is very thin and almost transparent.

6. Brush the dough with 4 oz/113 g of the remaining melted butter. Sprinkle half the bread crumbs evenly over the entire surface of the stretched dough and then place half of the sliced pears in a strip along one of the edges of the dough. Roll up the dough, starting by lifting one edge of the linen, then continuing to use the linen to help you roll so that the pastry forms a tight log. Transfer to a sheet pan and repeat with the remaining dough and filling.

7. Brush the tops of the strudels with the rest of the melted butter. Vent the top of the strudel by making a 1-in/3-cm cut in the dough at 2-in/5-cm intervals.

8. Bake at 350°F/177°C until light golden brown. Brush the strudels again with butter and bake until golden brown, about 25 minutes.

9. Serve immediately.

CHAPTER 15

Filled and Assembled Cakes and Tortes

WHEN SELECTING COMPONENTS TO BUILD A CAKE OR TORTE, IT IS IMPORTANT TO CONSIDER THE COMBINATION OF FLAVORS AND TEXTURES. CLASSICAL CAKES AND TORTES ARE FINE EXAMPLES OF FLAVOR COMBINATIONS AND APPEALING DESIGNS AND OFFER A FOUNDATION OF INSPIRATION FOR CONTEMPORARY APPLICATIONS. CONTEMPORARY CAKES AND TORTES EXPLORE NEW FLAVOR COMBINATIONS GENERATED FROM THE GLOBALIZATION OF CUISINE AND CULTURE.

Bavarian Cream Torte

Makes 1 torte (8 in/20 cm)

VANILLA SPONGE CAKE (8 in/20 cm) (page 302)	1 each	1 each
VANILLA SIMPLE SYRUP (page 820)	5 fl oz	150 mL
STRAWBERRY BAVARIAN CREAM (page 403)	1 lb	454 g
HEAVY CREAM, whipped	16 fl oz	480 mL
STRAWBERRIES, halved	5 each	5 each
DARK CHOCOLATE SHAVINGS (page 769)	1 oz	28 g

1. Place an 8-in/20-cm cake round on a sheet pan and place an 8-in/20-cm cake ring on top.

2. Slice the sponge cake into three even layers (between ¼ and ½ in/6 mm and 1 cm thick).

3. Place the layer cut from the bottom of the cake into the bottom of the cake ring with the cut side up and moisten it with simple syrup. Ladle 8 oz/227 g of the Bavarian cream on top of the sponge and spread it into an even layer. Top with a second sponge layer, cut from the center of the cake, and press down gently. Moisten the sponge with simple syrup. Ladle in the remaining 8 oz/227 g Bavarian cream and spread it evenly. Moisten the cut side of the remaining piece of cake with simple syrup, place it cut side down on top of the filling, and press down gently.

4. Cover the torte with plastic wrap and refrigerate until fully set.

5. To finish the torte, remove the plastic wrap. Warm the sides of the cake ring using a propane torch or a towel moistened with warm water and carefully remove the ring.

6. Coat the top and sides of the torte with whipped cream, reserving 6 oz/170 g for the finishing décor. Using a pastry bag fitted with a No. 5 plain tip, pipe 10 small domes of whipped cream around the outer edge of the top of the torte to mark portions. Place a strawberry half on each dome, resting it at a 45-degree angle pointing toward the center of the torte.

7. Garnish the bottom quarter edge of the side of the torte by gently pressing the chocolate shavings to adhere.

Basics of Cake Assembly

Fillings for cakes may complement or contrast the flavor of the cake. For example, a chocolate cake could be filled with either a chocolate or a raspberry filling. The chocolate filling would make a richer cake, while the raspberry filling, with its fresh berry flavor, would cut the richness of the chocolate cake.

Texture is also important when selecting a filling for a cake. The general rule is that the texture of the filling should match that of the cake. Lighter aerated fillings should be used with lighter cakes, such as sponge or chiffon; a mousse filling should never be paired with a pound cake. Richer fillings such as paddled hard ganache or cream fillings are better choices for pairing with rich creamed cakes. When filling a cake with a rich, heavy filling, use less than you would if using a lighter, more delicate filling.

Cakes should be allowed to cool completely before cutting into layers. Cut the cakes into layers between ¼ and ½ in/6 mm and 1 cm thick. Typically, thinner layers will make a better cake than thicker layers, creating a more uniform flavor and texture. Fillings that are spread onto layers should generally be less than ½ in/1 cm thick and should not exceed the thickness of the cake layers. However, poured fillings such as Bavarian cream can be applied in layers thicker than the cake layers, as they are usually less rich and have a lighter texture than spread fillings.

Before slicing a cake into layers, trim any uneven areas from the sides and top. For the best results, use a cake-decorating turntable and a knife with a long, thin, serrated blade. Set the cake on a cardboard cake round and then on the turntable. First divide the cake by eye into the desired number of layers. Then insert the knife into the side of the cake at the appropriate level and, holding the knife steady and level and slowly rotating the turntable, move the blade of the knife into the cake to cut the layer. Remove the layer and set aside; repeat as necessary.

Before assembling the cake, brush loose crumbs from the layers. Cake layers are often moistened with any of a variety of syrups, from plain simple syrup to one infused with spices or flavored with a liqueur. The syrup adds moisture to drier layers, such as sponge cakes, and adds flavor as well. Brush the syrup evenly over the cut surface of each layer as the cake is assembled. The layers should be moistened but not drowned. In assembly, the cut surfaces of the cake should be moistened with simple syrup and should face the interior of the cake. For ease of application of any glaze or icing and for serving, the top and bottom surfaces of a filled cake should never be a cut surface.

Trimming a cake and cutting it into layers for assembly

Functions of Garnish

The garnish for items in a bakery or pastry shop serves several important functions, one of which is that it adds visual appeal. Although a perfectly iced or glazed but otherwise unadorned cake can be a thing of beauty, it requires more interest and/or intricacy to entice most customers. Garnishing also displays the skill of the baker or pastry chef. They can use their imagination, creativity, and knowledge to garnish cakes and pastries, using techniques and ingredients in unique combinations to make items look enticing and exciting.

Garnish can also be used to indicate the flavors and ingredients in the cake or pastry item. This serves the customer, helping them make a selection by informing them of the flavors used in the cake or pastry. For example, a Black Forest cake is a chocolate cake with a filling of cherries, and the typical garnish is chocolate shavings and whole preserved cherries.

Classic cakes, tortes, and pastries often have a specific, traditional way in which they have been garnished since their inception. The décor (garnish) of an item like this is always the same, serving both as a way to identify these items and as an homage to the place or person responsible for the original cake or pastry.

In garnishing a cake or torte there are two basic approaches to the décor. The cake may be thought of as a whole, or it may be considered in terms of portions. Decorating a cake with portions in mind is an approach that developed in pastry shops where cakes are traditionally sold by the slice. Decorating cakes as a whole is the preferred approach where cakes are sold as a whole piece.

MOLDING CAKES

Cakes made with delicate fillings that must set before they can be sliced and served are assembled in some type of form or mold. Bavarian creams, almost any type of gelatin-based mousse, and even ice cream in a fairly fluid state (either taken directly from the machine or, if frozen hard, softened under refrigeration) are all examples of these types of fillings.

To make a molded cake, first prepare the mold. A cake ring, also known as an entremet ring, may be used, in which case the ring should be set on a cardboard cake round on a flat sheet pan so the cake has a stable, movable, level base. Closed molds, such as bowls used to prepare charlottes or bombes, or cake pans, may also be used. If a closed mold is used, the cake will be inverted onto a serving plate, platter, or board when unmolded. Closed molds are often lined with plastic to ease unmolding.

Cut the cake layers to fit the mold. If the mold has graduated or tapered sides, the layers should have varying diameters to fit the mold. The layers may be cut so they will touch the sides of the mold, in which case their edges will be exposed when the cake is unmolded, making it necessary to finish or ice the sides of the cake. Or the layers may be cut so that a gap is left between the edge of the cake and the mold, and in this case the filling will surround the layers, serving as both icing and filling.

In some instances, slices of cake may be used to line the sides of the mold as well. Used in this way, the cake adds an element of décor as well as flavor. Slices of roulade filled with jam are used to create the classic spiral finish for a charlotte royale. Layers of thin sponge cake tightly layered with jam may be sliced and used to create a basketweave or striped pattern. Other effects can be achieved using joconde cake and stenciled, spread, or piped décor batter. Ladyfingers are the classic finish for charlotte russe.

Usually a cake layer is placed into the mold first. The exception is for molds such as bombes, which are inverted in unmolding so that the bottom becomes the top of the cake. In either case, cake and filling are added to the mold in alternating layers.

Each layer of cake should be moistened before it is placed in the mold. Be sure to center the layers in the mold. The filling can be poured, spooned, or piped into the mold, but it is essential to add an equal amount each time to form layers of equal thickness.

You can add garnishes to the filling for additional flavor and textural interest. Fold the garnish ingredient into the filling to spread it evenly throughout the mixture, or sprinkle the garnish ingredients into the mold before adding the filling. The second technique is especially common with fresh fruit, to create a layer of garnish. Then the garnish is topped with filling (be sure the garnish remains evenly distributed and does not shift).

The top of a molded cake may be either filling or a cake layer. If a cake is to be iced, the top layer must be cake. When the top of the cake will be glazed with a clear, marbleized, or lightly colored glaze, the top layer of the cake should be filling. Be sure to leave enough space at the top of the mold (approximately ⅛ in/3 mm) for the glaze.

Molded cakes are generally frozen or refrigerated in the mold so the filling and structure of the cake will be firm enough to withstand unmolding. To release the cake from the mold or ring, warm the sides by either dipping the mold in warm water or carefully running a lighted propane torch around the sides.

FROM TOP LEFT:

Lining a cake ring with décor sponge

Ladling Bavarian cream over the first layer of sponge in a cake ring

Placing a second layer of sponge on top of the Bavarian cream

Smoothing the top of the final Bavarian cream layer

ICING CAKES

When icing a cake, you may wish to use a turntable. Some pastry chefs prefer to hold the cake (on its cardboard circle) on their fingertips and rotate it as they work. Either approach can yield excellent results, although holding the cake on your fingertips requires more control than using a turntable. The best and most consistent way to achieve a clean coat of icing is to apply two coats. First apply a thin seal coat or crumb

FROM TOP LEFT:
Spreading buttercream into even layers

Using a cake comb to smooth the sides of a cake

Using a spatula to create a cake with a smooth level top and sharp square edges coat and allow it to set completely. This coat does not necessarily have to be the same icing as the final coat; it is intended to attach any loose crumbs to the cake and prevent them from becoming incorporated in the final coat. Choose something that is a complementary flavor; it can be a jam or jelly, a buttercream, or ganache—anything that will seal the cake and ease the application of the final coat. This first coat should be very thin to ensure that there will not be too much icing applied to the cake overall; it may even be thin enough so that the layers of cake are visible through the coating on the side. After the first coat has set, apply the thicker second layer.

Use either a straight or an offset metal spatula to ice the cake. The appropriate length of the spatula depends on the size of the cake (and what feels most comfortable to you). Apply the icing generously to the top of the cake first, spreading it smoothly and evenly all the way out to the edges of the cake and slightly over them. Then ice the sides of the cake: Holding the spatula vertically so its tip points to the base of the cake, spread the icing onto the sides. Apply a generous amount of icing to the sides to ease smoothing and ensure a smooth finish. To smooth the sides of the cake, after applying the icing, hold the spatula vertically against the cake at a 45-degree angle, with the edge of the spatula touching the icing, and rotate the cake (by turning your hand or turning the turntable) against the spatula. (If you are holding the cake on your fingertips, hold the knife with the handle below the cake; if you are working on a turntable, the tip of the spatula should just touch its surface.) This will not only smooth the icing but will also cause some of the excess icing from the sides to rise above the top of the cake, making a lip or ridge. Working from the edges toward the center and holding the spatula parallel to the top of the cake at a 45-degree angle, with its edge touching the surface, smooth the lip over and across the top to create a perfectly smooth top and a sharp angled edge.

At this point, the cake can be marked into portions if desired, using a straight-edged knife or long straight metal spatula. A variety of simple garnishes or décor can also be applied to the top of the cake by piping the icing, filling, or glaze (such as a shell border or rosettes), with or without additional garnishes such as chocolate cutouts or cigarettes, tuiles, Florentines, fresh berries or jam, and the like. The side of the cake can be finished using a spatula to a smooth surface, or using a cake comb or other tool to leave a texture or pattern. Garnishes such as chopped nuts, cake crumbs, or chocolate shavings may be applied to the side of a cake by sprinkling or gently pressing to adhere. More intricate cakes are often adorned with piping or other fine décor work.

Working with Gelatin-Based Fillings

Gelatin-based fillings can be poured or piped to fill a wide variety of cakes and pastries. In either case, the fillings must be used immediately after they are made, before they set up.

Assemble all components, ingredients, and necessary equipment before beginning to make the filling. Be sure all advance preparation (e.g., whipping cream, slicing cake layers, cutting up fruit) is done. Then prepare the filling and assemble the cake or pastry.

Charlotte Royale

Makes 1 cake (8 in/20 cm)

FRANGIPANE CAKE (13½ by 17½ in/34 by 44 cm sheet) **(page 372)**	1 each	1 each
RASPBERRY JAM	2 lb	907 g
VANILLA SPONGE CAKE (8 in/20 cm) **(page 302)**	1 each	1 each
RASPBERRY BAVARIAN CREAM (page 403)	2 lb	907 g
VANILLA SIMPLE SYRUP (page 820)	3 fl oz	90 mL
APRICOT GLAZE, warm (page 429)	1 lb	454 g

1. Trim the edges of the frangipane and cut crosswise into three equal pieces. Spread a thin layer of jam on one strip and top with a second strip. Spread with jam and top with the final strip of frangipane. Cut the layered cake into 1-in/3-cm strips and cut each strip into slices ¼ in/6 mm thick.

2. Line a 48-fl-oz/1.44-L domed mold with plastic wrap, making sure some is hanging out of the mold. Line the mold with the frangipane slices to create a basketweave pattern.

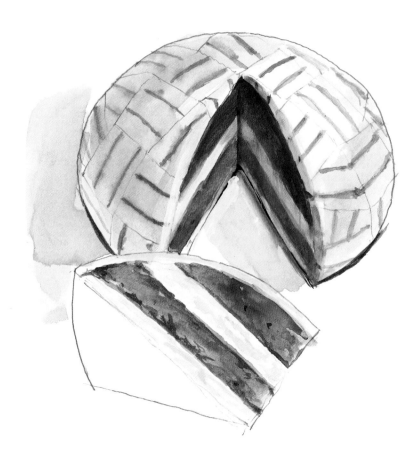

3. Slice the sponge cake into two even layers (between ¼ and ½ in/6 mm and 1 cm thick). Ladle 1 lb/454 g of the Bavarian cream into the mold. Trim one of the layers of sponge as necessary to fit, place it on top of the Bavarian cream, and moisten the layer with simple syrup. Ladle in the remaining 1 lb/454 g Bavarian cream, top with the second layer of sponge, and moisten it with simple syrup.

4. Cover with plastic wrap and refrigerate until the Bavarian cream has completely set.

5. Remove the plastic wrap and ease the cake out of the mold onto a serving platter or cardboard cake round by tugging carefully on the plastic. Invert onto a 10-in/25-cm cardboard round and carefully remove the mold. Using a pastry brush, coat the charlotte with the apricot glaze.

Charlotte Russe

Makes 1 cake (8 in/20 cm)

LADYFINGERS (page 370)	20–25 each	20–25 each
CHOCOLATE SPONGE CAKE (8 in/20 cm) (page 302)	1 each	1 each
VANILLA SIMPLE SYRUP (page 820)	5 fl oz	150 mL
CHOCOLATE BAVARIAN CREAM (page 403)	8 oz	227 g
VANILLA BAVARIAN CREAM (page 402)	8 oz	227 g
WHITE CHOCOLATE SHAVINGS	2 oz	57 g
DARK CHOCOLATE SHAVINGS	2 oz	57 g

1. Place an 8-in/20-cm cake ring on an 8-in/20-cm cardboard cake round. Trim the sponge to a 7½-in/19-cm round. Slice the sponge cake into three even layers (between ¼ and ½ in/6 mm and 1 cm thick). Place one of the sponge layers in the bottom of the mold and moisten with simple syrup.

2. Line the inside of the ring with the ladyfingers, flat sides facing in. Ladle the chocolate Bavarian cream on top of the sponge and spread it into an even layer. Top with the second layer of sponge and press down gently. Moisten the sponge layer with simple syrup. Ladle in the vanilla Bavarian cream and spread it evenly.

3. Cover with plastic wrap and refrigerate until the Bavarian cream has set completely.

4. Remove the plastic wrap and carefully lift away the cake ring.

5. Place a 4-in/10-cm ring in the center of the top of the cake and carefully fill it with the white chocolate shavings. Fill the space between the ring and the tops of the ladyfingers with the dark chocolate shavings. Remove the ring.

Chocolate Sabayon Torte

Makes 1 torte (8 in/20 cm)

CHOCOLATE SPONGE CAKE (8 in/20 cm) (page 302)	1 each	1 each
VANILLA SIMPLE SYRUP (page 820)	4 fl oz	120 mL
CHOCOLATE SABAYON MOUSSE (page 401)	1 lb 4 oz	567 g
SOFT GANACHE, whipped to medium peaks (page 424)	1 lb	454 g
CHOCOLATE TRIANGLES (page 764)	10 each	10 each
CHOCOLATE SHAVINGS	1 oz	28 g

1. Slice two even layers from the sponge cake (between ¼ and ½ in/6 mm and 1 cm thick). Moisten the sponge layers with simple syrup. Place one layer in the bottom of an 8-in/20-cm cake pan. Add 10 oz/284 g of the sabayon and spread it evenly. Place another sponge layer in the mold and top with the remaining 10 oz/284 g sabayon. Place the final sponge layer on top.

2. Cover and refrigerate until the sabayon has set completely.

3. To finish the cake, remove the plastic wrap. Warm the sides of the cake ring using a propane torch or a towel moistened with warm water and carefully remove the ring. Ice the cake with whipped ganache, reserving 4 oz/113 g for décor. Mark into 10 portions. Trim the edge with cake crumbs. Using a pastry bag fitted with a No. 5 plain tip, pipe 10 small domes of whipped ganache around the outer edge of the top of the cake to mark portions.

4. Fan the chocolate triangles around the cake, placing the base end of each at the center of the cake and fixing the opposite end to a piped dome so each stands at a 45-degree angle. Garnish the bottom quarter edge of the side of the cake by gently pressing the chocolate shavings to adhere.

Wine Cream Torte

Makes 1 torte (8 in/20 cm)

LARGE STRAWBERRIES	13 each	13 each
VANILLA SPONGE CAKE (8 in/20 cm) (page 302)	1 each	1 each
SIMPLE SYRUP (page 820)	3 fl oz	90 mL
WINE CREAM (page 40)	1 lb	454 g
HEAVY CREAM, whipped to medium peaks	16 fl oz	480 mL
DARK CHOCOLATE SHAVINGS	as needed	as needed

1. Place an 8-in/20-cm cake ring on an 8-in/20-cm cardboard round and then on a sheet pan.

2. Halve 8 of the strawberries. Line the inside of the cake ring with the strawberry halves, with the cut side facing out.

3. Slice two even layers from the sponge cake (between ¼ and ½ in/6 mm and 1 cm thick). Place one layer in the bottom of the cake ring and moisten with simple syrup. Ladle 8 oz/227 g of wine cream on top of the sponge and spread it into an even layer. Top with the second sponge layer and press down gently. Moisten the sponge with syrup. Ladle in the remaining 8 oz/227 g wine cream and spread it evenly.

4. Cover with plastic wrap and refrigerate until completely set.

5. Remove the plastic wrap. Warm the side of the cake ring using a propane torch or a towel moistened with warm water and carefully remove the ring.

6. Coat the top and sides of the cake with whipped cream, reserving 4 oz/113 g for garnish. Using a pastry bag fitted with a No. 5 plain tip, pipe 10 small domes of whipped cream around the outer edge of the top of the cake to mark portions. Slice the remaining strawberries in half and place a strawberry half on each dome.

7. Garnish the bottom quarter edge of the side of the cake by gently pressing the chocolate shavings to adhere.

Black Forest Cake

Makes 1 cake (8 in/20 cm)

CHOCOLATE SPONGE CAKE (8 in/20 cm) (page 302)	1 each	1 each
KIRSCH-FLAVORED SIMPLE SYRUP (page 820)	5 fl oz	150 mL
SOFT GANACHE, whipped (page 424)	1 lb	454 g
CHERRY FILLING (page 506)	12 oz	340 g
HEAVY CREAM, whipped	10 fl oz	300 mL
BRANDIED CHERRIES	10 each	10 each
CHOCOLATE SHAVINGS	2 oz	57 g

1. Slice three even layers from the sponge cake (between ¼ and ½ in/6 mm and 1 cm thick). Place one layer on an 8-in/20-cm cardboard cake round and moisten with simple syrup.

2. Using a pastry bag fitted with a No. 5 plain tip, pipe a ring of whipped ganache around the outer edge of the cake layer and then, leaving a gap of approximately 2 in/5 cm, pipe a circle of the ganache in the center of the layer. Fill the gap between the whipped ganache with cherry filling. Top with a second layer of sponge and pipe the remaining ganache evenly over it. Top with the last layer of sponge.

3. Finish the top and sides of the cake with whipped cream and mark into 10 portions. Using a No. 5 plain tip, pipe a dome of whipped cream on each portion. Garnish each dome with a brandied cherry.

4. Pile some chocolate shavings in the center of the cake and garnish the bottom edge of the side of the cake by gently pressing the chocolate shavings to adhere.

**COUNTER
CLOCKWISE
FROM TOP:**
Gâteau St.
Honoré, Black
Forest Cake,
Strawberry
Yogurt Torte
slice, Passion
Fruit Mousse
Cake Strawberry
Yogurt Torte

Assembling a Traditional Layer Cake

Traditional layer cakes call for different equipment and finishing techniques from molded cakes. Cake layers should be prepared according to the type of cake you are preparing. Filling options include jam, pudding, pastry cream, curd, buttercream, paddled ganache, whipped cream, mousse, and the like.

To assemble the cake, slice into layers and moisten with simple syrup if necessary. Place a dab of the filling or icing in the center of a cake round (the same diameter as the cake) and center the first cake layer on it. Spread a layer of filling evenly over the layer. The amount of filling is determined by the type of filling used, its consistency (i.e., its lightness or density), and the intensity of its flavor. If the filling is the right consistency for piping, a good way to ensure an even layer is to use a piping bag and pastry tip to fill the cake layers. Keep in mind that too much filling can cause the layers to slip as the cake is assembled and sliced. To keep certain types of fillings from oozing out between the layers as the cake is assembled or sliced, you can pipe a ring of buttercream or other icing around the edge of each layer before adding the filling.

As you assemble the cake, take time to straighten the layers if necessary. Brush away any excess crumbs from the sides of the cake. Once the cake is assembled, apply a thin layer of the icing, or, in some instances, the filling or a jam, to the top and sides of the cake for the seal coat, or crumb coat. This coat adheres any remaining crumbs onto the cake, preventing them from becoming incorporated in the final coating of icing or glaze and marring its appearance. The cake, with the crumb coat, is often refrigerated for an hour or so to allow the coating to set before applying the final coating of icing. This will ease the application of the final icing and ensure a smooth finished surface. (For more information on icing cakes see page 548.)

Dobos Torte

Makes 1 torte (8 in/20 cm)

DOBOS LAYERS (8 in/20 cm) (page 310)	7 each	7 each
BRANDY-FLAVORED SIMPLE SYRUP (page 820)	6 fl oz	180 mL
MOCHA BUTTERCREAM (page 419)	1 lb 8 oz	680 g
SUGAR	6 oz	170 g
LEMON JUICE	¼ tsp	1.25 mL
GLUCOSE SYRUP	1¼ oz	35 g
BUTTER, soft	1 oz	28 g
CHOCOLATE, tempered	8 oz	227 g

1. Trim the edges of 6 of the Dobos layers to make them 8 in/20 cm in diameter. Place one layer on an 8-in/20-cm cardboard cake round. Moisten with simple syrup and, reserving 8 oz/227 g of the buttercream for décor, apply a thin, even layer of buttercream. Top with a second Dobos layer, moisten with syrup, and spread with buttercream. Repeat the process with the remaining trimmed layers. Finish the top and sides of the cake with buttercream.

2. To prepare the caramel, combine the sugar, lemon juice, and glucose syrup in a heavy-bottomed saucepan set over medium heat and allow it to melt, stirring to dissolve. When all the sugar has dissolved, stop stirring and cook to the desired color. Remove from the heat and stir in the butter.

3. Spread the caramel in an even layer over the reserved Dobos layer. Cut into 10 even wedges and allow to cool completely.

4. Dip the rounded edge of each wedge in the tempered chocolate. Allow to set completely.

5. Mark the cake into 10 portions. Using a pastry bag fitted with a No. 5 plain tip, pipe a small dome of buttercream on each portion. Fan the caramel-coated wedges around the cake, placing the pointed tip of each wedge at the center of the cake and fixing the opposite end in a buttercream dome to create a "pinwheel" effect.

Hazelnut Torte

Makes 1 torte (8 in/20 cm)

HAZELNUT SPONGE CAKE (8 in/20 cm) (page 311)	1 each	1 each
BRANDY-FLAVORED SIMPLE SYRUP (page 820)	4 fl oz	120 mL
RASPBERRY JAM	1½ oz	43 g
HAZELNUT BUTTERCREAM (page 419)	2 lb	907 g
HAZELNUT FLORENTINE (8-in/20-cm round) (Recipe follows)	1 each	1 each
HAZELNUTS, toasted and ground	2 oz	57 g

1. Slice three even layers from the sponge cake (between ¼ and ½ in/6 mm and 1 cm thick). Place one layer on an 8-in/20-cm cardboard round and moisten with simple syrup. Spread the jam in a thin, even layer on the first layer of sponge and then apply an even coating of buttercream. Top with a second sponge layer and press down gently. Moisten with syrup, apply an even coating of buttercream, and top with the remaining sponge layer.

Cutting a hazelnut florentine into wedges for décor

2. Finish the top and sides of the cake with buttercream. Mark into 10 portions. Using a pastry bag fitted with a No. 5 plain tip, pipe a small dome of buttercream on each portion.

3. Cut the Florentine into 10 equal wedges. Fan the wedges around the cake, placing the pointed tip of each at the center of the cake and laying the opposite end on a dome to create a "pinwheel" effect.

4. Garnish the bottom quarter edge of the side of the cake by gently pressing the ground hazelnuts to adhere.

Hazelnut Florentine
Makes 6 circles (8 in/20 cm each)

HEAVY CREAM	7 fl oz	210 mL
SUGAR	8 oz	227 g
BUTTER	2 oz	57 g
HAZELNUTS, finely ground	12 oz	340 g
CAKE FLOUR	1/2 oz	14 g

1. Trace six 8-in/20-cm circles on parchment paper. Line sheet pans with the parchment paper. Combine the heavy cream, sugar, and butter in a saucepan and bring to a boil.

2. Blend in the hazelnuts and cake flour. Remove the pan from the heat.

3. Divide the mixture among the six 8-in/20-cm circles; spread thinly and evenly.

4. Bake at 300°F/149°C until golden brown, about 20 minutes.

5. Allow the florentines to rest on the sheet pans until they are set and no longer sticky, but still warm.

6. Place an 8-in/20-cm cardboard cake round on top of each florentine and trim the edges using a pastry wheel.

7. Immediately cut into 10 even wedges. Allow to cool completely before applying to a cake.

Variations   **Chocolate-Dipped Florentines** If desired, 1/4 in/6 mm of the end opposite the tip of each wedge can be dipped in tempered chocolate.

Confectioners' Sugar–Dusted Florentines If desired, place a 7-in/18-cm cardboard cake round on top of the florentine wedges while they are assembled in a circle and dust with confectioners' sugar.

Mocha Torte

Makes 1 torte (8 in/20 cm)

CHOCOLATE SPONGE CAKE (8 in/20 cm) (page 302)	1 each	1 each
VANILLA SPONGE CAKE (8 in/20 cm) (page 302)	1 each	1 each
COFFEE SIMPLE SYRUP (page 820)	8 fl oz	240 mL
CHOCOLATE BUTTERCREAM (page 419)	1 lb 6 oz	624 g
MARZIPAN COFFEE BEANS, for garnish	10 each	10 each
HARD GANACHE (page 425)	6 oz	170 g
CHOCOLATE SHAVINGS	2 oz	57 g

1. Slice two even layers from each of the sponge cakes (between ¼ and ½ in/6 mm and 1 cm thick).

2. Place a layer of the vanilla sponge on an 8-in/20-cm cardboard cake round and moisten with simple syrup. Apply an even coating of buttercream to the sponge layer, reserving 6 oz/170 g of the buttercream for décor. Top with a layer of chocolate sponge and press it down gently. Moisten with simple syrup and apply an even coating of buttercream. Top with the remaining vanilla sponge layer and apply an even coating of buttercream. Top with the remaining chocolate sponge layer.

3. Coat the top and sides of the cake with buttercream. Mark into 10 portions. Using a pastry bag fitted with a No. 5 plain tip, pipe a domed rosette of buttercream on each portion. Place a marzipan coffee bean in the center of each rosette. Using a parchment cone, pipe a small dome of ganache in the center of the cake. Then pipe a line of ganache on each marked portion, beginning at the center, looping around the rosette, and connecting again at the center to form a teardrop.

4. Garnish the bottom edge of the torte with the chocolate shavings.

Chocolate Almond Torte

Makes 1 torte (8 in/20 cm)

CHOCOLATE ALMOND CAKE (8 in/20 cm) (page 314)	1 each	1 each
APRICOT JAM	9 oz	255 g
HARD GANACHE (page 425)	10 oz	284 g

1. Cut the cake into two even layers. Place one layer on an 8-in/20-cm cake round. Spread a thin layer of jam on the layer and top with the second layer.

2. Coat the top and sides of the cake with the remaining jam.

3. Glaze the cake with the ganache, reserving 4 oz/113 g for décor. Chill for 15 minutes.

4. Mark the torte into 10 portions. Rewarm the reserved ganache and, using a parchment cone, decorate each portion with a filigree of ganache.

Spreading chocolate glaze to completely enrobe the top and sides of a cake

Glazing a Cake

To glaze a traditional layer cake, apply a thin seal coat layer with something such as paddled ganache or jam to the cake. Refrigerate until the seal coat is set.

To prepare a glazing setup, place a wire rack on a sheet pan. The rack will allow the glaze to run freely from the sides of the cake, while the sheet pan will catch the excess glaze, which, if it does not contain any crumbs, can be rewarmed and used on another item.

Have ready a straight or offset long metal spatula for spreading the glaze.

Place the cake on the center of the wire rack. Check the consistency and temperature of the glaze. If it is too thick, rewarm it or, for glazes such as fondant, adjust the fluidity and temperature as described on page 426. The glaze should not be too warm, or it will not coat properly. It may run too much and could cause the seal coat to begin to melt, making it difficult to achieve the glossy look of a properly applied glaze. Be careful not to stir the glaze too much, as this will incorporate air and cause bubbles in the glaze on the surface of the cake. Before you glaze, if you desire, reserve some of the glaze for décor.

Once you pour the glaze, it will have to be worked quickly. After it begins to set, it should not be touched, or the flat surface and glossy finish will be destroyed (with most glazes, it is difficult, if not impossible, to hide any markings created by touching the glaze after it has set). Pour enough glaze onto the center of the cake to enrobe it. Working quickly, spread the glaze over the entire top of the cake with three swipes of a long metal icing spatula, working across the top of the cake in one direction (always pushing or drawing the glaze away from you) from one side to the other and then off the cake. Do not lift the spatula while it is on the cake, or it will pull up the seal coat and cause crumbs to become mixed with the glaze, destroying the finish; pulling or drawing the spatula toward you can have the same effect. In addition to covering the top of the cake, this technique will cause the glaze to run down over the sides, covering them as well. Once the top of the cake is covered, use the spatula to spread glaze over any small portions of the sides of the cake that were not covered.

Check the finish on the top of the cake. If any air bubbles have formed, they can be removed if you act quickly, using a sharp skewer, or by moving the flame of a propane torch over the surface.

Havana Torte

Makes 1 torte (8 in/20 cm)

HAVANA BATTER CAKE (8 in/20 cm) (page 312)	1 each	1 each
CHOCOLATE BUTTERCREAM (page 419)	1 lb 8 oz	680 g
HARD GANACHE, warm (page 425)	1 lb	454 g
CHOCOLATE CIGARETTES (page 766)	10 each	10 each

1. Place the cake on an 8-in/20-cm cardboard cake round. Coat the top and sides of the cake with 1 lb/454 g of the buttercream. Refrigerate until the buttercream is firm.

2. Glaze the torte with the warm ganache. Allow to set.

3. Mark the torte into 10 portions. Using a pastry bag fitted with a No. 5 plain tip, pipe a small dome of ganache on each portion. Place a chocolate cigarette on each portion so that it rests on the dome of ganache.

Opera Torte

Makes 1 torte (8 in/20 cm)

JOCONDE SHEET (16½ by 24½ in/42 by 62 cm) (page 316)	1 each	1 each
DARK CHOCOLATE, melted	4 oz	113 g
VEGETABLE OIL	½ oz	14 g
COFFEE-FLAVORED SIMPLE SYRUP (page 820)	8 fl oz	240 mL
MEDIUM GANACHE, lightly whipped (Appendix A)	6 oz	170 g
COFFEE BUTTERCREAM (page 420)	8 oz	227 g
HARD GANACHE (page 425)	6 oz	170 g

1. Line a 10-in/25-cm cardboard cake round with a parchment circle of the same size. Cut the joconde sheet into three 8½-in/22-cm squares.

2. Combine the chocolate and vegetable oil. Turn one joconde layer upside down and thinly coat the top surface with the chocolate mixture. Place it chocolate side down on the parchment-lined cake round. Moisten the layer with simple syrup and spread with an even coating of ganache. Top with the next layer of cake, press it down gently, and coat evenly with 6 oz/170 g of the buttercream. Top with the final layer of cake, press down gently, and moisten with simple syrup.

3. Coat the top of the cake with the remaining buttercream. Refrigerate until the buttercream is firm.

4. Invert the cake carefully, peel the parchment circle off the bottom of the cake, and place the cake, buttercream-coated side up, on an 8-in/20-cm cardboard square. Glaze with the ganache using a warm knife, reserving 2 oz/57 g of the ganache for décor. Allow the glaze to set and trim the edges to make a perfect 8-in/20-cm square.

5. Using a parchment cone, pipe the word "Opera" with cooled ganache across the top of the torte.

Spanish Vanilla Torte

Makes 1 torte (8 in/20 cm)

SPANISH VANILLA CAKE (8 in/20 cm) (page 313)	1 each	1 each
BRANDY-FLAVORED SIMPLE SYRUP (page 820)	8 fl oz	240 mL
APRICOT JAM	6 oz	170 g
MARZIPAN (page 774)	13 oz	369 g
HARD GANACHE (page 425)	1 lb	454 g
CUT MARZIPAN FLOWERS (³/₄ in/2 cm diameter) (page 776)	10 each	10 each

1. Slice three even layers from the cake (between ¼ and ½ in/6 mm and 1 cm thick). Place one layer on an 8-in/20-cm cardboard cake round and moisten with simple syrup. Apply a thin coating of apricot jam to the layer. Top with a second layer and press down gently. Moisten with simple syrup, apply a thin coating of apricot jam, and top with the final layer of cake. Apply a thin coating of apricot jam to the top and sides of the cake, reserving 1 oz/28 g of the jam for décor.

2. On a work surface lightly dusted with sifted confectioners' sugar, roll out the marzipan to a circle about 15 in/38 cm in diameter and ⅛ in/3 mm thick. Carefully lift up the marzipan and drape it over the cake so that it completely covers it. Press the marzipan against the top and sides of the cake so that it adheres well. Using the palm of your hand in a rotating motion, smooth the marzipan as necessary. Using a sharp paring knife, trim the marzipan at the bottom edge of the cake.

3. Glaze the cake with the ganache, reserving 4 oz/113 g of the ganache for décor. Mark into 10 portions.

4. Using the paddle attachment, lightly beat the remaining ganache until light in color and texture. Using a pastry bag fitted with a No. 3 plain tip, pipe a small dome on each portion of cake. Place a marzipan flower on each dome. Using a parchment cone, pipe a small dot of apricot jam in the center of each flower.

Enrobing a Cake in Marzipan or Other Rolled Icing

Marzipan is often used as a covering for cakes. It may be used as the final coating, or it may be used as an undercoating that will be covered with an icing or glaze. If it is to be covered, roll the marzipan very thin (approximately 1/16 in/1.5 mm). If it is to be the finished covering, roll it to approximately 1/4 in/6 mm thick; this is thick enough to ensure a smooth finished surface.

Before applying the marzipan or other rolled icing, prepare the surface of the cake. Trim the sides so they are even, and apply a seal coat. The jam or buttercream coating should be thin so that the marizpan or icing will not slip or slide.

Apply the marzipan to the cake, using the palm of your hand in a circular motion to create a smooth, flat surface.

Zebra Torte
Makes 1 torte (8 in/20 cm)

VANILLA SPONGE CAKE (8 in/20 cm) (page 318)	1 each	1 each
VANILLA SIMPLE SYRUP (page 820)	5 fl oz	150 mL
CHOCOLATE ROULADE SHEET (11 1/2 by 16 1/2 in/29 by 42 cm) (page 307)	1 each	1 each
HEAVY CREAM	24 fl oz	720 mL
CONFECTIONERS' SUGAR, sifted	3/4 oz	21 g
RUM	3 fl oz	90 mL
ROUND DARK CHOCOLATE CUTOUTS (1 1/2 in/4 cm diameter) (page 765)	10 each	10 each
DARK CHOCOLATE, tempered	2 oz	57 g
CHOCOLATE CAKE CRUMBS	3 oz	85 g

1. Place an 8-in/20-cm cardboard cake round on a sheet pan and place an 8-in/20-cm cake ring on top. Slice the 8-in/20-cm round vanilla sponge cake into two even layers (between 1/4 and 1/2 in/6 mm and 1 cm thick), place one layer into the cake ring and moisten with simple syrup.

2. Moisten the chocolate roulade sheet with the simple syrup. Combine 12 fl oz/360 mL of the heavy cream with the confectioners' sugar and 2 fl oz/60 mL of the rum and whip to medium peaks. Spread evenly over the moistened roulade and cut into strips 1 1/2 in/4 cm wide.

3. Roll one of the strips, with the cream side in, into a spiral. Join the end of another strip to the end of the spiral and roll to continue the spiral. Repeat this process with the remaining strips to create a spiral approximately 8 in/20 cm in diameter. Carefully place the spiral into the cake ring. Moisten the remaining layer of the vanilla sponge with simple syrup and place on top of the spiral. Wrap the cake in the ring in plastic wrap and refrigerate for about 2 hours, or until the whipped cream layers have set.

4. Remove the plastic wrap and gently lift away the cake ring. Combine the remaining 12 fl oz/360 mL heavy cream with the remaining 1 fl oz/30 mL rum and whip to medium peaks. Finish the top and sides of the cake with the whipped cream, reserving 4 oz/113 g for décor.

5. Mark the torte into 10 portions. Using a pastry bag fitted with a No. 5 plain tip, pipe a small dome of whipped cream onto each portion. Place a chocolate cutout on each dome.

6. Mark the center of the cake with a 4-in/10-cm round cutter. Using a parchment cone, pipe a corneli design with the tempered chocolate into the marked circle. Garnish the bottom quarter edge of the side of the cake by gently pressing the chocolate cake crumbs to adhere.

Zuger Kirsch Torte
Makes 1 torte (8 in/20 cm)

JAPONAIS (8 in/20 cm) **(Appendix A)**	2 each	2 each
VANILLA SPONGE CAKE **(8 in/20 cm) (page 318)**	1 each	1 each
KIRSCH-FLAVORED **BUTTERCREAM** **(page 419)**	14 oz	397 g
KIRSCH-FLAVORED **SIMPLE SYRUP (page 820)**	3 fl oz	90 mL
SLICED ALMONDS, toasted	2 oz	57 g
CONFECTIONERS' **SUGAR**	1 oz	28 g
CANDIED CHERRIES	10 each	10 each

1. Using a serrated knife, cut one of the japonais layers into 10 even wedges. Cut one layer from the sponge (between ¼ and ½ in/6 mm and 1 cm thick).

2. Place the remaining japonais layer on an 8-in/20-cm cake round and apply a thin layer of buttercream. Thoroughly moisten the sponge layer with simple syrup and place on top of the japonais layer. Apply a thin layer of buttercream. Arrange the cut japonais wedges on top, carefully fitting them together.

3. Coat the sides of the torte with the remaining buttercream. Press the toasted almonds onto the buttercream.

4. Dust the top of the torte heavily with the confectioners' sugar, then mark with a lattice pattern, using the back of a knife. Mark the portions with a candied cherry at the outer edge of each one.

Gâteau St. Honoré

Makes 1 cake (8 in/20 cm)

PUFF PASTRY (page 260)	4 oz	113 g
PÂTE À CHOUX (page 255)	7½ oz	213 g
KIRSCH-FLAVORED PASTRY CREAM (page 388)	8 oz	227 g
SUGAR	12 oz	340 g
KIRSCH-FLAVORED DIPLOMAT CREAM (page 402)	1 lb	454 g

1. Roll the puff pastry into an 8-in/20-cm circle, dock, and place it on a parchment-lined sheet pan. Using a pastry bag fitted with a No. 8 plain tip, pipe a border of pâte à choux onto the puff pastry circle and a smaller ring in the center. Pipe approximately 12 small round cream puffs on a separate parchment-lined sheet pan.

2. Bake the puff pastry round and cream puffs at 375°F/191°C until golden brown, about 30 minutes. Allow to cool.

3. Fill each of the cream puffs with some of the pastry cream.

4. To prepare the caramel, add a small amount of the sugar to a medium-hot pan set over medium heat and allow it to melt, then add the remaining sugar in small increments, allowing each addition to fully melt before adding the next. Continue this process until all the sugar has been added to the pan and cook to the desired color. Dip the top of each cream puff into the caramel and place them caramel side down on a sheet pan that has been greased lightly. Once cool, dip the bottom of each puff into the caramel and stick it to the outside edge of the shell, spacing them evenly.

5. Fill the center of the gâteau with diplomat cream; it should come to within ½ in/1 cm of the tops of the cream puffs. Using a pastry bag fitted with a V-cut round tip or a large rose petal tip, pipe the diplomat cream in a wave pattern on top of the gâteau.

Pithivier

Makes 1 cake (8 in/20 cm)

BUTTER, soft	8 oz	227 g
SUGAR	8 oz	227 g
GROUND ALMONDS	3⅓ oz	94 g
VANILLA EXTRACT	1 tsp	5 mL
EGGS	4 oz	113 g
PUFF PASTRY (page 260)	1 lb	454 g
EGG WASH (page 825)	2 oz	57 g
LIGHT CORN SYRUP	1 oz	28 g

1. To prepare the filling, cream the butter and sugar in an electric mixer using the paddle attachment until light and fluffy, about 5 minutes.

2. Mix in the almonds and vanilla extract. Add the eggs one at a time, mixing until fully incorporated after each addition and scraping down the bowl as necessary.

3. Roll the puff pastry to a thickness of ⅛ in/3 mm. Cut out two 8-in/20-cm circles from the pastry.

4. Place one of the circles on a parchment-lined sheet pan and spread the filling in the center of the circle, leaving a 1½-in/4-cm border all around. Brush the border lightly with egg wash. Place the remaining puff pastry circle on top, carefully lining up the edges of the two circles. Gently press the edges together. Cover with plastic wrap and chill for 20 minutes.

5. Using a sharp paring knife, scallop the edges of the pastry. Brush the pastry with egg wash and cut a spiral sunburst pattern in the top, working from the center out and being careful not to cut through to the filling.

6. Bake at 375°F/191°C until golden brown, 35 to 40 minutes. Brush the top of the pithivier with the corn syrup. Turn the oven up to 425°F/218°C and bake until the corn syrup has become a golden glaze, about 3 minutes longer.

7. Allow the pithivier to cool slightly before serving.

The pattern of cuts atop a Pithivier

Almond Cake

Makes 1 cake (8 in/20 cm)

1-2-3 COOKIE DOUGH (page 249)	8 oz	227 g
ITALIAN BUTTERCREAM (page 418)	1 lb 10 oz	737 g
DARK CHOCOLATE, melted	2 oz	57 g
ALMOND EXTRACT	½ tsp	2.50 mL
BRANDY	2 fl oz	60 mL
VANILLA SPONGE CAKE (8 in/20 cm) (page 302)	1 each	1 each
RASPBERRY JAM	1 oz	28 g
VANILLA SIMPLE SYRUP (page 820)	4 fl oz	120 mL
MARZIPAN	2 oz	57 g
CHOCOLATE CIGARETTE (page 766)	1 each	1 each

1. Roll out the dough ⅛ in/3 mm thick and cut out an 8-in/20-cm round. Transfer to a parchment-lined sheet pan.

2. Bake at 350°F/177°C until golden brown, 10 to 12 minutes. Cool completely.

3. Flavor 6 oz/170 g of the buttercream with the melted chocolate. Flavor another 6 oz/170 g of the buttercream with the almond extract and 1 fl oz/30 mL of the brandy. Flavor the remaining buttercream with the remaining 1 fl oz/30 mL brandy. Reserve 6 oz/170 g of the brandy-flavored buttercream for décor.

4. Cut three even layers from the sponge cake (between ¼ and ½ in/6 mm and 1 cm thick).

5. Place the cookie round on a cardboard cake round and apply a thin coating of raspberry jam to the cookie round. Top with a sponge layer and moisten with simple syrup. Coat with the ginger chocolate buttercream. Top with the second sponge layer, moisten with simple syrup, and coat with the almond brandy buttercream. Top with the third layer of sponge cake and moisten with simple syrup.

6. Finish the top and sides of the cake with the brandy buttercream, reserving 4 oz/113 g for decor.

7. Dust a work surface with confectioners' sugar and roll the marzipan to a thickness of ¹⁄₁₆ in/1.5 mm. With a 1-in/3-cm cutter, cut out nine circles. Cut the circles in half. Press them against the base of the cake with the flat side down.

8. Using the reserved buttercream and a pastry bag fitted with a No. 3 plain tip, pipe a line of shells across the top of the cake, dividing the cake in half. Lay the chocolate cigarette at a 45-degree angle across the piped shell border.

Coffee Chantilly Torte

Makes 1 torte (8 in/20 cm)

1-2-3 COOKIE DOUGH (page 249)	8 oz	227 g
VANILLA CHIFFON CAKE (8 in/20 cm) (page 318)	1 each	1 each
SOFT GANACHE, whipped (page 424)	6 oz	170 g
KAHLÚA-FLAVORED SIMPLE SYRUP (page 820)	4 fl oz	120 mL
COFFEE CHANTILLY CREAM (page 422)	6 oz	170 g
CHANTILLY CREAM (page 422)	12 oz	340 g
ALMONDS, toasted and ground	4 oz	113 g
STRIPED CHOCOLATE TRIANGLES (page 764)	5 each	5 each
DARK CHOCOLATE, melted, tempered	2 oz	57 g

1. Roll out the dough ⅛ in/3 mm thick and cut out an 8-in/20-cm round. Transfer to a sheet pan.

2. Bake at 350°F/177°C until golden brown, 10 to 12 minutes. Cool completely.

3. Slice two ¼-in/6-mm layers from the chiffon cake.

4. Place the cookie round on an 8-in/20-cm cardboard cake round and coat with the whipped ganache. Top with a layer of chiffon cake and moisten with simple syrup. Coat with the coffee chantilly cream. Top with the second layer of chiffon cake and moisten with simple syrup.

5. Finish the top and sides of the cake with the plain Chantilly cream, reserving 4 oz/113 g for décor. Press the ground almonds onto the base of the cake.

6. Using the reserved Chantilly cream and a pastry bag fitted with a No. 4 star tip, cover one-third of the top of the cake with rosettes. Randomly layer the chocolate triangles in the center of the cake. Using a parchment cone, pipe a continuous swirl of the tempered chocolate around the triangles.

Chestnut Cake

Makes 1 paisley cake (8 in/20 cm)

VANILLA CHIFFON CAKE (8 in/20 cm) (page 318)	1 each	1 each
RUM-FLAVORED SIMPLE SYRUP (page 820)	5 fl oz	150 mL
CHESTNUT PURÉE	10 oz	284 g
ITALIAN MERINGUE (page 416)	8 oz	227 g
BUTTER, soft	10 oz	284 g
RUM	2 fl oz	60 mL
HARD GANACHE (page 425)	6 oz	170 g
CANDIED CHESTNUTS, for décor	3 each	3 each

1. Line the bottom of an 8-in/20-cm paisley mold (or an 8-in/20-cm ring mold) with a cardboard cake round, cutting it to fit. Line the sides of the paisley mold with a strip of acetate or plastic wrap, cutting it to fit.

2. Slice three even layers from the chiffon cake (between ¼ and ½ in/6 mm and 1 cm thick). Moisten each layer with simple syrup.

3. Blend the chestnut purée into the Italian meringue. Add the butter and rum and blend until well combined.

4. Place one cake layer in the mold and coat with a thin layer of the chestnut buttercream. Top with a second cake layer and coat with a thin layer of buttercream. Top with the final layer of cake.

5. Coat the top of the cake with the buttercream, reserving enough to coat the sides of the cake. Wrap in plastic wrap and refrigerate until the buttercream is firm, about 1 hour.

6. Unmold the cake. Coat the sides with the reserved buttercream. Refrigerate until the buttercream has set.

7. Glaze the cake with the ganache. Place the candied chestnuts in the center of the cake.

Chocolate Marquise Torte

Makes 1 hexagonal torte (6 by 10¼ in/15 by 26 cm)

ITALIAN BUTTERCREAM (page 418)	10 oz	284 g
GIANDUJA (page 742)	8 oz	227 g
JAPONAIS (6 by 10¼ in/ 15 by 26 cm) (Appendix A)	1 each	1 each
RASPBERRY JAM	2 oz	57 g
CHOCOLATE CHIFFON CAKE (6 by 10¼ in/15 by 26 cm) (page 318)	3 each	3 each
COINTREAU-FLAVORED SIMPLE SYRUP (page 820)	7 fl oz	210 mL
SOFT GANACHE, whipped (page 424)	5 oz	142 g
MARZIPAN	12 oz	340 g
HARD MILK CHOCOLATE GANACHE (Appendix A)	12 oz	340 g
WHITE CHOCOLATE TRIANGLES (2½ by 2½ by 2 in/6 by 6 by 5 cm) (page 764)	7 each	7 each

1. Blend together the buttercream and gianduja.

2. Line the bottom of a hexagonal bottomless mold (6 by 10¼ in/15 by 26 cm) with cardboard, cutting it to fit. Trim the japonais layer to fit inside the mold. Spread a thin coating of raspberry jam on the japonais and place it in the bottom of the mold. Top with a layer of chiffon cake and moisten with simple syrup. Coat with 5 oz/142 g of the gianduja buttercream. Top with a second layer of chiffon cake, moisten with simple syrup, and coat with the soft ganache. Top with the last layer of chiffon cake and moisten with simple syrup.

4. Coat the top of the torte with a thin layer of buttercream. Cover with plastic wrap and refrigerate until the buttercream is set.

5. Remove the plastic wrap. Warm the side of the cake ring using a propane torch or a towel moistened with warm water and carefully remove the ring. Coat the sides of the cake with the remaining buttercream, reserving 4 oz/113 g for décor.

6. Dust a work surface with confectioners' sugar and roll the marzipan to a rectangle ¹⁄₁₆ in/1.5 mm thick and large enough to cover the entire cake. Cover the torte with the marzipan. Smooth the top and sides and cut away the excess at the corners to create close, neat seams. Glaze the torte with the milk chocolate ganache. Refrigerate until firm.

7. Using a pastry bag fitted with a No. 4 plain tip, pipe a scrolled line of buttercream diagonally across the center of the cake. Place the white chocolate triangles in a line parallel to the left of the scrolled line, arranging them so that each triangle slightly overlaps the previous one.

Chocolate Dacquoise Torte

Makes 1 torte (8 in/20 cm)

JAPONAIS (8 in/20 cm) (Appendix A)	3 each	3 each
SOFT GANACHE, whipped (page 424)	26 oz	737 g
DARK CHOCOLATE RECTANGULAR CUTOUTS (1½ by 3 in/4 by 8 cm) (page 765)	25 each	25 each
HAZELNUTS, toasted, skins removed	4 oz	113 g

1. Trim each dacquoise layer to a perfect 8-in/20-cm round.

2. Smear a dollop of the ganache in the center of an 8-in/20-cm cardboard cake round and place one of the dacquoise rounds on top. Coat the dacquoise with 6 oz/170 g of the ganache. Top with a second dacquoise round and coat it with 6 oz/170 g of the ganache. Top with the remaining dacquoise round.

3. Coat the top and sides of the torte with 5 oz of the ganache and refrigerate for about 1 hour to set firm. Finish the top and sides of the torte with the remaining ganache, reserving 4 oz/113 g for décor.

4. Reserve three chocolate rectangles. Press the remaining rectangles onto the sides of the cake, slightly overlapping them and completely covering the sides of the cake.

5. Using a pastry bag fitted with a No. 3 plain tip, pipe small domes of chocolate whipped cream around the top edge of the cake. Place a hazelnut on each dome at intervals of 2 in/5 cm to mark the portions. Place a cluster of the remaining hazelnuts slightly off center on the top of the cake. Break up the reserved chocolate rectangles and place next to the cluster of hazelnuts.

Chocolate Mousse Torte

Makes 1 oval torte (5½ by 11 in/14 by 28 cm)

LADYFINGER STRIP (1½ by 24 in/4 by 61 cm), alternating vanilla and chocolate (page 370)	1 each	1 each
CHOCOLATE SPONGE CAKE SHEET (16½ by 24½ in/42 by 62 cm) (page 302)	1 each	1 each
ORANGE-FLAVORED SIMPLE SYRUP (page 820)	5 fl oz	150 mL
WHITE CHOCOLATE MOUSSE (page 400)	9 oz	255 g
DARK CHOCOLATE MOUSSE (page 398)	9 oz	255 g
HARD MILK CHOCOLATE GANACHE (Appendix A)	5 oz	142 g
WHITE AND DARK CHOCOLATE RUFFLES (page 769)	2 each	2 each

1. Line the bottom of an oval cake ring mold with cardboard, cutting it to fit. Line the sides of the mold with acetate. Line the inside of the mold with the ladyfinger strip with the flat side facing in.

2. Cut two ovals (5½ by 11 in/14 by 28 cm each) from the sheet of sponge cake. Place one in the mold and moisten with simple syrup. Spread the white chocolate mousse evenly over the layer. Top with the second layer of sponge cake, moisten, and spread evenly with the dark chocolate mousse.

3. Cover with plastic wrap and refrigerate until firm, at least 2 hours.

4. Glaze the top of the torte with a thin coating of milk chocolate ganache. Place the torte in the freezer for 30 minutes.

5. Warm the sides of the cake mold using a propane torch or a towel moistened with warm water and carefully remove the mold.

6. Garnish the top of the torte with the chocolate ruffles.

Chocolate Ruffle Cake

Makes 1 cake (8 in/20 cm)

CHOCOLATE HIGH-RATIO CAKE (8 in/20 cm) (page 299)	1 each	1 each
VANILLA SIMPLE SYRUP (page 820)	5 fl oz	150 mL
SOFT GANACHE, whipped (page 424)	12 oz	340 g
DARK CHOCOLATE, melted	1 lb 4 oz	567 g
CONFECTIONERS' SUGAR	3 oz	85 g

1. Slice three even layers from the cake (between ¼ and ½ in/6 mm and 1 cm thick). Place one of the cake layers on an 8-in/20-cm cardboard cake round. Moisten with simple syrup and coat with 4 oz/113 g of the ganache. Top with another layer of cake, moisten with simple syrup, and coat with 4 oz/113 g of the ganache. Top with the final layer of cake and moisten with simple syrup.

2. Coat the top and sides of the cake with the remaining ganache.

3. Warm two perfectly flat sheet pans in the oven until just warm to the touch (approximately 100°F/38°C). Ladle 10 oz/284 g of the melted chocolate onto the back of each sheet pan and spread evenly with an offset spatula.

4. Refrigerate the sheet pans for 15 minutes, then transfer to the freezer for 15 minutes.

5. Remove the pans from the freezer and let stand at room temperature until the chocolate becomes pliable, about 5 minutes.

6. With a small offset spatula pressing against the sheet pan, scrape a strip of chocolate approximately 3 in/8 cm wide and the length of the sheet pan in one continuous motion. Wrap the strip of chocolate around the cake.

7. With the same spatula, remove chocolate from the pans holding the tip of the spatula steady and rotating the handle end to create fans, or ruffles. Arrange the chocolate ruffles on the top of the cake in concentric circles, starting from the edge and working in, overlapping the circles to completely cover the top of the cake. Sprinkle lightly with confectioners' sugar.

Gâteau Praline

Makes 1 cake (8 in/20 cm)

1-2-3 COOKIE DOUGH (page 249)	8 oz	227 g
HAZELNUT SPONGE CAKE (8 in/20 cm) (page 311)	1 each	1 each
PRALINE PASTE	2 oz	57 g
FRENCH BUTTERCREAM (page 420)	1 lb 12 oz	794 g
NOUGATINE, crushed	2 oz	57 g
FRANGELICO-FLAVORED SIMPLE SYRUP (page 820)	6 fl oz	180 mL
DARK CHOCOLATE RECTANGULAR CUTOUTS (1½ by 3 in/ 4 by 8 cm) (page 765)	25 each	25 each
HAZELNUTS, roasted	8 oz	227 g

1. Roll out the dough ⅛ in/3 mm thick and cut out an 8-in/20-cm round. Transfer to a sheet pan.

2. Bake at 350°F/177°C until golden brown, 10 to 12 minutes. Cool completely.

3. Slice three even layers from the sponge cake (between ¼ and ½ in/6 mm and 1 cm thick).

4. Blend the praline paste into the buttercream. Add the crushed krokant to 10 oz/284 g of the praline buttercream and blend well. Reserve 6 oz/170 g of the buttercream for décor.

5. Place the cookie round on an 8-in/20-cm cardboard cake round and coat with 2 oz/57 g of the praline buttercream. Top with a layer of sponge cake, moisten with simple syrup, and coat with 5 oz/142 g of the krokant buttercream. Top with a second layer of sponge cake, moisten with simple syrup, and coat with the remaining krokant buttercream. Top with the remaining sponge layer.

6. Finish the top and sides of the cake with the praline buttercream. Press the chocolate rectangles onto the sides of the cake, overlapping them slightly and completely covering the sides of the cake.

7. Using a pastry bag fitted with a No. 3 star tip, pipe a shell border around the top edge of the cake. Place the caramelized hazelnuts on the border, spacing them evenly.

Gâteau Charlemagne

Makes 1 cake (8 in/20 cm)

JAPONAIS (8 in/20 cm) (Appendix A)	2 each	2 each
CHOCOLATE CHIFFON CAKE (8 in/20 cm) (page 318)	1 each	1 each
HAZELNUT LIQUEUR	2 fl oz	60 mL
HONEY	1 oz	28 g
DIPLOMAT CREAM (page 402)	10 oz	283 g
FRANGELICO-FLAVORED SIMPLE SYRUP (page 820)	3 fl oz	90 mL
CHANTILLY CREAM (page 822)	8 oz	227 g
WHITE CHOCOLATE ROUND CUTOUTS (3 in/8 cm) (page 765)	6 each	6 each
COCOA POWDER, for dusting	as needed	as needed

1. Trim each japonais layer to a perfect 8-in/20-cm round. Slice one layer from the chiffon cake (between ¼ and ½ in/6 mm and 1 cm thick).

2. Blend the hazelnut liqueur and honey into the diplomat cream.

3. Smear a dollop of the diplomat cream onto the center of an 8-in/20-cm cardboard cake round and place one of the japonais rounds on top. Coat with 5 oz/142 g of the diplomat cream. Top with the layer of chiffon cake, moisten it with simple syrup, and coat with the remaining diplomat cream. Top with the remaining japonais round.

4. Coat the top and sides of the cake with the Chantilly cream.

5. Reserve three of the white chocolate rounds. Press the remaining chocolate rounds onto the sides of the cake, overlapping them slightly and completely covering the sides of the cake.

6. Dust the top of the cake with cocoa powder, covering it completely.

7. Heat a small sharp knife and cut each of the reserved white chocolate circles in half. Place them around the top edge of the cake so they just touch one another, with the rounded side facing in.

Orange Mousseline Torte

Makes 1 torte (8 in/20 cm)

1-2-3 COOKIE DOUGH (page 249)	8 oz	227 g
ORANGE CHIFFON CAKE (8 in/20 cm) (page 318)	1 each	1 each
HEAVY CREAM, whipped to soft peaks	4 fl oz	120 mL
ORANGE CURD (page 394)	8 oz	227 g
ORANGE MARMALADE	2 oz	57 g
GRAND MARNIER–FLAVORED SIMPLE SYRUP (page 820)	6 fl oz	180 mL
SWISS MERINGUE (page 416)	1 lb	454 g

1. Roll out the dough ⅛ in/3 mm thick and cut out an 8-in/20-cm round. Transfer to a sheet pan.

2. Bake at 350°F/177°C until golden brown, 10 to 12 minutes. Cool completely.

3. Cut the chiffon cake into three layers (between ¼ and ½ in/6 mm and 1 cm thick). Fold one-third of the whipped cream into the orange curd to lighten it, and then fold in the remaining whipped cream.

4. Place an 8-in/20-cm cardboard cake round on a sheet pan and place an 8-in/20-cm cake ring on top. Line the sides of the cake ring with an acetate strip or plastic wrap. Apply a thin coating of marmalade to the cookie round and place it in the cake ring. Top with a layer of chiffon cake, moisten with simple syrup, and coat with 6 oz/170 g of the orange whipped cream. Top with a second layer of chiffon cake, moisten with simple syrup, and coat with the remaining 6 oz/170 g orange whipped cream. Top with the final layer of chiffon cake and moisten with simple syrup.

5. Coat the top and sides of the cake with meringue. Using a pastry bag fitted with a No. 5 star tip, pipe side-by-side columns of meringue all around the sides of the cake. Pipe swirls of meringue all over the top of the cake, then pipe a shell border around the base of the cake.

6. Using a propane torch, brown the meringue on the sides and top of the cake.

Parisian Gâteau

Makes 1 cake (8 in/20 cm)

SWISS MERINGUE (page 416)	1 lb	454 g
SOFT GANACHE (page 424)	1 lb 4 oz	567 g
DARK CHOCOLATE, melted	2 oz	57 g
COFFEE EXTRACT	½ fl oz	15 mL
KAHLÚA	1 fl oz	30 mL
CHOCOLATE SHAVINGS	4 oz	113 g
CONFECTIONERS' SUGAR	1 oz	28 g

1. Trace three 8-in/20-cm circles on a sheet of parchment paper and line a sheet pan with the parchment.

2. Using a pastry bag fitted with a No. 4 plain tip, pipe a spiral of meringue into each traced circle, starting in the middle and working outward to fill it completely.

3. Bake at 225°F/107°C until dry, about 40 minutes. Cool completely.

4. Combine the ganache, melted chocolate, coffee extract, and Kahlúa and blend well. Whip the ganache to firm peaks.

5. Place a meringue on an 8-in/20-cm cake round and coat with 5 oz/142 g of the ganache. Top with a second layer of meringue and coat it with 5 oz/142 g of ganache. Top with the last layer of meringue, with the smooth side facing out.

6. Coat the top and sides of the gâteau with the remaining ganache. Press the chocolate shavings onto the top and sides of the gâteau to cover it completely. Dust the top lightly with the confectioners' sugar.

Orange Torte
Makes 1 torte (8 in/20 cm)

ORANGE CHIFFON CAKE (8 in/20 cm) (page 318)	1 each	1 each
LADYFINGER STRIP (2 by 24 in/5 by 61 cm), striped vanilla and chocolate (page 370)	1 strip	1 strip
ORANGE-FLAVORED SIMPLE SYRUP (page 820)	3 fl oz	90 mL
ORANGE DIPLOMAT CREAM (page 422)	1 lb 10 oz	737 g
ORANGE MARMALADE	1 oz	28 g
MIRROR GLAZE (page 427)	3 oz	85 g
CANDIED ORANGE PEEL, julienned (page 726)	3 oz	85 g

1. Place an 8-in/20-cm cardboard cake round on a sheet pan and place an 8-in/20-cm cake ring on it. Line the ring with plastic wrap.
2. Slice two layers from the chiffon cake (between ¼ and ½ in/6 mm and 1 cm thick).

3. Line the inside of the cake ring with the ladyfinger strip so that the smooth side faces in. Place one layer of the chiffon cake in the bottom of the ring and moisten with simple syrup. Ladle 13 oz/369 g of the diplomat cream on top of the chiffon layer and spread it into an even layer. Top with a second layer of chiffon cake and press down gently. Moisten the chiffon layer with simple syrup, coat with a thin layer of orange marmalade, and ladle in the remaining 13 oz/369 g diplomat cream.

4. Wrap tightly in plastic wrap and refrigerate overnight. (The torte can be frozen for up to 1 month.)

5. Glaze the top of the torte with the mirror glaze. Refrigerate until the glaze has fully set, about 20 minutes.

6. Warm the sides of the cake ring using a propane torch or a towel moistened with warm water and carefully remove the ring.

7. Garnish the top of the cake with the julienned orange peel.

Passion Fruit Torte

Makes 1 torte (8 in/20 cm)

1-2-3 COOKIE DOUGH (page 249)	8 oz	227 g
VANILLA CHIFFON CAKE (8 in/20 cm) (page 318)	1 each	1 each
JOCONDE DÉCOR STRIP (2 by 24 in/5 by 61 cm) (page 316)	1 each	1 each
RASPBERRY JAM	2 oz	57 g
SIMPLE SYRUP (page 820)	3 fl oz	90 mL
PASSION FRUIT MOUSSE (page 397)	14 oz	397 g
PASSION FRUIT MIRROR GLAZE (page 427)	3 oz	85 g
PASSION FRUIT	½ each	½ each
KIWI, peeled and cut crosswise into slices ¼ in/6 mm thick	1 each	1 each
MANGO, peeled and thinly sliced	1 each	1 each
TWISTED DARK CHOCOLATE RIBBON, ⅓ by 6 in/1 by 15 cm (page 768)	1 each	1 each
TWISTED WHITE CHOCOLATE RIBBON, ⅓ by 6 in/1 by 15 cm (page 768)	1 each	1 each

1. Roll out the dough 1/8 in/3 mm thick and cut out an 8-in/20-cm round. Transfer to a sheet pan.

2. Bake at 350°F/177°C until golden brown, 10 to 12 minutes. Cool completely.

3. Slice two layers from the chiffon cake (between 1/4 and 1/2 in/6 mm and 1 cm thick).

4. Place an 8-in/20-cm cardboard cake round on a sheet pan and place an 8-in/20-cm cake ring on top. Line the inside of the cake ring with an acetate strip or plastic wrap. Line the inside of the ring with the strip of joconde. Coat the cookie round with raspberry jam and place in the bottom of the ring. Top with a layer of chiffon cake and moisten with simple syrup. Ladle 7 oz/198 g of the passion fruit mousse on top of the chiffon cake and spread it into an even layer. Top with the second layer of chiffon cake, press down gently, and moisten with simple syrup. Ladle in the remaining 7 oz/198 g passion fruit mousse.

5. Wrap tightly in plastic wrap and refrigerate overnight. (The torte can be frozen for up to 1 month.)

6. Glaze the top of the torte with the mirror glaze and refrigerate until the glaze has fully set.

7. Warm the sides of the cake ring using a propane torch or a towel moistened with warm water and carefully remove the ring.

8. Place the passion fruit half on top of the cake, slightly off center and seed side up. Place 2 kiwi slices next to the passion fruit half and fan the mango slices out from the kiwi slices. Place the chocolate ribbons to form an X over the fruit.

Notes   Fresh fruit can be added to the filling. Any fruit purée can be used to change the flavor.

Strawberry Yogurt Bavarian Torte

Makes 1 torte (8 in/20 cm)

1-2-3 COOKIE DOUGH (page 249)	8 oz	227 g
VANILLA CHIFFON CAKE (8 in/20 cm) (page 318)	1 each	1 each
STRAWBERRY JAM	1 oz	28 g
KIRSCH-FLAVORED SIMPLE SYRUP (page 820)	4 fl oz	120 mL
STRAWBERRY YOGURT BAVARIAN (page 404)	1 lb	454 g
STRAWBERRIES, thinly sliced	12 each	12 each
CHANTILLY CREAM (page 422)	8 oz	227 g
MARBLED WHITE AND DARK CHOCOLATE RECTANGULAR CUTOUTS (1 1/2 by 3 in/ 4 by 8 cm) (page 768)	25 each	25 each
STRAWBERRIES, quartered	2 each	2 each
CHOCOLATE FAN (page 768)	1 each	1 each
MARBLED CHOCOLATE CIGARETTE (page 767)	1 each	1 each

1. Roll out the dough 1/8 in/3 mm thick and cut out an 8-in/20-cm round. Transfer to a baking sheet. Bake at 350°F/177°C until golden brown, 10 to 12 minutes. Cool completely.

2. Place an 8-in/20-cm cardboard cake round on a sheet pan and place an 8-in/20-cm cake ring on top. Line the ring with plastic wrap.

3. Slice three layers from the chiffon cake (between 1/4 and 1/2 in/6 mm and 1 cm thick).

4. Spread a thin coating of strawberry jam on the cookie round and place it in the bottom of the ring. Place a layer of chiffon cake on the cookie base and moisten with simple syrup. Ladle 8 oz/227 g of the Bavarian cream on top of the chiffon and spread it into an even layer. Arrange half of the sliced strawberries in concentric circles over the cream. Top with a second layer of chiffon cake, press down gently, and moisten with simple syrup. Ladle in the remaining 8 oz/227 g Bavarian cream and cover in the same manner with the remaining strawberries. Top with the last layer of chiffon cake, press down gently, and moisten with simple syrup. Cover with plastic wrap and refrigerate until fully set.

5. Remove the plastic wrap. Warm the sides of the cake ring using a propane torch or a towel moistened with warm water and carefully remove the ring.

6. Coat the top and sides of the cake with the Chantilly cream. Press the chocolate rectangles onto the sides of the cake, overlapping them slightly and completely covering the sides of the cake. Arrange the quartered strawberries in the center of the cake. Place the chocolate fan in the center. Place the chocolate cigarette across the strawberries.

CHAPTER 16

Individual Pastries

INDIVIDUAL PASTRIES, CREATED FROM PASTRY DOUGHS, BATTERS, AND/OR FILLINGS, MAY BE CONSTRUCTED AS SINGLE PORTIONS OR AS A LARGER ITEM, SUCH AS A CAKE, WHICH IS INDIVIDUALLY GARNISHED AND PORTIONED. INDIVIDUAL PASTRIES ENCOMPASS A WIDE VARIETY OF BAKED GOODS, FROM VERY REFINED TO RUSTIC. DEPENDING ON THE TYPE OF PASTRY, IT MAY BE APPROPRIATE FOR SALE IN A RETAIL BAKESHOP, FOR SERVICE DURING BREAKFAST OR BRUNCH, WITH COFFEE OR TEA, AT RECEPTIONS, OR ON A DESSERT MENU.

Apple Galettes

Makes 12 galettes

CURRANTS	3 oz	85 g
BRANDY	3 fl oz	90 mL
BLITZ PUFF PASTRY (page 266)	1 lb 8 oz	680 g
APPLES	2 lb 8 oz	1.13 kg
BUTTER, melted	2 oz	57 g
SUGAR	1 oz	28 g
APRICOT GLAZE (page 429)	as needed	as needed

1. Combine the currants and brandy in a small bowl and let stand until the currants are fully plumped.

2. Roll out the puff pastry ⅛ in/3 mm thick. Transfer to a parchment-lined sheet pan, cover, and let rest for 30 minutes under refrigeration.

3. Using a 4¼-in/11-cm cutter, cut 12 rounds from the puff pastry. Dock the pastry rounds.

4. Peel, halve, and core the apples. Cut into slices ¹/₁₆ in/1.5 mm thick.

5. Arrange the apple slices in concentric rings on the puff pastry round, working from the outside in and overlapping the slices slightly; they should stack up in the center to a height of approximately 1 in/3 cm. Drizzle the melted butter over the galettes and sprinkle with the sugar.

6. Bake at 375°F/191°C until the pastry is golden brown and dry on the bottom, about 50 minutes.

7. Transfer the galettes to a 425°F/218°C convection oven and bake until the edges of the apples are golden brown, about 2 minutes. Cool to room temperature.

8. Brush the tops of the galettes with the apricot glaze. Drain the currants and scatter over the galettes before the glaze sets.

Tartlets

By scaling down the formulas for various pies and tarts, the pastry chef can prepare a number of individual pastries. Most of the tartlet formulas in this chapter were developed using a 3-in/8-cm ring mold or tartlet pan (with the exception of those that are "free-form"), but the formulas can be easily adapted to suit molds of other sizes or shapes. The same basic principles used for preparing large pies and tarts apply to tartlets. They can be baked in a mold or free-form, as with a galette. They may be made using short dough or puff pastry dough. Depending on the type of filling, the shells may be partially or completely prebaked. They may be filled with fresh or poached fruits, nuts, chocolate ganache, and/or custard. Fillings may be precooked and poured into a baked shell or baked with the crust. Many types of fillings contain components that combine techniques; for example, one component of a filling could be a frangipane filling, which would be baked with the crust, then a jam could be added in a thin, even layer, and the tart then finished by topping it with fresh berries and/or fruit. Combining elements in this way gives the pastry chef freedom to explore different flavor and textural profiles to create unique desserts.

Prebaked tartlet shells should be left in the ring molds while they are filled in order to support them during assembly and until the filling sets.

Fresh Fruit Tartlets

Makes 12 tartlets

I-2-3 COOKIE DOUGH (page 249)	1 lb 4 oz	567 g
ALMOND FILLING (page 831)	9 oz	255 g
ORANGE-FLAVORED SIMPLE SYRUP (page 821)	2 fl oz	60 mL
PASTRY CREAM (page 388)	3 oz	85 g
FRESH FRUIT, sliced, peeled, cored, as necessary	1 lb 8 oz	680 g
APRICOT GLAZE, warm (page 429)	as needed	as needed

1. Roll out the dough ⅛ in/3 mm thick. Using a 4-in/10-cm cutter, cut 12 rounds from the dough.

2. Place the rounds in 3-in/8-cm tart rings.

3. Dock the bottoms of the tartlet shells. Using a pastry bag fitted with a No. 5 plain tip, pipe the almond cream into the shells, filling them halfway.

4. Brush the almond cream with the syrup. Spread a thin coating of pastry cream in each tartlet shell. Arrange the fruit in the shells. Brush the fruit with the glaze.

5. Bake at 375°/191°C until the shells and filling are golden brown, about 30 minutes. Cool to room temperature.

Tartlet Shells

Makes 12 tartlet shells

1-2-3 COOKIE DOUGH (page 249)	1 lb 4 oz	567 g
EGG WASH (page 825)	as needed	as needed

1. Roll out the dough 1/8 in/3 mm thick. Using a 4-in/10-cm cutter, cut 12 rounds from the dough.

2. Assemble on a parchment-lined sheet pan if using rings. Fit the rounds into 3-in/8-cm tartlet rings or pans, pressing the dough into place against the sides of the rings or tartlet pans. Smooth and trim the top edges.

3. Place the shells under refrigeration or in the freezer until very firm. Line the frozen shells with foil or parchment and fill with pie weights or dry beans.

4. Bake at 375°F/191°C until the shells have just begun to brown, about 20 minutes (for more information on blind baking see page 511).

5. Remove the foil or parchment and weights. Lightly brush the pastry with egg wash. Bake until golden brown, about 10 minutes longer.

Bittersweet Chocolate Orange Tartlets

Makes 12 tartlets

HEAVY CREAM	6 fl oz	180 mL
SUGAR	2 oz	57 g
ORANGE ZEST, grated	1 tbsp	9 g
EGG YOLKS	6 oz	170 g
DARK CHOCOLATE, melted	3½ oz	99 g
ORANGE-FLAVORED LIQUEUR	1 fl oz	30 mL
TARTLET SHELLS, prebaked (page 590)	12 each	12 each
APRICOT GLAZE, warm (page 824)	as needed	as needed
CANDIED ORANGE ZEST (page 726)	2 oz	57 g

1. Combine the cream, 1 oz/28 g of the sugar, and the orange zest in a saucepan and bring to a boil. Remove from the heat, cover, and steep for 5 minutes.

2. Blend the egg yolks with the remaining 1 oz/28 g sugar to make a liaison. Temper by gradually adding about one-third of the hot cream mixture, whipping constantly. Add the remaining hot cream.

3. Add the melted chocolate and liqueur to the custard mixture, blending well. Strain the custard.

4. Divide the filling evenly among the tartlet shells, filling them to within ⅛ in/3 mm of the top.

5. Bake at 325°F/163°C just until the custard sets, about 15 minutes. Cool to room temperature.

6. Brush the tops of the tartlets with the warm glaze. Garnish each tartlet with a few strips of candied orange zest.

Citrus Tartlets

Makes 12 tartlets

HEAVY CREAM	4 fl oz	120 mL
LEMON JUICE	2 fl oz	60 mL
ORANGE JUICE	1 fl oz	30 mL
LEMON ZEST, grated	1 tsp	3 g
SUGAR	4 oz	113 g
EGGS	4 oz	113 g
EGG YOLKS	2 oz	57 g
TARTLET SHELLS, prebaked (page 590)	12 each	12 each
SUGAR	as needed	as needed
CHANTILLY CREAM (page 422)	3 oz	85 g
CANDIED LEMON ZEST (page 726)	1 oz	28 g

1. Combine the heavy cream, lemon juice, orange juice, lemon zest, and 3 oz/85g of the sugar in a saucepan and heat, stirring to dissolve the sugar, until the mixture reaches 180°F/82°C.

2. Meanwhile, blend the eggs and egg yolks with the remaining 1 oz/28 g sugar to make a liaison. Temper by gradually adding about one-third of the hot cream, whipping constantly. Add the remaining hot cream, and strain.

3. Divide the filling evenly among the tartlet shells, filling them to within 1/8 in/3 mm of the top.

4. Bake at 300°F/149°C until the custard is just set, about 20 minutes. Cool to room temperature.

5. Chill the tartlets until fully set.

6. Sprinkle a thin layer of sugar evenly on top of each tartlet. Caramelize the sugar using a torch. Allow to cool completely.

7. Using a pastry bag fitted with a No. 5 star tip, pipe a rosette of Chantilly cream onto each tartlet. Place several strips of candied lemon zest on each rosette.

Pear Custard Tartlets

Makes 12 tartlets

PEARS, fresh, halved	6 each	6 each
TARTLET SHELLS, prebaked (see Note) (page 590)	12 each	12 each
CRÈME BRULÉE MIXTURE (page 376)	12 oz	340 g
APRICOT GLAZE, warm (page 429)	as needed	as needed

1. Slice each pear half lengthwise into 1/4-in/6-mm slices, keeping the pear half intact. Place a sliced pear half in each of the tartlet shells and fan it slightly. Pour the custard mixture evenly over the fruit.

2. Bake at 325°F/163°C until the custard is set, about 20 minutes. Cool completely.

3. Unmold the tartlets, and brush with the glaze.

Note It is important to brush these shells particularly well with egg wash before prebaking.

Poached Fruits

Poached fruits may be featured as a main component of a plated dessert, or often used in fillings, toppings, or as garnish. Usually, fruits to be poached should be firm enough to hold their shape during cooking. Very tender fruits, such as berries and bananas, are generally not cooked using this technique. The greater the amount of sugar added to the poaching liquid, the more firm the end result will be. Using wine as part or all of the poaching liquid will have a similar effect. Poaching liquids that include some wine may be reduced and served as a sauce with the poached fruit or plated dessert.

Prepare the fruit as necessary. In some cases, it may be desirable to remove the peel, seeds, or pits before poaching the fruit. Combine the fruit with the poaching liquid, often a mixture of simple syrup, spices, and occasionally wine, and bring to a bare simmer. Reduce the heat and gently poach the fruit until it is tender. Test the fruit by piercing it with a sharp knife. There should be little to no resistance. Allow the fruit to cool in the poaching liquid, if possible. Poached fruits may be stored overnight or served immediately.

Poaching Liquid for Fruit

Makes 34 fl oz/1.02 L

WINE	20 fl oz	600 mL
WATER	10 fl oz	300 mL
SUGAR, optional (use with tart fruit)	4 oz	113 g
CINNAMON STICK	1 each	1 each
CLOVES	6 each	6 each

1. Combine all ingredients and bring to a simmer.

2. Peel fruit and shape, if necessary.

3. Cook the fruit in the poaching liquid until tender. Store, under refrigeration, in the poaching liquid.

Notes   To vary the flavor of the poaching liquid try different types of wine (red or white), or add fruit purée or juice to the poaching liquid. You can also use different types of spices: nutmeg, peppercorns, or allspice, for example. Add saffron to light-colored poaching liquids to impart flavor and a golden yellow color to the fruit.

Lemon Curd Tartlets

Makes 12 tartlets

LEMON CURD, just prepared (page 394)	1 lb 2 oz	510 g
TARTLET SHELLS, prebaked (page 590)	12 each	12 each
SWISS MERINGUE (page 416)	10 oz	284 g

1. Divide the warm lemon curd evenly among the tartlet shells. Chill for 1 hour, or until the curd sets.

2. Divide the meringue among the tartlets, mounding it on top of each one. Smooth the meringue using a palette knife, then create a pattern of parallel lines across the tartlet.

3. Brown the meringue using a torch or under a salamander.

Note   The lemon curd can be cooled before filling the shells, but it will fill the tartlet more easily and create a smoother top if it is used while still hot.

Raspberry Curd Tartlets

Makes 10 tartlets

GELATIN	1½ tsp	7 g
WATER	2 fl oz	60 mL
RED FOOD COLORING	2 drops	2 drops
ORANGE-FLAVORED LIQUEUR	½ fl oz	15 mL
RASPBERRY PURÉE	14 fl oz	420 mL
EGGS	5¼ oz	149 g
EGG YOLKS	4½ oz	128 g
SUGAR	3½ oz	99 g
BUTTER, cut into ½-in/1-cm cubes	5¼ oz	149 g
TARTLET SHELLS (6 in/15 cm diameter), prebaked (page 590)	10 each	10 each

1. Bloom the gelatin in the water and melt. Stir the food coloring into the liqueur.

2. Combine the raspberry purée, eggs, egg yolks, and sugar in a heavy-bottomed saucepan and bring to a boil, stirring frequently to dissolve the sugar.

3. Remove from the heat and whisk in the melted gelatin and butter. Add the liqueur. Strain the curd through a fine strainer.

4. Carefully pour 2½ oz/71 g of the curd into each of the tartlet shells; the curd should come to the top of the shells.

5. Place the tartlets in the freezer for 2 hours.

6. Wrap the tartlets and freeze until needed.

Margarita Chiffon Tartlets

Makes 10 tartlets

WATER	7 fl oz	210 mL
CORNSTARCH	¾ oz	21 g
SUGAR	8 oz	227 g
EGG YOLKS	3 oz	85 g
LIME JUICE	2 fl oz	60 mL
ORANGE JUICE CONCENTRATE	1 oz	28 g
TEQUILA	3 fl oz	90 mL
GELATIN	1½ tsp	7 g
EGG WHITES	4 oz	113 g
TARTLET SHELLS, prebaked (page 590)	10 each	10 each
SIMPLE SYRUP (page 820)	4 fl oz	120 mL
COARSE SUGAR	10 oz	284 g

1. In a bowl, combine 3 fl oz/90 mL of the water with the cornstarch to make a slurry. Add 2 oz/57 g of the sugar and the egg yolks and whisk together thoroughly.

2. Combine 2 oz/57 g of the sugar with the remaining 4 fl oz/120 mL water in a saucepan and bring to a boil, stirring to dissolve the sugar, creating a hot syrup.

3. Temper the egg mixture by gradually adding about one-third of the hot syrup, whisking constantly. Return the tempered egg mixture to the hot syrup in the saucepan and continue cooking until the mixture comes to a boil, whisking constantly.

4. Combine the lime juice, orange juice concentrate, and tequila.

5. Bloom and melt the gelatin using 2 fl oz/60 mL of the juice mixture.

6. Whisk the melted gelatin and the remaining juice into the warm egg mixture. Strain through a fine strainer.

7. Place the egg whites and remaining 4 oz/113 g of sugar in the bowl of an electric mixer and whisk until thoroughly combined.

8. Place the bowl over a pot of barely simmering water and slowly whisk the mixture until it reaches 165°F/74°C.

9. Transfer the mixture to the electric mixer and whip with the whip attachment on high until stiff peaks form.

10. Gently fold one-third of the meringue into the citrus mixture, then fold in the remaining meringue.

11. Brush the rim of each tartlet shell lightly with simple syrup, and dip the rim of each one in coarse sugar. Using a pastry bag fitted with a No. 6 plain tip, pipe 2 oz/57 g of the filling into each tartlet shell. Refrigerate the tartlets until fully chilled and set.

Fruit Tartlets, Victorias and other assorted individual pastries

Pecan Cranberry Tartlets

Makes 12 tartlets

DARK CORN SYRUP	8 oz	227 g
EGGS	6 oz	170 g
LIGHT BROWN SUGAR	4 oz	113 g
BUTTER	1¼ oz	35 g
ALL-PURPOSE FLOUR	½ oz	14 g
PECANS, toasted	6 oz	170 g
CRANBERRIES, fresh or frozen	3 oz	85 g
TARTLET SHELLS, prebaked (page 590)	12 each	12 each
APRICOT GLAZE, warm (page 429)	as needed	as needed
WHIPPED CREAM (page 423)	3 oz	85 g

1. Combine the corn syrup, eggs, sugar, and butter in a saucepan over medium heat. Warm the mixture until the sugar and butter are melted and all the ingredients are fully combined. Remove the pan from the heat. Stir in the flour and strain the mixture through a fine strainer.

2. Divide the pecans and cranberries among the tartlet shells, spreading them in an even layer.

3. Pour the corn syrup mixture over the nuts and cranberries, filling the shells to within ⅛ in/3 mm of the top.

4. Bake at 325°F/163°C just until the filling is set, about 25 minutes. Cool to room temperature.

5. Brush the tops of the tarts with the glaze. Using a pastry bag fitted with a No. 5 star tip, pipe a rosette of whipped cream onto each tartlet.

Pear Frangipane Tartlets

Makes 12 tartlets

I-2-3 COOKIE DOUGH (page 249)	1 lb 4 oz	567 g
FRANGIPANE FOR FILLINGS (Appendix A)	9 oz	255 g
SMALL PEARS, poached and halved (page 593–594)	12 each	12 each
APRICOT GLAZE, warm (page 429)	as needed	as needed
SLICED ALMONDS, toasted and chopped	3 oz	85 g

1. Roll out the dough ⅛ in/3 mm thick. Using a 4-in/10-cm cutter, cut 12 rounds from the dough.

2. Place the rounds in 3-in/8-cm tartlet rings.

3. Dock the bottoms of the tartlet shells. Using a pastry bag fitted with a No. 5 plain tip, pipe the frangipane into the shells, filling them halfway. Slice the pears and fan them on top of the frangipane.

4. Bake at 375°F/191°C until the shells and filling are golden brown, about 45 minutes. Cool to room temperature.

5. Brush the tops of the tartlets with the glaze. Arrange a thin border of toasted chopped almonds around the edge of each tartlet.

Pineapple Tartes Tatins

Makes 10 tartlets

SUGAR	1 lb 6 oz	624 g
LIGHT CORN SYRUP	4 oz	113 g
BUTTER	8 oz	227 g
WATER	2 fl oz	60 mL
PINEAPPLES	2 each	2 each
PÂTE BRISÉE (page 249)	1 lb 11 oz	765 g

1. Combine the sugar and corn syrup in a heavy-bottomed saucepan and bring to a boil over high heat, stirring to dissolve the sugar. Cook, covered, for 1 minute.

2. Remove the cover, reduce the heat to medium, and cook the caramel to a rich golden brown. Add the butter and water and stir until fully incorporated.

3. Divide the caramel evenly among ten 4¾-in/12-cm tartlet pans.

4. Peel and core the pineapples. Cut into ½-in/1-cm cubes. Place 3 oz/85 g diced pineapple on top of the caramel in each tartlet pan.

5. Roll the pâte brisée out ¹⁄₁₆ in/1.5 mm thick. Using a 4¾-in/12-cm fluted cutter, cut 10 rounds out of the pâte brisée.

6. Place a round of pâte brisée on top of each tartlet. The pâte brisée should be flush with the edges of the tartlet pan.

7. Bake at 375°F/191°C until the pastry is golden brown, about 15 minutes. Allow to cool slightly in the pans. Invert on a serving plate to unmold.

Strip Tartlets

Makes 12 portions

PUFF PASTRY DOUGH (page 260)	6 oz	170 g
EGG WASH (page 825)	as needed	as needed
PASTRY CREAM (page 388)	6 oz	170 g
ASSORTED FRUIT, peeled, trimmed, and cut, as necessary	8 oz	227 g
APRICOT GLAZE, warm (page 429)	as needed	as needed

1. Roll the puff pastry dough into a rectangle 4 by 16 in/10 by 41 cm. Transfer to a parchment-lined sheet pan, cover, and let rest, refrigerated, for 30 minutes or more.

2. Remove the dough from the sheet pan and cut it lengthwise into one strip 3½ in/9 cm wide and two strips ¾ in/2 cm wide.

3. Place the 3½-in/9-cm-wide strip on a parchment-lined sheet pan, dock, and brush with egg wash. Lay the ¾-in/2-cm-wide strips on top of the edges of the larger strip and brush them with egg wash.

4. Bake at 375°F/191°C until the pastry has risen and begun to brown, about 30 minutes. Turn the oven down to 325°F/163°C and bake until golden brown, about 20 minutes more. Cool to room temperature.

5. Cut most of the pastry out of the center of the strip, if necessary, leaving only a thin bottom layer. Pipe the pastry cream evenly over the center of the strip. Arrange the fruit on top of the pastry cream.

6. Brush the fruit with the glaze and allow to set.

7. Using a serrated knife, cut the strip into 12 even portions.

Placing the side "wall" on a puff pastry tart shell

Pecan Passions

Makes 12 tartlets

CHOCOLATE SHORT DOUGH (page 251)	12 oz	340 g
SOFT CARAMEL (page 729)	12 oz	340 g
PECANS, toasted and chopped	6 oz	170 g
SOFT GANACHE (page 424)	8 oz	227 g
HEAVY CREAM	4 fl oz	120 mL
WHIPPED CREAM (page 423)	6 oz	170 g

1. Roll out the dough into a rectangle 10 by 14 in/25 by 36 cm.

2. Lay the rectangle of dough carefully over twelve 3-in/8-cm tartlet pans that have been arranged closely together. Gently press the dough into the molds. Run a rolling pin across the molds to cut away the excess.

3. Blind bake the shells at 375°F/191°C until fully baked, about 15 minutes. Cool completely.

4. Divide half of the caramel evenly among the tartlet shells. Scatter half of the pecans over the caramel. Allow to cool completely.

5. Whip the soft ganache with the cream, using the whip attachment, to a mousselike consistency.

6. Using a palette knife, spread a layer of ganache into each shell. Freeze the tartlets until the filling is firm.

7. Divide the remaining caramel among the tartlets, spreading it over the ganache in a thin layer. Scatter the remaining pecans over the top. Using a pastry bag fitted with a No. 5 star tip, pipe a rosette of whipped cream on top of each tartlet.

Victorias

Makes 36 pastries

PUFF PASTRY (page 260)	2 lb	907 g
EGG WASH (page 820)	as needed	as needed
PÂTE À CHOUX (page 255)	2 lb 8 oz	1.13 kg
SLICED ALMONDS	4 oz	113 g
RUM	as needed	as needed
HEAVY CREAM, whipped	48 fl oz	1.44 L
PASTRY CREAM (page 388)	2 lb 4 oz	1.02 kg
STRAWBERRIES	1 lb 4 oz	567 g
CONFECTIONERS' SUGAR, for dusting	as needed	as needed

1. Roll the puff pastry out ¹⁄₁₆ in/1.5 mm thick. Transfer to a parchment-lined sheet pan, cover, and allow to rest under refrigeration for 1 hour.

2. Dock the pastry. Using a 4-in/10-cm cutter, cut 36 rounds from the dough. Fit them into individual brioche molds. Trim the excess dough from the tops of the molds.

3. Brush the inside of the puff shells lightly with egg wash. Using a pastry bag fitted with a No. 5 plain tip, pipe the pâte à choux into each shell, filling one-third full. Using a small palette knife, spread the pâte à choux so it reaches up the sides to the top of the molds, making the surface concave. Toss the almonds with just enough rum to moisten and sprinkle over the pâte à choux.

4. Bake at 375°F/191°C until the puff pastry is dry and the pâte à choux is golden brown, about 50 minutes. Cool completely.

5. Unmold the pastries. Using a serrated knife, slice the tops from the finished shells; reserve the tops.

6. Fold half of the whipped cream into the pastry cream. Fill the shells two-thirds full with the pastry cream. Arrange the berries on the cream.

7. Using a pastry bag fitted with a No. 5 star tip, pipe the remaining whipped cream on top of the berries. Place the reserved pastry tops on the whipped cream and dust with confectioners' sugar.

Classic Napoleons

Makes 16 napoleons (2 by 3¼ by 1½ in/5 by 8 by 4 cm each)

PUFF PASTRY (page 260)	1 lb 5½ oz	610 g
DIPLOMAT CREAM (page 402)	2 lb 2¼ oz	971 g
APRICOT GLAZE, warm (page 824)	as needed	as needed
FONDANT	8 oz	227 g
SIMPLE SYRUP (page 820)	2 fl oz	60 mL
BITTERSWEET CHOCOLATE, melted	2 oz	57 g

1. Roll the puff pastry to a rectangle 16½ by 24½ in/42 by 62 cm and ⅛ in/3 mm thick. Place the puff pastry on a parchment-lined sheet pan and allow it to rest under refrigeration for at least 1 hour.

2. Dock the puff pastry generously. Place a piece of parchment on top of the puff pastry dough and a sheet pan or a cooling rack on top of the parchment paper to control the rise of the puff pastry dough.

3. Bake the dough in a 375°F/191°C oven for 20 minutes. Rotate the pan and continue to bake for 7 to 10 minutes, or until golden brown and dry throughout. If necessary, remove the sheet pan from the top of the puff pastry during the final 10 minutes of baking to allow the puff pastry to brown. Cool the puff pastry to room temperature.

4. Trim the edges of the puff pastry using a long, flat, serrated knife. Cut the puff pastry into three strips 6½ by 16 in/17 by 41 cm long.

5. Spread half of the diplomat cream in a smooth, even layer on one of the puff pastry strips using a medium offset spatula.

6. Gently place a puff pastry strip on top of the diplomat cream. Spread the remaining diplomat cream on top of the puff pastry sheet in a smooth, even layer. Place the final puff pastry sheet upside down on top of the diplomat cream. Smooth the sides of the napoleon with an offset spatula to remove any excess diplomat cream.

7. Wrap the napoleon and freeze overnight.

8. To finish, allow the napoleon to thaw for 10 to 15 minutes. Brush the apricot glaze in a thin, even layer on top of the napoleon.

9. Gently warm the fondant over a double boiler to 100°F/38°C. Thin the fondant with the simple syrup until it is fluid and only slightly viscous. Pour the fondant on top of the napoleon in the center of the puff pastry and spread the fondant in a thin, even layer over the entire puff pastry.

10. Pour the melted chocolate into a parchment paper cone with a very thin tip. Pipe thin lines of chocolate lengthwise along the fondant ¼ in/6 mm apart.

11. Drag the tip of a paring knife horizontally across the chocolate lines in alternating directions ¼ in/6 mm apart. The chocolate lines may be piped closer together to create a more finely marbled look. Allow the fondant to set completely before slicing.

12. Fill a large bain marie with hot water. Using a long, serrated knife warmed in the hot water, trim the edges of the napoleon.

13. Slice the napoleon in half lengthwise. Using a warm, serrated knife, slice each napoleon strip into 8 pieces. Clean the knife in between each cut.

CLOCKWISE FROM LEFT: Puff pastry for napoleons and other layered pastries must be weighted down during baking to ensure flat, even layers.

Layering puff pastry sheets and diplomat cream to make Classic Napoleons

Dragging the tip of a paring knife across the chocolate lines in alternating directions to create the décor for napoleons

Layered Pastries and Roulades

Layered individual pastries can be composed of various types of cake or pastry that are baked as sheets, so they can be layered or rolled with a complementary filling. Properly assembled, the evenly filled, level layers make a dramatic and visually appealing pastry when sliced. A variety of icings, such as ganache, buttercream, whipped cream, fondant, or a clear glaze, may be applied to the assembled pastry. These large layered pastries can be cut into a variety of shapes, such as triangles or rectangles, to make individual pastries. Assembling pastries in this manner results in very little loss or trim, making them an economical choice for production. Many traditional, classical, and contemporary cakes can be adapted with only minor modifications to suit this style of assembly.

Roulades are made from a sheet of sponge cake or other cake that is flexible enough to be rolled without splitting. The sheet of cake is spread with an even layer of filling and then rolled, chilled, iced, and decorated. The roulade is then sliced into individual portions for service. Roulades are easy to prepare and can be made ahead and finished as needed.

Strawberry Napoleons
Makes 16 napoleons (2 by 3¼ in/5 by 8 cm)

PUFF PASTRY (page 260)	1 lb 5½ oz	610 g
APRICOT GLAZE, warm (page 429)	4 fl oz	120 mL
FONDANT	1 lb	454 g
SIMPLE SYRUP (page 820)	5 fl oz	150 mL
PINK FOOD COLORING	as needed	as needed
STRAWBERRIES, whole, roughly the same size	50 each	50 each
GRAND MARNIER DIPLOMAT CREAM (page 402)	2 lb 4 oz	1.02 kg
VANILLA SPONGE CAKE CRUMBS, for garnish	as needed	as needed
CHOCOLATE CIGARETTES (page 766)	16 each	16 each

1. Roll the puff pastry to a rectangle 16½ by 24½ in/42 by 62 cm and ⅛ in/3 mm thick. Place the puff pastry on a parchment-lined sheet pan and allow it to rest, under refrigeration, for at least 1 hour.

2. Cut one-third (8 by 16 in/20 by 41 cm) of the puff pastry dough off and place it on a separate sheet pan. Reserve the remaining puff pastry dough in the refrigerator.

3. Score the dough with the lattice wheel and gently pull the puff pastry apart to create the lattice pattern. Place a piece of parchment paper on top of the puff pastry dough. Place a sheet pan on top of the paper to control the rise of the dough.

4. Bake the dough in a 375°F/191°C oven for 10 to 15 minutes, or until golden brown. Allow to cool to room temperature before trimming.

5. Using a long, serrated knife, trim the lattice into 16 rectangles, 2 by 3¼ in/5 by 8 cm each. Brush a thin layer of apricot glaze over the top of the lattice puff pastry.

6. Gently warm the fondant over a water bath to 100°F/38°C. Thin the fondant with the simple syrup until it is very fluid and only slightly viscous. Add the food coloring.

7. Place the lattice puff pastry on a rack. Slowly pour the fondant over the puff pastry. Remove the lattice puff pastry from the rack so that the fondant does not stick to the rack. Reserve.

8. To assemble the napoleon, dock the remaining puff pastry generously using a dough docker. Place a piece of parchment on top of the puff pastry dough. Place a sheet pan on top of the parchment paper to control the rise of the puff pastry dough.

9. Bake the dough in a 375°F/191°C oven for 20 to 25 minutes, or until golden brown. If necessary, remove the sheet pans from the top of the puff pastry during the final 10 minutes of baking to allow the puff pastry to brown. Allow the puff pastry to cool to room temperature.

10. Using a long, serrated knife, trim the edges of the puff pastry. Cut the puff pastry into two strips 6½ by 16 in/17 by 41 cm. Brush a thin layer of apricot glaze onto one of the puff pastry strips to help the strawberries adhere to the puff pastry better.

11. Cut the tops off of the strawberries. Place 36 whole strawberries in three rows of 12 on the puff pastry strip. Cut 6 strawberries in half and place the strawberries, cut side facing out, along the long edge of the puff pastry strip. Make sure that the cut strawberries come right up to the edge of the puff pastry.

12. Using a No. 8 plain tip, pipe approximately half of the diplomat cream on top of the strawberries, making sure to fill in the crevices in between the strawberries. The diplomat cream should come ½ in/1 cm above the layer of strawberries.

13. Place the second plain strip of puff pastry on top of the diplomat cream. Spread the remaining diplomat cream on top of the puff pastry in a smooth, even layer. Be sure to come right up to the edge of the puff pastry without going over the edge. Gently smooth the sides of the napoleon using an offset spatula.

14. Refrigerate the napoleon for 1 hour to allow the diplomat cream to set.

15. Fill a large bain marie with hot water. Using a long, serrated knife warmed in the hot water, trim the edges of the napoleon.

16. Using a warm, long, serrated knife, slice the napoleon in half lengthwise. Gently press vanilla sponge cake crumbs into the longer sides of the napoleon.

17. Cut each strip of napoleon into 8 pieces. Be sure to clean the knife in between each slice. Using a long, straight spatula, gently place one lattice top on each of the napoleon slices. Garnish each slice with a strawberry half and a chocolate cigarette.

Mocha Mousse Slices

Makes 45 slices (1¼ by 3 in/3 by 8 cm each)

1-2-3 COOKIE DOUGH (page 249)	1 lb 4 oz	567 g
MOCHA MOUSSE (page 401)	5 lb 5 oz	2.41 kg
CHOCOLATE SPONGE SHEET (11½ by 16½ in/ 29 by 42 cm) (page 302)	1 each	1 each
COFFEE-FLAVORED SIMPLE SYRUP (page 820)	4 fl oz	120 mL
ULTRA SHINY CHOCOLATE GLAZE (page 427)	16 fl oz	480 mL
HEAVY CREAM, whipped	12 fl oz	360 mL
CHOCOLATE-COVERED ESPRESSO BEANS	45 each	45 each

1. Roll the dough out to a rectangle 13 by 17 in/33 by 43 cm. Trim to precisely 12 by 16 in/30 by 41 cm. Dock the dough.

2. Bake at 375°F/191°C until light golden brown, about 25 minutes.

3. Place a rectangular frame or mold of the same dimensions with sides 2 in/5 cm high around the baked cookie sheet. Ladle half of the mousse onto the cookie sheet and spread it evenly. Place the sponge on the mousse and press down lightly. Brush the sponge generously with the syrup. Ladle the remaining mousse over the sponge, filling the mold to the top, and spread it evenly.

4. Freeze the assembled mold until the mousse is firm enough to cut.

5. Pour the chocolate glaze evenly over the top of the frozen mousse. Allow the glaze to set.

6. Remove the frame and trim the edges of the assembled slab. Slice it crosswise into strips 3 in/8 cm wide and then cut each strip into pieces 1¼ in/3 cm wide.

7. Using a pastry bag fitted with a No. 5 plain tip, pipe a small dome of whipped cream on one side of the top of each slice. Place a marzipan coffee bean on each whipped cream dome. Refrigerate until ready to serve.

Chocolate Roulade Slices

Makes 24 slices

SOFT GANACHE (page 424)	10 oz	284 g
HEAVY CREAM	6 fl oz	180 mL
VANILLA ROULADE (16½ by 24½ in/ 42 by 62 cm) (page 307)	1 each	1 each
CONFECTIONERS' SUGAR, for dusting	as needed	as needed

1. Combine the ganache and cream and, using the whip attachment, whip to medium-stiff peaks.

2. Spread the ganache mixture evenly over the roulade sheet.

3. Cut the sheet lengthwise in half. Roll each roulade up tightly.

4. Chill the roulades for 30 minutes, or until the ganache is set.

5. Lay a strip of parchment ¾ in/2 cm wide over the middle of the length of each roulade and dust it with confectioners' sugar. Remove the strip.

6. Slice each roulade into 12 portions.

Using parchment paper to roll the roulade

Frangipane Triangle Slices

Makes 12 slices

FRANGIPANE FOR PETITS FOURS (page 372)	½ sheet pan	½ sheet pan
BITTERSWEET CHOCOLATE, melted	3 oz	85 g
ITALIAN BUTTERCREAM (page 418)	1 lb	454 g
HARD GANACHE, melted(page 425)	12 oz	340 g

1. Cut three strips (3 by 16 in/8 by 41 cm each) lengthwise from the frangipane.

2. Blend the melted chocolate into the buttercream. Spread 3 oz/85 g of the buttercream onto one strip of frangipane. Place a second strip on top of the buttercream and spread with 3 oz/85 g buttercream. Place the third strip of frangipane on top.

3. Refrigerate the strip until the buttercream is firm, at least 1 hour.

4. Cut the assembled strip lengthwise in half on the diagonal to create two triangular strips. Spread 4 oz/113 g of the buttercream onto the frangipane side of one of the triangular strips, and place the frangipane side of the other strip against the buttercream, pressing to adhere, creating a triangular, vertically layered cake.

5. Chill the assembled strip until the buttercream has set.

6. Seal the outside of the strip with the remaining buttercream. Chill until set, about 1 hour.

7. Place the strip on a wire rack set in a sheet pan. Glaze the strip with the ganache, spreading it along the sides to completely cover as you ladle the glaze. Chill until set, about 1 hour.

8. Slice the strip into 12 portions.

Mango Raspberry Slices

Makes 12 slices

VANILLA SPONGE SHEET (11½ by 16½ in/ 29 by 42 cm) (page 302)	1 each	1 each
RASPBERRY JAM	4 oz	113 g
JOCONDE SPONGE RECTANGLE (9 by 16 in/ 23 by 41 cm) (page 316)	1 each	1 each
JOCONDE SPONGE STRIP (4¼ by 16 in/ 11 by 41 cm) (page 316)	1 each	1 each
MANGO MOUSSE (page 397)	3 lb	1.36 kg

1. Cut the sponge crosswise into 3 strips. Spread the jam evenly over one strip and roll up, starting from a long side.

2. Line a 12-in/30-cm triangular terrine mold with plastic wrap.

3. Place the larger rectangle of joconde into the mold so that the sides are flush with the edges of the mold. Pour half of the mousse into the mold.

4. Lay the roulade in the center of the mousse. Pour the remaining mousse into the mold to within ¼ in/6 mm of the top.

5. Lay the remaining layer of joconde on the mousse, lining it up so that the edges are flush with the edges of the other sponge.

6. Cover and refrigerate overnight.

7. Unmold and slice into 12 portions.

1 Placing the joconde sponge in the mold

2 Placing the roulade in the center of the half-filled mold

Praline Slices

Makes 12 slices

HAZELNUT SPONGE SHEET (11½ by 16½ in/ 29 by 42 cm) (page 311)	1 each	1 each
ITALIAN BUTTERCREAM (page 418)	1 lb 4 oz	567 g
PRALINE PASTE	2 oz	57 g
RUM-FLAVORED SIMPLE SYRUP (page 820)	3 fl oz	90 mL
HAZELNUTS, toasted and finely ground	3 oz	85 g
DRAGÉED HAZELNUTS (page 723)	12 each	12 each

1. Slice three strips (3 by 16 in/8 by 41 cm each) lengthwise from the hazelnut sponge.

2. Combine the buttercream with the praline paste and mix until smooth.

3. Moisten one of the sponge strips with one-third of the syrup, and spread 4 oz/113 g of the buttercream over it. Place a second strip on top of the buttercream, moisten with another one-third of the syrup, and spread 4 oz/113 g of the buttercream over it. Top with the final strip of sponge and moisten with the remaining syrup.

4. Chill the assembled strip until the buttercream is set, about 1 hour.

5. Trim the sides of the assembled strip. Coat the top and sides with the remaining buttercream, reserving 4 oz/113 g for décor. Mark into 12 portions. Using a pastry bag fitted with a No. 3 star tip, pipe a rosette of buttercream off center on each slice.

6. Press the ground hazelnuts onto the frosted sides of each slice to completely cover the bottom half of each side. Garnish each slice by placing a dragéed hazelnut on the buttercream rosette.

Raspberry Marzipan Slices

Makes 12 slices

VANILLA SPONGE SHEET (11½ by 16½ in/ 29 by 42 cm) (page 302)	1 each	1 each
FRAMBOISE-FLAVORED SYRUP (page 820)	3 fl oz	90 mL
RASPBERRY JAM	1 oz	28 g
ITALIAN BUTTERCREAM (page 418)	12 oz	340 g
MARZIPAN, colored pale pink	1 lb	454 g
TEMPERED CHOCOLATE, for garnish	as needed	as needed

1. Slice three strips (3 by 16 in/8 by 41 cm each) lengthwise from the vanilla sponge.

2. Moisten one of the sponge strips with the syrup. Spread with a thin coat of jam and then with 3 oz/85 g of the buttercream. Place a second strip on top of the buttercream. Moisten with the syrup and spread with a thin coat of jam and then with 3 oz/85 g of the buttercream. Top with the final strip of sponge and moisten with the remaining syrup. Wrap the strip in plastic wrap.

3. Place the assembled strip on a parchment-lined sheet pan and place another piece of parchment on top of the strip. Weight by placing a second sheet pan on top of the strip and a heavy pan or two 1-lb/454-g weights on top, and refrigerate overnight.

4. Coat the top and sides of the strip with the remaining buttercream.

5. Roll the marzipan into a rectangle ¹⁄₁₆ in/1.5 mm thick. Texture the rolled marzipan with a textured rolling pin.

6. Drape the marzipan over the strip and gently press the marzipan to remove all wrinkles and to attach it to the strip. Trim the excess from the bottom edges.

7. Mark the strip into 12 portions. Garnish each piece by piping a stylish R or filigree of tempered chocolate using a parchment cone.

8. Chill until firm enough to slice, about 1 hour.

Raspberry Wine Cream Slices

Makes 45 slices (1¼ by 3 in/3 by 8 cm each)

1-2-3 COOKIE DOUGH (page 424)	1 lb 4 oz	567 g
RASPBERRY JAM	4 oz	113 g
VANILLA SPONGE SHEET (page 302)	1 each	1 each
RASPBERRY-FLAVORED SIMPLE SYRUP (page xxx)	4 fl oz	120 mL
WINE CREAM (page 403)	4 lb 14 oz	2.21 kg
RASPBERRY MIRROR GLAZE (page 427)	1 lb	454 g
WHIPPED CREAM (page 423)	12 oz	340 g
CHOCOLATE CIGARETTES (page 766)	45 each	45 each

1. Roll the cookie dough into a rectangle 13 by 17 in/33 by 43 cm. Trim to precisely 12 by 16 in/30 by 41 cm. Dock the dough.

2. Bake at 375°F/191°C until light golden brown, about 25 minutes. Cool completely.

3. Spread the raspberry jam onto the baked cookie sheet. Place a frame (12 by 16 by 1¾ in/30 by 41 by 4.5 cm) around it. Place the sponge cake on the jam and press down gently. Moisten the sponge with the syrup. Pour the wine cream into the frame, filling it to the top, and spread it evenly.

4. Freeze the assembled frame until the wine cream is set.

5. Pour the glaze over the frozen wine cream to coat it. Allow the glaze to set.

6. Remove the frame and trim the edges of the assembled strip. Slice into 45 portions.

7. Using a pastry bag fitted with a No. 5 star tip, pipe a domed rosette of whipped cream slightly off center on top of each slice. Place a chocolate cigarette on each slice, resting one end on the whipped cream rosette.

8. Refrigerate until ready to serve.

Pastries Formed in Molds

You can use a variety of small portion-size molds to shape such pastry components as mousse, Bavarian cream, and other stable creams. In most cases, gelatin is added to the cream to give it enough structure to hold its shape after it is unmolded.

There are several styles and materials to choose from. One option is flexible molds made of silicone, produced in hemisphere, pyramid, and other shapes. Cups, bowls, and other small containers also work well.

Combine components in a variety of colors, flavors, and textures, as we have done here. To add texture, consider small cookies, ladyfingers, sponge cake, or fresh fruit. To add color, include a garnish of a contrasting color.

Chocolate Caramel Bombes

Makes 24 bombes

CHOCOLATE SPONGE SHEET CAKE (page 302)	1 each	1 each
CHOCOLATE MOUSSE (page 617)	2 lb 8 oz	1.13 kg
SOFT CARAMEL FILLING (page 473)	12 oz	340 g
SIMPLE SYRUP) (page 820	4 fl oz	120 mL
ULTRA SHINY CHOCOLATE GLAZE (page 427)	36 fl oz	1.08 L
1-2-3 COOKIE DOUGH CUTOUTS, fluted (3¼ in/8 cm diameter), baked (page 249)	24 each	24 each
STRIPED CHOCOLATE CIGARETTES (page 766)	24 each	24 each

1. Using a 2-in/5-cm cutter, cut 24 rounds from the chocolate sponge.

2. Using a pastry bag fitted with a No. 5 plain tip, pipe the chocolate mousse into twenty-four 3-in/8-cm hemispherical flexible silicone molds, filling them two-thirds full.

3. Using a No. 5 plain tip, pipe ½ oz/14 g of the caramel into the center of each chocolate bombe. Be careful not to pipe the caramel too far down into the mousse, or it may leach through the mousse and show when unmolded.

4. Place a sponge round on top of each mousse and gently press to bring the cake flush with the top of the mold. Brush each sponge lightly with the syrup.

5. Freeze the bombes until they are solid.

6. Unmold the bombes and place them, dome side up, on a wire rack set over a sheet pan. Ladle the chocolate glaze over each bombe to coat completely. Let stand until the glaze sets.

7. Place each bombe on a fluted cookie. Garnish each one with a chocolate cigarette.

Chocolate Mousse Bombes

Makes 24 bombes

VANILLA SAUCE (page 430)	8 fl oz	240 mL
HARD GANACHE, melted (page 425)	8 oz	227 g
GELATIN	½ oz	14 g
WATER	4 fl oz	120 mL
EGG WHITES, pasteurized	2 oz	57 g
SUGAR	2 oz	57 g
HEAVY CREAM, whipped to very soft peaks	16 fl oz	480 mL
ULTRA SHINY CHOCOLATE GLAZE (page 427)	36 fl oz	1.08 L
1-2-3 COOKIE DOUGH CUTOUTS, fluted (3¼ in/8 cm diameter), baked (page 766)	24 each	24 each
DARK CHOCOLATE FANS (page 768)	24 each	24 each

1. Combine the vanilla sauce with the melted ganache.

2. Bloom and melt the gelatin in the water. Blend the gelatin into the vanilla sauce mixture. Set aside.

3. Beat the egg whites until frothy. Slowly add the sugar and whip to a stiff-peak meringue.

4. Stir the vanilla sauce mixture over an ice bath just until it begins to thicken. Fold in the meringue. Fold in the whipped cream.

5. Using a pastry bag fitted with a No. 5 plain tip, immediately pipe the mixture into twenty-four 3-in/8-cm hemispherical flexible silicone molds.

6. Freeze the bombes until they solid.

7. Unmold the bombes and place them, dome side up, on a wire rack set over a sheet pan. Ladle the chocolate glaze over each bombe to coat completely. Let stand until the glaze sets.

8. Place each bombe on a fluted cookie. Gently press a chocolate fan to the side of each bombe to adhear.

Chocolate Peanut Butter Bombes

Makes 10 bombes

DEVIL'S FOOD CAKE SHEET (11½ by 16½ in/ 29 by 42 cm) (page 300)	1 each	1 each
PEANUT BUTTER	10 oz	284 g
MILK CHOCOLATE BAVARIAN MOUSSE (page 403)	2 lb 8 oz	1.13 kg
CHOCOLATE SHORT DOUGH (page 257)	1 lb	454 g
ULTRA SHINY CHOCOLATE GLAZE (page 427)	20 fl oz	600 mL

1. Using a 2-in/5-cm cutter, cut 10 rounds from the devil's food cake.

2. Using a pastry bag fitted with a No. 6 plain tip, pipe 1 oz/28 g of peanut butter onto each round of cake.

3. Using a No. 5 plain tip, pipe 4 oz/113 g of the mousse into each of ten 3-in/8-cm hemispherical flexible molds, filling them to within ½ in/1 cm of the top. Flip a cake round upside down onto each mold and push the peanut butter into the mousse; push down until the devil's food cake is flush with the top of the mold.

4. Level the top of each bombe by scraping off any excess mousse. Freeze the bombes for 8 hours, or until firm.

5. Roll out the tart dough ⅛ in/3 mm thick. Using a 3¼-in/8-cm fluted cutter, cut 10 rounds from the dough.

6. Bake the pastry rounds in a 350°F/177°C deck oven until golden brown, 8 to 10 minutes. Cool.

7. Warm the glaze to 120°F/49°C.

8. Unmold the bombes and flip them upside down onto a wire rack set over a parchment-lined sheet pan. Enrobe each bombe with 2 fl oz/60 mL of the glaze.

9. Place each bombe on a cookie base. Place the bombes in the refrigerator to set the glaze.

Lemon Bombes with Macerated Raspberries

Makes 24 bombes

RASPBERRIES (fresh or frozen)	6 oz	170 g
ORANGE-FLAVORED LIQUEUR	4 fl oz	120 mL
VANILLA SPONGE CAKE SHEET (page 302)	1 each	1 each
LEMON MOUSSE (page 399)	2 lb 4 oz	1.02 kg
APRICOT GLAZE, warm (page 429)	72 fl oz	2.16 L
1-2-3 COOKIE DOUGH SHELLS, cutouts, fluted (3 1/4 in/8 cm diameter), prebaked (page 249)	24 each	24 each
CHOCOLATE FANS (page 768)	24 each	24 each

1. Combine the raspberries with the liqueur and allow to macerate for 1 hour or longer.

2. Using a 2-in/5-cm cutter, cut 24 rounds from the sponge cake.

3. Using a pastry bag fitted with a No. 5 plain tip, pipe the lemon mousse into 3-in/8-cm hemispherical flexible molds, filling them two-thirds full.

4. Remove the raspberries from the liqueur, reserving the liqueur, and drain them on a towel. Place 3 or 4 berries in each mold, and press them lightly into the mousse. Be careful not to press them in too far, or they will show when the bombes are unmolded.

5. Place a sponge round on top of each bombe, and press gently into the mousse to bring the level of the mousse up to the top of the molds. Brush each sponge lightly with the reserved liqueur.

6. Freeze the bombes until they are firm.

7. Place the bombes on an icing screen and glaze with the apricot glaze, using a fondant dropper or ladle. Let the glaze set.

8. Place each bombe on a fluted cookie. Garnish each one with a chocolate fan.

Melon Sherry Cream

Makes 12 pastries

OPERA SPONGE SHEET CAKE (page 565)	1 each	1 each
TIRAMISÙ FILLING (page 405)	9 fl oz	270 mL
MELON BALLS, 1/4 in/ 6 mm diameter	12 oz	340 g
GELATIN	1 oz	28 g
WATER	17 fl oz	510 mL
CREAM SHERRY	16 fl oz	480 mL
SORBET SYRUP (page 480)	1 lb 4 oz	567 g
LIME JUICE	1/2 fl oz	15 mL
SLICED ALMONDS, toasted and chopped	4 oz	113 g

1. Using a 2¾-in/7-cm cutter, cut 12 rounds from the opera sponge. Place each round in an oiled and sugared ring mold of the same diameter and at least 1½ in/4 cm high that has been placed on a parchment-lined sheet pan.

2. Using a pastry bag fitted with a No. 5 plain tip, pipe the tiramisù filling into the molds, filling them to ½ in/1 cm from the top. Put a single layer of melon balls in each mold.

3. Bloom and melt the gelatin in 8 fl oz/240 mL of the water.

4. Combine the sherry, sorbet syrup, lime juice, and the remaining 9 fl oz/270 mL water in a stainless-steel bowl. Blend in the gelatin. Stir gently over an ice bath, using a rubber spatula so as not to create air bubbles, until the mixture begins to thicken.

5. Immediately pour the gelatin mixture over the melon balls, covering them completely and filling the molds to the top.

6. Refrigerate or freeze until thoroughly set, at least 2 hours.

7. Remove from the molds. Gently press the chopped almonds onto the side of each dessert to adhear.

Summer Pudding

Makes 10 portions

BUTTER, soft	4 oz	113 g
BRIOCHE DOUGH (page 142)	2 lb	907 g
EGG WASH (page 825)	2 oz	57 g
STRAWBERRIES	12 oz	340 g
CRÈME DE CASSIS	6 fl oz	180 mL
LEMON JUICE	1 fl oz	30 mL
SUGAR	8 oz	227 g
RASPBERRIES	11 oz	312 g
BLUEBERRIES	11 oz	312 g
BLACKBERRIES	11 oz	312 g

1. Bake the brioche in two cylindrical molds, 6¾ in/17 cm in diameter and 8 in/20 cm tall. Brush each mold with 2 oz/57 g of the softened butter.

2. Divide the brioche dough into two 1-lb/454-g pieces. Round each one into a ball and place in one of the prepared molds.

3. Allow the dough to proof, covered, until it springs back lightly to the touch, 45 minutes to 1 hour; there should be a small indentation left in the dough, but it should not collapse. Brush the dough lightly with egg wash.

4. Bake in a 325°F/163°C deck oven until the brioche is dark golden brown on top and golden brown in the center cracks, about 45 minutes. Toward the end of baking, if the brioche is a deep brown but requires a little additional baking time, it may be necessary to remove the brioche from the molds and dry it out slightly in the oven. Cool to room temperature.

5. Unmold the brioche if necessary, and slice crosswise into rounds ⅜ in/1 cm thick. Using a 2½-in/6-cm round cutter, cut 30 disks out of the brioche slices.

6. Cut the strawberries in halves or quarters, depending on size; the pieces should be about the same size.

7. Combine the crème de cassis, lemon juice, and sugar in a large pot and bring to a boil. Reduce the heat to a low simmer, add the strawberries, and poach just until they begin to release their juices. Add the remaining fruit and poach it until it is tender. (This will only take a few minutes, depending on the ripeness of the berries.) Remove from the heat.

8. Place 1 brioche disk in the bottom of each of ten 4-fl-oz/120-mL soufflé cups. Place 1 oz/28 g fruit on each brioche disk and top with another brioche disk. Place another 1 oz/28 g fruit on each one, and place the remaining brioche disks on top.

9. Cover the puddings with a sheet of parchment paper and place a sheet pan on top. Weight down the sheet pan with a heavy pan or two 1-lb/454-g weights. Refrigerate overnight.

10. Carefully unmold the puddings. Serve chilled.

Containers

Pastry chefs are often on the lookout for unusual and attractive containers for presenting and serving special pastries and other desserts. Glass containers have several appealing qualities. Clear glass gives a pastry an immediate visual impact. Stemmed coupe glasses, hurricane glasses, and oversized martini glasses automatically give the pastry height.

Natural and edible containers, including hollowed-out citrus fruits and containers such as puff pastry cases (known as vol-au-vents or bouchées), pâte à choux puffs, and tuile cups, are all part of the classic pastry repertoire and can be other attractive choices.

White and Dark Chocolate Mousse in Glasses

Makes 12 portions (5 fl oz/140 mL each)

HARD GANACHE, melted (page 425)	6 oz	170 g
WHITE CHOCOLATE MOUSSE (page 400)	1 lb 8 oz	680 g
DARK CHOCOLATE MOUSSE (page 398)	1 lb 8 oz	680 g
WHIPPED CREAM (page 423)	3 oz	85 g
STRIPED CHOCOLATE CIGARETTES (page 766)	12 each	12 each

1. One at a time, put ½ oz/14 g of the melted ganache in the bottom of each of twelve 5-fl-oz/150-mL martini glasses and rapidly tip each glass in four different directions to create 4 arcs of ganache on the inside of the glass.

2. Using a pastry bag fitted with a No. 5 plain tip, pipe the white chocolate mousse into the glasses, filling each halfway and making the top of the mousse as even and level as possible. Using a No. 5 plain tip, pipe the dark chocolate mousse on top of the white chocolate mousse, filling each glass to the top. Using a palette knife, smooth the top of the mousse level with the top of the glasses.

3. Using a No. 3 star tip, pipe a small rosette of whipped cream on top of each mousse-filled glass. Lean a chocolate cigarette on each rosette of whipped cream.

4. Refrigerate until ready to serve.

Raspberry Mousse in Glasses

Makes 12 portions

RASPBERRY SAUCE (page 439)	6 fl oz	180 mL
RASPBERRY MOUSSE (page 396)	1 lb 8 oz	680 g
WHIPPED CREAM (page 423)	3 oz	85 g
WHITE CHOCOLATE FANS (page 768)	12 each	12 each
RASPBERRIES	36 each	36 each

1. Put 1 tbsp/15 mL of the raspberry sauce into each of twelve 4-fl-oz/120-mL cordial glasses. Using a pastry bag fitted with a No. 5 plain tip, pipe the mousse into the glasses, filling them to the top. Using a palette knife, smooth the mousse level with the tops of the glasses.

2. Using a No. 3 plain tip, pipe a small dome of whipped cream onto the center of each mousse. Lean a chocolate fan against each dome and stack 3 raspberries at the base of each fan.

3. Refrigerate until ready to serve.

Tiramisù in Glasses

Makes 12 portions

LADYFINGERS (3 in/8 cm) (page 370)	36 each	36 each
COFFEE-FLAVORED SIMPLE SYRUP (page 820)	4 fl oz	120 mL
TIRAMISÙ FILLING (page 405)	1 lb 5 oz	595 g
CHOCOLATE SHAVINGS	3 oz	85 g
CONFECTIONERS' SUGAR	as needed	as needed
GROUND CINNAMON	as needed	as needed

1. Brush the backs of the ladyfingers with the espresso syrup. Stand 3 ladyfingers each in twelve 4-fl-oz/120-mL cordial glasses so that the domed side of the ladyfingers is pressed against the side of the glasses.

2. Using a pastry bag fitted with a No. 5 plain tip, pipe the tiramisù filling into the glasses, filling them to within ½ in/1 cm of the tops of the ladyfingers. Scatter the chocolate shavings over the filling, covering it completely. Dust with confectioners' sugar and cinnamon.

3. Refrigerate until ready to serve.

Trifles

Makes 12 trifles

CURRANT JELLY	8 oz	227 g
RUM-FLAVORED SIMPLE SYRUP (page 820)	6 fl oz	180 mL
SHERRY	3 fl oz	90 mL
VANILLA SPONGE CAKE, cut into ¹/₂-in/1-cm cubes (page 302)	9 oz	255 g
FRESH FRUIT, cut into ¹/₂-in/1-cm cubes	1 lb 2 oz	510 g
DIPLOMAT CREAM (made without gelatin) (page 402)	3 lb	1.36 kg
WHIPPED CREAM (page 423)	6 oz	170 g
CHOCOLATE CIGARETTES (page 766)	12 each	12 each

1. Divide the jelly evenly among twelve 9-fl-oz/270-mL stemmed glasses.

2. Combine the syrup and sherry.

3. Place the sponge cake cubes in a bowl, add the syrup mixture, and toss to moisten evenly. Divide half of the sponge cubes evenly among the glasses. Top with half of the fruit, dividing it evenly.

4. Using a pastry bag fitted with a No. 5 plain tip, pipe a layer of diplomat cream on top of the fruit. Divide the remaining sponge cubes among the glasses, then divide the remaining fruit among them. Pipe the remaining diplomat cream on top; the glasses should be filled to within ¹/₄ in/6 mm of the top.

5. Using a No. 4 star tip, pipe a rosette of whipped cream on top of each trifle. Garnish each with a chocolate cigarette.

6. Refrigerate until ready to serve.

Phyllo Cups

Makes 12 cups

PHYLLO DOUGH SHEETS, 4 in/10 cm square	48 each	48 each
BUTTER, melted	as needed	as needed

1. Lay out 12 phyllo sheets on a work surface, brush each with melted butter, and top with a second phyllo sheet. Repeat this process two more times, rotating the sheet of phyllo slightly each time so that the corners do not align.

2. Place each stack of phyllo in a 6-fl-oz/180-mL ramekin or other ovenproof container, pressing it to the bottom and sides.

3. Bake in a 375°F/191°C oven for 10 minutes or until golden brown.

4. To serve, fill the cups as desired with a mousse, cream, or poached pear.

Phyllo Dough

Phyllo dough is made only of flour and water and occasionally a small amount of oil. The dough is stretched and rolled until it is extremely thin and then cut into sheets. The sheets are brushed with melted butter and layered to create many flaky layers of pastry (much like the layers of a laminated dough such as puff pastry) that encase or hold a filling, which may be anything from fruit to a mousse or cream. The butter, instead of being rolled into the dough as it is for laminated doughs, is melted and brushed onto the dough sheets before they are baked, as is done with strudel.

Many bakeshops purchase frozen phyllo dough sheets. This dough must thaw and come to room temperature before it can be worked with. Phyllo dough can dry out quickly and become brittle enough to shatter, so after it is removed from its wrapping, it is important to cover it with dampened towels and plastic wrap. Use a pastry brush to apply the butter in an even coat and then, if desired, sprinkle with cake or bread crumbs to keep the layers separate as they bake.

Meringue Swans

Makes 20 swan halves

EGG WHITES	6 oz	170 g
SALT	pinch	pinch
VANILLA EXTRACT	½ tsp	2.50 mL
SUGAR	12 oz	340 g

1. Place the egg whites, salt, and vanilla in a bowl and whisk until frothy.

2. Gradually add the sugar while continuing to whip, then whip to stiff peaks.

3. Trace 20 swans on a piece of parchment paper, using the template in Appendix D, making 10 left halves and 10 right halves.

4. Using a pastry bag fitted with a No. 3 plain tip, pipe meringue into the traced body of each swan, using the same motion that you would use to pipe a shell border; start at the tip of the wing and end at the bottom, making sure that the bottom edge is smooth. Fill in the head of each stencil with meringue.

5. Cut the parchment paper into rectangles so that there are two swan halves, one on top of another, on each. Drape the swan halves over a dowel 3 in/8 cm in diameter, so they will have a slight curve when dry.

6. Place the swans in a turned-off oven with a pilot light. Allow the swans to dry overnight. Alternatively, bake the meringue in a 200°F/93°C oven for several hours or until dry. Allow to cool to room temperature and peel off the parchment paper. Store in an airtight container until ready to assemble.

7. For finishing instructions see page 692.

Vacherins

Makes 12 vacherins

SWISS MERINGUE (page 416)	10 oz	284 g

1. Trace 12 ovals, 1½ by 3½ in/4 by 9 cm each, on a full sheet of parchment paper, leaving 3 in/8 cm between them.

2. Flip the parchment paper over and place on a sheet pan, so that the side with the tracing is against the pan.

3. Using a pastry bag fitted with a No. 3 plain tip, pipe meringue into each traced oval in a spiral motion, beginning at the center and moving out toward the edge, keeping the tip just above the parchment paper while piping. Once each oval is filled in, pipe a second layer of meringue all around the outer edge and a third layer if necessary or desired, building a "wall" for the container. The finished vacherins should be 1¼ in/3 cm tall.

4. Place the sheet pan in a turned-off oven with a pilot light. Allow the vacherins to dry out overnight.

Notes To finish vacherins, fill them with a sorbet, mousse, or cream and garnish with anything from chocolate shavings to fresh or poached fruit. Vacherins should be filled "à la minute" to prevent them from absorbing too much moisture from the filling and losing their crisp texture. If vacherins must be filled in advance, brush the inside and top rim with tempered white or dark chocolate. You can make the vacherins any shape that you like.

Piped Pastries

A variety of individual pastries can be made using baked meringue or pâte à choux. Both of these elements are shaped by piping, then baked and filled. Meringues can be piped into containers, filled, and served, or piped into disks and assembled like a sandwich. The fillings paired with meringue are usually high in fat to contrast with the lean, crisp flavor and mouth feel of the meringue.

Pâte à choux can be piped into oblongs for éclairs, into rings for paris breast, into domes for cream puffs, or into more intricate shapes to create the classic swan. After baking, a filling is piped into the pâte à choux either by slicing it open or by using a small pastry tip to puncture the shell and inject the filling. Pastries of this type are typically glazed or dusted with confectioners' sugar to finish. It is important when preparing either type of shell (meringue or pâte à choux) that it be baked until dry and crisp and allowed to cool completely before filling.

Piping éclairs

Chocolate Éclairs

Makes 12 éclairs

PÂTE À CHOUX (page 255)	1 lb	454 g
EGG WASH (page 825)	as needed	as needed
DIPLOMAT CREAM (see Note) (page 402)	1 lb	454 g
FONDANT (page 426)	8 oz	227 g
DARK CHOCOLATE, melted	3 oz	85 g
LIGHT CORN SYRUP	as needed	as needed
CHOCOLATE FONDANT, warm (page 426)	12 oz	340 g

1. Pipe the pâte à choux into cylinders 4 in/10 cm long on parchment-lined sheet pans, using a No. 8 plain piping tip, and lightly brush with egg wash.

2. Bake at 360°F/182°C for 50 minutes, or until the cracks formed in the pastries are no longer yellow. Allow to cool to room temperature.

3. Pierce each end of the éclairs using a skewer or similar instrument.

4. Fill the éclairs with the diplomat cream from each end using a No. 1 plain piping tip.

5. Warm the fondant over a hot water bath, add the melted chocolate, and thin to the proper viscosity using the corn syrup.

6. Top the filled éclairs with the chocolate fondant either by dipping or by enrobing using the back of a spoon.

Note   Gelatin is optional in the diplomat cream for this application.

Praline Éclairs

Makes 12 éclairs

PÂTE À CHOUX (page 255)	1 lb	454 g
EGG WASH (page 825)	as needed	as needed
PASTRY CREAM (page 388)	12 oz	340 g
PRALINE PASTE	2 oz	57 g
CHANTILLY CREAM (page 422)	9 oz	255 g
SLICED ALMONDS	48 slices	48 slices
TOPPING		
SUGAR	8 oz	227 g
WATER	3 fl oz	90 mL
LIGHT CORN SYRUP	1¾ oz	50 g

1. Pipe the pâte à choux into cylinders 4 in/10 cm long using a No. 5 plain pastry tip.

2. Brush with egg wash and bake at 360°F/182°C for 50 minutes, or until the cracks are no longer yellow. Allow to cool to room temperature.

3. Stretch plastic wrap tightly over the back of a sheet pan.

4. Place, for each éclair, 4 almond slices onto the sheet pan in a row the length of the éclairs.

5. To make the topping, cook the sugar, water, and corn syrup until it turns light golden brown. Shock the pan of sugar in a bowl of cool water.

6. Dip the top quarter of each éclair into the caramel. Place each éclair caramel side down onto the lines of almonds, and press down lightly. Allow to cool until the caramel hardens.

7. Remove the éclairs from the sheet pan, and slice off the caramel-coated tops.

8. Combine the pastry cream with the praline paste and mix until well combined.

9. Fill the bottoms of the éclairs with the praline pastry cream.

10. Using a No. 5 star pastry tip, pipe a spiral of Chantilly cream onto each éclair base.

11. Place the caramel-coated tops on the cream at an angle to expose the cream.

Cream Puffs

Makes 12 cream puffs

PÂTE À CHOUX (page 255)	1 lb	454 g
EGG WASH (page 825)	as needed	as needed
SLICED ALMONDS	2 oz	57 g
SUGAR	1 oz	28 g
PASTRY CREAM (page 388)	12 oz	340 g
CHANTILLY CREAM (page 422)	9 oz	255 g
CONFECTIONERS' SUGAR	as needed	as needed

1. Pipe the pâte à choux into bulbs 1½ in/4 cm in diameter onto parchment-lined sheet pans using a No. 5 plain piping tip and brush lightly with egg wash.

2. Stick several almond slices into the top of each bulb so that they protrude from the top and sprinkle each lightly with the granulated sugar.

3. Bake at 360°F/182°C for 50 minutes, or until the cracks formed in the pastries are no longer yellow. Allow to cool to room temperature. Slice the top off each of the baked pastries.

4. Pipe the pastry cream into the bases using a No.5 plain pastry tip, being careful not to overfill them.

5. Pipe a double rosette of Chantilly cream on top of the pastry cream using a No. 5 star tip.

6. Place the tops of the pastries on the Chantilly cream, and lightly dust with confectoners' sugar.

Variation Place strawberries or other fruit on top of the pastry cream and the Chantilly cream piped onto the fruit.

Filling cream puffs

Croissants

Makes 12 croissants

CROISSANT DOUGH (page 267)	2 lb 4 oz	1.02 kg
EGG WASH (page 825)	as needed	as needed

1. Roll the dough into a rectangle 9 by 24 in/23 by 61 cm.

2. Cut 12 isosceles triangles, 9 in/23 cm high and 4 in/10 cm at the base, from the dough.

3. Make a ¾-in/2-cm slit in the center of the base of each triangle. Working with one triangle at a time, gently stretch each of the three points of the triangle to elongate them. Place the triangle on an unfloured table with the narrow point directly away from you. Roll the triangle up from the base, exerting gentle pressure with your fingertips. Place seam side down on a parchment-lined sheet pan, making four rows of 5 croissants each. Shape the croissants into crescents, so that the ends curve inward at the front.

4. Brush the croissants with egg wash. Proof at 85°F/29°C for 1 hour, or until doubled in size.

5. Brush the croissants with egg wash a second time. Bake at 375°F/191°C until well browned, about 15 minutes.

Variation **Almond Croissants** Before rolling up the croissants, using a pastry bag fitted with a No. 4 plain tip, pipe ½ oz/14 g Almond Filling (page 831) onto the base of each triangle. Leave the rolled croissants straight rather than making crescent shapes. After the second egg wash, sprinkle untoasted sliced almonds onto the croissants.

Gently stretching each of the three points of the triangle to elongate them

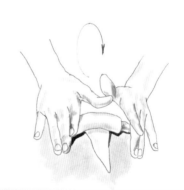
Curving the ends of the finished croissant inward

Rolling up the triangle from the base, exerting gentle pressure with the fingertips

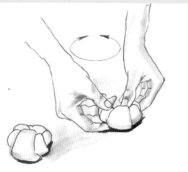

Croissant and Danish Doughs

Croissant and Danish doughs have many similarities in ingredients and preparation method. They are both yeast-leavened doughs produced using lamination (to learn more about lamination see pages 261–264). They differ, however, in ratios of ingredients and application. Danish dough contains a higher percentage of fat and other enriching ingredients, which gives finished pastries using this dough flakier layers. Danish dough is commonly used to prepare individual as well as larger cake-style pastries, while croissant dough is used only to produce individually sized items.

To work with croissant and Danish doughs after they are completely prepared, keep the dough chilled, taking out only the amount you can cut, fill, and shape in a relatively short amount of time. If the dough starts to warm as you work with it, you may lose some of the flaky, delicate texture that is the hallmark of a well-made Danish or croissant.

Use a sharp knife when shaping or cutting the dough. Clean cuts will ensure that the baked item rises evenly. Croissant dough may be cut using specialty cutters. To keep cuts even and straight when cutting by hand, use a straightedge as a guideline. Pastry wheels are helpful when cutting large quantities of dough.

After Danish or croissant doughs have been filled as desired and shaped, they are pan-proofed until nearly double in volume. Typically, they are lightly coated with egg wash. Depending upon the shaping and filling technique, Danish dough may be brushed with a clear fruit glaze or gel after baking for even greater moisture, flavor, and visual appeal.

Pain au Chocolate
Makes 12 pastries

CROISSANT DOUGH (page 267)	1 lb 14 oz	851 g
EGG WASH (page 825)	as needed	as needed
CHOCOLATE BATONS (3 in/8 cm long)	24 each	24 each

1. Roll the croissant dough into a rectangle 5 by 36 in/13 by 91 cm. Trim the edges so they are even.

2. With a long edge of the rolled dough facing you, brush the bottom half of the rectangle with egg wash. Place the chocolate batons in pairs the entire length of the dough, starting one-third of the way from the top of the rectangle. Fold the top of the dough over the batons, leaving 1½ in/4 cm of dough at the bottom. Fold the folded dough containing the chocolate over again, so that the seam is centered on the bottom of the dough.

3. Brush the dough with egg wash. Cut into 12 segments 3 in/8 cm long, so that each pair of chocolate batons is contained within one pastry. Place on a parchment-lined sheet pan, making four rows of 5 pastries each.

4. Proof at 85°F/29°C for 1 hour, or until doubled in size.

5. Brush the pastries with egg wash a second time. Bake at 375°F/191°C until well browned, about 15 minutes.

Bear Claws

Makes 12 pastries

DANISH DOUGH (page 268)	2 lb	907 g
EGG WASH (page 825)	as needed	as needed
ALMOND FILLING (page 831)	1 lb 2 oz	510 g
SLICED ALMONDS	4 oz	113 g
APRICOT GLAZE, warm (page 824)	as needed	as needed

1. Roll the dough into a rectangle 5 by 48 in/13 by 122 cm.

2. Brush the dough lightly with egg wash. Using a pastry bag fitted with a No. 9 plain tip, pipe a cylinder of filling lengthwise down the center of the dough. Fold the dough over the filling, lining up the edges carefully. Press the edges together to seal them.

3. Cut the dough crosswise into strips 4 in/10 cm wide.

4. Using a bench scraper, make four cuts in the seamed edge of each pastry. Curve the pastry back to open the cuts. Place the pastries on a parchment-lined sheet pan, making four rows of 5 pastries each.

5. Brush the pastries lightly with egg wash. Proof at 85°F/29°C for 1 hour, or until doubled in size.

6. Brush the pastries lightly with egg wash again and sprinkle with the sliced almonds.

7. Bake at 375°F/191°C until golden brown, about 17 minutes.

8. Brush the pastries with the warm glaze while they are still hot. Cool completely before serving.

CLOCKWISE FROM TOP: Cherry Cheese Pockets, Bear Claws, Schnecken, Croissants

Cheese Pockets

Makes 12 pockets

DANISH DOUGH (page 268)	1 lb 8 oz	680 g
EGG WASH (page 825)	as needed	as needed
CHEESE FILLING (page 831)	12 oz	340 g
SLICED ALMONDS	4 oz	113 g
APRICOT GLAZE, warm (page 824)	as needed	as needed

1. Roll the dough into a rectangle 12 by 16 in/30 by 41 cm. Cut the dough into twelve 4-in/10-cm squares.

2. Brush each square lightly with egg wash. Using a pastry bag fitted with a No. 5 plain tip, pipe 1 oz/28 g of the cheese filling onto the center of each square. One at a time, fold the corners of the dough over the filling into the center, so that each corner overlaps the previous one. Seal the pocket by pressing gently on the overlapped corners. Pierce the center of the pocket with the almonds to ensure they stay closed.

3. Brush the pockets lightly with egg wash. Proof at 85°F/29°C for 1 hour, or until doubled in size.

4. Brush the pockets lightly with egg wash again. Bake at 350°F/177°C until golden brown, about 17 minutes.

5. Brush the pastries with the warm glaze while they are still hot.

Cherry Half-Pockets

Makes 12 pastries

DANISH DOUGH (page 268)	1 lb 8 oz	680 g
EGG WASH (page 825)	as needed	as needed
CHERRY FILLING (page 506)	12 oz	340 g
APRICOT GLAZE, warm (page 824)	as needed	as needed

1. Roll the dough into a rectangle 12 by 16 in/30 by 41 cm. Cut the dough into twelve 4-in/10-cm squares.

2. Brush each square lightly with egg wash. Place 1 oz/28 g cherry filling at the center of each square. Fold one corner of the dough over just so it covers the filling, and press to seal. Stretch the opposite corner of dough over the first folded corner and around to go under the finished pocket. Pinch lightly to seal.

3. Brush the pockets lightly with egg wash. Proof at 85°F/29°C for 1 hour, or until doubled in size.

4. Brush the pockets lightly with egg wash again. Bake in a 375°F/191°C oven until golden brown, about 17 minutes.

5. Brush the pockets with the warm glaze while they are still hot.

Cherry Cheese Baskets

Makes 12 pastries

DANISH DOUGH (page 268)	1 lb 8 oz	680 g
EGG WASH (page 825)	as needed	as needed
CHEESE FILLING (page 831)	8 oz	227 g
CHERRY FILLING (page 506)	8 oz	227 g
APRICOT GLAZE, warm (page 824)	as needed	as needed

1. Roll the dough into a rectangle 12 by 16 in/30 by 41 cm. Cut the dough into twelve 4-in/10-cm squares.

2. Fold each square diagonally in half. Position a folded square so that the corner opposite the fold is pointing away from you. Insert the tip of the knife about $1/4$ in/6 mm from the corner and $1/2$ in/1 cm from the edge of the dough and cut down through the dough, parallel to the edge, going through the folded side. Repeat on the opposite side, being careful not to cut through the corner.

3. Open out the square and brush lightly with egg wash. Fold over one of the cut corners so that its outside edge aligns with the newly cut inside edge on the opposite side. Repeat with the opposite side. Place on a parchment-lined sheet pan, and repeat with the remaining squares of dough.

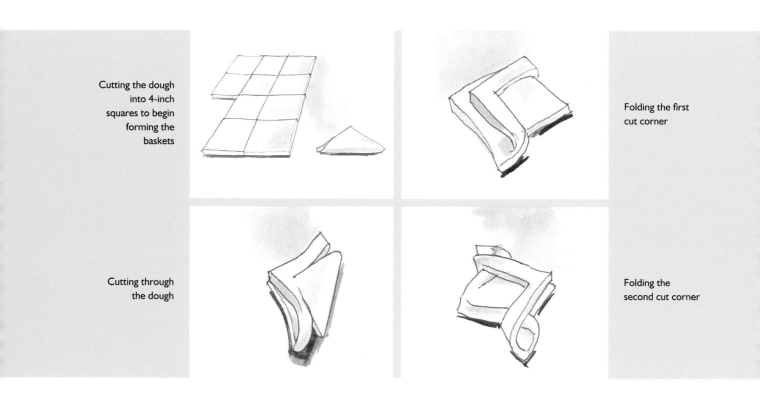

Cutting the dough into 4-inch squares to begin forming the baskets

Folding the first cut corner

Cutting through the dough

Folding the second cut corner

4. Brush the pastries lightly with egg wash. Proof at 85°F/29°C for 1 hour.

5. Dock the centers of the pastries. Using a pastry bag fitted with a No. 6 plain tip, pipe ½ oz/14 g of the cheese filling onto the center of each pastry, Then, using a No. 8 plain tip, pipe ½ oz/14 g of the cherry filling on top of the cheese on each pastry.

6. Brush the dough lightly with egg wash again. Bake at 350°F/177°C until golden brown, about 17 minutes.

7. Brush the pastries with the warm glaze while they are still hot.

Braided Coffee Cake

Makes 1 cake (12 in/30 cm long) or 8 slices (1½ in/4 cm each)

DANISH DOUGH (page 268)	1 lb	454 g
EGG WASH (page 825)	as needed	as needed
APPLE FILLING (page 502)	12 oz	340 g
COARSE SUGAR, for sprinkling	as needed	as needed
APRICOT GLAZE, warm (page 824)	as needed	as needed

1. Roll the dough into a rectangle 9 by 12 in/23 by 30 cm. Make a fringe down each long side of the dough by making cuts 3 in/8 cm long at intervals of 1 in/3 cm, leaving an uncut portion of dough in the center 3 in/8 cm wide.

2. Brush the dough lightly with egg wash. Place the filling in the middle of the uncut center portion of dough. One strip of dough at a time, fold the fringes over the filling at a 45-degree angle, alternating the sides and overlapping them.

3. Place on a parchment-lined sheet pan. Proof at 85°F/29°C for 1½ hours.

4. Lightly brush the pastry with egg wash again. Sprinkle with coarse sugar, and bake at 350°F/177°C until golden brown, about 40 minutes.

5. Brush the pastry with the warm glaze while it is still hot.

Schnecken

Makes 12 pastries

DANISH DOUGH (page 268)	1 lb 4 oz	567 g
PASTRY CREAM (page 388)	5 oz	142 g
CINNAMON SUGAR (page 826)	½ oz	14 g
PECANS, toasted and chopped	3 oz	85 g
DRIED CURRANTS	3 oz	85 g
EGG WASH (page 825)	as needed	as needed
APRICOT GLAZE, warm (page 824)	as needed	as needed

1. Roll the dough into a rectangle 8 by 16 in/20 by 41 cm.

2. Spread the pastry cream over the dough, leaving a bare strip of dough 1 in/3 cm wide along one of the long sides. Sprinkle the cinnamon sugar onto the pastry cream. Sprinkle the pecans and currants evenly over the cream. Roll lightly over the top with a rolling pin to press the nuts and currants into the cream.

3. Starting from the long side with the filling, roll up the dough into a roulade 16 in/41 cm long and press gently to seal.

4. Cut the roulade into 12 equal pieces. Place cut side down on a parchment-lined sheet pan, making four rows of 5 pastries each.

5. Brush the pastries lightly with egg wash. Proof at 85°F/29°C for 1 hour.

6. Lightly brush the pastries with egg wash again. Bake in a 375°F/191°C convection oven until golden brown, about 17 minutes.

7. Brush the pastries with the warm glaze while they are still hot.

Twist Coffee Cake

Makes 1 cake (14 in/36 cm long) or 9 slices (1½ in/4 cm each)

DANISH DOUGH (page 268)	1 lb 8 oz	680 g
RASPBERRY JAM	8 oz	227 g
EGG WASH (page 825)	as needed	as needed
APRICOT GLAZE, warm (page 824)	as needed	as needed

1. Roll the dough into a rectangle 8 by 14 in/20 by 36 cm.

2. Spread the jam over the dough, leaving bare a strip of dough 1 in/3 cm wide along one of the long sides.

3. Starting from the long side with the filling, roll up the dough into a roulade 14 in/36 cm long and press gently to seal. Using a sharp paring knife, cut 3 parallel lines down the length of the roulade, to within 1 in/3 cm of each end of the roulade.

4. Holding the roulade at each end, gently twist it, then shape it loosely into a spiral and place on a parchment-lined sheet pan.

5. Brush the spiral lightly with egg wash. Proof at 85°F/29°C for 1½ hours.

6. Brush with egg wash again and bake at 350°F/177°C until golden brown, about 45 minutes.

7. Brush the spiral with the warm glaze while it is still hot. Allow to cool completely before serving.

Danish Twists

Makes 12 pastries

DANISH DOUGH (page 268)	2 lb 2 oz	964 g
BUTTER, melted	1 oz	28 g
CINNAMON SUGAR (page 826)	1 oz	28 g
EGG WASH (page 825)	as needed	as needed
RASPBERRY JAM	8 oz	227 g
APRICOT GLAZE, warm (page 824)	as needed	as needed

1. Roll the dough into a rectangle 12 by 24 in/30 by 61 cm.

2. Brush the dough with the melted butter. Sprinkle the cinnamon sugar over the dough. Roll over the dough lightly with a rolling pin so the sugar adheres to it. Fold the dough crosswise in half to make a 12-in/30-cm square. Roll the dough to seal and slightly stretch it.

3. Cut the dough into 12 even strips. One at a time, hold each strip and both ends and twist it, then shape it loosely into a spiral and place on a parchment-lined sheet pan, leaving a 2-in/5-cm space between pastries.

4. Brush the spirals lightly with egg wash. Proof at 85°F/29°C for 1 hour, or until doubled in size.

5. Brush the spirals lightly again with egg wash, stipple the centers, and, using a No. 3 plain tip, pipe jam into the center of each Danish twist.

6. Bake in a 375°F/191°C convection oven until golden brown, about 17 minutes.

7. Brush the Danish twists with the warm glaze while they are still hot.

Wreath Coffee Cake

Makes 1 cake or 9 slices (1½ in/4 cm each)

DANISH DOUGH (page 268)	1 lb 8 oz	680 g
HAZELNUT FILLING (page 832)	12 oz	340 g
EGG WASH (page 825)	as needed	as needed
SLICED ALMONDS	4 oz	113 g
APRICOT GLAZE, warm (page 824)	as needed	as needed

1. Roll the dough into a rectangle 8 by 14 in/20 by 36 cm.

2. Spread the filling over the dough. Starting from a long side, roll the dough up into a roulade 14 in/36 cm long and transfer to a parchment-lined sheet pan, placing the roulade seam side down.

3. Using a bench scraper, cut almost all the way through one side of the roulade at intervals of 1 in/3 cm, and join the ends to form a wreath. Twist each sliced portion outward to expose the interior.

4. Brush the wreath lightly with egg wash. Proof at 85°F/29°C for 1½ hours.

5. Brush the wreath lightly again with egg wash, and sprinkle with the almonds. Bake at 350°F/177°C until golden brown, about 45 minutes.

6. Brush the wreath with the warm glaze while it is still hot.

Cutting slits almost through the roulade

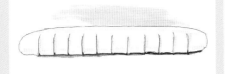

Forming the log into a wreath and twisting each section outward so that the spiral of dough and filling is exposed

CHAPTER 17

Plated Desserts

WHEN DESIGNING A PLATED DESSERT THE PASTRY CHEF MUST CONSIDER THE COMPOSITION; EXPLORING THE POSSIBILITIES OF CONTRASTING AND COMPLEMENTING FLAVORS AND TEXTURES, AS WELL AS COLOR AND STYLE. EQUALLY IMPORTANT TO CONSIDER ARE THE CUSTOMER BASE, SPECIFIC EVENT OR MENU NEEDS, AND THE ENVIRONMENT FOR PREPARATION AND SERVICE.

Chocolate Peanut Butter Bombe

Makes 10 desserts

CINNAMON MARSHMALLOWS (½ in/1 cm thick) (page 750)	½ sheet pan	½ sheet pan
VANILLA SAUCE (page 430)	15 fl oz	450 mL
CHOCOLATE PEANUT BUTTER BOMBES (page 618)	10 each	10 each
PEANUT BRITTLE (1-oz/28-g pieces) (page 732)	10 each	10 each
CHOCOLATE FANS (page 768)	10 each	10 each

1. Cut the marshmallows into 1-in/3-cm squares.

2. Ladle 1½ fl oz/45 mL vanilla sauce into the center of each chilled 10-in/25-cm plate. Place the bombes in the center of the plates. Stand a piece of peanut brittle in the side of each bombe, about one-third of the way from the top. Stick a chocolate fan into each bombe next to the peanut brittle.

3. Place 3 marshmallows around each bombe.

Trends in Plated Desserts

When designing a dessert menu, it is essential to consider current trends to keep your menu fresh and interesting. Among current trends is the use of "architectural style" in constructing plated desserts. Sophisticated customers will likely expect to see such cutting-edge desserts on the menu.

Current trends also include a return to more rustic-style desserts such as galettes and "comfort-food" such as pies and cobblers. The appeal of these desserts lies in their simplicity of flavor, style, and presentation.

It's also important to look at classic desserts with a contemporary eye and perhaps introduce ingredients that are not typical for the particular preparation to give them new life.

The Contrast Wheel

The pastry contrast wheel is a visual guide to understanding the basic contrasting flavors, temperatures, and textures that can be utilized by the pastry chef in the creation of a plated dessert. Use the contrast wheel when conceptualizing desserts. Think about incorporating a number of contrasting characteristics into a dessert by using different components, but never add components just to have another contrasting element. The number of components should make sense for the dessert.

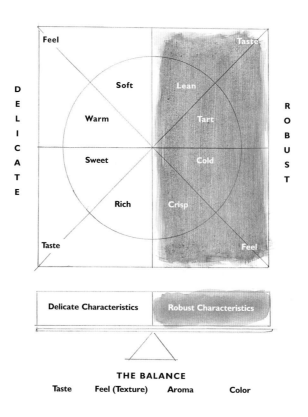

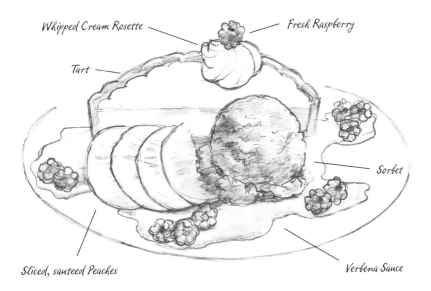

Whipped Cream Rosette

Fresh Raspberry

Tart

Sorbet

Sliced, sautéed Peaches

Verbena Sauce

This sketch of Raspberry Curd Tartlet with Peach Sorbet and Lemon Verbena Sauce (page 678) is an example of how a pastry chef utilizes the contrast wheel and visualizes a dessert before execution.

The contrast wheel is divided between delicate and robust tastes and mouth feels. Combining contrasting elements on one dessert plate will keep the palate interested and excited. The classic apple pie à la mode is a perfect example. Think of how it relates to the contrast wheel.

An exceptional apple pie will have a crisp, flaky crust and perhaps a filling that still retains a little tartness from the apples, while the ice cream will lend its creamy, soft characteristics. For the best pie à la mode, the pie should be served warm to bring out its flavors and aromas, as well as to provide temperature contrast with the cold ice cream.

Keep the idea of the contrast wheel in mind when adding new desserts to a current menu or designing a new menu. A balanced menu should contain warm and cold, sweet and tart, and rich and lean desserts.

Dessert Station Mise en Place

When setting up a dessert station, whether for a large banquet kitchen or a small restaurant, there are several important considerations. The size and configuration of the work area, as well as its location in relationship to the ovens, refrigerators, and freezers, determines how certain jobs are accomplished. For example, if you are preparing a hot soufflé, the location of the oven is an important factor in determining how and/or where the soufflés will be plated. In the same vein, if you are plating frozen desserts, the location of and access to freezer space must be considered. Keep often-used items within easy reach and easy to see. Keep efficient workflow in mind too—plates should move in a single direction.

The station must typically be able to accommodate a variety of service pieces. Some pieces may need to be kept hot or cold for service. During service, you will also need to have a variety of nonfood items at hand: paper and side towels, skewers or toothpicks, latex gloves, and equipment such as palette knives and pastry bags. Returning items to their rightful position each time you use them will help you become more efficient and avoid lost time spent searching for missing items.

To keep the station clean and sanitary, have a container of sanitizing solution available, as well as clean cloths or paper towels and hot water to wipe plates before they leave the station.

Plated Desserts at Banquets

In most cases, any dessert that can be prepared and served for 10 can also be served for 100. However, for larger-volume plating, equipment, storage, timing of service, and labor must all be considered.

When planning a dessert for a banquet menu, consider the final presentation of the dessert. Certain restrictions may immediately become apparent. Lack of equipment (not enough of a particular mold, for example) might force you to change the shape or look of a dessert. Timing can sometimes be a restrictive element for preparations such as hot soufflés, and in some cases you may want to reformulate the dessert to increase its stability.

Keep sauces that are to be used in plastic squeeze bottles. These give you more control over the amount and location of the sauce on the plate or dessert and make it easy to store the sauces at the station.

Molten New York Cheesecake

Makes 10 desserts

HEAVY CREAM	6 fl oz	180 mL
WHITE CHOCOLATE, melted	12 oz	340 g
CREAM CHEESE, melted	8 oz	227 g
BUTTER, soft	3 oz	85 g
SUGAR	3 oz	85 g
CHEESECAKE BATTER (page 320)	3 lb 12 oz	1.70 kg
1-2-3 COOKIE DOUGH WITH GRAHAM CRACKER CRUMBS (page 249)	1 lb	454 g
NUT TUILES (2 in/5 cm diameter) (page 350)	10 each	10 each
CHUNKY STRAWBERRY SAUCE (page 441)	10 fl oz	300 mL
CHAMPAGNE, chilled	10 fl oz	300 mL

1. Bring the heavy cream to a simmer. Combine with the white chocolate and cream cheese using a whisk, creating a ganache. Allow the ganache mixture to set up at room temperature.

2. Brush the inside of ten 8-fl-oz/240-mL ramekins lightly with the softened butter. Dust the ramekins with the sugar and tap out the excess.

3. Fill each ramekin with 6 oz/170 g of the cheesecake batter.

4. Bake the cheesecakes in a water bath in a 300°F/149°C oven until just barely set, about 40 minutes. Allow to cool to room temperature. Refrigerate overnight.

5. Roll out the dough 1/4 in/6 mm thick. Using a 3-in/8-cm round cutter, cut 10 disks out of the dough and place on a parchment-lined sheet pan.

6. Bake the cookies in a 350°F/177°C oven until they are golden brown at the edges, 8 to 10 minutes. Allow to cool to room temperature.

7. Work the ganache with a metal spatula on a marble work surface until it is of piping consistency. Using a pastry bag fitted with a No. 5 tip, pipe the ganache into 2-oz/57-g bulbs. Let the ganache set.

8. Gently roll the ganache balls into perfect rounds.

9. Using a 3/4-in/2-cm melon baller, make a hole in the center of each cheesecake that is big enough to hold a ball of ganache. Place a ball of ganache in each cheesecake.

10. Flip each cheesecake upside down onto one of the cookie bases, centering it on the cookie.

11. Warm the cheesecakes until hot but not weepy.

12. Place each cheesecake in a chilled 10-in/25-cm soup bowl and place a pistachio tuile on top. Place 1 fl oz/30 mL of strawberry sauce around each cheesecake. Just before serving, pour 1 fl oz/30 mL Champagne into each bowl.

Sautéed Apple Crêpes with Poached Cranberries, Calvados Caramel Sauce, and Vanilla Ice Cream

Makes 10 desserts

GOLDEN DELICIOUS APPLES	13 each	13 each
SUGAR	6 oz	170 g
BUTTER	3 oz	85 g
CRÊPES (6 in/15 cm diameter) (page 259)	20 each	20 each
CLEAR APPLE CARAMEL SAUCE (page 453)	20 fl oz	600 mL
POACHED CRANBERRIES (page 823)	80 each	80 each
VANILLA ICE CREAM (page 464)	20 fl oz	600 mL

1. Peel, quarter, and tourné the apples. Toss the apples with the sugar.

2. Melt 1 oz/28 g of the butter in a 10-in/25-cm sauté pan over medium-high heat. Add one-third of the apples and sauté until golden brown on all sides. Transfer to a hotel pan. Sauté the remaining apples in two batches, using 1 oz/28 g butter each time.

3. Fold the crêpes into quarters.

4. Ladle 2 fl oz/60 mL caramel sauce onto each warm 10-in/25-cm plate. Place 2 folded crêpes in the center of each plate, overlapping them slightly and pointing them toward the top of the plate.

5. Place 5 sautéed apples pieces on the bottom half of each plate, arranging them in an arc around the crêpes, pointing out and evenly spaced. Scatter 8 cranberries around the apples and crêpes.

6. Using a No. 30 scoop, place a 2-fl-oz/60-mL scoop of ice cream onto the center of the crêpes on each plate.

Blueberry and Cream Cheese Crêpes

Makes 10 desserts

CREAM CHEESE	1 lb	454 g
CONFECTIONERS' SUGAR	4 oz	113 g
VANILLA EXTRACT	1 fl oz	30 mL
LEMON ZEST	1 tsp	3 g
CRÊPES (6 in/15 cm diameter) (page 259)	20 each	20 each
BLUEBERRY FILLING (page 507)	1 lb 14 oz	851 g
CALVADOS SABAYON (page 433)	20 fl oz	600 mL
BUTTERMILK ICE CREAM (page 476)	20 fl oz	600 mL
BRANDY SNAP FANS (3 in/8 cm long) (page 341)	10 each	10 each

1. Cream together the cream cheese, confectioners' sugar, vanilla extract, and lemon zest using an electric mixer fitted with a paddle attachment on medium speed, scraping down the bowl periodically until smooth in texture and light in color, about 5 minutes.

2. Lay out the crêpes. Spread 1 oz/28 g cream cheese filling evenly over each crêpe. Spoon 1½ oz/43 g blueberry filling in the center of each crêpe. Fold one edge of each crêpe over the blueberry filling and roll the crêpe into a cylinder.

3. Place 2 crêpes in each 8-in/20-cm crêpe dish.

4. Spoon 2 fl oz/60 mL sabayon over the middle third of each pair of crêpes. Using a No. 30 scoop, place a 2-fl-oz/60-mL scoop of ice cream to the left of the crêpes. Place a brandy snap fan between the ice cream and crêpes.

Pumpkin Crème Brûlée

Makes 10 desserts

JACK BE LITTLE PUMPKINS, scrubbed	10 each	10 each
PUMPKIN CRÈME BRÛLÉE BASE (page 380)	60 fl oz	1.80 L
BRÛLÉE SUGAR BLEND (page 824)	10 oz	284 g
SPICE MIX (page 824)	1 lb 4 oz	567 g
HONEY TUILES, (page 353), Scarecrow Template (Appendix D)	10 each	10 each
CINNAMON STICKS	50 each	50 each
WHOLE CLOVES	½ oz	14 g
STAR ANISE	30 each	30 each

1. Cut the top ½ in/1 cm off each pumpkin; reserve these lids. Scoop the seeds and membranes out of each pumpkin. If necessary, shave a very thin layer off the bottom of the pumpkins so they stand perfectly upright. (Be careful to shave off as little flesh as possible; if there are any holes in the bottom of the pumpkin, the base will leak out.)

2. Fill each pumpkin with 6 fl oz/180 mL of crème brûlée base. Place the pumpkins in a hotel pan. Add water to come halfway up the side of the pumpkins.

3. Bake in a 300°F/149°C deck oven until the custard is set, about 40 minutes. Remove the pumpkins from the water bath and allow to cool to room temperature.

4. Cover the pumpkins and refrigerate them overnight.

5. Sprinkle ½ oz/14 g brûlée sugar over each crème brûlée. Caramelize the sugar evenly with a torch (be careful not to burn the edges of the pumpkins).

6. Sprinkle 2 oz/57 g of the spice mix in the center of each chilled 10-in/25-cm plate. Place the pumpkins on top of the spice mix (the spice mix will anchor the pumpkins in place).

7. Place a scarecrow body in each crème brûlée, toward the back of the pumpkin. Place a scarecrow leg in front of each body, draping it over the side of the pumpkin. Lean the reserved lids against the pumpkins, opposite the scarecrow legs.

8. Place 5 cinnamon sticks, 12 cloves, and 3 star anise around the pumpkin on each plate in a decorative fashion.

Chocolate Mousse in Tuiles with Chocolate Pyramid

Makes 10 desserts

CHOCOLATE MOUSSE (page 798)	2 lb 12 oz	1.25 kg
HONEY TUILES (2 in/5 cm diameter, slightly concave) (page 353)	30 each	30 each
HEAVY CREAM	5 fl oz	150 mL
SUGAR	1½ tsp	7.50 g
STRIPED CHOCOLATE TRIANGLES (3 in/8 cm tall and 1 in/3 cm wide at the base) (page 765)	30 each	30 each
RASPBERRY SAUCE (page 439)	15 fl oz	450 mL
CRÈME FRAÎCHE	5 oz	142 g

1. Using a pastry bag fitted with a No. 4 plain tip, pipe 1½ oz/43 g of the chocolate mousse into each tuile in a spiral.

2. Whip the heavy cream with the sugar until it holds soft peaks.

3. Using a No. 6 plain tip, pipe ½ oz/14 g whipped cream in a mound in the center of each chilled 10-in/25-cm plate; the whipped cream should be ¾ in/2 cm across at the base and 1¼ in/3 cm tall.

4. Lean 3 chocolate triangles against each mound of whipped cream to form a chocolate pyramid. There should be very little whipped cream showing. Place a mousse-filled tuile 1 in/3 cm away from the base of each chocolate triangle, pointing outward.

5. Pool ½ fl oz/15 mL raspberry sauce between each of the 3 tuiles. Using a No. 3 plain tip, pipe a ½-in/1-cm dot of crème fraîche in the center of each pool of raspberry sauce. Use a toothpick to create a paisley design in the raspberry sauce.

Tropical Fruit Vacherin with Passion Fruit Sauce

Makes 10 desserts

KIWIS	5 each	5 each
POMEGRANATES	3 each	3 each
PINEAPPLE	1 each	1 each
PAPAYAS	3 each	3 each
VACHERINS (3½ in/9 cm long by 1½ in/4 cm wide by 1¼ in/3 cm tall) (page 627)	10 each	10 each
DARK CHOCOLATE, tempered	10 oz	284 g
MANGO SORBET (page 482)	15 fl oz	450 mL
PASSION FRUIT SAUCE (page 439)	10 fl oz	300 mL

1. Peel the kiwis. Cut each kiwi into 6 wedges.

2. Cut the pomegranates in half. Gently scoop out all of the seeds.

3. Cut 1 in/3 cm off the top and bottom of the pineapple. Carefully cut the peel off the pineapple and remove the "eyes." Core the pineapple. Cut it into slices 1 by 2 in/3 by 5 cm and ¼ in/6 mm thick.

4. Peel the papayas, cut them in half, and remove the seeds. Cut the papayas into 1-in/3-cm cubes. Wrap all fruit in plastic wrap and refrigerate until ready to assemble.

5. Brush the inside of each vacherin with 1 oz/28 g tempered chocolate. Allow the chocolate to set completely.

6. Using a No. 50 scoop, place a 1½-fl-oz/45-mL scoop of sorbet in the left side of each vacherin. Arrange about 1½ oz/43 g pineapple, 1½ oz/43 g papaya, 1 oz/28 g pomegranate seeds, and 4 kiwi wedges next to the mango sorbet.

7. Ladle 2 fl oz/60 mL passion fruit sauce into the center of each chilled 10-in/25-cm plate. Place a vacherin slightly above the center of each plate.

Port-Poached Pear Stuffed with Roquefort and Walnuts

Makes 10 desserts

FORELLE PEARS	10 each	10 each
PORT POACHING LIQUID (page 823)	32 fl oz	960 mL
ROQUEFORT CHEESE	10 oz	284 g
WALNUTS, lightly toasted and finely chopped	5 oz	142 g
LADYFINGERS (page 370)	5 each	5 each
MANDARIN ORANGES	6 each	6 each
CORNSTARCH	1/2 oz	14 g
WATER	2 fl oz	60 mL
BUTTER	1/2 oz	14 g
PHYLLO DOUGH SHEETS (14 by 18 in/36 by 46 cm)	6 each	6 each
BUTTER, melted	4 oz	113 g

1. Peel the pears, leaving the stems on. Using a melon baller, core the pears from the bottom, making an opening 1/2 in/1 cm in diameter. Using a clean scouring pad, sand the outside of the pears to smooth the sides and remove any lines or ridges from peeling.

2. Put the pears in a pot and cover with the poaching liquid. Poach until tender, about 30 minutes. Let cool, then refrigerate the pears overnight in the poaching liquid.

3. Blend together the Roquefort and walnuts.

4. Remove the pears from the poaching liquid; reserve the liquid.

5. Spoon 1 1/2 oz/43 g Roquefort filling into each pear. Cut the ladyfingers in pieces crosswise, so they fit into the opening of each pear to seal it.

6. Cut the oranges into suprême segments. Reserve.

7. Reduce 16 fl oz/480 mL of the poaching liquid by one-third. Meanwhile, make a slurry with the cornstarch and water. Gradually whisk the slurry into the reduced poaching liquid and bring back to a boil, whisking until the sauce thickens enough to coat the back of a spoon. Finish the sauce with the 1/2 oz/14 g butter. Keep the sauce warm.

8. Cut each sheet of phyllo into twelve 4-in/10-cm squares. Brush one square lightly with melted butter. Top with another phyllo square, placing it so that the corners of the top square are over the centers of the sides of the square below. Brush the phyllo lightly with melted butter. Repeat this process with 2 more phyllo dough squares so that there are 4 layers. Repeat the process with the remaining phyllo and melted butter, to make 10 phyllo stacks in all.

(continued)

9. Stand a stuffed pear in the center of each phyllo dough stack. Gently bring the edges of the phyllo up and around the pear so that the pear is sitting in a phyllo dough cup. Transfer to a parchment-lined sheet pan.

10. Bake at 375°F/191°C until the phyllo dough is golden brown, about 10 minutes. Let cool slightly.

11. Make an incision ¼ in/6 mm long in the top of each pear, next to the stem.

12. Ladle 2 fl oz/60 mL port sauce into each warm 10-in/25-cm soup bowl. Place a pear in the center of each plate. Place 5 orange segments around each pear, pointing outward, like the spokes of a wheel.

Chocolate Soufflé with Strawberry Sauce

Makes 10 desserts

CHUNKY STRAWBERRY SAUCE (page 441)	10 fl oz	300 mL
CHOCOLATE SOUFFLÉS (page 407)	10 each	10 each
SWEDISH OATMEAL COOKIES (1½ in/4 cm diameter) (page 331)	30 each	30 each

1. Pour 1 fl oz/30 mL strawberry sauce into each of 10 small sauceboats. Refrigerate until needed.

2. Line ten 10-in/25-cm warm plates with folded napkins or underliners.

3. Remove the soufflés from the water bath immediately after they finish baking, gently dry off the bottoms of the ramekins, and place each ramekin on a lined plate.

4. Shingle 3 cookies to the lower right of each ramekin. Serve the soufflés with the sauce-boats of strawberry sauce.

Dates and Pistachios in Kataifi with Lemon Sorbet and Honey Cardamom Sauce

Makes 10 desserts

DATES, pitted and coarsely chopped	10 oz	284 g
PISTACHIOS, coarsely chopped	6¼ oz	177 g
ALMOND CREAM FILLING (page 831)	1 lb 4 oz	567 g
PERNOD	1½ fl oz	45 mL
KATAIFI	1 lb 4 oz	567 g
BUTTER, melted	5 oz	142 g
HONEY CARDAMOM SAUCE (page 456)	20 fl oz	600 mL
LEMON SORBET (page 478)	20 fl oz	600 mL
1-2-3 COOKIES (2 in/5 cm diameter, ⅛ in/3 mm thick) (page 249)	10 each	10 each

1. Mix together 8½ oz/241 g of the dates, 5 oz/142 g of the pistachios, the almond cream filling, and Pernod until thoroughly combined.

2. Lay out two pieces of plastic wrap, each 24 in/61 cm long. On one piece, use 12 oz/340 g of the kataifi to make a rectangle 6 by 18 in/15 by 46 cm. On the other piece, use the remaining 8 oz/227 g kataifi to make a rectangle 6 by 12 in/15 by 30 cm. Brush the longer rectangle with 3 oz/85 g of the melted butter. Brush the shorter rectangle with the remaining 2 oz/57 g melted butter.

3. Using a pastry bag fitted with a No. 5 plain tip, pipe 1 lb 4 oz/567 g of the pistachio-date filling over the long edge of the longer rectangle that is closest to you, about 1 in/3 cm from the edge. Using a No. 5 plain tip, pipe the remaining 13 oz/369 g filling over the long edge of the shorter rectangle that is closest to you. Use the plastic wrap to help roll the kataifi around the filling, like a jelly roll. Carefully transfer both rolls onto a parchment-lined sheet pan.

4. Bake in a 400°F/204°C oven until golden brown, about 30 minutes. Allow to cool slightly, but make sure they are warm for serving. Cut the rolls into 3-in/8-cm slices.

5. Ladle 2 fl oz/60 mL honey sauce onto each warm 10-in/25-cm plate. (The sauce should come out to the rim of the plate.) Place one kataifi slice toward the top of each plate, angling it slightly so that it is pointing toward the left side of the plate. Lean another slice of kataifi across the first slice, pointing toward the right side of the plate.

6. Using a No. 30 scoop, place a 2-fl-oz/60-mL scoop of sorbet below the kataifi slices on each plate. Sprinkle a pinch of the reserved pistachios on top of the sorbet, sprinkle a pinch of dates on the sauce, and lean a cookie against the sorbet.

Poached Pear with Dried Cherry Sauce and Vanilla Bean Ice Cream

Makes 10 desserts

ANJOU PEARS	10 each	10 each
POACHING LIQUID (page 823)	64 fl oz	1.92 L
BUTTER GANACHE (page 714)	1 lb 8 oz	680 g
CHOCOLATE CURLS (page 766)	10 each	10 each
DRIED CHERRY SAUCE (page 447)	10 oz	284 g
HONEY TUILE CUPS (page 353)	10 each	10 each
VANILLA ICE CREAM (page 464)	15 fl oz	450 mL

1. Peel the pears, leaving the stems on. Using a melon baller, core the pears from the bottom, making an opening ½ in/1 cm in diameter. Using a clean scouring pad, sand the outside of the pears to smooth the sides and remove any lines or ridges from peeling.

2. Put the pears in a pot, cover with the poaching liquid, and cover the pears with cheesecloth. Poach until tender, about 30 minutes. Let cool, then refrigerate overnight in the poaching liquid.

3. Remove the pears from the poaching liquid and place them on a wire rack to drain. Prepare the butter ganache.

4. Dip each pear in the ganache, holding it at a 45-degree angle so the ganache coats the pear at an angle, and place on a parchment-lined sheet pan. Refrigerate the pears to allow the ganache to set.

5. Snip the stems off the pears. Place a chocolate curl on each pear where the stem was.

6. Ladle 1 oz/28 g cherry sauce onto the bottom left section of each 10-in/25-cm chilled plate. Place a poached pear inside each tuile cup, and place the cup slightly below the center of each plate.

7. Using an oval scoop, place a 1½-fl-oz/45-mL scoop of ice cream to the lower right of each tuile cup.

Brown Sugar–Roasted Pear

Make 10 desserts

ANJOU PEARS	10 each	10 each
BROWN SUGAR–BUTTER RUB (page 461)	1 lb 4 oz	567 g
CREAM CHEESE FILLING (page 830)	15 oz	425 g
LADYFINGERS (page 370)	5 each	5 each
CRANBERRY SAUCE (page 448)	10 fl oz	300 mL
PHYLLO CUPS (page 626)	10 each	10 each
BUTTERSCOTCH SAUCE, warmed (page 626)	20 fl oz	600 mL
POACHED CRANBERRIES (page 823)	50 each	50 each

1. Peel the pears, leaving the stems on. Using a melon baller, core the pears from the bottom, making an opening ½ in/1 cm in diameter. Using a clean scouring pad, sand the outside of the pears to smooth the sides and remove any lines or ridges from peeling.

2. Rub each pear with 2 oz/57 g of the brown sugar–butter rub. Place the pears in a hotel pan.

3. Bake in a 350°F/177°C deck oven, basting the pears every 10 minutes with the melted brown sugar–butter mixture, until tender, 30 to 45 minutes, depending on the ripeness of the pears. Place the pears on a wire rack to cool to room temperature.

4. Using a pastry bag fitted with a No. 6 plain tip, pipe 1½ oz/43 g cream cheese filling into the cavity in each pear. Cut the ladyfingers so that they fit over the opening in each pear to seal it.

5. Cover and refrigerate the pears until ready to serve.

6. Warm the pears in a 350°F/177°C oven for 3 to 4 minutes.

7. Using a plastic squeeze bottle, drizzle 1 fl oz/30 mL cranberry sauce over the center of each warm plate in a spiral pattern.

8. Place a phyllo cup in the center of each plate. Place a roasted pear in the cup. Drizzle 2 fl oz/60 mL warm butterscotch sauce over the pear and arrange 5 poached cranberries around the phyllo cup.

Gratin of Lemon-Lime Chibouste

Makes 10 desserts

ROULADE SHEET (11½ by 16½ in/29 by 42 cm) (page 307)	1 each	1 each
LEMON SIMPLE SYRUP (page 820)	6 fl oz	180 mL
LEMON-LIME CHIBOUSTE (page 406)	1 lb 14 oz	851 g
RASPBERRIES	1 lb	454 g
BRÛLÉE SUGAR BLEND (page 824)	5 oz	142 g
SWISS MERINGUE (page 416)	10 fl oz	300 mL
LEMON CHIPS (Appendix D)	20 each	20 each
PAPAYA SAUCE (page 430)	20 fl oz	600 mL

1. Using a 3-in/8-cm cutter, cut 10 disks out of the roulade. Place a disk in the bottom of each of 10 rings, 3 in/8 cm in diameter and 1½ in/4 cm tall.

2. Brush each roulade disk with ½ fl oz/15 mL lemon syrup. Using a pastry bag fitted with a No. 6 plain tip, pipe 1½ oz/43 g chibouste in an even layer on top of each roulade disk.

3. Arrange 8 raspberries in a ring on top of the chibouste in each mold, placing them ½ in/1 cm from the outer edge of the chibouste. Press them down slightly. Pipe 1½ oz/43 g chibouste on top of the raspberries in each mold. Using a small offset spatula, level off the top of the chibouste so that it is flush with the top of the ring.

4. Freeze the chibouste overnight.

5. Remove the rings from the chibouste. Sprinkle ½ oz/14 g brûlée sugar blend evenly on top of each chibouste. Caramelize the brûlée sugar evenly using a torch. Allow the molten sugar to cool.

6. Using a No. 6 plain tip, pipe 3 mounds of Swiss meringue onto the center of each chibouste. Toast the meringue lightly with a torch.

7. Stand one lemon chip in the center of the toasted meringues so that they are at an angle to each other.

8. Ladle 2 fl oz/60 mL papaya sauce onto each chilled plate. Using a small offset spatula, place a chibouste in the center of each plate. Place 8 raspberries around each chibouste.

Sautéed Apples with Ginger Cake and Calvados Sabayon Sauce

Makes 10 desserts

CURRANTS	4 oz	113 g
BRANDY	8 fl oz	240 mL
GRANNY SMITH APPLES	5 each	5 each
BUTTER	3 oz	85 g
CALVADOS	1 fl oz	30 mL
CINNAMON SUGAR (page 826)	2 oz	57 g
GINGER CAKES (page 277)	10 each	10 each
VANILLA CONFECTIONERS' SUGAR (page 827)	½ oz	14 g
CALVADOS SABAYON (page 433)	20 fl oz	600 mL

1. Soak the currants in the brandy overnight. Drain.

2. Peel and core the apples. Cut each apple into 16 wedges.

3. Melt 1 oz/28 g of the butter in a large sauté pan over medium-high heat. Add one-third of the apples and sauté until golden brown and tender. Transfer to a hotel pan. Sauté the remaining apples in two batches, using 1 oz/28 g butter each time.

4. Deglaze the pan with the Calvados. Reduce the brandy until it has almost all evaporated, then add to the apples.

5. Toss the apples with the cinnamon sugar, then toss with the macerated currants. Keep warm.

6. Dust the tops of the ginger cakes with the vanilla sugar.

7. Place a ginger cake in the center of each warm 10-in/25-cm plate. Place 8 apple wedges to the lower right of each cake, and ladle 2 fl oz/60 mL sabayon sauce on top of the apples.

8. Lightly caramelize the sauce using a torch.

Honey Tangerine Angel Food Cake

Makes 10 desserts

ANGEL FOOD CAKE BATTER (page 300)	40 fl oz	1.20 L
HEAVY CREAM, whipped to soft peaks	10 fl oz	300 mL
HONEY TANGERINES, cut into suprême segments	15 each	15 each
APRICOT GLAZE, warmed (page 429)	5 fl oz	150 mL
RASPBERRIES	80 each	80 each
ORANGE VANILLA BEAN SAUCE (page 451)	20 fl oz	600 mL
MINT SPRIGS	10 each	10 each

1. Place 10 rings 4 in/10 cm in diameter and 1½ in/4 cm tall on a parchment-lined sheet pan. Scoop the angel food cake batter into the rings, filling them nearly full.

2. Bake in a 350°F/177°C deck oven until golden brown, about 30 minutes. Allow to cool to room temperature.

3. Remove the angel food cakes from the rings and refrigerate overnight. (Note: Angel food cake that is sliced the same day it is baked tends to be rubbery.)

4. Using a serrated slicing knife, slice each angel food cake horizontally in half. Using a pastry bag fitted with a No. 4 plain tip, pipe the whipped cream onto the bottom layer of each cake. Place the top layers of cake on top of the whipped cream.

5. Arrange 15 to 20 tangerine suprêmes in a spiral on top of each angel food cake. Glaze each spiral of tangerine suprêmes with ½ fl oz/15 mL warm apricot glaze. Place 8 raspberries in the empty center of each spiral.

6. Ladle 2 fl oz/60 mL orange sauce onto each chilled plate. Using a small offset spatula, place the angel food cakes in the center of the sauce. Place a mint sprig on top of each cake.

Toasted Brioche with Drunken Fruits

Makes 10 desserts

MANDARIN ORANGES, cut into suprême segments (page 517)	3 each	3 each
BLACKBERRIES	8 oz	227 g
STRAWBERRIES	8 oz	227 g
RASPBERRIES	8 oz	227 g
POMEGRANATE SEEDS	6 oz	170 g
GRAND MARNIER	16 fl oz	480 mL
FRAMBOISE	16 fl oz	480 mL
RUBY PORT	16 fl oz	480 mL
SUGAR	1 lb 8 oz	680 g
BUTTER, soft	1 lb 8 oz	680 g
BRIOCHE DOUGH (page 142)	2 lb	907 g
EGG WASH (page 825)	as needed	as needed
HEAVY CREAM, whipped to soft peaks	10 fl oz	300 mL

1. Combine the mandarin oranges, blackberries, strawberries, raspberries, pomegranate seeds, liqueurs, port, and 8 oz/227 g of the sugar in a large container. Allow the fruits to marinate overnight.

2. Bake the brioche in two cylindrical molds that are 6¾ in/17 cm in diameter and 8 in/20 cm tall. Brush each mold generously with 2 oz/57 g of the softened butter.

3. Divide the brioche dough into two 1-lb/454-g pieces. Round each one into a ball and place in one of the prepared molds.

4. Allow the dough to proof, covered, until it springs back lightly to the touch, 45 minutes to 1 hour; there should be a small indentation left in the dough, but it should not collapse. Brush the dough lightly with egg wash.

5. Bake in a 325°F/163°C deck oven until the brioche is dark golden brown on the outside and golden brown in the center of any cracks, about 45 minutes. If the brioche has browned sufficiently but is still not quite baked through toward the end of baking, it may be necessary to remove the brioche from the molds and dry it out slightly in the oven. Allow to cool to room temperature.

6. Drain the fruit.

7. Slice the brioche crosswise into rounds 1 in/3 cm thick. You will require two slices for each plated dessert. Brush each brioche slice on both sides with the remaining butter. Sprinkle on both sides with the remaining sugar.

8. Sauté the brioche slices over medium heat until golden brown on the first side. Flip the brioche slices over and sauté until the other side is golden brown.

9. Cut a paisley shape 3½ in/9 cm long and 2½ in/6 cm wide out of the center of each slice of brioche (the width is measured at the base of the paisley shape). Cut an identical paisley shape out of the brioche, facing in the opposite direction. (The cutouts should resemble a yin-yang symbol.) Reserve the cut slices as well as the cutouts.

10. Place each cut brioche slice in a warm 12-in/30-cm soup bowl. Place 2 oz/57 g of fruit in each opening in the brioche. Lean 1 cutout paisley shape on each mound of fruit.

11. Place a quenelle of whipped cream on top of each mound of fruit, in front of the brioche cutout.

Summer Pudding with Fruit-Filled Honey Tuile Basket and Raspberry Frozen Yogurt
Makes 10 desserts

SUMMER PUDDINGS (page 621)	10 each	10 each
HEAVY CREAM, lightly whipped	10 fl oz	300 mL
LINZER COOKIES (1¼ in/3 cm diameter, fluted) (page 344)	10 each	10 each
RASPBERRY FROZEN YOGURT (page 478)	10 fl oz	300 mL
HONEY TUILE BASKETS (page 353)	10 each	10 each
BLUEBERRIES	5 oz	142 g
RASPBERRIES	5 oz	142 g
BLACKBERRIES	5 oz	142 g

1. Place a summer pudding toward the top of each chilled plate. Spoon 1 fl oz/30 mL underwhipped cream over the lower half of each pudding, so it cascades off the sides of the pudding.

2. Place a linzer cookie 3 in/8 cm from the lower right of each summer pudding. Using a No. 60 scoop, place a 1-fl-oz/30-mL scoop of frozen yogurt on each cookie.

3. Place a honey tuile basket 4 in/10 cm from the lower left of each pudding. Place ½ oz/14 g of each berry in each basket.

Warm Citrus in Orange Brioche with Champagne Beurre Blanc

Makes 10 desserts

BLOOD ORANGES	5 each	5 each
NAVEL ORANGES	5 each	5 each
PINK GRAPEFRUITS	2 each	2 each
CLEMENTINES	5 each	5 each
SIMPLE SYRUP (page 820)	10 fl oz	300 mL
RIESLING	10 fl oz	300 mL
MINT LEAVES, cut into chiffonade	10 each	10 each
ORANGE BRIOCHE À TÊTE (page 220)	10 each	10 each
CHAMPAGNE BEURRE BLANC (page 460)	20 fl oz	600 mL

1. Segment the oranges, grapefruits, and clementines into suprêmes (see page xxx). Cut the grapefruit suprêmes in half.

2. Combine the citrus suprêmes, simple syrup, Riesling, and mint in a saucepan. Heat over medium-low heat for 15 minutes. Remove from the heat.

3. Cut off the top of each brioche at its widest point; reserve the tops. Scoop out the centers of the brioche.

4. Toast the brioche tops and bottoms in a 350°F/177°C deck oven for 5 minutes.

5. Ladle 2 fl oz/60 mL beurre blanc into the center of each warm 10-in/25-cm plate. Place a brioche bottom in the center of the plate. Spoon 4 oz/113 g of the warm citrus mix into the center of each brioche, so some of the citrus suprêmes are cascading out onto the sauce. Lean a brioche top against each filled brioche at a 45-degree angle.

Funnel Cake with Maple Syrup and Summer Fruit Sauces

Makes 10 desserts

MILK, room temperature	24 fl oz	720 mL
YEAST	²⁄₃ oz	19 g
ALL-PURPOSE FLOUR	1 lb 5 oz	595 g
SALT	pinch	pinch
EGG YOLKS	1½ oz	43 g
CONFECTIONERS' SUGAR	3 oz	85 g
MAPLE SYRUP	10 fl oz	300 mL
RASPBERRY SAUCE (page 439)	10 fl oz	300 mL
KIWI COULIS (page 436)	10 fl oz	300 mL
MANGO COULIS (page 436)	10 fl oz	300 mL
TOASTED ANISE ICE CREAM (page 469)	20 fl oz	600 mL

1. To make the funnel cakes, combine the milk and yeast with 10 oz/284 g of the flour. Cover and allow to ferment for 45 minutes.

2. Add the remaining flour, salt, and egg yolks and mix. Allow to ferment until double in size.

3. Stir the batter and pipe using a pastry bag with a No. 3 plain tip into 360°F/182°C oil to form 10 small individual cakes. Fry until golden, turning once. Remove from the hot oil and allow to drain on towels.

4. Dust the funnel cakes liberally with confectioners' sugar.

5. Using a plastic squeeze bottle, drizzle 1 fl oz/30 mL maple syrup in a spiral pattern over the center of each warm plate. Using a squeeze bottle, place 12 drops of raspberry sauce around the inner rim of the plate. (Note: Do not use more than 1 fl oz/30 mL of each fruit sauce per plate.) Using a squeeze bottle, place a drop of kiwi sauce to the left of each raspberry sauce drop, leaving space for the mango sauce. Using a squeeze bottle, place a drop of mango sauce to the left of each kiwi sauce drop. The sauces should run together slightly.

6. Place a funnel cake in the center of each plate. Using a No. 30 scoop, place a 2-fl-oz/60-mL scoop of ice cream on the center of each funnel cake.

Caramelized Pineapple with Ginger Rum Sauce and Coconut Sorbet in Honey Tuile Cup

Makes 10 desserts

PINEAPPLES	2 each	2 each
SUGAR	10 oz	284 g
BUTTER	4 oz	113 g
GINGER RUM SAUCE (page 444)	20 fl oz	600 mL
HONEY TUILE CUPS (page 353)	10 each	10 each
COCONUT SORBET (page 486)	20 fl oz	600 mL
COCONUT, lightly toasted	2½ oz	71 g

1. Cut the top and bottom of the pineapples. Carefully cut the peel off the pineapples, and cut out the "eyes." Cut 10 slices ³⁄₈ in/1 cm thick from the pineapples and remove the core.

2. Lightly coat both sides of each slice of pineapple with sugar.

3. Melt 1 oz/28 g of the butter in a large sauté pan over medium-high heat. Add a single layer of pineapple slices and sauté until golden brown on the first side. Flip the pineapple slices over gently and sauté until golden brown on the other side. Transfer to a hotel pan. Repeat this process with the remaining pineapple slices, cooking them in three batches and using 1 oz/28 g butter for each batch.

4. Ladle 2 fl oz/60 mL rum sauce onto each warm 10-in/25-cm plate. Place a sautéed pineapple slice in the center of each plate, and place a honey tuile cup in the center of the pineapple slice.

5. Using a No. 30 scoop, place a 2-fl-oz/60-mL scoop of sorbet in the center of each honey tuile cup. Sprinkle toasted coconut around the edges of the sauce on each plate.

Strawberry Rhubarb Soup

Makes 10 desserts

STRAWBERRIES, cleaned	5 qt	4.75 L
RHUBARB, cleaned	12 lb	5.44 kg
SUGAR	1 lb 4 oz plus as needed	567 g plus as needed
VANILLA BEANS, split and scraped	3 each	3 each
LEMONS, cut in half	3 each	3 each
CINNAMON STICKS	3 each	3 each
WHITE CHOCOLATE ICE CREAM (page 468)	15 fl oz	450 mL
WHITE CHOCOLATE FANS (3 in/8 cm long) (page 768)	10 each	10 each

1. Using a ¼-in/6-mm melon baller, scoop balls out of the strawberries. Set the balls aside, and reserve the strawberry scraps for the soup.

2. Cut 10 lb 8 oz/4.76 kg of the rhubarb into 1-in/3-cm slices.

3. Combine the strawberry scraps, sliced rhubarb, sugar, vanilla beans (seeds and pods), lemons, and cinnamon sticks in a saucepan. Add enough water so that all but the top ¼ in/6 mm of the fruit is covered. Bring to just under a simmer. Simmer gently for 1½ to 2 hours to extract all of the flavor from the fruit.

4. Set up an ice bath using two large stainless-steel bowls. Line the top bowl with a large square of cheesecloth. Pour the fruit mixture into the bowl and gently strain it through the cheesecloth. The soup should be very clear, similar to a consommé.

5. Slice the remaining 1 lb 8 oz/680 g rhubarb on the bias into ¼-in/6-mm slices.

6. Adjust the sweetness of the soup with additional sugar if necessary, and bring 48 fl oz/ 1.44 L of the soup to a boil. Remove from the heat and add the sliced rhubarb. Let cool, checking the rhubarb periodically to see if it is tender. (Note: Rhubarb overcooks very easily and should not be left unattended for any length of time.) If the rhubarb is not tender after the soup has cooled to room temperature, heat the soup very gently and poach the rhubarb until it is just tender; do not overcook.

7. Meanwhile, set up another ice bath using two large stainless-steel bowls. Once the rhubarb is tender, pour the mixture into the top bowl and cool in the ice bath so that the rhubarb does not overcook.

8. Once it has cooled, add the mixture to the soup base.

9. Ladle 10 fl oz/300 mL of the soup into each chilled 10-in/25-cm soup bowl (there should be about 12 poached rhubarb slices in each portion of soup). Add approximately 18 strawberry balls to each bowl.

10. Place a quenelle of approximately 1½ fl oz/45 mL of white chocolate ice cream in the center of each bowl of soup. Stand a white chocolate fan in the center of the ice cream.

Margarita Chiffon Tartlet with Orange Sauce and Candied Lime Zest

Makes 10 desserts

MARGARITA CHIFFON TARTLETS (page 596)	10 each	10 each
ORANGE VANILLA BEAN SAUCE (page 451)	20 fl oz	600 mL
HEAVY CREAM, whipped to soft peaks	10 fl oz	300 mL
CANDIED LIME ZEST, minced (page 726)	½ oz	14 g
CANDIED ORANGE ZEST, minced (page 726)	½ oz	14 g
HONEY TUILES (page 353), stenciled as a cactus	10 each	10 each

1. Cut out one-quarter of each tartlet; reserve the cut-out slices.

2. Ladle 2 fl oz/60 mL orange sauce over each chilled 10-in/25-cm plate. Place a tartlet in the center of each plate, and place the slice of tartlet near the bottom of the plate, pointing toward the tartlet.

3. Using a No. 6 plain tip, pipe a ½-fl-oz/15-mL dome of whipped cream 1 in/3 cm above the center of each tartlet. Pipe an identical rosette of whipped cream in the center of each slice of tartlet.

4. Sprinkle a pinch of lime zest over the sauce on each plate. Sprinkle a pinch of orange zest over each whipped cream rosette. Lean a tuile against the cut center of each tartlet so that it adheres to the exposed filling.

Raspberry Curd Tartlet with Peach Sorbet and Lemon Verbena Sauce

Makes 10 desserts

PEACHES	3 each	3 each
BUTTER	3 oz	85 g
SUGAR	4 oz, or as needed to taste	113 g, or as needed to taste
RASPBERRY CURD TARTLETS (6 in/15 cm diameter) (page 394)	5 each	5 each
HEAVY CREAM, whipped to soft peaks	5 fl oz	150 mL
RASPBERRIES	50 each	50 each
LEMON VERBENA SAUCE (page 443)	5 fl oz	150 mL
PEACH SORBET (page 482)	13 fl oz	390 mL

1. Slice the peaches in half and remove the pits. Cut each peach half into 8 slices.

2. Melt 1 oz/28 g of the butter in a large sauté pan over medium-high heat. Add one-third of the peaches and sprinkle sugar to taste over the peaches. (Note: The amount of sugar necessary depends on the ripeness of the fruit.) Sauté the peaches until golden brown on both sides. Transfer to a hotel pan. Sauté the remaining peaches in two batches, using 1 oz/28 g butter each time. Keep the peaches warm.

3. Slice the raspberry tartlets in half. Using a pastry bag fitted with a No. 8 plain tip, pipe a mound of whipped cream near the rounded edge of each tartlet half. Place a raspberry on top of each mound of whipped cream.

4. Drizzle ½ fl oz/15 mL lemon verbena sauce over each chilled 10-in/25-cm plate. Place one half of a raspberry curd tartlet slightly above the center of each plate, with the cut sides facing toward you.

5. Place 4 sautéed peach slices just below and to the left of each tartlet. Using a No. 30 scoop, place a 1¼-fl-oz/38-mL scoop of peach sorbet just below and to the right of the tartlet.

6. Place a raspberry to the left of the sautéed peaches on each plate. Place another raspberry to the right of the peach sorbet, and place a third raspberry at the bottom of the plate, where the peaches and the peach sorbet intersect.

Warm Caramelized Apple Tart

Makes 10 desserts

GRANNY SMITH APPLES	8 each	8 each
CLEAR CARAMEL SAUCE (page 453)	20 fl oz	600 mL
APPLE GALETTES (page 388)	10 each	10 each
CONFECTIONERS' SUGAR	1 oz	28 g
VANILLA ICE CREAM (page 464)	20 fl oz	600 mL
MINT SPRIGS	10 each	10 each

1. Peel the apples. Using a ¾-in/2-cm melon baller, scoop 50 balls out of the apples, being careful to avoid the cores.

2. Bring the caramel sauce to a boil. Add the apple balls, remove from the heat, and allow the sauce to cool to room temperature.

3. If the apple balls are not tender when the sauce has cooled, gently rewarm the sauce and poach the apple balls until they are tender.

4. Gently remove the apple balls from the caramel sauce using a slotted spoon. Strain and reserve the sauce.

5. Just before serving, warm the apple galettes in a 350°F/177°C deck oven for 5 to 7 minutes. Meanwhile, lightly dust one side of each apple chip decoration with confectioners' sugar.

6. Using a plastic squeeze bottle, drizzle 1½ fl oz/45 mL caramel sauce onto each warm 10-in/25-cm plate in a spiral pattern. Place an apple galette in the center of each plate.

7. Using a No. 30 scoop, place a 2-fl-oz/60-mL scoop of ice cream in the center of each galette. Place a mint sprig in front of the confectioners' sugar–dusted side of the apple chip decoration. Place 5 poached apple balls around each galette.

Grapefruit Mousse and Sauternes Cream

Makes 10 desserts

PINK GRAPEFRUITS	4 each	4 each
ROSE PETALS, red, untreated	10 each	10 each
VANILLA SPONGE CAKE (1/4 in/6 mm thick) (page 302)	1/2 sheet	1/2 sheet
SAUTERNES SIMPLE SYRUP (page 828)	5 fl oz	150 mL
SAUTERNES CREAM (page 405)	1 lb 4 oz	567 g
GRAPEFRUIT MOUSSE (page 397)	1 lb 9 oz	709 g
SAUTERNES MIRROR GLAZE (page 427)	6 fl oz	180 mL
PASSION FRUIT SAUCE (page 439)	15 fl oz	450 mL
VANILLA SAUTERNES REDUCTION (page 457)	6 fl oz	180 mL
WHITE CHOCOLATE FANS (2 in/5 cm tall) (page 768)	10 each	10 each
CANDIED ROSE PETALS (Appendix D)	10 each	10 each
CANDIED MINT LEAVES (Appendix D)	10 each	10 each

1. Line 10 paisley molds, 3½ in/9 cm long, 2½ in/6 cm wide, and 1½ in/4 cm tall, with acetate (the width is measured at the widest point of the base of the paisley).

2. Segment the grapefruits into suprêmes (see page 517). Cut the rose petals into chiffonade.

3. Cut out 10 pieces from the sponge cake to fit into the bottom of the paisley molds.

4. Place the sponge cake cutouts in the bottom of the molds; they should fit very snugly in the molds. Brush each sponge cake with ½ fl oz/15 mL simple syrup. Pipe 2 oz/57 g Sauternes cream into each mold.

5. Refrigerate for 1 hour to allow the cream to set.

6. Pipe 2½ oz/71 g grapefruit mousse into each mold. Using a small offset spatula, level off the mousse so that it is flush with the top of the molds.

7. Freeze the molds for 2 to 3 hours to set the mousse. Cover the molds and refrigerate them overnight.

8. Blot any condensation off the mousse with a paper towel. Carefully lift the molds away from the desserts and place on a wire rack set over a parchment-lined sheet pan. Ladle ½ fl oz/15 mL mirror glaze over the top of each dessert.

9. Refrigerate for 20 minutes to allow the glaze to set.

10. Peel off the acetate from the mousse.

11. Ladle 1½ fl oz/45 mL passion fruit sauce onto each chilled 10-in/25-cm plate. (The sauce should come out to the rim of the plate.) Place a mousse in the center of each plate.

12. Using a squeeze bottle, drizzle approximately ½ fl oz/15 mL Sauternes reduction in a ring around each mousse. Sprinkle a pinch of chiffonade rose petals at the base of each mousse. Stand a white chocolate fan, a candied rose petal, and a mint leaf in the center of each mousse. Lay 3 grapefruit segments in a ring around each mousse.

Warm Red Plum and Almond Cake

Makes 10 desserts

ALMOND FLOUR	3½ oz	99 g
SUGAR	10 oz	284 g
ALL-PURPOSE FLOUR	2½ oz	71 g
EGG WHITES	4 oz	113 g
BUTTER, melted	3½ oz	99 g
RED PLUMS	13 each	13 each
APRICOT GLAZE, warmed (page 429)	5 fl oz	150 mL
ORANGE ZEST, grated	1 tsp	3 g
VANILLA BEAN, split and scraped	1 each	1 each
GROUND CINNAMON	pinch	pinch
BUTTER	1 oz	28 g
LEMON VANILLA SAUCE (page 430)	20 fl oz	600 mL
CINNAMON ICE CREAM (page 464)	20 fl oz	600 mL

1. Combine the almond flour, 7 oz/198 g of the sugar, and the all-purpose flour. Add the egg whites and melted butter and blend thoroughly. Using a pastry bag fitted with a No. 6 plain tip, pipe 4 oz/113 g of the batter into each of 10 cake rings, 4 in/10 cm in diameter and 1½ in/4 cm tall.

2. Cut 10 of the plums into 6 slices each. Lay 6 plum slices in a spiral on the center of the financier batter in each cake ring, leaving space between the plums so that the batter will rise up around them when it bakes.

3. Bake the cakes in a 385°F/196°C oven until golden brown and a tester inserted in the center of each cake comes out clean, 15 to 20 minutes. Brush the plums lightly with apricot glaze, using ½ fl oz/15 mL glaze per cake.

4. Slice the remaining 3 plums into quarters or eighths, depending on their size. The pieces should be relatively the same size. Toss the plums with the remaining 3 oz/85 g sugar, orange zest, vanilla bean seeds, and cinnamon.

5. Melt the butter in a medium sauté pan over medium-high heat. Add the plum mixture and cook until the plums release their juices and are tender, 5 to 8 minutes. Allow to cool to room temperature.

6. Ladle 2 fl oz/60 mL crème anglaise onto each warm 10-in/25-cm plate.

7. Warm the cakes slightly by placing them in a 350°F/177°C oven for about 2 minutes. Place a cake in the center of each plate.

8. Using a No. 30 scoop, place a 2-fl-oz/60-mL scoop of ice cream on the center of each cake. Place 5 sautéed plum slices around each cake in a ring.

Pineapple Tarte Tatin with Coconut Sorbet

Makes 10 desserts

PINEAPPLE TARTES TATINS, warm (page 600)	10 each	10 each
NUT TUILES (2¹/₂ in/6 cm diameter) (page 350)	10 each	10 each
COCONUT SORBET (page 486)	15 fl oz	450 mL
COCONUT SHAVINGS (2 in/5 cm long) (Appendix D)	60 each	60 each

1. Unmold each warm tarte tatin onto a warm 10-in/25-cm plate.

2. Place a tuile in the center of each tarte tatin. Using a No. 30 scoop, place a 1¹/₂-fl-oz/45-mL scoop of sorbet in the center of each tuile. Scatter 6 coconut shavings around each tarte tatin.

Chocolate Orange Tartlet with Blood Orange Sorbet and Orange Sauce

Makes 10 desserts

BITTERSWEET CHOCOLATE ORANGE TARTLETS (page 591)	10 each	10 each
1-2-3 COOKIES (1¹/₄ in/ 3 cm diameter and ¹/₈ in/ 3 mm thick, fluted) (page 249)	10 each	10 each
BLOOD ORANGE SORBET (page 479)	15 fl oz	450 mL
BLOOD ORANGE SAUCE (page 440)	20 fl oz	600 mL
CANDIED ORANGE ZEST (page 726)	1 oz	28 g
CHOCOLATE CIGARETTES	10 each	10 each

1. Place a tartlet slightly above the center of each chilled 10-in/25-cm plate. Place a cookie 3 in/8 cm to the lower right of each tartlet. Using a No. 50 scoop, place a 1¹/₂-fl-oz/45-mL scoop of sorbet on each cookie.

2. Pool 2 fl oz/60 mL blood orange sauce to the lower left of each tartlet. Sprinkle a pinch of orange zest over each tartlet and place a chocolate cigarette on each plate.

Walnut Cheesecake with Dried Cherry Sauce and Vanilla Bean Sherbet

Makes 10 desserts

WALNUT CHEESECAKE, frozen (page 323)	1 each	1 each
NOUGATINE TUILE TRIANGLES (3 in/8 cm long and 1 1/2 in/4 cm wide at the base) (page 352)	10 each	10 each
DRIED CHERRY SAUCE (page 447)	5 fl oz	150 mL
WALNUT TUILES (2 in/5 cm diameter) (page 350)	10 each	10 each
VANILLA BEAN SHERBET (page 487)	10 fl oz	300 mL
STRIPED CHOCOLATE CIGARETTES (page 766)	10 each	10 each

1. While the cheesecake is semifrozen, cut it into 12 portions. Place a nougatine tuile triangle on 10 portions.

2. Drizzle 1/2 fl oz/15 mL cherry sauce over each chilled 10-in/25-cm plate. Place a slice of cheesecake in the right section of each plate, pointing down.

3. Place a tuile 1 in/3 cm to the left of each slice of cheesecake. Using a No. 50 scoop, place a 1-fl-oz/30-mL scoop of sherbet in the center of each tuile. Place a chocolate cigarette on top of each scoop of sherbet.

Raspberry Wine Cream Slice with Chocolate Sorbet and Raspberry Sauce

Makes 10 desserts

RASPBERRY WINE CREAM CAKE (page 614)	½ sheet pan	½ sheet pan
HEAVY CREAM, whipped to soft peaks	2½ fl oz	75 mL
STRIPED CHOCOLATE CIGARETTES (page 766)	10 each	10 each
1-2-3 COOKIES (1¾ in/4 cm diameter and ⅛ in/3 mm thick, fluted) (page 249)	10 each	10 each
CHOCOLATE SORBET (page 485)	10 fl oz	300 mL
RASPBERRY SAUCE (page 439)	10 fl oz	300 mL

1. Cut the raspberry cream cake into slices 1 by 3 in/3 by 8 cm.

2. Using a pastry bag fitted with a No. 4 plain tip, pipe whipped cream over the left side of each slice, ½ in/1 cm from the edge. Lean a chocolate cigarette against the whipped cream on each slice.

3. Place a raspberry cream slice in the upper left section of each chilled 10-in/25-cm plate, with one end near the top of the plate and the other end pointing toward the left side of the plate.

4. Place a cookie 4 in/10 cm from the lower right of each raspberry cream slice. Using a No. 60 scoop, place a 1-fl-oz/30-mL scoop of sorbet on each cookie.

5. Using a plastic squeeze bottle, pipe 1 fl oz/30 mL raspberry sauce between the raspberry cream slice and the cookie on each plate. Pipe the sauce in parallel lines from left to right, gradually increasing the length of the lines to make a triangular pattern; leave space between each line so that the triangle extends from the center to the bottom of the plate.

Plated Frozen Desserts

Frozen desserts are an important component of any dessert menu. While frozen desserts are commonly used as complementary components of various plated desserts, they can also serve as the main component. They can be produced in many and varied flavors, are suitable for use with different types of containers, such as tuile cookies or molded chocolate cups, and can be molded in any variety of forms. They work well in an endless number of combinations. Of course, successful plated frozen desserts rely on conveniently located freezer space for storage and service.

Tropical Banana Split with Selection of Ice Creams and Sorbets

Makes 10 desserts

BANANAS	10 each	10 each
BRÛLÉE SUGAR BLEND (page 824)	5 oz	142 g
FLOURLESS CHOCOLATE CAKE (page 304)	½ sheet pan	½ sheet pan
MANGO SORBET (page 482)	15 fl oz	450 mL
COCONUT SORBET (page 486)	15 fl oz	450 mL
BITTERSWEET CHOCOLATE ICE CREAM (page 468)	15 fl oz	450 mL
CLASSIC CARAMEL SAUCE (page 451)	10 fl oz	300 mL
RASPBERRY SAUCE (page 439)	10 fl oz	300 mL
CHOCOLATE SAUCE (page 435)	10 fl oz	300 mL
HEAVY CREAM, whipped to soft peaks	5 fl oz	150 mL
BRANDIED CHERRIES	10 each	10 each
HONEY TUILES (page 353), monkey template (Appendix D)	10 each	10 each
HONEY TUILES (page 353), Palmtree template (Appendix D)	10 each	10 each

1. Split the bananas in half. Sprinkle ½ oz/14 g brûlée sugar over each of the banana halves. Caramelize the sugar evenly with a torch. Set aside. Using a 2-in/5-cm cutter, cut 30 disks out of the chocolate cake. Place 3 disks of cake in a row in each chilled banana split dish. Place a caramelized banana half on either side of the cake disks in each dish.

2. Using a No. 50 scoop, place a 1½-fl-oz/45-mL scoop of mango sorbet on the left disk of cake in each dish. Place a 1½-fl-oz/45-mL scoop of coconut sorbet onto the center disk. Place a 1½-fl-oz/45-mL scoop of ice cream onto the right disk of cake.

3. Drizzle 1 fl oz/30 mL caramel sauce over the mango sorbet and bananas. Drizzle 1 fl oz/30 mL raspberry sauce over the coconut sorbet and bananas. Drizzle 1 fl oz/30 mL chocolate sauce over the ice cream and the bananas.

4. Using a pastry bag fitted with a No. 6 star tip, pipe a rosette of whipped cream onto each scoop of sorbet. Top with a brandied cherry. Place a monkey tuile on the left scoop of sorbet in each dish. Place a palm tree tuile on the scoop of ice cream in each dish.

Root Beer Ice Cream Float

Makes 10 desserts

VANILLA ICE CREAM (page 464)	30 fl oz	900 mL
ROOT BEER	80 fl oz	2.40 L
TRICOLOR CHOCOLATE CIGARETTES (8 in/20 cm long) (page 766)	10 each	10 each
MACADAMIA SHORTBREAD (diamond shaped) (page 346)	20 each	20 each

1. Using a No. 60 scoop, scoop three 1-fl-oz/30-mL portions of ice cream into each chilled ice cream soda glass. Pour 8 fl oz/240 mL root beer over the ice cream, and place a chocolate cigarette in each glass.

2. Place each glass on a chilled 5-in/13-cm plate. Place 2 pieces of shortbread next to each glass.

Chocolate Hazelnut Parfait with Orange Caramel Sauce

Makes 10 desserts

CLEMENTINES	6 each	6 each
ORANGE MARINADE (page 445)	12 fl oz	360 mL
CHOCOLATE HAZELNUT PARFAITS (page 497)	10 each	10 each
BUTTER GANACHE (page 714)	1 lb 8 oz	680 g
WHITE CHOCOLATE SHAVINGS	2 oz	57 g
CLEAR ORANGE CARAMEL SAUCE (page 453)	8 fl oz	240 mL
HONEY TUILE CUPS (page 353)	10 each	10 each
DRAGÉE HAZELNUTS (page 259)	60 each	60 each

1. Segment the clementines into suprêmes (see page 517). Put in a container and pour the orange marinade over them. Allow the clementines to macerate overnight.

2. Unmold the hazelnut parfaits. Place them on a wire rack set over a parchment-lined sheet pan. Glaze each parfait with butter ganache.

3. Refrigerate the parfaits to allow the ganache to set.

4. Garnish the bottom edge of each parfait with white chocolate shavings.

5. Ladle ¾ fl oz/23 mL caramel sauce into the center of each chilled 10-in/25-cm plate. Use the back of the ladle to create a space in the center of the sauce for the parfaits, and place a parfait on each plate.

6. Place 4 clementine segments around the base of each parfait in a ring. Place a tuile cookie at the base of each parfait. Scatter 6 dragée hazelnuts around each plate.

Frozen Lemon Savarin with Limoncello-Spiked Citrus Sauce
Makes 10 desserts

NOUGATINE TUILES (2 in/5 cm diameter) (page 352)	10 each	10 each
FROZEN LEMON SAVARINS (page 499)	10 each	10 each
BUTTER GANACHE (page 714)	3 oz	85 g
RASPBERRIES	60 each	60 each
VANILLA CONFECTIONERS' SUGAR (page 827)	½ oz	14 g
ORANGE VANILLA BEAN SAUCE (page 451)	5 fl oz	150 mL
RED CURRANTS	5 oz	142 g
CANDIED ORANGE ZEST, fine julienne (page 726)	1 oz	28 g
CANDIED LEMON ZEST, fine julienne (page 726)	1 oz	28 g

1. Drape the nougatine tuiles over a dowel 2 in/5 cm in diameter immediately after they come out of the oven.

2. Unmold the frozen savarins and place them on a wire rack set over a parchment-lined sheet pan.

3. Place 1 oz/28 g of the butter ganache in a medium parchment paper cone. Pipe thin parallel lines of butter ganache on the sides of the lemon savarins, leaving a ¼-in/6-mm space between lines. Refill the parchment cone with the remaining ganache as necessary.

4. Refrigerate the savarins to allow the ganache to set.

5. Place 6 raspberries in each tuile. Dust the raspberries lightly with the vanilla sugar.

6. Ladle ½ fl oz/15 mL citrus sauce into the center of each chilled 10-in/25-cm plate. Place a savarin in the center of each plate. Place a tuile on top of each savarin.

7. Scatter ½ oz/14 g currants around the pool of sauce on each plate. Sprinkle a pinch each of the candied orange and lemon zest over the currants.

Grand Marnier Soufflé Glacé in Meringue Swans

Makes 10 desserts

NAVEL ORANGES	5 each	5 each
ORANGE MARINADE (page 445)	8 fl oz	240 mL
CORNSTARCH	½ oz	14 g
WATER	1 fl oz	30 mL
1-2-3 COOKIES (2 in/5 cm diameter) (page 249)	10 each	10 each
FROZEN ORANGE LIQUEUR SOUFFLÉ (page 493)	28 fl oz	840 mL
SPUN SUGAR BALLS (page 781)	10 each	10 each
MERINGUE SWANS (left and right half pairs) (page 627)	10 each	10 each
RASPBERRY SAUCE (page 439)	5 fl oz	150 mL
RASPBERRIES	40 each	40 each

1. Segment the oranges into suprêmes (see page 517). Put the oranges in a container and pour the orange marinade over them. Allow the orange segments to macerate overnight.

2. Drain the oranges, and reserve the marinade.

3. Bring the marinade to a boil. Make a slurry with the cornstarch and water. Whisking constantly, add some of the hot marinade to the slurry and then add the slurry to the remaining marinade in the pan. Return to a boil, stirring constantly, and cook for 2 minutes. Remove from the heat and reserve.

4. Place a cookie in the center of each chilled 10-in/25-cm plate. Using a No. 16 scoop, place a 2¾-fl-oz/83-mL scoop of soufflé glacé on top of each cookie (the parfait should extend beyond the edges of the cookies).

5. Place a spun sugar ball on the right side of each parfait. Place one left and one right meringue swan half on either side of the parfait, with the head facing away from the spun sugar ball.

6. Drizzle ½ fl oz/15 mL each of raspberry sauce and orange sauce around each swan. Scatter 4 raspberries and 4 orange segments around each swan.

Granité Dessert Sampler

Makes 10 desserts

HONEY	3 oz	85 g
FRAMBOISE	3 oz	85 g
RASPBERRIES	40 each	40 each
BANANAS	3 each	3 each
SUGAR	2 oz	57 g
NOUGATINE TUILES (2¹⁄₂ in/6 cm diameter) (page 352)	30 each	30 each
MANGO GRANITÉ (page 488)	15 fl oz	450 mL
FRESH GINGER GRANITÉ (page 490)	15 fl oz	450 mL
RASPBERRY GRANITÉ (page 489)	15 fl oz	450 mL
FRUIT SALSA (page 445)	5 oz	142 g
SPUN SUGAR BALLS (page 781)	10 each	10 each

1. Gently warm the honey and framboise together. Pour over the raspberries and allow them to macerate for 1 hour.

2. Cut the bananas into ¹⁄₄-in/6-mm slices and lay out on a sheet pan. Sprinkle a pinch of sugar on top of each banana slice. Caramelize the sugar evenly with a torch. Reserve the banana slices.

3. Place three tuiles equidistant from each other in a circular fashion on each chilled 10-in/25-cm plate, so that the ends point in to the center and out to the edge of the plate.

4. Using an oval scoop, scoop 1¹⁄₂ fl oz/45 mL mango granité into the top tuile on each plate. Scoop 1¹⁄₂ fl oz/45 mL melon granité into the right tuile. Scoop 1¹⁄₂ fl oz/45 mL raspberry granité into the left tuile.

5. Place 3 caramelized banana slices in between the tuiles in the top left section of the plate. Place ¹⁄₂ oz/14 g fruit salsa in between the tuiles in the top right section of the plate. Place 4 macerated raspberries in between the tuiles in the bottom section of the plate.

6. Place a spun sugar ball where the tuiles meet in the center of each plate.

Red Wine and Citrus Granité in Cinnamon Tortilla Shell

Makes 10 desserts

FLOUR TORTILLAS (10 in/25 cm diameter)	5 each	5 each
OIL FOR DEEP FRYING	as needed	as needed
CINNAMON SUGAR (page 826)	2 oz	57 g
FRUIT SALSA (page 446)	1 lb 14 oz	851 g
RED WINE CITRUS GRANITÉ (page 491)	25 fl oz	750 mL
CANDIED ORANGE ZEST, minced (page 726)	1 oz	28 g
CANDIED LEMON ZEST, minced (page 726)	¾ oz	21 g

1. Using a 5-in/13-cm cutter, cut 10 rounds out of the flour tortillas.

2. Deep fry the tortillas in 350°F/177°C vegetable oil between two 8-fl-oz/240-mL ladles to make tortilla shell "bowls." Allow to drain on paper towels. Toss the tortilla shells in the cinnamon sugar.

3. Place 3 oz/85 g fruit salsa in each chilled 10-in/25-cm soup bowl, leaving a space in the middle for a tortilla shell. Place a tortilla shell in the center of each portion of salsa.

4. Using a No. 12 scoop, place a 2½-fl-oz/75-mL scoop of granité in the center of each tortilla shell. Sprinkle a pinch of candied orange zest and a pinch of candied lemon zest on top of each scoop of granité.

CHAPTER 18

Chocolates and Confections

THIS CHAPTER INTRODUCES PRINCIPLES AND TECHNIQUES INVOLVED IN WORKING WITH CHOCOLATE AND SUGAR. THESE TECHNIQUES ARE USED TO MAKE GANACHES, GIANDUJA, CARAMELS, CANDIED FRUIT, FONDANT, MARZIPAN, AND GELÉES, AS WELL AS AERATED, MOLDED, AND DEPOSITED CANDIES, CHOCOLATES, AND OTHER CONFECTIONS.

Classic Truffles

Makes 50 truffles

HEAVY CREAM	8 fl oz	240 mL
CORN SYRUP	1 oz	28 g
DARK CHOCOLATE, finely chopped	1 lb	454 g
BUTTER, soft	1 oz	28 g
DARK CHOCOLATE, melted, tempered, for coating	as needed	as needed

1. Bring the cream and corn syrup to a boil.

2. Pour the hot cream mixture over the chocolate and allow to sit, without stirring, for 2 minutes. Gently stir the mixture using a wooden spoon or rubber spatula until fully blended and smooth. If necessary, heat the ganache over a hot water bath to melt all of the chocolate. Add the butter and stir until melted and smooth. Allow to set until the ganache has reached room temperature.

3. To table the ganache, work it with a metal spatula on a clean marble work surface until it is piping consistency.

4. Once the ganache has been tabled, fill a pastry bag fitted with a No. 4 plain tip and pipe out truffles onto parchment-lined sheet pans. Allow the truffles to set until firm.

5. Roll the truffles in the palms of your hands to make them perfectly round and place on a clean parchment-lined sheet pan. Cover and allow to set until firm. Depending on the ambient temperature and the consistency of the ganache, it may be necessary to refrigerate the truffles at this point just until they are firm enough to coat.

6. To finish the truffles, spread a small amount of tempered chocolate at a time in the palm of your hand and gently roll each chilled truffle in the chocolate to coat. Place the coated truffles on a clean parchment-lined sheet pan. Allow the chocolate to set completely, then repeat the process. (For other finishing techniques for truffles, see page 706.)

Cream Ganache

Cream ganache has a wide range of uses, including centers for confections and glazing and filling cakes and pastries. Its consistency can be soft or hard or any variation in between (depending on the ratio of chocolate to cream). Soft ganache and medium ganache are not firm enough nor do they have an adequate enough shelf life to be used in confectionery work (see page 429 for more information on soft and medium ganache). In confectionery work, cream ganache is most commonly used as the center for truffles, but other confections are made with ganache as well. As a rule, hard ganache is required for piped and rolled truffle centers. A 2:1 ratio of dark chocolate to heavy cream is typically used to produce hard ganache. To achieve a similar consistency with milk chocolate or white chocolate, use a ratio of $2\frac{1}{2}$ parts chocolate to 1 part

heavy cream. Milk chocolate and white chocolate contain fewer cocoa solids and less cocoa butter than dark chocolate, making the additional chocolate necessary to produce a hard ganache. In addition, percentages of cocoa butter and cocoa solids may vary in chocolates from different manufacturers, making it necessary to adjust the ratios to achieve the desired results.

To make ganache, chop the chocolate into small pieces of uniform size so the pieces will melt quickly and at the same rate. When combining the chocolate and cream, some pastry chefs add the chocolate directly to the pan of hot cream. However, this practice risks scorching the chocolate on the bottom of the hot pan. It is best, instead, to pour the hot cream over the chocolate. Let the mixture stand undisturbed for a few minutes to allow the hot cream to begin melting the chocolate. Then stir the mixture gently to blend and melt the chocolate completely without incorporating air. If the chocolate is not fully melted at this point, warm the ganache over simmering water, stirring gently. When making ganache to be slabbed, it is advisable to allow the boiled cream to cool to 170°F/77°C in order not to melt all the stable cocoa butter crystals.

Chocolate and cream are the basic ingredients for making ganache, but other ingredients may be added for flavoring and to provide a smoother texture. The addition of butter and/or corn syrup or glucose syrup can yield a superior finished product in both flavor and texture. Butter is added to the ganache to increase fat content when some of the cream in the formula is replaced with liqueur. Typically, the amount of butter to be added is half the weight of the liqueur. The butter is usually added to the ganache after the chocolate is fully melted.

Corn syrup or glucose syrup may be added to ganache to help prevent recrystallization of the sugar and maintain a smooth texture. The weight of the added corn syrup generally should not exceed 10 percent of the total weight of the ganache. Corn syrup is typically added to the cream before it is boiled.

Flavoring Ganache for Truffles

Infusion is an effective method of flavoring ganache. Bring the cream to a boil, add the flavoring, and remove the pan from the heat. Cover and allow to stand until the flavor has been infused into the cream (5 to 10 minutes). After steeping, aromatics, such as teas, and/or herbs and spices may be strained out of the cream. After straining, water or milk should be added as necessary to bring the liquid to its original weight so the finished ganache will be the proper consistency. Before the infused cream is added to the chocolate, it should be rewarmed so it is hot enough to melt the chocolate. A liqueur or other spirit may be added for flavoring. Pastes and compounds may also be used to flavor ganache. Because these are strongly flavored, they are usually added to taste to the finished ganache.

Forming Truffles and Other Ganache Confections

Ganache that is to be used as a center for a confection must be agitated (through stirring or tabling) so that it is firm enough to be piped or shaped. When the ganache has the proper consistency, it is piped, then rolled into perfect spheres, which will be coated with tempered chocolate or otherwise finished.

To scoop truffles, the ganache must be chilled until it has firmly set. A very small ice cream scoop or a Parisian scoop may be used. Dip the scoop in hot water, scoop the ganache, and then release the truffle onto a parchment-lined sheet pan. Scooping may be the easiest method for portioning ganache for truffles, but it has certain disadvantages. The moisture added to the ganache by dipping the scoop in hot water changes the texture and flavor. In addition, although scooping requires less skill, it is much more time-consuming than piping.

Ganache that will be portioned by piping should not be refrigerated because it will become too firm. Instead, the ganache should be agitated by stirring it in a bowl or working it on a marble surface (tabling) to bring it to piping consistency. Care must be taken not to overwork the ganache, or it will separate, resulting in a grainy texture.

For piping truffles, a No. 3 or 4 plain tip is most commonly used. Sometimes the ganache is piped onto tempered chocolate disks to form a teardrop or peak shape; in this case the confection is allowed to set until firm and then dipped. For truffles, pipe the ganache into even rows of small round domes onto parchment-lined sheet pans.

After it has been portioned, the ganache must be allowed to set at room temperature until firm. Centers should never be dipped when cold, as the chocolate coating will be thick and will not have the desired shine.

An alternative method for portioning ganache is to pour it into a frame made by metal caramel rulers, spread it evenly if necessary, and allow it to set until firm. After the ganache has set, the bars are removed and the ganache is spread with a thin coat of tempered chocolate. Once the chocolate has set, the slab of ganache is then inverted onto a guitar (see page 749). The slab is cut using the guitar cutter, dipped in tempered chocolate, and finished. Ganache that is slabbed may also be cut by hand using a sharp knife or small cutters.

1 Piping truffles
2 Rolling truffles
3 Precoating truffles

Melting Chocolate

Chocolate that is to be melted should be finely chopped. The smaller the pieces, the more surface area is exposed, and the quicker the chocolate melts, helping to prevent overheating. This is an important consideration, as overheating chocolate will render it unusable. A heavy chef's knife is generally best for chopping chocolate, but some pastry chefs prefer to use a long serrated knife because the serrated blade breaks the chocolate into fine shards ideal for melting.

A hot water bath is usually used for melting chocolate, but it is important that moisture (steam, water, or condensation) never comes in contact with the chocolate. Moisture causes chocolate to "seize," or to become thick and grainy, rendering it unfit for tempering and most other uses. For this reason, it is important that the bowl (or the top of a double boiler) is completely dry and that the bowl (or top) fits snugly over the pan of water, forming a tight seal. The water should be steaming hot but not simmering. Gently stir the chocolate occasionally as it melts, and remove it from the heat promptly after it is fully melted.

A microwave may also be used to melt chocolate. Some pastry chefs consider it the best choice because the chocolate does not come in close proximity to water. The chocolate must be chopped or broken into small pieces about the same size. Use medium power rather than high and heat the chocolate for 30-second intervals, removing and stirring it after each one to ensure even heating and melting.

Working with Couverture

Couverture is chocolate that contains a minimum of 32 percent cocoa butter. This means it is thinner when melted than other chocolates and can easily form a thin coating, making it ideal for dipping and enrobing confections.

The temperature of the work space and the temperature of the items to be coated are important factors in ensuring that tempered chocolate retains its smooth, glossy appearance when set. When coating or dipping items in couverture, recrystallization must take place within a specific period of time. The ambient temperature should be between 65° and 70°F/18° and 21°C. (To find out more about tempering chocolate, see the following section.) The item to be dipped or enrobed should also be at room temperature. Confections that are too warm could cause the chocolate to bloom or to have a matte finish, while items that are too cold could "shock" the couverture, resulting in a dull finish.

Tempering Chocolate

Chocolate is purchased in temper, but in order to work with it, it must be melted and then tempered again, so that as it cools and sets it will return to the same state as when purchased. Tempered chocolate has the snap and gloss associated with good chocolate and will store better and for a longer period of time. Tempering is accomplished through a specific process of cooling and agitation. When tempering chocolate, it is best to melt more than you will need, as it is easier to keep larger amounts of chocolate in temper.

1 Melting
chocolate over a
water bath

2 Tabling
chocolate on
marble

3 Testing
chocolate for
temper

4 Flashing
chocolate over a
flame

Dipping or coating confections in tempered chocolate adds flavor, improves appearance, and helps to preserve them, as the tempered chocolate prevents moisture migration and keeps the filling from coming in contact with the air, which can cause spoilage.

There are several different methods of tempering chocolate, but all are based on the same general principles. Chocolate contains different types of fat crystals. When tempering chocolate, the object is to get the right type of crystals to form. Otherwise, when the chocolate sets, it will lack hardness, snap, and shine and will bloom when set. First, the chocolate must be heated to the following temperatures to ensure that all the different types of fat crystals melt: 110° to 120°F/43° to 49°C for dark chocolate, 105° to 110°F/41° to 43°C for milk chocolate and white chocolate. A portion of chocolate that is already in temper is then added to "seed" the untempered chocolate and begin the formation of the beta crystals (the desirable stable fat crystals). Then the chocolate must be cooled to about 80°F/27°C while being constantly agitated; it is gradually brought back up to the appropriate working temperature.

WORKING TEMPERATURES FOR TEMPERED CHOCOLATE

Dark Chocolate: 86° to 90°F/30° to 32°C

Milk Chocolate: 84° to 87°F/29° to 31°C

White Chocolate: 84° to 87°F/29° to 31°C

The temperatures given above are ranges because different brands of chocolate vary in terms of tempering. Each chocolate manufacturer, in fact, has specific recommended working temperatures for the couvertures it produces.

With the seed method of tempering chocolate, chopped tempered chocolate—approximately 25 percent of the weight of the melted chocolate to be tempered—is added to the warm (110°F/43°C) melted chocolate and gently stirred to melt and incorporate it. The stable crystals in the chopped chocolate help stimulate the formation of stable beta crystals in the untempered chocolate. The whole mass is then brought to the appropriate working temperature.

With the block method of chocolate tempering, a single block of tempered chocolate is added to warm, melted chocolate and gently stirred until the desired temperature is reached. The block of chocolate not only reduces the temperature of the melted chocolate but also provides the seed crystals necessary for tempering. After the chocolate is brought into temper, the seed, or block of chocolate, is removed and can be used again. This method is simple and effective but slightly more time-consuming than other methods of tempering.

With the tabling method of tempering chocolate, approximately one-third of the melted chocolate (at 110°F/43°C) is poured onto a marble surface and spread back and forth with a spatula and scraper until it begins to thicken. As it begins to set, the beta crystals form and the tabled chocolate becomes dull and takes on a pastelike consistency. This resulting mass is then added to the remaining melted chocolate and gently stirred so as to seed the couverture with the stable beta crystals. The entire mass is then gradually brought back up to the appropriate working temperature.

When the chocolate has reached the proper temperature, test it to be sure it is in full temper. Dip a tool, such as a small metal spatula, into the chocolate, then set it aside to allow the chocolate to set while you continue to gently stir the tempered chocolate. If the chocolate is in temper, the chocolate on the spatula will set within 3 to 5 minutes at normal room temperature and show a satiny shine with no streaks. If the chocolate is not in full temper, it will set more slowly, look speckled, slightly dull or streaky, and have a weak or crumbly structure. If this is the case, the chocolate must be seeded further until it sets properly.

Tempered chocolate sets quickly. Working with relatively large amounts helps to keep it from cooling and setting too rapidly. If tempered chocolate begins to set and thicken as you work, act quickly so the chocolate will not have to be melted and retempered: While stirring constantly, hold the bowl of chocolate directly over the burner of a stove for 2 or 3 seconds, then remove the chocolate from the heat while continuing to stir. Repeat the process, checking the temperature of the chocolate each time after removing the bowl from the heat so the chocolate does not overheat and come out of temper, until the chocolate is again at the optimal working temperature and consistency. Be careful not to return the bowl to the heat until the bottom of the bowl feels cooler than body temperature.

COATING TRUFFLES IN TEMPERED CHOCOLATE

One of the distinguishing characteristics of a high-quality truffle is a thin outer coating of tempered couverture. Two coats of chocolate should always be applied, a precoat and a final coat. As the outer shell of tempered chocolate coating hardens, it contracts and tightens around the ganache center, sometimes developing small cracks that allow the ganache or sugar within to seep out of the shell. Precoating truffles can prevent this from happening; it also makes the centers easier to handle and prolongs the shelf life of the final product.

To precoat a truffle, smear a small amount of tempered chocolate over the palm of your hand and gently roll the ganache center in the chocolate. It is important, with each coat, to use only enough chocolate for a thin coating; this reduces the chance of the truffles developing feet (chocolate that pools around the base). Set the coated truffle on a parchment-lined sheet pan and repeat the process with the remaining truffles. Allow the precoat to set completely before applying the second, final coating. Apply the final coat of chocolate in the same manner as the precoat, but make a thicker coat by using more chocolate.

LEFT TO RIGHT:
Dipping mint fondants—note the chocolate dipping station setup

Spiking chocolate truffles

Dipping Confections

To dip confections in tempered chocolate, you must have a bowl of chocolate large enough to immerse them easily. Have the confections to be dipped on a parchment-lined sheet pan next to the bowl, and have a clean parchment-lined sheet pan on the other side of the bowl for receiving the confections after dipping.

To dip a center, place it in the tempered chocolate, slip the dipping fork under the confection in the chocolate, and, with a scooping motion, pick it up so that it is sitting right side up on the fork. Gently raise and lower the confection on the fork a few times, allowing the base to just touch the surface of the melted chocolate (this removes excess chocolate from the dipped confection, so a foot does not form); then remove the confection from the bowl, gently scraping it on the edge of the bowl to remove any remaining excess chocolate from the base and to slide the confection so that one edge is hanging over the end of the fork. Carefully lower that edge of the confection onto the clean parchment-lined sheet pan and gently pull the fork out from under the confection.

FINISHING TRUFFLES AND CONFECTIONS

Décor is important in confectionery not only for eye and taste appeal, but also as a means of differentiating one filling from another. A dusting of cocoa powder is the classic finishing technique for truffles, but they can also be dusted with confectioners' sugar. Truffles and other round confections can also be rolled in a garnish, such as chocolate shavings or curls, chopped nuts, or toasted flaked coconut. Rolling a just-dipped truffle on a wire screen is another option, which creates an erratic but aesthetically pleasing spiked surface. When spiking truffles be sure to remove them from the screen before the chocolate sets completely.

Decorated transfer sheets can be applied to the top of any smooth flat confection. After the confection has been dipped, immediately lay the transfer sheet on its surface

Marking the top of a dipped fondant with a dipping fork

(see page 65 for more information on transfer sheets). After the coating is completely set, remove the sheet. Another common décor for flat confections is made with a dipping fork. After the confection has been dipped, allow it to set for a moment, then touch the fork to its surface, lifting the chocolate up to create small waves.

Tea Truffles

Makes 52 pieces

HEAVY CREAM	4 fl oz	120 mL
MILK	4 fl oz	120 mL
EARL GREY TEA	½ oz	14 g
DARK CHOCOLATE, finely chopped	8 oz	227 g
MILK CHOCOLATE, finely chopped	8 oz	227 g
BUTTER, soft	2 oz	57 g
DARK CHOCOLATE, melted, tempered, for coating	as needed	as needed

1. Bring the cream and milk to a boil. Remove the pan from the heat, add the tea, and allow to steep for 10 minutes.

2. Strain the milk mixture through a dampened cheesecloth and wring out thoroughly. Add water if necessary to return the liquid to 8 fl oz/240 mL.

3. Bring the liquid back to a boil and pour it over the chopped chocolate. Allow to sit for 3 minutes, then stir until well blended and smooth. If necessary, heat the ganache over a hot water bath to melt all of the chocolate. Gently stir the butter into the ganache until melted and smooth. Allow to set until the ganache has reached room temperature.

4. To table the ganache, work it with a metal spatula on a clean marble work surface until it is piping consistency.

5. Once the ganache has been tabled, fill a pastry bag fitted with a No. 3 or 4 plain tip and pipe out truffles onto parchment-lined sheet pans. Allow the truffles to set until firm.

6. Roll the truffles in the palms of your hands to make them perfectly round and place on a clean parchment-lined sheet pan. Allow to set until firm. Depending on the ambient temperature and the consistency of the ganache, it may be necessary to refrigerate the truffles at this point just until they are firm enough to coat.

7. To finish the truffles, spread a small amount of tempered chocolate at a time in the palm of your hand and gently roll each chilled truffle in the chocolate to coat. Place the coated truffles on a clean parchment-lined sheet pan. Allow the chocolate to set completely, then repeat the process. (For other finishing techniques for truffles, see page 706.)

Pear Ganache Confections

Makes 195 pieces

PEAR PURÉE	6 fl oz	180 mL
HEAVY CREAM	4 fl oz	120 mL
MILK CHOCOLATE, finely chopped	1 lb 9 oz	709 g
BUTTER, soft	2 oz	57 g
PEAR LIQUEUR	2 fl oz	60 mL
MILK CHOCOLATE, melted, tempered, for coating	as needed	as needed

1. Boil the pear purée until reduced by one-half its volume.

2. Bring the cream to a boil. Remove from the heat and let sit, covered, for 5 minutes.

3. Pour the cream over the chopped chocolate. Add the hot pear purée. Allow to sit until cooled to 170°F/77°C, then stir gently with a wooden spoon or rubber spatula until well blended and smooth. If necessary, heat the ganache over a hot water bath to melt all of the chocolate. Gently stir the butter and liqueur into the ganache until melted and smooth.

4. Emulsify the ganache using an immersion blender until completely smooth. Check to ensure the temperature of the finished ganache is 82°F/28°C.

5. Pour the ganache into a ½-in/1-cm frame (9 by 12 in/23 by 30 cm), cover, and allow to set overnight.

6. Brush a thin coating of the tempered milk chocolate on one side of the slab.

7. Cut the slab into rectangles ½ by 1¼ in/1 by 3 cm.

8. Dip the confections in tempered milk chocolate and apply a single diagonal line to the top surface of each confection using the tine of the dipping fork.

Anise Sticks

Makes 150 truffles

HEAVY CREAM	8 fl oz	240 mL
MILK CHOCOLATE, finely chopped	1 lb	454 g
BUTTER, soft	1 oz	28 g
PERNOD	2 oz	57 g
MILK CHOCOLATE, melted, tempered, for dipping	as needed	as needed

1. Bring the cream to a boil.

2. Pour over the chopped chocolate. Allow to sit for 3 minutes, then gently stir using a wooden spoon or rubber spatula until well blended and smooth. If necessary, heat the ganache over a hot water bath to melt all of the chocolate. Gently stir the butter and Pernod into the ganache until melted and smooth. Pour into a half hotel pan and allow to cool to room temperature.

3. To table the ganache, work it with a metal spatula on a clean marble work surface until it is piping consistency.

4. Fill a pastry bag fitted with a No. 3 or 4 plain tip and pipe out the ganache into logs onto parchment-lined sheet pans. Allow to set until firm. Precoat the logs with tempered milk chocolate and cut into 2-in/5-cm sections.

5. Dip in tempered milk chocolate. After dipping, place the confections on a wire screen and roll them to create a spiked finish. Place on a parchment-lined sheet pan.

Dark and Stormy Ganache Confections

Makes 184 pieces

HEAVY CREAM	4 fl oz	120 mL
GINGER ROOT, sliced	2 oz	57 g
VANILLA BEAN, split and scraped	½ each	½ each
WHITE CHOCOLATE, finely chopped	1 lb 8 oz	680 g
BUTTER, soft	1 oz	28 g
DARK RUM	2 fl oz	60 mL
DARK CHOCOLATE, melted, tempered, for coating	as needed	as needed

1. Bring the cream to a boil with the ginger root and the seeds and pod from the vanilla bean. Remove the pan from the heat, cover, and allow to steep for 10 minutes.

2. Strain the cream mixture through dampened cheesecloth and wring out thoroughly. Add water if necessary to return the liquid to 4 fl oz/120 mL.

3. Bring the liquid back to a boil and pour over the chopped chocolate. Allow to sit for 3 minutes, then stir gently with a wooden spoon or rubber spatula until well blended and smooth. If necessary, heat the ganache over a hot water bath to melt all of the chocolate. Gently stir the butter and rum into the ganache until melted and smooth. Emulsify the ganache using an immersion blender until completely smooth.

4. Pour the ganache into a ½-in/1-cm frame (10½ by 12 in/27 by 30 cm), cover, and allow to set overnight. Brush a thin coating of the tempered chocolate on one side of the slab.

5. Cut the slab into rectangles using the ½- and 1½-in/1- and 4-cm guitar attachments.

6. Dip the confections in tempered dark chocolate and mark the top of each confection with a three-pronged dipping fork.

Milk Chocolate Truffles

Makes 120 truffles

VANILLA BEAN	1 each	1 each
HEAVY CREAM	8 fl oz	240 mL
MILK CHOCOLATE, finely chopped	1 lb 5 oz	595 g
BUTTER, soft	2½ oz	71 g
MILK CHOCOLATE, melted, tempered, for coating	as needed	as needed

1. Split the vanilla beans and scrape the seeds into the cream. Add the pods to the cream and bring to a boil. Allow to steep for 10 minutes.

2. Strain the cream mixture through a dampened cheesecloth and wring out thoroughly. Add water if necessary to return the liquid to 8 fl oz/240 mL.

3. Bring the liquid back to a boil and pour over the chopped chocolate. Allow to sit for 3 minutes, then stir gently with a wooden spoon or rubber spatula until well blended and smooth. If necessary, heat the ganache over a hot water bath to melt all of the chocolate. Gently stir the butter into the ganache until melted and smooth. Pour into a half hotel pan and cover. Allow the ganache to set until it has reached room temperature.

4. To table the ganache, work it with a metal spatula on a clean marble work surface until it is piping consistency.

5. If the ganache has been tabled, fill a pastry bag fitted with a No. 3 or 4 plain tip and pipe out truffles onto parchment-lined sheet pans. Allow the truffles to set until firm.

6. Roll the truffles and place on a clean parchment-lined sheet pan. Allow the truffles to set until firm. Depending on the ambient temperature and the consistency of the ganache, it may be necessary to refrigerate the truffles at this point just until they are firm enough to coat.

7. To finish the truffles, spread a small amount of tempered milk chocolate at a time in the palm of your hand and gently roll each chilled truffle in the chocolate to coat. Place the coated truffles on a clean parchment-lined sheet pan. Allow the chocolate to set completely, then repeat the process. (For other finishing techniques for truffles, see page 706.)

Premade Chocolate Truffle Shells

Purchased premade chocolate shells can be used to make truffles. Typically they are used for fillings that are too soft to be formed by piping or rolling. The shells must be filled carefully and completely because any small air pockets will allow mold to grow. Additionally, although hollow shells permit the use of soft fillings, you must be mindful of the water content of fillings and their potential for spoilage.

After the shells are filled, they are capped with chocolate. The cap should extend over the edges of the hole in the shell so that as it hardens and contracts it will remain attached to the shell.

Premade shells guarantee consistent shape and size, are time-efficient, and make packaging easier due to their uniformity. Of course, the cost and quality of the shells must be taken into consideration.

Rum Truffles
Makes 85 truffles

HEAVY CREAM	5 fl oz	150 mL
MILK CHOCOLATE, finely chopped	11 oz	312 g
BUTTER, soft	½ oz	14 g
RUM	1¼ fl oz	38 mL
MILK CHOCOLATE TRUFFLE SHELLS	85 each	85 each
MILK CHOCOLATE, melted, tempered, for coating	as needed	as needed

1. Bring the heavy cream to a boil.
2. Pour the cream over the chopped chocolate. Allow to sit for 3 minutes, then stir with a wooden spoon or rubber spatula until well blended and smooth. If necessary, heat the ganache over a hot water bath to melt all of the chocolate. Gently stir in the butter until melted and smooth, then stir in the rum. Pour the ganache into a half hotel pan, cover, placing plastic wrap directly on the surface, and allow to cool to 85°F/29°C.
3. Pipe into premade milk chocolate truffle shells (see page 711). Seal and dip in tempered milk chocolate. After dipping, place the confections on a wire screen and roll them to create a spiked finish. Place on a parchment-lined sheet pan.

Orange Truffles

Makes 120 truffles

HEAVY CREAM	8 fl oz	240 mL
CORN SYRUP	1 oz	28 g
WHITE CHOCOLATE, finely chopped	1 lb 12 oz	794 g
BUTTER, soft	1 oz	28 g
COINTREAU	2 oz	57 g
CANDIED ORANGE PEEL, finely minced (page 726)	4 oz	113 g
MILK CHOCOLATE, melted, tempered, for coating	as needed	as needed

1. Bring the heavy cream to a boil. Add the corn syrup and stir until incorporated.

2. Pour the hot cream mixture over the chopped chocolate. Allow to sit for 3 minutes, then stir gently with a wooden spoon or rubber spatula until fully blended and smooth. If necessary, heat the ganache over a hot water bath to melt all of the chocolate. Stir in the butter and liqueur until smooth and completely melted. Add the candied orange peel and blend thoroughly.

3. Pour the ganache into a half hotel pan and cover, placing plastic wrap directly on the surface. Allow the ganache to cool.

4. Table the ganache by working it with a metal spatula on a clean marble work surface until it is piping consistency.

5. Fill a pastry bag fitted with a No. 3 or 4 plain tip and pipe out truffles onto parchment-lined sheet pans.

6. Roll the truffles and place on a clean parchment-lined sheet pan. Allow the truffles to set until firm. Depending on the ambient temperature and the consistency of the ganache, it may be necessary to refrigerate the truffles at this point just until they are firm enough to coat.

7. To finish the truffles, spread a small amount of tempered milk chocolate at a time in the palm of your hand and gently roll each chilled truffle in the chocolate to coat. Allow the chocolate to set completely, then repeat the process. (For other finishing techniques for truffles, see page 706.)

Pistachio Ganache Confections

Makes 120 pieces

MARZIPAN, for base	as needed	as needed
DARK CHOCOLATE, tempered, for coating	as needed	as needed
HEAVY CREAM	8 fl oz	240 mL
DARK CHOCOLATE, finely chopped	1 lb	454 g
PISTACHIO PASTE	2½ oz	71 g
DARK RUM	1 fl oz	30 mL
PISTACHIOS, peeled, finely chopped	as needed	as needed

1. Roll out the marzipan to 4 by 6 in/10 by 15 cm and ⅛ in/3 mm thick. Brush the marzipan with a thin layer of tempered dark chocolate and allow the chocolate to set completely.

2. Cut the marzipan lengthwise into strips ⅜ in/9.5 mm wide.

3. Bring the cream to a boil.

4. Pour the hot cream over the chopped chocolate. Allow to sit for 3 minutes, then stir gently with a wooden spoon or rubber spatula until fully blended and smooth. If necessary, heat the ganache over a hot water bath to melt all of the chocolate. Stir in the pistachio paste and dark rum until fully blended. Cool to room temperature.

5. To table the ganache, work it with a metal spatula on a clean marble work surface until it is piping consistency.

6. Fill a pastry bag fitted with a No. 2 plain tip with the ganache and pipe in a spiral onto the marzipan strips. Allow the ganache to set completely.

7. Cut the marzipan strips into 1-in/3-cm lengths. Dip in tempered dark chocolate.

8. Sprinkle with finely chopped pistachios before the chocolate sets.

Butter Ganache Confections

Makes 100 pieces

DARK CHOCOLATE, tempered	as needed	as needed
BUTTER, soft	4½ oz	128 g
GLUCOSE SYRUP	1¼ oz	35 g
WHITE CHOCOLATE, melted, tempered	8 oz, plus as needed for coating	227 g, plus as needed for coating
COCOA BUTTER, melted and cooled to 86°F/30°C	½ oz	14 g
DARK RUM	2¾ fl oz	83 mL
COARSE SUGAR	as needed	as needed

1. Spread a thin layer of tempered dark chocolate on a sheet of parchment paper and allow to set until firm but still malleable. Using a ¾-in/2-cm round cutter, cut out 100 disks, leaving them attached to the parchment paper. Allow the chocolate to set completely.

2. Cream together the butter and glucose syrup on medium speed, scraping down the bowl periodically, until smooth, fluffy, and lighter in color, about 5 minutes. Using a handheld whip, vigorously blend in the tempered white chocolate and cocoa butter until fully combined and creamy. Blend in the liqueur.

3. Allow the mixture to cool until it is firm enough to hold its shape when piped, about 3 minutes.

4. Fill a pastry bag fitted with a No. 6 plain tip with the ganache and pipe a teardrop shape onto each chocolate disk. Allow the ganache to set completely.

5. Dip each confection in tempered white chocolate and place on a parchment-lined sheet pan.

6. Decorate the tip of each chocolate with a sprinkling of coarse sugar.

Butter Ganache

Butter ganache for confection centers is made by mixing a sweetener with softened butter and adding tempered chocolate and flavoring. Butter ganache may be either piped or spread into a slab and cut to form confections. The butter is treated differently depending on which of the two techniques is used. If the ganache is to be piped, the butter is creamed with the sweetener until light and aerated. If the ganache is to be spread out into a slab to harden and be cut, the butter is blended with the sweetener, incorporating as little air as possible. (If too much air is incorporated into the butter, the ganache is likely to crack when cut.)

Tempered chocolate must be used for making butter ganache. The chocolate must be in temper when it is added to the butter or the butter ganache will not set properly. The basic ratios for butter ganache are 2:1 and 2½:1 chocolate to butter.

The sweetener used for butter ganache must be smooth—that is, its texture must not be discernible on the palate because the mixture does not contain enough moisture to melt the sweetener. Examples of sweeteners well suited for making butter ganache are jam, corn syrup, glucose syrup, and fondant. The amount of sweetener used may equal as much as half the weight of the butter. Spirits and liqueurs added for flavoring should be added last. When adding spirits be careful to maintain the 2:1 or 2½:1 ratio. The spirit is calculated as part of the butter. To maintain the ratio you can reduce the amount of butter or recalculate the quantity of chocolate based on the new value of butter plus spirit.

Butter ganache must be worked with quickly and in small batches. Once it has set, it is very difficult to bring butter ganache back to a working consistency, as softening would require heat, and that would ruin the structure by melting the butter.

If butter ganache is piped, it requires a base because it will not be rolled; instead, small, thin chocolate stencils or cutouts are used. The ganache is piped and allowed to set completely, then it is dipped in tempered chocolate.

Making Stencils

The stencil (also known as a cutout or base) is a component of many different types of confections. A stencil provides a base for piped fillings.

To form stencils, spread a thin, even layer of tempered chocolate onto a sheet of parchment paper laid out on a wooden work surface or countertop (a marble, metal, or other cold surface would cause the chocolate to set too quickly). Allow the chocolate to set until it begins to firm, then cut disks, typically with a ¾-in/2-cm round cutter. Allow the chocolate to set completely on the parchment paper.

Honey–Passion Fruit Butter Ganache Pralines

Makes 120 pieces

PASSION FRUIT CONCENTRATE	6 oz	170 g
BUTTER, soft	5 oz	142 g
HONEY	4 oz	113 g
MILK CHOCOLATE, melted, tempered	1 lb 6 oz, plus as needed for dipping	624 g, plus as needed for dipping

1. Boil the passion fruit concentrate until reduced by half its volume.
2. Mix together the butter and honey.
3. Blend in the chocolate and then the passion fruit concentrate.
4. Pour the ganache into a ½-in/1-cm frame (6 by 12 in/15 by 30 cm), cover, and allow to set overnight.
5. Brush a thin coating of tempered milk chocolate on one side of the slab.
6. Cut the slab into rectangles ½ by 1¼ in/1 by 3 cm and dip in tempered milk chocolate.

Fujiyamas

Makes 100 pieces

DARK CHOCOLATE, melted, tempered	as needed	as needed
BUTTER, soft	4½ oz	128 g
CORN SYRUP	½ oz	14 g
COCOA BUTTER, melted	1 oz	28 g
WHITE CHOCOLATE, melted	9 oz	255 g
CRÈME DE CASSIS	3½ oz	99 g
DARK CHOCOLATE, Melted, tempered, for dipping	as needed	as needed
WHITE CHOCOLATE, tempered, for garnish	as needed	as needed

1. Spread a thin layer of tempered dark chocolate onto a sheet of parchment paper and allow to set until firm but still malleable. Using a ¾-in/2-cm round cutter, cut out 100 disks, leaving them attached to the parchment paper. Allow the chocolate to set completely.

2. Cream together the butter and corn syrup on medium speed, scraping down the bowl periodically, until smooth, fluffy, and lighter in color, about 5 minutes.

3. Blend together the cocoa butter and white chocolate and temper. Using a handheld whip, vigorously blend the white chocolate and cocoa butter into the butter mixture until fully combined and creamy. Blend in the liqueur.

4. Allow the mixture to cool until it is firm enough to hold its shape when piped, about 3 minutes.

5. Fill a pastry bag fitted with a No. 5 plain tip with the ganache and pipe a peak shape onto each chocolate disk. Allow to set until firm.

6. Dip in tempered dark chocolate and allow the chocolate to set completely.

7. Decorate each chocolate with a "snowcap" of white chocolate by piping tempered white chocolate on the tip.

Piping butter ganache onto circle stencils of chocolate

Apricot Pralines

Makes 100 pieces

DARK CHOCOLATE, melted, tempered	as needed	as needed
BUTTER, soft	4½ oz	128 g
APRICOT JAM	3 oz, plus as needed for filling	85 g, plus as needed for filling
GLUCOSE SYRUP	1¼ oz	35 g
MILK CHOCOLATE, melted, tempered	8 oz, plus as needed for dipping	227 g, plus as needed for dipping
COCOA BUTTER, melted and cooled to 86°F/30°C	½ oz	14 g
APRICOT BRANDY	2¾ fl oz	83 mL
COARSE SUGAR, for garnish	as needed	as needed

1. Spread a thin layer of tempered dark chocolate onto a sheet of parchment paper and allow to set until firm but still malleable. Using a ¾-in/2-cm round cutter, cut out 100 disks, leaving them attached to the parchment paper. Allow the chocolate to set completely.

2. Cream together the butter, 3 oz/85 g of the apricot jam, and the glucose syrup on medium speed, scraping down the bowl periodically, until smooth, fluffy, and lighter in color, about 5 minutes. Vigorously blend in the tempered milk chocolate and cocoa butter until fully combined and creamy. Blend in the apricot brandy.

3. Allow the ganache to cool until it is firm enough to hold its shape when piped, about 3 minutes.

4. Fill a small parchment piping bag with apricot jam and pipe a small dot onto the center of each chocolate disk.

5. Fill a pastry bag fitted with a No. 2 plain tip with the ganache and pipe a teardrop shape over each jam dot. Allow the ganache to set completely.

6. Dip each disk in tempered milk chocolate, allow the chocolate to set until tacky, and sprinkle with coarse sugar.

Egg Ganache

Makes 144 pieces

HEAVY CREAM	2²/₃ fl oz	80 mL
BUTTER, soft	4¹/₂ oz	128 g
VANILLA BEAN	¹/₂ each	¹/₂ each
EGG YOLKS	2³/₄ oz	78 g
SUGAR	1 oz	28 g
FRUIT PURÉE	2³/₄ oz	78 g
ORANGE LIQUEUR	1¹/₄ fl oz	38 mL
MILK CHOCOLATE, finely chopped	9 oz	255 g
WHITE CHOCOLATE, finely chopped	9 oz	255 g
MILK CHOCOLATE, melted, tempered, for dipping	as needed	as needed

1. On a parchment-lined sheet tray, set up a frame made of caramel bars that measures 1 by 12 in/3 by 30 cm.

2. Combine the cream and butter in a heavy-bottomed saucepan. Split the vanilla bean and scrape the seeds into the cream. Add the pod and bring to a boil.

3. Meanwhile, combine the egg yolks, sugar, and fruit purée and blend well. Temper the egg yolk mixture by gradually adding one-third of the hot cream mixture while stirring constantly with a whip. Add the tempered egg yolk mixture back to the hot cream mixture in the pan. Return to the heat and continue cooking until the mixture coats a spoon (195°F/91°C), about 3 minutes. Strain through a fine strainer.

4. Cool the mixture over an ice water bath to about 85°F/29°C, then blend in the liqueur.

5. Meanwhile, combine the milk chocolate and white chocolate in a stainless-steel bowl. Pour the mixture over the chopped chocolates and allow to sit for 3 minutes. Gently stir with a wire whip until well blended and smooth.

6. Pour the mixture into the prepared frame. Cover and refrigerate until firm.

7. Using a pastry brush, apply a thin layer of tempered milk chocolate to the top of the ganache. Allow to set until firm.

8. Cut into ¹/₂-in/1-cm squares and dip in tempered milk chocolate.

Egg Ganache

Egg ganache is made in much the same way as cream ganache: melting the chocolate by blending it with a hot liquid. The difference is the type of hot liquid. For egg ganache, cream is heated with butter; then egg yolks, which have been blended with sugar, and often flavoring in the form of a fruit purée are tempered in and the mixture is cooked to the stage of nappé. The hot liquid is strained over the finely chopped chocolate, allowed to stand briefly, and then gently blended together until fully melted and combined. Any liqueur is added last for full flavor retention. Egg ganache, like cream ganache, may also be flavored by infusion.

Molding Chocolates

Chocolate molds should be completely clean and at room temperature before use. They should always be polished with a clean soft cloth to remove any debris or water spots, which would give the surface of the unmolded chocolate a blotchy and/or dull appearance. The temperature of the mold is also important. If a mold is cold, the chocolate will set too quickly; if the mold is warm, it may bring the chocolate out of temper.

Very fluid tempered chocolate should be used for molding. If the chocolate is not fluid enough, it will be difficult to fill and/or coat the surface of the mold without developing air pockets or streaks. Couverture is always used for molding; its high percentage of cocoa butter makes for a more fluid melted chocolate. The tempered chocolate should be as warm as possible, within, of course, the ideal working temperature range.

When using molds that have an intricate design, first brush in some of the tempered chocolate to coat the mold. The brush forces chocolate into the crevices of the design, ensuring that the sharp detail of any mold will be shown perfectly in relief when the chocolate is unmolded.

After brushing an intricate mold, or when using a mold that does not have an intricate design, pour the tempered chocolate into the mold, completely filling it. Then, working quickly, tap or vibrate the mold to release any air pockets and to ensure that the chocolate fills all the crevices. Immediately invert the mold, pouring the excess chocolate back into the container of tempered chocolate, leaving only a thin coating in the mold. Do not reinvert the mold, or chocolate may pool, creating a layer of chocolate that is too thick. Instead, suspend the mold upside down by balancing the edges on two containers or bars over a sheet of clean parchment paper and let stand until the chocolate in the mold reaches a semisolid consistency.

To clean the surface of the mold, hold the mold at a 45-degree angle, bracing one edge against a flat surface; starting halfway up the mold, push a bench scraper down the mold, removing any chocolate on or above the surface of the mold. (The edges of the chocolate must be flush with the surface of the mold so that the chocolate can be properly sealed after filling. If the chocolates are not properly sealed, they will have a shorter shelf life.) Turn the mold around and remove excess chocolate from the other half.

Fill the mold 80 to 90 percent full with the desired filling, which must be liquid enough so that there is no possibility of creating air pockets. Once it is filled, tap or vibrate the mold to release any air bubbles and settle the filling. To ensure that the mold is not overfilled, hold the mold up at eye level and look across the surface; there should be no filling visible above the surface. Any excess filling should be removed before the seal coat of chocolate is applied, or the filling will become mixed into the chocolate and it will not harden or effectively seal the confection.

1 Brushing chocolate into molds

2 Suspending a mold upside down and scraping its surface

3 Drizzling a chocolate seal over a filled mold

Coat and seal the molded confections by drizzling on a thin layer of tempered chocolate and then gently spreading the chocolate out to cover and completely seal. Let stand until the chocolate is in a semisolid state (it should be wet and tacky but not fluid) and then clean the surface of the mold using a bench scraper as described above.

Chill molded chocolates under refrigeration for 5 to 10 minutes; do not freeze. To test whether the chocolates are ready to be unmolded, give the tray a slight twist; you should hear a crackle. With clear plastic molds you can check the underside to see if the chocolates are releasing. To unmold, turn the mold upside down and, holding it at a 45-degree angle, gently but firmly tap it once.

Molded chocolates must be handled carefully at every step of the process. Even when finished, the chocolates can be damaged easily; picking up fingerprints, smudges, scratches, and the like will render a delicious product visually unappealing.

Rochers

Makes 100 pieces

ALMONDS, sliced or slivered	1 lb	454 g
LIQUEUR OR SPIRIT	3 fl oz	90 mL
SUGAR	3 oz	85 g
MILK CHOCOLATE, melted, tempered	12 oz	340 g

1. Toss the almonds together with the liqueur and sugar.

2. Toast in a 350°F/177°C oven, turning the mixture several times to ensure even color, until golden brown, about 10 minutes. Allow to cool completely.

3. Combine one-third of the chocolate with one-third of the nut mixture, toss together to coat the nuts evenly, and spoon out into high little mounds on a parchment-lined sheet pan. Repeat with the remaining chocolate and nuts in two batches.

Notes   Any variety of nuts may be used.

Any type of chocolate may be used in place of milk chocolate.

Chopped dried fruit may be used with the nuts.

Rochers

The ideal rocher is shaped like a haystack. The individual shapes of the nuts and/or candied fruit should be clearly visible through the chocolate. Tossing the nuts or fruit with melted cocoa butter before adding the chocolate will act to thin the chocolate and give more definition to the shape of the nuts or fruits.

Work quickly and in small batches when making rochers. If the chocolate is too firm when it is deposited, the confections will not hold together and will have a dull finish.

Almond Dragées

Makes 110 pieces

SUGAR	5 oz	142 g
WATER	1½ fl oz	45 mL
ALMONDS, whole, blanched	1 lb	454 g
BUTTER	½ oz	14 g
DARK CHOCOLATE, melted, tempered	12 oz	340 g
COCOA POWDER	½ oz	14 g

1. Combine the sugar and water in a heavy-bottomed saucepan and stir to ensure that all the sugar is moistened. Bring to a boil over high heat, stirring constantly. When the syrup comes to a boil, stop stirring and skim the surface to remove any scum. Continue to cook, without stirring, until the syrup reaches the thread stage. Remove from the heat.

2. Immediately add the nuts and stir until the sugar crystallizes. Return to the heat and stir constantly until the sugar melts and caramelizes on the nuts.

3. Stir in the butter. Pour the mixture onto a marble slab and immediately separate the clusters of nuts. Allow to cool on the slab, then place in a bowl and chill for 3 minutes in the refrigerator.

4. Add 4 oz/113 g of the tempered chocolate and stir, so the nuts don't stick together, until the chocolate sets. Repeat with another 4 oz/113 g chocolate. Add the remaining 4 oz/113 g chocolate and stir until it is almost set. Add the cocoa powder and stir to coat. Toss the nuts in a strainer to sift off the excess cocoa powder.

Variation   **Hazelnut Dragées** Substitute whole blanched hazelnuts for the almonds.

Dragées

To ensure the desirable thin coating of caramel, only a relatively small amount of sugar is used when making dragées. The larger the nut, the less sugar you should use. Typical proportions by weight vary from 3 parts nuts to 1 part sugar for small nuts, to 6 parts nuts to 1 part sugar for large nuts.

The nuts used for dragées should not be toasted, as they will roast as the sugar caramelizes.

Garnishing
Knackerli

Knackerli

Makes 50 pieces

DARK CHOCOLATE, melted, tempered	8 oz	227 g
PISTACHIOS, peeled	50 each	50 each
DRIED CRANBERRIES	50 each	50 each
DRIED APRICOTS, coarsely chopped	10 each	10 each

1. Fill a parchment cone with the tempered chocolate and pipe onto a parchment-lined sheet pan in 1-in/3-cm disks.

2. When the chocolate has begun to set, place 1 pistachio, 1 dried cranberry, and 1 piece of a dried apricot onto each disk.

3. Allow the chocolate to fully set before removing the disks from the parchment paper.

Notes Tempered milk or white chocolate may be substituted for the dark chocolate. The chocolate may be piped in larger or smaller disks if desired. Any type of nuts or dried fruit may be substituted for the pistachios, dried cranberries, and apricots.

It is important to remember when making knackerli that the size of the nuts and dried fruits corresponds to the size of the chocolate disk and that the colors and flavors complement each other.

Knackerli

For knackerli, as with rochers, it is important to work in small, manageable batches to ensure the chocolate disks do not set too much or completely before the garnish is added.

Praline-Filled Chocolate Cups

Makes 120 confections

BUTTER, soft	8 oz	227 g
FONDANT, for glazing	8 oz	227 g
PRALINE PASTE	8 oz	227 g
DARK CHOCOLATE, melted, tempered	as needed	as needed

1. Cream the butter, fondant, and praline paste on medium speed, scraping down the bowl periodically, until smooth and lighter in color, about 5 minutes.

2. Fill a pastry bag fitted with a No. 2 plain tip with the praline mixture and pipe into foil cups ⅞ in/2 cm in diameter by ⅝ in/1.5 cm high, lined with set tempered dark chocolate, filling the cups 80 percent full. Allow to set until firm.

3. Fill a parchment cone with tempered dark chocolate and pipe onto the top of each filled cup in a spiral motion, creating a seal. Tap each cup to smooth the top.

4. Allow the chocolate to set.

Candied Orange Peel

Makes 9½ oz/269 g

ORANGE PEELS, cut into strips ¼ by 2 in/6 mm by 5 cm	8 oz	227 g
WATER	12 fl oz	360 mL
CORN SYRUP	4 oz	113 g
SUGAR	1 lb	454 g

1. Place the orange peels in a pan of cold water to cover and bring to a boil; drain. Repeat this process three times, using fresh cold water each time, to remove some of the bitter flavor from the pith.

2. Combine the water, corn syrup, and sugar in a heavy-bottomed saucepan and bring to a boil, stirring to dissolve the sugar. Reduce to a very low simmer, add the peels, and poach until translucent, about 1 hour.

3. At this point, store the peels in the syrup in a tightly covered container under refrigeration, or dry and toss them in sugar and/or dip in tempered chocolate.

Lemon, lime, or grapefruit peels may be used in place of the orange peels.

To dry the peels, drain them and spread on a wire rack set on a parchment-lined sheet pan. Allow to dry and crystallize overnight at room temperature. Or place the peels on a parchment-lined sheet pan in a 280°F/138°C convection oven for 1½ hours.

If the peels are not to be dipped in chocolate, toss them in granulated sugar before drying.

Candied orange peel is opaque before cooking and translucent afterward.

Cooking Sugar to Different Stages

Of the two techniques for cooking sugar (wet and dry), only the wet method allows the sugar to be cooked to and used at the various stages that are vital for countless preparations. The dry method of sugar cooking melts the sugar crystals by the application of heat, resulting in sugar that caramelizes almost as soon as it melts. The wet method of sugar cooking, however, dissolves the sugar in water; then, as the solution cooks, water evaporates, acting to increase the concentration of sugar and resulting in a supersaturated, noncrystalline sugar solution. The concentration of the sugar solution increases as the solution is cooked, the temperature increases, and more of the water evaporates.

To cook sugar by the wet method, use a heavy-bottomed pot to ensure even heat conduction. The water should equal approximately 30 percent of the weight of the sugar; a small measure of an acid ingredient may also be added. If too little water is used, there may be undissolved sugar crystals in the syrup, which may cause recrystallization.

Bring the mixture to a boil, stirring constantly. When the mixture comes to a boil, stop stirring. Skim the impurities that rise to the surface. Brush down the sides of the pan using a pastry brush moistened with cool water. Add the acid ingredient (cream of tartar, lemon juice, etc.), if using.

If making hard candies, flavors should be added during the cool-down and may be folded or pulled in. Many flavors for hard candies are not heat-stable and should not be added until the sugar has cooled somewhat. Liquid and powdered colors, however, must be added to the sugar syrup at the end of the cooking process, but before it begins to cool down. Powdered colors should be dissolved in a small amount of water before being added to the sugar syrup.

SUGAR STAGES AND TEMPERATURES

STAGE	DEGREES FAHRENHEIT	DEGREES CELSIUS
THREAD	215–230	102–110
SOFT BALL	240	116
FIRM BALL	245	118
HARD BALL	250–260	121–127
SOFT CRACK	265–270	129–132
HARD CRACK	295–310	146–154
CARAMEL	320	160

Soft Caramels

Makes 126 pieces

EVAPORATED MILK	14 fl oz	420 mL
SUGAR	14 oz	397 g
VANILLA BEAN, split and scraped	¾ each	¾ each
ORANGE ZEST, grated	½ oz	14 g
GLUCOSE SYRUP	4 oz	113 g
BUTTER	½ oz	14 g
DARK CHOCOLATE, melted, tempered, for coating and dipping	as needed	as needed

1. On a piece of lightly oiled parchment papter, set up a frame of metal bars that measures 6 by 12 in/15 by 30 cm.

2. Combine the evaporated milk, sugar, vanilla bean seeds and pod, and orange zest in a heavy-bottomed saucepan and bring to a boil, stirring constantly. Add the glucose syrup, while continuing to stir, and continue cooking, stirring, to 245°F/118°C (the consistency should resemble the firm ball stage). Stir in the butter.

3. Immediately pour the mixture into the prepared frame. Remove the vanilla bean and allow to cool completely.

4. Brush the caramel with a thin layer of tempered dark chocolate and allow the chocolate to set completely.

5. Using caramel cutters, cut the slab into ⅞-in/2-cm squares. Dip in tempered dark chocolate and allow to set.

Pouring soft caramel into a frame

Soft Caramels

If the mixture for caramels is undercooked, they will be too soft and will not have the proper caramel flavor. If it is overcooked, they will be too firm. Although a thermometer is helpful in making caramels, the final assessment of whether the caramel is ready should be determined by testing the batch using ice water and a spoon. If the caramel is too firm, more liquid can be added to adjust the consistency.

Soft caramels may be flavored in any number of ways. Strong flavorings such as coffee beans, hazelnut paste, or spices can be added to the cream at the beginning of the cooking process. To make fruit caramels, replace up to half of the liquid in the recipe with a fruit purée. When using a fruit purée, it is advisable to cut the amount of glucose syrup by half, and it is likely that you will have to cook the caramels to a higher temperature to achieve the same consistency, due to the acidity of the fruit and the reduced amount of milk solids in the formula.

Raspberry Caramels
Makes 160 pieces

EVAPORATED MILK	9 fl oz	270 mL
SEEDLESS RASPBERRY PURÉE	6 fl oz	180 mL
SUGAR	14 oz	397 g
LEMON ZEST, grated	1 tbsp	9 g
GLUCOSE SYRUP	4 oz	113 g
BUTTER	2/3 oz	19 g
DARK CHOCOLATE, melted, tempered, for dipping	as needed	as needed

1. On a silicone baking mat, set up a frame of metal bars that measures 6½ by 12 in/17 by 30 cm.

2. Combine the evaporated milk, raspberry purée, sugar, and lemon zest in a heavy-bottomed saucepan and bring to a boil, stirring constantly. Add the glucose syrup, while continuing to stir, and cook, stirring, to 230°F/110°C.

3. Add the butter and continue cooking to 245°F/118°C, or firm ball stage. Immediately pour the caramel into the prepared frame and allow to cool.

4. Brush the cooled caramel with a thin layer of tempered dark chocolate and allow the chocolate to set completely.

5. Using caramel cutters, cut into ⅞-in/2-cm squares. Dip in tempered dark chocolate and allow to set.

Toffee

Makes 400 pieces

HEAVY CREAM	13 fl oz	390 mL
SUGAR	1 lb 6 oz	624 g
GLUCOSE SYRUP	4 oz	113 g
VANILLA BEAN, seeds only	¾ each	¾ each

1. Combine all the ingredients in a heavy-bottomed saucepan and cook over medium heat, stirring constantly and occasionally washing down the sides of the pan with a wet pastry brush, until the mixture reaches 293°F/145°C.

2. Pour the toffee onto a 12 by 16 in/30 by 41 cm silicone baking mat; it should be about ⅛ in/3 mm thick. Allow to cool slightly until the toffee begins to set, but not so much that it is brittle.

3. Using caramel cutters, score the toffee into ⅞-in/2-cm squares. Allow to cool completely.

4. Break the toffee apart at the scored marks. If the plain toffee is to be stored, it should be immediately wrapped tightly in plastic wrap or placed in an airtight container.

Peanut Brittle

Makes 6 lb/2.72 kg

SUGAR	1 lb 12 oz	794 g
WATER	12 fl oz	360 mL
GLUCOSE SYRUP	1 lb 4 oz	567 g
RAW PEANUTS	2 lb	907 g
SALT	½ oz	14 g
BUTTER	2 oz	57 g
VANILLA EXTRACT	½ fl oz	15 mL
BAKING SODA	2 tsp	8 g

1. Combine the sugar, water, and glucose syrup in a heavy-bottomed saucepan and stir to ensure all the sugar is moistened. Bring to a boil over high heat, stirring constantly. When the syrup comes to a boil, stop stirring and skim the surface to remove any impurities. Continue to cook, without stirring, occasionally washing down the sides of the pan using a wet pastry brush, to 264°F/129°C.

2. Add the peanuts and salt. Increase the heat to high and continue cooking, stirring gently with a wooden spoon, until the mixture reaches 318°F/159°C.

3. Remove from the heat and stir in the butter and vanilla until incorporated. Add the baking soda. Pour the mixture onto a lightly oiled marble work surface. Allow to cool slightly, to a plastic texture. Wearing latex gloves to protect your hands, pull the brittle from the edges, working from the edges and breaking off pieces as they harden. (This must be done quickly, before the brittle hardens, so it's best to have two people work on it.) The pieces will be all different shapes and sizes.

Peanut Brittle

Some caution is necessary when making peanut brittle. Temperature and color must be carefully monitored to achieve the characteristic flavor and texture. If your peanut brittle is pale or is milky white and granular, it probably was either not cooked to a high enough temperature or was stirred too much and/or too rapidly during cooking. Peanut brittle demands a slow, steady stir, especially after the peanuts have been added. As a general rule, if the mixture has reached the proper temperature but the color is not fully developed, continue cooking to the desired color.

Pecan Butter Crunch

Makes 4 lb 11 oz/2.13 kg

BUTTER	1 lb	454 g
SUGAR	1 lb	454 g
WATER	3 fl oz	90 mL
SALT	⅔ oz	19 g
PECANS, lightly toasted and coarsely chopped	12 oz	340 g
DARK CHOCOLATE, melted, tempered	14 oz	397 g

1. Melt the butter in a heavy-bottomed saucepan. Add the sugar, water, and 1 tsp/5 g of the salt. Bring to a rolling boil over high heat. Cook, stirring constantly with a wooden spoon, until the mixture reaches 295°F/146°C and is light golden brown.

2. Pour the mixture onto a full-size silicone baking mat and, using an offset metal spatula, spread evenly over the baking mat; the mixture should be about ⅛ in/3 mm thick. Allow to cool completely.

3. Toss the pecans with the remaining ½ oz/14 g salt.

4. Spread the cooled toffee with a thin layer of tempered dark chocolate. While the chocolate is still fluid, scatter half of the salted pecans over the top. Allow the chocolate to set completely.

5. Turn the slab of toffee over and brush with a thin layer of tempered chocolate. While the chocolate is still fluid, scatter the remaining pecans over the top. Allow to set completely, then break the toffee into pieces.

Leaf Croquant

Makes 70 pieces

ALMONDS, lightly toasted	1 lb	454 g
CONFECTIONERS' SUGAR	2 oz	57 g
SUGAR	1 lb	454 g
GLUCOSE SYRUP	2 oz	57 g
DARK CHOCOLATE, melted, tempered, for dipping	as needed	as needed

1. Grind the almonds and confectioners' sugar to a thick paste in a food processor.

2. Place the sugar in a heavy-bottomed saucepan and cook over medium heat, stirring constantly, to a rich golden brown. Blend in the glucose syrup.

3. Immediately pour the caramel into a rectangle on a sheet pan lined with a silicone baking mat, spreading it evenly over the mat. Allow to cool just enough to be handled: It should still be very warm; if it cools too much, it will crack.

4. Spread the almond paste over two-thirds of the caramel. Warm the slab if necessary to make it malleable. Make a three-fold (see page 263 for instructions on making a three-fold), folding the third with no almond paste over first.

5. Warm the slab if necessary and roll it into a rectangle. Make another three-fold, and roll the slab out again. Repeat for a total of 5 three-folds. Cut the croquant into 7/8-in/2-cm squares. If it has cooled too much to cut, rewarm it.

6. Allow the pieces to cool completely, then dip in tempered dark chocolate and allow it to set.

Folding the almond paste into the caramel for Leaf Croquant

Hard Candies

Makes 120 pieces

WATER	10 fl oz	300 mL
SUGAR	1 lb 11 oz	765 g
GLUCOSE SYRUP	5½ oz	156 g
CREAM OF TARTAR	¼ tsp	1 g
COLORING	as desired	as desired
FLAVORING	as desired	as desired

1. Lightly oil a ½-in/1-cm frame (8 by 12 in/20 by 30 cm).

2. Combine the water and sugar in a heavy-bottomed saucepan and bring to a boil, stirring constantly. Stir in the glucose syrup and cream of tartar and, if using, add powdered or liquid coloring as desired. Return the syrup to a boil.

3. Continue to cook, without stirring, occasionally washing down the sides of the pan using a wet pastry brush, until the mixture reaches 293°F/145°C.

4. Immediately pour into the prepared frame. Allow to cool for 3 minutes, then add paste coloring, if using, and the desired flavoring and fold it into the sugar.

5. While still hot and pliable pull out and twist the sugar until satiny in appearance (twisting multiple colors is also possible). Snip into small candies with sharp scissors. Allow to cool.

6. Store in an airtight container.

Note   Add the flavoring according to the manufacturer's instructions.

Snipping hard candies with scissors

Hard Candies

Oils, extracts, and concentrated synthetic or natural flavors are the most common flavorings used for hard candies. These flavorings are added at the end of the cooking process because they are often not heat-stable and because any acid they contain will prevent the finished product from becoming completely hard. Hard candies can be poured onto a slab, partially cooled, and then pulled and cut, or they can be cast in starch molds or other types of molds.

Raspberry Creams

Makes 100 pieces

BUTTER, soft	4 oz	113 g
SEEDLESS RASPBERRY JAM	6 oz	170 g
MILK CHOCOLATE, melted	4 oz	113 g
SEMISWEET CHOCOLATE, melted	3½ oz	99 g
COCOA BUTTER, melted	1 oz	28 g
RASPBERRY LIQUEUR	1 fl oz	30 mL
DARK OR MILK CHOCOLATE, melted, tempered, for coating	as needed	as needed

1. Place a ½-in/1-cm metal frame (9 by 12 in/23 by 30 cm) on parchment paper or a silicone baking mat.
2. Mix together the butter and jam by hand, scraping down the bowl periodically, just until homogeneous.
3. Blend together the chocolates and cocoa butter. Temper the chocolate mixture.
4. Gently fold the chocolate mixture into the butter mixture. Blend in the liqueur.
5. Spread the mixture evenly in the prepared frame. Allow to set until firm.
6. Brush the raspberry cream with a thin layer of tempered milk chocolate and allow the chocolate to set completely.
7. Remove the frame and cut the slab into strips ½ in/1 cm wide. Cut the strips into ¾-in/2-cm diamonds. Dip in tempered dark or milk chocolate. Allow the chocolate to set completely, about 30 minutes.

Mint Fondant

Makes 100 pieces

MINT LEAVES	35 each	35 each
FONDANT	1 lb 13 oz	822 g
BRANDY	as needed	as needed
PEPPERMINT OIL	1 drop	1 drop
DARK CHOCOLATE, melted, tempered, for dipping	as needed	as needed

1. Grind the mint leaves with 8 oz/227 g of the fondant in a food processor until smooth.

2. Transfer the mint mixture to a bowl, stir in the remaining 1 lb 5 oz/595 g fondant, and heat over a water bath until the mixture reaches 175°F/79°C. Adjust the consistency with brandy; the fondant should be thin enough to be deposited with the fondant funnel but should not be runny. Blend in the peppermint oil.

3. Dispense with a fondant funnel into molds on a parchment-lined sheet tray. The finished fondant should be ¾ in/2 cm in diameter and ¼ in/6 mm thick. Allow to set until firm, about 10 minutes.

4. Dip the fondant into tempered dark chocolate, transfer to parchment-lined sheet pans, and, when the chocolate has begun to set, use a three-pronged dipping fork to make three lines across the surface of each confection.

Fudge

Makes 4 lb 4 oz/1.93 kg

MILK	8 fl oz	240 mL
HEAVY CREAM	12 fl oz	360 mL
SUGAR	2 lb	907 g
CORN SYRUP	6 oz	170 g
BUTTER	1 oz	28 g
SALT	½ tsp	2.50 g
UNSWEETENED CHOCOLATE, finely chopped	8 oz	227 g
VANILLA EXTRACT	½ fl oz	15 mL
WALNUTS	5 oz	142 g

1. Line the bottom and sides of a half sheet pan with aluminum foil.

2. Combine the milk and cream. Pour 8 fl oz/240 mL of the mixture into a heavy-bottomed saucepan, add the sugar and corn syrup, and bring to a boil, stirring constantly to dissolve. Continue to cook and stir until the mixture reaches 230°F/110°C.

3. Add the butter and salt and stir to blend. Slowly add the remaining milk-cream mixture and continue to cook to 236°F/113°C.

4. Add the chocolate and vanilla. Stir twice, and pour onto a clean marble surface. Do not stir again. Allow to cool to 120°F/49°C.

5. Agitate the fudge by working it with a metal spatula on a marble surface until it begins to thicken. Quickly add the nuts, before the fudge becomes too thick, and pour onto the prepared sheet pan.

6. Allow to set completely before cutting.

Notes You can substitute any of the following for the unsweetened chocolate: white or dark chocolate, peanut butter, or pistachio or praline paste. You can also add 1 oz/28 g of garnish for every 8 oz/227 g fudge. For example, for white chocolate and dried cherry fudge, substitute white chocolate for the unsweetened chocolate and add 8½ oz/241 g dried cherries.

Frappe Chocolate Fudge

Makes 1 half sheet pan

FRAPPE		
GELATIN	2 tsp	7 g
WATER, cold	1½ fl oz	45 mL
VANILLA EXTRACT	1 tsp	5 mL
SUGAR	14 oz	397 g
GLUCOSE SYRUP	8 oz	227 g
MOLASSES	1½ oz	43 g
WATER	1½ fl oz	45 mL
FUDGE		
SEMISWEET CHOCOLATE, finely chopped	2 lb	907 g
UNSWEETENED CHOCOLATE, chopped	4 oz	113 g
VANILLA EXTRACT	¾ fl oz	23 mL
FRAPPE	1 lb 10½ oz	751 g
EVAPORATED MILK	18 fl oz	540 mL
SUGAR	3 lb 12 oz	1.70 kg
BUTTER, cut into ¼-in/6-mm slices	12 oz	340 g
WALNUTS, chopped	12 oz	340 g

1. To prepare the frappe, bloom the gelatin in the cold water and vanilla extract. Melt over a pan of hot water.

2. Cook the sugar, glucose syrup, molasses, and water to 241°F/116°C, stirring constantly. Allow the mixture to cool to 208°F/98°C and stir in the gelatin solution.

3. Whip the mixture using the whip attachment on high speed until medium peaks form.

4. To prepare the fudge, line a half sheet pan with aluminum foil. Place the chopped chocolate, vanilla extract, and frappe in a large bowl.

5. Warm the evaporated milk, stir in the sugar, and cook, stirring constantly, to 235°F/113°C. Turn off the heat, add the butter, and stir for 10 seconds to incorporate.

6. Pour the hot sugar mixture onto the chocolate and frappe in the bowl and stir for 1 minute to dissolve the frappe and chocolate.

7. Continue to stir the mixture until completely blended and smooth. Fold in the chopped nuts.

8. Pour the mixture immediately into the prepared sheet pan and allow to set to room temperature. Chill before removing from the pan and cutting.

Nuss Bonbon

Makes 85 pieces

FONDANT	8 oz	227 g
ALMOND PASTE	10 oz	284 g
HEAVY CREAM, hot	8 fl oz	240 mL
SUGAR	5 oz	142 g
WALNUTS, finely chopped	10 oz	284 g
DARK CHOCOLATE, melted, tempered, for coating and dipping	as needed	as needed
WALNUT HALVES	85 each	85 each

1. Grind together the fondant and almond paste in a food processor until smooth.

2. Place the sugar in a heavy-bottomed saucepan and cook over medium heat, stirring constantly, to a rich golden brown, occasionally washing down the sides of the pan using a wet pastry brush.

3. Add the hot cream to the caramel, stirring until blended. Add the almond paste mixture and the chopped walnuts. Cook, stirring constantly, until the mixture reaches 248°F/120°C; it will pull away from the sides of the saucepan.

4. Immediately pour onto a lightly oiled sheet of parchment paper. Place another lightly oiled parchment sheet on top and roll into a slab ½ in/1 cm thick.

5. Brush the bonbon slab with a thin layer of tempered dark chocolate and allow the chocolate to set completely.

6. Cut into pieces using a 1-in/3-cm oval praline cutter. Top each bonbon with a walnut half and dip in thinned tempered dark chocolate.

Gianduja

Makes 1 lb 8 oz/680 g

HAZELNUTS, toasted	8 oz	227 g
CONFECTIONERS' SUGAR	8 oz	227 g
DARK CHOCOLATE, coarsely chopped	8 oz	227 g

1. Process the nuts and 2 oz/57 g of the sugar together in a food processor to an oily paste. Add the chocolate and remaining sugar and process for 1 to 2 more minutes, until as smooth as possible.

2. Table the gianduja until it begins to thicken.

3. Allow to cool completely. Wrap tightly in plastic wrap and store in a cool, dry place.

Variations   **White Chocolate Gianduja** Substitute white chocolate for the dark chocolate and very lightly toasted almonds for the hazelnuts. Reduce the confectioners' sugar to 6 oz/170 g.

Milk Chocolate Gianduja Substitute milk chocolate for the dark chocolate and very lightly toasted almonds for the hazelnuts. Reduce the confectioners' sugar to 6 oz/170 g.

Gianduja

Gianduja may be made with any variety of chocolate—dark, milk, or white. It is traditionally made with either hazelnuts or almonds, but other nuts may be substituted in part or whole. The nuts can be roasted to any degree desired.

The final variable in the production of gianduja is the ratio of nuts to sugar to chocolate. For a firmer gianduja, use more chocolate. For a softer gianduja, use less. The basic ratio for a medium-consistency gianduja that is suitable for candy centers is 1 part nuts to 1 part sugar to 1 part dark chocolate (or 1.25 parts milk or white chocolate). If possible, gianduja should be ground in a mélangeur for the smoothest texture, but a food processor will make an acceptable gianduja. When using a food processor, always use confectioners' sugar, not granulated.

Because of its low moisture content, gianduja is not prone to spoilage and has a long shelf life.

Branchli (Branches)

Makes 55 pieces

GIANDUJA, melted (page 742)	8 oz	227 g
PRALINE PASTE	4 oz	113 g
CONFECTIONERS' SUGAR	4 oz	113 g
DARK CHOCOLATE, melted	5 oz	142 g
COCONUT OIL, melted (92°F/33°C)	2½ oz	71 g
NOUGATINE COUVERTURE, tempered, for dipping	as needed	as needed

1. Combine all the ingredients except for the nougatine couverture in a bowl, and blend thoroughly. Allow to set.

2. Table the mixture until it reaches a piping consistency.

3. Fill a pastry bag fitted with a No. 5 plain tip with the mixture and pipe into strips 16 in/41 cm long and ¼ in/6 mm thick. Allow to set until firm.

4. Cut into pieces 2 in/5 cm long. Dip into tempered nougatine couverture and allow to set completely.

Three Brothers

Makes 100 pieces

GIANDUJA (page 742)	1 lb	454 g
HAZELNUT DRAGÉES (page 259)	1 lb	454 g
DARK CHOCOLATE, melted, tempered, for dipping	as needed	as needed

1. Table the gianduja until it reaches a piping consistency.
2. Fill a pastry bag fitted with a No. 3 straight tip with the gianduja and pipe into ¾-in/2-cm bulbs on a parchment-lined sheet tray.
3. Place 3 dragéed hazelnuts together on each bulb of gianduja. Allow to set.
4. Dip in thinned tempered dark chocolate and allow the chocolate to set completely.

Note To thin the tempered chocolate for dipping, use 10 percent cocoa butter per weight of chocolate; blend in and temper before dipping.

Grouping three dragéed hazelnuts for Three Brothers

Tremors

Makes 120 pieces

DRIED CHERRIES, chopped	3 oz	85 g
SLICED ALMONDS, toasted and coarsely chopped	5 oz	142 g
GIANDUJA, melted (page 742)	1 lb	454 g
MILK CHOCOLATE, melted, tempered	1 lb	454 g

1. Line four triangle molds with plastic wrap.

2. Combine the cherries and almonds with the gianduja, folding them in with a rubber spatula.

3. Table the mixture until it is very cool to the touch.

4. Spread the mixture into the prepared molds. Allow to set at room temperature. Refrigerate for 10 minutes to allow the mixture to release from the mold.

5. Remove the triangular strips from the molds. Brush with a thin layer of the tempered milk chocolate and allow it to set completely.

6. Remove the strips from the molds and place coated sides down on a wire rack. Enrobe one strip in tempered milk chocolate. (Note: Enrobe and slice only one strip at a time; if the chocolate sets too hard, it will crack when cut.) Immediately remove the strip from the rack. When the chocolate is just set, place on a parchment-lined sheet pan, and slice into 1/2-in/1-cm pieces. Repeat with the remaining strips.

Pistachio Marzipan

Makes 1 lb 9 oz/709 g

BLANCHED ALMONDS	4½ oz	128 g
BLANCHED PISTACHIOS	4½ oz	128 g
SUGAR	1 lb	454 g
WATER	5 fl oz	150 mL
GLUCOSE SYRUP	2 oz	57 g
KIRSCH, RUM, OR OTHER SPIRITS	as needed	as needed

1. Lightly oil a marble surface or a silicone baking mat.

2. Combine the almonds and pistachios in a food processor and pulse just until coarsely ground. Set aside.

3. Combine the sugar, water, and glucose syrup in a heavy-bottomed saucepan and stir to ensure all the sugar is moistened. Bring to a boil over high heat, stirring to dissolve the sugar. Stop stirring and skim the surface of the syrup to remove any impurities. Continue to cook, without stirring, occasionally washing down the sides of the pan using a wet pastry brush, to 250°F/121°C, or hard ball stage.

4. Add the ground nuts to the syrup, stir only twice, and immediately pour the mixture onto the prepared marble surface or baking mat. Allow to cool to room temperature.

5. Grind the mixture to a paste in a food processor, adding only as much of the spirit as necessary for processing. Add a little spirit if the marzipan starts to separate.

6. If storing the marzipan, wrap tightly in plastic wrap and store in a cool, dry place.

Walnut Marzipan

Makes 1 lb 9 oz/709 g

BLANCHED ALMONDS	4½ oz	128 g
WALNUTS	4½ oz	128 g
SUGAR	1 lb	454 g
WATER	5 fl oz	150 mL
GLUCOSE SYRUP	2 oz	57 g
KIRSCH, RUM, OR OTHER SPIRITS	as needed	as needed

1. Lightly oil a clean marble surface or a silicone baking mat.

2. Combine the almonds and walnuts in a food processor and pulse just until coarsely ground. Set aside.

3. Combine the sugar, water, and glucose syrup in a heavy-bottomed saucepan and stir to ensure all the sugar is moistened. Bring to a boil over high heat, stirring to dissolve the sugar. Stop stirring and skim the surface of the syrup to remove any impurities. Continue to cook, without stirring, occasionally washing down the sides of the pan using a wet pastry brush, to 250°F/127°C, or hard ball stage.

4. Add the ground nuts to the syrup, stir only twice, and immediately pour the mixture onto the prepared marble surface or baking mat. Allow to cool to room temperature.

5. Grind the mixture to a paste in a food processor, adding only as much of the spirit as necessary for processing. Add a little more spirit if the marzipan starts to separate.

6. If storing the marzipan, wrap tightly in plastic wrap and store in a cool, dry place.

Note Alternatively, to finish, roll the marzipan out to ⅜ in/9.5 mm thick. Cut into 1-in/3-cm diamonds. Dip in tempered dark chocolate. When the chocolate is almost set but still tacky, place a toasted walnut half on top of each diamond.

Tree Trunks

Makes 118 pieces

GIANDUJA, melted (page 742)	1 lb	454 g
PISTACHIO MARZIPAN (page 746)	1 lb	454 g
COCOA BUTTER, melted	as needed	as needed
DARK CHOCOLATE, melted, tempered, for coating	as needed	as needed

1. Table the gianduja until it is firm enough to hold its shape when piped.

2. Fill a pastry bag fitted with a No. 5 or 6 straight tip with the gianduja and pipe cylinders 16 in/41 cm long onto a parchment-lined sheet pan. Allow to set until firm, 10 to 15 minutes.

3. Roll the marzipan out on a clean marble surface into a rectangle 16 in/41 cm long and 1/4 in/6 mm thick. Brush with a thin layer of cocoa butter.

4. Place one cylinder of gianduja on the marzipan and roll up the marzipan to encase the gianduja, overlapping the seam slightly; cut the marzipan at that point. Smooth the seam, then roll until as smooth as possible.

5. Brush the log with tempered dark chocolate to coat. Continue to brush until the chocolate starts to set, creating a bark-like pattern. Slice 1/2 in/1 cm thick on a slight bias. Do not let the chocolate set completely before cutting.

Pectin Gelées

Makes 125 pieces

FRUIT PURÉE OF CHOICE	1 lb	454 g
APPLESAUCE	11 oz	312 g
GLUCOSE SYRUP	3 oz	85 g
PECTIN POWDER	1 oz	28 g
SUGAR	3 lb 3½ oz, plus as needed for coating	1.46 kg, plus as needed for coating
LEMON JUICE	1 fl oz	30 mL

1. Spread the applesauce in a hotel pan and place in a 200°F/93°C oven for 30 minutes to remove moisture.

2. Line a half sheet pan with parchment paper.

3. Combine the fruit purée, applesauce, and glucose syrup in a heavy-bottomed saucepan. Blend the pectin with 3½ oz/99 g of the sugar and, off the heat, whisk into the fruit purée mixture. Bring to a rolling boil over medium heat, stirring constantly.

4. Add 1 lb 8 oz/680 g of the sugar and return to a rolling boil. Add the remaining 1 lb 8 oz/680 sugar, return to a rolling boil, and boil for 2½ minutes.

5. Stir in the lemon juice. Pour onto the prepared half sheet pan and allow to set overnight.

6. Sprinkle the fruit slab with granulated sugar. Using a guitar, cut into 1¼-in/3-cm squares. Toss the gelées in sugar to coat.

Cutting Pectin Gelées on a guitar

Marshmallows

Makes 1 half sheet pan

GELATIN	1¼ oz	35 g
WATER, cold	16 fl oz	480 mL
SUGAR	1 lb 8 oz	680 g
GLUCOSE SYRUP	12 oz	340 g
HONEY	12 oz	340 g
VANILLA EXTRACT	½ fl oz	15 mL

1. Line a half sheet pan with parchment paper.

2. Bloom the gelatin in 8 fl oz/240 mL cold water.

3. Meanwhile, combine the sugar, glucose syrup, honey, and the remaining 8 fl oz/240 mL water in a heavy-bottomed saucepan and stir to ensure all the sugar is moistened. Bring to a boil over high heat, stirring to dissolve the sugar. Stop stirring and skim the surface of the syrup to remove any impurities. Continue to cook, without stirring, occasionally washing down the sides of the pan using a wet pastry brush, to 252°F/122°C. Remove from the heat and cool to approximately 210°F/99°C.

4. While the sugar is cooling, dissolve the gelatin over simmering water. Remove from the heat and stir in the vanilla.

5. Stir the gelatin into the cooled sugar syrup. Using the whip attachment on high speed, whip the mixture until medium peaks form.

6. Spread the mixture evenly in the prepared sheet pan; the easiest way to do this is to place the mixture in the frame, place a sheet of oiled parchment paper on top of the marshmallow mixture, and roll the marshmallow into the pan.

7. Remove the slab from the pan, inverting onto a work surface, and peel off the paper.

8. Cut the marshmallows into 1-in/3-cm squares.

Variation **Cinnamon Marshmallows** Add 1 tbsp/6 g ground cinnamon to the mixture in Step 5 after the gelatin is added. Follow the remaining method as stated.

Cutting
marshmallows
coated with
cornstarch

Seafoam

Makes 125 pieces

SUGAR	3 lb	1.36 kg
GLUCOSE SYRUP	1 lb 10 oz	737 g
WATER	14 fl oz	420 mL
HONEY	1½ oz	43 g
GELATIN SOLUTION (page 826)	¼ oz	7 g
BAKING SODA	1½ oz	43 g

1. Butter and lightly flour two disposable aluminum half hotel pans.
2. Cook the sugar, glucose syrup, and water to 280°F/138°C, stirring constantly just until the sugar has dissolved. Stop stirring once the mixture comes to a boil.
3. Add the honey and continue to cook to 302°F/150°C.
4. Remove the pan from the heat and allow to cool for 5 minutes.
5. Blend in the gelatin solution. Blend in the baking soda and allow the mixture to rise to the top of the pan.
6. Pour into the prepared pans. Allow to cool overnight. Remove the slab from the pan, inverting onto a work surface, and peel off the paper.
7. Cut into 1-in/3-cm pieces.

Note   These confections may be dipped in tempered dark chocolate after cutting.

Soft Chocolate Nougat

Makes 100 pieces

SUGAR	1 lb 6 oz	624 g
WATER	6 fl oz	180 mL
GLUCOSE SYRUP	1 lb 9 oz	709 g
EGG WHITES	2 oz	57 g
VANILLA EXTRACT	½ fl oz	15 mL
NONFAT DRY MILK	4½ oz	128 g
CONFECTIONERS' SUGAR	1½ oz	43 g
DARK CHOCOLATE, melted	4 oz	113 g
COCOA BUTTER, melted	1½ oz	43 g
DARK CHOCOLATE, melted, tempered, for dipping	as needed	as needed

1. Combine the sugar, water, and 1 lb 7 oz/652 g of the glucose syrup in a heavy-bottomed saucepan and stir to ensure all the sugar is moistened. Bring to a boil over high heat, stirring to dissolve the sugar. Stop stirring and skim the surface of the syrup to remove any scum. Continue to cook, without stirring, occasionally washing down the sides of the pan using a wet pastry brush, to 252°F/122°C.

2. Meanwhile, when the mixture reaches 230°F/110°C, begin to whip the egg whites and the remaining 2 oz/57 g glucose syrup until the whites form medium peaks. Add the vanilla extract.

3. Using the whip attachment, with the mixer on medium speed, pour the hot sugar syrup into the egg whites in a fine stream, whipping until fully incorporated. Let cool slightly.

4. Sift together the dry milk and confectioners' sugar. Slowly fold the dry milk mixture into the meringue until fully incorporated. Cool until just warm to the touch.

5. Blend the melted dark chocolate and cocoa butter together. Add to the meringue and fold to combine.

6. Pour the mixture onto a sheet of oiled parchment paper. Place another sheet of oiled parchment paper on top and roll the mixture to ⅜ in/9.5 mm thick. Allow to cool completely.

7. Brush the nougat with a thin layer of tempered dark chocolate and allow the chocolate to set completely.

8. Cut the nougat into 1-in/3-cm squares with a hot knife, wiping the knife clean after each cut. Dip in tempered dark chocolate and let set completely.

Note   The texture of this nougat improves after dipping, as it crystallizes.

Nougat Montélimar

Makes 100 pieces

SUGAR	11½ oz	326 g
WATER	3½ fl oz	105 mL
GLUCOSE SYRUP	2 oz	57 g
HONEY, boiling	8 oz	227 g
EGG WHITES	2 oz	57 g
VANILLA BEAN, seeds only	½ each	½ each
BLANCHED ALMONDS, toasted	7 oz	198 g
HAZELNUTS, peeled and toasted	2½ oz	71 g
BLANCHED PISTACHIOS	2½ oz	71 g
ASSORTED DRIED FRUIT	5 oz	142 g
SLICED ALMONDS, toasted	2½ oz	71 g
COCOA BUTTER, melted	3½ oz	99 g
DARK CHOCOLATE, melted, tempered, for dipping	as needed	as needed

1. Sift confectioners' sugar lightly onto a marble slab.

2. Combine 11 oz/312 g of the sugar, the water, and glucose syrup in a heavy-bottomed saucepan and stir to ensure all the sugar is moistened. Bring to a boil over high heat, stirring to dissolve the sugar. Stop stirring and skim the surface of the syrup to remove any impurities. Continue to cook, without stirring, occasionally washing down the sides of the pan using a wet pastry brush, to 310°F/154°C.

3. Add the honey and bring once more to 310°F/154°C.

4. Meanwhile, whip the egg whites and the remaining ½ oz/14 g sugar to soft peaks.

5. With the mixer on medium speed, pour the hot sugar syrup into the egg whites in a fine stream, beating until fully incorporated. Continue to whip until lighter in color, about 4 minutes; the meringue should still be warm.

6. Warm the vanilla bean seeds, blanched almonds, hazelnuts, pistachios, dried fruit, and sliced almonds together in a low oven. Fold into the meringue.

7. Transfer the nougat onto an oiled sheet of parchment paper and roll out to ¼ in/6 mm thick. Allow to cool completely.

8. Cut the slab into strips ¾ in/2 cm wide. Cut the strips into 1-in/3-cm pieces. Stand the pieces of nougat on end (that is, on one short end). Brush the top edge of each one with melted cocoa butter to seal it. Dip only to the upper edge in tempered dark chocolate, so that the top surface is uncoated nougat.

Note   For a different finish, the slab of nougat can be coated on both sides with tempered dark chocolate and then cut into pieces.

CHAPTER 19

Décor

DÉCOR IS THE FINISHING TOUCH GIVEN TO ANY PASTRY OR CAKE. THE PASTRY CHEF EMPLOYS A VARIETY OF TECHNIQUES AND MATERIALS TO CRAFT A LOOK THAT NOT ONLY DISPLAYS CREATIVITY AND SKILL BUT ALSO SETS HIS OR HER PASTRIES, CAKES, AND OTHER DESSERTS APART.

Buttercream for Décor

Makes 1 lb 10 oz/737 g

VEGETABLE SHORTENING	8 oz	227 g
SALT	1 tsp	5 g
VANILLA EXTRACT	1 tsp	5 mL
WATER	3 fl oz	90 mL
CONFECTIONERS' SUGAR	2 lb	907 g

1. Combine the shortening, salt, vanilla, and 2 fl oz/60 mL of the water in the bowl of an electric mixer and blend together using the paddle attachment on low speed.

2. Add the confectioners' sugar and the remaining 1 fl oz/30 mL water and mix until fully blended, scraping the side of the bowl as necessary.

PIPING A SHELL BORDER

1. Fit a pastry bag with a star tip. Holding the piping bag at a 45-degree angle, place the tip close to the surface of the cake.

2. Squeeze the bag, allowing the icing to fan forward in a rounded shape while lifting the tip slightly.

3. Lower the tip back to the surface while slowly relaxing the pressure on the bag. Stop squeezing the bag and pull the tip away from the rounded head of the shell, keeping the tip on the surface of the cake to form the "tail" of the shell.

4. To form the next shell, place the star tip at the end of the first shell and repeat.

Using a Pastry Bag and Coupler

Buttercream or icing décor work requires many different and specialized pastry tips. When working with many different tips or colors of buttercream or icing, it is most efficient to use a coupler with the pastry bag. A coupler is a two-piece attachment that allows piping tips to be easily interchanged without having to empty the bag.

Piping Borders and Flowers

The technique for piping buttercream is similar to that for piping spritz cookies. The pastry bag is placed in the starting position, pressure is applied to pipe out the buttercream, and then the pressure is released just before the bag is lifted away, leaving the finished décor. By combining different tips and different motions—for example, by moving the tip in an up-and-down, circular, or back-and-forth motion—you can create many different patterns and effects.

PIPING A BUTTERCREAM LEAF

1. Fit a piping bag with a leaf tip.

2. Place the tip close to the surface and pipe out icing to form a base for the leaf.

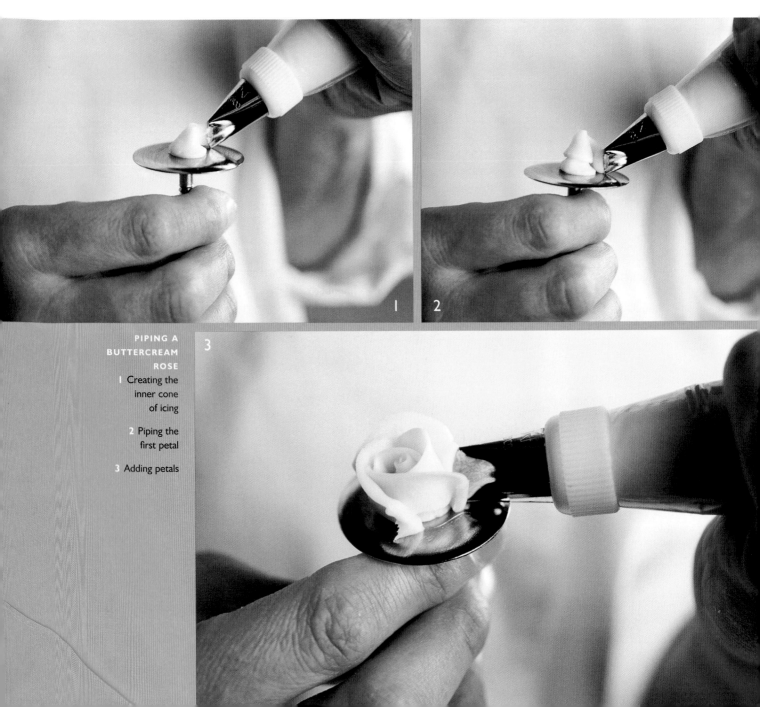

PIPING A
BUTTERCREAM
ROSE
1 Creating the
inner cone
of icing

2 Piping the
first petal

3 Adding petals

3. Relaxing the pressure on the piping bag, pull the tip up and away from the leaf base to form the rest of the leaf. Then stop exerting pressure on the bag as you pull the tip away to form the tip of the leaf.

PIPING A BUTTERCREAM ROSE

1. Fit a piping bag with a rose tip. Attach a small square of parchment paper to the top of a rose nail with a small dot of icing to make it easier to remove the rose once the icing has set. Hold the piping bag in your dominant hand and the rose nail in the other. Hold the bag so that the opening in the piping tip is vertical and the wider end is at the bottom.

2. The rose will be built on a cone of icing. To make the cone, place the wide end of the piping tip on the surface of the nail, with the narrower end angled slightly inward. Squeeze the bag while turning the nail clockwise, keeping the piping bag and tip in the same position.

3. To form the first inner petal of the rose, place the wide end of the tip on the cone of icing, with the narrower end angled slightly inward. Squeeze the piping bag while pulling it away from the cone, creating a ribbon of icing; at the same time, turn the rose nail counterclockwise, wrapping the ribbon of icing up and around the inner cone, ending by overlapping the point at which you began piping.

4. To form the first row of three petals, place the wide end of the piping tip near the base of the inner petal, with the narrow end pointing straight up. Position the first petal over the opening of the inner petal: Pipe a ribbon of icing around and down, turning the nail counterclockwise one-third of a turn at the same time. Then form the next two petals following the same procedure, beginning each petal near the center of the previous one.

5. For a larger rose, keep adding rows of petals in the same manner, increasing the number in each row and always adding an odd number of petals to keep the rose from looking square or boxy.

6. Once the icing is set, remove the rose from the nail. Use a small metal spatula to remove the rose from the paper and place it as desired.

PIPING CHOCOLATE FILIGREES AND WRITING

1. Make a parchment cone and fill it no more than halfway with piping chocolate. Fold over the top and cut a tiny hole in the tip of the cone.

2. Touch the tip of the cone to the surface on which you are piping and, exerting even pressure, pull the cone up and away from the surface to create a string of chocolate. Keeping the piped string of chocolate constant and even, move the parchment cone slowly and evenly to control the way in which the string falls onto the surface. To create small loops in the filigree or writing, for example, pause at the top of the piped element and allow the string to fall in a small loop.

3. To end a motif or word, touch the tip of the parchment cone back to the surface.

Making a Parchment Piping Cone

Preparing and using a parchment piping cone is an important part of décor work. To make a parchment cone, it is easiest to use a precut sheet of parchment paper (16 by 24 in/41 by 61 cm). Otherwise, cut a sheet of parchment paper this size from a roll of parchment paper. Place the parchment sheet on a flat surface with the length running parallel to the edge of the work surface. Take the lower left-hand corner and bring it up so that the point of the corner is adjacent to and level with the upper right-hand corner; it should look like two peaks of identical height. Firmly crease the fold. Insert a long, sharp knife (preferably not a serrated slicer) into the folded paper with the edge of the blade toward the creased edge and carefully cut the paper in half at the crease, using a single smooth stroke. The cut edge of each sheet will form the point of each piping cone, so it must be sharp and exact. A clean cut, not possible when tearing the paper or cutting it with scissors, enables piped icings or glazes to fall in a clean, straight line. The cone will also last longer because the clean edge will not absorb moisture as quickly as a ragged one would.

A small piping cone permits closer and tighter control, necessary for the fine work of piping letters, borders, and individual piped designs. Cut the parchment paper into quarters and use the four rectangles (8 by 12 in/20 by 30 cm) to make smaller cones as desired.

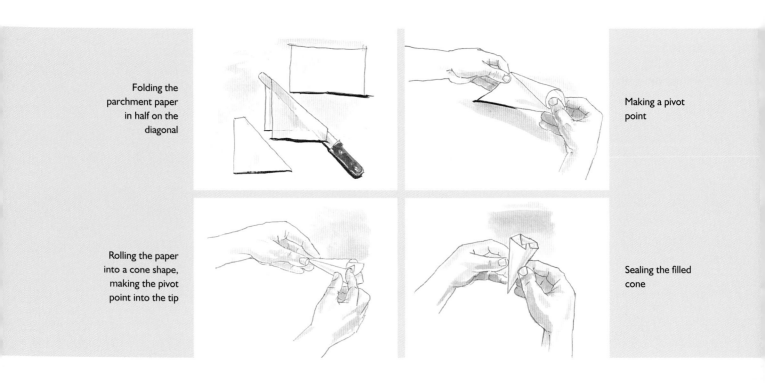

Folding the parchment paper in half on the diagonal

Making a pivot point

Rolling the paper into a cone shape, making the pivot point into the tip

Sealing the filled cone

Piping Tempered Chocolate

Using tempered chocolate, which will harden, rather than melted chocolate for piping enables the confectioner or pastry chef to pipe designs onto parchment paper, allow them to set firm, and then remove them from the paper and place them as desired on finished products for ornamentation and garnish. Because the piped details will become rigid once set, they can be made ahead and stored for later use. In addition, tempered chocolate designs can be used for numerous décor effects, as they do not have to lay flat. When piping tempered chocolate, use a small parchment cone because the chocolate can easily harden in the cone if the environment is cool.

MAKING CHOCOLATE TRIANGLES
(SPREAD-AND-CUT METHOD)

1. Pour tempered chocolate onto a sheet of parchment paper. With an offset spatula, spread the chocolate into a thin, even layer. Allow the chocolate to set slightly.

2. Run a cake comb lengthwise through the chocolate in a wave pattern, slightly overlapping each pass so that there are no uncombed areas of chocolate. Try to keep the thickness of the chocolate even throughout.

1 Combing the chocolate

2 Cutting triangles when the chocolate is almost set

3. Allow the chocolate to set until it becomes fudgy. It should be soft enough that you can draw a knife point through it without cracking but set enough so that the cut does not refill with chocolate.

4. Using a ruler and the point of a paring knife, cut the chocolate into triangles with 1¾-in/4-cm sides and 4-in/10-cm base: First, cut the sheet of chocolate lengthwise into strips 4 in/10 cm wide. Then mark the edges of each strip at intervals of 1¾ in/4 cm. Using the ruler, connect the marks on the diagonal to make triangles.

5. Slide the sheet of chocolate onto the back of a sheet pan. Place another sheet of parchment paper on top of the chocolate. Place a second sheet pan, bottom side down, on top of the parchment paper. Grasp both sheet pans firmly and flip the sheet pan sandwich over. Remove what is now the top sheet pan. The parchment paper on which you spread the chocolate is now facing up. Carefully peel this parchment paper away from the chocolate triangles, starting at one corner. Removing the parchment paper at this point allows the chocolate to set completely without curling.

Notes   For a very shiny finished surface, spread the chocolate onto a sheet of acetate rather than parchment paper. When cutting the partially set chocolate into triangles, cut completely through the acetate. Leave the chocolate triangles on the acetate until time for service so that the surface does not become marred. Do not touch the shiny surface of the chocolate, as it will pick up fingerprints readily.

Any shapes can be cut out of spread chocolate, with or without combing it first. You can use cutters or templates made out of stiff plastic or paper.

If desired, stripe the chocolate in the same manner as for Striped Chocolate Cigarettes (Below).

Striped Chocolate Triangles
Makes 32 triangles

WHITE CHOCOLATE, tempered	6 oz	170 g
DARK CHOCOLATE, tempered	10 oz	284 g

1. Cut two strips of acetate 6 by 18 in/15 by 46 cm.

2. Spread the white chocolate ¹⁄₁₆ in/1.5 mm thick over one of the strips. Using the smallest side of a square-toothed cake comb, comb through the white chocolate to create a zigzag pattern. Allow the chocolate to set slightly.

3. Spread the dark chocolate thinly and evenly over the white chocolate. Transfer the acetate strip to a cutting board and allow the chocolate to set for 10 seconds.

4. Place the other acetate strip on top of the dark chocolate. Cut the strip lengthwise in half to make two strips 3 in/8 cm wide. Cut triangles with a base 1 in/3 cm wide out of each strip.

5. Place another cutting board on top of the triangles to keep them flat. Allow the triangles to set for a minimum of 3 hours. Remove the acetate from the triangles when you are ready to use them.

Tempered Chocolate Stencils and Cutouts

Stencils and cutouts have many applications. They can be used as a garnish for a pastry, cake, or plated dessert, as the base for piped confections, or, in décor work, as either the focal point or a component of a larger display piece.

Stencils and cutouts may be made of white, milk, or dark chocolate. Generally, the chocolate should be spread thin, but the exact thinness will depend on the intended use.

MARBLEIZED CHOCOLATE PLAQUES

1. Drizzle tempered white chocolate, milk chocolate, and dark chocolate onto a sheet of acetate, overlapping the different colors of chocolate. With a long offset spatula, spread the chocolates into thin, even layers, allowing them to merge and flow together. Do not mix the chocolates too vigorously, or the finished plaques will look muddy instead of attractively marbled.

2. Allow the chocolate to set until it becomes fudgy. It should be soft enough that you can draw a knife point through it without cracking but set enough so that the cut does not refill with chocolate.

3. Using a ruler and the point of a paring knife, cut the chocolate into rectangles 2 by 2¾ in/5 by 7 cm: First, cut the sheet of chocolate lengthwise into strips 2¾ in/7 cm wide. Then mark the edges of the strips at intervals of 2 in/5 cm. Using the ruler, connect the marks from top to bottom.

4. Slide the sheet of chocolate onto the back of a sheet pan. Place another sheet of parchment paper on top of the chocolate. Place a second sheet pan, bottom side down, on top of the parchment paper. Grasp both sheet pans firmly and flip the sheet pan sandwich over. Leave the sheet pans stacked until the chocolate is completely set. Leave the chocolate rectangles on the acetate until you are ready to use them.

CHOCOLATE CIGARETTES

1. Drizzle a thin line of tempered chocolate onto a marble surface, parallel to the edge of the marble. Using an offset spatula, spread the chocolate in a thin, even layer. Let the chocolate set slightly.

2. When the chocolate is somewhat set, place a Plexiglas strip the width of the desired finished length of the cigarettes on top of the chocolate and evenly trim the edges of the chocolate strip with a bench scraper or putty knife.

3. With the bench scraper or putty knife, begin scraping cigarettes from one short end of the chocolate strip with a quick, abrupt motion; it should feel as though you are trying to scrape off a thin layer of marble. If the chocolate is not set enough, the cigarettes will not curl properly; and if the chocolate has set too much, the cigarettes will crack and break. Chocolate that is just slightly too cool can be warmed with the palm of your hand.

4. To trim the cigarettes, warm a sharp knife. Place the blade at the desired point and allow the heat of the knife to melt the chocolate.

Making dark chocolate cigarettes

MAKING MINI-CIGARETTES

1. Spread tempered chocolate on a marble surface no wider that the width of the tool you will be using to form the cigarettes, or, when the chocolate is somewhat set, use the tip of a paring knife to score the chocolate into narrow strips. Let the chocolate set briefly.

2. Using the same motion as described above, scrape the chocolate into mini-cigarettes. It is important to scrape the chocolate with a motion directly parallel to the length of the strip; otherwise, the mini-cigarettes will curl into each other and be difficult to separate.

STRIPED CHOCOLATE CIGARETTES

1. Drizzle a small amount of tempered white chocolate onto a marble surface. With an offset spatula, spread the chocolate in a strip parallel to the edge of the marble. Allow the chocolate to set until thick in consistency.

2. Draw a square-toothed cake comb firmly through the chocolate, scraping all the way down to the marble to make thin lines of chocolate. Try to keep the lines of chocolate straight and parallel to the edge of the marble.

3. Working quickly, drizzle dark chocolate over the white chocolate and spread it thinly and evenly with an offset spatula. The dark chocolate should fill the channels left in the white chocolate by the comb; spread it thin enough so that the white chocolate shows through the dark chocolate.

MAKING STRIPED WHITE AND DARK CHOCOLATE FOR DÉCOR Backing striped white chocolate with dark chocolate

4. When the chocolate is no longer tacky but still pliable and somewhat soft, place a Plexiglas strip the width of the desired finished length of the cigarettes on top of the chocolate and evenly trim the edges of the chocolate strip with a bench scraper or putty knife.

5. With the bench scraper or putty knife, begin scraping cigarettes from one short end of the chocolate strip with a quick, scraping motion; it should feel as though you are trying to scrape off a thin layer of marble. If the chocolate is too warm, the cigarettes will not curl properly; and if the chocolate is too cool, the cigarettes will crack and break. Chocolate that is just slightly too cool can be warmed with the palm of your hand.

6. To trim the cigarettes, warm a sharp knife. Place the blade at the desired point and allow the heat of the knife to melt the chocolate.

Variation   **Marbled Cigarettes**   Marble the chocolate as for Marbleized Chocolate Plaques, then shape as for Chocolate Cigarettes.

CHOCOLATE FANS

1. Fill a parchment piping cone with tempered chocolate. Pipe four or five quarter-size rounds of chocolate onto a parchment-lined sheet pan, spacing the rounds about 4 in/10 cm apart.

2. With the back of a spoon, spread chocolate across the parchment paper in an arc away from one round of chocolate. Repeat the motion four more times, beginning each arc at approximately the same point and making each arc shorter than the one before it, slightly overlapping the arcs. This motion creates a "fan" of chocolate with two ridges in it. Do not make the chocolate too thin or the fan will break. The base of the fan should be thicker than the top edges. Repeat with the remaining rounds of chocolate. Allow the chocolate to set completely.

3. The fans can be used as they are, or the top edges can be neatened with a warmed round metal cutter.

CHOCOLATE BANDS

1. Place a strip of acetate the desired width of the chocolate band on a marble surface or piece of parchment paper. Drizzle tempered chocolate onto the acetate. With an offset spatula, spread the chocolate thinly and evenly over the entire surface of the acetate; some of the chocolate should go over the long sides of the acetate.

2. Allow the chocolate to set slightly, so that the acetate can be picked up without the chocolate running. The chocolate should still be fluid enough to adhere to the surface or item where it is applied.

3. Pull up a corner of the acetate, then carefully lift up the acetate strip and apply the chocolate band to the desired surface. Place the band carefully, starting with one end; once it touches the surface, it cannot be moved without damaging the chocolate.

4. Peel away ½ in/1 cm of the acetate from the end you first attached, and overlap the other end of the band so that the chocolate adheres to itself. While the chocolate is still slightly tacky, use scissors to trim the acetate and the chocolate where it overlaps.

5. To preserve its shiny finish, leave the acetate on the chocolate until time for service.

CHOCOLATE SHAVINGS

1. Brace a large block of tempered chocolate against the near edge of a parchment-lined sheet pan.

2. Hold a sharp chef's knife so that the flat of the blade is straight up and down and the tip of the blade is pointing to your left. Using a smooth scraping motion, pull the blade across the surface of the chocolate, without digging the blade into the chocolate. To create small shavings, use a short scraping motion; for larger shavings, use a longer motion.

3. Use an offset spatula to move the shavings. Do not pick up the shavings with your hands or they will melt.

CHOCOLATE RUFFLES

1. Place a sheet pan in a low-temperature oven until it is just warm. Have ready a bowl of melted but not tempered chocolate that is also warm (just above body temperature). The chocolate and the sheet pan should be approximately the same temperature.

2. Pour the chocolate onto the back of the sheet pan and spread it thinly and evenly with an offset spatula, covering the back of the pan completely.

3. Place the sheet pan in the freezer until the chocolate is set but still malleable. (If the chocolate becomes too hard, remove the pan from the freezer and allow it to sit at room temperature until the chocolate is malleable.)

4. Brace the sheet pan against a wall or the backsplash of a counter. Using a bench scraper or putty knife, begin scraping the chocolate off the sheet pan in long strips. As you scrape, use your other hand to gather one of the long edges of the chocolate strip to create a ruffle.

5. Store the ruffles in a cool, dry place.

Spraying Chocolate

Makes 3 lb/1.36 kg

DARK CHOCOLATE, melted	2 lb	907 g
COCOA BUTTER, melted	1 lb	454 g

1. Combine the chocolate and cocoa butter and warm to 120°F/49°C over a hot water bath. Allow the mixture to cool to approximately 90°F/32°C, stirring frequently.

2. Strain the mixture through cheesecloth. Pour into a warmed spray gun canister. Spray onto finished chocolate pieces, or use to finish chocolates and desserts or to decorate dessert plates.

Note   A velvety texture can be achieved by placing the pieces to be sprayed in the freezer for 30 to 45 minutes before spraying.

Royal Icing

Makes 1 lb 3 oz/539 g

EGG WHITES	3 oz	85 g
CREAM OF TARTAR	1/8 tsp	0.50 g
CONFECTIONERS' SUGAR, sifted	1 lb	454 g

1. Place the egg whites in a clean, grease-free mixer bowl and mix on low speed with the wire whisk attachment just until the whites begin to break up.

2. Add the cream of tartar and continue mixing on low speed until the whites become frothy.

3. Gradually add the confectioners' sugar and continue to mix until the icing holds a peak and is dull in appearance.

4. Transfer to a glass container and press a moist towel directly on the surface of the icing. Store, covered tightly with plastic wrap, under refrigeration.

Note   The amount of egg whites used to make royal icing can be increased or decreased depending on the desired consistency.

Working with Royal Icing

Royal icing décor is typically piped on parchment or plastic sheets, allowed to dry, and stored in airtight containers for later use. Royal icing is easily colored using food coloring or by airbrushing it. Generally, royal icing is not intended to be consumed, at least in any measurable quantity, as it has no flavor and is only sweet.

Care must be used in handling royal icing. When exposed to air, the icing dries quickly, becoming hard and brittle. If any of the dried icing gets incorporated into the icing being used for décor work, the hardened particles will block the piping tip. For this reason, it is always good practice to keep the sides of the container holding the icing clean. Remove any dried particles of icing from the sides of the container promptly with a clean damp cloth before they can fall back into the icing. While you work, keep a clean, damp paper towel directly on the surface of the icing in the container to prevent a crust form forming.

Store royal icing under refrigeration with a piece of plastic wrap or a dampened paper towel placed directly on the surface. Cover the bowl or container tightly with plastic wrap to keep it airtight.

For piping royal icing, a small parchment cone may be used, but for intricate work, a very fine round writing pastry tip is usually best. The tip facilitates the production of a perfectly formed bead of icing, which will, in turn, enhance the quality of the décor.

Royal icing is often used to execute elaborate designs that are then dried and fitted or otherwise secured onto cakes and décor pieces. Usually a template or pattern is used to make this type of décor. Place the template or pattern under a piece of acetate or other food-safe plastic and secure it with tape or paper clips so it does not slip as you pipe the figure by tracing the template. When making large or very intricate patterns, it is usually necessary to pipe more than one layer of royal icing. Pay close attention to any connecting points or joints to ensure the finished piece will be strong enough to be lifted from the plastic and secured to the finished cake or other object. As you are planning the pattern of loops, keep in mind that loops that cross, intersect, or lie on top of one another result in greater stability of the sugar work. Using a template ensures consistent results, and the technique is especially useful when the same pattern is to be repeated on a cake or décor piece.

Another technique often used with royal icing is called flood work. To do flood work or to make a run-out, an outline of a pattern or motif is piped onto acetate and allowed to dry until firm. Then thinned royal icing is used to fill in the interior of the pattern. This icing should be thin enough to fill in the design easily, with little extra manipulation or spreading necessary, minimizing the chance that any lines or imprints will be left in the finished piece. A good way to test the consistency of royal icing for flood work is to have the icing in a container, spoon some out, and allow it to drip back into the container. The drips going back into the container should disappear without a trace at the count of ten.

ROYAL ICING
FLOOD WORK
Filling in an
outlined shape
with royal icing

FLOOD WORK AND RUN-OUTS WITH ROYAL ICING

1. Outline each shape with a thin line of piped royal icing. Allow the icing to dry.

2. Thin the remaining royal icing with water until a small amount dropped back into the bowl from the tip of a spoon flattens back into the surface in 10 seconds. Color the icing as desired.

3. Fit a piping bag with a No. 2 plain tip. Fill the bag halfway with the royal icing. To fill the outlines with icing, begin at the edges of each one and work toward the center. At the edge of the shape, hold the tip a short distance away from the piped outline and allow the icing to flow toward the outline, creating a rounded edge. Continue piping, allowing each successive pass of icing to flow into the previous one, creating a smooth surface.

5. Place the shapes under a heat lamp or other heat source to dry. The more quickly the icing dries, the shinier the finish.

STRING WORK WITH ROYAL ICING

1. Thin the royal icing until it is of a medium-thick consistency. Strain it through a double layer of cheesecloth.

2. Fit a pastry bag with a No. 0 or 00 plain tip. Fill the bag halfway with the royal icing. Test the consistency of the icing by piping a string. If the icing is too soft, it will sag and break under its weight; if the icing is too stiff, it will not fall into a smooth string. Adjust the consistency of the icing if necessary with confectioners' sugar, water, or additional egg whites.

3. Touch the tip of the pastry tip to the first attachment point, then pull the bag away while applying even pressure to it, allowing the string of icing to fall away from the tip. Do not move the tip downward; simply allow the icing to fall in a smooth curve. When the loop of icing is the desired length, touch the tip of the pastry tip to the next point to attach the string.

4. Repeat the process, using care to produce loops of the same length each time. As you are planning the pattern of loops, keep in mind that loops that cross, intersect, or lie on top of one another result in greater stability of the sugar work.

ROYAL ICING STRING WORK
Creating a string with royal icing

Marzipan for Modeling and Cake Covering

Makes 15 lb 2 oz/6.86 kg

ALMOND PASTE	7 lb	3.18 kg
CONFECTIONERS' SUGAR	7 lb	3.18 kg
FONDANT	2 lb	907 g
GLUCOSE SYRUP	1 lb	454 g
BRANDY	2 fl oz	60 mL

1. Blend together the almond paste and confectioners' sugar using the paddle attachment on low speed, about 2 minutes.

2. Add the fondant, glucose syrup, and brandy and mix just until the mixture is smooth.

3. Store in an airtight container under refrigeration.

Notes   You will need approximately 1 lb 4 oz/567 g marzipan to cover a 10-in/25-cm cake.

The consistency of marzipan can be adjusted as necessary. Molded marzipan fruits and similar items require a firmer consistency so they hold their shape. Knead additional confectioners' sugar into the marzipan by hand until the desired consistency is achieved.

Overworked marzipan becomes excessively oily and loses its characteristic smooth, clay-like texture. If this happens, knead in a small measure of simple syrup. This will rebind the oils and solids. Additional confectioners' sugar may be added to achieve the original consistency again as well.

Marzipan

Marzipan is a paste made of ground almonds and sugar. The best-quality marzipan, made with fresh nuts and the proper proportion of sugar, has a fresh natural flavor. Marzipan can be used as a center (to be enrobed in chocolate) or as a confection by itself.

There are a number of methods for making marzipan, but for the small-scale confectioner, the classic French method is the most practical. The nuts are coarsely ground, and a syrup of sugar, water, and glucose is boiled to the appropriate temperature. The cooked syrup is poured over the nuts and they are spread on a lightly oiled marble surface to cool. Once cooled, the sugar-coated nuts are ground to a paste consistency. The ratio of almonds to sugar varies depending on the intended use of the finished product, as does the temperature to which the syrup is cooked—the hotter the syrup, the firmer the marzipan. For confectionery work, the syrup is usually cooked to 257°F/125°C to make a firm marzipan. The syrup for a pâtisserie marzipan, which is used for fine décor work, is cooked only to 246°F/119°C, resulting in a softer marzipan. Marzipan should be ground in a mélangeur, a special machine with adjustable marble rollers. The mélangeur produces the smoothest possible finished product. However, if a mélangeur is unavailable, a food processor is acceptable.

When marzipan is ground without sufficient moisture, it will separate and appear oily. If this occurs, add a small amount of liquid, either a spirit or syrup, to the marzipan to return it to the proper consistency. The liquid enables the marzipan to reabsorb the oil that has separated out. It may also be necessary to add a small amount of confectioners' sugar.

Marzipan should be firm but not dry or brittle. To fix marzipan that is too hard or dry, massage in a few drops of liquor or glucose. To fix marzipan that is too brittle, for each kilogram of marzipan, massage in a piece of fondant approximately the size of a walnut. If the marzipan is so soft that it sticks to your hands or the work surface, massage in confectioners' sugar or a mixture of equal parts powdered milk and cornstarch.

You can replace from 25 to 50 percent of the almonds in marzipan with other nuts, such as hazelnuts or pistachios.

MARZIPAN FLOWER CUTOUTS

1. On a surface dusted with confectioners' sugar, roll a piece of marzipan with a small rolling pin to between ¹⁄₁₆ and ⅛ in/1.5 and 3 mm thick.

2. With a small flower cutter, cut out flower shapes from the marzipan. With the small end of a marzipan ball tool, press the center of each flower into a piece of urethane foam to create an indentation in the center of the flower.

3. To make centers for the flowers, shape small pieces of marzipan into tiny balls and place one in the indentation in each flower. Position the centers while the marzipan is still soft so that they will stay in place.

4. To create layered flowers, cut flower shapes with different sizes of cutters and different colors of marzipan. Stack the shapes and press them into the foam at the same time.

MAKING A MARZIPAN ROSE

1. Form a small piece of marzipan into a cylinder about 1½ in/4 cm long and ½ in/ 1 cm in diameter. Make an indentation in the cylinder approximately two-thirds of the way down the cylinder. Taper the cylinder to a point. Stand this cone on your work surface, pressing gently so that the bottom adheres to the surface.

2. Form a piece of marzipan into a rope approximately ½ in/1 cm in diameter. Cut it into four pieces and roll them into small balls about ½ in/1 cm in diameter.

3. Place the balls on a marble surface, about 2 in/5 cm away from the front edge of the marble. Using a plastic bowl scraper, flatten the front edge of each ball with three short strokes. Use a smooth motion, pushing down on the marzipan and pulling the scraper toward you in one motion. The front edge of the marzipan petals should be very thin but the back edge should remain quite thick. (The difference in thickness will allow you to form a delicate-looking rose that will still support its own weight.)

4. Holding the blade of a clean, sharp slicer flat against the marble, cut each petal off the marble. Make a small cut in the center of the thick edge of each petal, then overlap the resulting two sections and press them together to form a cupped shape.

5. To form the first inner petal of the flower, place one petal on the prepared marzipan cone, with the thin edge at the top and the thick edge at the indentation in the cone. Hold the petal tightly against the cone and wrap it all the way around the cone so that the edges overlap. The highest point of the petal should be just above the tip of the cone. There should be a tiny hole at the top of the wrapped petal, but the cone should no longer be visible. Use your fingers to gently turn back a small section of the top edge of the petal. Gently squeeze the bottom of the petal into the indentation in the cone.

6. Use the remaining three petals to form the first layer of rose petals. Place one of these petals on the rose, with its center in line with the edge of the first petal. The top of this petal and the subsequent ones should be even with or just slightly above the top of the inner petal. Press the bottom left side of the petal into the rose, leaving the right side open.

7. Position the other two petals in the same fashion, so that their centers line up with the previous petal's left edge, and gently curl the thin right edge of each petal back with your finger. The third petal's left edge should nestle inside the first petal's open right side. Gently press all the petals' bottom edges together and squeeze the bottom of the rose into the indentation in the cone, forming a rounded bottom to the rose.

8. Make another slightly thicker snake out of marzipan and cut it into five pieces. Form these into balls and then petals in the same fashion as above.

9. Use these five petals to form the second layer of rose petals. Place them on the rose in the same fashion, but with each petal overlapping the previous one by only about one-third. The tops of these petals should also be even with or just slightly above those of the previous petals. Gently curl each side of these five petals back and create a crease or point in the middle of the petal.

10. If desired, add another layer of seven petals to the rose.

11. Gently squeeze the bottom of the rose to create a rounded base. Cut the extra marzipan away from the base. Allow the rose to dry at room temperature.

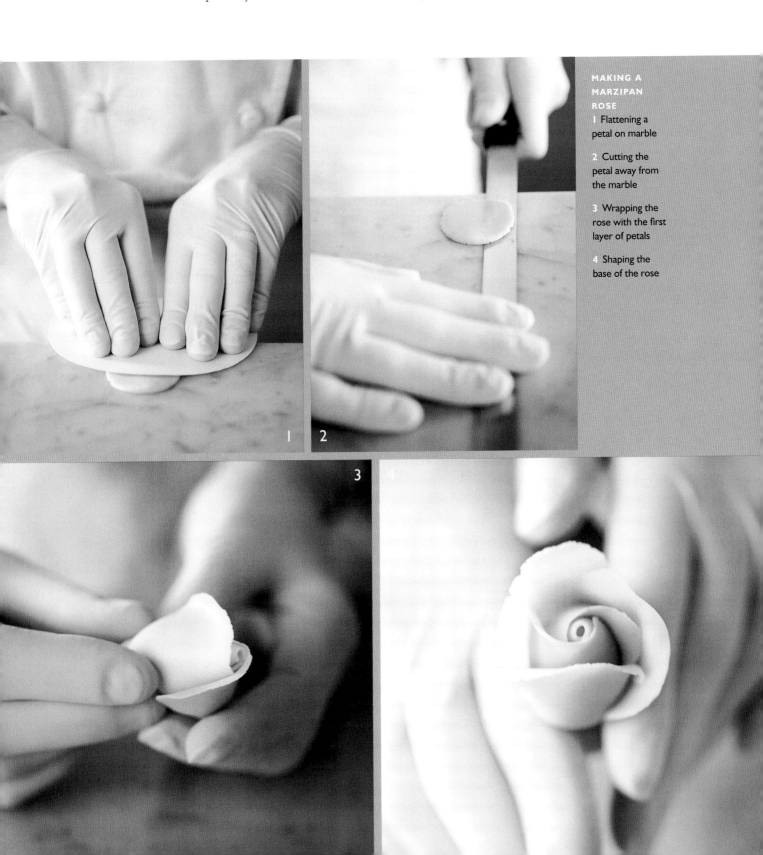

MAKING A MARZIPAN ROSE

1 Flattening a petal on marble

2 Cutting the petal away from the marble

3 Wrapping the rose with the first layer of petals

4 Shaping the base of the rose

1. Dust a work surface with confectioners' sugar. Roll a piece of marzipan to 1/16 in/1.5 mm thick using a small rolling pin.

2. Using a cutter or a cardboard template, cut a circle, oval, or other desired shape out of the marzipan.

3. Lay the plaque on a flat surface and, using your fingers and the palm of your hand, buff and smooth the cut edges and the top surface of the plaque, being careful not to crack or break the marzipan.

4. Place the plaque on a parchment-lined sheet pan and allow to dry at room temperature until it is completely hard. Use an emery board or very fine sandpaper to smooth any rough edges.

5. Pipe lettering on the plaque or decorate as desired.

Modeling Chocolate
Makes 10 oz/284 g

CORN SYRUP, warm	12 oz	340 g
DARK CHOCOLATE, melted and still warm	3 lb	1.36 kg

1. Add the warm corn syrup to the warm chocolate and blend into a smooth paste, then knead lightly.

2. Spread the chocolate mixture on a tray to cool, then refrigerate for at least 1 hour.

3. Store the modeling chocolate well wrapped at room temperature.

4. To use the modeling chocolate, knead it until smooth and pliable, using a light dusting of sifted cocoa powder if necessary to prevent sticking. Be careful not to overwork the chocolate or it will become oily.

White Modeling Chocolate

Makes 4 lb 6 oz/1.98 kg

COCOA BUTTER, melted	14 oz	397 g
CONFECTIONERS' SUGAR	2 lb 3 oz	992 g
GUM TRAGACANTH	½ oz	14 g
CORN SYRUP	1 lb 5 oz	595 g

1. Combine all the ingredients and mix gently until evenly blended. Roll and fold the mixture until workable. Spread the chocolate on a tray to cool, cover, and then refrigerate for at least 1 hour.

2. Store the modeling chocolate well wrapped at room temperature.

3. To use the modeling chocolate, knead it until smooth and pliable, using a light dusting of sifted cocoa powder if necessary to prevent sticking. Be careful not to overwork the chocolate or it will become oily.

Mixing White Modeling Chocolate

Poured Sugar

Makes 8 lb/3.63 kg

SUGAR	5 lb	2.27 kg
WATER	32 fl oz	960 mL
GLUCOSE SYRUP	1 lb 1½ oz	496 g

1. Combine the sugar and water in a copper or heavy-bottomed pot and bring to a boil, stirring to dissolve the sugar. Wash down the sides of the pan with a wet pastry brush to remove any sugar crystals.

2. Once the mixture has come to a boil, stop stirring. Add the glucose syrup and cook, continuing to wash down the sides of the pot as necessary, until the syrup comes to the proper temperature (see notes below).

3. Shock the pot in a bowl of cold water. Allow the surface bubbles to dissipate, then pour the syrup into a prepared frame or mold.

Notes   Final cooking temperatures of the syrup will range from 309°F/154°C to 320°F/160°C, depending on the size of the piece as well as the color desired.

When the sugar reaches 266°F/130°C, to control crystallization, add 1 drop of an acid for every 2 lb/907 g of sugar syrup, along with any desired color or whitening.

For pure white sugar, add whitening and cook the sugar syrup to 295°F/146°C.

Various marbleized effects can be achieved by swirling a small amount of food coloring into the sugar syrup before pouring it into the frame or mold.

Rock Sugar

Makes 1 lb 8 oz/680 g

SUGAR	1 lb	454 g
WATER, cold	8 fl oz	240 mL
ROYAL ICING (page 770)	1 oz	28 g

1. Combine the sugar and water in a heavy-bottomed saucepan and bring to a boil, stirring to dissolve the sugar. Wash down the sides of the pan with a wet pastry brush to remove any sugar crystals. Once the mixture comes to a boil, stop stirring and cook, continuing to wash down the sides of the pan as necessary, until the syrup reaches 298°F/148°C.

2. Remove from the heat and whip in the royal icing. The syrup will rise and then collapse.

3. Return to the heat and let it rise again. Pour the sugar syrup into an oiled, foil-lined mold and let cool.

4. Break the sugar into pieces. Store in an airtight container.

Note   To color rock sugar, either add the color when the syrup reaches 266°F/130°C or apply color with an airbrush when the sugar is cool.

Spun Sugar Ball

Makes 1 lb 8½ oz/695 g

SUGAR	1 lb	454 g
WATER	5 fl oz	150 mL
CORN SYRUP	3½ oz	99 g

1. Set up two metal bars 8 in/20 cm apart from each other and resting on containers so they are above the work surface. Combine the sugar and water in a heavy-bottomed saucepan and stir to ensure all the sugar is moistened. Bring to a boil over high heat, stirring frequently to dissolve the sugar.

2. When the mixture has come to a boil, add the corn syrup and cook, occasionally washing down the sides of the pan with a wet pastry brush, until the syrup reaches 293°F/145°C.

3. Shock the pan in an ice bath for 10 seconds. Allow the sugar syrup to cool undisturbed at room temperature until it reaches the consistency of honey.

4. Use a fork to drizzle the sugar quickly back and forth over the metal bars until you've formed a netting of sugar.

5. Gather the sugar into a ball.

Note   For caramel-colored spun sugar, cook the sugar until it reaches a light golden brown.

Making Spun Sugar

Makes 1 lb 3 oz/539 g

SUGAR	1 lb	454 g
WATER	5 fl oz	150 mL
CORN SYRUP	3½ oz	99 g

1. Combine the sugar and water in a heavy-bottomed saucepan and stir to ensure all the sugar is moistened. Bring to a boil over high heat, stirring frequently to dissolve the sugar. Wash down the sides of the pan with a wet pastry brush to remove any sugar crystals. When the mixture has come to a boil, stop stirring and skim the surface to remove any scum that has formed.

2. Add the corn syrup and cook, occasionally washing down the sides of the pan with a wet pastry brush, until the syrup reaches 293°F/145°C.

3. Shock the pan in an ice bath for 10 seconds. Allow the sugar to cool undisturbed at room temperature until it reaches the consistency of honey.

4. Lightly oil a foil-covered template and set it on a small measuring cup, so that it is raised above the surface of the table, on a silicone baking mat.

FROM LEFT TO RIGHT:
Drizzling sugar syrup over a template

Cutting away the excess sugar

5. With a fork, gently drizzle the sugar back and forth in one direction over the template, allowing the sugar to fall over the sides. Then drizzle more sugar back and forth across the first strands, creating a grid of sugar strands on the template.

6. Cut away the excess sugar that has fallen over the sides of the template with scissors. Remove the spun sugar from the template and warm it briefly under a heat lamp until it is pliable enough to bend or curve as desired.

Note   Isomalt may be substituted for the corn syrup to ensure that the sugar syrup remains clear.

Pulled and Blown Sugar
Makes 4 lb 8 oz/2.04 kg

LIGHT CORN SYRUP	1 lb 14 oz	851 g
SUGAR	2 lb	907 g
GLUCOSE SYRUP	7 oz	198 g
TARTARIC ACID	20 drops	20 drops

1. Combine the corn syrup and sugar in a heavy-bottomed pot and bring to a boil over high heat, stirring constantly to dissolve the sugar. Wash down the sides of the pot with a wet pastry brush to remove any sugar crystals.

2. When the mixture has come to a boil, stop stirring and add the glucose syrup and tartaric acid. Cook, continuing to wash down the sides of the pot, until the mixture comes to the proper temperature.

3. Pour the sugar syrup onto a lightly oiled marble slab.

Notes   Add the acid and any color at 266°F/130°C and cook to 315°F/157°C.

Alternatively, ½ tsp/2 g of cream of tartar may be substituted for the tartaric acid, but it must be fresh for optimum strength.

The final cooking temperature as well as the amount of acid used may be adjusted according to one's skill level as well as the weather conditions, such as high humidity and warm days.

FROM LEFT TO RIGHT: Shaping a blown sugar strawberry

Cutting the strawberry off the pipe

BLOWN SUGAR STRAWBERRIES

1. Warm a piece of red sugar in the microwave until it is hot and pliable but not so hot that it is fluid; check it frequently to ensure that it does not become too hot in one place while it is still hard in another.

2. Place the sugar under a heat lamp. Knead a small amount of crystal sugar into it to create the look of strawberry seeds.

3. Make a "foot" of sugar on the pipe by wrapping a small piece of sugar around the tip of the pipe, so the sugar strawberry will adhere to the pipe. Knead and pull the remaining sugar with your hands until it is a consistent texture and temperature. With your open right hand, grasp the piece of sugar and then close your hand, forcing a round ball of sugar out through your closed thumb and forefinger. Cut this ball away from the main piece of sugar.

4. Push your finger down into the center of the ball of sugar, creating an indentation. Make sure the thickness of the sugar is the same all the way around the indentation; if it varies in thickness, the sugar is more likely to blow out in a thin spot.

5. Heat the foot of sugar on the sugar pump over a Sterno flame, then place the ball of sugar on the tip of the pipe, being sure to leave enough space inside the indentation above the end of the pipe so that air will be able to come out of the pipe. Squeeze and press the base of the sugar ball around the end of the pipe, attaching it to the sugar foot.

6. Hold the ball of sugar in one hand and squeeze the pump with the other until the ball of sugar expands. Stop pumping and shape the sugar into a strawberry with your hands; at the same time, mold a thick stem at the base of the strawberry that protrudes above the end of the pipe. Continue to alternately pump air into the strawberry and shape it until it is the shape and thickness desired. The thinner the walls of the strawberry, the shinier the sugar will be when it cools.

7. Cool the strawberry under a blow dryer. To cut the strawberry away from the pump, heat just the thick stem over the Sterno flame. Place the open blades of a pair of scissors around the stem and slowly and gently close them until the sugar cracks.

MAKING A PULLED SUGAR BLOSSOM

1. Warm a piece of white sugar in the microwave until it is hot and pliable but not so hot that it is fluid; check frequently to ensure that it does not become too hot in one place while it is still hard in another.

2. Place the sugar under a heat lamp. With both hands, grasp the sugar firmly at the opposite ends of the piece and pull your hands apart, pulling the sugar to form a thin edge. This thin edge is important because it is the thinness of the petals' edges that will give the flowers a delicate appearance.

3. Place the piece of sugar on the edge of a sugar workbox with the thin pulled edge protruding over the edge. With the index finger and thumb of your right hand, grasp the thin edge of sugar and pull it down. With the index finger and thumb of your left hand, pin the sugar directly above your right thumb. With a short, sharp movement, pull your right hand away while pinning hard with your left. This will create a tapered, rounded petal. Repeat the process until you have five matching petals.

4. To assemble the flower, heat the tapered end of one petal over a flame. Place it next to another petal, overlapping the edges. Repeat with the remaining petals, overlapping them evenly. Heat the last petal until it is pliable enough that its edge can be slipped under the edge of the first petal. Cool the flower with a blow dryer.

5. To make the stamen for the flower, warm a piece of light yellow or gold sugar in the microwave. Cut off a small piece of sugar with scissors. Pull the piece of sugar into a very thin strand. Working quickly, bring the ends of the strand together to create a large loop. Loop the strands twice more, and pin them together about ½ to ¾ in/1 to 2 cm below the tops of the loops. The sugar should still be warm enough so that the strands adhere to one another. Cut the loops open with scissors.

6. Place the blades of the scissors at the point where the strands are pinned together and use the scissors to gently break the sugar. Heat this pinned end in the Sterno flame and attach it to the center of the flower.

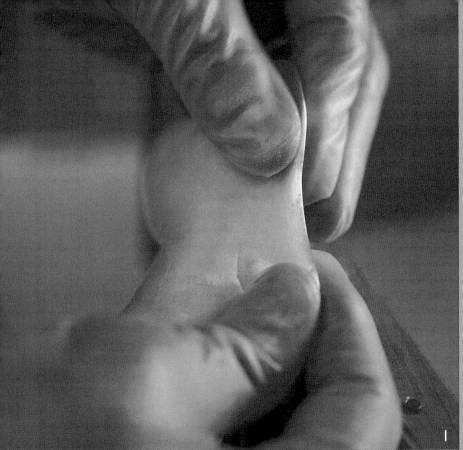

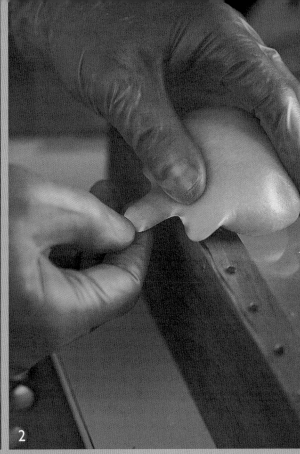

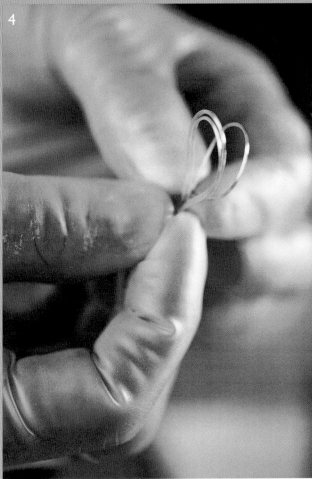

1 Pulling the sugar into a thin edge

2 Pulling the thin edge down and away from the sugar

3 Placing the petals on the flower

4 Pulling the flower stamen

1 Cutting the pulled sugar on an angle

2 Removing a leaf from the mold

3 Attaching the leaf to the sugar piece

1

2

3

MAKING PULLED SUGAR LEAVES

1. Warm a piece of light green sugar in the microwave until it is hot and pliable but not so hot that it is fluid; check frequently to ensure that it does not become too hot in one place while it is still hard in another.

2. Place the sugar under a heat lamp. With both hands, grasp the sugar firmly at the opposite ends of the piece and pull your hands apart, pulling the sugar to form a thin edge. This thin edge is important because it is the thinness of the leaves' edge that will give them a delicate appearance.

3. Place the piece of sugar on the edge of a sugar workbox with the thin pulled edge protruding over the edge. With the index finger and thumb of your left hand, grasp the thin edge of sugar and pull it down and away. Cut the sugar strip at an angle with scissors to create a leaf shape.

4. Immediately place the sugar piece into the bottom half of a silicone leaf mold and press down on it firmly with the top of the mold. Then remove the leaf from the mold and, while it is still warm, pin the thicker end of the leaf slightly. Curve the leaf slightly to make it look more realistic. Cool under a blow dryer. Repeat to make more leaves as needed.

5. To attach the leaves, heat the thicker end of each leaf over a flame. Press the heated end of the leaf to a base stem or petal and cool the joint with a blow dryer.

MAKING STRAW SUGAR

1. Warm a piece of sugar in the microwave until it is hot and pliable but not so hot that it is fluid; check it frequently to ensure that it does not become too hot in one place while it is still hard in another.

2. Place the sugar under a heat lamp. Cut a piece approximately 1½ by 6 in/4 by 15 cm from the piece of sugar. Pull it into a long cylinder. Fold the cylinder in half and bring the ends together, allowing the two halves to touch along their long sides and adhere to each other. Repeat two or three times.

3. Holding the piece of sugar at either end, fold it into a tube, allowing the long sides to adhere. From this point on, it is important to handle the sugar gently and touch the center of the piece as little as possible to retain the long tubes of air that you are building into the sugar. Fold the tube in half, as in Step 2, and allow the long sides to adhere to each other. Repeat two or three times.

4. Repeat Step 3 two more times, handling the sugar by the ends as much as possible.

5. Pull the sugar into a long cylinder and bend and shape it as desired. If the sugar is still warm enough, you can cut the ends with scissors. If it is too cool, warm the section to be cut over a Sterno flame and then cut carefully with scissors. Cool the sugar with a blow dryer.

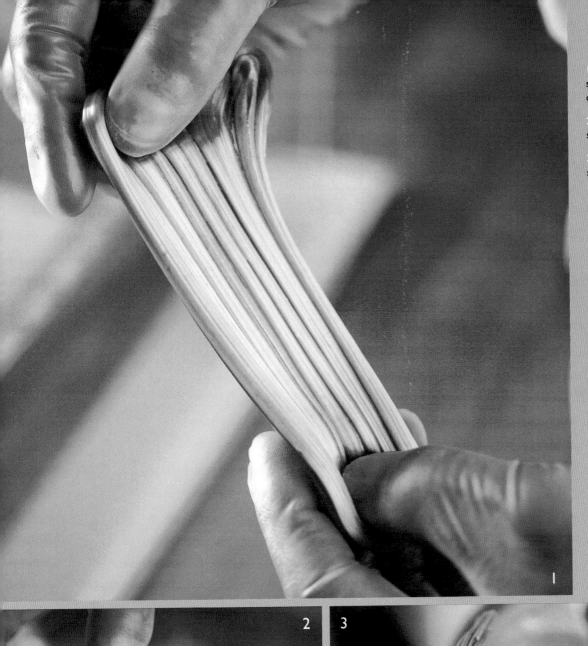

1 Joining the long sides of the sugar cylinder

2 Forming the sugar into a tube

3 Shaping the straw sugar

2

3

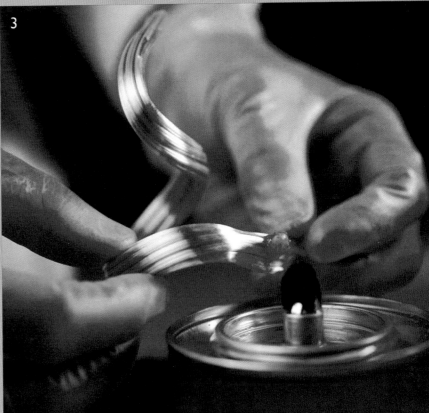

CLOCKWISE:
Beginning to pull the ribbon

Lengthening the ribbon

Shaping the ribbon

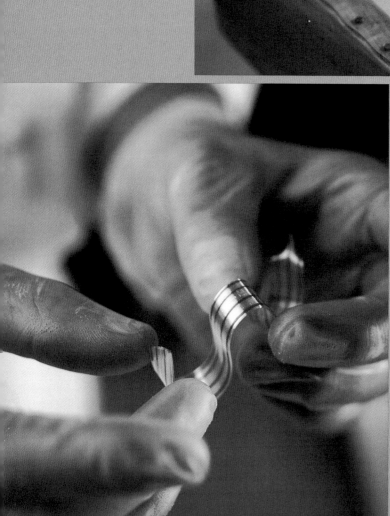

MAKING A PULLED SUGAR RIBBON

1. Warm one piece of white sugar and one piece of red sugar in the microwave until they are hot and pliable but not so hot that they are fluid; check frequently to ensure that the sugar does not become too hot in one place while it is still hard in another.

2. Place both pieces of sugar under a heat lamp. Cut off five pieces of white sugar, each approximately ¾ by 3 in/2 by 8 cm. Cut off two pieces of red sugar of approximately the same size. Lay the pieces of sugar in a row in this order: white, red, white, white, white, red, white; place the pieces close together so that they adhere to one another.

3. Pull the sugar band lengthwise until it is long enough to double back on itself. Bring the two ends of the sugar together and allow the long sides of the sugar to adhere to each other. Flatten the piece of sugar into a wide, thick ribbon.

4. Grasping one end of the ribbon in your left hand, begin pulling the ribbon out with your right hand. Apply pressure evenly, using your right hand to smooth out the length of the ribbon until you have created a very thin, delicate ribbon.

5. When the ribbon is the desired length and thickness, trim the ends at an angle with scissors. If necessary, warm the ribbon slightly under the heat lamp to shape and curve it as desired.

Note   For ribbons of three or more colors, simply add more colors of sugar in the same manner. The colors can be arranged in any sequence, but ribbons tend to look prettier if the different colors are separated by white sugar.

Pastillage

Makes 1 lb 2 oz/510 g

CONFECTIONERS' SUGAR	1 lb	454 g
GUM TRAGACANTH	1 tbsp	4 g
WATER	2 fl oz	60 mL

1. Sift 12 oz/340 g of the confectioners' sugar into a bowl. Blend in the gum tragacanth. Make a well in the center of the mixture and pour in the water. Stir with a wooden spoon until the sugar paste is a kneadable consistency.

2. Transfer the dough to a work surface and knead in the remaining 4 oz/113 g confectioners' sugar, continuing to knead until it is smooth and firm but not dry.

3. Form the pastillage into a log. Coat it lightly with vegetable shortening, wrap tightly in plastic wrap, and let set overnight. (Note: The dough will tighten overnight.)

MAKING A PASTILLAGE LINK TWIST

1. Roll out the pastillage ¹⁄₁₆ in/1.5 mm or thinner on a nonstick surface.

2. Using the template on page 795, cut teardrop shapes from the pastillage.

3. Carefully cut a slit down the center of each cut piece, leaving ¹⁄₄ in/6 mm uncut at each end. Lift up one piece and flip the flat end in through the slit.

4. Insert a pin into a piece of foam. Lean the flat end of the pastillage piece against the pin so that it is propped perpendicular to the rest of the piece, which should be lying flat on the foam. Repeat with the remaining cut pieces.

5. Allow to dry until stiff.

Working with Sugar Pastes

Pastillage is a pure white sugar paste. It is not sensitive to ambient humidity, making it possible to assemble pieces well in advance and hold them at room temperature. Pastillage should not be refrigerated. Sugar paste décor may be made in advance and stored almost indefinitely in controlled conditions of temperature and humidity.

Gum paste and pastillage are essentially the same medium; however, gum paste is more elastic and may be rolled thinner and manipulated more easily without cracking. Most gum paste and pastillage décor elements should be dried overnight before use.

When working with sugar pastes, the work surface and all tools must be kept clean and free of any debris, as the white paste accentuates any impurities. Keep sugar paste covered with plastic wrap as much as possible as it is being worked with because it dries out quickly.

1 Cutting a slit in the middle of the pastillage piece

2 Twisting the base of the pastillage piece through the cut

3 Letting the pastillage dry in the final shape

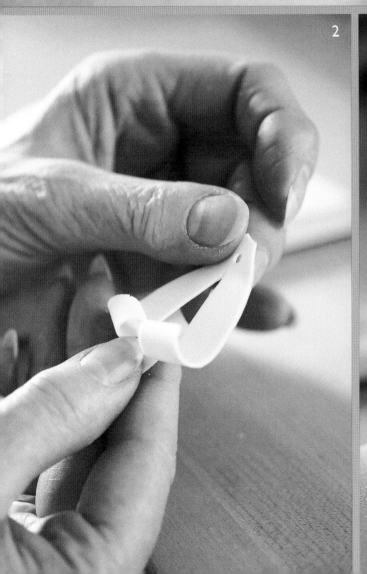

Gum Paste

Makes 2 lb 9 oz/1.16 kg

CONFECTIONERS' SUGAR	2 lb	907 g
GUM TRAGACANTH	3/4 oz	21 g
GELATIN	3/4 oz	21 g
WATER	4 fl oz	120 mL
GLUCOSE SYRUP	1 1/2 oz	43 g

1. Sift 1 lb 12 oz/794 g of the confectioners' sugar into a bowl. Blend in the gum tragacanth, and make a well in the center of the mixture.

2. Bloom and melt the gelatin in the water. Remove from the heat and stir in the glucose syrup.

3. Pour the gelatin mixture into the well in the sugar mixture and stir with a wooden spoon until the dough is a kneadable consistency.

4. Transfer the dough to a work surface and knead in the remaining 4 oz/113 g confectioners' sugar, continuing to knead until it is smooth and firm but not dry.

5. Form the gum paste into a log. Coat it lightly with vegetable shortening, wrap tightly in plastic wrap, and let set overnight. (Note: The dough will tighten overnight.)

MAKING A GUM PASTE ROSE

1. Roll a piece of gum paste with a small rolling pin to 1/16 in/1.5 mm or thinner. Keep the gum paste covered with a piece of plastic wrap when you are not working with it. Have ready a prepared cotton cone for the center of the flower.

2. Cut a set of petals out of the gum paste with a five-petal cutter. Cut the petals apart into one group of two petals and one of three petals. Roll the large end of a gum paste ball tool over the edges of the two-petal group to thin them. With a toothpick or a thin knitting needle, roll up one side of each petal. Roll the toothpick firmly across the surface of the petal to draw up and curl the edge of the petal.

3. Turn the petals over and brush the base with gum glue (see page 801). Without separating the petals, wrap the first petal around the cotton inner cone: The uncurled side of the petal should be wrapped around the cone and the curled side of the petal should be slightly open. Fit the uncurled side of the second petal into the open side of the first petal and wrap the second petal around the first. Press gently to attach the petals to each other and to the cotton cone; the top of the petals should form a tight spiral. (Note: For a rosebud, follow the procedure to this point, but do not add any more petals.)

1 Thinning the edges of the petals with a ball tool

2 Curling the edges of the petals

3 Wrapping the first layer of petals

4 Adding another layer of petals

4. Thin the edges, curl, and brush glue on the three-petal group in the same fashion. Wrap these petals around the first two, overlapping the petals and fitting the third petal inside the uncurled edge of the first. Press gently to attach the petals to one another.

5. For a larger rose, cut another group of five petals. Separate them again into one group of two petals and one of three petals. Thin the edges of the two-petal group as above and curl back both edges of each petal. Turn the petals over and brush the base with gum glue. Wrap the petals around the rose as before, overlapping them slightly.

6. Thin the edges, curl, and brush glue on the three-petal group in the same fashion. Wrap these petals around the rose, overlapping them; the last petal should overlap the first one of the two-petal group. Press gently to attach the petals to one another.

7. Form a hook out of the end of the wire attached to the inner cotton cone and hang the rose upside down to dry.

MAKING A GUM PASTE MAGNOLIA

1. Massage together equal parts of gum paste and pastillage.

2. Roll approximately 1 tsp of the mixture into a ball, then roll half of the ball into a point. Attach the rounded base of the pointed ball to a piece of floral wire. Attach twisted paper strands to the wire at the base of the ball.

3. Using sharp, pointed scissors, cut V-shaped snips into the sides of the pointed ball.

4. Roll out the remaining gum paste mixture $^1/_{16}$ in/1.5 mm thick.

5. Using the templates in Appendix D, cut three large and three small petals from the paste.

6. Attach the small petals to the wire so that the pointed ball rests in the center (for detailed instructions see Making a Marzipan Rose, page 776). Attach the large petals so that each fills a space between two of the smaller petals.

MOLDING A GUM PASTE–PASTILLAGE MIXTURE

1. Massage together equal parts of gum paste and pastillage. Roll out $^1/_4$ in/6 mm thick.

2. Place the desired mold over the rolled sugar paste and cut to the shape with a sharp paring knife using the mold as a template.

3. Place the cut shape in the mold and press it down firmly with the top of the mold. Carefully peel the molded shape away from the mold and drape it over a curved object, such as a rolling pin, or a flat work surface. Allow to dry for approximately 1 hour.

4. Shift the shape slightly to ensure that it does not stick to the rolling pin or other surface. Allow to dry completely.

Unmolding a gum
paste–pastillage
piece

Rolled Fondant

Makes 2 lb 7 oz/1.11 kg

GELATIN	1 tbsp	4 g
WATER	2 fl oz	60 mL
CORN SYRUP	4 oz	113 g
GLYCERIN	1½ tsp	7.50 mL
CONFECTIONERS' SUGAR	2 lb	907 g

1. Bloom and melt the gelatin in the water. Remove from the heat and add the corn syrup and glycerin.

2. Add the gelatin mixture to the confectioners' sugar and blend until fully incorporated. Knead to the consistency of a soft dough.

3. Form the fondant into a log. Coat lightly with vegetable shortening, wrap tightly in plastic wrap, and let set overnight. (Note: The fondant will tighten overnight.)

Covering a cake with rolled fondant

Gum Glue
Makes 8 fl oz/240 mL

GUM ARABIC	1 heaping tbsp	6 g
WATER	8 fl oz	240 mL

1. Combine the gum arabic with the water in a small bowl. Cover with a damp cloth and let stand until the gum arabic has completely dissolved.

2. Store under refrigeration.

Note Brush onto finished gum paste items to give them a shiny surface. Also used as an adhesive for sugar paste work.

CHAPTER 20

Wedding and Specialty Cakes

WEDDING AND SPECIALTY CAKES ARE A CULMINATION OF THE TALENT, SKILLS, AND KNOWLEDGE OF THE PASTRY CHEF OR BAKER. TO MAKE A BEAUTIFUL AND FLAVORFUL CAKE, THE PASTRY CHEF OR BAKER MUST HAVE HONED HIS OR HER SKILLS IN ALMOST ALL ASPECTS OF THE BAKING AND PASTRY ARTS. CREATION AND DEVELOPMENT OF CAKES SUCH AS THE ONES IN THIS CHAPTER ARE LIMITED ONLY BY THE CREATIVITY OF THE INDIVIDUAL.

Traditional Wedding Cakes

Traditional British-style wedding cakes are perhaps the quintessential wedding cakes, from which most other wedding cake styles are derived. These are, in general, unfilled dark fruitcakes. The richness of the cake reflects a time when refrigeration was unavailable. Dried fruit, sugar, suet, and thick layers of coatings and icings helped the cakes stay fresh for one year, as the top layer would be saved and eaten on the couple's first anniversary. The cakes are traditionally coated with a layer of jam, then with marzipan, and finally with several coats of royal icing. The jam and marzipan keep the white icing from absorbing oils or moisture from the cake while protecting the cake itself from moisture loss and staling.

Traditional British-style cakes consist of three tiers supported by pillars, generally pastillage, and both the icing and the decoration, which consists of royal icing piping and pastillage, are pure white.

To some traditionalists, the British cake remains the only true wedding cake. Because the cake does not require refrigeration, which would damage sugar décor work, very detailed decorations, often baroque or gothic in style, can be applied. However, the labor-intensive nature of this style of cake is a drawback for most pastry chefs and bakers today—nor are these cakes to everyone's taste. In addition, the royal icing used for décor is very hard and brittle, making it difficult to cut such a cake cleanly or easily.

The British cultural influence is reflected in the styles of wedding cakes that evolved in countries colonized by Britain. The Australian and South African styles are shining examples of this influence. Decoration consists of minute royal icing piping and gum paste flowers. Colors, if used at all, are the softest of pastels. Although these cakes may be quite ornate, their overall appearance is very soft and delicate. The tiers may simply be stacked, may be supported on pillars, or, often, may be displayed on offset asymmetrical cake stands.

In the Australian-style wedding cake, as with the British, it is not uncommon for tiers to be octagons, squares, or horseshoe shapes. The primary appeal of Australian cakes is their ornate yet delicate appearance. Beautiful realistic flowers are created from gum paste, and royal icing embroidery, string work, flood work, and ornaments are used to create stunning and intricate effects. The very detailed style of decoration, however, can be a disadvantage to the pastry chef or baker, in that they are labor-intensive and therefore expensive to produce.

The South African–style cake is very similar, but it can be distinguished from the Australian style by the large yet delicate wings made of royal icing filigree and flood work that extend over the cake.

The British cake also spawned American-style cakes. American wedding cakes are most clearly defined by the use of buttercream icing, buttercream piping décor, and buttercream roses, often colored. There is no single cake type of choice in American cakes, but pound cakes, high-ratio cakes, génoise, and carrot cakes are most common.

Regardless of the style of cake, good judgment and craftsmanship are a requirement for the production of a cake that is cost-effective and attractive. Highly decorated cakes such as these should always be made with high-quality ingredients so that the finished cake can be both a delicious dessert and an impressive showpiece.

The Modern Wedding Cake

Clean, straight lines and simple decorations in the form of cutouts of chocolate, pastillage, marzipan, or nougatine define contemporary wedding cakes. Fresh flowers or fresh fruits are frequently used. The cake itself may be almost any variety, from cheesecake to mousse cake to sponge cake with fruit, or even a charlotte. Almost any type of icing may be used, with whipped cream and good-quality buttercream most common. Offset cake stands are the rule for modern cakes, since they are too light and fragile to be stacked.

The advantages of modern-style cakes are efficiency in production and their visual and taste appeal. Simple elegance and a light, fresh appearance are the objectives, in contrast to the baroque ornamentation of more traditional styles. Cutouts can be made in advance, then placed on the cake relatively quickly for decoration. Fresh fruit and flowers are beautiful in their own right and require little assistance from the pâtissier.

The taste of the finished product is an important factor in favor of the modern-style wedding cake, with virtually no restrictions on the type of cake or fillings. Generally, as with modern cuisine, fresh and seasonal products are employed to their best advantage. If a customer loves fresh strawberry charlotte, there is no reason the pâtissier cannot create a festive, attractive wedding cake composed of charlottes. Many people seek out the unusual, and a modern-style wedding cake can be tailored to their liking.

Specialty Cakes

Specialty cakes employ many of the same techniques as do wedding cakes. There are two elements that distinguish wedding cakes from specialty cakes: Specialty cakes are typically not tiered or stacked as are wedding cakes, and they are most often less ornately decorated. In some respects, however, the creation of a specialty cake presents fewer restrictions for the pastry chef or baker's creativity. Specialty cakes are less limited by shape, color, and type of décor. Types of décor for these cakes will be restricted only by ambient temperature and humidity.

Building a Properly Supported Cake

Adequate support for a tiered cake is, of course, an important consideration in the construction of the cake. If the tiers are to be stacked without pillars, they will generally require added support (possible exceptions are British- and Australian-style cakes, which are often solid enough not to require additional support). This added support can be supplied by wooden dowels or pipes cut to length and inserted into each tier prior to placing the next tier on top. Thus, the weight of the tiers above is supported by the dowels rather than by the cake below. If pillars or columns are used, each type has its own system for providing strength and support to the layers above.

Scheduling the Production of a Wedding or Specialty Cake

The timetable for cake production varies widely depending on the style of cake being produced. A sample schedule is given below.

Prior to Day 1   Design and produce decorations; prepare hardware

Day 1   Bake cake layers

Day 2   Fill cake layers and seal-coat the cake

Day 3   Ice and decorate cake

Day 4   Transport cake and set it up

This schedule is designed for lighter, freshly made cakes. Rich, dense British- or Australian-style cakes are often allowed to mature and ripen for weeks, meaning that the cake can be baked well ahead of time. For any cake, most of the time-consuming decorations can be made well in advance as long as there are adequate dry storage facilities. Creating the décor for the cake generally must begin several days prior to assembling and serving both because of the time involved in the decoration and the time required for royal icing string work to dry. Do not refrigerate this type of cake or the sugar decorations will melt.

Sketching the design on paper

Transporting the Cake

Cakes that are to be transported to job sites require special packaging to ensure their safe arrival. In general, the farther the cake must travel, the less finished it should be prior to arrival at the site. For tiered cakes, each tier can be assembled as much as possible. However, stacking the cake on site will make the cake easier to maneuver. Once stacked, a cake will become very heavy and cumbersome. To transport, place each tier in a box on a nonskid carpet pad and then place each box on the floor of the vehicle to be used for transportation, again on a nonskid carpet pad. Fragile gum paste or pulled sugar flowers and ornaments are best placed on the cake after it reaches its destination.

Costing Wedding Cakes

Wedding cakes are generally priced by the portion. There are many factors influencing the price, including:

Labor cost: This is by far the highest expense, especially for fancy cakes. An Australian-style cake will cost more per portion than an American-style cake, as it requires many more hours of skilled labor to produce. It is also a more unusual product.

Market segment/location: Price will be dictated in part by who the customer is, what the ticket for a wedding averages in a given locale, and whether the wedding cake is sold retail (private) or wholesale (caterer).

Food cost: Originally a relatively small expense, becoming more crucial for modern cakes with fresh and high-quality ingredients.

What features make your cake unique? If you are selling to an affluent market segment, you will be able to charge more for something as important as a wedding cake. Customers are willing to pay extra for a product they cannot get elsewhere.

Heart-Shaped Wedding Cake

Makes 60 servings

CARROT CAKE: 6-, 8-, and 10-in/15-, 20-, and 25-cm heart-shaped layers (page 306)	1 of each	1 of each
CREAM CHEESE ICING (page 422)	4 lb 8 oz	2.04 kg
ROLLED FONDANT, colored peach (page 800)	5 lb	2.27 kg
BUTTERCREAM, for Décor (page 758)	10 oz	284 g
GUM PASTE ROSES (full) (page 796)	9 each	9 each
GUM PASTE ROSES (half open) (page 796)	12 each	12 each
GUM PASTE ROSEBUDS (page 796)	14 each	14 each
GUM PASTE LEAVES (page 798)	34 each	34 each
ROYAL ICING (page 770)	8 oz	227 g

1. Place the 10-in/25-cm cake layer on a heart-shaped cake board, the same diameter as the cake. Slice the cake into three even layers and fill with cream cheese icing. (Each of the assembled layers should be 4 in/10 cm high.) Crumb coat the cake with icing. Insert 6 dowels in the cake: 1 in the center, 2 at the top, 1 at each side, and 1 at the base. Roll the fondant out 1/8 in/3 mm thick. Carefully cover the cake with the fondant and smooth the top and sides. Trim the fondant from the bottom edge of the cake.

2. Repeat the process with the 8-in/20-cm cake and then with the 6-in/15-cm cake, using 4 dowels for the 8-in/20-cm cake and none for the 6-in/15-cm cake.

3. Place the 8-in/20-cm cake on top of the first layer, with the right side and right rear corner aligned with the 10-in/25-cm layer so that the assembled cake is offset. Place the 6-in/15-cm cake on top of the second layer, aligning the right sides and right rear corners.

4. Using a pastry bag fitted with a No. 3 star tip, pipe a shell border of buttercream around the base of each tier.

5. Arrange a spray of roses and leaves in the center of the top tier of the cake, using 5 full roses, 5 half-open roses, 7 rosebuds, and 8 leaves and attaching each with a small dab of royal icing.

6. Arrange a spray on the left side of the middle and bottom tiers and one on the cake board, placing each spray slightly in front of the previous one to create a cascading effect: Use 2 full roses, 2 half-open roses, 3 rosebuds, and 10 leaves for the spray on the 8-in/20-cm cake. Use 1 full rose, 3 half-open roses, 3 rosebuds, and 10 leaves for the spray on the 10-in/25-cm cake. Use the remaining 1 full rose, 2 half-open roses, 1 rosebud, and 6 leaves for the spray on the cake board.

Heart-Shaped
Wedding Cake
and details

Bell Wedding Cake

Makes 40 servings

WHITE MODELING CHOCOLATE (page 779)	10 lb	4.54 kg
CHOCOLATE HIGH-RATIO CAKE: 5-in/13-cm, 6-in/15-cm, 7-in/18-cm, 8-in/20-cm, 9-in/23-cm, 10-in/25-cm, and 12-in/30-cm layers (page 299)	1 of each	1 of each
SOFT GANACHE, whipped (page 424)	4 lb	1.81 kg
WHITE CHOCOLATE, tempered	2 lb	907 g

1. Roll out 1 lb 10 oz/737 g of the modeling chocolate ⅛ in/3 mm thick on a silicone décor mat with a floral design. Cover an 18-in/46-cm round cake base with the rolled chocolate, smooth the top and sides, and trim the rolled chocolate from the bottom edge.

2. Slice the 12-in/30-cm cake into three 1-in/3-cm layers. Place one layer on a 12-in/30-cm cardboard cake round. Coat evenly with 8 oz/227 g of the soft ganache. Top with the second layer and coat evenly with 8 oz/227 g of the soft ganache. Top with the third layer of cake. Seal coat the cake with an additional 8 oz/227 g of ganache.

3. Roll out 1 lb 10 oz/737 g of the white modeling chocolate ⅛ in/3 mm thick. Carefully cover the cake with the rolled chocolate and smooth the top and sides. (The finished cake should be 2¼ in/6 cm high.)

4. Place the cake in the center of the base of the cake stand so the curved 54-in/137-cm arm of the stand hangs directly over the center of the cake.

5. Slice each of the remaining cakes into three 1-in/3-cm layers. Place one of the 10-in/25-cm layers on the 10-in/25-cm Plexiglas round that will form the base of the bell and coat evenly with 4 oz/113 g of the ganache. Top with the second cake layer and coat it with ganache. Top with the third layer and coat evenly with ganache. Continue this process of filling and layering the cakes, stacking one on top of the other as you work, so as to end with the 5-in/13-cm cake at the top.

6. Carve the edges of the stacked and filled cakes with the rod through the center of the cakes to prevent them from shifting, using a serrated knife to form them into the shape of a bell. The finished cakes should be 9 in/23 cm in height with the bottom 10-in/25-cm layer 1 in/3 cm in height.

7. Roll out 1 lb 10 oz/737 g of the white modeling chocolate ⅛ in/3 mm thick. Carefully cover the bell-shaped cake with the rolled chocolate and smooth the sides.

8. Roll out another 1 lb 10 oz/737 g of the modeling chocolate ⅛ in/3 mm thick. Cut thirty strips 2³/₁₆ by 5½ in/6 by 14 cm from the chocolate.

9. Pick up a strip of modeling chocolate, pinch the ends together, and loop them around to connect them to form what looks like the loop of a bow. Repeat with the remaining 29 strips.

10. Fasten the looped strips to the sides of the 12-in/30-cm cake, using a dab of tempered chocolate to attach each one: The smooth looped end should be facing outward, the

crimped ends should be attached to the cake, and the smooth sides of each loop should touch the sides of the next one, to completely cover the sides of the cake.

11. Roll out the remaining white modeling chocolate ⅛ in/3 mm thick on the same silicone décor mat. Cut two strips 4 by 12 in/10 by 30 cm from the chocolate. Crimp one end of each of the strips and attach them to the top of the bell so that they overlap slightly. Cut a V in the other end of each of the strips to form what looks like the tails of a bow.

12. Cut two strips 4 by 8 in/10 by 20 cm from the rolled chocolate. Pinch the ends of one strip together and loop them around to connect to form what looks like the top of a bow. Repeat with the second strip. Join the crimped ends of the two loops together, using tempered chocolate, to form a bow.

13. Cut a strip 2 by 4 in/5 by 10 cm from the rolled chocolate and wrap it around the center of the bow to form a knot.

14. Cut two 4-in/10-cm squares from the modeling chocolate. Cut a V in one side of each square. Using tempered chocolate, attach the side of each square that is opposite the V to the top of the bell at the same point where the other longer strips are attached, so that the V points up.

15. Using tempered chocolate, attach the bow to the top of the bell at the same point, forming a bow with ribbon tails.

LEFT:
Bell Wedding Cake

RIGHT:
Modeling chocolate bow

White Buttercream Magnolia Wedding Cake

Makes 80 servings

VANILLA CHIFFON CAKE: 4 in/10 cm, 8 in/20 cm, and 12 in/30 cm layers (page 318)	1 of each	1 of each
STRAWBERRY MOUSSE (page 397)	3 lb 8 oz	1.59 kg
BUTTERCREAM (page 418)	3 lb	1.36 kg
PASTILLAGE/MARZIPAN LEAVES (½ by 2 in/1 by 5 cm) (page 794)	16 each	16 each
PASTILLAGE/MARZIPAN LEAVES (1 by 2½ in/3 by 6 cm) (page 794)	16 each	16 each
GUM PASTE MAGNOLIAS (page 798)	7 each	7 each

1. Slice each of the cakes into three 1-in/3-cm layers. Place one of the 4-in/10-cm layers on a cardboard cake round of the same size. Apply an even coating of mousse, using 6 oz/170 g. Top with a second layer, apply the same amount of mousse, and top with the third layer. Coat the top and sides of the cake with buttercream. Refrigerate until the filling has set, at least 2 hours.

2. Repeat the process with the two remaining cakes, using 10 oz/284 g mousse for each of the layers of the 8-in/20-cm cake and 12 oz/340 g mousse for each of the layers of the 12-in/30-cm cake.

3. Place the large cake on a 16-in/41-cm hexagonal cake board. Insert 9 dowels in the cake: 1 directly in the center and the other 8 around the center to form a circle 5 in/13 cm in diameter.

4. Coat a circular drum separator (3 by 6 in/8 by 15 cm) with buttercream. Place it in the center of the cake, directly over the dowels. Place the 8-in/20-cm cake on a 9-in/23-cm cake board and place it on top of the drum separator. Insert four dowels in the 8-in/20-cm cake: one directly in the center and the remaining three 1½ in/4 cm from the center to form a triangle around the center dowel. Place the small cake on top, in the center of the cake.

5. Using a pastry bag fitted with a No. 4 shell tip, pipe a shell border of buttercream around the base of each cake and the drum separator. Using a No. 2 plain tip, pipe buttercream scrollwork on each of the bottom two layers: 6 scrolls on the 12-in/30-cm cake and 6 scrolls on the 8-in/20-cm cake, spacing them evenly.

6. Attach the small lace leaves to the sides of the top tier by gently pressing the ends into the buttercream, with the tips pointing directly up. Attach the large lace leaves to the sides of the drum separator by gently pressing the ends into the buttercream, with the tips pointing directly up.

7. Place one of the magnolias in the center of the top tier. Place the remaining magnolias around the sides of the bottom tier, centering them between the piped scrollwork designs.

White
Buttercream
Magnolia
Wedding Cake

Anniversary Cake

Makes 12 servings

VANILLA CHIFFON CAKE (10 in/25 cm) (page 318)	1 each	1 each
STRAWBERRY JAM	1 lb 8 oz	680 g
APRICOT JAM	1 lb	454 g
MARZIPAN (page 775)	1 lb 4 oz	567 g
FONDANT, warm (page 800)	3 lb	1.36 kg
STRAW SUGAR BASE (page 790)	1 each	1 each
WHITE POURED SUGAR BASE (4-in/10-cm round) (page 780)	1 each	1 each
BLOWN SUGAR STRAWBERRIES (page 785)	3 each	3 each
PULLED SUGAR BLOSSOMS (page 786)	3 each	3 each
SUGAR LEAVES (page 789)	10 each	10 each
PULLED SUGAR RIBBON, red and white (page 793)	1 each	1 each
SPUN SUGAR TRIANGLE (page 782)	1 each	1 each
DARK CHOCOLATE, tempered, for writing	as needed	as needed
OVAL PASTILLAGE PLAQUE (1 by 1½ in/3 by 4 cm) (page 794)	1 each	1 each

1. Slice the cake into three 1-in/3-cm layers. Place one layer on a cardboard cake round of the same size. Spread evenly with 12 oz/340 g of the strawberry jam. Top with a second cake layer and spread evenly with the remaining strawberry jam. Top with the last layer of cake.

2. Coat the top and sides of the cake with the apricot jam.

3. Roll out the marzipan ⅛ in/3 mm thick. Carefully cover the cake with the marzipan and smooth the top and sides.

4. Thin the warm fondant to the proper glazing consistency. Place the cake on a wire rack set over a sheet pan. Glaze the cake with the fondant.

5. Attach a white satin ribbon ½ in/1 cm wide to the base of the cake, gently pressing it onto the fondant while it is still slightly tacky to create a finished border.

6. Attach the straw sugar base to the poured sugar base by melting small nails of sugar for pulling or blowing and using them as glue. (See pages 783 to 793 for more information on working with pulled and blown sugar.)

7. Attach the sugar strawberries, blossoms, leaves, and sugar ribbon to the base in the same manner to form an attractive spray. Attach the spun sugar triangle to the back of this centerpiece.

8. Place the sugar centerpiece slightly off center on top of the cake.

9. Using a parchment cone filled with tempered dark chocolate, write "Happy Anniversary" on the pastillage plaque and place it on top of the cake next to the sugar centerpiece.

Congratulations Cake

Makes 12 servings

ROYAL ICING (page 770)	10 oz	284 g
OVAL DOBOS SPONGE (7 by 10 in/18 by 25 cm) (page 310)	7 each	7 each
SIMPLE SYRUP (page 820)	8 fl oz	240 mL
CHOCOLATE BUTTERCREAM (page 419)	2 lb 8 oz	1.13 kg
ROLLED FONDANT, colored pistachio green (page 800)	5 lb	2.27 kg
PASTILLAGE DÉCOR LINK TWISTS (page 794)	20 each	20 each
POURED SUGAR (page 780)	as needed	as needed

1. Using royal icing, pipe and flood the C for the "Congratulations," using the template in Appendix D. Let set for several hours, until completely dry. (See page 772 for more information on flood work.)

2. Place a Dobos layer on a cardboard cake oval of the same size. Moisten with simple syrup, apply a thin coating of buttercream, and top with another layer of sponge. Repeat the process with the remaining layers.

3. Coat the top and side of the cake with the remaining buttercream.

4. Roll out the fondant ¼ in/6 mm thick. Carefully cover the cake with the fondant and smooth the top and sides. Trim the fondant from the bottom edge of the cake. Cover the sides of an oval drum 4 by 7 in/10 by 18 cm with rolled fondant. Smooth and trim.

5. Roll out the remaining fondant ¼ in/6 mm thick and cover an oval cake board of the same dimensions as the cake with the rolled fondant. Place the drum on the cake board, then place the cake on the drum, being sure to center it perfectly.

6. Color a small portion of the royal icing the same green as the fondant. Using a pastry bag fitted with a No. 4 shell tip, pipe a small shell border around the base of the drum and the edges of the cake board.

7. Using small dabs of royal icing, attach the pastillage links to the sides of the cake, positioning them so that the untwisted ends hang from the bottom of the cake and the sides of the links just touch one another. Using a No. 1 plain pastry tip or a parchment cone, pipe royal icing strings to connect the pastillage links.

8. Place the royal icing C on the top left side of the cake. Color a small portion of royal icing gold. Using a parchment cone, pipe the rest of the word "Congratulations," then pipe some small accents on the C. Using a parchment cone, pipe spirals of plain royal icing on top of the cake.

9. Pour some liquid poured sugar (see page 780) into small silicone jewel molds. Allow them to cool completely and solidify. Using small dabs of royal icing, attach the sugar jewels to the C in the Congratulations.

Mother's Day Butterfly Cake

Makes 30 servings

PASTILLAGE (page 794)	2 lb	907 g
ROYAL ICING (page 770)	1 lb 8 oz	680 g
WHITE MODELING CHOCOLATE (page 779)	2 lb	907 g
LEMON CHIFFON CAKE (12 in/30 cm) (page 318)	1 each	1 each
SIMPLE SYRUP (page 820)	as needed	as needed
WHITE CHOCOLATE BUTTERCREAM (page 419)	3 lb	1.36 kg
ROLLED FONDANT (page 800)	2 lb	907 g

1. Roll out the pastillage ¼ in/6 mm thick. Using the template in Appendix D, cut two butterfly wings from the cake and slice each into three layers. Allow to dry completely.

2. Using a pastry bag fitted with a No. 1 plain tip, pipe and flood the design on top of the pastillage wings with royal icing, according to the diagram in Appendix D. (Have a straight pin handy to pop any air bubbles that form while piping.) Immediately place the wings under a heat lamp and allow to harden completely. (Note: The faster a crust forms, the higher the shine of the finished décor.)

3. Using the modeling chocolate, form the body of the butterfly; it should be 8 in/20 cm long and ¾ in/2 cm wide. Use food coloring markers to make markings on the body using the photo on the facing page as a guide. Attach two wires 2 in/5 cm long to the head for antennae.

4. Using the butterfly wing template, cut six layers of lemon chiffon cake. Place one of the layers on a cake board cut to the same dimensions. Moisten it with simple syrup, coat it lightly with buttercream, and top with a second layer. Moisten the the second layer with simple syrup, coat lightly with buttercream, and top with a third layer. Repeat the process with the remaining three layers, so that you have a left wing and a right wing. Coat the top and sides of each wing with buttercream.

5. Roll out the fondant ¼ in/6 mm thick. Carefully cover each of the wings with fondant and smooth the top and sides. Trim the fondant from the base of the cake.

6. Cover a cake board cut into a butterfly shape 2 in/5 cm larger than the cake with rolled fondant. Place the wings side by side on the board.

7. Place a pastillage wing on each half of the cake, securing them with royal icing. Using royal icing, attach the butterfly body between the two wings.

8. Using a No. 4 star tip, pipe a shell border of buttercream around the edges of the wings and around the base of the cake.

Elemental Recipes

Basic Ratios by Weight for Cream Ganache

TYPE OF GANACHE	PARTS CHOCOLATE	PARTS CREAM
DARK CHOCOLATE HARD GANACHE	2	1
MILK AND WHITE CHOCOLATE HARD GANACHE	2½	1
DARK CHOCOLATE MEDIUM GANACHE	1	1
MILK AND WHITE CHOCOLATE MEDIUM GANACHE	2	1
DARK CHOCOLATE SOFT GANACHE	1	2
MILK AND WHITE CHOCOLATE SOFT GANACHE	1½	2

Simple Syrup

Makes 32 fl oz/960 mL

SUGAR	1 lb	454 g
WATER	16 fl oz	480 mL

1. Combine the sugar and water in a saucepan and stir to ensure all the sugar is moistened. Bring to a boil, stirring to dissolve the sugar.

Variations **Vanilla Simple Syrup** After the sugar and water comes to a boil, add 1 vanilla bean, split and scraped. Remove the pan from the heat, cover, and allow to steep for 20 minutes. Strain to remove the pod.

Coffee Simple Syrup After the sugar and water comes to a boil, add 1 oz/28 g ground coffee. Remove the pan from the heat, cover, and allow to steep for 20 minutes. Strain to remove the grounds.

Liquor-Flavored Simple Syrup To flavor simple syrup with a liquor such as brandy or rum, add 2 fl oz/60 mL of the desired liquor to the syrup after it has cooled completely.

Liqueur-Flavored Simple Syrup To flavor simple syrup with a liqueur such as framboise, kirsch, or Kahlúa, add 4 fl oz/120 mL of the desired liqueur to the syrup after it has cooled completely.

Note Simple syrup may be made with varying ratios of sugar to water depending on the desired use and the sweetness and flavor of the cake or pastry to which it is to be applied.

Citrus-Flavored Syrup

Makes 192 fl oz/5.76 L

WATER	128 fl oz	3.84 L
SUGAR	4 lb	1.81 kg
ORANGE, halved	1 each	1 each
LEMON, halved	1 each	1 each
VANILLA BEAN, split and scraped	1 each	1 each

1. Combine all the ingredients in a saucepan and stir to ensure all the sugar is moistened. Bring to a boil. Simmer over medium heat for 15 minutes. Remove from the heat and allow to cool completely.

2. Strain the syrup. Store, tightly covered, under refrigeration.

Variation **Spiced Flavored Syrup for Cakes** Add 1 nutmeg, 1 cinnamon stick, and 1 tablespoon black peppercorns to the mixture along with the vanilla bean.

Coconut Shavings

Makes 1 lb 4 oz/567 g

COCONUTS, halved	2 each	2 each
SIMPLE SYRUP (page 820)	8 fl oz	240 mL

1. Place the coconut halves on a sheet pan. Bake in a 350°F/177°C oven until the flesh just begins to pull away from the shells, 5 to 7 minutes. Allow to cool completely.

2. Remove the coconut flesh from the shells. Using a vegetable peeler, shave strips 2 in/5 cm long from the flesh.

3. Toss the coconut shavings with the simple syrup, then drain any excess syrup.

4. Spread the coconut shavings on a parchment-lined sheet pan. Bake in a 350°F/177°C deck oven until lightly toasted, 8 to 10 minutes.

5. Allow the coconut shavings to cool to room temperature. Store in an airtight container at room temperature.

Savarin Syrup

Makes 96 fl oz/2.88 L (enough for 30 savarins)

WATER	48 fl oz	1.44 L
ORANGE JUICE	16 fl oz	480 mL
SUGAR	2 lb	907 g
CINNAMON STICKS	2 each	2 each
VANILLA EXTRACT	1 tsp	5 mL
WHITE RUM	to taste	to taste

1. Combine the water, orange juice, sugar, and cinnamon sticks in a saucepan and bring to a boil, stirring to dissolve the sugar. Simmer over medium heat for 5 minutes.

2. Remove the pan from the heat and add the vanilla extract. Add rum to taste. Strain.

3. Allow to cool completely. Store, tightly covered, under refrigeration.

Saffron Poaching Liquid

Makes 32 fl oz/960 mL

WHITE WINE	36 fl oz	1.08 L
LEMON JUICE	1½ fl oz	45 mL
CINNAMON STICK	1 each	1 each
CLOVES	6 each	6 each
SUGAR	5 oz	142 g
SAFFRON THREADS	pinch	pinch

1. Combine all the ingredients in a saucepan and bring to a simmer, stirring to dissolve the sugar.

Note   Add peeled and prepped fruit to the simmering liquid and poach until slightly underdone. Cool the fruit in the liquid.

Port Poaching Liquid

Makes 52 fl oz/1.56 L

PORT	32 fl oz	960 mL
SUGAR	1 lb 4 oz	567 g
CINNAMON STICK	½ each	½ each
VANILLA BEAN, split	1 each	1 each
ORANGE ZEST, grated	⅔ oz	19 g

1. Combine all the ingredients in a saucepan and bring to a simmer, stirring to dissolve the sugar.

Note Add peeled and prepped fruit to the simmering liquid and poach until slightly underdone. Cool the fruit in the liquid.

Poached Cranberries

Makes 1 lb 8 oz/680 g

SIMPLE SYRUP (page 820)	48 fl oz	1.44 L
CRANBERRIES	1 lb	454 g

1. Heat the simple syrup to a simmer.

2. Add the cranberries and continue to simmer for 10 minutes.

3. Remove from the heat and cool completely. Store the cranberries in the syrup, under refrigeration, until ready to use.

Apricot Glaze

Makes 25½ fl oz/765 mL

APRICOT JAM	9 oz	255 g
WATER	6 fl oz	180 mL
CORN SYRUP	9 oz	255 g
LIQUOR (such as rum)	1½ fl oz	45 mL

1. Combine all the ingredients in a saucepan and stir to ensure all the sugar is moistened. Bring to a boil, stirring to dissolve the sugar.

Note   Use the glaze while it is still warm, applying it to the items with a pastry brush.

Brûlée Sugar Blend

Makes 1 lb/454 g

SUGAR	8 oz	227 g
LIGHT BROWN SUGAR	8 oz	227 g

1. Combine the two sugars and spread out on a sheet pan. Allow to air-dry overnight.
2. Process the sugar mixture in a food processor until very fine. Sift through a fine strainer.
3. Store, tightly covered, in a cool, dry place.

Spice Mix for Pumpkin Crème Brûlée

Makes 1 lb 2 oz/510 g

BRÛLÉE SUGAR BLEND (see above)	8 oz	227 g
LIGHT BROWN SUGAR	8 oz	227 g
GROUND CINNAMON	1 oz	28 g
GROUND CLOVES	1 oz	28 g

1. Thoroughly combine all of the ingredients.
2. Store in an airtight container.

Egg Wash
Makes 16 fl oz/480 mL

EGGS	8 oz	227 g
MILK	8 fl oz	240 mL
SALT	pinch	pinch

1. Combine the eggs, milk, and salt using a wire whip.

Note   There are infinite variations possible from these basic egg washes to best suit different uses and tastes. For example, water or cream can be substituted for some or all of the milk. Egg yolks can be substituted for all or a portion of the whole eggs. Sugar can also be added.

Candied Rose Petals
Makes 20 petals

ROSE PETALS, untreated	20 each	20 each
PASTEURIZED EGG WHITES	2 oz	57 g
SUPERFINE SUGAR	as needed	as needed

1. Lightly brush both sides of the petals with the egg whites.
2. Make an even layer of sugar approximately 1/4 in/6 mm deep in a half sheet pan.
3. Arrange the petals in the sugar, making sure they do not touch.
4. Sprinkle additional sugar over the petals to cover completely.
5. Remove the petals from the sugar and place them on a clean parchment-lined sheet pan. Allow to air-dry, then use or store in an airtight container.

Note   Mint leaves or other edible untreated flowers may be substituted for the rose petals.

Pan Grease

Makes 3 lb/1.36 kg

SHORTENING	1 lb	454 g
BREAD FLOUR	1 lb	454 g
VEGETABLE OIL	1 lb	454 g

1. Blend the shortening and flour using an electric mixer fitted with a paddle attachment on low speed until a smooth paste forms. Gradually add the oil and blend until smooth.

Note   Coat the inside of cake and loaf pans with the mixture to create a nonstick surface.

Gelatin Solution

Makes 7 oz/198 g

WATER, cold	6 fl oz	180 mL
GELATIN	1 oz	28 g

1. Bloom the gelatin in the water for 5 minutes. Heat the bloomed gelatin over a warm water bath until fully dissolved.
2. Store, tightly covered, under refrigeration.

Note   Use this solution to stabilize whipped cream used for filling or icing cakes and pastries.

Cinnamon Sugar

Makes 9 oz/255 g

SUGAR	8 oz	227 g
GROUND CINNAMON	1 oz	28 g

1. Blend the sugar and cinnamon until fully combined.

Variation   **Cinnamon Sugar (strong)** Reduce the sugar to 5 oz/142 g.

Vanilla Sugar

Makes 1 lb/454 g

VANILLA BEAN, split	1 each	1 each
SUGAR	1 lb	454 g

1. Place the vanilla bean and sugar in a lidded jar, cover tightly, and shake well. Let stand for at least 1 week before using.

Notes Vanilla sugar can also be made using confectioners' sugar.

Vanilla beans used to infuse custards, sauces, and other liquids can be used to make vanilla sugar if first rinsed and allowed to thoroughly air-dry.

Japonais Meringue

Makes 4 lb/1.81 kg

HAZELNUTS, finely ground	1 lb	454 g
CONFECTIONERS' SUGAR	1 lb	454 g
EGG WHITES	1 lb	454 g
GRANULATED SUGAR	1 lb	454 g

1. Combine the hazelnuts and confectioners' sugar; rub together well.
2. Place the egg whites in a bowl and whisk until frothy. Gradually add the granulated sugar while continuing to whip, then whip to stiff peaks.
3. Fold the hazelnut mixture into the meringue.
4. Pipe into the desired shapes and dry or bake as needed.

Lebkuchen Spice (or Gingerbread Spice)

Makes 2 oz/57 g

GROUND CINNAMON	1½ tbsp	9 g
GROUND CLOVES	1 tbsp plus ½ tsp	7 g
GROUND NUTMEG	2 tsp	4 g
GROUND ANISE	1½ tbsp	9 g
GROUND GINGER	1 tbsp plus ½ tsp	7 g
GROUND FENNEL	1½ tbsp	9 g
GROUND CORIANDER	1½ tbsp	9 g

1. Combine all the spices. Store in an airtight container at room temperature.

Bieber Spice

Makes 2 lb 6 oz/1.08 kg

GROUND CINNAMON	12 oz	340 g
GROUND CORIANDER	12 oz	340 g
GROUND NUTMEG	3 oz	85 g
GROUND ANISE	6 oz	170 g
GROUND CLOVES	4 oz	113 g
GROUND GINGER	1 oz	28 g

1. Combine all the spices. Store in an airtight container at room temperature.

Streusel Topping

Makes 4 lb/1.81 kg

BUTTER	1 lb	454 g
SUGAR	1 lb	454 g
BREAD FLOUR	2 lb	907 g
GROUND CINNAMON	1 tbsp	6 g

1. Cream the butter and sugar together using an electric mixer fitted with a paddle attachment until light and fluffy.
2. Add the flour and cinnamon and mix to a rough crumb.

Coffee Concentrate

Makes 64 fl oz/1.92 L

DARK-ROAST COFFEE BEANS, coarsely ground	1 lb	454 g
WATER	64 fl oz, plus more as needed	1.92 L, plus more as needed
SUGAR	2 lb	907 g

1. Combine the coffee and water in a saucepan, bring to a boil, and boil for 10 minutes. Strain through a sieve set over a bowl, then return the volume of the liquid to 64 fl oz/1.92 L by pouring additional hot water through the coffee grounds.
2. Combine the sugar and 16 fl oz/480 mL of the coffee mixture in a saucepan and bring to a boil, stirring to dissolve the sugar. Continue cooking until the sugar caramelizes.
3. Gradually add the remaining coffee mixture to the caramel. Continue cooking the mixture until it reaches 325°F/163°C. Cool completely.
4. Store, tightly covered, at room temperature.

Note Use the concentrate sparingly to flavor buttercreams, syrups, and mousses.

Walnut Praline Paste

Makes 4 lb/1.81 kg

WALNUTS, roughly chopped and lightly toasted	2 lb	907 g
SUGAR	2 lb	907 g

1. Spread the walnuts out on a marble surface.

2. Place the sugar in a heavy-bottomed saucepan and cook over medium heat, stirring constantly, to a rich golden brown.

3. Pour the caramel over the walnuts. Allow to cool to room temperature.

4. Break up the praline and grind to a soft paste in a food processor.

Cream Cheese Filling

Makes 1 lb 4 oz/567 g

CREAM CHEESE	1 lb	454 g
CONFECTIONERS' SUGAR	4 oz	113 g
VANILLA EXTRACT	1 fl oz	30 mL
LEMON ZEST	1 tsp	3 g

1. Cream together the cream cheese, confectioners' sugar, vanilla extract, and lemon zest in an electric mixer fitted with a paddle attachment on medium speed, scraping down the bowl periodically, until smooth in texture and light in color, about 5 minutes.

2. Pipe or otherwise deposit to fill pastries before baking.

Cheese Danish Filling

Makes 4 lb 10 oz/2.10 kg

CREAM CHEESE	3 lb	1.36 kg
SUGAR	12 oz	340 g
CORNSTARCH	6 oz	170 g
LEMON ZEST	1 tsp	3 g
ORANGE ZEST	1 tsp	3 g
VANILLA EXTRACT	1 tbsp	15 mL
EGGS	8 oz	227 g

1. Cream together the cream cheese, sugar, cornstarch, lemon and orange zest, and vanilla in an electric mixer fitted with a paddle attachment on medium speed until light and smooth.

2. Add the eggs gradually, one at a time, scraping down the bowl periodically, until fully blended.

3. Fill pastries as desired and bake.

Almond Filling

Makes 1 lb 5 oz/595 g

ALMOND PASTE	6 oz	170 g
BUTTER, unsalted	6 oz	170 g
EGGS	6 oz	170 g
GROUND CINNAMON	½ tsp	1 g
CAKE FLOUR, sifted	3 oz	85 g

1. Blend the almond paste with 3 oz/85 g of the butter in an electric mixer fitted with a paddle attachment on medium speed until light and smooth.

2. Add the remaining 3 oz/85 g butter, the eggs, cinnamon, and cake flour and mix on medium speed until fully blended.

3. Fill pastries as desired and bake.

Hazelnut Filling

Makes 6 lb/2.72 kg

ALMOND PASTE	1 lb	454 g
SUGAR	1 lb	454 g
BUTTER	1 lb	454 g
HAZELNUTS, slightly toasted, finely ground	3 lb	1.36 kg
GROUND CINNAMON	½ oz	14 g

1. Blend the almond paste with the sugar in an electric mixer fitted with a paddle attachment on medium speed until light and smooth.

2. Add the butter and blend on medium speed until smooth.

3. Add the hazelnuts and cinnamon and blend until fully combined.

4. Fill pastries as desired and bake.

Frangipane for Filling

Makes 2 lb 5.50 oz/1.06 kg

ALMOND PASTE	1 lb	454 g
SUGAR	2½ oz	71 g
EGGS	8 oz	227 g
BUTTER	8 oz	227 g
CAKE FLOUR	3 oz	85 g

1. Cream together the almond paste and sugar; add a small amount of egg to be sure there are no lumps. Add the butter and cream well.

2. Gradually add the remaining eggs.

3. Add the flour and mix until just combined.

4. Use only as a filling for tart shells or pithivier.

Tomato Sauce

Makes 2 lb 5 oz/1.05 kg

OLIVE OIL	2 oz	57 g
YELLOW ONIONS, cut into small dice	4 oz	113 g
GARLIC, minced	1¼ oz	35 g
TOMATOES, concasséed	1 lb 12 oz	794 g
SUGAR	½ oz	14 g
DRIED BASIL	1 tbsp plus ½ tsp	7 g
DRIED ROSEMARY, crushed	1 tbsp plus ½ tsp	7 g
DRIED OREGANO	1 tbsp plus ½ tsp	7 g
DRIED TARRAGON	1 tbsp plus ½ tsp	7 g
SALT	to taste	to taste
BLACK PEPPER	to taste	to taste

1. Heat the oil in a sauteuse over medium heat. Sauté the onions until translucent and tender. Add the garlic and sauté for 2 minutes.

2. Add the remaining ingredients and simmer for 25 minutes.

3. Cool the tomato sauce over an ice bath. Store, covered, under refrigeration.

Pesto

Makes 18 oz/510 g

PINE NUTS	2½ oz	71 g
GARLIC, fresh	½ oz	14 g
BASIL LEAVES	6 oz	170 g
PARMESAN CHEESE	3½ oz	99 g
BLACK PEPPER	1 tsp	2 g
SALT	2 tsp	10 g
OLIVE OIL	6 fl oz	180 mL

1. Combine the pine nuts, garlic, basil, Parmesan, pepper, and salt in a food processor fitted with a metal chopping blade. Process to blend.

2. Add the olive oil with the processor running and process until smooth.

Conversions, Equivalents, and Calculations

Weight Conversions

To convert ounces to grams, multiply the number of ounces by 28.349.	
¼ oz	7 g
½ oz	14 g
1 oz	28 g
4 oz (¼ lb)	113 g
8 oz (½ lb)	227 g
16 oz (1 lb)	454 g
24 oz (1½ lb)	680 g
32 oz (2 lb)	907 g
40 oz (2½ lb)	1.13 kg
48 oz (3 lb)	1.36 kg

Metric values have been rounded.

Volume Conversions

To convert fluid ounces to milliliters, multiply the number of ounces by 30.	
1 tsp	5 mL
½ fl oz (1 tbsp)	15 mL
1 fl oz (2 tbsp)	30 mL
8 fl oz (1 cup)	240 mL
16 fl oz (1 pt)	480 mL
32 fl oz (1 qt)	960 mL
128 fl oz (1 gal)	3.84 L

Metric values have been rounded.

Length Conversions

To convert inches to centimeters, multiply the number of inches by 2.54.	
¼ in	6 mm
½ in	1 cm
1 in	3 cm
2 in	5 cm
4 in	10 cm
6 in	15 cm
7 in	18 cm
8 in	20 cm
9 in	23 cm
10 in	25 cm
12 in (1 ft)	30 cm

Metric values have been rounded.

Hints and Tips for Calculations

1 gal = 4 qt = 8 pt = 16 cups (8 fl oz per cup) = 128 fl oz

1 fifth bottle = approximately 1½ pt = exactly 25.6 fl oz

1 liquid measuring cup holds 8 fl oz (a coffee cup generally holds 6 fl oz)

1 large egg white = 2 fl oz (average)

1 lemon = 1 to 1¼ fl oz juice

1 orange = 3 to 3¼ fl oz juice

To round to whole numbers, round up if the final decimal is 5 or greater; round down if less than 5.

Metric Conversions

Dash	less than $1/8$ tsp
3 tsp	1 tbsp ($1/2$ fl oz)/15 mL
2 tbsp	$1/8$ cup (1 fl oz)/30 mL
4 tbsp	$1/4$ cup (2 fl oz)/60 mL
$5\frac{1}{3}$ tbsp	$1/3$ cup ($2\frac{2}{3}$ fl oz)/80 mL
8 tbsp	$1/2$ cup (4 fl oz)/120 mL
$10\frac{2}{3}$ tbsp	$2/3$ cup ($5\frac{1}{3}$ fl oz)/160 mL
12 tbsp	$3/4$ cup (6 fl oz)/180 mL
14 tbsp	$7/8$ cup (7 fl oz)/210 mL
16 tbsp	1 cup
1 gill	$1/2$ cup
1 cup	8 fl oz/240 mL
2 cups	1 pt/480 mL
2 pt	1 qt/960 mL
4 qt	1 gal/3.84 L
8 qt	1 peck/7.68 L
4 pecks	1 bushel/30.72 L

Metric values have been rounded.

Temperature Conversions

To convert Fahrenheit to Celsius: $F - 32 \div 1.8 = C$	
32°F	0°C
40°F	4°C
140°F	60°C
150°F	66°C
160°F	71°C
170°F	77°C
212°F	100°C
275°F	135°C
300°F	149°C
325°F	163°C
350°F	177°C
375°F	191°C
400°F	204°C
425°F	218°C
450°F	232°C
475°F	246°C
500°F	260°C

Approximate Volumes to Weights

ITEM	VOLUME Tablespoons/Cups	OUNCES
Allspice, ground	T	1/4
Almonds, blanched	C	5 1/3
Apples, peeled, 1/2-in/1-cm cubes	C	3 1/3
Apples, pie, canned	C	6
Applesauce, canned	C	8
Apricots, canned, drained	C	5 1/3
Apricots, cooked	C	3 1/3
Apricots, halved	C	8
Baking powder	T	1/2
Baking powder	C	8
Baking soda	T	2/5
Bananas, diced	C	6 1/2
Blueberries	C	7
Blueberries, canned	C	6 1/2
Bread crumbs, dried	C	4
Bread crumbs, soft	C	2
Butter	C	8
Cake crumbs, soft	C	2 3/4
Cheese, cottage or cream	C	8
Cheese, hard, grated	C	4
Cherries, glacéed	C	6 1/2
Chocolate, grated	C	4 1/2
Chocolate, melted	C	8
Cinnamon, ground	T	1/4
Citron, dried, chopped	C	6 1/2

ITEM	VOLUME Tablespoons/Cups	OUNCES
Cloves, ground	T	1/4
Cloves, whole	C	3
Cocoa powder	C	4
Coconut, shredded	C	2 1/2
Cornmeal	C	5 1/3
Cornstarch	T	1/4
Cornstarch	C	4 1/2
Corn syrup	C	12
Cranberries, raw	C	4
Cream, whipping	C	8
Cream, whipped	C	4
Cream of tartar	T	1/3
Currants, dried	C	5 1/3
Dates, pitted	C	6 1/5
Eggs, fresh, whites (9)	C	8
Eggs, fresh, yolks (10)	C	8
Eggs, raw, shelled (5)	C	8
Figs, dried, chopped	C	6 1/2
Flour, all-purpose	C	4
Flour, bread, sifted	C	4
Flour, bread, unsifted	C	4 1/2
Flour, cake/pastry, sifted	C	3 1/3
Flour, rye	C	2 3/4
Flour, whole wheat	C	4 1/4
Gelatin, granulated	T	1/4

ITEM	VOLUME Tablespoons/Cups	OUNCES
Gelatin, granulated	C	5⅓
Ginger, ground	T	⅕
Grapes, halved, seeded	C	5¾
Grapes, whole	C	4
Honey	C	12
Jam	C	12
Jelly	C	10⅔
Lard	C	8
Margarine	C	8
Milk, condensed	C	10⅔
Milk, evaporated	C	9
Milk, liquid	C	8½
Milk, nonfat dry	T	¼
Milk, nonfat dry	C	4
Molasses	C	12
Nutmeg, ground	T	¼
Oil, vegetable	C	8
Peaches, chopped	C	8
Peanut butter	C	9
Peanuts	C	5
Pears, canned, drained, diced	C	6½
Pecans	C	4½
Pineapple, crushed	C	8
Poppy seeds	C	5
Prunes, dried	C	6½
Prunes, pitted, cooked	C	5

ITEM	VOLUME Tablespoons/Cups	OUNCES
Pumpkin, cooked	C	6½
Raisins	C	5⅓
Raisins, plumped	C	7
Raspberries	C	4¾
Rhubarb, cooked	C	6½
Rhubarb, raw, 1-in/3-cm dice	C	4
Rice, raw	C	8
Salt	T	⅔
Sesame seed	T	⅓
Sesame seed	C	5⅜
Shortening, vegetable	C	7
Strawberries	C	7
Sugar, brown, lightly packed	C	5⅓
Sugar, brown, solidly packed	C	8
Sugar, confectioners', sifted	C	5⅓
Sugar, granulated	C	8
Tapioca, pearl	C	5¾
Tapioca, quick-cooking	C	5⅓
Tea, instant	C	2
Tea, loose-leaf	C	2⅔
Vanilla extract	T	½
Vinegar	C	8
Walnuts	C	4
Water	C	8
Yeast, active dry, envelope	each	¼
Yeast, cake	each	⅗

Pan Sizes and Volumes

PAN SIZE	VOLUME
¾ by 1¾ in mini muffin cup	1 oz
1¼ by 2¾ in muffin cup	4 oz (½ c)
1½ by 8 in pie or cake	32 oz (1 qt)
2 by 8 in cake	48 oz (3 pt)
1½ by 9 in pie or cake	40 oz (5 c)
1½ by 8 in square	48 oz (6 c)
7 by 11 by 2 in rectangle	48 oz (6 c)
3 by 7½ in Bundt	48 oz (6 c)
4½ by 8 ½ by 2½ in loaf	48 oz (6 c)
5 by 9 by 3 in loaf	64 oz (2 qt)
2 by 9 in pie or cake	64 oz (2 qt)
2 by 8 in square	64 oz (2 qt)
1½ by 9 in square	64 oz (2 qt)
3 by 9 in Bundt	72 oz (9 c)
3 by 8 in tube	72 oz (9 c)
2 by 9 in square	80 oz (5 pt)
2½ by 9½ in springform	80 oz (5 pt)
2 by 10 in cake	88 oz (11 c)
3½ by 10 in Bundt	96 oz (3 qt)
3 by 9 in tube	96 oz (3 qt)
2½ by 10 in springform	96 oz (3 qt)
9 by 13 by 2 in rectangle	120 oz (15 c)
4 by 10 in tube	128 oz (1 gal)

Sugar Solution Equivalents

DEGREES BRIX	DEGREES BAUMÉ	SUGAR IN 1 QT WATER
20	11.10	6.40 oz
21	11.70	6.72 oz
22	12.20	7.04 oz
23	12.80	7.36 oz
24	13.30	7.68 oz
25	13.90	8 oz
26	14.40	8.32 oz
27	15	8.64 oz
28	15.60	8.96 oz
29	16.10	9.28 oz
30	16.70	9.60 oz
31	17.20	9.92 oz
32	17.80	10.24 oz
33	18.30	10.56 oz
34	18.90	10.88 oz
35	19.40	11.20 oz
36	20	11.52 oz
37	20.60	11.84 oz
38	21.10	12.16 oz
39	21.70	12.48 oz
40	22.20	12.80 oz
41	22.80	13.12 oz

DEGREES BRIX	DEGREES BAUMÉ	SUGAR IN 1 QT WATER
42	23.30	13.44 oz
43	23.90	13.76 oz
44	24.40	14.08 oz
45	25	14.40 oz
46	25.60	14.72 oz
47	26.10	15.04 oz
48	26.70	15.36 oz
49	27.20	15.68 oz
50	27.80	16 oz
51	28.30	16.32 oz
52	28.90	16.64 oz
53	29.40	16.96 oz
54	30	17.28 oz
55	30.60	17.60 oz
56	31.10	17.92 oz
57	31.70	18.24 oz
58	32.20	18.56 oz
59	32.80	18.88 oz
60	33.30	19.20 oz
61	34.40	19.52 oz
62	33.90	19.84 oz
63	35	20.16 oz

DEGREES BRIX	DEGREES BAUMÉ	SUGAR IN 1 QT WATER
64	35.60	20.48 oz
65	36.10	20.80 oz
66	36.70	21.12 oz
67	37.20	21.44 oz
68	37.80	21.76 oz
69	38.30	22.08 oz
70	38.90	22.40 oz
71	39.40	22.72 oz
72	40	23.04 oz
73	40.60	23.36 oz
74	41.10	23.68 oz
75	41.70	24 oz

Values for degrees Baumé have been rounded to the nearest tenth.
To convert brix to Baumé, the number of degrees brix by 1.8.

Readings and Resources

Books

BAKING AND PASTRY ARTS

The Baker's Manual. 5th ed. Joseph Amendola and Nicole Rees. John Wiley & Sons, 2003.

The Baker's Trade. Zachary Y. Schat. Acton Circle, 1998.

Baking with Julia: Based on the PBS Series Hosted by Julia Child. Julia Child and Dorie Greenspan. William Morrow, 1996.

The Bread Bible: Beth Hensperger's 300 Favorite Recipes. Beth Hensperger. Chronicle, 1999.

The Bread Builders: Hearth Loaves and Masonry Ovens. Daniel Wing and Alan Scott. Chelsea Green, 1999.

Buffets Sucres. [Sweet Buffets.] Lenôtre. C.H.I.P.S., 1997.

The Cake Bible. Rose Levy Beranbaum. William Morrow, 1988.

The Chocolate Bible. Christian Teubner. Penguin Books, 1997.

Chocolate Desserts by Pierre Hermé. Pierre Hermé and Dorie Greenspan. Little, Brown, 2001.

The Classic and Contemporary Recipes of Yves Thuriès: French Pastry. Yves Thuriès. John Wiley & Sons, 1997.

The Classic and Contemporary Recipes of Yves Thuriès: Modern French Pastry. Yves Thuriès. John Wiley & Sons, 1997.

The Classic and Contemporary Recipes of Yves Thuriès: Restaurant Pastries and Desserts. Yves Thuriès. John Wiley & Sons, 1997.

Creams, Confections, and Finished Desserts. Roland Bilheux and Alain Escoffier. John Wiley & Sons, 1997.

Desserts by Pierre Hermé. Pierre Hermé and Dorie Greenspan. Little, Brown, 1998.

Doughs, Batters, and Meringues. Roland Bilheux and Alain Escoffier. John Wiley & Sons, 1997.

English Bread and Yeast Cookery. Elizabeth David. National Book Network, 1995.

Flatbreads and Flavors: A Culinary Atlas. Jeffrey Alford and Naomi Duguid. Morrow, 1995.

Four-Star Desserts. Emily Luchetti. HarperCollins, 1996.

French Professional Pastry Series: Decorations, Borders and Letters, Marzipan, Modern Desserts. Roland Bilheux and Alain Escoffier. John Wiley & Sons, 1998.

Grand Finales: The Art of the Plated Dessert. Tish Boyle and Timothy Moriarty. John Wiley & Sons, 1996.

Grand Finales: A Neoclassic View of Plated Desserts. Tish Boyle and Timothy Moriarty. John Wiley & Sons, 2000.

Les Recettes Fruitées. [Recipes for Fruit from l'Ecole Lenôtre.]. Lenôtre School. C.H.I.P.S., 1998.

The Making of a Pastry Chef. Andrew MacLauchlan. John Wiley & Sons, 1999.

Grand Finales: A Modernist View of Plated Desserts. Tish Boyle and Timothy Moriarty. John Wiley & Sons, 1997.

Nancy Silverton's Breads from the La Brea Bakery: Recipes for the Connoisseur. Nancy Silverton, with Laurie Ochoa. Random House, 1996.

The New International Confectioner. 5th ed. Wilfred J. France. Virtue, 1987.

Pains et Viennoiseries [Bread and Viennese Breads]. Lenôtre. C.H.I.P.S., 1995.

Pastries, Cakes, and Desserts. Rossano Boscolo. C.H.I.P.S., 1996.

Petits Fours, Chocolate, Frozen Desserts, and Sugar Work. Roland Bilheux and Alain Escoffier. John Wiley & Sons, 1997.

The Pie and Pastry Bible. Rose Levy Beranbaum. Simon & Schuster, 1998.

Practical Baking. William J. Sultan. John Wiley & Sons, 1996.

The Professional Pastry Chef . 3rd ed. Bo Friberg. John Wiley & Sons, 1996.

Recettes et Glacées. [Ice Cream and Iced Desserts.] Lenôtre. C.H.I.P.S., 1995.

Simply Sensational Desserts: 140 Classics for the Home Baker from New York's Famous Pâtisserie and Bistro. François Payard, with Tim Moriarty and Tish Boyle. Broadway Books, 1999.

Special and Decorative Breads: Basic Bread-making Techniques—46 Special Breads, Fancy Breads—Viennese Breads, Decorative Breads—Presentation Pieces. Roland Bilheux, Alain Escoffier, Daniel Hervé, and Jean-Marie Pouradier. John Wiley & Sons, 1998.

Special and Decorative Breads: Traditional, Regional and Special Breads, Fancy Breads—Viennese Pastries—Croissants, Brioches—Decorative Breads—Presentation Pieces. Alain Couet and Eric Kayser. John Wiley & Sons, 1997.

Understanding Baking. 3rd ed. Joseph Amendola and Nicole Rees. John Wiley & Sons, 2003.

The Village Baker. Joe Ortiz. Ten Speed Press, 1993.

GENERAL COOKERY

Escoffier: The Complete Guide to the Art of Modern Cookery. Auguste Escoffier. John Wiley & Sons, 1995.

Escoffier Cook Book. Auguste Escoffier. Crown, 1941.

Le Répertoire de la Cuisine. Louis Saulnier. Barron's, 1977.

Ma Gastronomie. Ferdinand Point. Translated by Frank Kulla and Patricia S. Kulla. Lyceum, 1974.

The Professional Chef. 7th ed. The Culinary Institute of America. John Wiley & Sons, 2002.

EQUIPMENT AND MISE EN PLACE

The Chef's Book of Formulas, Yields, and Sizes. 2nd ed. Arno Schmidt. John Wiley & Sons, 1996.

Food Equipment Facts: A Handbook for the Foodservice Industry. 2nd ed. Carl Scriven and James Stevens. John Wiley & Sons, 1989.

The New Cook's Catalogue: The Definitive Guide to Cooking Equipment. Burt Wolf, Emily Aronson, and Florence Fabricant, eds. Knopf, 2000.

The Professional Chef's Knife Kit. 2nd ed. The Culinary Institute of America. John Wiley & Sons, 1999.

GENERAL PRODUCT IDENTIFICATION

The Book of Coffee and Tea. 2nd ed. Joel Schapira, David Schapira, and Karl Schapira. St. Martin's, 1996.

Cheese Primer. Steven Jenkins. Workman, 1996.

Cheeses of the World. U.S. Department of Agriculture. Peter Smith, 1986.

The Chef's Companion: A Concise Dictionary of Culinary Terms. 2nd ed. Elizabeth Riely. John Wiley & Sons, 1996.

The Complete Book of Spices: A Practical Guide to Spices and Aromatic Seeds. Jill Norman. Viking, 1995.

A Concise Encyclopedia of Gastronomy. André Louis Simon. Overlook, 1983.

The Cook's Ingredients. Philip Dowell and Adrian Bailey. Reader's Digest, 1990.

Food Lover's Companion. 3rd ed. Sharon Tyler Herbst. Barron's, 2001.

Larousse Gastronomique. Jenifer Harvey Lang, ed. Crown, 1988.

The Master Dictionary of Food and Wine. 2nd ed. Joyce Rubash. John Wiley & Sons, 1996.

The Oxford Companion to Food. Alan Davidson. Oxford University Press, 1999.

Pâtisserie: An Encyclopedia of Cakes, Pastries, Cookies, Biscuits, Chocolate, Confectionery, and Desserts. Aaron Maree. HarperCollins, 1994.

Spices, Salt, and Aromatics in the English Kitchen. Elizabeth David. Penguin, 1972.

The World Encyclopedia of Food. Patrick L. Coyle. Facts-on-File, 1982.

Uncommon Fruits & Vegetables: A Commonsense Guide. Elizabeth Schneider. William Morrow, 1998.

Vegetables from Amaranth to Zucchini. Elizabeth Schneider. William Morrow, 2001.

FOOD SCIENCE AND MATH

CookWise: The Secrets of Cooking Revealed. Shirley Corriher. William Morrow, 1997.

Culinary Math. Linda Blocker, Julia Hill, and The Culinary Institute of America. John Wiley & Sons, 2002.

The Curious Cook. Harold McGee. Hungry Minds, 1992.

Food Science. 3rd ed. Helen Charley. Macmillan, 1994.

On Food and Cooking: The Science and Lore of the Kitchen. Harold McGee. Simon & Schuster, 1997.

SANITATION AND SAFETY

Applied Foodservice Sanitation Textbook. 4th ed. Educational Foundation of the National Restaurant Association, 1993.

Basic Food Sanitation. The Culinary Institute of America, 1993.

HACCP: Reference Book. Educational Foundation of the National Restaurant Association, 1993.

FOOD HISTORY

Culture and Cuisine: A Journey Through the History of Food. Jean-François Revel. Translated by Helen R. Lane. DaCapo, 1984.

Food and Drink Through the Ages, 2500 B.C. to 1937 A.D. Barbara Feret. Maggs Brothers, 1937.

Food in History. Reay Tannahill. Random House, 1995.

Periodicals

AMERICAN CAKE DECORATING
4215 White Bear Parkway, Suite100
St. Paul, MN 55110-7635
Tel: 651-293-1544
Fax: 651-653-4308
www.americancakedecorating.com

ART CULINAIRE
40 Mills Street
Morristown, NJ 07960
Tel: 800-SO-TASTY
Fax: 973-993-8779
www.getartc.com

BAKERS JOURNAL
222 Argyle Avenue
Delhi, Ontario N4B 2Y2
Canada
Tel: 519-582-2513
Fax: 519-582-4040

THE BAKING SHEET
King Arthur Flour Company
P.O. Box 1010
Norwich, VT 05055
Tel: 800-827-6836
www.kingarthurflour.com

BAKING AND SNACK
4800 Main Street, Suite 100
Kansas City, MO 64112
Tel: 816-756-1000
Fax: 816-756-0494
bakesnack@sosland.com
www.bakingbusiness.com

BON APPÉTIT
6300 Wilshire Boulevard
Los Angeles, CA 90048
Tel: 800-765-9419
www.bonappetit.com

CAKE: CRAFT AND DECORATION
Cake Magazine Subscription Dept.
Tower House
Sovereign Park
Market Harborough LE16 9EF
UK
Tel: 01858-439605
www.cake-craft.com

CAKES AND SUGARCRAFT
Squires Kitchen Magazine
Publishing Ltd.
Alfred House
Hones Business Park
Farnham, Surrey GU9 8BB
UK
Tel: 01252-727572
Fax: 01252-714714
www.squires-group.co.uk

CHEF MAGAZINE
20 West Kinzie Street, 12th floor
Chicago, IL 60610
Tel: 888-545-3676, ext. 10
www.chefmagazine.com

CHEF EDUCATOR TODAY
20 West Kinzie, 12th floor
Chicago, IL 60610
Tel: 888-545-3676, ext.10
Fax: 800-444-9745
www.chefedtoday.com

CHOCOLATIER
P.O. Box 333
Mt. Morris, IL 61054
Tel: 815-734-5816

CONFECTIONER MAGAZINE
155 Pfingsten Road, Suite 205
Deerfield, IL 60015
Tel: 847-205-5660
Fax: 847-205-5680

COOK'S ILLUSTRATED
P.O. Box 7446
Red Oak, IA 51591-0446
Tel: 617-232-1000
Fax: 617-232-1572

FANCY FOOD AND CULINARY PRODUCTS
20 North Wacker Drive, Suite 1865
Chicago, IL 60606
Tel: 312-849-2220, ext. 48
Fax: 312-849-2174

FINE COOKING
The Taunton Press
Newtown, CT 06470-5506
Tel: 203-426-8171
www.finecooking.com

FOOD ARTS
387 Park Avenue South
New York, NY 10016
Tel: 212-684-4224
Fax: 212-779-3334

FOOD & WINE
1120 Avenue of the Americas
New York, NY 10036
Tel: 800-333-6569
www.foodandwine.com

GOURMET
4 Times Square
New York, NY 10036-6563
Tel: 800-365-2454

MODERN BAKING
P.O. Box 9400
Collingswood, NJ 08108-0940
www.bakery-net.com

NATION'S RESTAURANT NEWS
Tel: 800-944-4676
Fax: 212-756-5215
www.nrn.com

PASTRY ART & DESIGN
P.O. Box 333
Mt. Morris, IL 61054
Tel: 815-734-5816

SAVEUR
P.O. Box 420235
Palm Coast, FL 32142-0235
Tel: 877-717-8925
Saveur@palmcoastd.com

TEA AND COFFEE
26 Broadway, Floor 9M
New York, NY 10004
Tel: 212-391-2060
Fax: 212-827-0945
www.teaandcoffee.net

WINE AND SPIRITS
2 West 32nd Street, Suite 601
New York, NY 10001
Tel: 212-695-4660
Info@wineandspiritsmagazine.com

WINE SPECTATOR
P.O. Box 37367
Boone, IA 50037-0367
Tel: 800-752-7799

Organizations

AMERICAN CULINARY FEDERATION (ACF)
P.O. Box 3466
St. Augustine, FL 32085
Tel: 904-824-4468

AMERICAN INSTITUTE OF BAKING
1213 Bakers Way
Manhattan, KS 66502
Tel: 785-537-4750
www.aibonline.org

BREAD BAKERS GUILD OF AMERICA
3203 Maryland Avenue
North Versailles, PA 15137
Tel: 412-322-8275
www.bbga.org

CHEFS COLLABORATIVE 2000
282 Moody Street, Suite 207
Waltham, MA 02453
Tel: 781-736-0635
www.chefnet.com/cc2000

INTERNATIONAL COUNCIL ON HOTEL/RESTAURANT AND INSTITUTIONAL EDUCATION (CHRIE)
3205 Skipwith Road
Richmond, VA 23294
Tel: 804-747-4971
www.chrie.org

INTERNATIONAL ASSOCIATION OF CULINARY PROFESSIONALS (IACP)
304 West Liberty, Suite 201
Louisville, KY 40202
Tel: 502-581-9786
www.iacp.com

JAMES BEARD FOUNDATION
167 West 12th Street
New York, NY 10011
Tel: 212-675-4984
www.jamesbeard.org

MID-ATLANTIC BAKERS ASSOCIATION
P.O. Box 4141
Harrisburg, PA 17111-4141
Tel: 717-561-4155
www.midatlanticbakers.org

NATIONAL RESTAURANT ASSOCIATION (NRA)
1200 17th Street, NW
Washington, DC 20036
Tel: 202-331-5900
www.restaurant.org

RETAILER'S BAKERY ASSOCIATION
14239 Park Center Drive
Laurel, MD 20707-5261
Tel: 800-638-0924
www.rbanet.com

ROUNDTABLE FOR WOMEN IN FOODSERVICE
3022 West Eastwood Street
Chicago, IL 60625
Tel: 800-898-2849

WOMEN CHEFS AND RESTAURATEURS (WCR)
304 West Liberty, Suite 201
Louisville, KY 40202
Tel: 502-581-0300
www.chefnet.com/wcr

Décor Templates

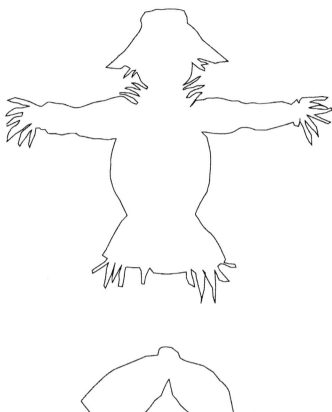

Monkey Template

Scarecrow Template

Palm Tree Template

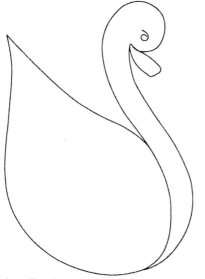

Swan Template

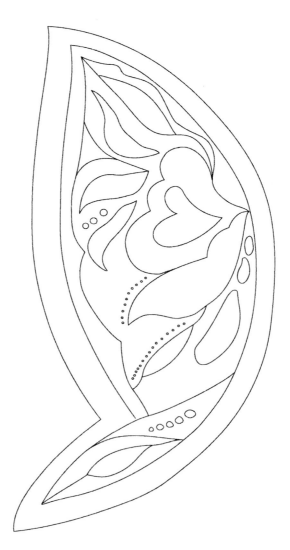

Butterfly Cake Template

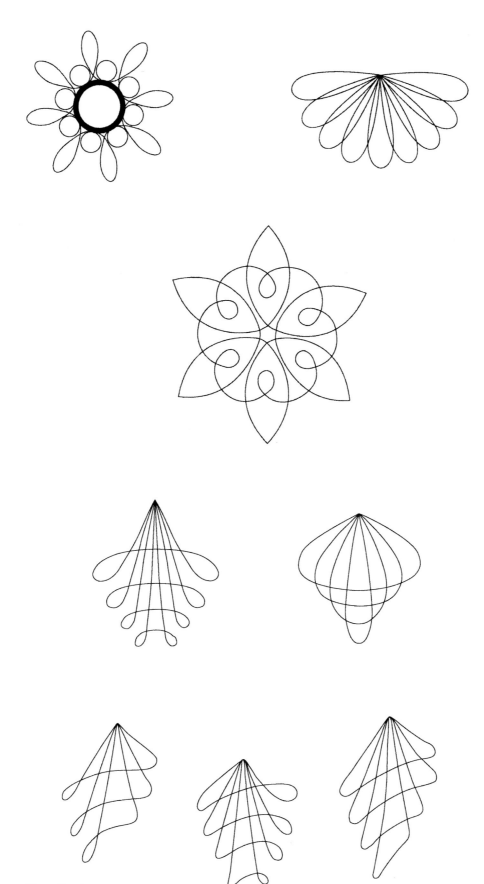

Filigree Templates

Congratulations "C" Template

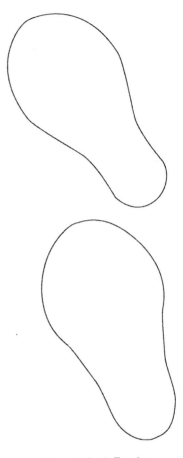

Magnolia Petals Template

Glossary

ACID: A substance having a sour or sharp flavor. Foods generally referred to as acids include citrus juice, vinegar, and wine. A substance's degree of acidity is measured on the pH scale; acids have a pH of less than 7.

ACTIVE DRY YEAST: A dehydrated form of yeast that needs to be hydrated in warm water (105°F/41°C) before using it. It contains about one-tenth of the moisture of compressed yeast.

ADULTERATED FOOD: Food that has been contaminated to the point that it is considered unfit for human consumption.

AERATION: To incorporate air by beating or whipping the ingredients together.

AEROBIC BACTERIA: Bacteria that require the presence of oxygen to function.

AGAR-AGAR: A substance derived from certain sea vegetables. It is eight times stronger than gelatin.

ALBUMIN: A water-soluble protein found in egg whites.

ALKALI: A substance that tests at higher than 7 on the pH scale. Baking soda is an example of an alkaline ingredient.

ALMOND PASTE: A mass of ground almonds and sugar.

ALPHA CRYSTALS: Large crystals in untempered chocolate. They are not uniform or stable and are melted at 83°F/28°C to properly temper chocolate.

AMYLOPECTIN: A component of starch composed of irregularly branched molecules. With a high presence of amylopectin, a starch will act to increase viscosity to a greater extent without causing a gel to form.

AMYLOSE: A component of starch composed of long, linear molecules. The higher the presence of amylose, the more the substance is prone to gel.

ANAEROBIC BACTERIA: Bacteria that do not require oxygen to function.

ASH CONTENT: The mineral content in flour.

AUTOLYSE: A resting period for dough after mixing the flour and water. This rest allows the dough to fully hydrate and to relax the gluten.

BACTERIA: Microscopic organisms. Some have beneficial properties; others can cause food-borne illnesses when contaminated foods are ingested.

BAKING POWDER: A chemical leavening agent composed of sodium bicarbonate, an acid, and a moisture absorber such as cornstarch. When moistened and/or exposed to heat, it releases carbon dioxide to raise a batter or dough.

BAKING SODA: A chemical leavening agent. Sodium bicarbonate is an alkali that when combined with an acid breaks down and releases carbon dioxide. This reaction causes the product to leaven as it is baked.

BATTER: A pourable mixture of combined ingredients, high in liquefiers.

BAUMÉ (BÉ): A scale for expressing the specific gravity of a liquid or the method for measuring the density of sugar syrups. It is expressed in degrees.

BENCH REST: In yeast dough production, the stage that allows the preshaped dough to rest before its final shaping. Also known as secondary fermentation.

BETA CRYSTALS: The small, stable fat crystals that give chocolate its shine and snap.

BIGA: Italian for an aged dough. A type of pre-ferment containing 50 to 60 percent water and ⅓ to ½ percent instant yeast.

BITTERSWEET CHOCOLATE: Chocolate containing a minimum of 35 percent chocolate liquor with varying amounts of sweeteners and cocoa butter.

BLANCH: To remove the skins from nuts by scalding.

BLEND: To fold or mix ingredients together.

BLIND BAKE: To partially or completely bake an unfilled pastry crust.

BLOCK METHOD: A method for tempering chocolate in which a block of tempered chocolate is added to melted chocolate and agitated until the proper temperature is reached, at which time the block is removed.

BLOOMING: (1) The process of allowing gelatin to soften in (sheet gelatin) or soak up (granulated gelatin) cold water. (2) For chocolate, see Fat bloom and Sugar bloom.

BOULANGER: The French word for baker.

BRAN: The tough outer layer of a grain kernel and the part highest in fiber.

BRIX SCALE: A scale of measurement (decimal system) used to determine the density and concentration of sugar in a solution.

CARAMELIZATION: The process of cooking sugar in the presence of heat. The temperature range in which sugar caramelizes is approximately 320° to 360°F/160° to 182°C. The browning of sugar enhances the flavor and appearance of food.

CHEMICAL LEAVENER: An ingredient (such as baking soda or baking powder) whose chemical action is used to produce carbon dioxide gas to leaven baked goods.

CHOCOLATE LIQUOR: The product made by grinding cocoa beans without adding sugar or cocoa butter.

COATING CHOCOLATE: Chocolate made with fats other than cocoa butter, which does not require tempering to use.

COCOA BUTTER: The fat extracted from the cacao bean.

COMMON MERINGUE: A mixture of stiffly beaten egg whites and sugar.

COMPOUND CHOCOLATE: See Coating chocolate.

COMPRESSED FRESH YEAST: This type of yeast is moist and must be refrigerated because it is extremely perishable.

COUVERTURE: A type of chocolate specifically designed for coating or incorporation with other ingredients. Extra cocoa butter is added to increase its smoothness, flexibility, and gloss after tempering. The cocoa butter content of couverture should be at least 32 percent.

CREAMING: To blend fats and sugar together to incorporate air.

CROSS CONTAMINATION: The transference of disease-causing elements from one source to another through physical contact.

CRUMB: A term used to describe the interior texture of baked goods.

CRYSTALLIZATION: A process that occurs when sugar is deposited from a solution.

DENATURE: To alter the original form of a substance. In proteins, exposure to heat or acid will "cook" or denature the protein.

DEXTROSE: A simple sugar made by the action of acids or enzymes on starch. Also known as corn sugar.

DISACCHARIDE: A complex or double sugar. When fructose and dextrose are bonded together, this is called sucrose, or table sugar. Maltose is another example of a disaccharide.

DISSOLVING: The process of heating bloomed gelatin until it is transparent and liquid.

DOCK: To pierce dough lightly with a fork or dough docker (resembles a spiked paint roller) to allow steam to escape during baking. This helps the dough to remain flat and even.

DOCTOR: A substance that is added to a sugar solution to help prevent crystallization. Common doctors are acids and glucose.

DOUGH: A mixture of ingredients high in stabilizers and often stiff enough to cut into shapes.

DUTCH PROCESS COCOA: Cocoa made by adding alkali to nibs or to cocoa powder to develop certain flavors, reduce acidity, and make it more soluble.

EMULSION: The suspension of two ingredients that do not usually mix. Butter is an emulsion of water in fat.

ENDOSPERM: The inside portion of a grain, usually the largest portion, composed primarily of starch and protein.

ENRICHED DOUGH: Dough that is enriched with ingredients that add fat or vitamins. Examples of these ingredients are sugar, eggs, milk, and fats.

FACULTATIVE BACTERIA: Bacteria that can survive both with and without oxygen.

FAT BLOOM: The white cast and soft texture that is the result of poor tempering or exposure of chocolate to high temperatures. Although fat bloom is visually and texturally unappealing, the chocolate is safe to eat.

FERMENTATION: A process that happens in any dough containing yeast. It begins as soon as the ingredients are mixed together and continues until the dough reaches an internal temperature of 138°F/59°C during baking. As the yeast eats the sugars present in the dough, carbon dioxide is released, which causes the dough to expand. Fermentation alters the flavor and appearance of the final product.

FOAMING: The process of beating eggs (the yolks and/or whites) to incorporate air until they form a foam.

FOLDING: (1) To incorporate a lighter mixture into a heavier one. (2) The process of folding a dough over itself during the bulk fermentation stage to redistribute the available food supply for the yeast, to equalize the tempera-

ture of the dough, to expel gases, and to further develop the gluten in the dough.

FONDANT: Sugar cooked with corn syrup, which is induced to crystallize by constant agitation, in order to produce the finest possible crystalline structure. Fondant is used as centers in chocolate production, or as a glaze in pastries.

FOOD-BORNE ILLNESS: An illness in humans caused by the consumption of an adulterated food product. In order for a food-borne illness to be considered official, it must involve two or more people who have eaten the same food, and it must be confirmed by health officials.

FORMULA: A recipe in which measurements for each ingredient are given as percentages of the weight for the main ingredient.

FRUCTOSE: A monosaccharide that occurs naturally in fruits and honey. Also known as fruit sugar or levulose.

GANACHE: An emulsion of chocolate and cream. Ganache may also be made with butter or other liquids in place of the cream.

GÂTEAU: The French word for cake.

GELATIN: A protein derived from the skins and tendons of animals. Gelatin is used as a binder and stabilizer. It is available in granulated and sheet/leaf forms.

GELATINIZATION: The process in which starch granules, suspended in liquid, are heated; they begin to absorb liquid and swell in size.

GERM: The embryo of a cereal grain that is usually separated from the endosperm during milling because it contains oils that accelerate the spoilage of flours and meals.

GLIADIN: A protein found in wheat flour. The part of gluten that gives it extensibility and viscosity.

GLUCOSE: (1) A monosaccharide that occurs naturally in fruits, some vegetables, and honey. Also known as dextrose. (2) A food additive used in confections.

GLUTEN: The protein component in wheat flour that builds structure and strength in baked goods. It is developed when the proteins glutenin and gliadin are moistened and agitated (kneaded). It provides the characteristic elasticity and extensibility of dough.

GLUTENIN: A protein found in wheat flour. The part of gluten that gives it strength and elasticity.

GRAIN: (1) To crystallize. Fondant is agitated until it grains. (2) A seed or fruit of a cereal grass.

GUM ARABIC: A water-soluble vegetable gum obtained from the stems and branches of various species of acacia trees. It is used to thicken, emulsify, and stabilize foods such as candy and ice cream.

GUM PASTE: A white modeling substance made from gum tragacanth or gelatin, water, glucose, and sugar.

GUM TRAGACANTH: A substance obtained from the Asian shrub *Astragalus gummifier* that is used like gum arabic to thicken, emulsify, and stabilize foods.

HOMOGENIZE: To take ingredients and mix them together so they become the same in structure.

HUMECTANT: A type of food additive used to promote moisture retention.

HYDRATE: To combine ingredients with water.

HYDROGENATION: The process in which hydrogen atoms are added to an unsaturated fat molecule, making it partially or completely saturated at room temperature. Vegetable oils are hydrogenated to create shortening.

HYDROLYZE: To chemically split one compound into other compounds by taking up the elements of water. Cornstarch is hydrolyzed to produce corn syrup.

HYGROSCOPIC: Absorbing moisture from the air. Sugar and salt are both hygroscopic ingredients.

INFECTION: Contamination by disease-causing agents, such as bacteria, consumed via foods.

INFUSE: To flavor by allowing an aromatic to steep in the substance to be flavored. Infusions may be made either hot or cold.

INTOXICATION: Poisoning. A state of being tainted with toxins, particularly those produced by microorganisms that have infected food.

INVERT SUGAR: Sucrose that has been broken down (inverted) into a mix of dextrose (glucose) and levulose (fructose). It is sweeter, more soluble, and does not crystallize as easily as sucrose.

ITALIAN MERINGUE: A mixture of egg whites and sugar syrup (140°F/60°C) whipped until shiny, fluffy, and cool.

KUCHEN: The German word for cake or pastry.

LACTIC ACID: An acid produced when lactose is fermented. It occurs naturally when milk is soured.

LACTOSE: The simple sugar found in milk.

LAMINATION: The technique of layering fat and dough through a process of rolling and folding to create alternating layers.

LEAN DOUGH: A yeast dough that does not contain fats or sugar.

LEAVENING: Raising or lightening by air, steam, or gas (carbon dioxide). In baking, leavening occurs with yeast (organic), baking powder or baking soda (chemical), and steam (physical/mechanical).

LECITHIN: A naturally occurring emulsifier found in egg yolks and legumes.

LEVULOSE: A simple sugar found in honey and fruits. It is also known as fructose or fruit sugar.

LIQUEFIER: An ingredient that helps to loosen or liquefy a dough or batter. Sugar, fats, and water or milk are examples of liquefiers in baking.

MAILLARD REACTION: A complex browning reaction that results in the particular flavor and color of foods that do not contain much sugar, such as bread. The reaction, which involves carbohydrates and amino acids, is named after the French scientist who first discovered it.

MARZIPAN: A pliable dough of almonds and sugar. Marzipan may also be flavored by the addition of nuts other than almonds.

MASKING: Covering a cake with icing, frosting, or glaze.

MERINGUE: A white, frothy mass of beaten egg whites and sugar.

MIGNARDISES: An assortment of small, two-bite-size pastries.

MILK CHOCOLATE: Sweet chocolate to which whole and/or skim milk powder has been added. It must contain at least 10 percent chocolate liquor by weight, although premium brands contain more.

MILLE-FEUILLE: French for "a thousand leaves." This pastry is known in America as a napoleon.

MISE EN PLACE: French for "put in place." The preparation and assembly of ingredients, pans, utensils, and plates or serving pieces needed for a particular dish or service period.

MIXING: The blending of ingredients.

MONOSACCHARIDE: A single or simple sugar and the basic building block of sugars and starches. Fructose, glucose, levulose, and dextrose are examples of monosaccharides.

NAPPÉ: The consistency of a liquid that will coat or cover the back of a spoon.

ORGANIC LEAVENER: Yeast. A living organism operates by fermenting sugar to produce carbon dioxide gas, causing the batter or dough to rise.

OVEN SPRING: The rapid initial rise of yeast doughs when placed in a hot oven. Heat accelerates the growth of the yeast, which produces more carbon dioxide gas and also causes this gas to expand. This continues until the dough reaches a temperature of 140°F/60°C.

OVERRUN: The increase in volume of ice cream caused by the incorporation of air during the freezing process.

PAIN: The French word for bread.

PAR BAKE: To start the baking process, and to finish it at a later time.

PASTILLAGE: See Gum paste.

PATHOGEN: A disease-causing microorganism.

PATISSIER: The French word for pastry chef.

PECTIN: A gelling agent or thickener found in fruits, particularly in apples, quince, and the skins of citrus fruits.

PETIT FOUR: A small bite-size cake, pastry, cookie, or confection. The term is French for "small oven."

PH SCALE: A scale with values from 0 to 14 representing degrees of acidity. A measurement of 7 is neutral, 0 is most acidic, and 14 is most alkaline. Chemically, pH measures the concentration and activity of the element hydrogen.

PHYSICAL LEAVENING: occurs when air and/or moisture that is trapped during the mixing process expands as it is heated. This can occur through foaming, creaming, or lamination. Also known as mechanical leavening.

POLYSACCHARIDE: A complex carbohydrate such as a starch, which consists of long chains of saccharides, amylose, and amylopectin.

POOLISH: A semiliquid starter dough with equal parts, by weight, of flour and water that are blended with yeast and allowed to ferment for 3 to 15 hours.

PRE-FERMENT: A piece of dough that is saved from the previous day's production to be used in the following day's dough.

PRESHAPING: The gentle, first shaping of dough. Also known as rounding.

PROOF: To allow yeast dough to rise.

PROTEASES: Enzymes that break down the collagen in gelatin and do not allow it to set or "gel." This destructive enzyme is in kiwi, pineapple, papaya, and other fruits.

RATIOS: A general formula of ingredients that can be varied.

RECIPE: A specific formula of ingredients and amounts.

RETROGRADATION: The process in which starches high in amylose revert back to their insoluble form after they are gelatinized and then undergo freezing, refrigeration, or aging. This reaction causes changes in texture and appearance.

SACCHARIDE: A sugar molecule.

SANITATION: The preparation and distribution of food in a clean environment by healthy food workers.

SANITIZE: To kill pathogenic organisms chemically and/or by moist heat.

SCALE: To measure ingredients by weight.

SCALING: Portioning batter or dough according to weight or size.

SCORE: To make incisions into dough to allow steam to escape and the crust to expand. Also known as slashing or docking.

SECONDARY FERMENTATION: See Bench rest.

SEED: (1) In chocolate tempering, a portion of tempered chocolate added to begin the formation of beta crystals. (2) Anything that acts as a surface to which sugar will adhere and crystallize.

SEED METHOD: A method of tempering chocolate. Chopped tempered chocolate, or seeds, are added to the melted chocolate and agitated until the desired temperature is reached.

SEMISWEET CHOCOLATE: Chocolate that contains between 15 and 35 percent chocolate liquor. Other than chocolate liquor, it contains added cocoa butter, sugar, vanilla or vanillin, and often lecithin.

SHORTENING AGENTS: Fats and oils. This term is derived from their ability to split the long, elastic gluten strands that can toughen dough and batters. This tenderizing effect renders the strands more susceptible to breaking or "shortening," resulting in a more tender and less dense crumb.

STABILIZER: An ingredient that helps to develop the solid structure or "framework" of a finished product. Flour and eggs act as stabilizers in baking.

STARTER: A mixture of flour, liquid, and commercial or wild yeast that is allowed to ferment. The starter must be "fed" with flour and water to keep it active.

STEEP: To allow to infuse.

SUCROSE: Table sugar. A disaccharide extracted from sugarcane or sugar beets and consisting of glucose and fructose joined together in the molecule.

SUGAR BLOOM: The result of damp storage conditions in milk or dark chocolate. When the moisture evaporates, a white crust of sugar crystals is left behind. Like fat bloom, it is visually and texturally unappealing, but the chocolate is still safe to eat.

SWISS MERINGUE: A mixture of stiffly beaten egg whites and sugar heated over simmering water until it reaches 140°F/60°C; it is then whipped until cool.

TABLING METHOD: A method of tempering chocolate. A percentage of the chocolate is poured onto a marble slab and agitated until it begins to set. It is then added back to the remaining chocolate and stirred until it reaches the proper working temperature.

TART: A shallow, usually open-faced pastry shell with filling.

TARTLET: A small, single-serving tart.

TEMPER: (1) To melt, agitate, and cool chocolate to ensure that it retains its smooth gloss, crisp "snap" feel, and creamy texture. (2) To heat gently and gradually, as in the process of incorporating hot liquid into a liaison to gradually raise its temperature.

TEXTURE: The interior grain or structure of a baked product as shown by a cut surface; the feeling of a substance under the fingers.

TORTE: The German word for cake. It can be multilayered or a single, dense layer.

TOXIN: A naturally occurring poison, particularly those produced by the metabolic activity of living organisms such as bacteria.

TRUFFLE: A ganache center that is usually coated with chocolate. Truffles are round and are named after the fungus that they resemble.

UNSWEETENED CHOCOLATE: Chocolate liquor without added sugar or flavorings.

VIRUS: A type of pathogenic microorganism that can be transmitted in food. Viruses cause such illnesses as measles, chicken pox, infectious hepatitis, and colds.

WHIP: To beat an item, such as cream or egg whites, to incorporate air.

WHITE CHOCOLATE: True white chocolate, like that found in Europe, is made from cocoa butter, milk, sugar, and flavorings, and it contains no chocolate liquor. In the United States, white confectionery coating, made with vegetable fat instead of cocoa butter, is more readily available.

Recipe and Title Index

Subject Index

Acetate sheets, 66
Acidity, 81
Active dry yeast, 31, 126
Adulterated food, 89
Aerobic bacteria, 90
Agar-agar, 23, 86
Airbrush, 66
Alkalinity, 81
All-purpose flour, 19, 246, 276
Allspice, 33
Almonds, 34
  in marzipan, 775
Alpha crystals, in chocolate, 89
American Culinary Federation
    (ACF), 8–9
Americans with Disabilities Act
    (ADA), 104
American-style wedding cakes, 804
Amylopectin, 85
Amylose, 85
Anaerobic bacteria, 90
Angel food cake, 273, 274, 301
Anise seeds, 33, 36
Apple corers, 57, 518
Apples
  pitting and coring, 518
  varieties of, 40
Apricots, 45
Architectural style plated desserts,
    648
Arrowroot, 24, 86
Ash content, in flour, 18
Asian pears, 45
As-purchased quantity (APQ), 115,
    116
Australian-style wedding cakes, 804,
    806
Autolyse, 130–131

Bacteria, 90–92
Bagels, 211
Bain-marie (hot water bath), 381,
    702
Baker's balance, 52
Baker's cheese, 26
Bakers' percentages, 117–118
Bakeware, 66–69
Baking pans
  preparation of, 273, 328
  sizes and volumes, 838
  types of, 66, 68
Baking and pastry professionals. See
    also Management
  career opportunities for, 3–7
  certification of, 8–9
  character traits of, 13
  education of, 7–8
  historical background, 2
  networking, 9
  organizations of, 844
  periodicals for, 843
  reading list for, 840–841
Baking powder, 31, 81
Baking science
  browning reactions, 84–85
  emulsions, 88
  information sources on, 842
  leaveners, 79–82
  liquefiers, 77–79
  stabilizers, 76
  sugar crystallization, 82–84
  tempering chocolate, 89

thickeners, 85–88
Baking soda, 31, 80–81
Banana, 47, 87
Bands, chocolate, 768
Bannetons, 62, 188
Banquets, plated desserts at, 650
Bar cookies, 337
Bartlett pears, 45
Basil, 32
Basket-weave pattern, 546
Basket-weave rolling pin, 63
Batters. See Mixing methods
Baumé scale, 480, 838–839
Bavarian cream, 403, 545, 546
Beam balance, 52
Bench knives, 60
Bench rest, 187
Berries
  for pies and tarts, 516
  varieties of, 40–42
Beta crystals, in chocolate, 89, 704
Biga, 149
Biological food contaminants, 90, 97
Bittersweet chocolate, 29
Blackberries, 41
Black Friar plums, 46
Blenders, 70
Blending mixing method, 276
Blind baking, 511
Blitz puff pastry, 266
Block method of tempering choco-
    late, 704
Blood oranges, 42
Bloom, in chocolate, 29, 702, 703
Bloomed gelatin, 87, 392
Blow dryer, 66
Blown sugar pump, 66
Blown sugar strawberries, 785
Blueberries, 42
Bombes, 495
Bosc pears, 45
Boysenberries, 41
Bramble berries, 41
Bran, 16, 130
Brandy, 49
Brazil nuts, 34
Bread flour, 19, 246, 258, 503
Bread knives, 56
Bread making
  autolyse step in, 130–131
  bagels, 211
  baking, 187, 190, 199, 209, 225
  bulk fermentation period in, 127
  cooling loaves, 190
  desired dough temperature
    (DDT), 118–119, 126–127
  direct fermentation method of,
    122, 127
  enriched dough, 133
  equipment and tools, 60, 62, 72,
    188
  fiber-enriched dough, 130, 151
  flavorings and garnishes, 171
  flavor and texture in, 122, 130,
    149
  folding process in, 126, 171
  indirect fermentation method of,
    149
  leaveners, 79–80
  mixing, 123–124
  pre-ferments, 149
  preshaping dough, 184, 186

proofing (final fermentation), 186,
    188, 198, 208, 224
  resting (intermediate) fermenta-
    tion, 187
  retarding dough, 127
  scaling dough, 183
  scoring dough, 187, 189, 199, 209,
    224
  soakers in, 151
  with sourdough starter, 165–167
  washes, 189
  with wet dough, 163
  yeast to flour ratio, 126
Bread pudding, 391
Brigade system, 2
British-style wedding cakes, 804, 806
British Thermal Units (BTUs), 127
Brix scale, 480, 838–839
Browning reactions, 84–85
Brown sugar, 21
Buckwheat, 20, 130
Bulk fermentation, 127
Butter
  cold foaming method, 302
  combination mixing method, 315
  creaming mixing method, 283–284
  ganache, 715
  quality of, 26–27
  in rubbed dough, 246–247
  in short dough, 250
  as shortening agent, 78
Buttercream icing and filling
  flavorings for, 419–420
  types of, 419
  in wedding cakes, traditional, 804
Buttercream piping
  in American-style wedding cakes,
    804
  leaf, 760–761
  with pastry bag and coupler, 759
  rose, 761, 804
  shell border, 758
Buttermilk, 25

Cake. See also Cake fillings; Décor;
    Specialty cakes; Wedding
    cakes
  assembling and filling layers,
    544–545, 556
  basic principles of, 273
  cooling, 274
  glazing, 547
  high-ratio, 297–298
  icing, 547, 548–549, 556
  in layered pastries, 606
  marzipan covering for, 566
  mixing methods
    angel food, 301
    blending, 276
    chiffon, 273, 319
    combination, 314–315
    creaming, 273, 283–284
    foaming, 273, 302–303, 308
    two-stage, 273, 297–298
  molded cakes, 546–547
  pan preparation, 273
  for petits fours, 372
Cake-decorating combs, 64, 549
Cake-decorating turntable, 64, 545,
    548
Cake fillings
  Bavarian cream, 403, 545

buttercream, 419–420
  chocolate, 544
  ganache, 545
  gelatin-based, 549
  layer cake assembly, 544–545, 556
  meringue, 414–415
  molded cakes, 546
  mousse, 544–545, 546
  raspberry, 544
  whipped cream, 423
Cake flour, 19, 246, 250
Cake pans
  materials and sizes, 66
  preparation of, 273
Cake ring, 68, 546
Cake stands, 805
Candies. See also Confections
  hard, 728, 737
Candy thermometers, 54
Cantaloupes, 44
Caramel
  dragées, 723
  ice cream variegation with, 473
  sauce, 428, 452
  soft caramels, 730
  sugar stages and temperatures, 728
Caramelizing sugar
  browning reaction, 84
  dry method, 385, 728
  wet method, 384–385, 728
Caramel rulers, 65, 700
Caraway seeds, 33, 36
Cardamom, 33
Career opportunities, 3–7
Carême, Marie-Antoine, 2
Casaba melons, 44
Cashews, 34
Cassava, 24, 86
Catering, 4
Certification, 8–9
Certified Executive Pastry Chef
    (CEPC), 9
Certified Master Baker (CMB), 9
Charlotte royale, 546
Charlotte russe, 546
Cheddar cheese, 26
Cheese
  in bread dough, 171
  in custards, baked, 380
  types of, 26
Cheesecake
  cooling, 274
  crumb crust for, 255
  toppings, 322
Cheesecloth, 60
Chef's knives, 55
Chemical food contaminants, 89
Chemical leaveners, 31, 80–81, 273
Cherries, varieties of, 47
Chestnuts, 34
Chiffon mixing method, 273, 319
Chives, 32
Chocolate. See also Chocolate con-
    fections; Chocolate décor;
    Ganache; Tempered chocolate
  couverture, 29, 702
  filling, 544
  fondant, 426
  melting, 702
  molds, 64, 720
  sabayon, 432
  sauce, 428, 434

peelers, reamers, and corers, 57
pots and pans, 69
refrigeration, 72–73
safe handling of, 101
sanitation procedures for, 92, 99
scales, 52
scoops and ladles, 59, 700
for sifting, straining, and puréeing, 60
spatulas and scrapers, 58
spoons and tongs, 57–58
sugar density, measuring, 480–481
for tempering chocolate, 704
thermometers, 53–54
for truffle making, 700
whips, 58
Evaporated milk, 25
Extraction rate, in flour refinement, 18
Extracts, 34, 49

Facultative bacteria, 90
Fans, chocolate, 768
Farmers cheese, 26
Fats
blending mixing method, 276
in bread dough, 133
creaming mixing method, 283–284
functions in baking, 78
in laminated dough, 261
in rubbed dough, 246
in short dough, 250
types of, 28–29
Fermentation
bulk, 127
defined, 79–80
direct, 122
final (proofing), 62, 186, 188, 198
indirect, 149
resting (intermediate), 187
temperature for, 80
Fiber-enriched bread dough, 130–131
Filigree, piped, 373, 761
Fillings
Bavarian cream, 403, 545
buttercream, 419–420
fruit, for pies and tarts, 516–518
fruit, poached, in plated desserts, 593
gelatin-based, 549
for layer cakes, 544–545, 556
meringue, 414–415
for molded cakes, 546
in pâte à choux, 622, 628
for tartlets, 589
whipped cream, 423
Fire extinguishers, 102
Fire safety, 101–102, 104
First in, first out (FIFO) system, 94
Flaky dough, 247–248
Flan rings, 68
Flavorings. See also Herbs, Spices
for bread dough, 171
for butter ganache, 715
for caramel sauce, 452
for cream ganache, 699, 700
for egg ganache, 720
extracts, 34, 49
fruit purée as, 409, 471, 720
for granita, 489
for hard candies, 728, 737
for ice cream, 467, 471
infusion method, 49, 452, 700, 720
for sorbet, 480
tea and coffee as, 49, 452
for truffles, 700

wine and liqueur as, 49, 700, 715, 720
Floating egg test, 481
Flood work, with royal icing, 771–772
Flour
in bakers' percentages, 117–118
gluten-content, 76, 77
grain, 19, 20
high-gluten, 211
high-protein, 257, 258
for pâte à choux, 256–257
for quick breads and cakes, 276
for rubbed dough, 246
sifted, 273, 276, 284
as stabilizer, 77
as thickener, 86
wheat, 16, 17–18, 76, 130
whole wheat/whole grain, 19, 130
yeast to flour ratio, 126
Flowers, décor
buttercream rose, 761
gum paste magnolia, 798
gum paste rose, 796–798
marzipan cutouts, 775
marzipan rose, 776–777
pulled sugar blossom, 786–787
Foaming mixing method, 81, 273
cold, 302–303
separated, 308
warm, 303
Folding of laminated dough, 261–263
Folding method
bread dough, 126, 171
cakes, 303, 308, 315, 319
mousse, 397–398
Fondant
on doughnuts, 243
on layer cake, 562
on petits fours, 373
preparing, 426
Fondant funnel, 64
Food-borne illness, 89–92
Food chopper, 71
Food and Drug Administration (FDA), 94–95, 97, 467
Food mill, 60
Food processor, 71, 742, 775
Food safety
contaminant sources, 89–91
in cooling food, 94–95
cross-contamination, 92–93
hand-washing practices for, 90, 92
Hazard Analysis Critical Control Points (HACCP), 96–99
hazardous foods and, 91–92
hot- and cold-holding equipment, 94
information sources on, 842
pest control, 99–100
in receiving process, 93
in reheating food, 95
during service, 96
storage conditions for, 93–94
temperature controls and, 93, 94, 97–98
in thawing frozen foods, 95
Food science. See Baking science
Formulas
in bakers' percentages, 117–118
cost calculations, 115, 117
desired dough temperature (DDT), 118–119
scaling and, 108
standardized, 110–111

U.S./metric system conversions, 114
volume to weight conversions, 113–114
yield calculations, 115
yield conversions, 111–112
yield percentage, 115–116
Frangipane
for petits fours, 372
for tartlets, 589
Freezing, laminated dough, 264
French buttercream, 419
French ice cream, 466
French knives, 55
French meringue, 415
French method of marzipan making, 775
Frozen dessert. See also Ice cream
granita, 480, 489
molded, 492
plated, 688
sorbet and sherbet, 480–481
still-frozen, 495
Frozen foods, thawing, 95
Fructose, 82
Fruit
apple varieties, 40
berries, 40–42
candied, in rochers, 722
citrus, 42
cutting and peeling, 517–518
exotic/tropical, 47–49
gelatin-based applications, 87
in ice cream, 471
melons, 43–45
pear varieties, 45
for pies and tarts, 516
pitting and coring, 518
poached, 471, 593
rhubarb, 49
sauces, 428, 436
selecting and handling, 37
in sorbets and sherbets, 480, 481
stone fruits, 45–47
yield calculation, 115–116
Fruit, dried
blending mixing method, 276, 284
in bread dough, 171
macerating, 295
Fruitcake, for traditional wedding cake, 804
Fruit purées
in egg ganache, 720
in ice cream, 471
in soufflés, 409
Fungi, in food-borne illnesses, 90

Ganache
butter, 715
cream, 698–699, 833
egg, 719–720
fillings, 545
flavorings, 699, 700
glazing with, 426
hard, 698–699
ice cream variegation with, 473
soft and medium, 698
truffle centers, 698, 700
Ganache rulers, 65
Garlic, roasted, in bread dough, 171
Garnishes
for breads, 171
for cakes. See Décor
for doughnuts, 243
Gelatin
in Bavarian cream, 403
in fillings, 546, 549

forms of, 23
with fruits, 87
melted, 393
in mirror glaze, 426
in mousse, 397, 546
rehydrated (bloomed), 87, 392
in sherbets, 481
uses of, 23, 85, 86
Gelatinization of starches, 16, 85
Gelling agents, 23, 86
Germ, wheat kernel, 16
German buttercream, 419
Gianduja, 742
Ginger, 34
Glass containers, 622
Glazes, glazing
bar cookies, 337
doughnuts, 243
fondant, 243, 372–373, 426, 562
layer cakes, 562
molded cakes, 547
petits fours, 372–373
types of, 426
Gliadin, in flour, 76
Glucose syrup, 21, 22, 82
in butter ganache, 715
in confections, 84
in cream ganache, 699
Gluten, in flour, 76, 211
Gluten development, in bread-making process, 127, 128, 130, 131, 163
Glutenin, in flour, 76
Golden syrup, 23
Gooseberries, 42
Grains
rye flour, 19
types of, 20
wheat flour, 16, 18–19
whole, soakers for, 151
whole and milled, 16
Granita, 480, 489
Granulated sugar, 20
Grapefruit, 42
Grapes, 42
Graters, 57
Grating cheese, 26
Greengage plums, 46
Guava, 47
Guitar cutter, 65, 700
Gum paste
magnolia, 798
modeling tools, 66
pastillage link twist, 794
rose, 796–797
in traditional wedding cake décor, 804
working with, 794

Hand-washing practices, 90, 92
Hard candies, 728, 737
Hat, chef's, 102
Hazard Analysis Critical Control Points (HACCP), 96–99
Hazardous foods, 91–92, 96–97
Hazelnuts, 34
Heat gun, 66
Heimlich maneuver, 101
Herbs
in bread dough, 171
storage of, 32
varieties of, 32–33
High-gluten flour, 19
High-ratio cakes, 297–298
Homogenized milk and cream, 25
Honey, 23
Honeydew melon, 44–45, 87

in rochers, 722
varieties of, 34–35

Oat flour, 20, 130
Oat groats, 20
Oats, 20
Oblique mixers, 71
Occupational Safety and Health
  Administration (OSHA), 103
Oils
  as shortening agent, 78
  types of, 28
Oil sprays, 28
Oligosaccharides, 82
Olive oil, 28
Olives, in bread dough, 171
Omelet pans, 69
On-site refrigeration units, 72
Oranges, varieties of, 42
Oregano, 33
Organizations, culinary, 844
Ovens, types of, 71–72
Oven spring, 190

Paddles, 58
Pan preparation
  cakes and quick breads, 273
  cookies, 328
  custards, 382
  soufflés, 409
Pans
  baking, 66, 68
  for bread making, 62
  for caramelizing sugar, 384
  sizes and volumes, 838
  stovetop, 69
Papaya, 47, 87
Parasites, in food-borne illnesses, 90
Parchment paper
  collar, for frozen soufflés, 495
  cones, 63–64, 762
  lining baking pans with, 273
  removal from cooled cakes, 274
  stencils, making, 715
  uses of, 69
Parfaits, 495
Paring knives, 56
Paris brest, 628
Parmesan cheese, 26
Parsley, 33
Passion fruit, 47
Pastes
  nut, 467
  sugar. See Gum paste
Pasteurized milk, 25
Pastillage link twist, 794
Pastries, individual
  from croissant and Danish dough,
    633
  fruits, poached in, 593
  in glass and natural containers, 622
  layered, 606
  in molds, 615
  in phyllo dough, 626
  piped, 628
  roulades, 606
  tartlets, 588–589
Pastry bag, 63, 760, 761
  with coupler, 759
Pastry brush, 63
Pastry chefs (pâtissier), 2, 3
Pastry cream, 409, 410
Pastry dough
  flaky, 248
  laminated. See Laminated dough;
    Puff pastry
  mealy, 248

pâte à choux, 256–257
phyllo, 626
rolling out, 504
rubbed, 246–248
short, 250
strudel, 258, 539
tools for, 62–63
Pastry flour, 19, 246, 276
Pastry professionals. See Baking and
  pastry professionals
Pastry shells, blind baking, 511
Pastry wheel, 63
Pâte à choux
  cooking and baking, 256–257
  piped pastries, 622, 628
Pâte fermentée, 149
Pâtisserie Pittoresque (Carême), 2
Pâtisserie Royal (Carême), 2
Peaches, 45
Peanut brittle, 732
Peanuts, 34, 35
Pears
  pitting and coring, 518
  varieties of, 45
Pecans, 35
Pectin, 23, 86, 87, 481
Peelers, swivel-bladed, 57
Peels (paddles), 62
Peppercorns, 33
Periodicals, culinary, 843
Persian limes, 42
Persian melons, 45
Persimmon, 47
Pest control, 99–100
Petits fours, 372–373
pH scale, 81, 91
Phyllo dough, 626
Physical assets management, 10
Physical food contaminants, 89
Pie pans, 68
  lining with dough, 503, 504
Pies. See also Pastry dough; Tarts
  blind baking shells, 511
  crimping edges of, 505
  crumb crust, 255
  fruit preparation for, 516–518
  rolled dough for, 503–504
  toppings for, 505
Pineapple
  in gelatin-based applications, 87
  peeling and cutting, 518
Piping
  buttercream, 758–761
    leaf, 760–761
    rose, 761
    shell border, 758
  butter ganache, 715
  chocolate, tempered, 763
  chocolate filigrees and writing, 761
  cookies, 360, 366
  gelatin-based fillings, 549
  pâte à choux, 628
  royal icing, 771–773
  tools for, 63–64, 759, 762
  truffles, 700
Piping cones, parchment, 63–64,
  762, 771
Piping tips, 63, 700, 759, 760, 761,
  771
Pistachio nuts, 35
Planetary mixers, 71
Plaques
  chocolate, marbleized, 765
  marzipan, 778
Plastic bowl scrapers, 58
Plated desserts
  at banquets, 650

contrast wheel, 648–649
dessert station setup for, 649–650
frozen, 688
fruits, poached, in, 593
trends in, 648
Plum pudding, 396
Plums, varieties of, 46
Poached fruits, 471, 593
Polysaccharides, 82, 85
Pomegranate, 47
Poolish, 149
Poppy seeds, 36
Portable refrigeration, 73
Portion size
  converting formula, 112
  standardized formula, 110
Potassium bromate, in flour, 18
Potato starch, 24, 86
Pots and pans, stovetop, 69
Praline paste, 467
Pre-ferment, 149
Preshaping bread dough, 184, 186
Pretzels, in lye solution, 233
Probe thermometers, 53
Professionals. See Baking and pastry
  professionals
Proofers, 72, 188
Proofing bread dough, 62, 186, 188,
  198, 208, 224
Proteases, gelatin and, 87
Protein
  bacterial growth and, 91
  coagulation of, 87–88
  denatured, 88
Prune plums, 46
Psychrophilic bacteria, 91
Puddings
  bread, 391
  steamed, 396
  stirred, 389
Puff pastry
  blitz, 266
  cases, 622
  inverted, 264
  rolling and folding method (lami-
    nated dough), 261–263
  for tarts, 515
Pulled sugar
  blossom, 786–787
  leaves, 788–789
  ribbon, 792–793
Pullman loaf pan, 62
Pumpkin seeds, 37
Purchasing system, 10
Puréeing equipment and tools
  large, 69–71
  small, 60

Quick breads
  basic principles of, 273
  blending mixing method, 276
  cooling, 274
  creaming mixing method, 273,
    283–284
  pan preparation, 273
  storage of, 274

Ramekins, soufflés in, 409, 495
Rapid rise yeast, 31
Rasp, 57
Raspberry(ies), 41
  filling, 544
Reach-in refrigerators, 72
Reading list, 840–841
Reamers, 57
Recipes. See Formulas
Reduction sauces, 428, 458

Refractometer, 480–481
Refrigeration
  of frozen desserts, 649, 688
  of ice cream, 466
  of royal icing, 771
  sanitary conditions in, 93
  of sourdough starter, 167
  temperature, 93–94
  thawing, 95–96
  types of equipment, 72–73
Reheating foods, safety in, 95
Research-and-development kitchens,
  6
Restaurants, career opportunities in,
  4
Resting fermentation, 187
Retailer's Bakery Association (RBA),
  8, 9
Retarding yeast dough, 72, 127
Retrogradation of starches, 85–86
Rhubarb, 49
Ribbon, pulled sugar, 792–793
Rice, 20
Rice flour, 20, 130
Ricotta cheese, 26
Ring molds, 68, 588
Ripeness of fruit
  melons, 43
  in sorbets and sherbets, 481
Rochers, 722
Rock salt, 31
Rolled dough
  cookie dough, 342–343
  laminated dough, 82, 261–263
  for pies and tarts, 503, 515
  puff pastry, 515
Rolled icing, 566
Rolling pins, 62–63
Rose
  buttercream, 761, 804
  gum paste, 796–798
  marzipan, 776–777
Rosemary, 33
Roulades, 546, 606
Royal icing
  flood work and run-outs with,
    771–772
  string work with, 773
  in wedding cakes, traditional, 804
  working with, 771
Rubbed dough, 246–248
Rubber spatulas, 58
Ruffles, chocolate, 769
Run-outs, with royal icing, 771–772
Rye flour, 19, 130
Rye sourdough starter, 167

Sabayon, 428, 432
Saccharometer, 480
Safety. See also Food safety; Kitchen
  safety
  disabled access and, 104
  regulations, 103
  smoking and, 104
Salt
  in bread baking, 80
  hygroscopic properties of, 84
  types of, 31
Salted butter, 27
Sanding sugar, 20
Sanitation and cleaning
  in dessert station, 650
  equipment and tools for, 99
  hand washing, 90, 92
  information sources on, 842
  uniforms, 103
Saturated sugar solutions, 83

Saucepots, 69
Sauces
  in banquet service, 650
  caramel, 452
  chocolate, 428, 434
  fruit, 428, 436
  reduction, 428, 458
  sabayon, 428, 432
  types of, 428
  vanilla (crème anglaise), 430–431
Sauté pans, 69
Scaling
  bread dough, 183
  cookie dough, 328
  measurement conventions, 108
  tools, 52, 108
Scoops, 59, 700
Scoring bread dough, 187, 189, 198, 209, 224
Scrapers, 58
Sea salt, 31
Seckel pears, 45
Seed method of tempering chocolate, 704
Seeds, varieties of, 36–37
Semisweet chocolate, 29
Semolina, 19
Servers, safe food-handling practices of, 96
Sesame seeds, 37
Shavings, chocolate, 769
Sheet pans, 66
Shell border, buttercream, 758
Sherbet, 480–481
Short dough, 250
Shortening agents, 78
Shortenings, 28, 78, 246
Sieves, 60
Sifting dry ingredients, 273
Sifting tools, 60
Silicone mats, flexible, 69, 328
Silicone molds, flexible, 68, 615
Skimmers, 58
Slicers, 56
Smoking, as safety hazard, 104
Soakers, in bread making, 151
Sorbet, 480–481
Soufflés
  frozen (soufflés glacés), 495
  hot, 409–410
Sour cream, 25
Sourdough, 149
  starter, 165–167
South African–style wedding cakes, 804
Soybean oil, 28
Spatulas, 58, 549, 562, 704
Specialty cakes. See also Wedding cakes
  décor for, 805
  scheduling production of, 806
Spelt, 20
Spices
  in bread dough, 171
  infusing, 452, 467
  varieties of, 33
Spiders, 58
Spiral mixers, 71
Sponge cake, 273
Sponge method of fermentation, 149
Spoons, 57–58
Springerle rolling pin, 63
Springform pans, 68
Spring scales, 52
Spritz cookies, piping, 366
Stabilizers, 77
  in Bavarian cream, 403

gelatin, 392–393, 403
  in mousse, 397
Standardized formulas, 110–111
Starches
  retrogradation of, 85–86
  syrup manufacture from, 22
  as thickener, 23–24, 85, 86
Star fruit, 49
Starter, sourdough, 165–167
Steamed puddings, 396
Steam-injection ovens, 72
Steel-cut oats, 20
Stencils, for cookies, 350–351
Stencils and cutouts, tempered chocolate, 715
  bands, 768–769
  cigarettes, 766
    marbleized, 768
    mini-, 767
    striped, 767–768
  fans, 768
  plaques, marbleized, 765
  ruffles, 769
  shavings, 769
Still-frozen desserts, 495
Stone fruits
  pitting and coring, 518
  varieties of, 45–47
Storage
  of cakes, 274
  of chocolate, 29
  cross contamination in, 93
  of dairy products, 25
  of eggs, 27
  of extracts, 49
  first in, first out (FIFO) system, 94
  of fruits and vegetables, 37
  of herbs, 32
  of knives, 55
  of laminated dough, 264
  of nuts, 34
  of oils and shortenings, 28
  of quick breads, 274
  refrigeration equipment, 72–73
  of royal icing, 771
  sanitary conditions in, 93
  of sourdough starters, 167
  temperatures, 93–94
  of wines and liqueurs, 49
Straight mixing method, 123
Strainers, 60
Strawberries, 41
  blown sugar, 785
Straw sugar, 790–791
String work, with royal icing, 773
Strudels
  dough, 258
  stretching and assembly, 539
Substance-abuse problems, 104
Sucrose, 82, 83, 84
Sugar. See also Confections; Sugar décor
  in bread dough, 133
  caramelized
    browning reaction, 84
    dry method, 385, 728
    wet method, 384–385, 728
  coating, 409
  crystallization process, 82–84, 385
  functions in baking, 78–79
  hygroscopic properties of, 84
  invert, 23, 83, 84
  measuring density, 480–481, 838–839
  saturated and supersaturated, 83
  in sorbets and sherbets, 480–481
  stages of cooking, 728, 838

types of, 20–21
Sugar décor
  blown sugar strawberries, 785
  gum paste, 794
    magnolia, 798
    rose, 796–797
  pastillage, 794
    link twist, 794–795
  pulled sugar
    blossom, 786–787
    leaves, 788–789
    ribbon, 792–793
    straw sugar, 790–791
  in wedding cakes, traditional, 804
Sugar lamps, 66
Sugar paste. See Gum paste
Sugar thermometers, 54
Sunflower seeds, 37
Superfine sugar, 20
Supersaturated sugar solutions, 83
Swan, 628
Sweet chocolate, 30
Sweeteners. See also Sugar
  in ganache, 699, 715
  monosaccharides and oligosaccharides, 82
  types of, 20–21
Swiss meringue, 415
Syrup
  in cake layers, 545
  corn, 21, 22, 82
  glucose, 21, 22, 82, 84
  inverted, 23
  maple, 23

Table rest, 187
Table salt, 31
Tabling method of tempering chocolate, 704
Tangerines, 42
Tapioca, 24, 86
Tartlet pans, 68, 588
Tartlets, 588–589
Tart pans, 68
Tarts. See also Pastry dough; Pies
  blind baking shells, 511
  puff pastry, 515
  rolled dough for, 503–504
  tartlets, 588–589
  toppings for, 505
Tea, as flavoring, 49, 452, 700
Temperature
  in bread making
    baking, 187, 190, 199, 209, 225
    desired dough temperature (DDT), 118–119, 126–127
    for fermentation, 80
    proofing, 188
    total temperature factor (TTF), 118, 127
  conversions, 114, 835
  and food safety
    of cooled foods, 94–95
    critical limits and controls, 97–98
    danger zone, 93
    in refrigeration storage, 93–94
    of reheated foods, 95
  of pastry dough, 247
  in sugar cooking, 728
  in tempering chocolate, 89, 703–704
  thermometers, 53–54
Tempered chocolate. See also Chocolate confections
  in butter ganache, 715
  coating truffles in, 705

couverture, 705
  dipping confections in, 89, 702, 703, 706
  methods of tempering, 89, 702–704
  for molding, 720
  piping, 763
  stencils and cutouts, 715
    cigarettes, 766–768
    fans, 768
    plaques, marbleized, 765
    ruffles, 769
    shavings, 769
  tools for, 704
  triangles (spread-and-cut method), 763
Template, for royal icing, 771
Test kitchens, 6
Thawing frozen foods, 95–96
Thermometers, 53–54
Thermophilic bacteria, 91
Thickeners, 23–24, 85–88
  eggs, 86, 87–88
  gelling agents, 23, 86, 87
  starches, 23–24, 85, 86
Tiered cakes
  support for, 804, 805
  transporting, 807
Time management, 11–12
Tongs, 58
Tools. See Equipment and tools
Tortes, decoration of. See Décor
Total temperature factor (TTF), 118, 127
Toxins, 90
Transfer sheets, 65
Transporting tiered cakes, 807
Triangles, chocolate (spread-and-cut method), 763–764
Trichinella spiralis, 90
Trim loss, 115, 116
Tropical fruits, 47–49
Truffles
  chocolate coating for, 705
  décor, 706
  flavoring ganache for, 700
  piping, 700
  in premade shells, 711
Tube pans, 68
Turbinado sugar, 21
Turntable, cake decorating, 64, 545, 548
Two-stage mixing method, 273, 297–298

Uniforms, employee, 102–103
Unsalted butter, 27
Unsweetened chocolate, 29
Utility knives, 55

Vanilla (beans), 34, 377
  Bavarian cream, 403
  sauce (crème anglaise), 430–431
Vegetable oil, 28
Vegetables
  selecting and handling, 37
  yield calculation, 115–116
Vertical chopping machines (VCMs), 71
Vertical mixers, 71
Viruses, in food-borne illnesses, 90
Vital wheat gluten, 19
Volume measurement
  defined, 108
  pan sizes and, 838
  tools, 52–53
  U.S./metric conversions, 834